Popular Quotations
FOR ALL USES

Popular Quotations
FOR ALL USES

EDITED BY

Lewis Copeland

Garden City Publishing Company, Inc.
GARDEN CITY, NEW YORK

PRINTED IN THE UNITED STATES OF AMERICA
AMERICAN BOOK–STRATFORD PRESS, INC., NEW YORK

INTRODUCTION

THIS IS A BOOK "which hath been culled from the flowers of all other books." Quotations preserve for mankind not only the beauty of literature, but also the wisdom of philosophy, the counsel of experience, and the inspiration of achievement. These passages bring us in contact with the world's great authors, poets, thinkers, orators, and leaders. A volume of quotations is therefore a treasurehouse of gems of wit, argument, learning, and knowledge.

This collection has been planned primarily for those who need colorful and forceful quotations as effective aids to their speaking and writing. The book has been arranged alphabetically by subjects for ready reference. A comprehensive index at the beginning of the book gives cross references for each subject. This enables the reader to find additional quotations dealing with the topic in which he is interested. An index of authors at the end of the book provides biographical information as well as another means of locating the quotations desired.

A feature of this work is the inclusion of many contemporary quotations from the writings and speeches of outstanding men and women of our time, in addition to the carefully chosen best from the great works and utterances of the past. Here then is a reference work of useful quotations in poetry and prose which is virtually an anthology of the world's finest thought on the important problems of life.

L. C.

INDEX OF SUBJECTS

With Cross References

[Each subject entry given in this Index is followed by a list of related subject headings also found in this book. By referring to these related headings, the reader will find additional quotations dealing with the topic in which he is interested.]

C

D

E

Q

W

Y

Z

Popular Quotations

FOR ALL USES

A

ABILITY

Ability is found to consist mainly in a high degree of solemnity.
BIERCE—*The Devil's Dictionary.*

He could raise scruples dark and nice,
And after solve 'em in a trice:
As if Divinity had catch'd
The itch, on purpose to be scratch'd.
BUTLER—*Hudibras.*

I add this also, that natural ability without education has oftener raised man to glory and virtue, than education without natural ability.
CICERO—*Oratio Pro Licinio Archia.*

The dwarf sees farther than the giant, when he has the giant's shoulders to mount on.
COLERIDGE—*The Friend.*

As we advance in life, we learn the limits of our abilities.
FROUDE—*Short Studies on Great Subjects.*

We judge ourselves by what we feel capable of doing, while others judge us by what we have already done.
LONGFELLOW.

Ability is of little account without opportunity.
NAPOLEON.

Exigencies create the necessary ability to meet and to conquer them.
WENDELL PHILLIPS.

One thing, however, I must premise, that without the assistance of natural capacity, rules and precepts are of no efficacy.
QUINTILIAN—*Prooemium.*

The world is like a board with holes in it, and the square men have got into the round holes.
SYDNEY SMITH—*Sketches of Moral Philosophy.*

Read my little fable:
He that runs may read.
Most can raise the flowers now,
For all have got the seed.
TENNYSON—*The Flowers.*

They are able because they think they are able.
VERGIL—*Aeneid.*

ABSENCE

Absence makes the heart grow fonder.
THOMAS HAYNES BAYLY—*Isle of Beauty.*

Wives in their husbands' absences grow subtler,
And daughters sometimes run off with the butler.
BYRON—*Don Juan.*

Absent in body, but present in spirit.
I Corinthians. V. 3.

Achilles absent, was Achilles still.
HOMER—*Iliad.*

Ever absent, ever near;
Still I see thee, still I hear;
Yet I cannot reach thee, dear!
FRANCIS KAZINCZY—*Separation.*

What shall I do with all the days and hours
That must be counted ere I see thy face?
How shall I charm the interval that lowers
Between this time and that sweet time of grace?
FRANCES ANNE KEMBLE—*Absence.*

But when he (man) shall have been taken from sight, he quickly goes also out of mind.
THOMAS À KEMPIS—*Imitation of Christ.*

Oft in the tranquil hour of night,
When stars illume the sky,
I gaze upon each orb of light,
And wish that thou wert by.
GEORGE LINLEY—*Song.*

A short absence is safest.
OVID.

Let no one be willing to speak ill of the absent.
PROPERTIUS—*Elegiae.*

All days are nights to see till I see thee,
And nights bright days when dreams do show thee me.
SHAKESPEARE—*Sonnet.*

How like a winter hath my absence been
From thee, the pleasure of the fleeting year!
What freezings have I felt, what dark days seen!
What old December's bareness everywhere.
SHAKESPEARE—*Sonnet.*

ABSTINENCE

The more a man denies himself, the more shall he obtain from God.
HORACE.

Abstinence is as easy to me as temperance would be difficult.
SAMUEL JOHNSON.

ABSURDITY

Every absurdity has a champion to defend it.
GOLDSMITH.

Of all the authorities to which men can be called to submit, the wisdom of our ancestors is the most whimsically absurd.
JEREMY TAYLOR.

ABUNDANCE

Great abundance of riches cannot be gathered and kept by any man without sin.
ERASMUS.

Abundance kills more than hunger.
German Proverb.

If I have enough for myself and family, I am steward only for myself; if I have more, I am but a steward of that abundance for others.
GEORGE HERBERT.

ABUSE

Remember that it is not he who gives abuse or blows who affronts, but the view we take of these things as insulting. When, therefore, any one provokes you, be assured that it is your own opinion which provokes you.
EPICTETUS.

Abuse is often of service. There is nothing so dangerous to an author as silence. His name, like a shuttlecock, must be beat backward and forward, or it falls to the ground.
SAMUEL JOHNSON.

There are more people abusive to others than lie open to abuse themselves; but the humor goes round, and he that laughs at me to-day will have somebody to laugh at him tomorrow.
SENECA.

ACCIDENT

Accidents will occur in the best regulated families.
DICKENS—*David Copperfield.*

To what happy accident is it that we owe so unexpected a visit?
GOLDSMITH—*Vicar of Wakefield.*

Nothing under the sun is accidental, least of all that of which the intention is so clearly evident.
LESSING—*Emilia Galotti.*

At first laying down, as a fact fundamental,
That nothing with God can be accidental.
LONGFELLOW—*Christus.*

ACQUAINTANCE

A wise man knows everything; a shrewd one, everybody.
ANONYMOUS.

Make the most of the day, by determining to spend it on two sorts of acquaintances only—those by whom something may be got, and those from whom something may be learned.
COLTON.

Sudden acquaintance brings repentance.

THOMAS FULLER.

If a man is worth knowing at all, he is worth knowing well.

ALEXANDER SMITH—*Dreamthorp.*

ACTING

The most difficult character in comedy is that of the fool, and he must be no simpleton that plays that part.

CERVANTES.

When an actor has money, he doesn't send letters but telegrams.

ANTON CHEKHOV.

Remember that you are but an actor, acting whatever part the Master has ordained. It may be short or it may be long. If he wishes you to represent a poor man, do so heartily; if a cripple, or a magistrate, or a private man, in each case act your part with honor.

EPICTETUS.

Prologues precede the piece in mournful verse,
As undertakers walk before the hearse.

DAVID GARRICK—*Apprentice.*

On the stage he was natural, simple, affecting,
'Twas only that when he was off, he was acting.

GOLDSMITH—*Retaliation.*

Players, sir! I look upon them as no better than creatures set upon tables and joint-stools to make faces and produce laughter, like dancing dogs.—But, sir, you will allow that some players are better than others?—Yes, sir; as some dogs dance better than others.

SAMUEL JOHNSON.

The drama's laws, the drama's patrons give.
For we that live to please, must please to live.

SAMUEL JOHNSON—*Prologue.*

Who teach the mind its proper face to scan,
And hold the faithful mirror up to man.

ROBERT LLOYD—*The Actor.*

There still remains to mortify a wit
The many-headed monster of the pit.

POPE—*Horace.*

To wake the soul by tender strokes of art,
To raise the genius, and to mend the heart;
To make mankind, in conscious virtue bold,
Live o'er each scene, and be what they behold—
For this the tragic Muse first trod the stage.

POPE—*Prologue to Addison's Cato.*

If it be true that good wine needs no bush, 'tis true that a good play needs no epilogue.

SHAKESPEARE—*As You Like It. Epilogue.*

Like a dull actor now,
I have forgot my part, and I am out,
Even to a full disgrace.

SHAKESPEARE—*Coriolanus.* Act V. Sc. 3.

The play's the thing
Wherein I'll catch the conscience of the king.

SHAKESPEARE—*Hamlet.* Act II. Sc. 2.

Suit the action to the word, the word to the action, with this special observance, that you o'erstep not the modesty of nature.

SHAKESPEARE—*Hamlet.* Act III. Sc. 2.

A hit, a very palpable hit.

SHAKESPEARE—*Hamlet.* Act V. Sc. 2.

A beggarly account of empty boxes.

SHAKESPEARE—*Romeo and Juliet.* Act V. Sc. 1.

Lo, where the Stage, the poor, degraded Stage,
Holds its warped mirror to a gaping age!

CHARLES SPRAGUE—*Curiosity.*

The play is done; the curtain drops,
Slow falling to the prompter's bell:

A moment yet the actor stops,
And looks around, to say farewell.
It is an irksome word and task:
And, when he's laughed and said his say,
He shows, as he removes the mask,
A face that's anything but gay.
THACKERAY—*The End of the Play.*

ACTION

Of every noble action the intent
Is to give worth reward, vice punishment.
BEAUMONT AND FLETCHER—*The Captain.*

Let us do or die.
BURNS—*Scots, Wha Hae.*

Our grand business undoubtedly is, not to *see* what lies dimly at a distance, but to *do* what lies clearly at hand.
CARLYLE—*Essays. Signs of the Times.*

The best way to keep good acts in memory is to refresh them with new.
ATTRIBUTED TO CATO BY BACON—*Apothegms.*

What one has, one ought to use: and whatever he does he should do with all his might.
CICERO—*De Senectute.*

Actions of the last age are like almanacs of the last year.
SIR JOHN DENHAM—*The Sophy.*

Whatsoever thy hand findeth to do, do it with thy might.
Ecclesiastes. IX. 10.

Zeus hates busybodies and those who do too much.
EURIPIDES. *Quoted by Emerson.*

Do well and right, and let the world sink.
GEORGE HERBERT—*Country Parson.*

Attempt the end, and never stand to doubt;
Nothing's so hard but search will find it out.
HERRICK—*Seek and Find.*

Every event that a man would master must be mounted on the run, and no man ever caught the reins of a thought except as it galloped by him.
HOLMES.

That action which appears most conducive to the happiness and virtue of mankind.
FRANCIS HUTCHESON—*A System of Moral Philosophy.*

All the means of action—the shapeless masses, the materials—lie everywhere about us; what we need is the celestial fire to change the flint into transparent crystal, bright and clear.
LONGFELLOW.

Trust no future, howe'er pleasant!
Let the dead past bury its dead!
Act,—act in the living Present!
Heart within and God o'erhead.
LONGFELLOW—*Psalm of Life.*

Let us then be up and doing,
With a heart for any fate;
Still achieving, still pursuing,
Learn to labor and to wait.
LONGFELLOW—*Psalm of Life.*

Every man feels instinctively that all the beautiful sentiments in the world weigh less than a single lovely action.
LOWELL.

Go, and do thou likewise.
Luke. X. 37.

He nothing common did, or mean,
Upon that memorable scene.
ANDREW MARVELL—*Horatian Ode. Upon Cromwell's Return from Ireland.*

Therefore all things whatsoever ye would that men should do to you, do ye even so to them: for this is the law and the prophets.
Matthew. VII. 12.

Awake, arise, or be forever fall'n!
MILTON—*Paradise Lost.*

What the Puritans gave the world was not Thought, but *action.*
WENDELL PHILLIPS—*The Pilgrims.*

So much to do; so little done.
CECIL RHODES—*Last Words.*

I took the canal zone and let Congress debate, and while the debate goes on the canal does also.
THEODORE ROOSEVELT.

To live is not merely to breathe: it is to act; it is to make use of our organs, senses, faculties,—of all those parts of ourselves which give us the feeling of existence.

ROUSSEAU.

Get good counsel before you begin: and when you have decided, act promptly.

SALLUST—*Catilina.*

The Lord is a God of knowledge, and by Him actions are weighed.

I Samuel II. 3.

He that is overcautious will accomplish little.

SCHILLER—*Wilhelm Tell.*

I profess not talking: only this,
Let each man do his best.

SHAKESPEARE—*Henry IV.* Pt. I. Act V. Sc. 2.

We must not stint
Our necessary actions, in the fear
To cope malicious censurers.

SHAKESPEARE—*Henry VIII.* Act I. Sc. 2.

If it were done, when 'tis done, then 'twere well
It were done quickly.

SHAKESPEARE—*Macbeth.* Act I. Sc. 7.

But I remember now
I am in this earthly world; where, to do harm,
Is often laudable; to do good, sometime,
Accounted dangerous folly.

SHAKESPEARE—*Macbeth.* Act IV. Sc. 2.

What's done can't be undone.

SHAKESPEARE—*Macbeth.* Act V. Sc. 1.

Better that we should err in action than wholly refuse to perform. The storm is so much better than the calm, as it declares the presence of a living principle. Stagnation is something worse than death. It is corruption also.

SIMMS.

Heaven ne'er helps the men who will not act.

SOPHOCLES—*Fragment.*

Theirs not to make reply,
Theirs not to reason why,
Theirs but to do and die.

TENNYSON—*Charge of the Light Brigade.*

Said and done. Done as soon as said.

TERENCE—*Eunuchus.*

A slender acquaintance with the world must convince every man that actions, not words, are the true criterion of the attachment of friends; and that the most liberal professions of good-will are very far from being the surest marks of it.

WASHINGTON—*Social Maxims.*

Man, being essentially active, must find in activity his joy, as well as his beauty and glory; and labor, like everything else that is good, is its own reward.

WHIPPLE.

ADAM AND EVE

In *Adam's* fall—
We sinned all.

New England Primer.

Whilst Adam slept, Eve from his side arose:
Strange his first sleep would be his last repose.

ANONYMOUS.

Adam and Eve had many advantages, but the principal one was that they escaped teething.

S. L. CLEMENS (Mark Twain) *Pudd'nhead Wilson.*

Adam ate the apple, and our teeth still ache.

Hungarian Proverb.

ADMIRATION

Admiration is a very short-lived passion, that immediately decays upon growing familiar with its object.

ADDISON—*The Spectator.*

No nobler feeling than this of admiration for one higher than himself dwells in the breast of man.

CARLYLE.

Distance is a great promoter of admiration!

DIDEROT.

We always love those who admire us, and we do not always love those whom we admire.

LA ROCHEFOUCAULD.

For fools admire, but men of sense approve.

POPE—*Essay on Criticism.*

Season your admiration for awhile.

SHAKESPEARE—*Hamlet.* Act I. Sc. 2.

Admiration is a youthful fancy which scarcely ever survives to mature years.

H. W. SHAW.

ADVENTURE

The fruit of my tree of knowledge is plucked, and it is this: "Adventures are to the adventurous."

DISRAELI—*Ixion in Heaven.*

He who has not an adventure has not horse or mule, so says Solomon.—Who is too adventurous, said Echephron,—loses horse and mule, replied Malcon.

RABELAIS—*Gargantua.*

ADVERSITY

Adversity introduces a man to himself.

ANONYMOUS.

God brings men into deep waters, not to drown them, but to cleanse them.

AUGHEY.

Prosperity is not without many fears and distastes, and Adversity is not without comforts and hopes.

BACON—*Of Adversity.*

Adversity is sometimes hard upon a man; but for one man who can stand prosperity, there are a hundred that will stand adversity.

CARLYLE—*Heroes and Hero Worship.*

The brightest crowns that are worn in heaven have been tried and smelted and polished and glorified through the furnace of tribulation.

CHAPIN.

Constant success shows us but one side of the world; adversity brings out the reverse of the picture.

COLTON.

There is no education like adversity.

DISRAELI.

In the day of prosperity be joyful, but in the day of adversity consider.

Ecclesiastes. VIII. 14.

Adversity is the trial of principle. Without it a man hardly knows whether he is honest or not.

FIELDING.

It is often better to have a great deal of harm happen to one than a little; a great deal may rouse you to remove what a little will only accustom you to endure.

GREVILLE.

Prosperity is a great teacher; adversity is a greater. Possession pampers the mind; privation trains and strengthens it.

HAZLITT.

Adversity has the effect of eliciting talents, which, in prosperous circumstances, would have lain dormant.

HORACE.

Remember that there is nothing stable in human affairs; therefore avoid undue elation in prosperity, or undue depression in adversity.

ISOCRATES.

Great men rejoice in adversity just as brave soldiers triumph in war.

SENECA—*De Providentia.*

Sweet are the uses of adversity;
Which, like the toad, ugly and venomous,
Wears yet a precious jewel in his head.

SHAKESPEARE—*As You Like It.* Act II. Sc. 1.

The truly great and good, in affliction, bear a countenance more princely than they are wont; for it is the temper of the highest hearts, like the palm-tree, to strive most upwards when it is most burdened.

SIR PHILIP SIDNEY.

In all distresses of our friends
We first consult our private ends.

SWIFT—*On the Death of Dr. Swift.*

ADVICE

Never give advice in a crowd.
Arab Proverb.

Never give advice unless asked.
German Proverb.

Know when to speak; for many times it brings
Danger to give the best advice to kings.
HERRICK—*Caution in Councell.*

To attempt to advise conceited people is like whistling against the wind.
HOOD.

Whatever advice you give, be short.
HORACE—*Ars Poetica.*

Old men are fond of giving good advice, to console themselves for being no longer in a position to give bad examples.
LA ROCHEFOUCAULD.

We give advice, but we do not inspire conduct.
LA ROCHEFOUCAULD.

In great straits and when hope is small, the boldest counsels are the safest.
LIVY—*Annales.*

Agreeable advice is seldom useful advice.
MASSILLON.

Good counsel has no price.
MAZZINI.

In the multitude of counsellors there is safety.
Proverbs. XI. 14; XXIV. 6.

One can advise comfortably from a safe port.
SCHILLER—*Wilhelm Tell.*

Many receive advice, only the wise profit by it.
SYRUS.

Admonish your friends privately, but praise them openly.
SYRUS.

A dead father's counsel, a wise son heedeth.
TEGNER—*Fridthjof's Saga.*

We all, when we are well, give good advice to the sick.
TERENCE—*Andria.*

There is nothing of which men are more liberal than their good advice, be their stock of it ever so small; because it seems to carry in it an intimation of their own influence, importance, or worth.
YOUNG.

AFFECTATION

Affectation is the product of falsehood.
CARLYLE.

Almost every man wastes part of his life in attempts to display qualities which he does not possess, and to gain applause which he cannot keep; so that scarcely can two persons meet but one is offended or diverted by the ostentation of the other.
SAMUEL JOHNSON.

We are never so ridiculous from the habits we have as from those we affect to have.
LA ROCHEFOUCAULD.

All affectation is the vain and ridiculous attempt of poverty to appear rich.
LAVATER.

Affectation hides three times as many virtues as charity does sins.
HORACE MANN.

AFFECTION

Affection is the broadest basis of good in life.
GEORGE ELIOT.

Caresses, expressions of one sort or another, are necessary to the life of the affections as leaves are to the life of a tree. If they are wholly restrained love will die at the roots.
HAWTHORNE.

Talk not of wasted affection, affection never was wasted.
If it enrich not the heart of another, its waters, returning
Back to their springs, like the rain, shall fill them full of refreshment;
That which the fountain sends forth returns again to the fountain.
LONGFELLOW—*Evangeline.*

Affection is a coal that must be cool'd;
Else, suffer'd, it will set the heart on fire.
SHAKESPEARE—*Venus and Adonis.*

The affection of young ladies is of as rapid growth as Jack's beanstalk, and reaches up to the sky in a night.
THACKERAY.

AFFLICTION

The truest help we can render an afflicted man is not to take his burden from him, but to call out his best energy, that he may be able to bear the burden.
PHILLIPS BROOKS.

Affliction's sons are brothers in distress;
A brother to relieve, how exquisite the bliss!
BURNS—*A Winter Night.*

The eternal stars shine out as soon as it is dark enough.
CARLYLE.

It is the crushed grape that gives out the blood-red wine: it is the suffering soul that breathes the sweetest melodies.
GAIL HAMILTON.

Whom the Lord loveth he chasteneth.
Hebrews. XII. 6.

Be still, sad heart, and cease repining,
Behind the clouds the sun is shining;
Thy fate is the common fate of all;
Into each life some rain must fall,—
Some days must be dark and dreary.
LONGFELLOW.

Affliction till it do cry out itself,
Enough, enough, and die.
SHAKESPEARE—*King Lear.* Act IV. Sc. 6.

There is healing in the bitter cup.
SOUTHEY.

The Lord gets his best soldiers out of the highlands of affliction.
SPURGEON.

Patience cannot remove, but it can always dignify and alleviate, misfortune.
LAURENCE STERNE.

AGE

He who would pass the declining years of his life with honor and comfort, should when young, consider that he may one day become old, and remember, when he is old, that he has once been young.
ADDISON.

It is always in season for old men to learn.
AESCHYLUS—*Age.*

Old wood best to burn, old wine to drink, old friends to trust, and old authors to read.
QUOTED BY BACON—*Apothegm.*

Men of age object too much, consult too long, adventure too little, repent too soon, and seldom drive business home to the full period, but content themselves with a mediocrity of success.
BACON—*Of Youth and Age.*

My days are in the yellow leaf;
The flowers and fruits of love are gone;
The worm, the canker, and the grief
Are mine alone!
BYRON—*On this day I complete my thirty-sixth year.*

You must become an old man in good time if you wish to be an old man long.
CICERO—*De Senectute.*

There are three classes into which all the women past seventy years of age, that ever I knew, were to be divided: 1. That dear old soul; 2. That old woman; 3. That old witch.
COLERIDGE.

Youth is a blunder; Manhood a struggle; Old Age a regret.
DISRAELI—*Coningsby.*

The Disappointment of Manhood succeeds to the delusion of Youth; let us hope that the heritage of Old Age is not Despair.
DISRAELI—*Vivian Grey.*

Forsake not an old friend; for the new is not comparable to him: a new friend is as new wine; when it is old, thou shalt drink it with pleasure.
Ecclesiasticus. IX. 10.

Nature abhors the old.
EMERSON—*Essays.*

Nature is full of freaks, and now puts an old head on young shoulders, and then a young heart beating under fourscore winters.
EMERSON.

At 20 years of age the will reigns; at 30 the wit; at 40 the judgment.
FRANKLIN—*Poor Richard's Almanac.*

If wrinkles must be written upon our brows, let them not be written upon the heart. The spirit should not grow old.
JAMES A. GARFIELD.

They say women and music should never be dated.
GOLDSMITH.

I love everything that's old,—old friends, old times, old manners, old books, old wine.
GOLDSMITH—*She Stoops to Conquer.*

To be seventy years young is sometimes far more cheerful and hopeful than to be forty years old.
HOLMES—*On the seventieth birthday of Julia Ward Howe, May 27, 1889.*

When he's forsaken,
Wither'd and shaken,
What can an old man do but die?
HOOD—*Ballad.*

Ladies, stock and tend your hive,
Trifle not at thirty-five,
For, howe'er we boast and strive,
Life declines from thirty-five;
He that ever hopes to thrive
Must begin by thirty-five.
SAMUEL JOHNSON—*To Mrs. Thrale, when thirty-five.*

Few persons know how to be old.
LA ROCHEFOUCAULD.

Old age is a tyrant who forbids, upon pain of death, all the pleasures of youth.
LA ROCHEFOUCAULD.

The sunshine fails, the shadows grow more dreary,
And I am near to fall, infirm and weary.
LONGFELLOW—*Canzone.*

Whatever poet, orator, or sage
May say of it, old age is still old age.
LONGFELLOW—*Morituri Salutamus.*

Age is not all decay; it is the ripening, the swelling, of the fresh life within, that withers and bursts the husk.
GEORGE MACDONALD—*The Marquis of Lossie.*

So may'st thou live, till like ripe fruit thou drop
Into thy mother's lap, or be with ease
Gather'd, not harshly pluck'd for death mature.
MILTON—*Paradise Lost.*

How old I am! I'm eighty years!
I've worked both hard and long,
Yet patient as my life has been,
One dearest sight I have not seen—
It almost seems a wrong;
A dream I had when life was new,
Alas our dreams! they come not true;
I thought to see fair Carcassonne,
That lovely city—Carcassonne!
GUSTAVE NADAUD—*Carcassonne.*

When a man reaches the last stage of life,—without senses or mentality—they say that he has grown a child again.
PLAUTUS—*Mercator.*

Learn to live well, or fairly make your will;
You've played, and loved, and ate, and drank your fill.
Walk sober off, before a sprightlier age
Comes tittering on, and shoves you from the stage.
POPE—*Imitations of Horace.*

The days of our years are threescore years and ten; and if by reason of strength they be fourscore years, yet is their strength labour and sorrow; for it is soon cut off, and we fly away.
Psalms I. 3.

What makes old age so sad is, not that our joys but that our hopes cease.
JEAN PAUL RICHTER—*Titan.*

O, roses for the flush of youth,
And laurel for the perfect prime;
But pluck an ivy branch for me,
Grown old before my time.
CHRISTINA G. ROSSETTI—*Song.*

I'm growing fonder of my staff;
I'm growing dimmer in the eyes;
I'm growing fainter in my laugh;
I'm growing deeper in my sighs;
I'm growing careless of my dress;
I'm growing frugal of my gold;
I'm growing wise; I'm growing,—yes,—
I'm growing old.
JOHN GODFREY SAXE—*I'm Growing Old.*

The first forty years of life give us the text; the next thirty supply the commentary on it.
SCHOPENHAUER.

Nothing is more dishonourable than an old man, heavy with years, who has no other evidence of his having lived long except his age.
SENECA—*De Tranquillitate.*

Old age is an incurable disease.
SENECA—*Epistoloe Ad Lucilium.*

Age cannot wither her, nor custom stale
Her infinite variety.
SHAKESPEARE—*Antony and Cleopatra.* Act. II. Sc. 2.

All the world's a stage,
And all the men and women merely players:
They have their exits and their entrances;
And one man in his time plays many parts,
His acts being seven ages. At first the infant,
Mewling and puking in the nurse's arms.
And then the whining school-boy, with his satchel
And shining morning face, creeping like snail
Unwillingly to school. And then the lover,
Sighing like furnace, with a woeful ballad
Made to his mistress' eyebrow. Then a soldier,
Full of strange oaths and bearded like the pard,
Jealous in honour, sudden and quick in quarrel,
Seeking the bubble reputation
Even in the cannon's mouth. And then the justice,
In fair round belly with good capon lined,
With eyes severe and beard of formal cut,
Full of wise saws and modern instances;
And so he plays his part. The sixth age shifts
Into the lean and slipper'd pantaloon,
With spectacles on nose and pouch on side,
His youthful hose, well saved, a world too wide
For his shrunk shank; and his big manly voice,
Turning again toward childish treble, pipes
And whistles in his sound. Last scene of all,
That ends this strange eventful history,
Is second childishness and mere oblivion,
Sans teeth, sans eyes, sans taste, sans every thing.
SHAKESPEARE—*As You Like It.* Act II. Sc. 7.

An old man is twice a child.
SHAKESPEARE—*Hamlet.* Act II. Sc. 2.

A good old man, sir; he will be talking: as they say, When the age is in the wit is out.
SHAKESPEARE—*Much Ado About Nothing.* Act III. Sc. 5.

Give me a staff of honor for mine age,
But not a sceptre to control the world.
SHAKESPEARE—*Titus Andronicus.* Act I. Sc. 1.

"You are old, Father William," the young man cried,
"The few locks which are left you are gray;

You are hale, Father William,—a hearty old man:
Now tell me the reason, I pray."

SOUTHEY.

I swear she's no chicken; she's on the wrong side of thirty, if she be a day.

SWIFT—*Polite Conversation.*

Every man desires to live long; but no man would be old.

SWIFT.

When a noble life has prepared old age, it is not the decline that it reveals, but the first days of immortality.

MME. DE STAËL.

Old things are always in good repute, present things in disfavour.

TACITUS—*Dialogus de Oratoribus.*

Next to the very young, I suppose the very old are the most selfish. Alas! the heart hardens as the blood ceases to run.

THACKERAY.

The old believe everything: the middle-aged suspect everything: the young know everything.

OSCAR WILDE.

AGRICULTURE

The diligent farmer plants trees, of which he himself will never see the fruit.

CICERO—*Tusculanarum Disputationum.*

The first farmer was the first man, and all historic nobility rests on possession and use of land.

EMERSON—*Society and Solitude.*

Happy he who far from business, like the primitive race of mortals, cultivates with his own oxen the fields of his fathers, free from all anxieties of gain.

HORACE—*Epodon.*

Ye rigid Ploughmen! bear in mind
Your labor is for future hours.
Advance! spare not! nor look behind!
Plough deep and straight with all your powers!

RICHARD HENRIST HORNE—*The Plough.*

Earth is here so kind, that just tickle her with a hoe and she laughs with a harvest.

JERROLD—*A Land of Plenty.*

A field becomes exhausted by constant tillage.

OVID.

And he gave it for his opinion, "that whoever could make two ears of corn, or two blades of grass, to grow upon a spot of ground where only one grew before, would deserve better of mankind, and do more essential service to his country, than the whole race of politicians put together."

SWIFT—*Voyage to Brobdingnag.*

Praise a large domain, cultivate a small estate.

VERGIL—*Georgics.*

Blessed be agriculture! if one does not have too much of it.

CHARLES DUDLEY WARNER—*My Summer in a Garden.*

When tillage begins, other arts follow. The farmers, therefore, are the founders of human civilization.

DANIEL WEBSTER—*Remarks on Agriculture.*

Heap high the farmer's wintry hoard!
Heap high the golden corn!
No richer gift has Autumn poured
From out her lavish horn!

WHITTIER—*The Corn-Song.*

AMBITION

Ambition is a gilded misery, a secret poison, a hidden plague, the engineer of deceit, the mother of hypocrisy, the parent of envy, the original of vices, the moth of holiness, the blinder of hearts.

THOMAS BROOKS.

Ambition has no rest!

BULWER-LYTTON.

When you are aspiring to the highest place, it is honorable to reach the second or even the third rank.

CICERO—*De Oratore.*

On what strange stuff Ambition feeds!

ELIZA COOK—*Thomas Hood.*

By low ambition and the thirst of praise.
COWPER—*Table Talk.*

On the summit see,
The seals of office glitter in his eyes;
He climbs, he pants, he grasps them! At his heels,
Close at his heels, a demagogue ascends,
And with a dexterous jerk soon twists him down,
And wins them, but to lose them in his turn.
COWPER—*Task.*

Nothing is too high for the daring of mortals: we would storm heaven itself in our folly.
HORACE—*Carmina.*

Ambition is but avarice on stilts, and masked. God sometimes sends a famine, sometimes a pestilence, and sometimes a hero, for the chastisement of mankind; none of them surely for our admiration.
LANDOR.

The ambitious deceive themselves when they propose an end to their ambition; for that end, when attained, becomes a means.
LA ROCHEFOUCAULD.

Most people would succeed in small things if they were not troubled with great ambitions.
LONGFELLOW—*Drift-Wood.*

Ambition! deadly tyrant! inexorable master! what alarms, what anxious hours, what agonies of heart, are the sure portion of thy gaudy slaves?
MALLET.

The man who seeks one thing in life, and but one,
May hope to achieve it before life be done;
But he who seeks all things, wherever he goes,
Only reaps from the hopes which around him he sows
A harvest of barren regrets.
OWEN MEREDITH—*Lucile.*

Here may we reign secure, and in my choice
To reign is worth ambition, though in Hell.
Better to reign in hell than serve in heaven.
MILTON—*Paradise Lost.*

If at great things thou would'st arrive,
Get riches first, get wealth, and treasure heap,
Not difficult, if thou hearken to me;
Riches are mine, fortune is in my hand,
They whom I favor thrive in wealth amain,
While virtue, valor, wisdom, sit in want.
MILTON—*Paradise Regained.*

Be always displeased at what thou art, if thou desire to attain to what thou art not; for where thou hast pleased thyself, there thou abidest.
QUARLES—*Emblems.*

Ambition breaks the ties of blood, and forgets the obligations of gratitude.
SCOTT.

Ambition is no cure for love!
SCOTT—*Lay of the Last Minstrel.*

The noble Brutus
Hath told you Caesar was ambitious;
If it were so, it was a grievous fault;
And grievously hath Caesar answered it.
SHAKESPEARE—*Julius Caesar.* Act III. Sc. 2.

The very substance of the ambitious is merely the shadow of a dream.
SHAKESPEARE—*Hamlet.* Act II. Sc. 2.

Mark but my fall, and that that ruin'd me.
Cromwell, I charge thee, fling away ambition.
By that sin fell the angels; how can man then,
The image of his Maker, hope to win by it?
SHAKESPEARE—*Henry VIII.* Act III. Sc. 2.

If you wish to reach the highest, begin at the lowest.
SYRUS—*Maxims.*

Ambition destroys its possessor.
TALMUD—*Yoma.*

Ambition has but one reward for all:
A little power, a little transient fame,
A grave to rest in, and a fading name!

WILLIAM WINTER—*The Queen's Domain.*

AMERICA

America! half brother of the world!
With something good and bad of every land.

BAILEY—*Festus.*

Young man, there is America—which at this day serves for little more than to amuse you with stories of savage men and uncouth manners; yet shall, before you taste of death, show itself equal to the whole of that commerce which now attracts the envy of the world.

BURKE—*Speech on Conciliation with America.*

The breaking waves dashed high
On a stern and rock-bound coast;
And the woods, against a stormy sky,
Their giant branches tost.

FELICIA D. HEMANS—*Landing of the Pilgrim Fathers.*

It does not require a lawyer to interpret the provisions of the Bill of Rights. They are as clear as the Ten Commandments.

HERBERT HOOVER—*Speech, 1935.*

Hail, Columbia! happy land!
Hail, ye heroes! heavenborn band!
Who fought and bled in Freedom's cause.

JOSEPH HOPKINSON—*Hail Columbia.*

However great the hardships and the trials which loom ahead, our America will endure and the cause of human freedom will triumph.

CORDELL HULL—*Speech, 1940.*

America is a tune. It must be sung together.

GERALD STANLEY LEE—*Crowds.*

Thou, too, sail on, O Ship of State!
Sail on, O Union, strong and great!
Humanity with all its fears,
With all the hopes of future years,
Is hanging breathless on thy fate!

LONGFELLOW—*Building of the Ship.*

Only those Americans who are willing to die for their country are fit to live.

DOUGLAS MACARTHUR.

When you become used to never being alone you may consider yourself Americanized.

ANDRÉ MAUROIS.

More things than ships were sunk at Pearl Harbor.

WILLIAM MCFEE.

We should consider any attempt (by the European Powers) to extend their system to any portion of this hemisphere as dangerous to our peace and safety.

JAMES MONROE—*Message to Congress, 1823.*

America is a fortunate country. She grows by the follies of our European nations.

NAPOLEON.

These unhappy times call for the building of plans that rest upon the forgotten, the unorganized but indispensable units of economic power, for plans like those of 1917 that build from the bottom up and not from the top down, that put their faith once more in the forgotten man at the bottom of the economic pyramid.

FRANKLIN D. ROOSEVELT, *Address, 1932.*

The whole tendency over many years has been to view the interstate commerce clause in the light of present-day civilization, although it was written into the Constitution in the horse-and-buggy days of the eighteenth century.

F. D. ROOSEVELT, at a press conference at the White House, May 31, 1935.

With confidence in our armed forces, with unbounding determination of our people, we will gain the inevitable triumph. So help us God.

F. D. ROOSEVELT—*Speech,* December 8, 1941.

We have room but for one Language here and that is the English Language, for we intend to see that the crucible turns our people out as Americans of

American nationality and not as dwellers in a polyglot boarding-house.

THEODORE ROOSEVELT.

The American people never carry an umbrella. They prepare to walk in eternal sunshine.

ALFRED E. SMITH, 1931.

Gigantic daughter of the West
We drink to thee across the flood. . . .
For art not thou of English blood?

TENNYSON—*Hands All Round.*

I pledge allegiance to the flag of the United States and to the Republic for which it stands, one nation, indivisible, with liberty and justice for all.

JAMES B. UPHAM and FRANCIS BELLAMY—*Pledge to the Flag.*

So it's home again, and home again,
America for me!
My heart is turning home again, and
I long to be
In the land of youth and freedom beyond the ocean bars,
Where the air is full of sunshine, and
the flag is full of stars.

HENRY VAN DYKE—*America for Me.*

I was born an American; I live an American; I shall die an American.

DANIEL WEBSTER.

Lo! body and soul!—this land!
Mighty Manhattan, with spires, and
The sparkling and hurrying tides, and
the ships;
The varied and ample land—the South
And the North in the light—Ohio's
shores, and flashing Missouri,
And ever the far-spreading prairies,
covered with grass and corn.

WALT WHITMAN.

American liberty is a religion. It is a thing of the spirit. It is an aspiration on the part of the people for not only a free life but a better life.

WENDELL L. WILLKIE—*Speech, 1941.*

Some Americans need hyphens in their names, because only part of them has come over; but when the whole man has come over, heart and thought and all, the hyphen drops of its own weight out of his name.

WOODROW WILSON.

AMUSEMENT

If those who are the enemies of innocent amusements had the direction of the world, they would take away the spring, and youth, the former from the year, the latter from human life.

BALZAC.

I am a great friend to public amusements; for they keep people from vice.

SAMUEL JOHNSON—*Boswell's Life of Johnson.*

You can't live on amusement. It is the froth on water,—an inch deep, and then the mud!

GEORGE MACDONALD.

When I play with my cat, who knows whether I do not make her more sport than she makes me?

MONTAIGNE.

The mind ought sometimes to be amused, that it may the better return to thought, and to itself.

PHAEDRUS.

The real character of a man is found out by his amusements.

SIR JOSHUA REYNOLDS.

ANCESTRY

Those who depend on the merits of their ancestors may be said to search in the roots of the tree for those fruits which the branches ought to produce.

BARROW.

Some decent regulated pre-eminence, some preference (not exclusive appropriation) given to birth, is neither unnatural, nor unjust, nor impolitic.

BURKE—*Reflections on the Revolution in France.*

A degenerate nobleman, or one that is proud of his birth, is like a turnip. There is nothing good of him but that which is underground.

SAMUEL BUTLER—*Characters.*

Born in the garret, in the kitchen bred.

BYRON—*A Sketch.*

Great families of yesterday we show,
And lords whose parents were the
Lord knows who.

DANIEL DEFOE—*The True-Born Englishman.*

My father was a creole, his father a Negro, and his father a monkey; my family, it seems, begins where yours left off.

ALEXANDER DUMAS, PÈRE, on being asked "Who was your father?"

Breed is stronger than pasture.

GEORGE ELIOT.

Say, when the ground our father
Adam till'd,
And mother Eve the humble distaff
held,
Who then his pedigree presumed to
trace,
Or challenged the prerogative of
place?

GROBIANUS.

The brave are born from the brave and good. In steers and in horses is to be found the excellence of their sires; nor do savage eagles produce a peaceful dove.

HORACE—*Carmina.*

There is no king who has not had a slave among his ancestors, and no slave who has not had a king among his.

HELEN KELLER—*Story of My Life.*

People who take no pride in the noble achievements of remote ancestors will never achieve anything worthy to be remembered with pride by remote descendants.

MACAULAY.

Birth and ancestry, and that which we have not ourselves achieved, we can scarcely call our own.

OVID—*Metamorphoses.*

He who boasts of his descent, praises the deeds of another.

SENECA.

Our ancestors are very good kind of folks; but they are the last people I should choose to have a visiting acquaintance with.

SHERIDAN—*The Rivals.*

The Smiths never had any arms, and have invariably sealed their letters with their thumbs.

SYDNEY SMITH—*Lady Holland's Memoir.*

Whoever serves his country well has no need of ancestors.

VOLTAIRE.

Rank is a farce: if people Fools will
be
A Scavenger and King's the same to
me.

JOHN WOLCOT—*Peter's Prophecy.*

ANGEL

Like those of angels, short and far between.

ROBERT BLAIR—*The Grave.*

As the moths around a taper,
As the bees around a rose,
As the gnats around a vapour,
So the spirits group and close
Round about a holy childhood, as if
drinking its repose.

E. B. BROWNING—*A Child Asleep.*

What is the question now placed before society with the glib assurance which to me is most astonishing? That question is this: Is man an ape or an angel? I, my lord, I am on the side of the angels. I repudiate with indignation and abhorrence those newfangled theories.

DISRAELI—*Speech at Oxford Diocesan Conference.*

Be not forgetful to entertain strangers, for thereby some have entertained angels unawares.

Hebrews. XIII. 2.

Men would be angels, angels would be gods.

POPE—*Essay on Man.*

In Heaven an angel is nobody in particular.

GEORGE BERNARD SHAW.

What know we of the Blest above
But that they sing, and that they love?
WORDSWORTH—*Scene on the Lake of Brienz.*

ANGER

Men often make up in wrath what they want in reason.
W. R. ALGER.

Anger makes dull men witty, but it keeps them poor.
BACON.

Nursing her wrath to keep it warm.
BURNS—*Tam o'Shanter.*

An angry man opens his mouth and shuts up his eyes.
CATO.

When angry, count four; when very angry, swear.
SAMUEL L. CLEMENS—*Pudd'nhead Wilson.*

Heaven hath no rage like love to hatred turned, nor hell a fury like a woman scorned.
CONGREVE.

Beware the fury of a patient man.
DRYDEN—*Absalom and Achitophel.*

Anger is momentary madness, so control your passion or it will control you.
HORACE—*Epistles.*

Anger blows out the lamp of the mind. In the examination of a great and important question, every one should be serene, slow-pulsed, and calm.
INGERSOLL.

I never work better than when I am inspired by anger. When I am angry I can write, pray, and preach well; for then my whole temperament is quickened, my understanding sharpened, and all mundane vexations and temptations depart.
LUTHER.

He that is slow to anger is better than the mighty; and he that ruleth his spirit than he that taketh a city.
Proverbs. XVI. 32.

Anger begins with folly, and ends with repentance.
PYTHAGORAS.

Anger wishes that all mankind had only one neck; love, that it had only one heart; grief, two tear-glands; and pride, two bent knees.
JEAN PAUL RICHTER—*Flower, Fruit and Thorn Pieces.*

He that will be angry for anything will be angry for nothing.
SALLUST.

Anger's my meat; I sup upon myself,
And so shall starve with feeding.
SHAKESPEARE—*Coriolanus.* Act IV. Sc. 2.

Touch me with noble anger!
And let not women's weapons, water drops,
Stain my man's cheeks.
SHAKESPEARE—*King Lear.* Act II. Sc. 4.

Give not reins to your inflamed passions; take time and a little delay; impetuosity manages all things badly.
STATIUS—*Thebais.*

Our passions are like convulsion fits, which make us stronger for the time, but leave us weaker forever after.
SWIFT.

ANIMALS

Tiger, tiger, burning bright
In the forests of the night,
What immortal hand or eye,
Could frame thy fearful symmetry?
WILLIAM BLAKE—*The Tiger.*

Animals are such agreeable friends; they ask no questions, pass no criticisms.
GEORGE ELIOT.

If 't were not for my cat and dog,
I think I could not live.
EBENEZER ELLIOTT.

A mule has neither pride of ancestry nor hope of posterity.
ROBERT G. INGERSOLL.

The ox knoweth his owner, and the ass his master's crib.
Isaiah. I. 3.

Who drives fat oxen should himself be fat.

SAMUEL JOHNSON.

As an ox goeth to the slaughter.

Proverbs. VII. 22. *Jeremiah*. XI. 19.

Men show their superiority inside; animals, outside.

Russian Proverb.

There is in every animal's eye a dim image and gleam of humanity, a flash of strange light through which their life looks out and up to our great mystery of command over them, and claims the fellowship of the creature if not of the soul.

RUSKIN.

ANTICIPATION

Nothing is so good as it seems beforehand.

GEORGE ELIOT.

All earthly delights are sweeter in expectation than enjoyment; but all spiritual pleasures more in fruition than expectation.

FELLTHAM.

He who foresees calamities suffers them twice over.

PORTEUS.

Anticipation and Hope are born twins.

ROUSSEAU.

There is nothing so wretched or foolish as to anticipate misfortunes. What madness is it in expecting evil before it arrives?

SENECA.

It is expectation makes a blessing dear; heaven were not heaven if we knew what it were.

SUCKLING.

We expect everything, and are prepared for nothing.

MME. SWETCHINE.

ANTIQUITY

I do by no means advise you to throw away your time in ransacking, like a dull antiquarian, the minute and unimportant parts of remote and fabulous times. Let blockheads read what blockheads wrote.

CHESTERFIELD.

How cunningly Nature hides every wrinkle of her inconceivable antiquity under roses and violets and morning dew!

EMERSON.

Antiquity! I like its ruins better than its reconstructions.

JOUBERT.

Let others praise ancient times; I am glad that I was born in these.

OVID.

Remove not the ancient landmark.

Proverbs. XXII. 28; XXIII. 10.

ANXIETY

It is not work that kills men; it is worry. Work is healthy; you can hardly put more upon a man than he can bear. Worry is rust upon the blade. It is not the revolution that destroys the machinery, but the friction. Fear secretes acids; but love and trust are sweet juices.

HENRY WARD BEECHER.

Better to be despised for too anxious apprehensions than ruined by too confident a security.

BURKE.

Anxiety never yet successfully bridged over any chasm.

RUFFINI.

APOLOGY

No sensible person ever made an apology.

EMERSON.

Apology is only egotism wrong side out.

HOLMES.

APPAREL

Dresses for breakfasts, and dinners, and balls.
Dresses to sit in, and stand in, and walk in;

Dresses to dance in, and flirt in, and talk in,
Dresses in which to do nothing at all;
Dresses for Winter, Spring, Summer, and Fall;
All of them different in color and shape.
Silk, muslin, and lace, velvet, satin, and crape,
Brocade and broadcloth, and other material,
Quite as expensive and much more ethereal.

WILLIAM ALLEN BUTLER—*Nothing to Wear.*

Beauty when most unclothed is clothed best.

PHINEAS FLETCHER—*Sicelides.*

It's like sending them ruffles, when wanting a shirt.

GOLDSMITH—*The Haunch of Venison.*

Old Grimes is dead, that good old man,
We ne'er shall see him more;
He used to wear a long black coat
All button'd down before.

ALBERT G. GREENE—*Old Grimes.*

It is not linen you're wearing out,
But human creatures' lives.

HOOD—*Song of the Shirt.*

Apes are apes though clothed in scarlet.

BEN JONSON—*Poetaster.*

The soul of this man is his clothes.

SHAKESPEARE—*All's Well That Ends Well.* Act II. Sc. 5.

Costly thy habit as thy purse can buy,
But not express'd in fancy; rich, not gaudy;
For the apparel oft proclaims the man.

SHAKESPEARE—*Hamlet.* Act I. Sc. 3.

She wears her clothes as if they were thrown on her with a pitchfork.

SWIFT—*Polite Conversation.*

APPARITION

I can call spirits from the vasty deep.
Why, so can I, or so can any man;
But will they come when you do call for them?

SHAKESPEARE—*Henry IV.* Pt. I. Act III. Sc. 1.

A dagger of the mind, a false creation,
Proceeding from the heat-oppressed brain?

SHAKESPEARE—*Macbeth.* Act. II. Sc. 1.

APPEARANCE

O wad some power the giftie gie us
To see oursel's as ithers see us!

BURNS—*To a Louse.*

All that glisters is not gold.

CERVANTES—*Don Quixote.*

Polished brass will pass upon more people than rough gold.

CHESTERFIELD.

Handsome is that handsome does.

FIELDING—*Tom Jones.*

By outward show let's not be cheated.
An ass should like an ass be treated.

GAY—*Fables.*

Things are seldom what they seem,
Skim milk masquerades as cream.

W. S. GILBERT—*H. M. S. Pinafore.*

An emperor in his nightcap will not meet with half the respect of an emperor with a crown.

GOLDSMITH.

We take less pains to be happy than to appear so.

LA ROCHEFOUCAULD.

Even when the bird walks one feels that it has wings.

LEMIERRE.

Men in general judge more from appearances than from reality. All men have eyes, but few have the gift of penetration.

MACHIAVELLI.

Whited sepulchres, which indeed appear beautiful outward, but are within full of dead men's bones.

MATTHEW. XXIII. 27.

To succeed in the world, we must be foolish in appearance, but really wise.

MONTESQUIEU.

The dress does not make the monk.
RABELAIS—*Prologue.*

She looks as if butter wouldn't melt in her mouth.
SWIFT—*Polite Conversation.*

APPETITE

My soul tasted that heavenly food, which gives new appetite while it satiates.
DANTE—*Purgatorio.*

All philosophy in two words,—sustain and abstain.
EPICTETUS.

The chief pleasure in eating does not consist in costly seasoning or exquisite flavor, but in yourself. Seek you for sauce in sweating.
HORACE.

Govern well thy appetite, lest Sin
Surprise thee, and her black attendant
Death.
MILTON—*Paradise Lost.*

My appetite comes to me while eating.
MONTAIGNE—*Essays.*

Put a knife to thy throat, if thou be a man given to appetite.
Proverbs. XXIII. 2.

When the belly is empty, the body becomes spirit; when it is full, the spirit becomes body.
SAADI.

Animals feed, man eats; the man of intellect alone knows how to eat.
BRILLAT SAVARIN.

If you are surprised at the number of our maladies, count our cooks.
SENECA.

Now good digestion wait on appetite,
And health on both!
SHAKESPEARE—*Macbeth.* Act III. Sc. 4.

APPLAUSE

The echo of a platitude.
BIERCE—*The Devil's Dictionary.*

Applause is the spur of noble minds, the end and aim of weak ones.
COLTON—*Lacon.*

O Popular Applause! what heart of man
Is proof against thy sweet, seducing charms?
COWPER—*Task.*

The silence that accepts merit as the most natural thing in the world, is the highest applause.
EMERSON.

The applause of a single human being is of great consequence.
SAMUEL JOHNSON—*Boswell's Life of Johnson.*

APPRECIATION

Contemporaries appreciate the man rather than the merit; posterity will regard the merit rather than the man.
BUXTON.

It is a matter of the simplest demonstration, that no man can be really appreciated but by his equal or superior.
RUSKIN.

By appreciation we make excellence in others our own property.
VOLTAIRE.

APRIL

Oh, to be in England
Now that April's there.
ROBERT BROWNING—*Home Thoughts from Abroad.*

The April winds are magical,
And thrill our tuneful frames;
The garden-walks are passional
To bachelors and dames.
EMERSON—*April.*

Oh, the lovely fickleness of an April day!
W. H. GIBSON—*Pastoral Days.*

Make me over, Mother April,
When the sap begins to stir!
When thy flowery hand delivers
All the mountain-prisoned rivers,
And thy great heart beats and quivers,
To revive the days that were.
RICHARD HOVEY—*April.*

The first of April, some do say
Is set apart for All Fools' day;
But why the people call it so,
Nor I, nor they themselves, do know.
Poor Robin's Almanac.

Sweet April showers
Do bring May flowers.
TUSSER—*Five Hundred Points of Good Husbandry.*

Again the blackbirds sing; the streams
Wake, laughing, from their winter dreams,
And tremble in the April showers
The tassels of the maple flowers.
WHITTIER—*The Singer.*

ARCADIA

I, too, was born in Arcadia.
GOETHE.

ARCHITECTURE

Houses are built to live in, not to look on; therefore, let use be preferred before uniformity, except where both may be had.
BACON—*Essays.*

Old houses mended,
Cost little less than new, before they're ended.
COLLEY CIBBER.

Earth proudly wears the Parthenon
As the best gem upon her zone.
EMERSON—*The Problem.*

The hand that rounded Peter's dome
And groined the aisles of Christian Rome,
Wrought in a sad sincerity:
Himself from God he could not free;
He builded better than he knew;
The conscious stone to beauty grew.
EMERSON—*The Problem.*

Architecture is frozen music.
GOETHE.

Ah, to build, to build!
That is the noblest of all the arts.
LONGFELLOW—*Michelangelo.*

No person who is not a great sculptor or painter, *can* be an architect. If he is not a sculptor or painter, he can only be a *builder.*
RUSKIN—*True and Beautiful.*

ARGUMENT

Arguments out of a pretty mouth are unanswerable.
ADDISON.

Many can argue; not many converse.
ALCOTT.

Wise men argue causes, and fools decide them.
ANACHARSIS.

When Bishop Berkeley said, "there was no matter,"
And proved it—'twas no matter what he said.
BYRON—*Don Juan.*

Neither irony nor sarcasm is argument.
RUFUS CHOATE.

Silence is less injurious than a weak reply.
COLTON.

I am bound to furnish my antagonists with arguments, but not with comprehension.
DISRAELI.

How agree the kettle and the earthen pot together?
Ecclesiasticus. XIII. 2.

There is no arguing with Johnson; for if his pistol misses fire, he knocks you down with the butt end of it.
GOLDSMITH.

Be calm in arguing; for fierceness makes
Error a fault, and truth discourtesy.
HERBERT—*Temple.*

Strong and bitter words indicate a weak cause.
VICTOR HUGO.

Insolence is not logic; epithets are the arguments of malice.
INGERSOLL.

Myself when young did eagerly frequent
Doctor and Saint, and heard great argument

About it and about: but evermore
Came out by the same door wherein
I went.

OMAR KHAYYÁM—*Rubaiyat.*

In arguing one should meet serious pleading with humor, and humor with serious pleading.

GORGIAS LEONTINUS.

There is no good in arguing with the inevitable. The only argument available with an east wind is to put on your overcoat.

LOWELL—*Democracy.*

Agreeing to differ.

OVID—*Metamorphoses.*

One single positive weighs more,
You know, than negatives a score.

PRIOR—*Epistle to Fleetwood Shepherd.*

The first the Retort Courteous; the second the Quip Modest; the third the Reply Churlish; the fourth the Reproof Valiant; the fifth the Countercheck Quarrelsome; the sixth the Lie with Circumstance; the seventh the Lie Direct.

SHAKESPEARE—*As You Like It.* Act V. Sc. 4.

For they are yet but ear-kissing arguments.

SHAKESPEARE—*King Lear.* Act II. Sc. 1.

When people agree with me I always feel that I must be wrong.

OSCAR WILDE—*The Critic as an Artist.*

ART

What is art? Nature concentrated.

BALZAC.

Art is I; science is we.

CLAUDE BERNARD.

No work of art is worth the bones of a Pomeranian Grenadier.

BISMARCK.

Nature hath made one world, and art another.

SIR THOMAS BROWNE.

Art for art's sake.

VICTOR COUSIN.

Art, as far as it is able, follows nature, as a pupil imitates his master; thus your art must be, as it were, God's grandchild.

DANTE—*Inferno.*

There is an art of reading, as well as an art of thinking, and an art of writing.

ISAAC D'ISRAELI—*Literary Character.*

All passes, Art alone
Enduring stays to us;
The Bust out-lasts the throne,—
The coin, Tiberius.

AUSTIN DOBSON—*Ars Victrix.*

Art is the stored honey of the human soul, gathered on wings of misery and travail.

THEODORE DREISER—*Life, Art and America.*

Every artist was first an amateur.

EMERSON.

Many persons feel art, some understand it; but few both feel and understand it.

HILLARD.

A picture is a poem without words.

HORACE.

Painters and poets have equal license in regard to everything.

HORACE.

Art hath an enemy called ignorance.

BEN JONSON.

We have learned to whittle the Eden Tree to the shape of a surplice peg,
We have learned to bottle our parents twain in the yelk of an addled egg.
We know that the tail must wag the dog, for the horse is drawn by the cart,
But the devil whoops, as he whooped of old;
It's clever, but is it art?

KIPLING—*The Conundrum of the Workshops.*

Ah! would that we could at once paint with the eyes! In the long way, from

the eye, through the arm to the pencil, how much is lost!
LESSING.

Art is the child of Nature; yes,
Her darling child in whom we trace
The features of the mother's face,
Her aspect and her attitude.
LONGFELLOW—*Keramos.*

Dead he is not, but departed,—for the artist never dies.
LONGFELLOW—*Nuremburg.*

Art does not imitate, but interpret.
MAZZINI.

Great art is as irrational as great music. It is mad with its own loveliness.
GEORGE JEAN NATHAN—*House of Satan.*

Art is more godlike than science. Science discovers; art creates.
JOHN OPIE.

Art is a kind of illness.
GIACOMO PUCCINI.

The perfection of art is to conceal art.
QUINTILIAN.

Art is indeed not the bread but the wine of life.
JEAN PAUL RICHTER.

Art is difficult, transient is her reward.
SCHILLER.

ASSOCIATE

My friends! There are no friends.
ARISTOTLE.

Constant companionship is not enjoyable, any more than constant eating. We sit too long at the table of friendship, when we outsit our appetites for each other's thoughts.
BOVEE.

When a dove begins to associate with crows its feathers remain white but its heart grows black.
German Proverb.

If you always live with those who are lame, you will yourself learn to limp.
Latin Proverb.

He that walketh with wise men shall be wise.
SOLOMON.

ASTRONOMY

The narrow sectarian cannot read astronomy with impunity. The creeds of his church shrivel like dried leaves at the door of the observatory.
EMERSON.

Astronomy is one of the sublimest fields of human investigation. The mind that grasps its facts and principles receives something of the enlargement and grandeur belonging to the science itself. It is a quickener of devotion.
HORACE MANN.

At night astronomers agree.
PRIOR—*Phillis's Age.*

ATHEISM

I am an atheist, thank God!
ANONYMOUS.

I don't believe in God because I don't believe in Mother Goose.
CLARENCE DARROW.

The fool hath said in his heart, There is no God.
Psalm CIV. 1.

O Reader! hast thou ever stood to see
The Holly-tree?
The eye that contemplates it well perceives
Its glossy leaves
Ordered by an Intelligence so wise
As might confound the Atheist's sophistries.
SOUTHEY—*The Holly-Tree.*

That the universe was formed by a fortuitous concourse of atoms, I will no more believe than that the accidental jumbling of the alphabet would fall into a most ingenious treatise of philosophy.
SWIFT.

By night an atheist half believes in God.
YOUNG.

AUDACITY

Fear made the gods; audacity has made kings.
CRÉBILLON, *during French Revolution.*

Audacity, more audacity, always audacity.
DANTON, *during French Revolution.*

Fortune favors the audacious.
ERASMUS.

AUTHORITY

I appeal unto Caesar.
Acts. XXV. 11.

Authority intoxicates,
And makes mere sots of magistrates;
The fumes of it invade the brain,
And make men giddy, proud, and vain.
BUTLER—*Miscellaneous Thoughts.*

All authority belongs to the people.
JEFFERSON.

Thou hast seen a farmer's dog bark at a beggar,
And the creature run from the cur:
There, thou might'st behold the great image of authority;
A dog's obeyed in office.
SHAKESPEARE—*King Lear.* Act IV. Sc. 6.

Those he commands, move only in command,
Nothing in love: now does he feel his title
Hang loose about him, like a giant's robe
Upon a dwarfish thief.
SHAKESPEARE—*Macbeth.* Act V. Sc. 2.

But man, proud man,
Drest in a little brief authority,
Most ignorant of what he's most assur'd,
His glassy essence, like an angry ape,
Plays such fantastic tricks before high heaven,
As make the angels weep.
SHAKESPEARE—*Measure for Measure.* Act II. Sc. 2.

AUTHORSHIP

Write to the mind and heart, and let the ear
Glean after what it can.
BAILEY—*Festus.*

But words are things, and a small drop of ink,
Falling, like dew, upon a thought produces
That which makes thousands, perhaps millions think.
BYRON—*Don Juan.*

Dear authors! suit your topics to your strength,
And ponder well your subject, and its length;
Nor lift your load, before you're quite aware
What weight your shoulders will, or will not, bear.
BYRON—*Hints from Horace.*

The pen is the tongue of the mind.
CERVANTES—*Don Quixote.*

Apt Alliteration's artful aid.
CHURCHILL — *The Prophecy of Famine.*

When I want to read a book I write one.
DISRAELI.

The author who speaks about his own books is almost as bad as a mother who talks about her own children.
DISRAELI.

The most original modern authors are not so because they advance what is new, but simply because they know how to put what they have to say, as if it had never been said before.
GOETHE.

Written with a pen of iron, and with the point of a diamond.
Jeremiah. XVII. 1.

An incurable itch for scribbling takes possession of many, and grows inveterate in their insane breasts.
JUVENAL—*Satires.*

A man of moderate Understanding, thinks he Writes divinely: A man of

good Understanding, thinks he writes reasonably.
La Bruyère.

He who writes prose builds his temple to Fame in rubble; he who writes verses builds it in granite.
Bulwer-Lytton.

You do not publish your own verses, Laelius; you criticise mine. Pray cease to criticise mine, or else publish your own.
Martial.

The ink of the scholar is more sacred than the blood of the martyr.
Mohammed—*Tribute to Reason.*

It is the rust we value, not the gold;
Authors, like coins, grow dear as they grow old.
Pope—*Second Book of Horace.*

E'en copious Dryden wanted, or forgot,
The last and greatest art—the art to blot.
Pope—*Second Book of Horace.*

Let him be kept from paper, pen, and ink;
So may he cease to write, and learn to think.
Prior.

Write till your ink be dry, and with your tears
Moist it again, and frame some feeling line
That may discover such integrity.
Shakespeare—*Two Gentlemen of Verona.* Act III. Sc. 2.

Ah, ye knights of the pen! May honour be your shield, and truth tip your lances! Be gentle to all gentle people. Be modest to women. Be tender to children. And as for the Ogre Humbug, out sword, and have at him!
Thackeray—*Roundabout Papers.*

AUTUMN

O Autumn, laden with fruit, and stained
With the blood of the grape, pass not, but sit
Beneath my shady roof; there thou mayest rest
And tune thy jolly voice to my fresh pipe,
And all the daughters of the year shall dance!
Sing now the lusty song of fruits and flowers.
Blake—*To Autumn.*

The melancholy days have come, the saddest of the year,
Of wailing winds, and naked woods, and meadows brown and sear.
Bryant — *The Death of the Flowers.*

Yellow, mellow, ripened days,
Sheltered in a golden coating;
O'er the dreamy, listless haze,
White and dainty cloudlets floating;
Winking at the blushing trees,
And the sombre, furrowed fallow;
Smiling at the airy ease,
Of the southward flying swallow.
Sweet and smiling are thy ways,
Beauteous, golden Autumn days.
Will Carleton—*Autumn Days.*

The year's in the wane;
There is nothing adoring;
The night has no eve,
And the day has no morning;
Cold winter gives warning!
Hood—*Autumn.*

Every season hath its pleasures;
Spring may boast her flowery prime,
Yet the vineyard's ruby treasures
Brighten Autumn's sob'rer time.
Moore—*Spring and Autumn.*

O, it sets my heart a clickin' like the tickin' of a clock,
When the frost is on the punkin and the fodder's in the shock.
James Whitcomb Riley—*When the Frost Is on the Punkin.*

Cold autumn, wan with wrath of wind and rain,
Saw pass a soul sweet as the sovereign tune
That death smote silent when he smote again.
Swinburne—*Autumn and Winter.*

AVARICE

If you wish to remove avarice you must remove its mother, luxury.
CICERO—*De Oratore.*

Avarice has ruined more men than prodigality, and the blindest thoughtlessness of expenditure has not destroyed so many fortunes as the calculating but insatiable lust of accumulation.
COLTON.

Poverty wants some, luxury many, and avarice all things.
COWLEY.

Avarice is generally the last passion of those lives of which the first part has been squandered in pleasure, and the second devoted to ambition.
SAMUEL JOHNSON.

The avaricious man is kind to no person, but he is most unkind to himself.
JOHN KYRLE.

That disease
Of which all old men sicken, avarice.
THOMAS MIDDLETON—*The Roaring Girl.*

In plain truth, it is not want, but rather abundance, that creates avarice.
MONTAIGNE.

The lust of avarice has so totally seized upon mankind that their wealth seems rather to possess them than they possess their wealth.
PLINY.

AWKWARDNESS

Men lose more conquests by their own awkwardness than by any virtue in the woman.
NINON DE LENCLOS.

God may forgive sins, he said, but awkwardness has no forgiveness in heaven or earth.
EMERSON—*Society and Solitude.*

B

BABYHOOD

Oh those little, those little blue shoes!
Those shoes that no little feet use.
Oh, the price were high
That those shoes would buy,
Those little blue unused shoes!
WILLIAM C. BENNETT—*Baby's Shoes.*

Sweet babe, in thy face
Soft desires I can trace,
Secret joys and secret smiles,
Little pretty infant wiles.
WILLIAM BLAKE—*A Cradle Song.*

He smiles, and sleeps!—sleep on
And smile, thou little, young inheritor
Of a world scarce less young: sleep on and smile!
Thine are the hours and days when both are cheering
And innocent!
BYRON—*Cain.*

He is so little to be so large!
Why, a train of cars, or a whale-back barge
Couldn't carry the freight
Of the monstrous weight
Of all of his qualities, good and great.
And tho' one view is as good as another,
Don't take my word for it. Ask his mother!
EDMUND VANCE COOKE—*The Intruder.*

What is the little one thinking about?
Very wonderful things, no doubt;
Unwritten history!
Unfathomed mystery!
Yet he laughs and cries, and eats and drinks,
And chuckles and crows, and nods and winks,
As if his head were as full of kinks
And curious riddles as any sphinx!
J. G. HOLLAND—*Bitter-Sweet.*

He seemed a cherub who had lost his way
And wandered hither, so his stay

With us was short, and 'twas most meet
That he should be no delver in earth's clod,
Nor need to pause and cleanse his feet
To stand before his God:
O blest word—Evermore!
LOWELL—*Threnodia.*

Where did you come from, baby dear?
Out of the Everywhere into here.
GEORGE MACDONALD—*Song in "At the Back of the North Wind."*

Rock-a-bye-baby on the tree top,
When the wind blows the cradle will rock,
When the bough bends the cradle will fall,
Down comes the baby, cradle and all.
Old nursery rhyme.

As living jewels dropped unstained from heaven.
POLLOCK.

Out of the mouth of babes and sucklings hast thou ordained strength.
Psalms. VIII. 2.

Sweetest li'l feller, everybody knows;
Dunno what to call him, but he's mighty lak' a rose;
Lookin' at his mammy wid eyes so shiny blue
Mek' you think that Heav'n is comin' clost ter you.
FRANK L. STANTON—*Mighty Lak' a Rose.*

A little soul scarce fledged for earth
Takes wing with heaven again for goal,
Even while we hailed as fresh from birth
A little soul.
SWINBURNE—*A Baby's Death.*

Beat upon mine, little heart! beat, beat!
Beat upon mine! you are mine, my sweet!
All mine from your pretty blue eyes to your feet,
My sweet!
TENNYSON—*Romney's Remorse.*

A babe in a house is a well-spring of pleasure, a messenger of peace and love, a resting-place for innocence on earth, a link between angels and men.
TUPPER.

Hush, my dear, lie still and slumber,
Holy angels guard thy bed!
Heavenly blessings without number
Gently falling on thy head.
ISAAC WATTS—*A Cradle Hymn.*

BALLAD

The farmer's daughter hath soft brown hair
(*Butter and eggs and a pound of cheese*)
And I met with a ballad, I can't say where,
That wholly consisted of lines like these.
CHARLES S. CALVERLY—*Ballad.*

I knew a very wise man that believed that . . . if a man were permitted to make all the ballads, he need not care who should make the laws of a nation.
ANDREW FLETCHER—Quoting the Earl of Cromarty. *Letters to the Marquis of Montrose.*

I have a passion for ballads. . . . They are the gypsy children of song, born under green hedgerows in the leafy lanes and bypaths of literature,—in the genial Summertime.
LONGFELLOW—*Hyperion.*

For a ballad's a thing you expect to find lies in.
SAMUEL LOVER—*Paddy Blake's Echo.*

BANISHMENT

The bitter bread of banishment.
SHAKESPEARE—*Richard II.*

No, my good lord: banish Peto, banish Bardolph, banish Poins; but for sweet Jack Falstaff, kind Jack Falstaff, true Jack Falstaff, valiant Jack Falstaff, and therefore more valiant, being as he is old Jack Falstaff, banish not him thy

Harry's company: banish plump Jack and banish all the world.
SHAKESPEARE—*Henry IV*. Pt. I. Act II.

BEAUTY

Beauty soon grows familiar to the lover,
Fades in his eye, and palls upon the sense.
ADDISON—*Cato*.

What is lovely never dies,
But passes into other loveliness,
Star-dust, or sea-foam, flower or winged air.
T. B. ALDRICH—*A Shadow of the Night*.

The beautiful are never desolate;
But some one always loves them—God or man.
If man abandons, God himself takes them.
BAILEY—*Festus*.

The essence of all beauty, I call love,
The attribute, the evidence, and end,
The consummation to the inward sense
Of beauty apprehended from without,
I still call love.
E. B. BROWNING—*Sword Glare*.

Thou who hast
The fatal gift of beauty.
BYRON—*Childe Harold*.

She walks in beauty like the night
Of cloudless climes and starry skies;
And all that's best of dark and bright
Meet in her aspect and her eyes:
Thus mellowed to that tender light
Which heaven to gaudy day denies.
BYRON—*She Walks in Beauty*.

Beauty is the lover's gift.
CONGREVE—*The Way of the World*.

When beauty fires the blood, how love exalts the mind!
DRYDEN—*Cymon and Iphigenia*.

Each ornament about her seemly lies,
By curious chance, or careless art composed.
EDWARD FAIRFAX—*Godfrey of Bouillon*.

The dimple that thy chin contains has beauty in its round,
That never has been fathomed yet by myriad thoughts profound.
HAFIS—*Odes*.

There's beauty all around our paths, if but our watchful eyes
Can trace it 'midst familiar things, and through their lowly guise.
FELICIA D. HEMANS—*Our Daily Paths*.

Nothing is beautiful from every point of view.
HORACE—*Carmina*.

The beautiful attracts the beautiful.
LEIGH HUNT.

Rare is the union of beauty and purity.
JUVENAL—*Satires*.

A thing of beauty is a joy forever;
Its loveliness increases; it will never
Pass into nothingness; but still will keep
A bower quiet for us, and a sleep
Full of sweet dreams, and health, and quiet breathing.
KEATS—*Endymion*.

Beauty is truth, truth beauty.
KEATS—*Ode on a Grecian Urn*.

The common foible of women who have been handsome is to forget that they are no longer so.
LA ROCHEFOUCAULD.

That which is striking and beautiful is not always good, but that which is good is always beautiful.
NINON DE LENCLOS.

Blue were her eyes as the fairy-flax,
Her cheeks like the dawn of day,
And her bosom white as the hawthorn buds,
That ope in the month of May.
LONGFELLOW—*Wreck of the Hesperus*.

O, thou art fairer than the evening air
Clad in the beauty of a thousand stars.
MARLOWE—*Dr. Faustus*.

Beauty is the first present Nature gives to women, and the first it takes away.
MÉRÉ.

Too fair to worship, too divine to love.
HENRY HART MILMAN—*Belvedere Apollo.*

She fair, divinely fair, fit love for gods.
MILTON—*Paradise Lost.*

Not more the rose, the queen of flowers,
Outblushes all the bloom of bower,
Than she unrivall'd grace discloses;
The sweetest rose, where all are roses.
MOORE—*Odes of Anacreon.*

A pleasing countenance is no slight advantage.
OVID.

Beauty and wisdom are rarely conjoined.
PETRONIUS ARBITER—*Satyricon.*

When the candles are out all women are fair.
PLUTARCH—*Conjugal Precepts.*

Beauties in vain their pretty eyes may roll;
Charms strike the sight, but merit wins the soul.
POPE—*Rape of the Lock.*

For, when with beauty we can virtue join,
We paint the semblance of a form divine.
PRIOR—*To the Countess of Oxford.*

Beauty is power; a smile is its sword.
CHARLES READE.

Remember that the most beautiful things in the world are the most useless; peacocks and lilies, for instance.
RUSKIN.

The saying that beauty is but skin deep is but a skin deep saying.
RUSKIN—*Personal Beauty.*

A handsome woman is a jewel; a good woman is a treasure.
SAADI.

Beauty is a fairy; sometimes she hides herself in a flower-cup, or under a leaf, or creeps into the old ivy, and plays hide-and-seek with the sunbeams, or haunts some ruined spot, or laughs out of a bright young face.
G. A. SALA.

The beauty that addresses itself to the eyes is only the spell of the moment; the eye of the body is not always that of the soul.
GEORGE SAND.

What is really beautiful needs no adorning. We do not grind down the pearl upon a polishing stone.
SATAKA.

It is only through the morning gate of the beautiful that you can penetrate into the realm of knowledge. That which we feel here as beauty we shall one day know as truth.
SCHILLER.

Truth exists for the wise, beauty for the feeling heart.
SCHILLER—*Don Carlos.*

Beauty is such a fleeting blossom, how can wisdom rely upon its momentary delight?
SENECA.

Beauty provoketh thieves sooner than gold.
SHAKESPEARE—*As You Like It.* Act I. Sc. 3.

Of Nature's gifts thou may'st with lilies boast
And with the half-blown rose.
SHAKESPEARE—*King John.* Act III. Sc. 1.

Beauty doth varnish age.
SHAKESPEARE—*Love's Labour's Lost.* Act IV. Sc. 3.

Beauty is a witch,
Against whose charms faith melteth into blood.
SHAKESPEARE—*Much Ado About Nothing.* Act II. Sc. 1.

Beauty is but a vain and doubtful good;
A shining gloss that fadeth suddenly;
A flower that dies when first it 'gins to bud;
A brittle glass that's broken presently;
A doubtful good, a gloss, a glass, a flower,
Lost, faded, broken, dead within an hour.
SHAKESPEARE—*The Passionate Pilgrim.*

Thoughtless of beauty, she was Beauty's self.
THOMSON—*Seasons.*

All the beauty of the world, 'tis but skin deep.
RALPH VENNING—*Orthodox Paradoxes.*

Trust not too much to an enchanting face.
VERGIL.

True beauty dwells in deep retreats,
Whose veil is unremoved
Till heart with heart in concord beats,
And the lover is beloved.
WORDSWORTH—*Let Other Bards of Angels Sing.*

BED

Matthew, Mark, Luke and John,
The bed be blest that I lye on.
THOMAS ADY—*A Cradle in the Dark.*

In bed we laugh, in bed we cry;
And born in bed, in bed we die;
The near approach a bed may show
Of human bliss to human woe.
ISAAC DE BENSERADE.

As you make your bed you must lie in it.
English Proverb.

Rise with the lark and with the lark to bed.
JAMES HURDIS—*The Village Curate.*

The bed has become a place of luxury to me! I would not exchange it for all the thrones in the world.
NAPOLEON.

BEE

Seeing only what is fair,
Sipping only what is sweet.
EMERSON—*The Humble-Bee.*

Bees work for man, and yet they never bruise
Their Master's flower, but leave it having done,
As fair as ever and as fit to use;
So both the flower doth stay and honey run.
GEORGE HERBERT—*The Church.*

As busie as a Bee.
LYLY—*Euphues and His England.*

How doth the little busy bee
Improve each shining hour,
And gather honey all the day
From every opening flower.
ISAAC WATTS—*Against Idleness.*

BEGGING

Beggars must be no choosers.
BEAUMONT AND FLETCHER—*Scornful Lady.*

Set a beggar on horseback, and he will ride a gallop.
BURTON—*Anatomy of Melancholy.*

Better a living beggar than a buried emperor.
LA FONTAINE.

Borrowing is not much better than begging.
LESSING—*Nathan the Wise.*

A beggar through the world am I,
From place to place I wander by.
Fill up my pilgrim's scrip for me,
For Christ's sweet sake and charity.
LOWELL—*The Beggar.*

I'd just as soon be a beggar as king,
And the reason I'll tell you for why;
A king cannot swagger, nor drink like a beggar,
Nor be half so happy as I.
Old English Folk Song.

He who begs timidly courts a refusal.
SENECA—*Hippolytus.*

Beggar that I am, I am even poor in thanks.
SHAKESPEARE—*Hamlet.*

BEGINNING

Begin; to begin is half the work. Let half still remain; again begin this, and thou wilt have finished.
AUSONIUS—*Epigrams.*

In all matters, before beginning, a diligent preparation should be made.
CICERO.

Whatever begins, also ends.
SENECA.

It is the beginning of the end.
TALLEYRAND.

The first step, my son, which one makes in the world, is the one on which depends the rest of our days.
VOLTAIRE.

BELIEF

Men willingly believe what they wish.
CAESAR.

No iron chain, or outward force of any kind, could ever compel the soul of man to believe or to disbelieve: it is his own indefeasible light, that judgment of his; he will reign and believe there by the grace of God alone!
CARLYLE—*Heroes and Hero Worship.*

There is no unbelief;
Whoever plants a seed beneath the sod
And waits to see it push away the clod,
He trusts in God.
ELIZABETH YORK CASE—*Unbelief.*

Belief consists in accepting the affirmations of the soul; unbelief, in denying them.
EMERSON—*Montaigne.*

Better trust all and be deceived,
And weep that trust, and that deceiving,
Than doubt one heart that, if believed,
Had blessed one's life with true believing.
FANNY KEMBLE.

Nothing is so firmly believed as what we least know.
MONTAIGNE.

BELLS

How soft the music of those village bells,
Falling at intervals upon the ear
In cadence sweet; now dying all away,
Now pealing loud again, and louder still,
Clear and sonorous, as the gale comes on!
With easy force it opens all the cells
Where Memory slept.
COWPER—*The Task.*

Bell, thou soundest merrily,
When the bridal party
To the church doth hie!
Bell, thou soundest solemnly,
When, on Sabbath morning,
Fields deserted lie!
LONGFELLOW.

Those evening bells! those evening bells!
How many a tale their music tells!
MOORE—*Those Evening Bells.*

Hear the sledges with the bells,
Silver bells!
What a world of merriment their melody foretells!
How they tinkle, tinkle, tinkle,
In the icy air of night,
While the stars that oversprinkle
All the Heavens seem to twinkle
With a crystalline delight:
Keeping time, time, time,
In a sort of Runic rhyme
To the tintinnabulation that so musically wells
From the bells, bells, bells, bells,
Bells, bells, bells—
From the jingling and the tinkling of the bells.
POE—*The Bells.*

Like sweet bells jangled, out of tune and harsh.
SHAKESPEARE—*Hamlet.*

Ring in the valiant man and free,
The larger heart, the kindlier hand;
Ring out the darkness of the land;
Ring in the Christ that is to be.
TENNYSON—*In Memoriam.*

Ring out the old, ring in the new,
Ring, happy bells, across the snow.
TENNYSON—*In Memoriam.*

Curfew must not ring to-night.
ROSA H. THORPE—*Poem.*

BIBLE

A noble book! all men's book!
CARLYLE.

I call the Book of Job, apart from all theories about it, one of the grandest things ever written with pen.

CARLYLE.

A glory gilds the sacred page,
Majestic like the sun,
It gives a light to every age;
It gives, but borrows none.

COWPER.

Whence but from Heaven, could men unskill'd in arts,
In several ages born, in several parts,
Weave such agreeing truths? or how, or why
Should all conspire to cheat us with a lie?

DRYDEN.

The Bible is a window in this prison-world, through which we may look into eternity.

TIMOTHY DWIGHT.

A Bible and a newspaper in every house, a good school in every district—all studied and appreciated as they merit—are the principal support of virtue, morality and civil liberty.

FRANKLIN.

The inspiration of the Bible depends upon the ignorance of the gentleman who reads it.

R. G. INGERSOLL—*Speech, 1881.*

The Bible is to religion what the Iliad is to poetry.

JOUBERT.

The English Bible—a book which, if every thing else in our language should perish, would alone suffice to show the whole extent of its beauty and power.

MACAULAY.

The most learned, acute, and diligent student cannot, in the longest life, obtain an entire knowledge of this one volume.

SCOTT.

If there be any thing in my style of thought to be commended, the credit is due to my kind parents in instilling into my mind an early love of the Scriptures.

DANIEL WEBSTER.

BIGOTRY

A man must be excessively stupid, as well as uncharitable, who believes there is no virtue but on his own side.

ADDISON.

Bigotry dwarfs the soul by shutting out the truth.

CHAPIN.

To follow foolish precedents, and wink
With both our eyes is easier than to think.

COWPER

The superstition in which we were brought up never loses its power over us, even after we understand it.

LESSING.

BIOGRAPHY

Biography is the only true history.

CARLYLE.

One anecdote of a man is worth a volume of biography.

CHANNING.

Of all studies, the most delightful and the most useful is biography. The seeds of great events lie near the surface; historians delve too deep for them. No history was ever true. Lives I have read which, if they were not, had the appearance, the interest, and the utility of truth.

LANDOR.

To be ignorant of the lives of the most celebrated men of antiquity is to continue in a state of childhood all our days.

PLUTARCH.

BIRDS

Vainly the fowler's eye
Might mark thy distant flight to do thee wrong,
As, darkly painted on the crimson sky,
Thy figure floats along.

BRYANT—*To a Water Fowl.*

A bird in the hand is worth two in the bush.

CERVANTES—*Don Quixote.*

Never look for birds of this year in the nests of the last.
CERVANTES—*Don Quixote.*

One day in the bluest of summer weather,
Sketching under a whispering Oak,
I heard five bobolinks laughing together,
Over some ornithological joke.
C. P. CRANCH—*The Bobolinks.*

The crack-brained bobolink courts his crazy mate,
Poised on a bulrush tipsy with his weight.
O. W. HOLMES—*Spring.*

St. Agnes' Eve—Ah, bitter chill it was!
The owl, for all his feathers, was a-cold.
KEATS—*The Eve of St. Agnes.*

To Paradise, the Arabs say,
Satan could never find the way
Until the peacock led him in.
LELAND—*The Peacock.*

Sweet bird! thy bower is ever green,
Thy sky is ever clear;
Thou hast no sorrow in thy song,
No winter in thy year.
JOHN LOGAN—*To the Cuckoo.*

Then from the neighboring thicket the mocking-bird, wildest of singers,
Swinging aloft on a willow spray that hung o'er the water,
Shook from his little throat such floods of delirious music,
That the whole air and the woods and the waves seemed silent to listen.
LONGFELLOW—*Evangeline.*

The swallow is come!
The swallow is come!
O, fair are the seasons, and light
Are the days that she brings,
With her dusky wings,
And her bosom snowy white!
LONGFELLOW—*Hyperion.*

The sparrows chirped as if they still were proud
Their race in Holy Writ should mentioned be.
LONGFELLOW—*Tales of a Wayside Inn.*

The wailing owl
Screams solitary to the mournful moon.
MALLET—*Excursion.*

The Raven's house is built with reeds,—
Sing woe, and alas is me!
And the Raven's couch is spread with weeds,
High on the hollow tree;
And the Raven himself, telling his beads
In penance for his past misdeeds,
Upon the top I see.
THOMAS D'ARCY MCGEE—*The Penitent Raven.*

Birds of a feather will flock together.
MINSHEU.

The screech-owl, with ill-boding cry,
Portends strange things, old women say;
Stops every fool that passes by,
And frights the school-boy from his play.
LADY MONTAGU—*The Politicians.*

O thrush, your song is passing sweet,
But never a song that you have sung
Is half so sweet as thrushes sang
When my dear love and I were young.
WILLIAM MORRIS—*Other Days.*

Sing away, ay, sing away,
Merry little bird
Always gayest of the gay,
Though a woodland roundelay
You ne'er sung nor heard;
Though your life from youth to age
Passes in a narrow cage.
D. M. MULOCK—*The Canary in His Cage.*

And the Raven, never flitting,
Still is sitting, still is sitting
On the pallid bust of Pallas
Just above my chamber door;
And his eyes have all the seeming
Of a demon's that is dreaming,
And the lamplight o'er him streaming
Throws his shadow on the floor,
And my soul from out that shadow,
That lies floating on the floor,
Shall be lifted—nevermore.
POE—*The Raven.*

Hear how the birds, on ev'ry blooming spray,
With joyous musick wake the dawning day!
Pope—*Pastorals.*

A little bird told me.
Shakespeare—*King Henry IV*. Pt. II.

Between two seas the sea-bird's wing makes halt,
Wind-weary; while with lifting head he waits
For breath to reinspire him from the gates
That open still toward sunrise on the vault
High-domed of morning.
Swinburne—*Songs of the Spring Tides.*

A flash of harmless lightning,
A mist of rainbow dyes,
The burnished sunbeams brightening
From flower to flower he flies.
John Bannister Tabb—*Humming Bird.*

Hush!
With sudden gush
As from a fountain sings in yonder bush
The Hermit Thrush.
John Bannister Tabb—*Overflow.*

O Blackbird! sing me something well:
While all the neighbors shoot thee round,
I keep smooth plats of fruitful ground,
Where thou may'st warble, eat and dwell.
Tennyson—*The Blackbird.*

The Redbreast, sacred to the household gods,
Wisely regardful of the embroiling sky,
In joyless fields and thorny thickets leaves
His shivering mates, and pays to trusted Man
His annual visit.
Thomson—*The Seasons. Winter.*

Hail to thee, far above the rest
In joy of voice and pinion!
Thou, linnet! in thy green array,
Presiding spirit here to-day,
Dost lead the revels of the May;
And this is thy dominion.
Wordsworth—*The Green Linnet.*

Art thou the bird whom Man loves best,
The pious bird with the scarlet breast,
Our little English Robin;
The bird that comes about our doors
When autumn winds are sobbing?
Wordsworth — *The Redbreast Chasing the Butterfly.*

And hark! how blithe the throstle sings!
He, too, is no mean preacher:
Come forth into the light of things,
Let Nature be your teacher.
Wordsworth—*The Tables Turned.*

BIRTH

Born on Monday, fair in the face;
Born on Tuesday, full of God's grace;
Born on Wednesday, sour and sad;
Born on Thursday, merry and glad;
Born on Friday, worthily given;
Born on Saturday, work hard for your living;
Born on Sunday, you will never know want.
Anonymous.

Believing hear, what you deserve to hear:
Your birthday as my own to me is dear.
Blest and distinguish'd days! which we should prize
The first, the kindest bounty of the skies.
But yours gives most; for mine did only lend
Me to the world; yours gave to me a friend.
Martial—*Epigrams.*

Man alone at the very moment of his birth, cast naked upon the naked earth, does she abandon to cries and lamentations.
Pliny the Elder—*Natural History.*

BLACKSMITH

Curs'd be that wretch (Death's factor sure) who brought
Dire swords into the peaceful world, and taught
Smith (who before could only make
The spade, the plough-share, and the rake)
Arts, in most cruel wise
Man's left to epitomize!
COWLEY.

Under a spreading chestnut tree
The village smithy stands:
The smith, a mighty man is he,
With large and sinewy hands;
And the muscles of his brawny arms
Are strong as iron bands.
LONGFELLOW—*The Village Blacksmith.*

BLESSING

God bless me and my son John,
Me and my wife, him and his wife,
Us four, and no more.
ANONYMOUS.

Prosperity is the blessing of the Old Testament;
Adversity is the blessing of the New.
BACON.

Blessings star forth forever; but a curse
Is like a cloud—it passes.
BAILEY—*Festus.*

Blessings never come in pairs; misfortunes never come alone.
Chinese Proverb.

For blessings ever wait on virtuous deeds,
And though a late, a sure reward succeeds.
CONGREVE.

Blessed shall be thy basket and thy store.
Deuteronomy. XXVII. 5.

God bless us every one.
DICKENS—*Christmas Carol.*

To heal divisions, to relieve the oppress'd,
In virtue rich; in blessing others, bless'd.
HOMER.

We mistake the gratuitous blessings of heaven for the fruits of our industry.
L'ESTRANGE.

Blessings be with them, and eternal praise
Who gave us nobler loves, and nobler cares,
The poets, who on earth have made us heirs
Of truth and pure delight, by heavenly lays.
WORDSWORTH.

BLINDNESS

Ye have a world of light,
When love in the loved rejoices;
But the blind man's home is the house of night
And its beings are empty voices.
BULWER-LYTTON.

In the country of the blind the one-eyed man is king.
ERASMUS.

If the blind lead the blind, both shall fall into the ditch.
Matthew. XV. 14.

O dark, dark, dark, amid the blaze of noon,
Irrecoverable dark; total eclipse,
Without all hope of day.
MILTON.

O loss of sight, of thee I most complain!
Blind among enemies, O worse than chains,
Dungeon, or beggary, or decrepit age!
MILTON—*Samson Agonistes.*

There's none so blind as they that won't see.
SWIFT—*Polite Conversation.*

BLISS

To bliss unknown my lofty soul aspires,
My lot unequal to my vast desires.
J. ARBUTHNOT—*Gnothi Seauton.*

Vain, very vain, my weary search to find
That bliss which only centres in the mind.
GOLDSMITH.

Alas! by some degree of woe
We every bliss must gain;
The heart can ne'er a transport know,
That never feels a pain.
LORD LYTTLETON—*Song*.

The sum of earthly bliss.
MILTON—*Paradise Lost*.

Every one speaks of it,—who has known it?
MME. NECKER.

Condition, circumstance, is not the thing;
Bliss is the same in subject or in king.
POPE—*Essay on Man*.

BLOOD

Whoso sheddeth man's blood, by man shall his blood be shed.
Genesis. IX. 6.

Blood is thicker than water.
Attributed to COMMODORE TATTNALL.

The blood of the martyrs is the seed of the church.
TERTULLIAN.

The old blood is bold blood, the wide world round.
BYRON WEBBER—*Hands across the Sea*.

BLUSHES

Girls blush, sometimes, because they are alive,
Half wishing they were dead to save the shame.
The sudden blush devours them, neck and brow;
They have drawn too near the fire of life, like gnats,
And flare up bodily, wings and all.
E. B. BROWNING—*Aurora Leigh*.

So sweet the blush of bashfulness,
E'en pity scarce can wish it less!
BYRON—*Bride of Abydos*.

We griev'd, we sigh'd, we wept; we never blushed before.
COWLEY.

Blushing is the colour of virtue.
MATTHEW HENRY—*Commentaries*.

From every blush that kindles in thy cheeks,
Ten thousand little loves and graces spring
To revel in roses.
NICHOLAS ROWE—*Tamerlane*.

He blushes: all is safe.
TERENCE—*Adelphi*.

The man that blushes is not quite a brute.
YOUNG—*Night Thoughts*.

BOATING

But oars alone can ne'er prevail
To reach the distant coast;
The breath of Heaven must swell the sail,
Or all the toil is lost.
COWPER—*Human Frailty*.

The Owl and the Pussy-Cat went to sea
In a beautiful pea-green boat.
EDWARD LEAR—*The Owl and the Pussy-Cat*.

BOLDNESS

We make way for the man who boldly pushes past us.
BOVEE.

Fortune befriends the bold.
DRYDEN.

Fools rush in where angels fear to tread.
POPE.

BOOKS

That is a good book which is opened with expectation and closed with profit.
ALCOTT—*Table Talk*.

Some books are to be tasted, others to be swallowed, and some few to be chewed and digested.
BACON—*Of Studies*.

Worthy books
Are not companions—they are solitudes:
We lose ourselves in them and all our cares.

BAILEY—*Festus.*

That place that does contain
My books, the best companions, is to me
A glorious court, where hourly I converse
With the old sages and philosophers;
And sometimes, for variety, I confer
With kings and emperors, and weigh their counsels.

BEAUMONT and FLETCHER—*The Elder Brother.*

Books are embalmed minds.

BOVEE.

Laws die, Books never.

BULWER-LYTTON—*Richelieu.*

Some said, John, print it, others said, Not so;
Some said, It might do good, others said, No.

BUNYAN—*Apology for his Book.*

All that Mankind has done, thought, gained or been it is lying as in magic preservation in the pages of Books. They are the chosen possession of men.

CARLYLE—*Heroes and Hero Worship.*

The true University of these days is a collection of Books.

CARLYLE—*Heroes and Hero Worship.*

God be thanked for books. They are the voices of the distant and the dead, and make us heirs of the spiritual life of past ages.

CHANNING.

A book is the only immortality.

RUFUS CHOATE.

He who loves not books before he comes to thirty years of age will hardly love them enough afterwards to understand them.

CLARENDON.

Beware of the man of one book.

ISAAC D'ISRAELI—*Curiosities of Literature.*

Golden volumes! richest treasures,
Objects of delicious pleasures!
You my eyes rejoicing please,
You my hands in rapture seize!
Brilliant wits and musing sages,
Lights who beam'd through many ages!
Left to your conscious leaves their story,
And dared to trust you with their glory;
And now their hope of fame achiev'd,
Dear volumes! you have not deceived!

ISAAC D'ISRAELI—*Curiosities of Literature.*

Of making many books there is no end; and much study is a weariness of the flesh.

Ecclesiastes. XII. 12.

How pure the joy when first my hands unfold
The small, rare volume, black with tarnished gold.

JOHN FERRIAR—*Bibliomania.*

Dear little child, this little book
Is less a primer than a key
To sunder gates where wonder waits
Your "Open Sesame!"

RUPERT HUGHES—*With a First Reader.*

My desire is . . . that mine adversary had written a book.

Job. XXXI. 35.

Everywhere I have sought rest and found it not except sitting apart in a nook with a little book.

THOMAS À KEMPIS.

The writings of the wise are the only riches our posterity cannot squander.

LANDOR.

Books are sepulchres of thought.

LONGFELLOW—*Wind over the Chimney.*

All books are either dreams or swords,
You can cut, or you can drug, with words.

AMY LOWELL—*Sword Blades and Poppy Seed.*

Every great book is an action, and every great action is a book.

LUTHER.

A good book is the precious life-blood of a master-spirit imbalmed and treasured up on purpose to a life beyond life.

MILTON—*Areopagitica.*

As good almost kill a man as kill a good book; who kills a man kills a reasonable creature, God's image; but he who destroys a good book kills reason itself, kills the image of God, as it were, in the eye.

MILTON—*Areopagitica.*

I had rather than forty shillings,
I had my Book of Songs and Sonnets here.

SHAKESPEARE—*Merry Wives of Windsor.*

Books, the children of the brain.

SWIFT—*Tale of a Tub.*

All the known world, excepting only savage nations, is governed by books.

VOLTAIRE.

A small number of choice books are sufficient.

VOLTAIRE.

Beware you be not swallowed up in books.

JOHN WESLEY.

Camerado, this is no book.
Who touches this, touches a man.

WHITMAN—*So Long.*

There is no such thing as a moral or an immoral book. Books are well written or badly written. That is all.

WILDE—*The Picture of Dorian Gray.*

BORE

Bore: A person who talks when you wish him to listen.

AMBROSE BIERCE—*The Devil's Dictionary.*

Society is now one polished horde,
Formed of two mighty tribes, the *Bores* and *Bored.*

BYRON—*Don Juan.*

He says a thousand pleasant things,—
But never says "Adieu."

J. G. SAXE—*My Familiar.*

BORROWING

Debt is a bottomless sea.

CARLYLE.

Borrowing from Peter to pay Paul.

CICERO.

He who prefers to give Linus the half of what he wishes to borrow, rather than to lend him the whole, prefers to lose only the half.

MARTIAL—*Epigrams.*

The reason why borrowed books are so seldom returned to their owners is that it is much easier to retain the books than what is in them.

MONTAIGNE.

The borrower is servant to the lender.

Proverbs. XXII. 7

Let us have the courage to stop borrowing to meet continuing deficits. Stop the deficits.

F. D. ROOSEVELT, 1932.

Neither a borrower nor a lender be:
For loan oft loses both itself and friend,
And borrowing dulls the edge of husbandry.

SHAKESPEARE—*Hamlet.* Act I. Sc. 3.

BOSTON

If you hear an owl hoot: "To whom" instead of "To who," you can make up your mind he was born and educated in Boston.

ANONYMOUS.

And this is good old Boston,
The home of the bean and the cod,
Where the Lowells talk to the Cabots,
And the Cabots talk only to God.

J. C. BOSSIDY—*On the Aristocracy of Harvard.*

Then here's to the City of Boston,
The town of the cries and the groans,
Where the Cabots can't see the Kabotschniks,
And the Lowells won't speak to the Cohns.

FRANKLIN P. ADAMS—*Revised.*

A Boston man is the east wind made flesh.

THOMAS APPLETON.

A hundred thousand men were led
By one calf near three centuries dead;
They followed still his crooked way
And lost a hundred years a day;
For thus such reverence is lent
To well-established precedent.

SAM WALTER FOSS—*The Calf-Path.*

Boston State-house is the hub of the solar system. You couldn't pry that out of a Boston man if you had the tire of all creation straightened out for a crow-bar.

HOLMES—*Autocrat of the Breakfast Table.*

A solid man of Boston;
A comfortable man with dividends,
And the first salmon and the first green peas.

LONGFELLOW—*New England Tragedies.*

BRAIN

With curious art the brain, too finely wrought,
Preys on herself, and is destroyed by thought.

CHARLES CHURCHILL.

The brain is the palest of all the internal organs, and the heart the reddest. Whatever comes from the brain carries the hue of the place it came from, and whatever comes from the heart carries the heat and color of its birthplace.

HOLMES.

The human brain is the highest bloom of the whole organic metamorphosis of the earth.

SCHELLING.

BRAVERY

How sleep the brave, who sink to rest,
By all their country's wishes blest!

ANONYMOUS.

A brave man is clear in his discourse, and keeps close to truth.

ARISTOTLE.

At the bottom of a good deal of bravery that appears in the world there lurks a miserable cowardice. Men will face powder and steel because they cannot face public opinion.

CHAPIN.

Bravery is a cheap and vulgar quality, of which the brightest instances are frequently found in the lowest savages.

CHATFIELD.

No man can be brave who thinks pain the greatest evil; nor temperate, who considers pleasure the highest good.

CICERO—*De Officiis.*

None but the brave deserves the fair.

DRYDEN.

The brave man seeks not popular applause,
Nor, overpower'd with arms, deserts his cause;
Unsham'd, though foil'd, he does the best he can,
Force is of brutes, but honor is of man.

DRYDEN—*Palamon and Arcite.*

The brave
Love mercy, and delight to save.

GAY.

Without a sign his sword the brave man draws,
And asks no omen but his country's cause.

HOMER—*Iliad.*

Many brave men lived before Agamemnon; but, all unwept and unknown, are lost in the distant night, since they are without a divine poet (to chronicle their deeds).

HORACE—*Odes.*

The brave are parsimonious of threats.

KOSSUTH.

True bravery is shown by performing without witness what one might be capable of doing before all the world.

LA ROCHEFOUCAULD.

'Tis more brave
To live, than to die.

OWEN MEREDITH—*Lucile.*

Fortune and love favour the brave.

OVID.

Physical bravery is an animal instinct; moral bravery is a much higher and truer courage.
WENDELL PHILLIPS.

God helps the brave.
SCHILLER—*Wilhelm Tell.*

BREVITY

Rather to excite your judgment briefly than to inform it tediously.
BACON.

The more you say, the less people remember. The fewer the words, the greater the profit.
FÉNELON.

The fewer words, the better prayer.
LUTHER.

The wisdom of nations lies in their proverbs, which are brief and pithy.
WILLIAM PENN.

A downright fact may be briefly told.
RUSKIN.

Brevity is the soul of wit.
SHAKESPEARE—*Hamlet.* Act II. Sc. 2.

When a man has no design but to speak plain truth, he may say a great deal in a very narrow compass.
STEELE.

BRIBERY

The universe would not be rich enough to buy the vote of an honest man.
ST. GREGORY.

Our supple tribes repress their patriot throats,
And ask no questions but the price of votes.
SAMUEL JOHNSON—*Vanity of Human Wishes.*

Alas! the small discredit of a bribe
Scarce hurts the lawyer, but undoes the scribe.
POPE—*Essay on Man.*

Judges and senates have been bought for gold;
Esteem and love were never to be sold.
POPE—*Essay on Man.*

There is thy gold, worse poison to men's souls,
Doing more murders in this loathsome world,
Than these poor compounds that thou mayst not sell.
I sell thee poison, thou hast sold me none.
SHAKESPEARE—*Romeo and Juliet.* Act. V. Sc. I.

Every man has his price.
SIR ROBERT WALPOLE.

Few men have virtue to withstand the highest bidder.
WASHINGTON—*Moral Maxims.*

BROOK

I chatter, chatter, as I flow
To join the brimming river,
For men may come and men may go,
But I go on forever.
TENNYSON—*The Brook.*

BROTHERHOOD

The universe is but one great city, full of beloved ones, divine and human by nature endeared to each other.
EPICTETUS.

The era of Christianity—peace, brotherhood, the Golden Rule as applied to governmental matters—is yet to come, and when it comes, then, and then only, will the future of nations be sure.
KOSSUTH.

Man, man, is thy brother, and thy father is God.
LAMARTINE.

To live is not to live for one's self alone; let us help one another.
MENANDER.

Give bread to a stranger, in the name of the universal brotherhood which binds together all men under the common father of nature.
QUINTILIAN.

However wretched a fellow-mortal may be, he is still a member of our common species.
SENECA.

BUILDING

Old houses mended cost little less than new before they're ended.

CIBBER.

Never build after you are five and forty; have five years' income in hand before you lay a brick; and always calculate the expense at double the estimate.

KETT.

BUSINESS

Nation of shopkeepers.

Attributed to SAMUEL ADAMS.

Business is religion, and religion is business. The man who does not make a business of his religion has a religious life of no force, and the man who does not make a religion of his business has a business life of no character.

MALTBIE BABCOCK.

The nature of business is swindling.

AUGUST BEBEL.

Business despatched is business well done, but business hurried is business ill done.

BULWER-LYTTON.

When we speak of the commerce with our colonies, fiction lags after truth, invention is unfruitful, and imagination cold and barren.

BURKE—*Speech on the Conciliation of America.*

Keep thy shop, and thy shop will keep thee. Light gains make heavy purses.

GEORGE CHAPMAN—*Eastward Ho.*

There are two times in a man's life when he should not speculate: when he can't afford it, and when he can.

SAMUEL L. CLEMENS (Mark Twain).

They (corporations) cannot commit treason, nor be outlawed, nor excommunicated, for they have no souls.

COKE—*The Case of Sutton's Hospital.*

The business of America is business.

CALVIN COOLIDGE.

Success in business is seldom owing to uncommon talents or original power which is untractable and self-willed, but to the greatest degree of commonplace capacity.

HAZLITT.

Ill ware is never cheap.

GEORGE HERBERT—*Jacula Prudentum.*

I attend to the business of other people, having lost my own.

HORACE—*Satires.*

Whose merchants are princes.

Isaiah. XXII. 8.

A man's success in business today turns upon his power of getting people to believe he has something that they want.

GERALD STANLEY LEE—*Crowds.*

Wist ye not that I must be about my Father's business?

Luke. II. 49.

There can be no profit, if the outlay exceeds it.

PLAUTUS—*Poenulus.*

Shoemaker, stick to your last.

PLINY.

Let every one engage in the business with which he is best acquainted.

PROPERTIUS.

We demand that big business give people a square deal; in return we must insist that when any one engaged in big business honestly endeavors to do right, he shall himself be given a square deal.

THEODORE ROOSEVELT.

To things of sale a seller's praise belongs.

SHAKESPEARE—*Love's Labour's Lost.*

That which is everybody's business, is nobody's business.

IZAAK WALTON—*Compleat Angler.*

Call on a business man at business times only, and on business, transact your business and go about your business, in order to give him time to finish his business.

DUKE OF WELLINGTON.

The way to stop financial "joy-riding" is to arrest the chauffeur, not the automobile.

WOODROW WILSON.

BUTTERFLY

I'd be a butterfly, born in a bower,
Where roses and lilies and violets meet.

THOMAS HAYNES BAYLY—*I'd Be a Butterfly.*

With the rose the butterfly's deep in love,
A thousand times hovering round;
But round himself, all tender like gold,
The sun's sweet ray is hovering found.

HEINE—*Book of Songs.*

Much converse do I find in thee,
Historian of my infancy!
Float near me; do not yet depart!
Dead times revive in thee:
Thou bring'st, gay creature as thou art!
A solemn image to my heart.

WORDSWORTH—*To a Butterfly.*

C

CALAMITY

Times of general calamity and confusion have ever been productive of the greatest minds. The purest ore is produced from the hottest furnace, and the brightest thunderbolt is elicited from the darkest storm.

COLTON.

A vulgar man, in any ill that happens to him, blames others; a novice in philosophy blames himself; and a philosopher blames neither the one nor the other.

EPICTETUS.

When any calamity has been suffered the first thing to be remembered is, how much has been escaped.

SAMUEL JOHNSON.

Calamity is the test of integrity.

RICHARDSON.

It is from the level of calamities, not that of every-day life, that we learn impressive and useful lessons.

THACKERAY.

CALUMNY

Calumniate, calumniate; there will always be something which sticks.

BEAUMARCHAIS—*Barber of Seville.*

Nothing is so swift as calumny; nothing is more easily uttered; nothing more readily received; nothing more widely dispersed.

CICERO.

Calumny is only the noise of madmen.

DIOGENES.

One triumphs over calumny only by disdaining it.

MME. DE MAINTENON.

He that lends an easy and credulous ear to calumny is either a man of very ill morals or has no more sense and understanding than a child.

MENANDER.

I never listen to calumnies, because if they are untrue I run the risk of being deceived, and if they be true, of hating persons not worth thinking about.

MONTESQUIEU.

There are calumnies against which even innocence loses courage.

NAPOLEON.

Calumny is a vice of curious constitution; trying to kill it keeps it alive; leave it to itself and it will die a natural death.

THOMAS PAINE.

Cutting honest throats by whispers.

SCOTT.

Be thou as chaste as ice, as pure as snow, thou shalt not escape calumny.

SHAKESPEARE—*Hamlet.* Act III. Sc. I.

To persevere in one's duty and to be silent is the best answer to calumny.

WASHINGTON.

CANDOR

Candor may be considered as a compound of justice and the love of truth.
J. Abercrombie.

A man should never be ashamed to own he has been in the wrong, which is but saying, in other words, that he is wiser to-day than he was yesterday.
Pope.

CANT

Cant is the twin sister of hypocrisy.
Henry Ward Beecher.

Is not cant the materia prima of the devil, from which all falsehoods, imbecilities, abominations, body themselves, from which no true thing can come? For cant is itself properly a double-distilled lie, the second power of a lie.
Carlyle.

CAPITAL AND LABOR

Capital is a result of labor, and is used by labor to assist it in further production. Labor is the active and initial force, and labor is therefore the employer of capital.
Henry George — *Progress and Poverty.*

Labor is prior to, and independent of, capital. Capital is only the fruit of labor, and could never have existed if labor had not first existed. Labor is the superior of capital, and deserves much the higher consideration.
Abraham Lincoln—*Message to Congress, 1861.*

Each needs the other: capital cannot do without labor, nor labor without capital.
Pope Leo XIII.

CAPRICE

Woman is a miracle of divine contradictions.
Michelet.

There is a proverb in the South that a woman laughs when she can, and weeps when she pleases.
J. Petit-Senn.

There are women so hard to please that it would seem as if nothing less than an angel would suit them; and hence it comes that they often encounter devils.
Marguerite de Valois.

CARDS

With spots quadrangular of diamond form,
Ensanguined hearts, clubs typical of strife,
And spades, the emblems of untimely graves.
Cowper—*The Task.*

He's a sure card.
Dryden—*The Spanish Friar.*

Cards were at first for benefits designed,
Sent to amuse, not to enslave the mind.
David Garrick.

You do not play then at whist, sir! Alas, what a sad old age you are preparing for yourself!
Talleyrand.

CARE

Ye banks and braes o' bonny Doon,
How can ye bloom sae fresh and fair;
How can ye chant, ye little birds,
And I sae weary fu'o'care!
Burns—*The Banks o'Doon.*

To carry care to bed is to sleep with a pack on your back.
Haliburton.

He that taketh his own cares upon himself loads himself in vain with an uneasy burden. I will cast all my cares on God; He hath bidden me; they cannot burden Him.
Bishop Hall.

Light burdens, long borne, grow heavy.
HERBERT—*Jacula Prudentum.*

Eat not thy heart; which forbids to afflict our souls, and waste them with vexatious cares.
PLUTARCH.

Old Care has a mortgage on every estate,
And that's what you pay for the wealth that you get.
J. G. SAXE—*Gifts of the Gods.*

Care keeps his watch in every old man's eye,
And where care lodges, sleep will never lie;
But where unbruised youth with unstuff'd brain,
Doth couch his limbs, there golden sleep doth reign.
SHAKESPEARE—*Romeo and Juliet.* Act II. Sc. 3.

Providence has given us hope and sleep as a compensation for the many cares of life.
VOLTAIRE.

Care to our coffin adds a nail, no doubt;
And every Grin, so merry, draws one out.
JOHN WOLCOT—*Expostulatory Odes.*

CARELESSNESS

Carelessness does more harm than a want of knowledge.
FRANKLIN.

For want of a nail the shoe was lost; for want of a shoe the horse was lost; and for want of a horse the rider was lost; being overtaken and slain by the enemy, all for want of care about a horse-shoe nail.
FRANKLIN—*Poor Richard's Almanac.*

Carelessness is inexcusable, and merits the inevitable sequence.
FROUDE.

If you will fling yourself under the wheels, Juggernaut will go over you; depend upon it.
THACKERAY.

CARPENTER

A carpenter's known by his chips.
SWIFT—*Polite Conversation.*

CAT

Ding, dong, bell,
Pussy's in the well;
Who put her in?
Little Tommy Green.
Who pulled her out?
Little Johnny Stout.
ANONYMOUS.

Confound the cats! All cats—alway—
Cats of all colours, black, white, grey;
By night a nuisance and by day—
Confound the cats!
ORLANDO THOMAS DOBBIN—*A Dithyramb on Cats.*

The Cat in Gloves catches no Mice.
FRANKLIN—*Poor Richard's Almanac.*

It has been the providence of nature to give this creature nine lives instead of one.
PILPAY—*Fable.*

A cat may look at a king.
Title of a Pamphlet. (1652)

CAUSE

In war events of importance are the result of trivial causes.
CAESAR.

Christian Science explains all cause and effect as mental, not physical.
MARY BAKER EDDY—*Science and Health.*

The cause is hidden, but the result is known.
OVID—*Metamorphoses.*

God befriend us, as our cause is just!
SHAKESPEARE—*Henry IV.* Pt. I. Act V. Sc. 1.

Everything in nature is a cause from which there flows some effect.
SPINOZA.

The first springs of great events, like those of great rivers, are often mean and little.
SWIFT.

CAUTION

Hasten slowly.
AUGUSTUS CAESAR.

Be slow of tongue and quick of eye.
CERVANTES.

The cautious seldom err.
CONFUCIUS.

Among mortals second thoughts are wisest.
EURIPIDES.

Little boats should keep near shore.
FRANKLIN.

Caution is the eldest child of wisdom.
VICTOR HUGO.

The bird alighteth not on the spread net when it beholds another bird in the snare. Take warning by the misfortunes of others, that others may not take example from you.
SAADI.

Doctor Livingstone, I presume?
HENRY M. STANLEY to David Livingstone, on finding him in the African jungle, 1871.

It is a good thing to learn caution by the misfortunes of others.
SYRUS.

CELIBACY

"As to marriage or celibacy, let a man take which course he will," says Socrates, "he will be sure to repent."
COLTON.

Alas! many an enamored pair have courted in poetry, and after marriage lived in prose.
JOHN FOSTER.

God has set the type of marriage through creation. Each creature seeks its perfection in another.
LUTHER.

It happens, as with cages: the birds without despair to get in, and those within despair of getting out.
MONTAIGNE.

No man can either live piously or die righteous without a wife.
JEAN PAUL RICHTER.

CENSURE

There is no defense against reproach except obscurity.
ADDISON.

He that accuses all mankind of corruption ought to remember that he is sure to convict only one.
BURKE.

Censure is often useful, praise often deceitful.
CHARLES CHURCHILL.

It is harder to avoid censure than to gain applause; for this may be done by one great or wise action in an age. But to escape censure a man must pass his whole life without saying or doing one ill or foolish thing.
HUME.

Censure is the tax a man pays to the public for being eminent.
SWIFT.

CHANCE

Chance happens to all, but to turn chance to account is the gift of few.
BULWER-LYTTON.

I do not believe such a quality as chance exists. Every incident that happens must be a link in a chain.
DISRAELI.

Chance is a nickname for Providence.
CHAMFORT.

Chance is perhaps the pseudonym of God when He did not want to sign.
ANATOLE FRANCE.

Although men flatter themselves with their great actions, they are not so often the result of a great design as of chance.
LA ROCHEFOUCAULD.

I shot an arrow into the air
It fell to earth I knew not where;
For so swiftly it flew, the sight
Could not follow it in its flight.
LONGFELLOW—*The Arrow and the Song.*

Or that power
Which erring men call chance.
MILTON—*Comus.*

Chance is always powerful; let your hook always be cast. In a pool where you least expect it there will be a fish.
OVID.

Chance is blind and is the sole author of creation.
SAINTINE.

Chance never helps those who do not help themselves.
SOPHOCLES.

Chance is a word void of sense; nothing can exist without a cause.
VOLTAIRE—*A Philosophical Dictionary.*

CHANGE

Earth changes, but thy soul and God stand sure.
BROWNING—*Rabbi Ben Ezra.*

I am not now
That which I have been.
BYRON—*Childe Harold.*

And one by one in turn, some grand mistake
Casts off its bright skin yearly like the snake.
BYRON.

Today is not yesterday: we ourselves change; how can our Works and Thoughts, if they are always to be the fittest, continue always the same? Change, indeed, is painful; yet ever needful; and if Memory have its force and worth, so also has Hope.
CARLYLE—*Essays.*

Times change and we change with them. The stars rule men but God rules the stars.
CELLARIUS—*Harmonia Macrocosmica.*

Longing not so much to change things as to overturn them.
CICERO—*De Officiis.*

Good to the heels the well-worn slipper feels
When the tired player shuffles off the buskin;
A page of Hood may do a fellow good
After a scolding from Carlyle or Ruskin.
HOLMES—*How Not to Settle It.*

If matters go badly now, they will not always be so.
HORACE—*Carmina.*

I am not what I once was.
HORACE.

There is a certain relief in change, even though it be from bad to worse; as I have found in travelling in a stage-coach, that it is often a comfort to shift one's position and be bruised in a new place.
IRVING—*Tales of a Traveller.*

So many great nobles, things, administrations,
So many high chieftains, so many brave nations,
So many proud princes, and power so splendid,
In a moment, a twinkling, all utterly ended.
JACOPONE—*De Contemptu Mundi.*

Can the Ethiopian change his skin, or the leopard his spots?
Jeremiah. XIII. 23.

He is no wise man that will quit a certainty for an uncertainty.
SAMUEL JOHNSON—*The Idler.*

The world goes up and the world goes down,
And the sunshine follows the rain;
And yesterday's sneer and yesterday's frown
Can never come over again.
KINGSLEY—*Songs.*

I do not allow myself to suppose that either the convention or the League, have concluded to decide that I am either the greatest or the best man in America, but rather they have concluded it is not best to swap horses while crossing the river, and have further concluded that I am not so poor a horse that they might not make a botch of it in trying to swap.

LINCOLN, to a delegation who congratulated him on his nomination as the Republican candidate for President, June 9, 1864.

All things must change
To something new, to something strange.

LONGFELLOW.

Believe, if thou wilt, that mountains change their place, but believe not that man changes his nature.

MOHAMMED.

Revolutions are not made; they come.

WENDELL PHILLIPS.

Manners with Fortunes, Humours turn with Climes,
Tenets with Books, and Principles with Times.

POPE—*Moral Essays.*

As the blessings of health and fortune have a beginning, so they must also find an end. Everything rises but to fall, and increases but to decay.

SALLUST.

That we would do,
We should do when we would; for this "would" changes
And hath abatements and delays as many
As there are tongues, are hands, are accidents;
And then this "should" is like a spendthrift sigh,
That hurts by easing.

SHAKESPEARE—*Hamlet.* Act IV. Sc. 7.

Men must reap the things they sow,
Force from force must ever flow,
Or worse; but 'tis a bitter woe
That love or reason cannot change.

SHELLEY—*Lines Written among the Euganean Hills.*

Life may change, but it may fly not;
Hope may vanish, but can die not;
Truth be veiled, but still it burneth;
Love repulsed,—but it returneth.

SHELLEY—*Hellas.*

In this world of change, nought which comes stays, and nought which goes is lost.

MME. SWETCHINE.

The life of any one can by no means be changed after death; an evil life can in no wise be converted into a good life, or an infernal into an angelic life: because every spirit, from head to foot, is of the character of his love, and therefore, of his life; and to convert this life into its opposite, would be to destroy the spirit utterly.

SWEDENBORG—*Heaven and Hell.*

CHAOS

The chaos of events.

BYRON—*Prophecy of Dante.*

Nay, had I power, I should
Pour the sweet milk of concord into hell,
Uproar the universal peace, confound
All unity on earth.

SHAKESPEARE—*Macbeth.* Act. IV. Sc. 3.

CHARACTER

Many men build as cathedrals were built, the part nearest the ground finished; but that part which soars toward heaven, the turrets and the spires, forever incomplete.

HENRY WARD BEECHER—*Life Thoughts.*

He was not merely a chip of the old Block, but the old Block itself.

BURKE—*About William Pitt.*

Heroic, stoic Cato, the sententious,
Who lent his lady to his friend Hortensius.

BYRON—*Don Juan.*

Clever men are good, but they are not the best.

CARLYLE—*Goethe.*

We are firm believers in the maxim that, for all right judgment of any man or thing, it is useful, nay, essential, to see his good qualities before pronouncing on his bad.

CARLYLE—*Goethe.*

It is in general more profitable to reckon up our defects than to boast of our attainments.

CARLYLE—*Signs of the Times.*

Every one is as God made him, and often a great deal worse.

CERVANTES—*Don Quixote.*

Thou art a cat, and rat, and a coward to boot.

CERVANTES—*Don Quixote.*

The great hope of society is individual character.

CHANNING.

You must look into people as well as at them.

CHESTERFIELD.

For every inch that is not fool, is rogue.

DRYDEN—*Absalom and Achitophel.*

Character is not cut in marble; it is not something solid and unalterable. It is something living and changing, and may become diseased as our bodies do.

GEORGE ELIOT.

She was and is (what can there more be said?)
On earth the first, in heaven the second maid.

Tribute to Queen Elizabeth.

Human improvement is from within outward.

FROUDE.

Our thoughts and our conduct are our own.

FROUDE.

In every deed of mischief, he (Andronicus Comnenus) had a heart to resolve, a head to contrive, and a hand to execute.

GIBBON—*Decline and Fall of the Roman Empire.*

Talent is nurtured in solitude; character is formed in the stormy billows of the world.

GOETHE—*Torquato Tasso.*

Our Garrick's a salad; for in him we see
Oil, vinegar, sugar, and saltness agree.

GOLDSMITH—*Retaliation.*

Though equal to all things, for all things unfit;
Too nice for a statesman, too proud for a wit.

GOLDSMITH—*Retaliation.*

He were n't no saint—but at jedgment
I'd run my chance with Jim.
'Longside of some pious gentlemen
That wouldn't shook hands with him.
He seen his duty, a dead-sure thing—
And went for it thar and then;
And Christ ain't a-going to be too hard
On a man that died for men.

JOHN HAY—*Jim Bludso.*

O Douglas, O Douglas!
Tender and true.

SIR RICHARD HOLLAND—*The Buke of the Howlat.*

In death a hero, as in life a friend!

HOMER—*Iliad.*

Gentle of speech, beneficent of mind.

HOMER—*Odyssey.*

Wise to resolve, and patient to perform.

HOMER—*Odyssey.*

Only what we have wrought into our character during life can we take away with us.

HUMBOLDT.

He was worse than provincial—he was parochial.

HENRY JAMES—*Of Thoreau.*

The heart to conceive, the understanding to direct, or the hand to execute.

JUNIUS—*City Address and the King's Answer.*

No one ever became thoroughly bad all at once.

JUVENAL—*Satires.*

Every man has three characters—that which he exhibits, that which he has, and that which he thinks he has.

ALPHONSE KARR.

Oh, East is East, and West is West, and never the twain shall meet
Till earth and sky stand presently at God's great judgment seat;

But there is neither East nor West, border nor breed nor birth
When two strong men stand face to face, tho' they come from the ends of the earth!
KIPLING—*Ballad of East and West.*

E'en as he trod that day to God, so walked he from his birth,
In simpleness, and gentleness and honor and clean mirth.
KIPLING—*Barrack Room Ballads.*

The qualities we have do not make us so ridiculous as those which we affect to have.
LA ROCHEFOUCHAULD.

A tender heart; a will inflexible.
LONGFELLOW—*Christus.*

Sensitive, swift to resent, but as swift in atoning for error.
LONGFELLOW—*Courtship of Miles Standish.*

So mild, so merciful, so strong, so good,
So patient, peaceful, loyal, loving, pure.
LONGFELLOW—*The Golden Legend.*

In this world a man must either be anvil or hammer.
LONGFELLOW—*Hyperion.*

Not in the clamor of the crowded street,
Not in the shouts and plaudits of the throng,
But in ourselves, are triumph and defeat.
LONGFELLOW—*The Poets.*

Soft-heartedness, in times like these,
Shows sof'ness in the upper story.
LOWELL—*Biglow Papers.*

It is by presence of mind in untried emergencies that the native metal of a man is tested.
LOWELL—*My Study Windows.*

There thou beholdest the walls of Sparts, and every man a brick.
LYCURGUS.

We hardly know any instance of the strength and weakness of human nature so striking and so grotesque as the character of this haughty, vigilant, resolute, sagacious blue-stocking, half Mithridates and half Trissotin, bearing up against a world in arms, with an ounce of poison in one pocket and a quire of bad verses in the other.
MACAULAY—*Frederick the Great.*

In all thy humours, whether grave or mellow,
Thou'rt such a touchy, testy, pleasant fellow;
Hast so much wit, and mirth, and spleen about thee,
That there's no living with thee, or without thee.
MARTIAL—*Epigrams.*

Who knows nothing base,
Fears nothing known.
OWEN MEREDITH—*A Great Man.*

In men whom men condemn as ill
I find so much of goodness still,
In men whom men pronounce divine
I find so much of sin and blot
I do not dare to draw a line
Between the two, where God has not.
JOAQUIN MILLER—*Byron.*

He that has light within his own clear breast
May sit i' the centre, and enjoy bright day:
But he that hides a dark soul and foul thoughts
Benighted walks under the mid-day sun;
Himself his own dungeon.
MILTON—*Comus.*

Men, who are rogues individually, are in the mass very honorable people.
MONTESQUIEU—*De l'Esprit.*

To those who know thee not, no words can paint;
And those who know thee, know all words are faint!
HANNAH MORE—*Sensibility.*

He never unbuttons himself.
Said of SIR ROBERT PEEL.

Grand, gloomy and peculiar, he sat upon the throne, a sceptred hermit wrapped in the solitude of his awful originality.

Charles Phillips—*Character of Napoleon I.*

The highest of character, in my estimation, is his, who is as ready to pardon the moral errors of mankind, as if he were every day guilty of some himself; and at the same time as cautious of committing a fault as if he never forgave one.

Pliny the Younger—*Epistles.*

Of Manners gentle, of Affections mild;
In Wit a man; Simplicity, a child.

Pope—*Epitaph.*

In men we various ruling passions find;
In women two almost divide the kind;
Those only fixed, they first or last obey,
The love of pleasure, and the love of sway.

Pope—*Moral Essays.*

'Tis from high Life high Character are drawn;
A Saint in Crape is twice a Saint in Lawn:
A Judge is just, a Chanc'llor juster still;
A Gownman learn'd; a Bishop what you will;
Wise if a Minister; but if a King,
More wise, more learn'd, more just, more everything.

Pope—*Moral Essays.*

He that sweareth
Till no man trust him;
He that lieth
Till no man believe him;
He that borroweth
Till no man will lend him;
Let him go where
No man knoweth him.

Hugh Rhodes—*Cautions.*

Do you seek Alcides' equal? None is, except himself.

Seneca—*Hercules Furens.*

When he is best, he is a little worse than a man, and when he is worst, he is little better than a beast.

Shakespeare—*Merchant of Venice.* Act II. Sc. 2.

His heart as far from fraud as heaven from earth.

Shakespeare—*Two Gentlemen of Verona.* Act II. Sc. 7.

There are many persons of whom it may be said that they have no other possession in the world but their character, and yet they stand as firmly upon it as any crowned king.

Samuel Smiles.

Daniel Webster struck me much like a steam engine in trousers.

Sydney Smith—*Lady Holland's Memoir.*

It's the bad that's in the best of us
Leaves the saint so like the rest of us!
It's the good in the darkest-curst of us
Redeems and saves the worst of us!
It's the muddle of hope and madness;
It's the tangle of good and badness;
It's the lunacy linked with sanity
Makes up, and mocks, humanity!

Arthur Stringer—*Humanity.*

The true greatness of nations is in those qualities which constitute the greatness of the individual.

Charles Sumner.

It is in men as in soils where sometimes there is a vein of gold which the owner knows not of.

Swift.

In seasons of tumult and discord bad men have most power; mental and moral excellence require peace and quietness.

Tacitus—*Annales.*

Fame is what you have taken,
  Character's what you give;
When to this truth you waken,
  Then you begin to live.

Bayard Taylor—*Improvisations.*

He makes no friend who never made a foe.

Tennyson—*Idylls of the King.*

And one man is as good as another—and a great dale betther, as the Irish philosopher said.

THACKERAY—*Roundabout Papers.*

There are beauties of character which, like the night-blooming cereus are closed against the glare and turbulence of every-day life, and bloom only in shade and solitude, and beneath the quiet stars.

TUCKERMAN.

They attack this one man with their hate and their shower of weapons. But he is like some rock which stretches into the vast sea and which, exposed to the fury of the winds and beaten against by the waves, endures all the violence and threats of heaven and sea, himself standing unmoved.

VERGIL—*Aeneid.* X. 692.

I hope I shall always possess firmness and virtue enough to maintain what I consider the most enviable of all titles, the character of an "honest man."

WASHINGTON.

I celebrate myself, and sing myself,
And what I assume you shall assume,
For every atom belonging to me as good as belongs to you.

WALT WHITMAN—*Song of Myself.*

Formed on the good old plan,
A true and brave and downright honest man!
He blew no trumpet in the market-place,
Nor in the church with Hypocritic face
Supplied with cant the lack of Christian grace;
Loathing pretence, he did with cheerful will
What others talked of while their hands were still.

WHITTIER—*Daniel Neall.* II.

Whom neither shape of danger can dismay,
Nor thought of tender happiness betray.

WORDSWORTH—*Character of a Happy Warrior.*

CHARITY

Charity is the perfection and ornament of religion.

ADDISON.

Charity is a virtue of the heart, and not of the hands.

ADDISON—*The Guardian.*

The desire of power in excess caused the angels to fall; the desire of knowledge in excess caused man to fall; but in charity there is no excess, neither can angel or man come in danger by it.

BACON—*On Goodness.*

Every charitable act is a stepping stone toward heaven.

HENRY WARD BEECHER.

My poor are my best patients. God pays for them.

BOERHAAVE.

No sound ought to be heard in the church but the healing voice of Christian charity.

BURKE.

Though I have all faith, so that I could remove mountains, and have not charity, I am nothing.

I Corinthians. XIII. 2.

Charity suffereth long and is kind; charity envieth not; charity vaunteth not itself, is not puffed up.

I Corinthians. XIII. 4.

And now abideth faith, hope, charity, these three; but the greatest of these is charity.

I Corinthians. XIII. 13.

Better to expose ourselves to ingratitude than fail in assisting the unfortunate.

DU COEUR.

What we frankly give, forever is our own.

GRANVILLE.

As the purse is emptied the heart is filled.

VICTOR HUGO.

That charity which longs to publish itself, ceases to be charity.

HUTTON.

He who waits to do a great deal of good at once, will never do anything.
SAMUEL JOHNSON.

Prayer carries us half way to God, fasting brings us to the door of His palace and alms-giving procures us admission.
The Koran.

Liberality consists less in giving profusely than in giving judiciously.
LA BRUYÈRE.

In things essential, unity; in doubtful, liberty; in all things, charity.
RUPERTUS MELDENIUS.

Charity shall cover the multitude of sins.
I Peter. IV. 8.

Soft peace she brings, wherever she arrives:
She builds our quiet, as she forms our lives:
Lays the rough paths of peevish Nature even,
And opens in each heart a little Heaven.
PRIOR—*Charity.*

Charity,
Which renders good for bad, blessings for curses.
SHAKESPEARE—*Richard III.* Act I. Sc. 2.

Ah! what a divine religion might be found out if charity were really made the principle of it instead of faith!
SHELLEY.

Our charity begins at home,
And mostly ends where it begins.
HORACE SMITH—*Horace in London.*

Giving is true having.
SPURGEON.

Defer not charities till death. He who does so is rather liberal of another man's substance than his own.
STRETCH.

He gives a benefit twice who gives quickly.
SYRUS—*Proverbs of Seneca.*

Charity begins at home.
TERENCE—*Andria.*

CHASTITY

As pure as a pearl,
And as perfect: a noble and innocent girl.
OWEN MEREDITH—*Lucile.*

The most chaste woman may be the most voluptuous, if she truly loves.
MIRABEAU.

As chaste as unsunn'd snow.
SHAKESPEARE—*Cymbeline.* Act II. Sc. 5.

To the pure all things are pure.
SHELLEY.

CHEERFULNESS

He who sings frightens away his ills.
CERVANTES.

The creed of the true saint is to make the best of life, and make the most of it.
CHAPIN.

A cheerful look makes a dish a feast.
GEORGE HERBERT—*Jacula Prudentum.*

Cheer up, the worst is yet to come.
PHILANDER JOHNSON.

Mirth is like a flash of lightning that breaks through a gloom of clouds and glitters for a moment. Cheerfulness keeps up a daylight in the mind, filling it with a steady and perpetual serenity.
SAMUEL JOHNSON.

Let us be of good cheer, remembering that the misfortunes hardest to bear are those which never happen.
LOWELL.

A good laugh is sunshine in a house.
THACKERAY.

A cheerful life is what the Muses love,
A soaring spirit is their prime delight.
WORDSWORTH—*From the Dark Chambers.*

CHILDHOOD

Do ye hear the children weeping, O my brothers,
Ere the sorrow comes with years?

They are leaning their young heads against their mothers,
And that cannot stop their tears.
E. B. Browning—*The Cry of the Children.*

Diogenes struck the father when the son swore.
Burton—*Anatomy of Melancholy.*

A little curly-headed, good-for-nothing,
And mischief-making monkey from his birth.
Byron—*Don Juan.*

There's plenty of boys that will come hankering and gruvvelling around when you've got an apple, and beg the core off you; but when *they've* got one, and you beg for the core, and remind them how you give them a core one time, they make a mouth at you, and say thank you 'most to death, but there ain't a-going to be no core.
S. L. Clemens (Mark Twain)—*Tom Sawyer Abroad.*

When I was a child, I spake as a child, I understood as a child, I thought as a child; but when I became a man, I put away childish things.
I Corinthians. XIII. 11.

Better to be driven out from among men than to be disliked of children.
R. H. Dana—*The Idle Man.*

I love these little people; and it is not a slight thing when they, who are so fresh from God, love us.
Dickens.

Childhood has no forebodings; but then, it is soothed by no memories of outlived sorrow.
George Eliot—*Mill on the Floss.*

Wynken, Blynken and Nod one night
Sailed off in a wooden shoe—
Sailed on a river of crystal light
Into a sea of dew.
Eugene Field—*Wynken, Blynken and Nod.*

Teach your child to hold his tongue,
He'll learn fast enough to speak.
Franklin—*Poor Richard's Maxims.*

I think that saving a little child
And bringing him to his own,
Is a derned sight better business
Than loafing around the throne.
John Hay—*Little Breeches.*

It is a wise child that knows his own father.
Homer—*Odyssey.*

Rachel weeping for her children, and would not be comforted, because they are not.
Jeremiah. XXXI. 15; *Matthew.* II. 18.

Children have more need of models than of critics.
Joubert.

Children have neither past nor future; and that which seldom happens to us, they rejoice in the present.
La Bruyère.

A babe is fed with milk and praise.
Lamb—*The First Tooth.*

Oh, would I were a boy again,
When life seemed formed of sunny years,
And all the heart then knew of pain
Was wept away in transient tears!
Mark Lemon—*Oh, Would I Were a Boy Again.*

There was a little girl,
And she had a little curl,
Right in the middle of her forehead;
When she was good she was very, very good,
When she was bad she was horrid.
Longfellow.

Who can foretell for what high cause
This darling of the gods was born?
Andrew Marvell.

Lord, give to men who are old and rougher
The things that little children suffer,
And let keep bright and undefiled
The young years of the little child.
John Masefield—*The Everlasting Mercy.*

The childhood shows the man,
As morning shows the day.
Milton—*Paradise Regained.*

The children in Holland take pleasure in making
What the children in England take pleasure in breaking.
Old Nursery Rhyme.

The wildest colts make the best horses.
PLUTARCH—*Life of Themistocles.*

Behold the child, by Nature's kindly law,
Pleas'd with a rattle, tickled with a straw.
POPE—*Essay on Man.*

A wise son maketh a glad father.
Proverbs. X. 1.

Train up a child in the way he should go; and when he is old he will not depart from it.
Proverbs. XXII. 6.

Happy child! the cradle is still to thee a vast space; but when thou art a man the boundless world will be too small for thee.
SCHILLER.

It is a wise father that knows his own child.
SHAKESPEARE—*Merchant of Venice.* Act II. Sc. 2.

Every night my prayers I say,
And get my dinner every day,
And every day that I've been good,
I get an orange after food.
STEVENSON—*Child's Garden of Verses.*

It is very nice to think
The world is full of meat and drink
With little children saying grace
In every Christian kind of place.
STEVENSON—*Child's Garden of Verses.*

If there is anything that will endure
The eye of God, because it still is pure,
It is the spirit of a little child,
Fresh from his hand, and therefore undefiled.
R. H. STODDARD—*The Children's Prayer.*

As each one wishes his children to be, so they are.
TERENCE—*Adelphi.*

How dear to this heart are the scenes of my childhood,
When fond recollection presents them to view.
SAMUEL WOODWORTH—*The Old Oaken Bucket.*

The child is father of the man.
WORDSWORTH—*My Heart Leaps Up.*

CHOICE

Life often presents us with a choice of evils, rather than of goods.
COLTON—*Lacon.*

Betwixt the devil and the deep sea.
ERASMUS—*Adagia.*

Submit or resign.
GAMBETTA.

For many are called, but few are chosen.
Matthew. XXII. 14.

The difficulty in life is the choice.
GEORGE MOORE—*Bending of the Bough.*

If I were not Alexander, I should wish to be Diogenes.
PLUTARCH—*Life of Alexander.*

Or fight or fly,
This choice is left ye, to resist or die.
POPE—*Homer's Odyssey.*

There's small choice in rotten apples.
SHAKESPEARE—*Taming of the Shrew.* Act I. Sc. 1.

When to elect there is but one,
'Tis Hobson's Choice; take that or none.
THOMAS WARD—*England's Reformation.*

CHRIST

There is a green hill far away,
Without a city wall,
Where the dear Lord was crucified
Who died to save us all.
CECIL FRANCES ALEXANDER.

Star unto star speaks light, and world to world
Repeats the passage of the universe

To God; the name of Christ—the one
great word
Well worth all languages in earth or
heaven.
BAILEY.

Hail, O bleeding Head and wounded,
With a crown of thorns surrounded,
Buffeted, and bruised and battered,
Smote with reed by striking shattered,
Face with spittle vilely smeared!
Hail, whose visage sweet and comely,
Marred by fouling stains and homely,
Changed as to its blooming color,
All now turned to deathly pallor,
Making heavenly hosts affeared!
ST. BERNARD OF CLAIRVAUX—*Passion Hymn.*

In every pang that rends the heart
The Man of Sorrows had a part.
MICHAEL BRUCE—*Gospel Sonnets.*

The sages and heroes of history are receding from us, and history contracts the record of their deeds into a narrower and narrower page. But time has no power over the name and deeds and words of Jesus Christ.
CHANNING.

As to Jesus of Nazareth, my opinion of whom you particularly desire, I think the system of morals and His religion, as He left them to us, is the best the world ever saw, or is likely to see.
FRANKLIN.

Certainly, no revolution that has ever taken place in society can be compared to that which has been produced by the words of Jesus Christ.
MARK HOPKINS.

Thou hast conquered, O Galilean.
Attributed to JULIAN THE APOSTATE.

All His glory and beauty come from within, and there He delights to dwell, His visits there are frequent, His conversation sweet, His comforts refreshing; and His peace passing all understanding.
THOMAS À KEMPIS—*Imitation of Christ.*

The foxes have holes, and the birds of the air have nests; but the Son of Man hath not where to lay his head.
Matthew. VIII. 20.

Alexander, Caesar, Charlemagne and I myself have founded empires; but upon what do these creations of our genius depend? Upon force. Jesus alone founded His empire upon love; and to this very day millions would die for Him.
NAPOLEON.

Near, so very near to God,
Nearer I cannot be;
For in the person of his Son
I am as near as he.
CATESBY PAGET—*Hymn.*

But chiefly Thou,
Whom soft-eyed Pity once led down
from Heaven
To bleed for man, to teach him how
to live,
And, oh! still harder lesson! how to
die.
BISHOP PORTEUS—*Death.*

If the life and death of Socrates were those of a sage, the life and death of Jesus were those of a God.
ROUSSEAU.

CHRISTIAN

Almost thou persuadest me to be a Christian.
Acts. XXVI. 28.

Onward, Christian soldiers,
Marching as to war,
With the cross of Jesus
Going on before.
BARING-GOULD.

It is more to the honor of a Christian soldier, by faith to overcome the world, than by a monastical vow to retreat from it; and more for the honor of Christ, to serve Him in a city than to serve Him in a cell.
MATTHEW HENRY.

A Christian is God Almighty's gentleman.
J. C. and A. W. HARE—*Guesses at Truth.*

Servant of God, well done, well hast thou fought
The better fight.

MILTON—*Paradise Lost.*

If all were perfect Christians, individuals would do their duty; the people would be obedient to the laws, the magistrates incorrupt, and there would be neither vanity nor luxury in such a state.

ROUSSEAU.

The greatness of God is the true rebuke to the littleness of men. The greatness of Christ is the true rebuke of the littleness of Christians.

DEAN STANLEY.

I thank the goodness and the grace
Which on my birth have smiled,
And made me, in these Christian days
A happy Christian child.

JANE TAYLOR—*Child's Hymn of Praise.*

Whatever makes men good Christians, makes them good citizens.

DANIEL WEBSTER—*Speech at Plymouth.*

CHRISTIANITY

Ours is a religion jealous in its demands, but how infinitely prodigal in its gifts! It troubles you for an hour, it repays you by immortality.

BULWER-LYTTON.

Christianity is completed Judaism, or it is nothing.

DISRAELI.

His Christianity was muscular.

DISRAELI—*Endymion.*

God must have loved the plain people;
He made so many of them.

ABRAHAM LINCOLN.

Yes,—rather plunge me back in pagan night,
And take my chance with Socrates for bliss,
Than be the Christian of a faith like this,
Which builds on heavenly cant its earthly sway,
And in a convert mourns to lose a prey.

MOORE—*Intolerance.*

Christianity ruined emperors, but saved peoples.

ALFRED DE MUSSET.

Take up the cross if thou the crown would'st gain.

ST. PAULINUS, BISHOP OF NOLA.

Christianity is a battle, not a dream.

WENDELL PHILLIPS.

I desire no other evidence of the truth to Christianity than the Lord's Prayer.

MADAME DE STAËL.

Christianity, with its doctrine of humility, of forgiveness, of love, is incompatible with the state, with its haughtiness, its violence, its punishment, its wars.

TOLSTOY.

CHRISTMAS

No trumpet-blast profaned
The hour in which the Prince of Peace was born;
No bloody streamlet stained
Earth's silver rivers on that sacred morn.

BRYANT—*Christmas in 1875.*

Christians awake, salute the happy morn
Whereon the Saviour of the world was born.

JOHN BYROM—*Hymn for Christmas Day.*

For little children everywhere
A joyous season still we make;
We bring our precious gifts to them,
Even for the dear child Jesus' sake.

PHOEBE CARY—*Christmas.*

A good conscience is a continual Christmas.

FRANKLIN.

How bless'd, how envied, were our life,
Could we but 'scape the poulterer's knife!
But man, curs'd man, on Turkeys preys,
And Christmas shortens all our days:

Sometimes with oysters we combine,
Sometimes assist the savory chine;
From the low peasant to the lord,
The Turkey smokes on every board.
GAY—*Fables.*

Today the whole Christian world prostrates itself in adoration around the crib of Bethlehem and rehearses in accents of love a history which precedes all time and will endure throughout eternity.
CARDINAL GIBBONS.

What babe newborn is this that in a manger cries?
Near on her lowly bed his happy mother lies.
Oh, see the air is shaken with white and heavenly wings—
This is the Lord of all the earth, this is the King of Kings.
R. W. GILDER—*A Christmas Hymn.*

I heard the bells on Christmas Day
Their old, familiar carols play,
And wild and sweet
The words repeat
Of peace on earth, good-will to men!
LONGFELLOW—*Christmas Bells.*

"What means this glory round our feet,"
The Magi mused, "more bright than morn!"
And voices chanted clear and sweet,
"To-day the Prince of Peace is born."
LOWELL—*Christmas Carol.*

For unto you is born this day in the city of David a Saviour, which is Christ the Lord.
Luke. II. 11.

Let's dance and sing and make good cheer,
For Christmas comes but once a year.
G. MACFARREN (Before 1580)

This is the month, and this the happy morn,
Wherein the Son of Heaven's eternal King,
Of wedded maid and virgin mother born,
Our great redemption from above did bring,
For so the holy sages once did sing,
That He our deadly forfeit should release,
And with His Father work us a perpetual peace.
MILTON—*On the Morning of Christ's Nativity.*

'Twas the night before Christmas, when all through the house
Not a creature was stirring—not even a mouse:
The stockings were hung by the chimney with care,
In hopes that St. Nicholas soon would be there.
CLEMENT C. MOORE—*A Visit from St. Nicholas.*

God rest ye, little children; let nothing you affright,
For Jesus Christ, your Saviour, was born this happy night;
Along the hills of Galilee the white flocks sleeping lay,
When Christ, the Child of Nazareth, was born on Christmas day.
D. M. MULOCK—*Christmas Carol.*

As many mince pies as you taste at Christmas, so many happy months will you have.
Old English Saying.

England was merry England, when
Old Christmas brought his sports again.
'Twas Christmas broach'd the mightiest ale;
'Twas Christmas told the merriest tale;
A Christmas gambol oft could cheer
The poor man's heart through half the year.
SCOTT—*Marmion.*

Be merry all, be merry all,
With holly dress the festive hall;
Prepare the song, the feast, the ball,
To welcome merry Christmas.
W. R. SPENCER.

The time draws near the birth of Christ:
The moon is hid; the night is still;
The Christmas bells from hill to hill
Answer each other in the mist.
TENNYSON—*In Memoriam.*

Christmas is here:
Winds whistle shrill,
Icy and chill,
Little care we:
Little we fear
Weather without,
Sheltered about
The Mahogany-Tree.
THACKERAY—*The Mahogany-Tree.*

At Christmas play, and make good cheer,
For Christmas comes but once a year.
TUSSER.

Hark the herald angels sing,
"Glory to the new-born king."
Peace on earth, and mercy mild,
God and sinners reconciled!
CHARLES WESLEY—*Christmas Hymn.*

Blow, bugles of battle, the marches of peace;
East, west, north, and south let the long quarrel cease;
Sing the song of great joy that the angels began,
Sing the glory to God and of good-will to man!
WHITTIER—*Christmas Carmen.*

CHURCH

The nearer the church, the further from God.
BISHOP ANDREWS—*Sermon on the Nativity before James I.*

Oh! St. Patrick was a gentleman
Who came of decent people;
He built a church in Dublin town,
And on it put a steeple.
HENRY BENNETT.

Persecution has not crushed it, power has not beaten it back, time has not abated its force, and, what is most wonderful of all, the abuses and treasons of its friends have not shaken its stability.
HORACE BUSHNELL.

Steele has observed that there is this difference between the Church of Rome and the Church of England,—the one professes to be infallible, the other to be never in the wrong.
COLTON.

What is a church?—Our honest sexton tells,
'Tis a tall building, with a tower and bells.
CRABBE—*The Borough.*

Whenever God erects a house of prayer
The devil always builds a chapel there;
And 'twill be found, upon examination,
The latter has the largest congregation.
DEFOE—*True Born Englishman.*

It is common for those that are farthest from God, to boast themselves most of their being near to the Church.
MATTHEW HENRY—*Commentaries.*

Division has done more to hide Christ from the view of men than all the infidelity that has ever been spoken.
GEORGE MACDONALD.

It was founded upon a rock.
Matthew. VII. 25.

Who builds a church to God, and not to Fame,
Will never mark the marble with his Name.
POPE—*Moral Essays.*

It is not about the pasture of the sheep, but about their wool.
POPE PIUS II.

I never weary of great churches. It is my favourite kind of mountain scenery. Mankind was never so happily inspired as when it made a cathedral.
STEVENSON—*Inland Voyage.*

A beggarly people,
A church and no steeple.
Attributed to MALONE by SWIFT.

See the Gospel Church secure,
And founded on a Rock!
All her promises are sure;
Her bulwarks who can shock?
Count her every precious shrine;
Tell, to after-ages tell,
Fortified by power divine,
The Church can never fail.
CHARLES WESLEY.

The itch of disputing is the scab of the churches.

Sir Henry Wotton—*A Panegyric to King Charles.*

CIRCUMSTANCE

The trifles of our daily lives,
The common things, scarce worth recall,
Whereof no visible trace survives,
These are the mainsprings after all.

Anonymous.

I am the very slave of circumstance
And impulse—borne away with every breath.

Byron—*Sardanapalus.*

The long arm of coincidence.

Haddon Chambers—*Captain Swift.*

Thus neither the praise nor the blame is our own.

Cowper—*Letter to Mr. Newton.*

Man is not the creature of circumstances,
Circumstances are the creatures of men.

Disraeli—*Vivian Grey.*

Circumstances alter cases.

Haliburton—*The Old Judge.*

The happy combination of fortuitous circumstances.

Scott.

The circumstances of others seem good to us, while ours seem good to others.

Syrus—*Maxims.*

CITY

I live not in myself, but I become
Portion of that around me; and to me
High mountains are a feeling, but the hum
Of human cities torture.

Byron—*Childe Harold.*

This poor little one-horse town.

S. L. Clemens (Mark Twain)—*The Undertaker's Story.*

If you would know and not be known, live in a city.

Colton.

God made the country, and man made the town.

Cowper—*The Task.*

I always seem to suffer some loss of faith on entering cities.

Emerson.

Cities force growth, and make men talkative and entertaining, but they make them artificial.

Emerson.

I bless God for cities. Cities have been as lamps of life along the pathway of humanity and religion. Within them science has given birth to her noblest discoveries. Behind their walls freedom has fought her noblest battles. They have stood on the surface of the earth like great breakwaters, rolling back or turning aside the swelling tide of oppression. Cities, indeed, have been the cradles of human liberty. They have been the active centres of almost all church and state reformation.

Rev. Dr. Guthrie.

In the busy haunts of men.

Felicia D. Hemans—*Tale of the Secret Tribunal.*

Seven cities warr'd for Homer being dead,
Who living had no roofe to shroud his head.

Thomas Heywood—*Hierarchie of the Blessed Angells.*

Far from gay cities, and the ways of men.

Homer—*Odyssey.*

Before man made us citizens, great Nature made us men.

Lowell.

Ye are the light of the world. A city that is set on a hill cannot be hid.

Matthew. V. 14.

Dante might choose his home in all the wide beautiful world; but to be out of the streets of Florence was exile to him. Socrates never cared to go beyond the bounds of Athens. The great universal heart welcomes the city as a natural growth of the eternal forces.

F. B. Sanborn.

The people are the city.
SHAKESPEARE—*Coriolanus.* Act III. Sc. 1.

He (Caesar Augustus) found a city built of brick; he left it built of marble.
SUETONIUS.

The city of dreadful night.
JAMES THOMSON—*Current Literature for 1889.*

CIVILIZATION

Mankind's struggle upwards, in which millions are trampled to death, that thousands may mount on their bodies.
MRS. BALFOUR.

Increased means and increased leisure are the two civilizers of men.
DISRAELI.

The truest test of civilization is not the census, nor the size of cities, nor the crops; no, but the kind of man the country turns out.
EMERSON.

A sufficient measure of civilization is the influence of good women.
EMERSON.

The path of civilization is paved with tin cans.
ELBERT HUBBARD.

Nations, like individuals, live and die; but civilization cannot die.
MAZZINI.

Civilization, or that which is so called, has operated two ways to make one part of society more affluent and the other part more wretched than would have been the lot of either in a natural state.
THOMAS PAINE.

Extremes produce reaction. Beware that our boasted civilization does not lapse into barbarism.
RIVAROL.

CLEANLINESS

For cleanness of body was ever esteemed to proceed from a due reverence to God, to society, and to ourselves.
BACON—*Advancement of Learning.*

All will come out in the washing.
CERVANTES—*Don Quixote.*

He that toucheth pitch shall be defiled therewith.
Ecclesiasticus. XIII. 1.

God loveth the clean.
The Koran.

If dirt was trumps, what hands you would hold!
LAMB—*Lamb's Suppers.*

The doctrines of religion are resolved into carefulness; carefulness into vigorousness; vigorousness into guiltlessness; guiltlessness into abstemiousness; abstemiousness into cleanliness; cleanliness into godliness.
The Talmud.

Certainly this is a duty, not a sin. "Cleanliness is indeed next to godliness."
JOHN WESLEY.

CLERGYMAN

Politics and the pulpit are terms that have little agreement.
BURKE.

He was a shepherd and no mercenary,
And though he holy was and virtuous,
He was to sinful men full piteous;
His words were strong, but not with anger fraught;
A love benignant he discreetly taught.
To draw mankind to heaven by gentleness
And good example was his business.
CHAUCER.

There goes the parson, oh illustrious spark!
And there, scarce less illustrious, goes the clerk.
COWPER.

If you would lift me you must be on a higher ground.
EMERSON.

At church with meek and unaffected grace,
His looks adorn'd the venerable place;
Truth from his lips prevail'd with double sway,
And fools, who came to scoff, remain'd to pray.
GOLDSMITH.

As a career, the business of an orthodox preacher is about as successful as that of a celluloid dog chasing an asbestos cat through Hell.
ELBERT HUBBARD.

The life of a conscientious clergyman is not easy. I have always considered a clergyman as the father of a larger family than he is able to maintain. I would rather have chancery suits upon my hands than the cure of souls.
SAMUEL JOHNSON.

I do not envy a clergyman's life as an easy life, nor do I envy the clergyman who makes it an easy life.
SAMUEL JOHNSON.

The defects of a preacher are soon spied.
LUTHER.

I never saw, heard, nor read, that the clergy were beloved in any nation where Christianity was the religion of the country.
SWIFT.

CLOUDS

Were I a cloud I'd gather
My skirts up in the air,
And fly I well know whither,
And rest I well know where.
ROBERT BRIDGES—*Elegy*.

Our fathers were under the cloud.
I Corinthians. X. 1.

Though outwardly a gloomy shroud,
The inner half of every cloud
Is bright and shining:
I therefore turn my clouds about
And always wear them inside out
To show the lining.
ELLEN THORNEYCROFT FOWLER—*Wisdom of Folly*.

When clouds appear like rocks and towers,
The earth's refreshed by frequent showers.
Old Weather Rhyme.

If woolly fleeces spread the heavenly way
No rain, be sure, disturbs the summer's day.
Old Weather Rhyme.

Do you see yonder cloud, that's almost in shape of a camel?
By the mass, and 'tis like a camel, indeed.
Methinks it is like a weasel.
It is backed like a weasel.
Or, like a whale?
Very like a whale.
SHAKESPEARE—*Hamlet*. Act III. Sc. 2.

I bring fresh showers for the thirsting flowers,
From the seas and the streams;
I bear light shade for the leaves when laid
In their noonday dreams.
From my wings are shaken the dews that waken
The sweet buds every one,
When rocked to rest on their mother's breast,
As she dances about the sun.
I wield the flail of the lashing hail,
And whiten the green plains under,
And then again I dissolve it in rain,
And laugh as I pass in thunder.
SHELLEY—*The Cloud*.

Far clouds of feathery gold,
Shaded with deepest purple, gleam
Like islands on a dark blue sea.
SHELLEY—*Queen Mab*.

COACH

Go, call a coach, and let a coach be called;
And let the man who calleth be the caller;
And in the calling, let him nothing call,
But coach! coach! coach! O for a coach, ye gods!
HENRY CAREY.

COMFORT

Comfort and indolence are cronies.
HOOD.

Is there no balm in Gilead?
Jeremiah. VIII. 22.

Thy rod and thy staff they comfort me.
Psalms. XXIII. 4.

Of all created comforts, God is the lender; you are the borrower, not the owner.
RUTHERFORD.

And He that doth the ravens feed,
Yea, providently caters for the sparrow,
Be comfort to my age!
SHAKESPEARE—*As You Like It*. Act II. Sc. 3.

I want a sofa, as I want a friend, upon which I can repose familiarly. If you can't have intimate terms and freedom with one and the other, they are of no good.
THACKERAY.

COMMERCE

Commerce defies every wind, outrides every tempest, and invades every zone.
BANCROFT.

God is making commerce His missionary.
JOSEPH COOK.

More pernicious nonsense was never devised by man than treaties of commerce.
DISRAELI.

Commerce links all mankind in one common brotherhood of mutual dependence and interests.
JAMES A. GARFIELD.

Commerce is the equalizer of the wealth of nations.
GLADSTONE.

Whatever has a tendency to promote the civil intercourse of nations by an exchange of benefits is a subject as worthy of philosophy as of politics.
THOMAS PAINE.

COMMON SENSE

Common sense is very uncommon.
HORACE GREELEY.

Common sense is in spite of, not the result of, education.
VICTOR HUGO.

Common sense is instinct, and enough of it is genius.
H. W. SHAW.

Common sense is in spite of, not because of age.
LORD THURLOW.

COMMUNISM

What is a Communist? One who hath yearnings
For equal division of unequal earnings.
Idler or bungler, or both, he is willing,
To fork out his copper and pocket your shilling.
EBENEZER ELLIOTT.

The theory of Communism may be summed up in one sentence: Abolish all private property.
KARL MARX and FRIEDRICH ENGELS—*The Communist Manifesto*.

As soon as classes have been abolished, and the dictatorship of the proletariat has been done away with, the (Communist) party will have fulfilled its mission and can be allowed to disappear.
JOSEPH STALIN—*Speech, 1924*.

COMPANIONSHIP

Tell me thy company and I will tell thee what thou art.
CERVANTES—Quoted in *Don Quixote*.

We have been born to associate with our fellow-men, and to join in community with the human race.
CICERO.

We are in the same boat.
POPE CLEMENT I—*To the Church of Corinth*.

Ah, savage company; but in the church
With saints, and in the taverns with
the gluttons.
DANTE—*Inferno* XXII. 13.

The right hands of fellowship.
Galatians. II. 9.

It takes two for a kiss
Only one for a sigh,
Twain by twain we marry
One by one we die.
FREDERICK L. KNOWLES—*Grief and Joy.*

No possession is gratifying without a companion.
SENECA.

(Epicurus) says that you should rather have regard to the company with whom you eat and drink, than to what you eat and drink.
SENECA—*Epistles.*

Join the company of lions rather than assume the lead among foxes.
The Talmud.

No man can be provident of his time who is not prudent in the choice of his company.
JEREMY TAYLOR.

COMPARISON

About a donkey's taste why need we
fret us?
To lips like his a thistle is a lettuce.
ANONYMOUS.

'Tis light translateth night; 'tis in-
spiration
Expounds experience; 'tis the west ex-
plains
The east; 'tis time unfolds Eternity.
BAILEY—*Festus.*

Comparisons are odious.
ARCHBISHOP BOIARDO—*Orlando Innamorato.*

It's wiser being good than bad;
It's safer being meek than fierce:
It's fitter being sane than mad.
My own hope is, a sun will pierce
The thickest cloud earth ever stretched;
That, after Last, returns the First,
Though a wide compass round be
fetched;
That what began best, can't end
worst,
Nor what God blessed once, prove
accurst.
BROWNING—*Apparent Failure.*

Some say, compared to Bononcini,
That Mynheer Handel's but a ninny;
Others aver, that he to Handel
Is scarcely fit to hold a Candle:
Strange all this difference should be,
'Twixt Tweedle-dum and Tweedle-
dee!'
JOHN BYROM.

At whose sight, like the sun,
All others with diminish'd lustre
shone.
CICERO.

The bee and the serpent often sip from the selfsame flower.
METASTASIO—*Morte d'Abele.*

Crabbed age and youth cannot live together.
SHAKESPEARE—*The Passionate Pilgrim.*

Here and there a cotter's babe is royal
—born by right divine;
Here and there my lord is lower than
his oxen or his swine.
TENNYSON—*Locksley Hall.*

Thus I knew that pups are like dogs, and kids like goats; so I used to compare great things with small.
VERGIL.

COMPASSION

Compassion is an emotion of which we ought never to be ashamed. Graceful, particularly in youth, is the tear of sympathy, and the heart that melts at the tale of woe.
BLAIR.

Man may dismiss compassion from
his heart,
But God will never.
COWPER.

Compassion, the fairest associate of the heart.
PAINE.

COMPENSATION

There is a day of sunny rest
For every dark and troubled night;
And grief may hide an evening guest,
But joy shall come with early light.
BRYANT.

Each loss has its compensation
There is healing for every pain,
But the bird with a broken pinion
Never soars so high again.
HEZEKIAH BUTTERWORTH — *The Broken Pinion.*

Cast thy bread upon the waters; for thou shalt find it after many days.
Ecclesiastes. XI. 1.

Curses always recoil on the head of him who imprecates them. If you put a chain around the neck of a slave, the other end fastens itself around your own.
EMERSON.

If the poor man cannot always get meat, the rich man cannot always digest it.
HENRY GILES.

'Tis always morning somewhere in the world.
RICHARD HENGEST HORNE—*Orion.*

Nothing is pure and entire of a piece. All advantages are attended with disadvantages. A universal compensation prevails in all conditions of being and existence.
HUME.

Give unto them beauty for ashes, the oil of joy for mourning, the garment of praise for the spirit of heaviness.
Isaiah. LXI. 3.

The equity of Providence has balanced peculiar sufferings with peculiar enjoyments.
SAMUEL JOHNSON.

O weary hearts! O slumbering eyes!
O drooping souls, whose destinies
Are fraught with fear and pain,
Ye shall be loved again.
LONGFELLOW—*Endymion.*

Earth gets its price for what Earth gives us,
The beggar is taxed for a corner to die in,
The priest hath his fee who comes and shrives us,
We bargain for the graves we lie in;
At the devil's booth are all things sold,
Each ounce of dross costs its ounce of gold;
For a cap and bells our lives we pay,
Bubbles we buy with a whole soul's tasking,
'Tis heaven alone that is given away,
'Tis only God may be had for the asking,
No price is set on the lavish summer;
June may be had by the poorest comer.
LOWELL—*Vision of Sir Launfal.* Prelude to Pt. I.

Whoever makes great presents expects great presents in return.
MARTIAL.

Merciful Father, I will not complain.
I know that the sunshine shall follow the rain.
JOAQUIN MILLER — *For Princess Maud.*

The prickly thorn often bears soft roses.
OVID.

The rose does not bloom without thorns. True; but would that the thorns did not outlive the rose!
JEAN PAUL RICHTER.

I believe that every right implies a responsibility; every opportunity, an obligation; every possession, a duty.
JOHN D. ROCKEFELLER, JR.— *Speech, 1941.*

Long pains are light ones,
Cruel ones are brief!
J. F. SAXE—*Compensation.*

No evil is without its compensation.
SENECA.

And light is mingled with the gloom,
And joy with grief;
Divinest compensations come,
Through thorns of judgment mercies bloom
In sweet relief.
WHITTIER.

COMPLAINING

I have always despised the whining yelp of complaint, and the cowardly feeble resolve.

BURNS.

Constant complaint is the poorest sort of pay for all the comforts we enjoy.

FRANKLIN.

Those who complain most are most to be complained of.

MATTHEW HENRY.

The usual fortune of complaint is to excite contempt more than pity.

JOHNSON.

Complaint is the largest tribute Heaven receives.

SWIFT.

COMPLIMENT

Compliments are only lies in court clothes.

ANONYMOUS.

When two people compliment each other with the choice of anything, each of them generally gets that which he likes least.

POPE.

A woman . . . always feels herself complimented by love, though it may be from a man incapable of winning her heart, or perhaps even her esteem.

ABEL STEVENS—*Life of Madame de Stael.*

Current among men,
Like coin, the tinsel clink of compliment.

TENNYSON—*The Princess.*

Compliments and flattery oftenest excite my contempt by the pretension they imply; for who is he that assumes to flatter me? To compliment often implies an assumption of superiority in the complimenter. It is, in fact, a subtle detraction.

THOREAU.

COMPROMISE

All government—indeed, every human benefit and enjoyment, every virtue and every prudent act—is founded on compromise and barter.

EDMUND BURKE—*Speech on Conciliation.*

Compromise makes a good umbrella, but a poor roof; it is a temporary expedient, often wise in party politics, almost sure to be unwise in statesmanship.

LOWELL.

CONCEIT

Conceited men often seem a harmless kind of men, who, by an overweening self-respect, relieve others from the duty of respecting them at all.

HENRY WARD BEECHER.

An eagerness and zeal for dispute on every subject, and with every one, shows great self-sufficiency, that never-failing sign of great self-ignorance.

LORD CHATHAM.

No man was ever so much deceived by another as by himself.

LORD GREVILLE.

A man who is always well satisfied with himself is seldom so with others, and others as little pleased with him.

LA ROCHEFOUCAULD.

The art of making much show with little substance.

MACAULAY.

In men this blunder still you find,
All think their little set mankind.

HANNAH MORE—*Florio.*

Seest thou a man wise in his own conceit? There is more hope of a fool than of him.

Proverbs. XXVI. 12.

We go and fancy that everybody is thinking of us. But he is not; he is like us—he is thinking of himself.

CHARLES READE.

Conceit may puff a man up, but never prop him up.

RUSKIN—*True and Beautiful.*

Wind puffs up empty bladders; opinion, fools.

SOCRATES.

CONDUCT

As in walking it is your great care not to run your foot upon a nail, or to tread awry, and strain your leg; so let it be in all the affairs of human life, not to hurt your mind or offend your judgment. And this rule, if observed carefully in all your deportment, will be a mighty security to you in your undertakings.

EPICTETUS.

It is not enough that you can form, nay, and follow, the most excellent rules for conducting yourself in the world. You must also know when to deviate from them, and where lies the exception.

GREVILLE.

Be swift to hear, slow to speak, slow to wrath.

James. I. 19.

The integrity of men is to be measured by their conduct, not by their professions.

JUNIUS.

CONFIDENCE

He who believes in nobody knows that he himself is not to be trusted.

AUERBACH.

He who has lost confidence can lose nothing more.

BOISTE.

For they can conquer who believe they can.

DRYDEN.

The confidence which we have in ourselves gives birth to much of that which we have in others.

LA ROCHEFOUCAULD.

Society is built upon trust.

SOUTH.

Confidence is conqueror of men; victorious both over them and in them;
The iron will of one stout heart shall make a thousand quail;
A feeble dwarf, dauntlessly resolved, will turn the tide of battle,
And rally to a nobler strife the giants that had fled.

TUPPER.

Confidence is nowhere safe.

VERGIL—*Aeneid.*

CONQUEST

How grand is victory, but how dear!

BOUFFLERS.

He who surpasses or subdues mankind must look down on the hate of those below.

BYRON.

I came, I saw, I conquered.

CAESAR.

It is the right of war for conquerors to treat those whom they have conquered according to their pleasure.

CAESAR.

Yield to him who opposes you; by yielding you conquer.

OVID.

The more acquisitions the government makes abroad, the more taxes the people have to pay at home.

THOMAS PAINE.

Self-conquest is the greatest of victories.

PLATO.

I sing the hymn of the conquered, who fell in the battle of life,
The hymn of the wounded, the beaten who died overwhelmed in the strife;
Not the jubilant song of the victors for whom the resounding acclaim
Of nations was lifted in chorus whose brows wore the chaplet of fame,
But the hymn of the low and the humble, the weary, the broken in heart,
Who strove and who failed, acting bravely a silent and desperate part.

W. W. STORY—*Io Victis.*

CONSCIENCE

A good conscience is the palace of Christ; the temple of the Holy Ghost;

the paradise of delight; the standing Sabbath of the saints.
St. Augustine.

Nor ear can hear nor tongue can tell
The tortures of that inward hell!
Byron.

But at sixteen the conscience rarely gnaws
So much, as when we call our old debts in
At sixty years, and draw the accounts of evil,
And find a deuced balance with the devil.
Byron—*Don Juan*.

Liberty of conscience (when people have consciences) is rightly considered the most indispensable of liberties.
Chambers.

O faithful conscience, delicately pure, how doth a little failing wound thee sore!
Dante—*Purgatorio*.

Conscience is harder than our enemies,
Knows more, accuses with more nicety.
George Eliot.

The only incorruptible thing about us.
Fielding.

Conscience is a coward, and those faults it has not strength to prevent, it seldom has justice enough to accuse.
Goldsmith—*Vicar of Wakefield*.

Man, wretched man, whene'er he stoops to sin,
Feels, with the act, a strong remorse within.
Juvenal.

A still, small voice.
I Kings. XIX. 12.

Conscience is a sacred sanctuary where God alone may enter as judge.
Lamennais.

I am more afraid of my own heart than of the pope and all his cardinals. I have within me the great pope, self.
Luther.

Conscience is justice's best minister.
Lady Montagu.

What Conscience dictates to be done,
Or warns me not to do;
This teach me more than Hell to shun,
That more than Heav'n pursue.
Pope—*Universal Prayer*.

Live with men as if God saw you; converse with God as if men heard you.
Seneca.

Thus conscience does make cowards of us all;
And thus the native hue of resolution
Is sicklied o'er with the pale cast of thought.
And enterprises of great pith and moment,
With this regard, their currents turn awry,
And lose the name of action.
Shakespeare—*Hamlet*. Act III. Sc. 1.

The worm of conscience still begnaw thy soul!
Thy friends suspect for traitors while thou liv'st,
And take deep traitors for thy dearest friends!
Shakespeare—*Richard III*. Act. I. Sc. 3.

Conscience is but a word that cowards use,
Devised at first to keep the strong in awe.
Shakespeare—*Richard III*. Act V. Sc. 3.

Conscience warns us as a friend before it punishes us as a judge.
Stanislaus.

Trust that man in nothing who has not a Conscience in everything.
Laurence Sterne—*Tristram Shandy*. Bk. II.

And I know of the future judgment
How dreadful so'er it be
That to sit alone with my conscience
Would be judgment enough for me.
Charles William Stubbs.

Labor to keep alive in your breast that little spark of celestial fire, called Conscience.
WASHINGTON—*Moral Maxims.*

The soft whispers of the God in man.
YOUNG.

CONSERVATISM

A conservative young man has wound up his life before it was unreeled. We expect old men to be conservative; but when a nation's young men are so, its funeral bell is already rung.
HENRY WARD BEECHER.

A statesman who is enamored of existing evils, as distinguished from the Liberal, who wishes to replace them with others.
BIERCE—*The Devil's Dictionary.*

We are reformers in spring and summer; in autumn and winter we stand by the old; reformers in the morning, conservers at night. Reform is affirmative, conservatism negative; conservatism goes for comfort, reform for truth.
EMERSON.

A conservative is a man who will not look at the new moon, out of respect for that "ancient institution," the old one.
DOUGLAS JERROLD.

What is conservatism? Is it not adherence to the old and tried, against the new and untried?
LINCOLN, 1860.

A Conservative is a man with two perfectly good legs who, however, has never learned to walk.
F. D. ROOSEVELT, 1939.

CONSISTENCY

A foolish consistency is the hobgoblin of little minds, adored by little statesmen and philosophers and divines.
EMERSON—*Self-Reliance.*

Speak what you think to-day in words as hard as cannon balls, and to-morrow speak what to-morrow thinks in hard words again, though it contradict everything you said to-day.
EMERSON—*Self-Reliance.*

Inconsistency is the only thing in which men are consistent.
HORATIO SMITH—*Tin Trumpet.*

You are harping on the same string.
TERENCE.

CONSOLATION

For every bad there might be a worse; and when one breaks his leg, let him be thankful it was not his neck.
BISHOP HALL.

God has commanded time to console the unhappy.
JOUBERT.

Consolation indiscreetly pressed upon us, when we are suffering undue affliction, only serves to increase our pain, and to render our grief more poignant.
ROUSSEAU.

CONSTANCY

Without constancy, there is neither love, friendship, nor virtue in the world.
ADDISON.

True constancy no time no power can
more;
He that hath known to change, ne'er
knew to love.
GAY.

Changeless march the stars above,
Changeless morn succeeds to even;
And the everlasting hills,
Changeless watch the changeless
heaven.
KINGSLEY—*Saint's Tragedy.*

Then come the wild weather, come
sleet or come snow,
We will stand by each other, however
it blow.

Oppression, and sickness, and sorrow, and pain
Shall be to our true love as links to the chain.
LONGFELLOW.

Sigh no more, ladies, sigh no more,
Men were deceivers ever,
One foot in sea and one on shore;
To one thing constant never.
SHAKESPEARE—*Much Ado About Nothing*. Act II. Sc. 3.

The lasting and crowning privilege of friendship is constancy.
SOUTH.

Out upon it! I have lov'd
Three whole days together;
And am like to love three more,
If it prove fair weather.
SUCKLING—*Constancy*.

CONTEMPT

Speak with contempt of no man. Every one hath a tender sense of reputation. And every man hath a sting, which he may, if provoked too far, dart out at one time or another.
BURTON.

An Englishman fears contempt more than death.
GOLDSMITH.

No man can fall into contempt but those who deserve it.
SAMUEL JOHNSON.

None but the contemptible are apprehensive of contempt.
LA ROCHEFOUCAULD.

Contempt is the only way to triumph over calumny.
MADAME DE MAINTENON.

Who can refute a sneer?
PALEY.

CONTENTION

Let there be no strife, I pray thee, between thee and me.
Genesis. XIII. 8.

If a house be divided against itself, that house cannot stand.
Mark. III. 25.

CONTENTMENT

In Paris a queer little man you may see,
A little man all in gray;
Rosy and round as an apple is he,
Content with the present whate'er it may be,
While from care and from cash he is equally free,
And merry both night and day!
"Ma foi! I laugh at the world," says he,
"I laugh at the world, and the world laughs at me!"
What a gay little man in gray.
BÉRANGER—*The Little Man All in Gray*.

There was a jolly miller once,
Lived on the River Dee;
He worked and sang, from morn to night;
No lark so blithe as he.
And this the burden of his song,
Forever used to be,—
"I care for nobody, not I,
If no one cares for me."
BICKERSTAFF—*Love in a Village*.

Content is not happiness. An oyster may be contented. Happiness is compounded of richer elements.
BOVEE.

I would do what I pleased, and doing what I pleased, I should have my will, and having my will, I should be contented; and when one is contented, there is no more to be desired; and when there is no more to be desired, there is an end of it.
CERVANTES—*Don Quixote*.

Enjoy your own life without comparing it with that of another.
CONDORCET.

We'll therefore relish with content,
Whate'er kind Providence has sent,
Nor aim beyond our pow'r;
For, if our stock be very small,
'Tis prudent to enjoy it all,
Nor lose the present hour.
NATHANIEL COTTON.

Contentment, as it is a short road and pleasant, has great delight and little trouble.
EPICTETUS.

Happy the man, of mortals happiest he,
Whose quiet mind from vain desires is free;
Whom neither hopes deceive, nor fears torment,
But lives at peace, within himself content;
In thought, or act, accountable to none
But to himself, and to the gods alone.
GEORGE GRANVILLE.

Sweet are the thoughts that savour of content;
The quiet mind is richer than a crown;
Sweet are the nights in careless slumber spent;
The poor estate scorns fortune's angry frown:
Such sweet content, such minds, such sleep, such bliss,
Beggars enjoy, when princes oft do miss.
ROBERT GREENE—*Farewell to Folly.*

Where wealth and freedom reign, contentment fails,
And honour sinks where commerce long prevails.
GOLDSMITH—*The Traveller.*

Contentment is, after all, simply refined indolence.
HALIBURTON.

Let's live with that small pittance which we have;
Who covets more is evermore a slave.
HERRICK—*The Covetous Still Captive.*

Those who want much, are always much in need; happy the man to whom God gives with a sparing hand what is sufficient for his wants.
HORACE—*Carmina.*

Who can enjoy alone?
Or all enjoying what contentment find?
MILTON—*Paradise Lost.*

Contentment furnishes constant joy. Much covetousness, constant grief. To the contented, even poverty is joy. To the discontented, even wealth is a vexation.
MING SUM PAOU KEËN.

Happy am I; from care I'm free!
Why aren't they all contended like me?
Opera, La Bayadère.

I earn that I eat, get that I wear, owe no man hate, envy no man's happiness; glad of other men's good, content with my harm.
SHAKESPEARE—*As You Like It.* Act III. Sc. 2.

My crown is in my heart, not on my head;
Not deck'd with diamonds and Indian stones,
Nor to be seen: my crown is called content;
A crown it is that seldom kings enjoy.
SHAKESPEARE—*Henry VI.* Pt. III. Act III. Sc. 1.

He is well paid that is well satisfied.
SHAKESPEARE—*Merchant of Venice.* Act IV. Sc. 1.

'Tis not so deep as a well, nor so wide as a church door; but 'tis enough, 'twill serve.
SHAKESPEARE—*Romeo and Juliet.* Act III. Sc. 1.

Not on the outer world
For inward joy depend;
Enjoy the luxury of thought,
Make thine own self friend;
Not with the restless throng,
In search of solace roam
But with an independent zeal
Be intimate at home.
LYDIA SIGOURNEY—*Know Thyself.*

Contentment is natural wealth; luxury, artificial poverty.
SOCRATES.

It is not for man to rest in absolute contentment.
SOUTHEY.

The harvest song of inward peace.
WHITTIER.

CONTRAST

Strange as it may seem, the most ludicrous lines I ever wrote have been written in the saddest mood.
COWPER.

Shadow owes its birth to light.
GAY.

Men and statues that are admired in an elevated situation have a very different effect upon us when we approach them; the first appear less than we imagined them, the last bigger.
LORD GREVILLE.

The superiority of some men is merely local. They are great because their associates are little.
SAMUEL JOHNSON.

CONTROVERSY

No great advance has ever been made in science, politics, or religion, without controversy.
LYMAN BEECHER.

Where violence reigns, reason is weak.
CHAMFORT.

If a cause be good, the most violent attack of its enemies will not injure it so much as an injudicious defence of it by its friends.
COLTON.

He who is not open to conviction is not qualified for discussion.
WHATELY.

CONVERSATION

Egotists cannot converse, they talk to themselves only.
A. BRONSON ALCOTT.

Debate is masculine; conversation is feminine.
A. BRONSON ALCOTT.

In conversation avoid the extremes of forwardness and reserve.
CATO.

Never hold any one by the button or the hand in order to be heard out; for if people are unwilling to hear you, you had better hold your tongue than them.
CHESTERFIELD.

Conversation is the laboratory and workshop of the student.
EMERSON.

The great secret of succeeding in conversation is to admire little, to hear much; always to distrust our own reason, and sometimes that of our friends; never to pretend to wit, but to make that of others appear as much as possibly we can; to hearken to what is said, and to answer to the purpose.
FRANKLIN.

Conversation enriches the understanding, but solitude is the school of genius.
GIBBON.

Silence is one great art of conversation.
HAZLITT.

Questioning is not the mode of conversation among gentlemen.
SAMUEL JOHNSON.

Conceit causes more conversation than wit.
LA ROCHEFOUCAULD.

A single conversation across the table with a wise man is better than ten years' study of books.
LONGFELLOW.

The less men think, the more they talk.
MONTESQUIEU.

The first ingredient in conversation is truth, the next good sense, the third good humor, and the fourth wit.
SIR W. TEMPLE.

COOKING

To make a ragout, first catch your hare.
ANONYMOUS.

We may live without friends; we may live without books;
But civilized man cannot live without cooks.
BULWER-LYTTON.

Cookery is become an art, a noble science; cooks are gentlemen.
BURTON.

God sends meat, and the Devil sends cooks.
JOHN TAYLOR—*Works*.

CORRUPTION

Just for a handful of silver he left us,
Just for a ribbon to stick in his coat.
ROBERT BROWNING—*The Lost Leader.*

The time to guard against corruption and tyranny is before they shall have gotten hold of us. It is better to keep the wolf out of the fold than to trust to drawing his teeth and talons after he shall have entered.
JEFFERSON—*Notes on Virginia.*

The impious man, who sells his country's freedom
Makes all the guilt of tyranny his own.
His are her slaughters, her oppressions his;
Just heav'n! reserve your choicest plagues for him,
And blast the venal wretch.
MARTYN.

The men with the muck-rake are often indispensable to the well-being of society, but only if they know when to stop raking the muck.
THEODORE ROOSEVELT.

The more corrupt the state, the more laws.
TACITUS.

COUNTRY LIFE

I consider it the best part of an education to have been born and brought up in the country.
ALCOTT.

This pure air
Braces the listless nerves, and warms the blood:
I feel in freedom here.
JOANNA BAILLIE.

The town is man's world, but this (country life) is of God.
COWPER—*The Task.*

Sir, when you have seen one green field, you have seen all green fields. Let us walk down Cheapside.
SAMUEL JOHNSON.

Oh knew he but his happiness, of men
The happiest he! who far from public rage,
Deep in the vale, with a choice few retir'd
Drinks the pure pleasures of the rural life.
THOMSON.

COUNTRY, LOVE OF

Our country is wherever we are well off.
CICERO.

They love their land, because it is their own,
And scorn to give aught other reason why;
Would shake hands with a king upon his throne,
And think it kindness to his majesty.
FITZ-GREENE HALLECK—*Connecticut.*

To be really cosmopolitan a man must be at home even in his own country.
T. W. HIGGINSON.

Breathes there the man with soul so dead,
Who never to himself hath said,
This is my own, my native land!
Whose heart hath ne'er within him burn'd,
As home his footsteps he hath turn'd,
From wandering on a foreign strand!
SCOTT—*Lay of the Last Minstrel.*

COURAGE

He who loses wealth loses much; he who loses a friend loses more; but he that loses his courage loses all.
CERVANTES.

The moral courage that will face obloquy in a good cause is a much rarer gift than the bodily valor that will confront death in a bad one.
CHATFIELD.

A man of courage is also full of faith.
CICERO.

Life is not so short but that there is always time enough for courtesy.
EMERSON—*Social Aims.*

Tender handed stroke a nettle,
And it stings you for your pains;
Grasp it like a man of mettle,
And it soft as silk remains.
AARON HILL—*Verses Written on a Window.*

Courage is poorly housed that dwells in numbers; the lion never counts the herd that are about him, nor weighs how many flocks he has to scatter.
AARON HILL.

Truth wants no champion who is not ready to be struck as to strike for her.
J. G. HOLLAND.

O friends, be men, and let your hearts be strong,
And let no warrior in the heat of fight
Do what may bring him shame in others' eyes;
For more of those who shrink from shame are safe
Than fall in battle, while with those who flee
Is neither glory nor reprieve from death.
HOMER—*Iliad.*

When moral courage feels that it is in the right, there is no personal daring of which it is incapable.
LEIGH HUNT.

Write on your doors the saying wise and old,
"Be bold!" and everywhere—"Be bold;
Be not too bold!" Yet better the excess
Than the defect; better the more than less;
Better like Hector in the field to die,
Than like a perfumed Paris turn and fly.
LONGFELLOW—*Morituri Salutamus.*

Fortune and Love befriend the bold.
OVID.

Courage consists not in hazarding without fear, but being resolutely minded in a just cause.
PLUTARCH.

Women and men of retiring timidity are cowardly only in dangers which affect themselves, but the first to rescue when others are endangered.
JEAN PAUL RICHTER.

Courage consists not in blindly overlooking danger, but in seeing it and conquering it.
JEAN PAUL RICHTER.

Courage leads to heaven; fear to death.
SENECA.

Dissembling courtesy! How fine this tyrant
Can tickle where she wounds!
SHAKESPEARE—*Cymbeline.* Act I. Sc. 1.

Muster your wits: stand in your own defence;
Or hide your heads like cowards, and fly hence.
SHAKESPEARE — *Love's Labour's Lost.* Act V. Sc. 2.

Hail, Caesar, those who are about to die salute thee.
SUETONIUS.

I wonder is it because men are cowards in heart that they admire bravery so much, and place military valor so far beyond every other quality for reward and worship.
THACKERAY.

COURTESY

The small courtesies sweeten life; the greater ennoble it.
BOVEE.

A moral, sensible, and well-bred man
Will not affront me, and no other can.
COWPER.

COURTSHIP

What a woman says to her lover should be written on air or swift water.
CATULLUS.

A feast is more fatal to love than a fast.
COLTON.

If you cannot inspire a woman with love of you, fill her above the brim with love of herself; all that runs over will be yours.
COLTON.

COVETOUSNESS

If money be not thy servant, it will be thy master. The covetous man cannot so properly be said to possess wealth, as that it may be said to possess him.
BACON.

To think well of every other man's condition, and to dislike our own, is one of the misfortunes of human nature. "Pleased with each other's lot, our own we hate."
BURTON.

Thou shalt not covet thy neighbor's house, thou shalt not covet thy neighbor's wife, nor his manservant, nor his maidservant, nor his ox, nor his ass, nor anything that is thy neighbor's.
Exodus. XX. 17.

We covet what is guarded; the very care invokes the thief. Few love what they may have.
OVID.

He deservedly loses his own property, who covets that of another.
PHAEDRUS.

COW

I never saw a Purple Cow,
I never hope to see one;
But I can tell you, anyhow
I'd rather see than be one.
GELETT BURGESS—*The Purple Cow*.

A cow is a very good animal in the field; but we turn her out of a garden.
SAMUEL JOHNSON.

There was an old man who said, "How
Shall I flee from this horrible cow?
I will sit on this stile, and continue to smile,
Which may soften the heart of that cow."
LEAR—*The Book of Nonsense*.

COWARD

One who in a perilous emergency thinks with his legs.
BIERCE—*The Devil's Dictionary*.

The coward wretch whose hand and heart
Can bear to torture aught below,
Is ever first to quail and start
From slightest pain or equal foe.
ELIZA COOK.

He who fights and runs away
May live to fight another day.
But he who is in battle slain,
Can never rise to fight again.
GOLDSMITH.

Strange that cowards cannot see that their greatest safety lies in dauntless courage.
LAVATER.

A cowardly act! What do I care about that? You may be sure that I should never fear to commit one if it were to my advantage.
NAPOLEON.

All men would be cowards if they durst.
EARL OF ROCHESTER.

A cowardly cur barks more fiercely than it bites.
QUINTUS CURTIUS RUFUS.

CREATION

In the vast, and the minute, we see
The unambiguous footsteps of the God,
Who gives its lustre to an insect's wing
And wheels His throne upon the rolling worlds.
COWPER.

From harmony, from heavenly harmony,
This universal frame began:
From harmony, to harmony,
Through all the compass of the notes it ran,
The diapason closing full in man.
DRYDEN.

In the beginning God created the Heaven and the earth. And the earth was without form, and void; and darkness was upon the face of the deep. And the Spirit of God moved upon the face of the waters. And God said, Let there be light; and there was light.

Genesis. I. 3.

Nature they say, doth dote,
And cannot make a man
Save on some worn-out plan,
Repeating us by rote.

LOWELL—*Ode at Harvard Commemoration.*

Open, ye heavens, your living doors; let in
The great Creator from his work return'd
Magnificent, his six days' work, a world!

MILTON—*Paradise Lost.* Bk. VII.

All are but parts of one stupendous whole,
Whose body Nature is, and God the soul.

POPE.

It is easier to suppose that the universe has existed from all eternity than to conceive a Being beyond its limits capable of creating it.

SHELLEY—*Queen Mab.*

The world embarrasses me, and I cannot dream
That this watch exists and has no watchmaker.

VOLTAIRE.

CREDITOR

It takes a man to make a devil; and the fittest man for such a purpose is a snarling, waspish, red-hot, fiery creditor.

HENRY WARD BEECHER.

Creditors have better memories than debtors; and creditors are a superstitious sect, great observers of set days and times.

FRANKLIN.

CREDULITY

A man must have a good deal of vanity who believes, and a good deal of boldness who affirms, that all the doctrines he holds are true, and all he rejects are false.

FRANKLIN.

Let us believe neither half of the good people tell us of ourselves, nor half the evil they say of others.

J. PETIT-SENN.

You believe that easily which you hope for earnestly.

TERENCE.

I wish I was as sure of anything as Macaulay is of everything.

WILLIAM WINDHAM.

CRIME

Disgrace does not consist in the punishment, but in the crime.

ALFIERI—*Antigone.*

Society prepares the crime; the criminal commits it.

BUCKLE.

One crime is everything; two nothing.

MADAME DELUZY.

It is worse than a crime, it is a blunder.

JOSEPH FOUCHÉ.

Many commit the same crimes with a very different result. One bears a cross for his crime; another a crown.

JUVENAL—*Satires.*

If poverty is the mother of crimes, want of sense is the father.

LA BRUYÈRE.

There are crimes which become innocent and even glorious through their splendor, number and excess.

LA ROCHEFOUCALD.

Most people fancy themselves innocent of those crimes of which they cannot be convicted.

SENECA.

Yet each man kills the thing he loves,
By each let this be heard,
Some do it with a bitter look,
Some with a flattering word,
The coward does it with a kiss,
The brave man with a sword.

Oscar Wilde—*Ballad of Reading Gaol.*

CRISIS

In great straits, and when hope is small, the boldest counsels are the safest.

Livy.

These are the times that try men's souls.

Thomas Paine.

The nearer any disease approaches to a crisis, the nearer it is to a cure. Danger and deliverance make their advances together; and it is only in the last push that one or the other takes the lead.

Thomas Paine.

CRITICISM

It is much easier to be critical than to be correct.

Disraeli.

He was in Logic, a great critic,
Profoundly skill'd in Analytic;
He could distinguish, and divide
A hair 'twixt south and south-west side.

Butler—*Hudibras.*

The rule in carving holds good as to criticism; never cut with a knife what you can cut with a spoon.

Charles Buxton.

Said the pot to the kettle, "Get away, blackface."

Cervantes—*Don Quixote.*

Who shall dispute what the Reviewers say?
Their word's sufficient; and to ask a reason,
In such a state as theirs, is downright treason.
Though by whim, envy, or resentment led,
They damn those authors whom they never read.

Charles Churchill—*Apology.*

Charles Churchill—*The Candidate.*

If the present criticises the past, there is not much hope for the future.

Winston Churchill—*Speech, 1941.*

Reviewers are usually people who would have been poets, historians, biographers, etc., if they could: they have tried their talents at one or the other, and have failed; therefore tney turn critics.

Coleridge—*Lectures on Shakespeare and Milton.*

What a blessed thing it is that nature, when she invented, manufactured and patented her authors, contrived to make critics out of the chips that were left!

Holmes.

I had rather be hissed for a good verse than applauded for a bad one.

Victor Hugo.

Damn with faint praise, assent with civil leer,
And, without sneering, teach the rest to sneer:
Willing to wound, and yet afraid to strike,
Just hint a fault, and hesitate dislike.

Pope.

Reviewers, with some rare exceptions, are a most stupid and malignant race. As a bankrupt thief turns thief-taker in despair, so an unsuccessful author turns critic.

Shelley—*Fragments of Adonais.*

Of all the cants which are canted in this canting world—though the cant of hypocrites may be the worst—the cant of criticism is the most tormenting.

Laurence Sterne—*Tristram Shandy.*

CRUELTY

Man's inhumanity to man
Makes countless thousands mourn!

BURNS—*Man Was Made to Mourn.*

It is not linen you're wearing out,
But human creatures' lives.

HOOD—*Song of the Shirt.*

The Puritan hated bear-baiting, not because it gave pain to the bear, but because it gave pleasure to the spectators.

MACAULAY—*History of England.*

The man who prates about the cruelty of angling will be found invariably to beat his wife.

CHRISTOPHER NORTH.

All cruelty springs from weakness.

SENECA.

CULTURE

Culture is properly described as the love of perfection; it is a study of perfection.

MATTHEW ARNOLD—*Culture and Anarchy.*

Reading makes a full man, conference a ready man, and writing an exact man.

BACON.

Culture, with us, ends in headache.

EMERSON—*Experience.*

Man is born barbarous—he is ransomed from the condition of beasts only by being cultivated.

LAMARTINE.

The prosperity of a country depends, not on the abundance of its revenues, nor on the strength of its fortifications, nor on the beauty of its public building; but it consists in the number of its cultivated citizens, in its men of education, enlightenment and character.

LUTHER.

Culture is what your butcher would have if he were a surgeon.

MARY PETTIBONE POOLE—*A Glass Eye at the Keyhole.*

CUNNING

We take cunning for a sinister or crooked wisdom; and certainly there is a great difference between a cunning man and a wise man, not only in point of honesty, but in point of ability.

BACON.

A cunning man overreaches no one half as much as himself.

HENRY WARD BEECHER.

Cunning is the art of concealing our own defects, and discovering other people's weaknesses.

HAZLITT.

Nobody was ever so cunning as to conceal their being so; and everybody is shy and distrustful of crafty men.

LOCKE.

CURIOSITY

Curiosity killed the cat.

American Proverb.

Ask me no questions, and I'll tell you no fibs.

GOLDSMITH—*She Stoops to Conquer.*

Curiosity is one of the forms of feminine bravery.

VICTOR HUGO.

Curiosity is one of the permanent and certain characteristics of a vigorous intellect.

SAMUEL JOHNSON.

The knowledge that women lack stimulates their imagination; the knowledge that men possess blunts theirs.

MME. DE SARTORY.

CUSTOM

Men commonly think according to their inclinations, speak according to their learning and imbibed opinions; but generally act according to custom.

BACON.

There is no tyrant like custom, and no freedom where its edicts are not resisted.

BOVEE.

The slaves of custom and established mode,
With pack-horse constancy we keep the road
Crooked or straight, through quags or thorny dells,
True to the jingling of our leader's bells.

COWPER—*Tirocinium.*

The custom and fashion of to-day will be the awkwardness and outrage of to-morrow. So arbitrary are these transient laws.

DUMAS.

The ancients tell us what is best; but we must learn of the moderns what is fittest.

FRANKLIN.

But to my mind, though I am native here,
And to the manner born, it is a custom
More honor'd in the breach than the observance.

SHAKESPEARE—*Hamlet.* Act I. Sc. 4.

The old order changeth, yielding place to new;
And God fulfils himself in many ways,
Lest one good custom should corrupt the world.

TENNYSON—*Passing of Arthur.*

Custom is the law of fools.

VANBURGH.

CYNICISM

The cynic is one who never sees a good quality in a man, and never fails to see a bad one. He is the human owl, vigilant in darkness and blind to light, mousing for vermin, and never seeing noble game. The cynic puts all human actions into two classes—openly bad and secretly bad.

HENRY WARD BEECHER.

There is so much trouble in coming into the world, and so much more, as well as meanness, in going out of it, that it is hardly worth while to be here at all.

LORD BOLINGBROKE.

A cynic is a man who knows the price of everything, and the value of nothing.

WILDE—*Lady Windermere's Fan.*

D

DAISY

Not worlds on worlds, in phalanx deep,
Need we to prove a God is here;
The daisy, fresh from nature's sleep,
Tells of His hand in lines as clear.

DR. JOHN MASON GOOD.

All summer she scattered the daisy leaves;
They only mocked her as they fell.
She said: "The daisy but deceives;
'He loves me not,' 'he loves me well,'
One story no two daisies tell."
Ah foolish heart, which waits and grieves
Under the daisy's mocking spell.

HELEN HUNT JACKSON—*The Sign of the Daisy.*

Stars are the daisies that begem
The blue fields of the sky.

D. M. MOIR—*Dublin University Magazine.*

There is a flower, a little flower
With silver crest and golden eye,
That welcomes every changing hour,
And weathers every sky.

MONTGOMERY—*A Field Flower.*

DANCING

On with the dance! let joy be unconfin'd;
No sleep till morn, when Youth and Pleasure meet.

BYRON—*Childe Harold.*

No amusement seems more to have a foundation in our nature. The animation of youth overflows spontaneously in harmonious movements. The true idea of dancing entitles it to favor. Its end is to realize perfect grace in motion; and who does not know that a sense of the graceful is one of the higher faculties of our nature?

CHANNING.

No man in his senses will dance.

CICERO.

We are dancing on a volcano.

COMTE DE SALVANDY.

Come and trip it as ye go,
On the light fantastic toe.

MILTON—*L'Allegro.*

They who love dancing too much seem to have more brains in their feet than their head, and think to play the fool with reason.

TERENCE.

And beautiful maidens moved down in the dance,
With the magic of motion and sunshine of glance;
And white arms wreathed lightly, and tresses fell free
As the plumage of birds in some tropical tree.

WHITTIER—*Cities of the Plain.*

DANGER

We triumph without glory when we conquer without danger.

PIERRE CORNEILLE—*The Cid.*

Where, O king, destined to perish, are you directing your unavailing flight? Alas, lost one, you know not whom you flee; you are running upon enemies, whilst you flee from your foe. You fall upon the rock Scylla desiring to avoid the whirlpool Charybdis.

PHILLIPPE GAULTIER DE LILLE.

Danger for danger's sake is senseless.

LEIGH HUNT.

'Twas a dangerous cliff, as they freely confessed,
Though to walk near its crest was so pleasant,
But over its terrible edge there had slipped
A Duke and full many a peasant,
So the people said something would have to be done,
But their projects did not at all tally.
Some said: "Put a fence round the edge of the cliff."
Some: "An ambulance down in the valley."

JOSEPH MALINES—*Fence or Ambulance.*

A timid person is frightened before a danger, a coward during the time, and a courageous person afterwards.

JEAN PAUL RICHTER.

Constant exposure to dangers will breed contempt for them.

SENECA.

He is safe from danger who is on his guard even when safe.

SYRUS.

DARING

And what he greatly thought he nobly dared.

HOMER.

Who dares nothing, need hope for nothing.

SCHILLER—*Don Carlos.*

No one reaches a high position without daring.

SYRUS.

DARKNESS

It is always darkest just before the day dawneth.

THOMAS FULLER.

And out of darkness came the hands
That reach thro' nature, moulding men.

TENNYSON—*In Memoriam.*

DAUGHTER

My son is my son till he have got him a wife,
But my daughter's my daughter all the days of her life.

THOMAS FULLER.

A daughter is an embarrassing and ticklish possession.
MENANDER.

If thy daughter marry well, thou hast found a son; if not, thou hast lost a daughter.
QUARLES.

DAY

Think that day lost whose (low) descending sun
Views from thy hand no noble action done.
JACOB BOBART—*Krieg's Album in British Museum.*

Well, this is the end of a perfect day,
Near the end of a journey, too;
But it leaves a thought that is big and strong,
With a wish that is kind and true.
For mem'ry has painted this perfect day
With colors that never fade,
And we find at the end of a perfect day,
The soul of a friend we've made.
CARRIE JACOBS BOND—*A Perfect Day.*

What a day may bring a day may take away.
THOMAS FULLER.

Days should speak and multitude of years should teach wisdom.
Job. XXXII. 7.

He who has lived a day has lived an age.
LA BRUYÈRE.

Boast not thyself of to-morrow; for thou knowest not what a day may bring forth.
Proverbs. XXVII. 1.

No day is without its innocent hope.
RUSKIN.

One glance of Thine creates a day.
ISAAC WATTS.

DEATH

Call no man happy till he is dead.
AESCHYLUS—*Agamemnon.*

Though this may be play to you,
'Tis death to us.
AESOP—*Fables.*

Better die once for all than to live in continual terror.
AESOP—*Fables.*

Your lost friends are not dead, but gone before,
Advanced a stage or two upon that road
Which you must travel in the steps they trod.
ARISTOPHANES.

He who died at Azan sends
This to comfort all his friends:
Faithful friends! It lies I know
Pale and white and cold as snow;
And ye say, "Abdallah's dead!"
Weeping at the feet and head.
I can see your falling tears,
I can hear your sighs and prayers;
Yet I smile and whisper this:
I am not the thing you kiss.
Cease your tears and let it lie;
It was mine—it is not I.
EDWIN ARNOLD—*He Who Died at Azan.*

It is as natural to die as to be born; and to a little infant, perhaps, the one is as painful as the other.
BACON—*Of Death.*

Men fear Death, as children fear to go in the dark; and as that natural fear in children is increased with tales, so is the other.
BACON—*Of Death.*

The death-change comes.
Death is another life. We bow our heads
At going out, we think, and enter straight
Another golden chamber of the king's,
Larger than this we leave, and lovelier.
And then in shadowy glimpses, disconnect,
The story, flower-like, closes thus its leaves.
The will of God is all in all. He makes,
Destroys, remakes, for His own pleasure, all.
BAILEY—*Festus.*

But whether on the scaffold high,
Or in the battle's van,
The fittest place where man can die
Is where he dies for man.
MICHAEL J. BARRY—*The Place to Die.*

Earth to earth, ashes to ashes, dust to dust, in sure and certain hope of the resurrection.
Book of Common Prayer.

In the midst of life we are in death.
Book of Common Prayer.

Man that is born of a woman hath but a short time to live, and is full of misery. He cometh up, and is cut down, like a flower; he fleeth as it were a shadow, and never continueth in one stay.
Book of Common Prayer.

Sustained and soothed
By an unfaltering trust, approach thy grave
Like one that wraps the drapery of his couch
About him, and lies down to pleasant dreams.
BRYANT—*Thanatopsis.*

The fear of death is worse than death.
BURTON—*Anatomy of Melancholy.*

Death, so called, is a thing which makes men weep,
And yet a third of life is pass'd in sleep.
BYRON—*Don Juan.*

And I still onward haste to my last night;
Time's fatal wings do ever forward fly;
So every day we live, a day we die.
THOMAS CAMPION—*Divine and Moral Songs.*

O death, where is thy sting? O grave, where is thy victory?
I Corinthians. XV. 55.

Every moment of life is a step towards death.
CORNEILLE.

All has its date below; the fatal hour
Was register'd in Heav'n ere time began.
We turn to dust, and all our mightiest works
Die too.
COWPER—*Task.*

One short sleep past, we wake eternally,
And Death shall be no more; Death, thou shalt die.
DONNE—*Divine Poems.*

Heaven gave him all at once; then snatched away,
Ere mortals all his beauties could survey;
Just like the flower that buds and withers in a day.
DRYDEN—*On the Death of Amyntas.*

He thought it happier to be dead,
To die for Beauty, than live for bread.
EMERSON—*Beauty.*

The prince who kept the world in awe,
The judge whose dictate fix'd the law;
The rich, the poor, the great, the small,
Are levell'd; death confounds 'em all.
GAY—*Fables.*

Sit the comedy out, and that done,
When the Play's at an end, let the Curtain fall down.
THOMAS FLATMAN—*The Whim.*

Why fear death? It is the most beautiful adventure in life.
CHARLES FROHMAN.

Ere the dolphin dies
Its hues are brightest. Like an infant's breath
Are tropic winds before the voice of death.
FITZ-GREENE HALLECK—*Fortune.*

Death possesses a good deal of real estate, namely, the graveyard in every town.
HAWTHORNE.

Leaves have their time to fall,
And flowers to wither at the north wind's breath,

And stars to set—but all.
Thou hast all seasons for thine own,
O Death.
FELICIA D. HEMANS—*Hour of Death.*

So be my passing.
My task accomplished and the long day done,
My wages taken, and in my heart
Some late lark singing,
Let me be gathered to the quiet west,
The sundown splendid and serene,
Death.
W. E. HENLEY.

Now I am about to take my last voyage, a great leap in the dark.
THOMAS HOBBES.

We all do fade as a leaf.
Isaiah. LXIV. 6.

The Lord gave, and the Lord hath taken away; blessed be the name of the Lord.
Job. I. 21.

He shall return no more to his house, neither shall his place know him any more.
Job. VII. 10.

The land of darkness and the shadow of death.
Job. X. 21.

No one can obtain from the Pope a dispensation for never dying.
THOMAS À KEMPIS.

When I have folded up this tent
And laid the soiled thing by,
I shall go forth 'neath different stars,
Under an unknown sky.
FREDERIC L. KNOWLES—*The Last Word.*

If some men died and others did not, death would indeed be a most mortifying evil.
LA BRUYÈRE.

The young may die, but the old must!
LONGFELLOW—*Christus.*

And, as she looked around, she saw how Death, the consoler,
Laying his hand upon many a heart, had healed it forever.
LONGFELLOW—*Evangeline.*

There is no Death! What seems so is transition;
This life of mortal breath
Is but a suburb of the life elysian,
Whose portal we call Death.
LONGFELLOW—*Resignation.*

The gods conceal from those destined to live how sweet it is to die, that they may continue living.
LUCAN.

There is no such thing as death.
In nature nothing dies.
From each sad remnant of decay
Some forms of life arise.
CHARLES MACKAY.

We begin to die as soon as we are born, and the end is linked to the beginning.
MANILIUS.

There is no death! the stars go down
To rise upon some other shore,
And bright in Heaven's jeweled crown,
They shine for ever more.
JOHN L. MCCREERY.

He whom the gods love dies young.
MENANDER.

Death is delightful. Death is dawn,
The waking from a weary night
Of fevers unto truth and light.
JOAQUIN MILLER—*Even So.*

Strange—is it not?—that of the myriads who
Before us passed the door of Darkness through,
Not one returns to tell us of the road
Which to discover we must travel too.
OMAR KHAYYÁM—*Rubáiyat.*

Concerning the dead nothing but good shall be spoken.
PLUTARCH—*Life of Solon.*

Come! let the burial rite be read—
The funeral song be sung!—
A dirge for her, the doubly dead
In that she died so young.
POE—*Lenore.*

Till tired, he sleeps, and life's poor play is o'er.
POPE—*Essay on Man.*

But thousands die without or this or that,
Die, and endow a college or a cat.
Pope—*Moral Essays.*

And, oh! still harder lesson! how to die.
Bishop Porteus—*Death.*

Yet a little sleep, a little slumber, a little folding of the hands to sleep.
Proverbs. VI. 10; XXIV. 33.

I have said ye are gods . . . But ye shall die like men.
Psalms. LXXXII. 6. 7.

I am going to seek a great perhaps; draw the curtain, the farce is played.
Attributed to Rabelais.

When I am dead, my dearest,
Sing no sad songs for me;
Plant thou no roses at my head,
No shady cypress tree.
Christina G. Rossetti—*Song.*

If Socrates died like a sage, Jesus died like a God.
Rousseau.

Out of the chill and the shadow,
Into the thrill and the shine;
Out of the dearth and the famine,
Into the fulness divine.
Margaret E. Sangster — *Going Home.*

Is death the last sleep? No, it is the last final awakening.
Scott.

Like the dew on the mountain,
Like the foam on the river,
Like the bubble on the fountain,
Thou art gone, and for ever!
Scott—*Lady of the Lake.*

I have a rendezvous with Death
At some disputed barricade.
Alan Seeger.

Sometimes death is a punishment; often a gift; it has been a favor to many.
Seneca.

I am dying, Egypt, dying.
Shakespeare—*Antony and Cleopatra.* Act IV. Sc. 15.

To die:—to sleep:
No more; and, by a sleep to say we end
The heart-ache and the thousand natural shocks
That flesh is heir to, 'tis a consummation
Devoutly to be wished.
Shakespeare—*Hamlet.* Act III. Sc. 1.

Who would fardels bear,
To grunt and sweat under a weary life;
But that the dread of something after death,
The undiscover'd country from whose bourn
No traveller returns, puzzles the will
And makes us rather bear those ills we have
Than fly to others that we know not of?
Shakespeare—*Hamlet.* Act III. Sc. 1.

Why, what is pomp, rule, reign, but earth and dust?
And, live we how we can, yet die we must.
Shakespeare—*Henry VI.* Pt. III. Act V. Sc. 2.

Cowards die many times before their deaths;
The valiant never taste of death but once.
Of all the wonders that I yet have heard,
It seems to me most strange that men should fear;
Seeing that death, a necessary end,
Will come when it will come.
Shakespeare—*Julius Caesar.* Act II. Sc. 2.

Death, death; oh, amiable, lovely death!
Shakespeare—*Julius Caesar.* Act IV. Sc. 3.

Nothing in his life
Became him like the leaving it.
Shakespeare—*Macbeth.* Act I. Sc. 4.

If I must die
I will encounter darkness as a bride,
And hug it in mine arms.
SHAKESPEARE—*Measure for Measure.* Act III. Sc. 1.

The ripest fruit first falls, and so doth he;
His time is spent.
SHAKESPEARE—*Richard II.* Act II. Sc. 1.

Death lies on her, like an untimely frost
Upon the sweetest flower of all the field.
SHAKESPEARE—*Romeo and Juliet.* Act IV. Sc. 5.

First our pleasures die—and then
Our hopes, and then our fears—and when
These are dead, the debt is due,
Dust claims dust—and we die too.
SHELLEY—*Death.*

Yet it'll only be a sleep:
When, with songs and dewy light,
Morning blossoms out of Night,
She will open her blue eyes
'Neath the palms of Paradise,
While we foolish ones shall weep.
EDWARD ROWLAND SILL—*Sleeping.*

Hail Caesar, we who are about to die salute you.
SUETONIUS.

I shall be like that tree,—I shall die at the top.
SWIFT—*Scott's Life of Swift.*

Death, if thou wilt, fain would I plead with thee:
Canst thou not spare, of all our hopes have built,
One shelter where our spirits fain would be
Death, if thou wilt?
SWINBURNE—*A Dialogue.*

For tho' from out our bourne of Time and Place
The flood may bear me far,
I hope to see my Pilot face to face
When I have crossed the bar.
TENNYSON—*Crossing the Bar.*

Sunset and evening star,
And one clear call for me!
And may there be no moaning of the bar
When I put out to sea.
TENNYSON—*Crossing the Bar.*

Twilight and evening bell,
And after that the dark!
And may there be no sadness of farewell
When I embark.
TENNYSON—*Crossing the Bar.*

God's finger touched him, and he slept.
TENNYSON—*In Memoriam.*

I have lived, and I have run the course which fortune allotted me; and now my shade shall descend illustrious to the grave.
VERGIL—*Æneid.*

It is today, my dear, that I take a perilous leap.
Last words of VOLTAIRE.

Softly his fainting head he lay
Upon his Maker's breast;
His Maker kiss'd his soul away,
And laid his flesh to rest.
ISAAC WATTS—*Death of Moses.*

Joy, shipmate, joy
(Pleas'd to my soul at death I cry,)
Our life is closed, our life begins,
The long, long anchorage we leave,
The ship is clear at last, she leaps!
Joy, shipmate, joy!
WALT WHITMAN—*Joy, Shipmate, Joy.*

Nothing can happen more beautiful than death.
WALT WHITMAN—*Starting from Paumanok.*

For he who lives more lives than one
More deaths than one must die.
OSCAR WILDE—*Ballad of Reading Gaol.*

Early, bright, transient, chaste, as morning dew
She sparkled, was exhal'd, and went to heaven.
YOUNG—*Night Thoughts.*

DEBT

A church debt is the devil's salary.
HENRY WARD BEECHER.

Wilt thou seal up the avenues of ill?
Pay every debt as if God wrote the bill!
EMERSON.

A national debt, if it is not excessive, will be to us a national blessing.
ALEXANDER HAMILTON.

If I owe Smith ten dollars, and God forgives me, that doesn't pay Smith.
R. G. INGERSOLL.

The principle of spending money to be paid by posterity, under the name of funding, is but swindling futurity on a large scale.
JEFFERSON.

Small debts are like small shot,—they are rattling on every side, and can scarcely be escaped without a wound; great debts are like cannon, of loud noise but little danger.
SAMUEL JOHNSON.

Debt is the worst poverty.
M. G. LICHTWER.

Owe no man anything.
Romans. XII. 8.

He that dies pays all debts.
SHAKESPEARE—*Tempest*. Act III. Sc. 2.

If you want the time to pass quickly, just give your note for 90 days.
R. B. THOMAS—*Farmers' Almanack*.

DECENCY

No law reaches it, but all right-minded people observe it.
CHAMFORT.

Decency renders all things tolerable.
DE GERANDO.

DECEPTION

Many an honest man practices upon himself an amount of deceit sufficient, if practiced upon another, and in a little different way, to send him to the state prison.
BOVEE.

The surest way of making a dupe is to let your victim suppose you are his.
BULWER-LYTTON.

A delusion, a mockery, and a snare.
LORD DENMAN.

Of all the evil spirits abroad at this hour in the world, insincerity is the most dangerous.
FROUDE.

We are never deceived; we deceive ourselves.
GOETHE.

Pretexts are not wanting when one wishes to use them.
GOLDONI.

Which I wish to remark—
And my language is plain,—
That for ways that are dark
And for tricks that are vain,
The heathen Chinee is peculiar.
BRET HARTE—*Plain Language from Truthful James*.

Hateful to me as are the gates of hell,
Is he who, hiding one thing in his heart,
Utters another.
HOMER—*Iliad*.

It is double pleasure to deceive the deceiver.
LA FONTAINE.

You can fool some of the people all of the time, and all of the people some of the time, but you cannot fool all of the people all the time.
LINCOLN.

Where the lion's skin falls short it must be eked out with the fox's.
LYSANDER.

Men are so simple, and yield so much to necessity, that he who will deceive will always find him who will lend himself to be deceived.
MACHIAVELLI.

One is easily fooled by that which one loves.
MOLIÈRE—*Tartuffe*.

No one has deceived the whole world, nor has the whole world ever deceived any one.

PLINY THE YOUNGER.

The world is still deceiv'd with ornament,
In law, what plea so tainted and corrupt,
But, being season'd with a gracious voice,
Obscures the show of evil? In religion,
What damned error, but some sober brow
Will bless it and approve it with a text,
Hiding the grossness with fair ornament?

SHAKESPEARE—*Merchant of Venice*. Act III. Sc. 2.

O, that deceit should dwell
In such a gorgeous palace!

SHAKESPEARE—*Romeo and Juliet*. Act III. Sc. 2.

You should not live one way in private, another in public.

SYRUS.

DECISION

And her *yes,* once said to you,
Shall be Yes for evermore.

E. B. BROWNING—*The Lady's Yes.*

There is nothing more to be esteemed than a manly firmness and decision of character. I like a person who knows his own mind and sticks to it; who sees at once what is to be done in given circumstances and does it.

HAZLITT.

Once to every man and nation comes the moment to decide,
In the strife of Truth with Falsehood, for the good or evil side.

LOWELL—*The Present Crisis.*

Here I stand; I can do no otherwise. God help me. *Amen.*

LUTHER.

Advise well before you begin; and when you have decided, act promptly.

SALLUST.

There is no mistake; there has been no mistake; and there shall be no mistake.

DUKE OF WELLINGTON.

DEEDS

Anything done for another is done for oneself.

BONIFACE VIII.

We have left undone those things which we ought to have done; and we have done those things which we ought not to have done.

Book of Common Prayer.

Little deeds of kindness, little words of love,
Make our earth an Eden like the heaven above.

JULIA F. CARNEY—*Little Things.*

Whatever is worth doing at all is worth doing well.

EARL OF CHESTERFIELD.

Deeds are males, words females are.

SIR JOHN DAVIES.

Our deeds determine us, as much as we determine our deeds.

GEORGE ELIOT—*Adam Bede.*

Give me the ready hand rather than the ready tongue.

GARIBALDI.

Did nothing in particular,
And did it very well.

W. S. GILBERT—*Iolanthe.*

When a man dies they who survive him ask what property he has left behind. The angel who bends over the dying man asks what good deeds he has sent before him.

The Koran.

But the good deed, through the ages
Living in historic pages,
Brighter grows and gleams immortal,
Unconsumed by moth or rust.

LONGFELLOW—*Norman Baron.*

Noble deeds that are concealed are most esteemed.

PASCAL.

He who considers too much will perform little.
SCHILLER—*Wilhelm Tell.*

How far that little candle throws his beams!
So shines a good deed in a naughty world.
SHAKESPEARE—*Merchant of Venice.* Act V. Sc. 1.

Heaven ne'er helps the man who will not help himself.
SOPHOCLES.

DEFEAT

What is defeat? Nothing but education, nothing but the first step to something better.
WENDELL PHILLIPS.

Defeat should never be a source of discouragement, but rather a fresh stimulus.
SOUTH.

DELAY

All delays are dangerous in war.
DRYDEN.

He that riseth late must tread all day, and shall scarce overtake his business at night.
FRANKLIN.

When a man's life is at stake no delay is too long.
JUVENAL.

Do not delay,
Do not delay: the golden moments fly!
LONGFELLOW—*Masque of Pandora.*

Nothing is more annoying than a tardy friend.
PLAUTUS.

Late, late, so late! but we can enter still.
Too late, too late! ye cannot enter now.
TENNYSON—*Idylls of the King.*

DELICACY

A fine lady is a squirrel-headed thing, with small airs and small notions; about as applicable to the business of life as a pair of tweezers to the clearing of a forest.
GEORGE ELIOT.

Women could take part in the processions, the songs, the dances, of old religion; no one fancied their delicacy was impaired by appearing in public for such a cause.
MARGARET FULLER.

The finest qualities of our nature, like the bloom on fruits, can be preserved only by the most delicate handling.
THOREAU.

DELIGHT

Why, all delights are vain; and that most vain,
Which with pain purchas'd, doth inherit pain.
SHAKESPEARE — *Love's Labour's Lost.* Act I. Sc. 1.

DELUSION

The worst deluded are the self-deluded.
BOVEE.

When our vices quit us, we flatter ourselves with the belief that it is we who quit them.
LA ROCHEFOUCAULD.

DEMOCRACY

When everybody is somebody, then nobody is anybody.
ANONYMOUS.

A perfect democracy is therefore the most shameless thing in the world.
BURKE—*Reflections on the Revolution in France.*

The world is weary of statesmen whom democracy has degraded into politicians.
DISRAELI—*Lothair.*

Democracy is on trial in the world, on a more colossal scale than ever before.

CHARLES FLETCHER DOLE — *The Spirit of Democracy.*

Democracy is based upon the conviction that there are extraordinary possibilities in ordinary people.

HARRY EMERSON FOSDICK—*Democracy.*

While democracy must have its organization and controls, its vital breath is individual liberty.

CHARLES EVANS HUGHES—*Speech, 1939.*

Democracy is the government of the people, by the people, for the people.

LINCOLN.

Democ'acy gives every man
A right to be his own oppressor.

LOWELL—*Biglow Papers.*

Thus our democracy was from an early period the most aristocratic, and our aristocracy the most democratic.

MACAULAY—*History.*

Democracy means not "I am as good as you are," but "You are as good as I am."

THEODORE PARKER.

If there were a people consisting of gods, they would be governed democratically. So perfect a government is not suitable to men.

ROUSSEAU.

All the ills of democracy can be cured by more democracy.

ALFRED E. SMITH—*Speech, 1933.*

I believe in Democracy because it releases the energies of every human being.

WOODROW WILSON.

The world must be made safe for democracy. Its peace must be planted upon the tested foundations of political liberty. We have no selfish ends to serve. We desire no conquest, no dominion. We seek no indemnities for ourselves, no material compensation for the sacrifices we shall freely make. We are but one of the champions of the rights of mankind. We shall be satisfied when those rights have been made as secure as the faith and the freedom of nations can make them.

WOODROW WILSON—*War Address to Congress, 1917.*

DEPENDENCE

There is no one subsists by himself alone.

FELLTHAM.

The greatest man living may stand in need of the meanest, as much as the meanest does of him.

FULLER.

People may live as much retired from the world as they please; but sooner or later, before they are aware, they will find themselves debtor or creditor to somebody.

GOETHE.

He who imagines he can do without the world deceives himself much; but he who fancies the world cannot do without him is still more mistaken.

LA ROCHEFOUCAULD.

DESIRE

We trifle when we assign limits to our desires, since nature has set none.

BOVEE.

When our desires are fulfilled, we never fail to realize the wealth of imagination and the paucity of reality.

NINON DE LENCLOS.

It is easier to suppress the first desire than to satisfy all that follow it.

FRANKLIN.

Our desires always increase with our possessions. The knowledge that something remains yet unenjoyed impairs our enjoyment of the good before us.

SAMUEL JOHNSON.

He who desires naught will always be free.

E. R. LEFEBVRE LABOULAYE.

Ah love! could you and I with Him conspire
To grasp this sorry scheme of things entire,
Would not we shatter it to bits—and then
Re-mold it nearer to the heart's desire!
OMAR KHAYYÁM—*Rubaiyat.*

There are two tragedies in life. One is not to get your heart's desire. The other is to get it.
GEORGE BERNARD SHAW—*Man and Superman.*

DESPAIR

Despair is the conclusion of fools.
DISRAELI.

All hope abandon, ye who enter here.
DANTE—*Inferno.*

There is no despair so absolute as that which comes with the first moments of our first great sorrow, when we have not yet known what it is to have suffered and be healed, to have despaired and have recovered hope.
GEORGE ELIOT.

Alas for him who never sees
The stars shine through his cypress-trees
Who, hopeless, lays his dead away,
Nor looks to see the breaking day
Across the mournful marbles play!
WHITTIER—*Snow-Bound.*

DESPOTISM

Despotism can no more exist in a nation until the liberty of the press be destroyed than the night can happen before the sun is set.
COLTON.

Fear must rule in a despotism.
KOSSUTH.

Honor is unknown in despotic states.
MONTESQUIEU.

I will believe in the right of one man to govern a nation despotically when I find a man born into the world with boots and spurs, and a nation with saddles on their backs.
ALGERNON SIDNEY.

DESTINY

The scapegoat which we make responsible for all our crimes and follies; a necessity which we set down for invincible, when we have no wish to strive against it.
MRS. BALFOUR.

Life treads on life, and heart on heart;
We press too close in church and mart
To keep a dream or grave apart.
E. B. BROWNING—*A Vision of Poets.*

Our deeds determine us, as much as we determine our deeds.
GEORGE ELIOT.

We are all sure of two things, at least; we shall suffer and we shall all die.
GOLDSMITH.

No living man can send me to the shades
Before my time; no man of woman born,
Coward or brave, can shun his destiny.
HOMER—*Iliad.*

We are but as the instrument of Heaven.
Our work is not design, but destiny.
OWEN MEREDITH—*Clytemnestra.*

Every man meets his Waterloo at last.
WENDELL PHILLIPS.

A man may fish with the worm that hath eat of a king, and eat of the fish that hath fed of that worm.
SHAKESPEARE—*Hamlet.* Act V. Sc. 1.

Imperious Caesar, dead and turn'd to clay,
Might stop a hole to keep the wind away:
O, that that earth, which kept the world in awe,
Should patch a wall to expel the winter's flaw!
SHAKESPEARE—*Hamlet.* Act. V. Sc. 1.

There is a divinity that shapes our ends,
Rough-hew them how we will.
SHAKESPEARE—*Hamlet.* Act V. Sc 2.

The seed ye sow, another reaps;
The wealth ye find, another keeps;
The robes ye weave, another wears;
The arms ye forge, another bears.
SHELLEY—*To Men of England.*

DEVIL

The devil was sick, the devil a monk would be;
The devil was well, the devil a monk was he.
ANONYMOUS.

Where God hath a temple, the devil will have a chapel.
BURTON.

Here is the devil-and-all to pay.
CERVANTES—*Don Quixote.*

How art thou fallen from heaven, O Lucifer, son of the morning!
Isaiah. XIV. 12.

Resist the Devil, and he will flee from you.
James. IV. 7.

Every newspaper editor owes tribute to the devil.
LA FONTAINE.

It is Lucifer,
The son of mystery;
And since God suffers him to be,
He, too, is God's minister,
And labors for some good
By us not understood.
LONGFELLOW—*Christus.*

Tell your master that if there were as many devils at Worms as tiles on its roofs, I would enter.
LUTHER.

Get thee behind me, Satan.
Mark. VIII. 33.

Satan exalted sat, by merit raised
To that bad eminence.
MILTON—*Paradise Lost.*

Satan; so call him now, his former name
Is heard no more in heaven.
MILTON—*Paradise Lost.*

Be sober, be vigilant; because your adversary, the Devil, as a roaring lion, walketh about, seeking whom he may devour.
I Peter. V. 8.

He will give the devil his due.
SHAKESPEARE—*Henry IV.* Pt. I. Act I. Sc. 2.

The prince of darkness is a gentleman.
SHAKESPEARE—*King Lear.* Act III. Sc. 4.

The devil can cite Scripture for his purpose.
SHAKESPEARE—*Merchant of Venice.* Act I. Sc. 3.

DEW

'Tis of the tears which stars weep, sweet with joy.
BAILEY—*Festus.*

The dews of the evening most carefully shun;
Those tears of the sky for the loss of the sun.
CHESTERFIELD—*Advice to a Lady in Autumn.*

The dew-bead
Gem of earth and sky begotten.
GEORGE ELIOT — *The Spanish Gypsy.*

Every dew-drop and rain-drop had a whole heaven within it.
LONGFELLOW—*Hyperion.*

DIFFICULTY

The three things most difficult are—to keep a secret, to forget an injury, and to make good use of leisure.
CHILO.

The greatest difficulties lie where we are not looking for them.
GOETHE.

The illustration which solves one difficulty by raising another, settles nothing.
HORACE.

Many things difficult to design prove easy to performance.
SAMUEL JOHNSON.

It is the surmounting of difficulties that makes heroes.

KOSSUTH.

Every noble acquisition is attended with its risks; he who fears to encounter the one must not expect to obtain the other.

METASTASIO.

DIGNITY

As vivacity is the gift of woman, gravity is that of man.

ADDISON.

In order that she may be able to give her hand with dignity, she must be able to stand alone.

MARGARET FULLER.

There is a healthful hardiness about real dignity that never dreads contact and communion with others, however humble.

WASHINGTON IRVING.

All celebrated people lose on a close view.

NAPOLEON.

We have exchanged the Washingtonian dignity for the Jeffersonian simplicity, which was in truth only another name for the Jeffersonian vulgarity.

BISHOP HENRY C. POTTER.

Let none presume
To wear an undeserved dignity.

SHAKESPEARE—*Merchant of Venice.* Act II. Sc. 9.

DISAPPOINTMENT

The best-laid schemes o'mice an'men,
Gang aft a-gley,
And leave us nought but grief and pain,
For promised joy.

BURNS—*To a Mouse.*

Disappointment is the nurse of wisdom.

SIR BAYLE ROCHE.

Disappointments are to the soul what a thunder-storm is to the air.

SCHILLER.

Women suffer more from disappointment than men, because they have more of faith and are naturally more credulous.

MARGUERITE DE VALOIS.

DISCIPLINE

He that hath wife and children hath given hostages to fortune, for they are impediments to great enterprises, either of virtue or mischief. . . . Certainly wife and children are a kind of discipline of humanity.

BACON.

No pain, no palm; no thorns, no throne; no gall, no glory; no cross, no crown.

WILLIAM PENN.

No evil propensity of the human heart is so powerful that it may not be subdued by discipline.

SENECA.

A stern discipline pervades all nature, which is a little cruel that it may be very kind.

SPENSER.

DISCONTENT

Discontent is the source of all trouble, but also of all progress in individuals and in nations.

AUERBACH.

In such a strait the wisest may well be perplexed, and the boldest staggered.

BURKE.

Discontent is the want of self-reliance: it is infirmity of will.

EMERSON.

Men would be angels;
Angels would be gods.

POPE.

We love in others what we lack ourselves, and would be everything but what we are.

R. H. STODDARD—*Arcadian Idyl.*

I was *born* to other things.

TENNYSON—*In Memoriam.*

And from the discontent of man
The world's best progress springs.
ELLA WHEELER WILCOX.

Discontent is the first step in the progress of a man or a nation.
OSCAR WILDE—*Woman of No Importance.*

DISCRETION

Discretion in speech is more than eloquence.
BACON.

A sound discretion is not so much indicated by never making a mistake as by never repeating it.
BOVEE.

All persons are not discreet enough to know how to take things by the right handle.
CERVANTES.

Great ability without discretion comes almost invariably to a tragic end.
GAMBETTA.

What is denominated discretion in man we call cunning in brutes.
LA FONTAINE.

Some delicate matters must be treated like pins, because if they are not seized by the right end, we get pricked.
J. PETIT-SENN.

Let your own discretion be your tutor: suit the action to the word, the word to the action.
SHAKESPEARE—*Hamlet,* Act III. Sc. 2.

The better part of valour is discretion; in the which better part I have saved my life.
SHAKESPEARE—*Henry IV.* Pt. I. Act V. Sc. 4.

DISEASE

Disease is the retribution of outraged Nature.
HOSEA BALLOU.

Disease is an experience of so-called mortal mind. It is fear made manifest on the body.
MARY BAKER EDDY—*Science and Health.*

Desperate diseases require desperate remedies.
English Proverb.

He who cures a disease may be the skilfullest, but he that prevents it is the safest physician.
T. FULLER.

The canker which the trunk conceals is revealed by the leaves, the fruit, or the flower.
METASTASIO.

And as in men's bodies, so in government, that disease is most serious which proceeds from the head.
PLINY THE YOUNGER.

Some remedies are worse than the disease.
SYRUS.

DISGRACE

No one can disgrace us but ourselves.
J. G. HOLLAND.

Whatever disgrace we may have deserved, it is almost always in our power to re-establish our character.
LA ROCHEFOUCAULD.

Disgrace is immortal, and living even when one thinks it dead.
PLAUTUS.

DISPLAY

Display is as false as it is costly.
FRANKLIN.

Loud-dressing men and women have also loud characters.
HALIBURTON.

Display is like shallow water, where you can see the muddy bottom.
ALPHONSE KARR.

They that govern most make least noise.
SELDEN.

DISSENSION

And Doubt and Discord step 'twixt thine and thee.
BYRON—*The Prophecy of Dante.*

Dissensions, like small streams, are first begun,
Scarce seen they rise, but gather as they run:
So lines that from their parallel decline,
More they proceed the more they still disjoin.
SAMUEL GARTH—*The Dispensary.*

An old affront will stir the heart
Through years of rankling pain.
JEAN INGELOW—*Strife and Peace.*

Alas! how light a cause may move
Dissension between hearts that love!
Hearts that the world in vain had tried,
And sorrow but more closely tied;
That stood the storm when waves were rough,
Yet in a sunny hour fall off.
MOORE—*Lalla Rookh.*

Believe me, lords, my tender years can tell
Civil dissension is a viperous worm
That gnaws the bowels of the commonwealth.
SHAKESPEARE—*Henry VI.* Pt. I. Act IV. Sc. 1.

DISTRUST

A usurper always distrusts the whole world.
ALFIERI.

Doubt the man who swears to his devotion.
MME. LOUISE COLET.

Women distrust men too much in general, and too little in particular.
COMMERSON.

What loneliness is more lonely than distrust?
GEORGE ELIOT—*Middlemarch.*

When desperate ills demand a speedy cure,
Distrust is cowardice, and prudence folly.
SAMUEL JOHNSON—*Irene.*

Three things a wise man will not trust,
The wind, the sunshine of an April day,
And woman's plighted faith.
SOUTHEY—*Madoc in Aztlan.*

DOCTRINE

Doctrine is nothing but the skin of truth set up and stuffed.
HENRY WARD BEECHER.

What makes all doctrines plain and clear?—
About two hundred pounds a year.
And that which was prov'd true before
Prove false again? Two hundred more.
BUTLER—*Hudibras.*

How absurd to try to make two men think alike on matters of religion, when I cannot make two timepieces agree!
CHARLES V.

In religion as in politics it so happens that we have less charity for those who believe half our creed, than for those who deny the whole of it.
COLTON.

He was the word that spake it,
He took the bread and brake it;
And what that word did make it,
I do believe and take it.
DONNE—*Divine Poems.*

You can and you can't,
You will and you won't;
You'll be damn'd if you do,
You'll be damn'd if you don't.
LORENZO DOW—(*Definition of Calvinism*).

And after hearing what our Church can say,
If still our reason runs another way,
That private reason 'tis more just to curb,
Than by disputes the public peace disturb;
For points obscure are of small use to learn,
But common quiet is mankind's concern.
DRYDEN—*Religio Laici.*

All sects seem to me to be right in what they assert, and wrong in what they deny.

GOETHE.

Shall I ask the brave soldier, who fights by my side
In the cause of mankind, if our creeds agree?
Shall I give up the friend I have valued and tried,
If he kneel not before the same altar with me?
From the heretic girl of my soul should I fly,
To seek somewhere else a more orthodox kiss?
No! perish the hearts, and the laws that try
Truth, valour, or love, by a standard like this!

MOORE—*Irish Melodies.*

"Orthodoxy, my Lord," said Bishop Warburton, in a whisper,—"orthodoxy is my doxy,—heterodoxy is another man's doxy."

JOSEPH PRIESTLY—*Memoirs.*

As thou these ashes, little brook! will bear
Into the Avon, Avon to the tide
Of Severn, Severn to the narrow seas,
Into main ocean they, this deed accurst,
An emblem yields to friends and enemies
How the bold teacher's doctrine, sanctified
By truth, shall spread throughout the world dispersed.

WORDSWORTH—*Wicliffe.*

DOG

Do not disturb the sleeping dog.

ALESSANDRO ALLEGRI.

Who loves me will love my dog also.

ST. BERNARD OF CLAIRVAUX.

The cowardly dog barks more violently than it bites.

QUINTUS CURTIUS.

A living dog is better than a dead lion.

Ecclesiastes. IX. 4.

Old dog Tray's ever faithful;
Grief can not drive him away;
He is gentle, he is kind—
I shall never, never find
A better friend than old dog Tray!

STEPHEN C. FOSTER—*Old Dog Tray.*

And in that town a dog was found,
As many dogs there be,
Both mongrel, puppy, whelp and hound,
And curs of low degree.

GOLDSMITH—*Elegy on the Death of a Mad Dog.*

The more one comes to know men, the more one comes to admire the dog.

JOUSSENEL.

Is thy servant a dog, that he should do this great thing?

II Kings. VIII. 13.

There is sorrow enough in the natural way
From men and women to fill our day;
But when we are certain of sorrow in store
Why do we always arrange for more?
Brothers and sisters I bid you beware
Of giving your heart to a dog to tear.

KIPLING—*The Power of the Dog.*

The dogs eat of the crumbs which fall from their masters' table.

Matthew. XV. 27.

The dog is turned to his own vomit again.

II Peter. II. 22.

I am his Highness' dog at Kew;
Pray tell me, sir, whose dog are you?

POPE—*On the Collar of a Dog.*

I have a dog of Blenheim birth,
With fine long ears and full of mirth;
And sometimes, running o'er the plain,
He tumbles on his nose:
But quickly jumping up again
Like lightning on he goes!

RUSKIN.

Every dog must have his day.

SWIFT.

We are two travellers, Roger and I.
Roger's my dog—come here, you scamp!
Jump for the gentleman—mind your eye!
Over the table,—look out for the lamp!
The rogue is growing a little old;
Five years we've trampled through wind and weather,
And slept out-doors when nights were cold,
And ate and drank and starved together.

JOHN T. TROWBRIDGE—*The Vagabonds.*

Gentlemen of the Jury: The one, absolute, unselfish friend that man can have in this selfish world, the one that never deserts him, the one that never proves ungrateful or treacherous, is his dog.

SENATOR GEORGE GRAHAM VEST—*Eulogy on the Dog.*

DOUBT

Who never doubted, never half believed.
Where doubt there truth is—'tis her shadow.

BAILEY—*Festus.*

Galileo called doubt the father of invention; it is certainly the pioneer.

BOVEE.

He would not, with a peremptory tone,
Assert the nose upon his face his own.

COWPER.

Doubting charms me not less than knowledge.

DANTE—*Inferno.*

We know accurately only when we know little; with knowledge doubt increases.

GOETHE.

When in doubt, win the trick.

HOYLE.

He who dallies is a dastard,
He who doubts is damned.

Attributed to GEORGE MCDUFFLE.

I respect faith, but doubt is what gets you an education.

WILSON MIZNER.

People, when asked if they are Christians, give some of the strangest answers you ever heard. Some will say if you ask them: "Well—well—well, I—I hope I am." Suppose a man should ask me if I am an American. Would I say: "Well, I—well, I—I hope I am"?

D. L. MOODY.

Fain would I but dare not; I dare, and yet I may not;
I may, although I care not for pleasure when I play not.

SIR WALTER RALEIGH—*A Lover's Verses.*

And he that doubteth is damned if he eat.

Romans. XIV. 23.

To be, or not to be, that is the question:
Whether 'tis nobler in the mind to suffer
The slings and arrows of outrageous fortune;
Or to take arms against a sea of troubles,
And by opposing end them?

SHAKESPEARE—*Hamlet.* Act III. Sc. 1.

But now I am cabin'd, cribb'd, confin'd, bound in
To saucy doubts and fears.

SHAKESPEARE—*Macbeth.* Act. III. Sc. 4.

Our doubt are traitors
And make us lose the good we oft might win
By fearing to attempt.

SHAKESPEARE—*Measure for Measure.* Act I. Sc. 4.

To believe with certainty we must begin with doubting.

STANISLAUS—*Maxims and Moral Sentences.*

There lives more faith in honest doubt,
Believe me, than in half the creeds.

TENNYSON—*In Memoriam.*

When you doubt, abstain.

ZOROASTER.

DOVE

We roar all like bears, and mourn sore like doves.
Isaiah. LIX. 11.

See how that pair of billing doves
With open murmurs own their loves
And, heedless of censorious eyes,
Pursue their unpolluted joys:
No fears of future want molest
The downy quiet of their nest.
LADY MARY WORTLEY MONTAGU.

The Dove,
On Silver pinions, winged her peaceful way.
MONTGOMERY—*Pelican Island*.

Oh that I had wings like a dove! for then would I fly away, and be at rest.
Psalms. LV. 6.

DRAMA

A passion for the dramatic art is inherent in the nature of man.
EDWIN FORREST.

The drama's laws the drama's patrons give,
For we that live to please, must please to live.
DR. JOHNSON.

The business of the dramatist is to keep himself out of sight, and to let nothing appear but his characters. As soon as he attracts notice to his personal feelings, the illusion is broken.
MACAULAY.

The drama is the book of the people.
WILLMOTT.

The dramatist, like the poet, is born, not made. . . . There must be inspiration back of all true and permanent art, dramatic or otherwise, and art is universal: there is nothing national about it. Its field is humanity, and it takes in all the world.
WILLIAM WINTER.

DREAMS

When to soft Sleep we give ourselves away,
And in a dream as in a fairy bark
Drift on and on through the enchanted dark
To purple daybreak—little thought we pay
To that sweet bitter world we know by day.
T. B. ALDRICH—*Sleep*.

Sweet sleep be with us, one and all!
And if upon its stillness fall
The visions of a busy brain,
We'll have our pleasure o'er again,
To warm the heart, to charm the sight,
Gay dreams to all! good night, good night.
JOANNA BAILLIE—*The Phantom*.

If there were dreams to sell,
Merry and sad to tell,
And the crier rung his bell,
What would you buy?
T. L. BEDDOES—*Dream-Pedlary*.

As dreams are the fancies of those that sleep, so fancies are but the dreams of those awake.
T. P. BLOUNT.

I dreamt that I dwelt in marble halls,
With vassals and serfs at my side.
MICHAEL BRUCE—*Elegy on Spring*.

And dreams in their development have breath,
And tears, and tortures, and the touch of joy;
They take a weight from off our waking toils,
They do divide our being.
BYRON—*The Dream*.

Again let us dream where the land lies sunny
And live, like the bees, on our hearts' old honey,
Away from the world that slaves for money—
Come journey the way with me.
MADISON CAWEIN—*Song of the Road*.

My eyes make pictures, when they are shut.
COLERIDGE—*Fears in Solitude*.

Dreams are but interludes, which fancy makes;
When monarch reason sleeps, this mimic wakes.
DRYDEN—*The Cock and the Fox*.

In dreams we are true poets; we create the persons of the drama; we give them appropriate figures, faces, costumes; they are perfect in their organs, attitudes, manners; moreover they speak after their own characters, not ours; and we listen with surprise to what they say.
EMERSON.

In blissful dream, in silent night,
There came to me, with magic might,
With magic might, my own sweet love,
Into my little room above.
HEINE—*Youthful Sorrows.*

Abou Ben Adhem (may his tribe increase!)
Awoke one night from a deep dream of peace.
LEIGH HUNT—*Abou Ben Adhem.*

Your old men shall dream dreams, your young men shall see visions.
Joel. II. 28.

There's a long, long trail a-winding
Into the land of my dreams,
Where the nightingales are singing
And the white moon beams;
There's a long, long night of waiting
Until my dreams all come true,
Till the day when I'll be going down that
Long, long trail with you.
STODDARD KING—*There's a Long, Long Trail.*

Every one turns his dreams into realities as far as he can; man is cold as ice to the truth, hot as fire to falsehood.
LA FONTAINE.

'Twas but a dream,—let it pass,—let it vanish like so many others!
What I thought was a flower is only a weed, and is worthless.
LONGFELLOW—*Courtship of Miles Standish.*

For dhrames always go by conthraries, my dear.
SAMUEL LOVER.

A thousand creeds and battle cries,
A thousand warring social schemes,
A thousand new moralities
And twenty thousand, thousand dreams.
ALFRED NOYES—*Forward.*

That holy dream—that holy dream,
While all the world were chiding,
Hath cheered me as a lovely beam
A lonely spirit guiding.
POE—*A Dream.*

Some must delve when the dawn is nigh;
Some must toil when the noonday beams;
But when night comes, and the soft winds sigh,
Every man is a King of Dreams.
CLINTON SCOLLARD—*King of Dreams.*

I talk of dreams,
Which are the children of an idle brain,
Begot of nothing but vain fantasy,
Which is as thin of substance as the air.
And more inconstant than the wind.
SHAKESPEARE—*Romeo and Juliet.* Act I. Sc. 4.

We are such stuff
As dreams are made on, and our little life
Is rounded with a sleep.
SHAKESPEARE—*The Tempest.* Act IV. Sc. 1.

In the world of dreams, I have chosen my part.
To sleep for a season and hear no word
Of true love's truth or of light love's art,
Only the song of a secret bird.
SWINBURNE—*A Ballad of Dreamland.*

The chambers in the house of dreams
Are fed with so divine an air,
That Time's hoar wings grow young therein,
And they who walk there are most fair.
FRANCIS THOMPSON—*Dream Tryst.*

And yet, as angels in some brighter
dreams
Call to the soul when man doth sleep.
So some strange thought transcend
our wonted dreams,
And into glory peep.
VAUGHAN—*Ascension Hymn.*

DRESS

If a woman were about to proceed to her execution, she would demand a little time to perfect her toilet.
CHAMFORT.

Eat to please thyself, but dress to please others.
FRANKLIN.

In the indications of female poverty there can be no disguise. No woman dresses below herself from caprice.
LAMB.

The dress does not make the monk.
RABELAIS.

No man is esteemed for gay garments but by fools and women.
SIR WALTER RALEIGH.

DRINKING

There was an old hen
And she had a wooden leg,
And every damned morning
She laid another egg;
She was the best damned chicken
On the whole damned farm—
And another little drink
Wouldn't do us any harm.
American Folksong.

Drinking will make a man quaff,
Quaffing will make a man sing,
Singing will make a man laugh,
And laughing long life doth bring,
Says old Simon the King.
ANONYMOUS.

It's a long time between drinks.
ANONYMOUS.

Here
With my beer
I sit,
While golden moments flit:
Alas!
They pass
Unheeded by:
And as they fly,
I,
Being dry,
Sit, idly sipping here
My beer.
GEORGE ARNOLD—*Beer.*

Or merry swains, who quaff the nut-
brown ale,
And sing enamour'd of the nut-brown
maid.
BEATTIE—*The Minstrel.*

"Nose, nose, jolly red nose,
And who gave thee that jolly red
nose?
Nutmegs and ginger, cinnamon and
cloves;
And that gave me my jolly red nose!"
BEAUMONT AND FLETCHER—*Knight of the Burning Pestle.*

What harm in drinking can there be,
Since punch and life so well agree?
BLACKLOCK.

Inspiring bold John Barleycorn,
What dangers thou canst make us
scorn!
Wi' tippenny, we fear nae evil;
Wi' usquebae, we'll face the devil!
BURNS—*Tam o'Shanter.*

I drink when I have occasion, and sometimes when I have no occasion.
CERVANTES—*Don Quixote.*

Nothing in Nature's sober found,
But an eternal Health goes round.
Fill up the Bowl then, fill it high—
Fill all the Glasses there; for why
Should every Creature Drink but I?
Why, Man of Morals, tell me why?
COWLEY—*Drinking.*

Did you ever hear of Captain Wattle?
He was all for love and a little for
the bottle.
CHARLES DIBDIN—*Captain Wattle and Miss Rol.*

Drink to-day, and drown all sorrow;
You shall perhaps not do it to-morrow.
FLETCHER—*The Bloody Brother.*

The habit of using ardent spirits by men in office has occasioned more injury to the public, and more trouble to me, than all other causes. Were I to commence my administration again, the first question I would ask respecting candidate for office would be, Does he use ardent spirits?

JEFFERSON.

I would appeal to Philip, she said, but to Philip sober.

VALERIUS MAXIMUS.

If all be true that I do think,
There are five reasons we should drink;
Good wine—a friend—or being dry—
Or lest we should be by and by—
Or any other reason why.

Attributed to DE LA MONNOYE.

Drink! for you know not whence you came, nor why:
Drink! for you know not why you go, nor where.

OMAR KHAYYÁM—*Rubaiyat.*

All excess is ill, but drunkenness is of the worst sort. It spoils health, dismounts the mind, and unmans men. It reveals secrets, is quarrelsome, lascivious, impudent, dangerous and bad.

WILLIAM PENN.

There St. John mingles with my friendly bowl
The feast of reason and the flow of soul.

POPE—*Second Book of Horace.*

They never taste who always drink.

PRIOR.

There are more old drunkards than old physicians.

RABELAIS—*Gargantua.*

Drunkenness is temporary suicide: the happiness that it brings is merely negative, a momentary cessation of unhappiness.

BERTRAND RUSSELL—*The Conquest of Happiness.*

Drunkenness is nothing else than a voluntary madness.

SENECA.

DUTY

In doing what we ought we deserve no praise, because it is our duty.

ST. AUGUSTINE.

To do my duty in that state of life unto which it shall please God to call me.

Book of Common Prayer.

The reward of one duty is the power to fulfil another.

GEORGE ELIOT—*Daniel Deronda.*

So nigh is grandeur to our dust,
So near is God to man.
When Duty whispers low, *Thou must,*
The youth replies, *I can.*

EMERSON—*Voluntaires.*

No personal consideration should stand in the way of performing a public duty.

U. S. GRANT.

It is thy duty oftentimes to do what thou wouldst not; thy duty, too, to leave undone that thou wouldst do.

THOMAS À KEMPIS.

Duty is what goes most against the grain, because in doing that we do only what we are strictly obliged to, and are seldom much praised for it.

LA BRUYÈRE.

Let us have faith that right makes might, and in that faith let us, to the end, dare to do our duty as we understand it.

LINCOLN.

New occasions teach new duties.

LOWELL.

The things which must be, must be for the best,
God helps us do our duty and not shrink,
And trust His mercy humbly for the rest.

OWEN MEREDITH—*Imperfection.*

Knowledge is the hill which few may wish to climb;
Duty is the path that all may tread.

LEWIS MORRIS—*Epic of Hades.*

England expects every man to do his duty.

HORATIO NELSON.

Theirs not to make reply,
Theirs not to reason why,
Theirs but to do and die.
TENNYSON—*The Charge of the Light Brigade.*

Not once or twice in our rough island story,
The path of duty was the way to glory.
TENNYSON—*Ode on the Death of the Duke of Wellington.*

E

EAGLE

So, in the Libyan fable it is told
That once an eagle, stricken with a dart,
Said, when he saw the fashion of the shaft,
"With our own feathers, not by others' hand
Are we now smitten."
AESCHYLUS.

Wheresoever the carcass is, there will the eagles be gathered together.
Matthew. XXIV. 28.

Bird of the broad and sweeping wing,
Thy home is high in heaven,
Where wide the storms their banners fling,
And the tempest clouds are driven.
PERCIVAL—*To the Eagle.*

EARLY RISING

Next to temperance, a quiet conscience, a cheerful mind and active habits, I place early rising as a means of health and happiness.
FLINT.

The early morning has gold in its mouth.
FRANKLIN.

Early to bed and early to rise,
Makes a man healthy, wealthy and wise.
FRANKLIN—*Poor Richard's Almanac.*

He that from childhood has made rising betimes familiar to him will not waste the best part of his life in drowsiness.
LOCKE.

EARNESTNESS

A man in earnest finds means, or, if he cannot find, creates them.
WILLIAM ELLERY CHANNING.

Vigor is contagious; and whatever makes us either think or feel strongly adds to our power and enlarges our field of action.
EMERSON.

Earnestness is the salt of eloquence.
VICTOR HUGO.

Earnestness and sincerity are synonymous.
KANT.

Earnestness is enthusiasm tempered by reason.
PASCAL.

EASTER

All Christian worship is a witness of the resurrection of Him who liveth for ever and ever. Because He lives, "now abideth faith, hope, charity."
LYMAN ABBOTT.

Awake, thou wintry earth—
Fling off thy sadness!
Fair vernal flowers, laugh forth
Your ancient gladness!
Christ is risen.
THOMAS BLACKBURN—*An Easter Hymn.*

O Risen Christ! O Easter Flower!
How dear Thy Grace has grown!
From east to west, with loving power,
Make all the world Thine own.
PHILLIPS BROOKS.

Tomb, thou shalt not hold Him longer;
Death is strong, but Life is stronger;
Stronger than the dark, the light;
Stronger than the wrong, the right;

Faith and Hope triumphant say
Christ will rise on Easter Day.
PHILLIPS BROOKS—*An Easter Carol.*

Hail, Day of days! in peals of praise
Throughout all ages owned,
When Christ, our God, hell's empire trod,
And high o'er heaven was throned.
FORTUNATUS (Bishop of Poitiers).

Come, ye saints, look here and wonder,
See the place where Jesus lay;
He has burst His bands asunder;
He has borne our sins away;
Joyful tidings,
Yes, the Lord has risen to-day.
THOMAS KELLY.

Hallelujah! Hallelujah!
On the third morning He arose,
Bright with victory o'er his foes.
Sing we lauding,
And applauding,
Hallelujah!
From the Latin of the 12th Century.

In the bonds of Death He lay
Who for our offence was slain;
But the Lord is risen to-day,
Christ hath brought us life again,
Wherefore let us all rejoice,
Singing loud, with cheerful voice,
Hallelujah!
LUTHER.

Spring bursts to-day,
For Christ is risen and all the earth's at play.
CHRISTINA G. ROSSETTI—*Easter Carol.*

"Christ the Lord is risen to-day,"
Sons of men and angels say.
Raise your joys and triumphs high;
Sing, ye heavens, and earth reply.
CHARLES WESLEY.

EATING

When the Sultan Shah-Zaman
Goes to the city Ispahan,
Even before he gets so far
As the place where the clustered palm-trees are,
At the last of the thirty palace-gates,
The pet of the harem, Rose-in-Bloom,
Orders a feast in his favorite room—
Glittering square of colored ice,
Sweetened with syrup, tinctured with spice,
Creams, and cordials, and sugared dates,
Syrian apples, Othmanee quinces,
Limes and citrons and apricots,
And wines that are known to Eastern princes.
T. B. ALDRICH—*When the Sultan Goes to Ispahan.*

Acorns were good till bread was found.
BACON.

Eat, drink, and be merry, for tomorrow ye diet.
WILLIAM GILMORE BEYMER.

A warmed-up dinner was never worth much.
BOILEAU—*Lutrin.*

All human history attests
That happiness for man,—the hungry sinner!—
Since Eve ate apples, much depends on dinner.
BYRON—*Don Juan.*

Man is a carnivorous production,
And must have meals, at least one meal a day;
He cannot live, like woodcocks, upon suction,
But, like the shark and tiger, must have prey;
Although his anatomical construction
Bears vegetables, in a grumbling way,
Your laboring people think beyond all question,
Beef, veal, and mutton better for digestion.
BYRON—*Don Juan.*

Better halfe a loafe than no bread.
CAMDEN—*Remaines.*

The proof of the pudding is in the eating.
CERVANTES—*Don Quixote.*

Thou shouldst eat to live; not live to eat.
CICERO.

Man shall not live by bread alone.
Deuteronomy. VIII. 3; *Matthew*. IV. 4.

When I demanded of my friend what viands he preferred,
He quoth: "A large cold bottle, and a small hot bird!"
EUGENE FIELD—*The Bottle and the Bird*.

I want every peasant to have a chicken in his pot on Sundays.
HENRY IV OF FRANCE.

A cheerful look makes a dish a feast.
GEORGE HERBERT—*Jacula Prudentum*.

Let us eat and drink; for to-morrow we shall die.
Isaiah. XXII. 13.

Think of the man who first tried German sausage.
JEROME K. JEROME—*Three Men in a Boat*.

For a man seldom thinks with more earnestness of anything than he does of his dinner.
SAMUEL JOHNSON.

If you wish to grow thinner, diminish your dinner,
And take to light claret instead of pale ale;
Look down with an utter contempt upon butter,
And never touch bread till it's toasted—or stale.
HENRY S. LEIGH—*A Day for Wishing*.

Take no thought for your life, what ye shall eat, or what ye shall drink.
Matthew. VI. 25.

We may live without poetry, music and art;
We may live without conscience, and live without heart;
We may live without friends; we may live without books;
But civilized man cannot live without cooks.
He may live without books,—what is knowledge but grieving?
He may live without hope,—what is hope but deceiving?
He may live without love,—what is passion but pining?
But where is the man that can live without dining?
OWEN MEREDITH—*Lucile*.

Gluttony kills more than the sword, and is the kindler of all evils.
PATRICIUS, Bishop of Gaeta.

The way to a man's heart is through his stomach.
MRS. SARAH PAYSON—*Willis Parton*.

Better is a dinner of herbs where love is, than a stalled ox and hatred therewith.
Proverbs. XV. 17.

Tell me what you eat, and I will tell you what you are.
BRILLAT SAVARIN—*Physiologie du Gout*.

He hath eaten me out of house and home.
SHAKESPEARE—*Henry IV*. Pt. II. Act. II. Sc. 1.

Fat paunches have lean pates, and dainty bits
Make rich the ribs, but bankrupt quite the wits.
SHAKESPEARE — *Love's Labour's Lost*. Act I. Sc. 1.

Though we eat little flesh and drink no wine,
Yet let's be merry; we'll have tea and toast;
Custards for supper, and an endless host
Of syllabubs and jellies and mince-pies,
And other such ladylike luxuries.
SHELLEY—*Letter to Maria Gisborne*.

They say fingers were made before forks, and hands before knives.
SWIFT—*Polite Conversation*.

Bread is the staff of life.
SWIFT—*Tale of a Tub*.

ECCENTRICITY

Even beauty cannot always palliate eccentricity.

BALZAC.

Who affects useless singularities has surely a little mind.

LAVATER.

Eccentricity has always abounded when and where strength of character has abounded; and the amount of eccentricity in a society has been proportional to the amount of genius, mental vigor, and moral courage it contained. That so few now dare to be eccentric, marks the chief danger of the time.

JOHN STUART MILL.

ECHO

I came to the place of my birth and cried:
"The friends of my youth, where are they?"—and an echo answered, "Where are they?"

ROGERS—*Pleasures of Memory.*

Our echoes roll from soul to soul,
And grow for ever and for ever.
Blow, bugle, blow, set the wild echoes flying,
And answer, echoes, answer, dying, dying, dying.

TENNYSON—*The Princess.*

ECONOMY

Buy not what you want, but what you have need of; what you do not want is dear at a farthing.

CATO.

The injury of prodigality leads to this, that he who will not economize will have to agonize.

CONFUCIUS.

After order and liberty, economy is one of the highest essentials of a free government. . . . Economy is always a guarantee of peace.

CALVIN COOLIDGE—*Speech, 1923.*

If you know how to spend less than you get you have the philosopher's stone.

FRANKLIN.

Beware of little expenses; a small leak will sink a great ship.

FRANKLIN.

Many have been ruined by buying good Pennyworths.

FRANKLIN—*Poor Richard's Almanac.*

No man is rich whose expenditure exceeds his means; and no one is poor whose incomings exceed his outgoings.

HALIBURTON.

He will always be a slave, who does not know how to live upon a little.

HORACE—*Epistles.*

By robbing Peter he paid Paul, he kept the moon from the wolves, and was ready to catch larks if ever the heavens should fall.

RABELAIS.

Any government, like any family, can for a year spend a little more than it earns. But you and I know that a continuance of that habit means the poorhouse.

F. D. ROOSEVELT—*Speech, 1932.*

Have more than thou showest,
Speak less than thou knowest,
Lend less than thou owest,
Ride more than thou goest,
Learn more than thou trowest,
Set less than thou throwest.

SHAKESPEARE—*King Lear.* Act I. Sc. 4.

Economy is a savings-bank, into which men drop pennies, and get dollars in return.

H. W. SHAW.

Economy is half the battle of life; it is not so hard to earn money as to spend it well.

SPURGEON.

EDUCATION

Histories make men wise; poets, witty; the mathematics, subtile; natural phi-

losophy, deep; morals, grave; logic and rhetoric, able to contend.
BACON—*Essays.*

Education commences at the mother's knee, and every word spoken within the hearsay of little children tends towards the formation of character.
HOSEA BALLOU.

Education makes a people easy to lead, but difficult to drive; easy to govern, but impossible to enslave.
Attributed to LORD BROUGHAM.

Education is the cheap defence of nations.
BURKE.

"Reeling and Writhing, of course, to begin with," the Mock Turtle replied, "and the different branches of Arithmetic—Ambition, Distraction, Uglification, and Derision."
LEWIS CARROLL—*Alice in Wonderland.*

What greater or better gift can we offer the republic than to teach and instruct our youth?
CICERO.

Training is everything. The peach was once a bitter almond; cauliflower is nothing but cabbage with a college education.
SAMUEL L. CLEMENS (Mark Twain).

The foundation of every state is the education of its youth.
DIOGENES.

By education most have been misled.
DRYDEN—*Hind and Panther.*

The things taught in schools and colleges are not an education, but the means of education.
EMERSON—*Journal, 1831.*

Education is the process of driving a set of prejudices down your throat.
MARTIN H. FISCHER.

Next in importance to freedom and justice is popular education, without which neither justice nor freedom can be permanently maintained.
JAMES A. GARFIELD.

The best and most important part of every man's education is that which he gives himself.
GIBBON.

Much may be made of a Scotchman if he be caught young.
SAMUEL JOHNSON—*Boswell's Life of Johnson.*

It was in making education not only common to all, but in some sense compulsory on all, that the destiny of the free republics of America was practically settled.
LOWELL.

Schoolhouses are the republican line of fortifications.
HORACE MANN.

'Tis education forms the common mind;
Just as the twig is bent the tree's inclined.
POPE—*Moral Essays.*

There is nothing so stupid as an educated man, if you get off the thing that he was educated in.
WILL ROGERS.

The great difficulty in education is to get experience out of idea.
SANTAYANA—*The Life of Reason.*

Oh how our neighbour lifts his nose,
To tell what every schoolboy knows.
SWIFT—*Century Life.*

If we work upon marble, it will perish; if we work upon brass, time will efface it; if we rear temples, they will crumble into dust; but if we work upon immortal minds, if we imbue them with principles, with the just fear of God and love of our fellowmen, we engrave on those tablets something which will brighten to all eternity.
DANIEL WEBSTER.

Education is an admirable thing, but it is well to remember from time to time that nothing that is worth knowing can be taught.
OSCAR WILDE—*The Critic as Artist.*

EGOTISM

Be your character what it will, it will be known; and nobody will take it upon your word.
CHESTERFIELD.

The reason why lovers are never weary of one another is this—they are always talking of themselves.
LA ROCHEFOUCAULD.

When all is summed up, a man never speaks of himself without loss; his accusations of himself are always believed, his praises never.
MONTAIGNE.

Do you wish men to speak well of you? Then never speak well of yourself.
PASCAL.

Here is the egotist's code: everything for himself, nothing for others.
SANIAL-DUBAY.

Nothing is more to me than myself.
STIRNER—*The Ego and His Own.*

ELOQUENCE

No man ever did or ever will become truly eloquent without being a constant reader of the Bible, and an admirer of the purity and sublimity of its language.
FISHER AMES.

Eloquence is the poetry of prose.
BRYANT.

The manner of your speaking is full as important as the matter, as more people have ears to be tickled than understandings to judge.
CHESTERFIELD.

He is an eloquent man who can treat humble subjects with delicacy, lofty things impressively, and moderate things temperately.
CICERO.

Noise proves nothing. Often a hen who has merely laid an egg cackles as if she laid an asteroid.
SAMUEL L. CLEMENS (Mark Twain).

Thoughts that breathe and words that burn.
GRAY.

Eloquence, when in its highest pitch, leaves little room for reason or reflection.
HUME.

Talking and eloquence are not the same: to speak and to speak well are two things. A fool may talk, but a wise man speaks.
BEN JONSON.

There is as much eloquence in the tone of voice, in the eyes, and in the air of a speaker as in his choice of words.
LA ROCHEFOUCAULD.

True eloquence consists in saying all that is necessary, and nothing but what is necessary.
LA ROCHEFOUCAULD.

That besotting intoxication which verbal magic brings upon the mind.
SOUTH.

It is with eloquence as with a flame; it requires fuel to feed it, motion to excite it, and it brightens as it burns.
WILLIAM PITT THE YOUNGER.

EMULATION

Emulation admires and strives to imitate great actions; envy is only moved to malice.
BALZAC.

'Tis no shame to follow the better precedent.
BEN JONSON.

Emulation is a noble and just passion, full of appreciation.
SCHILLER.

END

The end must justify the means.
PRIOR—*Hans Carvel.*

All's well that ends well; still the fine's
the crown;
Whate'er the course, the end is the renown.
SHAKESPEARE—*All's Well That Ends Well.* Act IV. Sc. 4.

ENDURANCE

Endurance is patience concentrated.
CARLYLE.

What can't be cured must be endured.
English Proverb.

The greater the difficulty the more glory in surmounting it. Skilful pilots gain their reputation from storms and tempests.
EPICURUS.

To endure is the first thing a child ought to learn, and that which he will have most need to know.
ROUSSEAU.

Endurance is the prerogative of woman, enabling the gentlest to suffer what would cause terror to manhood.
WIELAND.

ENEMY

It is better to decide a difference between enemies than friends, for one of our friends will certainly become an enemy and one of our enemies a friend.
BIAS.

They love him most for the enemies that he has made.
GENERAL E. S. BRAGG—*Nominating Speech for Cleveland, 1884.*

Man is his own worst enemy.
CICERO.

He who has a thousand friends has not a friend to spare,
And he who has one enemy will meet him everywhere.
EMERSON—*Translations.*

If we could read the secret history of our enemies we should find in each man's life sorrow and suffering enough to disarm all hostility.
LONGFELLOW.

None but yourself who are your greatest foe.
LONGFELLOW.

If thine enemy hunger, feed him; if he thirst, give him drink: for in so doing thou shalt heap coals of fire on his head.
Romans. XII. 20.

A merely fallen enemy may rise again, but the reconciled one is truly vanquished.
SCHILLER.

A man cannot be too careful in the choice of his enemies.
WILDE—*Picture of Dorian Gray.*

ENERGY

Energy, even like the Biblical grain of mustard-seed, will remove mountains.
HOSEA BALLOU.

Energy and persistence conquer all things.
FRANKLIN.

Energy will do anything that can be done in this world; and no talents, no circumstances, no opportunities, will make a two-legged animal a man without it.
GOETHE.

ENGLAND

England! my country, great and free!
Heart of the world, I leap to thee!
BAILEY—*Festus.*

If I should die, think only this of me:
That there's some corner of a foreign field
That is forever England. There shall be
In that rich earth a richer dust concealed;
A dust whom England bore, shaped, made aware,
Gave, once, her flowers to love, her ways to roam,
A body of England's, breathing English air,
Washed by the rivers, blest by suns of home.
RUPERT BROOKE—*The Soldier.*

Oh, to be in England,
Now that April's there,
And whoever wakes in England
Sees some morning, unaware,

That the lowest boughs and the brushwood sheaf,
Round the elm-tree bole are in tiny leaf
While the chaffinch sings on the orchard bough
In England—now.

ROBERT BROWNING—*Home Thoughts from Abroad.*

In England there are sixty different religions, and only one sauce.

MARQUIS CARACCIOLI.

Be England what she will,
With all her faults, she is my country still.

CHARLES CHURCHILL—*The Farewell.*

I have nothing to offer but blood, toil, tears and sweat.

WINSTON CHURCHILL—*Speech,* May 28, 1940.

We shall go on to the end, we shall fight in France, we shall fight on the seas and oceans, we shall fight with growing confidence and growing strength in the air, we shall defend our Island, whatever the cost may be, we shall fight on the landing grounds, we shall fight in the fields and in the streets, we shall fight in the hills; we shall never surrender, and even if, which I do not for a moment believe, this Island or a large part of it were subjugated and starving, then our Empire beyond the seas, armed and guarded by the British Fleet, would carry on the struggle, until, in God's good time, the New World, with all its power and might, steps forth to the rescue and the liberation of the old.

WINSTON CHURCHILL—*Speech,* June 4, 1940.

Let us therefore brace ourselves to our duties, and so bear ourselves that, if the British Empire and its Commonwealth last for a thousand years, men will still say, "This was their finest hour."

WINSTON CHURCHILL—*Speech,* June 18, 1940.

Long, dark months of trials and tribulations lie before us. Not only great dangers, but many more misfortunes, many shortcomings, many mistakes, many disappointments will surely be our lot. Death and sorrow will be the companions of our journey; hardship our garment; constancy and valor our only shield. We must be united, we must be undaunted, we must be inflexible. Our qualities and deeds must burn and glow through the gloom of Europe until they become the veritable beacon of its salvation.

WINSTON CHURCHILL—*Speech,* October 8, 1940.

Never in the field of human conflict was so much owed by so many to so few.

WINSTON CHURCHILL, 1941, referring to England's debt to its Royal Air Force.

'Tis a glorious charter, deny it who can,
That's breathed in the words, "I'm an Englishman."

ELIZA COOK—*An Englishman.*

Bind her, grind her, burn her with fire,
Cast her ashes into the sea,—
She shall escape, she shall aspire,
She shall arise to make men free;
She shall arise in a sacred scorn,
Lighting the lives that are yet unborn,
Spirit supernal, splendour eternal,
England!

HELEN GRAY CONE—*Chant of Love for England.* (1915)

O, it's a snug little island!
A right little, tight little island!

THOMAS DIBDIN—*The Snug Little Island.*

We are indeed a nation of shopkeepers.

DISRAELI—*The Young Duke.*

The English nation is never so great as in adversity.

DISRAELI—*Speech, 1857.*

Hearts of oak are our ships,
Jolly tars are our men,
We always are ready, steady, boys, steady,
We'll fight and will conquer again and again.
David Garrick—*Hearts of Oak.*

For he might have been a Rooshian
A French or Turk or Proosian,
Or perhaps Itali-an.
But in spite of all temptations
To belong to other nations,
He remains an Englishman.
W. S. Gilbert—*H. M. S. Pinafore.*

What have I done for you,
England, my England?
What is there I would not do,
England, my own?
W. E. Henley—*England, My England.*

Winds of the World give answer! They are whimpering to and fro—
And what should they know of England who only England know?—
Kipling—*English Flag.*

This royal throne of kings, this scepter'd isle,
This earth of majesty, this seat of Mars,
This other Eden, demi-paradise,
This fortress built by nature for herself
Against infection and the hand of war;
This happy breed of men, this little world,
This precious stone set in the silver sea.
Shakespeare—*Richard II.* Act II. Sc. 1.

Oh, Britannia the pride of the ocean
The home of the brave and the free,
The shrine of the sailor's devotion,
No land can compare unto thee.
Davis Taylor Shaw—*Britannia.*

There is nothing so bad or so good that you will not find Englishmen doing it; but you will never find an Englishman in the wrong. He does everything on principle. He fights you on patriotic principles; he robs you on business principles; he enslaves you on imperial principles.
George Bernard Shaw—*The Man of Destiny.*

An Englishman thinks he is moral when he is only uncomfortable.
George Bernard Shaw.

When Britain first at Heaven's command,
Arose from out the azure main,
This was the charter of the land,
And Guardian angels sung this strain;
"Rule Britannia! rule the waves;
Britons never will be slaves."
James Thomson—*Masque of Alfred.*

Froth at the top, dregs at bottom, but the middle excellent.
Voltaire—*Description of the English Nation.*

ENTHUSIASM

In things pertaining to enthusiasm no man is sane who does not know how to be insane on proper occasions.
Henry Ward Beecher.

Nothing is so contagious as enthusiasm; it moves stones, it charms brutes. Enthusiasm is the genius of sincerity and truth accomplishes no victories without it.
Bulwer-Lytton.

Nothing great was ever achieved without enthusiasm.
Emerson—*On Circles.*

The same reason makes a man a religious enthusiast that makes a man an enthusiast in any other way, an uncomfortable mind in an uncomfortable body.
Hazlitt.

The sense of this word among the Greeks affords the noblest definition of it: enthusiasm signifies God in us.
Mme. de Staël.

Enthusiasm is that temper of the mind in which the imagination has got the better of the judgment.
Bishop Warburton—*Divine Legation.*

ENVY

As a moth gnaws a garment, so doth envy consume a man.

St. Chrysostom.

The hen of our neighbor appears to us a goose, says the Oriental proverb.

Mme. Deluzy.

Fools may our scorn, not envy, raise.
For envy is a kind of praise.

Gay—*The Hound and the Huntsman.*

Envy is the deformed and distorted offspring of egotism; and when we reflect on the strange and disproportioned character of the parent, we cannot wonder at the perversity and waywardness of the child.

Hazlitt.

It is better to be envied than pitied.

Herodotus.

No man likes to be surpassed by those of his own level.

Livy—*Annales.*

Envy assails the noblest: the winds howl around the highest peaks.

Ovid.

Envy feeds only on the living.

Ovid.

We ought to be guarded against every appearance of envy, as a passion that always implies inferiority wherever it resides.

Pliny.

Envy, to which th' ignoble mind's a slave,
Is emulation in the learn'd or brave.

Pope—*Essay on Man.*

It is the practice of the multitude to bark at eminent men, as little dogs do at strangers.

Seneca—*Of a Happy Life.*

When men are full of envy they disparage everything, whether it be good or bad.

Tacitus.

Base Envy withers at another's joy,
And hates that excellence it cannot reach.

Thomson—*The Seasons.*

EPIGRAM

A platitude with vine-leaves in its hair.

Anonymous.

What is an epigram? a dwarfish whole,
Its body brevity, and wit its soul.

Anonymous.

Some learned writers . . . have compared a Scorpion to an Epigram . . . because as the sting of the Scorpion lyeth in the tayl, so the force and virtue of an Epigram is in the conclusion.

Topsell—*Serpent.*

EPITAPH

Here lies the remains of James Pady, Brickmaker, in hope that his clay will be remoulded in a workmanlike manner, far superior to his former perishable materials.

Epitaph from Addiscombe Churchyard, Devonshire.

A tomb now suffices him for whom the whole world was not sufficient.

Epitaph on Alexander the Great.

If Paris that brief flight allow,
My humble tomb explore!
It bears: "Eternity, be thou
My refuge!" and no more.

Matthew Arnold—*Epitaph.*

Here lies Anne Mann; she lived an
Old maid and died an old Mann.

Bath Abbey.

Lie lightly on my ashes, gentle earthe.

Beaumont and Fletcher—*Tragedy of Bonduca.*

And be the Spartan's epitaph on me—
"Sparta hath many a worthier son than he."

Byron—*Childe Harold.*

Shrine of the mighty! can it be,
That this is all remains of thee?

Byron—*Giaour.*

It is so soon that I am done for,
I wonder what I was begun for!

Epitaph in Cheltenham Churchyard.

Peas to his Hashes.

Epitaph on a Cook (London).

O man! whosoever thou art, and whensoever thou comest, for come I know thou wilt, I am Cyrus, founder of the Persian empire. Envy me not the little earth that covers my body.
Epitaph of Cyrus.

"Let there be no inscription upon my tomb. Let no man write my epitaph. No man can write my epitaph. I am here ready to die. I am not allowed to vindicate my character; and when I am prevented from vindicating myself, let no man dare calumniate me. Let my character and motives repose in obscurity and peace, till other times and other men can do them justice."
ROBERT EMMET—*Speech on his Trial,* 1803.

The body of Benjamin Franklin, Printer, (Like the cover of an old book, its contents torn out and stript of its lettering and gilding), Lies here, food for worms; But the work shall not be lost, for it will (as he believed) appear once more in a new and more elegant edition, revised and corrected by the author.
BENJAMIN FRANKLIN—*Epitaph on Himself,* written in 1728.

Here lies Nolly Goldsmith, for shortness called Noll,
Who wrote like an angel, and talked like poor Poll.
DAVID GARRICK.

Life is a jest, and all things show it,
I thought so once, but now I know it.
GAY—*My Own Epitaph.*

Beneath these green trees rising to the skies,
The planter of them, Isaac Greentree, lies;
The time shall come when these green trees shall fall,
And Isaac Greentree rise above them all.
Epitaph at Harrow.

Man's life is like unto a winter's day,
Some break their fast and so depart away,
Others stay dinner then depart full fed;
The longest age but sups and goes to bed.
Oh, reader, then behold and see,
As we are now so must you be.
BISHOP HENSHAW.

Here she lies a pretty bud,
Lately made of flesh and blood;
Who, as soone fell fast asleep,
As her little eyes did peep.
Give her strewings, but not stir
The earth that lightly covers her.
HERRICK—*Upon a Child that Dyed.*

Sleep undisturbed within this peaceful shrine,
Till angels wake thee with a note like thine.
SAMUEL JOHNSON—*Epitaph on Claude Phillips.*

Underneath this stone doth lie
As much beauty as could die;
Which in life did harbor give
To more virtue than doth live.
If at all she had a fault,
Leave it buried in this vault.
BEN JONSON—*To Lady Elizabeth L. H.*

Here lies one whose name was writ in water.
Engraved on Keats' tombstone.

Satire does not look pretty upon a tombstone.
LAMB.

I strove with none, for none was worth my strife;
Nature I loved, and after Nature, Art;
I warmed both hands before the fire of life;
It sinks, and I am ready to depart.
LANDOR—*Epitaph on Himself.*

Emigravit, is the inscription on the tombstone where he lies;
Dead he is not, but departed,—for the artist never dies.
LONGFELLOW—*Nuremberg.*

The shameless Chloe placed on the tombs of her seven husbands the inscription. "The work of Chloe." How could she have expressed herself more plainly?

MARTIAL—*Epigrams.*

Here lie I, Martin Elginbrodde:
Have mercy o' my soul, Lord God;
As I wad do, were I Lord God,
And ye were Martin Elginbrodde.

GEORGE MCDONALD—*David Elginbrodde.*

Requiescat in pace.
May he rest in peace.

Order of the Mass.

Excuse my dust.

DOROTHY PARKER—*Her Own Epitaph.*

Statesman, yet friend to truth! of soul sincere,
In action faithful, and in honour clear;
Who broke no promise, served no private end,
Who gained no title, and who lost no friend,
Ennobled by himself, by all approved,
And praised, unenvied, by the muse he loved.

POPE—*Moral Essays.*

To this sad shrine, whoe'er thou art! draw near!
Here lies the friend most lov'd, the son most dear;
Who ne'er knew joy but friendship might divide,
Or gave his father grief but when he died.

POPE—*Epitaph on Harcourt.*

Heralds and statesmen, by your leave,
Here lies what once was Matthew Prior;
The son of Adam and of Eve;
Can Bourbon or Nassau go higher?

PRIOR—*Epitaph.*

I came at morn—'twas spring, I smiled,
The fields with green were clad;
I walked abroad at noon,—and lo!
'Twas summer,—I was glad;
I sate me down; 'twas autumn eve,
And I with sadness wept;
I laid me down at night, and then
'Twas winter,—and I slept.

MARY PYPER—*Epitaph.*

The world's a *book*, writ by th' *eternal Art*
Of the great Maker; printed in man's heart;
'Tis falsely *printed* though divinely penn'd,
And all the *Errata* will appear at th' end.

QUARLES—*Divine Fancies.*

Earth walks on Earth,
Glittering in gold;
Earth goes to Earth,
Sooner than it wold;
Earth builds on Earth,
Palaces and towers;
Earth says to Earth,
Soon, all shall be ours.

SCOTT—*Unpublished Epigram.*

After your death you were better have a bad epitaph than their ill report while you live.

SHAKESPEARE—*Hamlet.* Act II. Sc. 2.

These are two friends whose lives were undivided:
So let their memory be, now they have glided
Under the grave; let not their bones be parted,
For their two hearts in life were single-hearted.

SHELLEY—*Epitaph.*

Let no man write my epitaph; let my grave
Be uninscribed, and let my memory rest
Till other times are come, and other men,
Who then may do me justice.

SOUTHEY.

Here lies one who meant well, tried a little, failed much.

STEVENSON—*Christman Sermon.*

Under the wide and starry sky,
Dig the grave and let me lie;
Glad did I live and gladly die,
And I laid me down with a will.
This be the verse you grave for me:
"Here he lies, where he longed to be;

Home is the sailor, home from the sea,
And the hunter home from the hill."

STEVENSON. *Engraved on his tombstone.*

Warm summer sun shine kindly here;
Warm southern wind blow softly here;
Green sod above lie light, lie light—
Good night, dear heart, good night, good night.

On the tombstone of Susy Clemens by MARK TWAIN.

Here in this place sleep one whom love
Caused, through great cruelty to fall,
A little scholar, poor enough,
Whom François Villon men did call.
No scrap of land or garden small
He owned. He gave his goods away,
Table and treatles, baskets—all;
For God's sake say for him this Lay.

FRANÇOIS VILLON. *His own Epitaph.*

Here lies the first author of this sentence; "The itch of disputation will prove the scab of the Church." Inquire his name elsewhere.

IZAAK WALTON—*Life of Wotton.*

The poet's fate is here in emblem shown,
He asked for bread, and he received a stone.

SAMUEL WESLEY. *On Butler's Monument in Westminster Abbey.*

He first deceas'd; she for a little tri'd
To live without him, lik'd it not, and died.

SIR HENRY WOTTON—*Upon the Death of Sir Albertus Morton's Wife.*

If you would see his monument look around.

Inscription on the tomb of Sir Christopher Wren in St. Paul's, London.

EQUALITY

Men are made by nature unequal. It is vain, therefore, to treat them as if they were equal.

FROUDE—*Party Politics.*

The equal right of all men to the use of land is as clear as their equal right to breathe the air—it is a right proclaimed by the fact of their existence. For we cannot suppose that some men have a right to be in this world, and others no right.

HENRY GEORGE.

We hold these truths to be self-evident: that all men are created equal; that they are endowed by their Creator with inalienable rights; that among these are life, liberty and the pursuit of happiness.

THOMAS JEFFERSON.

For the colonel's lady an' Judy O'Grady,
Are sisters under their skins.

KIPLING—*Barrack Room Ballads.*

Equality is the share of every one at their advent upon earth, and equality is also theirs when placed beneath it.

NINON DE LENCLOS.

Fourscore and seven years ago, our fathers brought forth on this continent a new nation, conceived in liberty, and dedicated to the proposition that all men are created equal.

LINCOLN—*Gettysburg Address.*

For some must follow, and some command
Though all are made of clay!

LONGFELLOW—*Keramos.*

The sun shines even on the wicked.

SENECA.

Let's go hand in hand, not one before another.

SHAKESPEARE—*Comedy of Errors.* Act V. Sc. 1.

The trickling rain doth fall
Upon us one and all;
The south-wind kisses
The saucy milkmaid's cheek,
The nun's, demure and meek,
Nor any misses.

E. C. STEDMAN—*A Madrigal.*

Mortals are equal; their mask differs.

VOLTAIRE.

ERROR

The truth is perilous never to the true,
Nor knowledge to the wise; and to the fool,
And to the false, error and truth alike,
Error is worse than ignorance.
BAILEY—*Festus*.

Error is always more busy than truth.
HOSEA BALLOU.

Mistake, error, is the discipline through which we advance.
CHANNING—*Address on The Present Age*.

To stumble twice against the same stone is a proverbial disgrace.
CICERO.

By Hercules! I prefer to err with Plato, whom I know how much you value, than to be right in the company of such men.
CICERO.

The cautious seldom err.
CONFUCIUS.

Errors, like straws, upon the surface flow;
He who would search for pearls, must dive below.
DRYDEN—*All for Love*.

An error gracefully acknowledged is a victory won.
CAROLINE L. GASCOIGNE.

When every one is in the wrong, every one is in the right.
LA CHAUSSÉE.

The man who makes no mistakes does not usually make anything.
EDWARD J. PHELPS—*Speech at Mansion House*.

To err is human, to forgive divine.
POPE—*An Essay on Criticism*.

Error will slip through a crack, while truth will stick in a doorway.
H. W. SHAW.

From the errors of others, a wise man corrects his own.
SYRUS.

ESCAPE

I am escaped with the skin of my teeth.
Job. XIX. 20.

ETERNITY

Eternity is not an everlasting flux of time, but time is as a short parenthesis in a long period.
DONNE—*Book of Devotions Meditation*.

Eternity has no gray hairs! The flowers fade, the heart withers, man grows old and dies, the world lies down in the sepulchre of ages, but time writes no wrinkles on the brow of eternity.
BISHOP HEBER.

This is eternal life; a life of everlasting love, showing itself in everlasting good works; and whosoever lives that life, he lives the life of God, and hath eternal life.
KINGSLEY.

The thought of eternity consoles for the shortness of life.
MALESHERBES.

This speck of life in time's great wilderness
This narrow isthmus 'twixt two boundless seas,
The past, the future, two eternities!
MOORE—*Lalla Rookh*.

The time will come when every change shall cease,
This quick revolving wheel shall rest in peace:
No summer then shall glow, nor winter freeze;
Nothing shall be to come, and nothing past,
But an eternal now shall ever last.
PETRARCH—*Triumph of Eternity*.

In time there is no present,
In eternity no future,
In eternity no past.
TENNYSON — *The "How" and "Why."*

EVENING

It is the hour when from the boughs
The nightingale's high note is heard;
It is the hour when lovers' vows
Seem sweet in every whispered word;
And gentle winds, and waters near,
Make music to the lonely ear.
Each flower the dews have lightly wet,
And in the sky the stars are met,
And on the wave is deeper blue,
And on the leaf a browner hue,
And in the heaven that clear obscure,
So softly dark, and darkly pure.
Which follows the decline of day,
As twilight melts beneath the moon away.
BYRON—*Parisina.*

When day is done, and clouds are low,
And flowers are honey-dew,
And Hesper's lamp begins to glow
Along the western blue;
And homeward wing the turtle-doves,
Then comes the hour the poet loves.
GEORGE CROLY—*The Poet's Hour.*

The curfew tolls the knell of parting day,
The lowing herd winds slowly o'er the lea,
The ploughman homeward plods his weary way,
And leaves the world to darkness and to me.
GRAY—*Elegy in a Country Churchyard.*

Day hath put on his jacket, and around
His burning bosom buttoned it with stars.
HOLMES—*Evening.*

One by one the flowers close,
Lily and dewy rose
Shutting their tender petals from the moon.
CHRISTINA G. ROSSETTI—*Twilight Calm.*

The holy time is quiet as a Nun
Breathless with adoration.
WORDSWORTH—*It Is a Beauteous Evening.*

EVENTS

Coming events cast their shadows before.
CAMPBELL.

What wonderful things are events! The least are of greater importance than the most sublime and comprehensive speculations.
DISRAELI.

Events of great consequence often spring from trifling circumstances.
LIVY.

EVIDENCE

One eye-witness is of more weight than ten hearsays.
PLAUTUS.

Facts are stubborn things.
SMOLLETT.

Some circumstantial evidence is very strong, as when you find a trout in the milk.
THOREAU.

EVIL

Evil events from evil causes spring.
ARISTOPHANES.

Evil and good are God's right hand and left.
BAILEY—*Prelude to Festus.*

Often the fear of one evil leads us into a worse.
BOILEAU.

Every evil in the bud is easily crushed: as it grows older, it becomes stronger.
CICERO.

The doing an evil to avoid an evil cannot be good.
COLERIDGE.

Touch not; taste not; handle not.
Colossians. II. 21.

Evil communications corrupt good manners.
I Corinthians. XV. 33.

Of two evils choose the least.
ERASMUS.

How many men would be mute if they were forbidden to speak well of themselves and evil of others.
MME. DE FONTAINE.

There is no evil in human affairs that has not some good mingled with it.
GUICCIARDINI.

What has this unfeeling age of ours left untried, what wickedness has it shunned?
HORACE.

Woe unto them that call evil good, and good evil.
ISAIAH. V. 20.

A man has no more right to say an uncivil thing than to act one; no more right to say a rude thing to another than to knock him down.
SAMUEL JOHNSON.

What is evil?—Whatever springs from weakness.
NIETZSCHE—*The Antichrist.*

Never throw mud. You may miss your mark; but you must have dirty hands.
JOSEPH PARKER.

Ill gotten is ill spent.
PLAUTUS.

An evil-speaker differs from an evil-doer only in the want of opportunity.
QUINTILIAN.

Be not overcome of evil, but overcome evil with good.
Romans. XII. 21.

Evil often triumphs, but never conquers.
JOSEPH ROUX.

Multitudes think they like to do evil; yet no man ever really enjoyed doing evil since God made the world.
RUSKIN.

There is no evil in the world without a remedy.
SANNAZARO—*Ecloga Octava.*

If thou wishest to get rid of thy evil propensities, thou must keep far from evil companions.
SENECA.

The evil that men do lives after them;
The good is oft interred with their bones.
SHAKESPEARE—*Julius Caesar.* Act III. Sc. 2.

Never let man imagine that he can pursue a good end by evil means, without sinning against his own soul! Any other issue is doubtful; the evil effect on himself is certain.
SOUTHEY.

As sure as God is good, so surely there is no such thing as necessary evil.
SOUTHEY.

So far any one shuns evils, so far as he does good.
SWEDENBORG—*Doctrine of Life.*

There are times when it would seem as if God fished with a line, and the devil with a net.
MADAME SWETCHINE.

A bad heart, bad designs.
TERENCE.

But, by all thy nature's weakness,
Hidden faults and follies known,
Be thou, in rebuking evil,
Conscious of thine own.
WHITTIER—*What the Voice Said.*

EVOLUTION

Observe constantly that all things take place by change, and accustom thyself to consider that the nature of the Universe loves nothing so much as to change the things which are, and to make new things like them.
MARCUS AURELIUS—*Meditations.*

There is no more reason to believe that man descended from some inferior animal than there is to believe that a stately mansion has descended from a small cottage.
W. J. BRYAN, 1925.

A fire-mist and a planet,
A crystal and a cell,

A jellyfish and a saurian,
And caves where the cavemen dwell;
Then a sense of law and beauty,
And a face turned from the clod—
Some call it Evolution,
And others call it God.

W. H. CARRUTH—*Each in His Own Tongue.*

There was an ape in the days that were earlier,
Centuries passed and his hair became curlier;
Centuries more gave a thumb to his wrist—
Then he was a MAN and a Positivist.

MORTIMER COLLINS—*The British Birds.*

I have called this principle, by which each slight variation, if useful, is preserved, by the term of Natural Selection.

DARWIN—*Origin of Species.*

Said the little Eohippus,
"I am going to be a horse,
And on my middle fingernails
To run my earthly course!

. . .

I'm going to have a flowing tail!
I'm going to have a mane!
I'm going to stand fourteen hands high
On the Psychozoic plain!"

CHARLOTTE P. S. GILMAN—*Similar Cases.*

Or ever the knightly years were gone
With the old world to the grave,
I was a king in Babylon
And you were a Christian Slave.

W. F. HENLEY—*Echoes.*

Children, behold the Chimpanzee;
He sits in the ancestral tree
From which we sprang in ages gone.
I'm glad we sprang: had we held on,
We might, for aught that I can say,
Be horrid Chimpanzees to-day.

OLIVER HERFORD—*The Chimpanzee.*

We seem to exist in a hazardous time,
Driftin' along here through space;
Nobody knows just when we begun,
Or how fur we've gone in the race.

BEN KING—*Evolution.*

When you were a tadpole and I was a fish in the Palaeozoic time
And side by side in the sluggish tide, we sprawled in the ooze and slime.

LANGDON SMITH—*Evolution.*

This survival of the fittest, which I have here sought to express in mechanical terms, is that which Mr. Darwin has called "natural selection, or the preservation of favoured races in the struggle for life."

HERBERT SPENCER—*Principles of Biology.*

Civilization is a progress from an indefinite, incoherent homogeneity toward a definite, coherent heterogeneity.

HERBERT SPENCER—*First Principles.*

Out of the dusk a shadow,
Then a spark;
Out of the cloud a silence,
Then a lark;
Out of the heart a rapture,
Then a pain;
Out of the dead, cold ashes,
Life again.

JOHN BANISTER TABB—*Evolution.*

EXAMPLE

Example is the school of mankind, and they will learn at no other.

BURKE—*On a Regicide Peace.*

Men think they may justly do that for which they have a precedent.

CICERO.

None preaches better than the ant, and she says nothing.

FRANKLIN.

We can do more good by being good than in any other way.

ROWLAND HILL.

Example is more efficacious than precept.

SAMUEL JOHNSON.

Children have more need of models than of critics.

JOUBERT.

Example is a dangerous lure; where the wasp got through the gnat sticks fast.

LA FONTAINE.

Lives of great men all remind us
We can make our lives sublime,
And, departing, leave behind us
Footprints on the sands of time.

LONGFELLOW—*A Psalm of Life.*

He who would teach men to die, should at the same time teach them to live.

MONTAIGNE—*Essays.*

EXCESS

We cannot employ the mind to advantage when we are filled with excessive food and drink.

CICERO.

The excesses of our youth are drafts upon our old age, payable with interest, about thirty years after date.

COLTON.

There can be no excess to love, none to knowledge, none to beauty, when these attributes are considered in the purest sense.

EMERSON.

Excess always carries its own retribution.

"OUIDA."

Moderation is a fatal thing; nothing succeeds like excess.

WILDE—*A Woman of No Importance.*

EXCUSE

An excuse is worse and more terrible than a lie; for an excuse is a lie guarded.

POPE.

Oftentimes, excusing of a fault
Doth make the fault the worse by the excuse;
As patches, set upon a little breach,
Discredit more in hiding of the fault,
Than did the fault before it was so patched.

SHAKESPEARE.

EXILE

"Farewell, my Spain! a long farewell!" he cried.
"Perhaps I may revisit thee no more,
But die, as many an exiled heart hath died.
Of its own thirst to see again thy shore."

BYRON.

Home, kindred, friends, and country—these
Are ties with which we never part;
From clime to clime, o'er land and seas,
We bear them with us in our heart:
But, oh! 'tis hard to feel resign'd,
When these must all be left behind!

J. MONTGOMERY.

An exile, ill in heart and frame,—
A wanderer, weary of the way;—
A stranger, without love's sweet claim
On any heart, go where I may!

MRS. OSGOOD.

EXPECTATION

Great expectations are better than a poor possession.

CERVANTES.

Uncertainty and expectation are joys of life. Security is an insipid thing; and the overtaking and possessing of a wish discovers the folly of the chase.

CONGREVE.

I have known him (Micawber) come home to supper with a flood of tears, and a declaration that nothing was now left but a jail; and go to bed making a calculation of the expense of putting bow-windows to the house, "in case anything turned up," which was his favorite expression.

DICKENS—*David Copperfield.*

I suppose, to use our national motto, *something will turn up.*

DISRAELI.

Everything comes if a man will only wait.

DISRAELI—*Tancred.*

Those who live on expectation are sure to be disappointed.

JOACHIM MURAT.

'Tis Expectation makes a blessing dear;
Heaven were not heaven, if we knew what it were.

SUCKLING.

Blessed are those that nought expect,
For they shall not be disappointed.

JOHN WALCOT—*Ode to Pitt.*

It is folly to expect men to do all that they may reasonably be expected to do.

WHATELY—*Apophthegms.*

EXPERIENCE

By experience we find out a shorter way by a long wandering. Learning teacheth more in one year than experience in twenty.

ROGER ASCHAM—*Schoolmaster.*

Theories are very thin and unsubstantial; experience only is tangible.

HOSEA BALLOU.

Would they could sell us experience, though at diamond prices, but then no one would use the article second-hand!

BALZAC.

To most men, experience is like the stern lights of a ship, which illumine only the track it has passed.

COLERIDGE.

A sadder and a wiser man,
He rose the morrow morn.

COLERIDGE—*The Ancient Mariner.*

Experience cannot deliver to us necessary truths; truths completely demonstrated by reason. Its conclusions are particular, not universal.

DEWEY—*The Quest for Certainty.*

Only so much do I know, as I have lived.

EMERSON—*The American Scholar.*

Experience is no more transferable in morals than in art.

FROUDE—*Education.*

Experience teaches slowly, and at the cost of mistakes.

FROUDE—*Party Politics.*

Experience makes us wise.

HAZLITT.

Experience is the extract of suffering.

ARTHUR HELPS.

I have but one lamp by which my feet are guided, and that is the lamp of experience.

PATRICK HENRY.

One thorn of experience is worth a whole wilderness of warning.

LOWELL—*Among My Books.*

Every man's experience of to-day is that he was a fool yesterday and the day before yesterday. To-morrow he will most likely be of exactly the same opinion.

CHARLES MACKAY.

Experience is the name men give to their follies or their sorrows.

ALFRED DE MUSSET.

What man would be wise, let him drink of the river
That bears on his bosom the record of time;
A message to him every wave can deliver
To teach him to creep till he knows how to climb.

JOHN BOYLE O'REILLY.

Men are wise in proportion, not to their experience, but to their capacity for experience.

GEORGE BERNARD SHAW—*Maxims for Revolutionists.*

And others' follies teach us not,
Nor much their wisdom teaches,
And most, of sterling worth, is what
Our own experience preaches.

TENNYSON—*Will Waterproof.*

Is there any one so wise as to learn by the experience of others?

VOLTAIRE.

EXTRAVAGANCE

Prodigality is indeed the vice of a weak nature, as avarice is of a strong

one; it comes of a weak craving for those blandishments of the world which are easily to be had for money.
HENRY TAYLOR.

Extravagance is the rich man's pitfall.
TUPPER.

EXTREME

Extreme views are never just; something always turns up which disturbs the calculations formed upon their data.
DISRAELI.

All extremes are error. The reverse of error is not truth, but error still. Truth lies between these extremes.
CECIL.

There is danger in all extremes.
JAMES ELLIS.

Mistrust the man who finds everything good, the man who finds everything evil, and still more, the man who is indifferent to everything.
LEVATER.

Our senses will not admit anything extreme. Too much noise confuses us, too much light dazzles us, too great distance or nearness prevents vision, too great prolixity or brevity weakens an argument, too much pleasure gives pain, too much accordance annoys.
PASCAL.

In everything the middle course is best; all things in excess bring trouble.
PLAUTUS.

Avoid Extremes; and shun the fault of such
Who still are pleas'd too little or too much.
POPE—*Essay on Criticism.*

No one tries extreme remedies at first.
SENECA.

EYE

A gray eye is a sly eye,
And roguish is a brown one;
Turn full upon me thy eye,—
Ah, how its wavelets drown one!
A blue eye is a true eye;
Mysterious is a dark one,
Which flashes like a spark-sun!
A black eye is the best one.
W. R. ALGER—*Oriental Poetry.*

Among the blind the one-eyed man is king.
ANONYMOUS.

A wanton eye is a messenger of an unchaste heart.
ST. AUGUSTINE.

There are whole veins of diamonds in thine eyes,
Might furnish crowns for all the Queens of earth.
BAILEY—*Festus.*

The mind has a thousand eyes,
And the heart but one;
Yet the light of a whole life dies
When love is done.
F. W. BOURDILLON—*Light.*

The learned compute that seven hundred and seven millions of millions of vibrations have penetrated the eye before the eye can distinguish the tints of a violet.
BULWER-LYTTON—*What Will He Do With It?*

With eyes that look'd into the very soul—
BYRON—*Don Juan.*

There are eyes half defiant,
Half meek and compliant;
Black eyes, with a wondrous, witching charm
To bring us good or to work us harm.
PHOEBE CARY—*Dove's Eyes.*

The love light in her eye.
HARTLEY COLERIDGE.

In the twinkling of an eye.
I Corinthians. XV. 52.

He kept him as the apple of his eye.
Deuteronomy. XXXII. 10.

My life lies in those eyes which have me slain.
DRUMMOND—*Sonnet XXIX.*

An eye can threaten like a loaded and levelled gun, or can insult like hissing

or kicking; or, in its altered mood, by beams of kindness, it can make the heart dance with joy.
EMERSON—*Conduct of Life.*

Eyes so transparent,
That through them one sees the soul.
THÉOPHILE GAUTIER.

I everywhere am thinking
Of thy blue eyes' sweet smile;
A sea of blue thoughts is spreading
Over my heart the while.
HEINE—*New Spring.*

The ear is a less trustworthy witness than the eye.
HERODOTUS.

Her eyes the glow-worme lend thee,
The shooting starres attend thee;
And the elves also,
Whose little eyes glow
Like the sparks of fire, befriend thee.
HERRICK—*The Night Piece to Julia.*

Drink to me only with thine eyes, and
I will pledge with mine.
BEN JONSON.

Who has a daring eye tells downright truths and downright lies.
LAVATER.

Glances are the first billets-doux of love.
NINON DE LENCLOS.

As President, I have no eyes but constitutional eyes; I cannot see you.
LINCOLN *to the South Carolina Commissioners.*

I dislike an eye that twinkles like a star. Those only are beautiful which, like the planets, have a steady, lambent light,—are luminous, but not sparkling.
LONGFELLOW—*Hyperion.*

And the world's so rich in resplendent eyes,
'Twere a pity to limit one's love to a pair.
MOORE—*'Tis Sweet to Think.*

Her eyes, like marigolds, had sheath'd their light;
And, canopied in darkness, sweetly lay,
Till they might open to adorn the day.
SHAKESPEARE—*Rape of Lucrece.*

Her eyes in heaven
Would through the airy region stream so bright,
That birds would sing and think it were not night.
SHAKESPEARE—*Romeo and Juliet.* Act II. Sc. 2.

Alack, there lies more peril in thine eye
Than twenty of their swords.
SHAKESPEARE—*Romeo and Juliet.* Act II. Sc. 2.

If I could write the beauty of your eyes,
And in fresh numbers number all your graces,
The age to come would say, "This poet lies;
Such heavenly touches ne'er touch'd earthly faces."
SHAKESPEARE—*Sonnet.*

Her eyes are homes of silent prayer.
TENNYSON—*In Memoriam.*

F

FACE

The loveliest faces are to be seen by moonlight, when one sees half with the eye and half with the fancy.
BOVEE.

A face to lose youth for, to occupy age
With the dream of, meet death with.
BROWNING—*A Likeness.*

And to his eye
There was but one beloved face on earth,
And that was shining on him.
BYRON—*The Dream.*

He had a face like a benediction.
CERVANTES.

Look in the face of the person to whom you are speaking, if you wish to

know his real sentiments; for he can command his words more easily than his countenance.
LORD CHESTERFIELD.

Some women's faces are, in their brightness, a prophecy; and some, in their sadness, a history.
DICKENS.

A cheerful face is nearly as good for an invalid as healthy weather.
FRANKLIN.

How some they have died, and some they have left me,
And some are taken from me; all are departed;
All, all are gone, the old familiar faces.
LAMB—*The Old Familiar Faces.*

Faces are as legible as books, only with these circumstances to recommend them to our perusal, that they are read in much less time, and are much less likely to deceive us.
LAVATER.

The worst of faces still is human.
LAVATER.

The light upon her face
Shines from the windows of another world.
Saints only have such faces.
LONGFELLOW—*Michael Angelo.*

Oh! could you view the melody
Of every grace,
And music of her face,
You'd drop a tear,
Seeing more harmony
In her bright eye,
Than now you hear.
LOVELACE—*Orpheus to Beasts.*

Was this the face that launch'd a thousand ships,
And burnt the topless towers of Ilium?
Sweet Helen, make me immortal with a kiss.—
Her lips suck forth my soul; see, where it flies!—
MARLOWE—*Dr. Faustus.*

"What is your fortune, my pretty maid?"
"My face is my fortune, sir," she said.
Nursery Rhyme.

Lift thou up the light of thy countenance upon us.
Psalms. IV. 6.

Those faces which have charmed us most escape us the soonest.
SCOTT.

A countenance more in sorrow than in anger.
SHAKESPEARE—*Hamlet.* Act I. Sc. 2.

God has given you one face, and you make yourselves another.
SHAKESPEARE—*Hamlet.* Act III. Sc. 1.

Your face, my thane, is a book where men
May read strange matters. To beguile the time,
Look like the time.
SHAKESPEARE—*Macbeth.* Act I. Sc. 5.

Compare her face with some that I shall show;
And I will make thee think thy swan a crow.
SHAKESPEARE—*Romeo and Juliet.* Act I. Sc. 2.

Her face is like the Milky Way i' the sky,—
A meeting of gentle lights without a name.
SUCKLING—*A Ballad Upon a Wedding.*

White rose in red rose-garden
Is not so white;
Snowdrops, that plead for pardon
And pine for fright
Because the hard East blows
Over their maiden vows,
Grow not as this face grows from pale to bright.
SWINBURNE—*Before the Mirror.*

Fire burns only when we are near it, but a beautiful face burns and inflames, though at a distance.
XENOPHON.

My face. Is this long strip of skin
Which bears of worry many a trace,

Of sallow hue, of features thin,
This mass of seams and lines, my face?
EDMUND YATES—*Aged Forty.*

FACTS

I grow daily to honor facts more and more, and theory less and less.
CARLYLE.

There are no eternal facts, as there are no absolute truths.
NIETZSCHE—*Human All-too-Human.*

Some people have a peculiar faculty for denying facts.
G. D. PRENTICE.

Facts are stubborn things.
TOBIAS SMOLLETT.

Every fact that is learned becomes a key to other facts.
E. L. YOUMANS.

FAILURE

(Oxford) Home of lost causes, and forsaken beliefs and unpopular names and impossible loyalties.
MATTHEW ARNOLD — *Essays in Criticism.*

A failure establishes only this, that our determination to succeed was not strong enough.
BOVEE.

In the lexicon of youth, which
Fate reserves for a bright manhood, there is no such word
As—*fail!*
BULWER-LYTTON—*Richelieu.*

Half the failures in life come from pulling one's horse when he is leaping.
HOOD.

Albeit failure in any cause produces a correspondent misery in the soul, yet it is, in a sense, the highway to success, inasmuch as every discovery of what is false leads us to seek earnestly after what is true, and every fresh experience points out some form of error which we shall afterward carefully eschew.
KEATS.

"All honor to him who shall win the prize,"
The world has cried for a thousand years;
But to him who tries and fails and dies,
I give great honor and glory and tears.
JOAQUIN MILLER—*For Those Who Fail.*

How are the mighty fallen!
II Samuel. I. 25.

Here's to the men who lose!
What though their work be e'er so nobly plann'd
And watched with zealous care;
No glorious halo crowns their efforts grand—
Contempt is Failure's share!
G. L. SCARBOROUGH—*To the Vanquished.*

And each forgets, as he strips and runs
With a brilliant, fitful pace,
It's the steady, quiet, plodding ones
Who win in the lifelong race.
And each forgets that his youth has fled,
Forgets that his prime is past,
Till he stands one day, with a hope that's dead,
In the glare of the truth at last.
SERVICE—*The Men That Don't Fit In.*

We have scotch'd the snake, not killed it.
SHAKESPEARE—*Macbeth.* Act III. Sc. 2.

Not all who seem to fail have failed indeed,
Not all who fail have therefore worked in vain.
There is no failure for the good and brave.
Attributed to ARCHBISHOP TRENCH.

Failure is more frequently from want of energy than want of capital.
DANIEL WEBSTER.

He only is exempt from failures who makes no efforts.
WHATELY.

FAIRIES

Up the airy mountain,
Down the rushy glen,
We daren't go a-hunting
For fear of little men;
Wee folk, good folk,
Trooping all together,
Green jacket, red cap,
And white owl's feather!
WILLIAM ALLINGHAM — *The Fairies.*

When the first baby laughed for the first time, the laugh broke into a million pieces, and they all went skipping about. That was the beginning of fairies.
BARRIE—*Peter Pan.*

Nothing can be truer than fairy wisdom. It is as true as sunbeams.
DOUGLAS JERROLD.

Fairies, black, grey, green, and white,
You moonshine revellers, and shades of night.
SHAKESPEARE — *Merry Wives of Windsor.* Act V. Sc. 5.

FAITH

Faith is the continuation of reason.
WILLIAM ADAMS.

The person who has a firm trust in the Supreme Being is powerful in his power, wise by his wisdom, happy by his happiness.
ADDISON.

Faith is to believe what we do not see; and the reward of this faith is to see what we believe.
ST. AUGUSTINE.

There never was found in any age of the world, either philosopher or sect, or law or discipline, which did so highly exalt the public good as the Christian faith.
BACON.

Faith is a higher faculty than reason.
BAILEY—*Festus.*

There is one inevitable criterion of judgment touching religious faith in doctrinal matters. Can you reduce it to practice? If not, have none of it.
HOSEA BALLOU.

Faith is nothing but spiritualized imagination.
HENRY WARD BEECHER.

An outward and visible sign of an inward and spiritual grace.
Book of Common Prayer.

Strike from mankind the principle of faith, and men would have no more history than a flock of sheep.
BULWER-LYTTON.

Faith is love taking the form of aspiration.
WILLIAM ELLERY CHANNING.

We walk by faith, not by sight.
II Corinthians. V. 7.

Faith is a fine invention
For gentlemen who see;
But Microscopes are prudent
In an emergency.
EMILY DICKINSON—*Poems.*

To take up half on trust, and half to try,
Name it not faith but bungling bigotry.
DRYDEN—*The Hind and the Panther.*

All I have seen teaches me to trust the Creator for all I have not seen.
EMERSON.

The highest historical probability can be adduced in support of the proposition that, if it were possible to annihilate the Bible, and with it all its influences, we should destroy with it the whole spiritual system of the moral world.
EDWARD EVERETT.

It is by faith that poetry, as well as devotion, soars above this dull earth; that imagination breaks through its clouds, breathes a purer air, and lives in a softer light.
HENRY GILES.

If you have any faith, give me, for heaven's sake, a share of it! Your

doubts you may keep to yourself, for I have a plenty of my own.
GOETHE.

Faith is necessary to victory.
HAZLITT.

Faith is the substance of things hoped for, the evidence of things not seen.
Hebrews. XI. 1.

What sought they thus afar?
Bright jewels of the mine?
The wealth of seas, the spoils of war?—
They sought a faith's pure shrine!
MRS. HEMANS—*Landing of the Pilgrim Fathers*.

The German is the discipline of fear; ours is the discipline of faith—and faith will triumph.
GEN. JOFFRE, *at unveiling of a statue of Lafayette in Brooklyn, 1917*.

Let us have faith that right makes might; and in that faith, let us, to the end, dare to do our duty as we understand it.
LINCOLN.

The only faith that wears well and holds its color in all weathers is that which is woven of conviction and set with the sharp mordant of experience.
LOWELL—*My Study Windows*.

A perfect faith would lift us absolutely above fear.
GEORGE MACDONALD.

O welcome pure-ey'd Faith, white-handed Hope,
Thou hovering angel, girt with golden wings!
MILTON—*Comus*.

How many things served us yesterday for articles of faith, which to-day are fables to us!
MONTAIGNE—*Essays*.

But Faith, fanatic Faith, once wedded fast
To some dear falsehood, hugs it to the last.
MOORE—*Lalla Rookh*.

For modes of faith let graceless zealots fight;
His can't be wrong whose life is in the right.
POPE—*Essay on Man*.

Be thou faithful unto death.
Revelation. II. 10.

The saddest thing that can befall a soul
Is when it loses faith in God and woman.
ALEXANDER SMITH—*A Life Drama*.

Faith is the subtle chain
Which binds us to the infinite; the voice
Of a deep life within, that will remain
Until we crowd it thence.
ELIZABETH OAKES SMITH.

There lives more faith in honest doubt,
Believe me, than in half the creeds.
TENNYSON.

I have fought a good fight, I have finished my course, I have kept the faith.
II Timothy. IV. 7.

Faith is the force of life.
TOLSTOI.

Faith, mighty faith the promise sees
And rests on that alone;
Laughs at impossibilities,
And says it shall be done.
CHARLES WESLEY—*Hymns*.

Through this dark and stormy night
Faith beholds a feeble light
Up the blackness streaking;
Knowing God's own time is best,
In a patient hope I rest
For the full day-breaking!
WHITTIER—*Barclay of Ury*.

Faith builds a bridge across the gulf of Death,
To break the shock blind nature cannot shun,
And lands Thought smoothly on the further shore.
YOUNG—*Night Thoughts*.

FALSEHOOD

Not the least misfortune in a prominent falsehood is the fact that tradition is apt to repeat it for truth.
HOSEA BALLOU.

And none speaks false, when there is none to hear.

Beattie—*The Minstrel.*

There is no such thing as white lies; a lie is as black as a coal-pit, and twice as foul.

Henry Ward Beecher.

So near is falsehood to truth that a wise man would do well not to trust himself on the narrow edge.

Cicero.

Falsehood is never so successful as when she baits her hook with truth, and no opinions so fastly mislead us as those that are not wholly wrong, as no watches so effectually deceive the wearer as those that are sometimes right.

Colton.

Falsehood is so easy, truth so difficult.

George Eliot.

As ten millions of circles can never make a square, so the united voice of myriads cannot lend the smallest foundation to falsehood.

Goldsmith—*Vicar of Wakefield.*

Round numbers are always false.

Samuel Johnson.

False in one thing, false in everything.

Law Maxim.

To tell a falsehood is like the cut of a sabre; for though the wound may heal, the scar of it will remain.

Saadi.

Falsehoods not only disagree with truths, but usually quarrel among themselves.

Daniel Webster.

FAME

And what after all is everlasting fame?
Altogether vanity.

Marcus Aurelius Antoninus—*Med.* 4. 33.

Many have lived on a pedestal who will never have a statue when dead.

Béranger.

What is the end of Fame? 'tis but to fill
A certain portion of uncertain paper:
Some liken it to climbing up a hill,
Whose summit, like all hills, is lost in vapour:
For this men write, speak, preach, and heroes kill,
And bards burn what they call their "midnight taper,"
To have, when the original is dust,
A name, a wretched picture, and worse bust.

Byron—*Don Juan.*

I awoke one morning and found myself famous.

Byron—From Moore's *Life of Byron.*

To many fame comes too late.

Camoens.

Unlike the sun, intellectual luminaries shine brightest after they set.

Colton.

Fame is the beauty-parlor of the dead.

Benjamin De Casseres—*Fantasia Impromptu.*

If you would not be forgotten as soon as you are dead, either write things worth reading or do things worth writing.

Franklin.

Men think highly of those who rise rapidly in the world; whereas nothing rises quicker than dust, straw, and feathers.

Hare.

But sure the eye of time beholds no name,
So blest as thine in all the rolls of fame.

Homer—*Odyssey.*

The fame of great men ought always to be estimated by the means used to acquire it.

La Rochefoucauld.

Fame comes only when deserved, and then is as inevitable as destiny, for it is destiny.

Longfellow—*Hyperion.*

I do not like the man who squanders life for fame; give me the man who living makes a name.

Martial—*Epigrams.*

If fame comes after death, I am in no hurry for it.

MARTIAL—*Epigrams.*

It is pleasing to be pointed at with the finger and to have it said, "There goes the man."

PERSIUS—*Satires.*

Who grasp'd at earthly fame,
Grasped wind: nay, worse, a serpent grasped that through
His hand slid smoothly, and was gone; but left
A sting behind which wrought him endless pain.

POLLOK—*Course of Time.*

And what is Fame? the Meanest have their Day,
The Greatest can but blaze, and pass away.

POPE—*First Book of Horace.*

Time magnifies everything after death; a man's fame is increased as it passes from mouth to mouth after his burial.

PROPERTIUS.

Fame is but the breath of the people, and that often unwholesome.

ROUSSEAU.

I'll make thee famous by my pen,
And glorious by my sword.

SCOTT—*Legend of Montrose.*

He lives in fame, that died in virtue's cause.

SHAKESPEARE—*Titus Andronicus.* Act I. Sc. 1.

Fame is the perfume of heroic deeds.

SOCRATES.

No true and permanent Fame can be founded except in labors which promote the happiness of mankind.

CHARLES SUMNER — *Fame and Glory.*

Censure is the tax a man pays to the public for being eminent.

SWIFT.

Even the best things are not equal to their fame.

THOREAU.

What a heavy burden is a name that has become too famous.

VOLTAIRE.

In fame's temple there is always a niche to be found for rich dunces, importunate scoundrels, or successful butchers of the human race.

ZIMMERMANN.

FAMILIARITY

Familiarity breeds contempt.

ANONYMOUS.

A woman who throws herself at a man's head will soon find her place at his feet.

LOUIS DESNOYERS.

Though familiarity may not breed contempt, it takes off the edge of admiration.

HAZLITT.

The living together for three long, rainy days in the country has done more to dispel love than all the perfidies in love that have ever been committed.

ARTHUR HELPS.

Familiarity is a magician that is cruel to beauty, but kind to ugliness.

OUIDA.

FANATICISM

The downright fanatic is nearer to the heart of things than the cool and slippery disputant.

CHAPIN.

The false fire of an overheated mind.

COWPER.

Fanaticism is the child of false zeal and of superstition, the father of intolerance and of persecution.

J. W. FLETCHER.

What is fanaticism to-day is the fashionable creed to-morrow, and trite as the multiplication table a week after.

WENDELL PHILLIPS.

FANCY

Fancy runs most furiously when a guilty conscience drives it.

FULLER.

Fancy brings us as many vain hopes as idle fears.

HUMBOLDT.

She's all my fancy painted her,
She's lovely, she's divine.

WILLIAM MEE—*Alice Gray*.

Fancy tortures more people than does reality.

OUIDA.

The difference is as great between
The optics seeing as the objects seen.
All manners take a tincture from our own;
Or come discolor'd through our passions shown;
Or fancy's beam enlarges, multiplies,
Contracts, inverts, and gives ten thousand dyes.

POPE—*Moral Essays*.

Fancy rules over two thirds of the universe, the past and the future, while reality is confined to the present.

JEAN PAUL RICHTER.

FAREWELL

Fare thee well! and if for ever,
Still for ever, fare thee well.

BYRON—*Fare Thee Well*.

Farewell! "But not for ever."

COWPER.

Gude Nicht, and joy be wi' you a'.

LADY NAIRNE.

Sweets to the sweet; farewell!

SHAKESPEARE—*Hamlet*. Act V. Sc. 1.

Farewell, and stand fast.

SHAKESPEARE—*Henry IV*. Pt. I. Act II. Sc. 2.

FARMING

Some people tell us that there ain't no Hell,
But they never farmed, so how can they tell?

ANONYMOUS.

He that by the plow would thrive
Himself must either hold or drive.

FRANKLIN—*Poor Richard's Almanac*.

Those who labor in the earth are the chosen people of God, if He ever had a chosen people, whose breasts He has made His peculiar deposit for substantial and genuine virtue.

THOMAS JEFFERSON—*Notes on Virginia*.

Farming is a most senseless pursuit, a mere laboring in a circle. You sow that you may reap, and then you reap that you may sow. Nothing ever comes of it.

STOBÆUS.

Let us never forget that the cultivation of the earth is the most important labor of man. When tillage begins, other arts follow. The farmers, therefore, are the founders of civilization.

DANIEL WEBSTER.

FASHION

There would not be so much harm in the giddy following the fashions, if somehow the wise could always set them.

BOVEE.

Fashion—a word which knaves and fools may use,
Their knavery and folly to excuse.

CHARLES CHURCHILL—*Rosciad*

Ladies of fashion starve their happiness to feed their vanity, and their love to feed their pride.

COLTON.

The fashion of this world passeth away.

I Corinthians. VII. 31.

Women cherish fashion because it rejuvenates them, or at least renews them.

MADAME DE PREIZEUX.

Fashion is the bastard of vanity, dressed by art.

FUSELI.

Fashion is only the attempt to realize art in living forms and social intercourse.

HOLMES.

A fashionable woman is always in love—with herself.

La Rochefoucauld.

Be neither too early in the fashion, nor too long out of it; nor at any time in the extremes of it.

Lavater.

A glass of fashion and the mould of form,
The observ'd of all observers.

Shakespeare—*Hamlet*. Act III. Sc. 1.

I see that the fashion wears out more apparel than the man.

Shakespeare—*Much Ado About Nothing*. Act III. Sc. 3.

Ridiculous modes, invented by ignorance, and adopted by folly.

Smollett.

Fashion is a form of ugliness so intolerable that we have to alter it every six months.

Oscar Wilde.

FATE

The bow is bent, the arrow flies,
The wingèd shaft of fate.

Ira Aldridge—*On William Tell*.

Here's a sigh to those who love me,
And a smile to those who hate;
And whatever sky's above me,
Here's a heart for every fate.

Byron—*To Thomas Moore*.

To bear is to conquer our fate.

Campbell.

They are raised on high that they may be dashed to pieces with a greater fall.

Claudian.

He has gone to the demnition bow-wows.

Dickens—*Nicholas Nickleby*.

We make our fortunes and we call them fate.

Disraeli.

'Tis Fate that flings the dice,
And as she flings
Of kings makes peasants,
And of peasants kings.

Dryden.

A strict belief in fate is the worst of slavery, imposing upon our necks an everlasting lord and tyrant, whom we are to stand in awe of night and day.

Epicurus.

Thou must (in commanding and winning, or serving and losing, suffering or triumphing) be either anvil or hammer.

Goethe.

Though men determine, the gods do dispose: and oft times many things fall out between the cup and the lip.

Greene.

Toil is the lot of all, and bitter woe
The fate of many.

Homer—*Iliad*.

I do not know beneath what sky
Nor on what seas shall be thy fate;
I only know it shall be high,
I only know it shall be great.

Richard Hovey—*Unmanifest Destiny*.

No one is so accursed by fate,
No one so utterly desolate,
But some heart, though unknown,
Responds unto his own.

Longfellow—*Endymion*.

There is no good in arguing with the inevitable.

Lowell.

For him who fain would teach the world
The world holds hate in fee—
For Socrates, the hemlock cup;
For Christ, Gethsemane.

Don Marquis—*Wages*.

The Moving Finger writes; and having writ,
Moves on; nor all your Piety nor Wit
Shall lure it back to cancel half a Line,
Nor all your Tears wash out a Word of it.

Omar Khayyám—*Rubaiyat*.

Heaven from all creatures hides the book of fate.

Pope—*Essay on Man*.

He putteth down one and setteth up another.

Psalms. LXXV. 7.

The fates lead the willing, and drag the unwilling.
SENECA.

What fates impose, that men must needs abide;
It boots not to resist both wind and tide.
SHAKESPEARE—*Henry VI.* Pt. III. Act IV. Sc. 3.

Two shall be born, the whole wide world apart,
And speak in different tongues, and have no thought
Each of the other's being; and have no heed;
And these, o'er unknown seas to unknown lands
Shall cross, escaping wreck, defying death;
And, all unconsciously, shape every act to this one end:
That one day out of darkness they shall meet
And read life's meanings in each other's eyes.
SUSAN M. SPALDING—*Fate.*

The die is cast.—*Exclamation of Caesar as he crossed the Rubicon.*
SUETONIUS.

From too much love of living,
From hope and fear set free,
We thank with brief thanksgiving
Whatever gods may be
That no life lives forever;
That dead men rise up never;
That even the weariest river
Winds somewhere safe to sea.
SWINBURNE—*Garden of Proserpine.*

I saw him even now going the way of all flesh.
JOHN WEBSTER—*Westward Ho.*

FATHER

No one ever knew his own father.
BUCKLEY.

A father is a banker provided by nature.
French Proverb.

The fathers have eaten sour grapes, and the children's teeth are set on edge.
Jeremiah. XXXI. 29.

It is a wise father that knows his own child.
SHAKESPEARE.

The child is father of the man.
WORDSWORTH.

FAULT

There is so much good in the worst of us,
And so much bad in the best of us,
That it ill behooves any of us
To find fault with the rest of us.
ANONYMOUS.

The greatest of faults, I should say, is to be conscious of none.
CARLYLE—*Heroes and Hero-Worship.*

The great fault in women is to desire to be like men.
DE MAISTRE.

Why do we discover faults so much more readily than perfections?
MADAME DE SÉVIGNÉ.

The defects of great men are the consolation of the dunces.
ISAAC D'ISRAELI.

We blame in others only the faults by which we do not profit.
ALEXANDER DUMAS.

If the best man's faults were written on his forehead, he would draw his hat over his eyes.
GRAY.

It is well that there is no one without a fault, for he would not have a friend in the world. He would seem to belong to a different species.
HAZLITT.

We keep on deceiving ourselves in regard to our faults, until we at last come to look upon them as virtues.
HEINE.

Go to your bosom;
Knock there, and ask your heart what it doth know
That's like my brother's fault.
SHAKESPEARE—*Measure for Measure*. Act. II. Sc. 2.

They say, best men are moulded out of faults;
And, for the most, become much more the better
For being a little bad.
SHAKESPEARE—*Measure for Measure*. Act V. Sc. 1.

He who overlooks a fault, invites the commission of another.
SYRUS—*Maxims*.

Faults are beauties in a lover's eye.
THEOCRITUS.

FAVOR

A favor tardily bestowed is no favor; for a favor quickly granted is a more agreeable favor.
AUSONIUS.

He only confers favors generously who appears, when they are once conferred, to remember them no more.
SAMUEL JOHNSON.

That man is worthless who knows how to receive a favor, but not how to return one.
PLAUTUS.

To accept a favor is to sell one's freedom.
SYRUS.

FEAR

No one loves the man whom he fears.
ARISTOTLE.

Nothing is to be feared but fear.
BACON.

An aching tooth is better out than in,
To lose a rotten member is a gain.
RICHARD BAXTER—*Hypocrisy*.

Fear makes us feel our humanity.
DISRAELI.

God planted fear in the soul as truly as He planted hope or courage. Fear is a kind of bell, or gong, which rings the mind into quick life and avoidance upon the approach of danger. It is the soul's signal for rallying.
HENRY WARD BEECHER.

There is great beauty in going through life fearlessly. Half our fears are baseless, the other half discreditable.
BOVEE.

In politics, what begins in fear usually ends in folly.
COLERIDGE.

Fear always springs from ignorance.
EMERSON—*The American Scholar*.

Fear is the parent of cruelty.
FROUDE.

From a distance it is something; and nearby it is nothing.
LA FONTAINE.

No one but a poltroon will boast that he never was afraid.
MARSHAL LANNES.

They are slaves who fear to speak
For the fallen and the weak.
LOWELL—*Stanzas on Freedom*.

The thing in the world I am most afraid of is fear, and with good reason; that passion alone, in the trouble of it, exceeding all other accidents.
MONTAIGNE.

A lamb appears a lion, and we fear
Each bush we see's a bear.
QUARLES—*Emblems*.

The only thing we have to fear is fear itself.
F. D. ROOSEVELT—*Inaugural Address, 1933*.

If you wish to fear nothing, consider that everything is to be feared.
SENECA.

Fear in the world first created the gods.
STATIUS.

Even the bravest men are frightened by sudden terrors.
TACITUS—*Annales*.

Fear is the proof of a degenerate mind.
VERGIL—*Aeneid*.

I was astounded, my hair stood on end, and my voice stuck in my throat.
VERGIL—*Aeneid*.

FESTIVITIES

Why should we break up
  Our snug and pleasant party?
Time was made for slaves,
  But never for us so hearty.
    JOHN B. BUCKSTONE—*Billy Taylor.*

Let us have wine and woman, mirth and laughter,
Sermons and soda-water the day after.
    BYRON—*Don Juan.*

Then I commended mirth, because a man hath no better thing under the sun, than to eat, than to drink, and to be merry.
    Ecclesiastes. VIII. 15; *Luke.* XII. 19.

Feast, and your halls are crowded;
Fast, and the world goes by.
    ELLA WHEELER WILCOX—*Solitude.*

FICTION

Fiction may be said to be the caricature of history.
    BULWER-LYTTON.

Every novel is a debtor to Homer.
    EMERSON.

Man is a poetical animal, and delights in fiction.
    HAZLITT.

If you would understand your own age, read the works of fiction produced in it. People in disguise speak freely.
    ARTHUR HELPS.

FIDELITY

Nothing is more noble, nothing more venerable than fidelity. Faithfulness and truth are the most sacred excellences and endowments of the human mind.
    CICERO.

Be not the first by whom the new are tried,
Nor yet the last to lay the old aside.
    POPE—*Essay on Criticism.*

Ever keep thy promise, cost what it may; this it is to be "true as steel."
    CHARLES READE.

Fidelity bought with money is overcome by money.
    SENECA.

To God, thy country, and thy friend be true.
    VAUGHAN—*Rules and Lessons.*

FIRE

From little spark may burst a mighty flame.
    DANTE.

Some heart once pregnant with celestial fire.
    GRAY—*Elegy.*

A crooked log makes a straight fire.
    GEORGE HERBERT—*Jacula Prudentum.*

Well may he smell fire, whose gown burns.
    GEORGE HERBERT—*Jacula Prudentum.*

Your own property is concerned when your neighbor's house is on fire.
    HORACE.

The most tangible of all visible mysteries—fire.
    LEIGH HUNT.

The burnt child dreads the fire.
    BEN JONSON—*The Devil Is an Ass.*

There can no great smoke arise, but there must be some fire.
    LYLY.

All the fat's in the fire.
    MARSTON—*What You Will.*

A little fire is quickly trodden out;
Which, being suffer'd, rivers cannot quench.
    SHAKESPEARE—*Henry VI.* Pt. III. Act IV. Sc. 8.

FIRMNESS

Firmness of purpose is one of the most necessary sinews of character and one of the best instruments of suc-

cess. Without it, genius wastes its efforts in a maze of inconsistencies.
CHESTERFIELD.

That which is called firmness in a king is called obstinacy in a donkey.
LORD ERSKINE.

When firmness is sufficient, rashness is unnecessary.
NAPOLEON.

Stubbornness is not firmness.
SCHILLER.

FISH

As lacking in privacy as a goldfish.
ANONYMOUS.

"Will you walk a little faster?" said a whiting to a snail,
"There's a porpoise close behind us, and he's treading on my tail!
See how eagerly the lobsters and the turtles all advance:
They are waiting on the shingle—will you come and join the dance?"
LEWIS CARROLL—Song in *Alice in Wonderland*.

O scaly, slippery, wet, swift, staring wights,
What is't ye do? what life lead? eh, dull goggles?
How do ye vary your vile days and nights?
How pass your Sundays? Are ye still but joggles
In ceaseless wash? Still nought but gapes and bites,
And drinks, and stares, diversified with boggles.
LEIGH HUNT—*Sonnets*.

Ye monsters of the bubbling deep,
Your Maker's praises spout;
Up from the sands ye codlings peep,
And wag your tails about.
COTTON MATHER—*Hymn*.

Master, I marvel how the fishes live in the sea.
Why, as men do a-land: the great ones eat up the little ones.
PERICLES.

We have here other fish to fry.
RABELAIS—*Works*.

It's no fish ye're buying—it's men's lives.
SCOTT—*The Antiquary*.

FISHING

When the wind is in the East,
Then the fishes bite the least;
When the wind is in the West,
Then the fishes bite the best;
When the wind is in the North,
Then the fishes do come forth;
When the wind is in the South,
It blows the bait in the fish's mouth.
ANONYMOUS.

There are as good fish in the sea as ever came out of it.
English Proverb.

To fish in troubled waters.
MATTHEW HENRY—*Commentaries. Psalm* LX.

You must lose a fly to catch a trout.
GEORGE HERBERT—*Jacula Prudentum*.

We really cannot see what equanimity there is in jerking a lacerated carp out of the water by the jaws, merely because it has not the power of making a noise; for we presume that the most philosophic of anglers would hardly delight in catching shrieking fish.
LEIGH HUNT.

Canst thou draw out leviathan with an hook?
Job. XLI. 1.

A fishing-rod was a stick with a hook at one end and a fool at the other.
SAMUEL JOHNSON.

His angle-rod made of a sturdy oak;
His line, a cable which in storms ne'er broke;
His hook he baited with a dragon's tail,—
And sat upon a rock, and bobb'd for whale.
WILLIAM KING—*Upon a Giant's Angling*.

Angling is an innocent cruelty.
GEORGE PARKER.

In a bowl to sea went wise men three,
On a brilliant night in June:
They carried a net, and their hearts were set
On fishing up the moon.
THOMAS LOVE PEACOCK.

The pleasant'st angling is to see the fish
Cut with her golden oars the silver stream,
And greedily devour the treacherous bait.
SHAKESPEARE—*Much Ado About Nothing*. Act III. Sc. 1.

Angling may be said to be so like the mathematics that it can never be fully learnt.
IZAAK WALTON—*The Compleat Angler*.

As no man is born an artist, so no man is born an angler.
IZAAK WALTON—*The Compleat Angler*.

Doubt not but angling will prove to be so pleasant, that it will prove to be, like virture, a reward to itsellf.
IZAAK WALTON—*The Compleat Angler*.

We may say of angling as Dr. Boteler said of strawberries: "Doubtless God could have made a better berry, but doubtless God never did"; and so, (if I might be judge,) God never did make a more calm, quiet, innocent recreation than angling.
IZAAK WALTON—*The Compleat Angler*.

Idle time not idly spent.
SIR HENRY WOTTON.

FLAG

Uncover when the flag goes by, boys,
'Tis freedom's starry banner that you greet,
Flag famed in song and story
Long may it wave, old glory
The flag that has never known defeat.
CHARLES L. BENJAMIN AND GEORGE D. SUTTON.

Hats off!
Along the street there comes
A blare of bugles, a ruffle of drums,
A flash of color beneath the sky:
Hats off!
The flag is passing by.
HENRY H. BENNETT—*The Flag Goes By*.

Ye mariners of England!
That guard our native seas;
Whose flag has braved a thousand years,
The battle and the breeze!
CAMPBELL—*Ye Mariners of England*.

If any one attempts to haul down the American flag, shoot him on the spot.
JOHN A. DIX—*Speeches and Addresses*.

When Freedom from her mountain height
Unfurled her standard to the air,
She tore the azure robe of night,
And set the stars of glory there.
JOSEPH RODMAN DRAKE—*The American Flag*.

Oh! say can you see by the dawn's early light
What so proudly we hail'd at the twilight's last gleaming,
Whose broad stripes and bright stars, thro' the perilous fight,
O'er the ramparts we watch'd, were so gallantly streaming;
And the rocket's red glare, the bombs bursting in air,
Gave proof thro' the night that our flag was still there!
Chorus
Oh! say, does that star-spangled banner yet wave,
O'er the land of the free and the home of the brave.
FRANCIS SCOTT KEY—*The Star-Spangled Banner*.

Praise the Power that hath made and preserved us a nation!
Then conquer we must when our cause it is just.
And this be our motto, "In God is our trust!"

And the star-spangled banner in triumph shall wave
O'er the land of the free and the home of the brave.
FRANCIS SCOTT KEY—*The Star-Spangled Banner.*

"A song for our banner?"—The watchword recall
Which gave the Republic her station;
"United we stand—divided we fall!"
It made and preserves us a nation!
GEORGE P. MORRIS—*The Flag of Our Union.*

The flag of our Union forever!
GEORGE P. MORRIS—*The Flag of Our Union.*

Your flag and my flag,
And how it flies today
In your land and my land
And half a world away!
Rose-red and blood-red
The stripes forever gleam;
Snow-white and soul-white—
The good forefathers' dream;
Sky-blue and true-blue, with stars to gleam aright—
The gloried guidon of the day, a shelter through the night.
WILBUR D. NESBIT—*Your Flag and My Flag.*

Yes, we'll rally round the flag, boys, we'll rally once again,
Shouting the battle-cry of Freedom,
We will rally from the hill-side, we'll gather from the plain,
Shouting the battle-cry of Freedom.
GEORGE F. ROOT—*Battle-Cry of Freedom.*

Let it rise! let it rise, till it meet the sun in his coming: let the earliest light of the morning gild it, and the parting day linger and play on its summit.
DANIEL WEBSTER.

"Shoot, if you must, this old gray head,
But spare your country's flag," she said.
WHITTIER—*Barbara Frietchie.*

A star for every state, and a state for every star.
ROBERT C. WINTHROP.

FLATTERY

Very ugly or very beautiful women should be flattered on their understanding, and mediocre ones on their beauty.
CHESTERFIELD.

Imitation is the sincerest of flattery.
C. C. COLTON—*Lacon.*

He that is much flattered soon learns to flatter himself.
SAMUEL JOHNSON.

Men are like stone jugs—you may lug them where you like by the ears.
SAMUEL JOHNSON.

We sometimes think that we hate flattery, but we only hate the manner in which it is done.
LA ROCHEFOUCAULD.

No adulation; 'tis the death of virtue;
Who flatters, is of all mankind the lowest
Save he who courts the flattery.
HANNAH MORE—*Daniel.*

They who delight to be flattered, pay for their folly by a late repentance.
PHAEDRUS.

Their throat is an open sepulchre; they flatter with their tongue.
Psalms. V. 9.

It is easy to flatter; it is harder to praise.
JEAN PAUL RICHTER.

O, that men's ears should be
To counsel deaf, but not to flattery!
SHAKESPEARE—*Timon of Athens.* Act I. Sc. 2.

'Tis an old maxim in the schools,
That flattery's the food of fools;
Yet now and then your men of wit
Will condescend to take a bit.
SWIFT—*Cadenus and Vanessa.*

Flatterers are the worst kind of enemies.
TACITUS.

FLEA

Great fleas have little fleas upon their backs to bite 'em,
And little fleas have lesser fleas, and so ad infinitum.
And the great fleas themselves, in turn, have greater fleas to go on;
While these again have greater still, and greater still, and so on.
AUGUSTUS DE MORGAN—*A Budget of Paradoxes.*

"I cannot raise my worth too high;
Of what vast consequence am I!"
"Not of the importance you suppose,"
Replies a Flea upon his nose;
"Be humble learn thyself to scan;
Know, pride was never made for man."
GAY—*The Man and the Flea.*

It was many and many a year ago,
In a District styled E.C.,
That a monster dwelt whom I came to know
By the name of Cannibal Flea,
And the brute was possessed with no other thought
Than to live—and to live on me.
THOMAS HOOD, JR.—*The Cannibal Flea.*

I do honour the very flea of his dog.
BEN JONSON—*Every Man in His Humour.*

FLIRTATION

Never wedding, ever wooing,
Still a love-lorn heart pursuing,
Read you not the wrong you're doing,
In my cheek's pale hue?
All my life with sorrow strewing,
Wed, or cease to woo.
CAMPBELL.

Flirtation, attention without intention.
MAX O'RELL—*John Bull and His Island.*

Men seldom make passes
At girls who wear glasses.
DOROTHY PARKER.

It is the same in love as in war; a fortress that parleys is half taken.
MARGUERITE DE VALOIS.

Ye belles, and ye flirts, and ye pert little things,
Who trip in this frolicsome round,
Pray tell me from whence this impertinence springs,
The sexes at once to confound?
WHITEHEAD—*Song for Ranelagh.*

FLOWERS

Sweet letters of the angel tongue,
I've loved ye long and well,
And never have failed in your fragrance sweet
To find some secret spell,—
A charm that has bound me with witching power,
For mine is the old belief,
That midst your sweets and midst your bloom,
There's a soul in every leaf!
M. M. BALLOU—*Flowers.*

Flowers may beckon towards us, but they speak toward heaven and God.
HENRY WARD BEECHER.

Flowers have an expression of countenance as much as men or animals. Some seem to smile; some have a sad expression; some are pensive and diffident; others again are plain, honest and upright, like the broad-faced sunflower and the hollyhock.
HENRY WARD BEECHER—*A Discourse of Flowers.*

Flowers are Love's truest language; they betray,
Like the divining rods of Magi old,
Where precious wealth lies buried, not of gold,
But love—strong love, that never can decay!
PARK BENJAMIN—*Sonnet.*

And tulips, children love to stretch
Their fingers down, to feel in each
Its beauty's secret nearer.
E. B. BROWNING—*A Flower in a Letter.*

Brazen helm of daffodillies,
With a glitter toward the light.
Purple violets for the mouth,
Breathing perfumes west and south;

And a sword of flashing lilies,
Holden ready for the fight.
E. B. BROWNING—*Hector in the Garden.*

The lily of the vale, of flowers the queen,
Puts on the robe she neither sew'd nor spun.
MICHAEL BRUCE—*Elegy.*

The little windflower, whose just opened eye
Is blue as the spring heaven it gazes at.
BRYANT—*A Winter Piece.*

Where fall the tears of love the rose appears,
And where the ground is bright with friendship's tears,
Forget-me-not, and violets, heavenly blue,
Spring glittering with the cheerful drops like dew.
BRYANT—Trans. of N. Müller's *Paradise of Tears.*

Yet, all beneath the unrivall'd rose,
The lowly daisy sweetly blows;
Tho' large the forest's monarch throws
His army shade,
Yet green the juicy hawthorn grows,
Adown the glade.
BURNS—*Vision.*

The snowdrop and primrose our woodlands adorn,
And violets bathe in the wet o' the morn.
BURNS—*My Nannie's Awa'.*

Light-enchanted sunflower, thou
Who gazest ever true and tender
On the sun's revolving splendour.
CALDERON.

Ye field flowers! the gardens eclipse you 'tis true:
Yet wildings of nature, I dote upon you,
For ye waft me to summers of old,
When the earth teem'd around me with fairy delight,
And when daisies and buttercups gladden'd my sight,
Like treasures of silver and gold.
CAMPBELL—*Field Flowers.*

I know not which I love the most,
Nor which the comeliest shows,
The timid, bashful violet
Or the royal-hearted rose:

The pansy in her purple dress,
The pink with cheek of red,
Or the faint, fair heliotrope, who hangs,
Like a bashful maid her head.
PHOEBE CARY—*Spring Flowers.*

I lie amid the Goldenrod,
I love to see it lean and nod;
I love to feel the grassy sod
Whose kindly breast will hold me last,
Whose patient arms will fold me fast!—
Fold me from sunshine and from song,
Fold me from sorrow and from wrong:
Through gleaming gates of Goldenrod
I'll pass into the rest of God.
MARY CLEMMER—*Goldenrod.*

Not a flower
But shows some touch, in freckle, streak or strain,
Of his unrivall'd pencil.
COWPER—*The Task.*

Flowers are words
Which even a babe may understand.
BISHOP COXE—*The Singing of Birds.*

In the marsh pink orchid's faces,
With their coy and dainty graces,
Lure us to their hiding places—
Laugh, O murmuring Spring!
SARAH F. DAVIS—*Summer Song.*

The buttercups, bright-eyed and bold,
Held up their chalices of gold
To catch the sunshine and the dew.
JULIA C. R. DORR—*Centennial Poem.*

And all the meadows, wide unrolled,
Were green and silver, green and gold,
Where buttercups and daisies spun
Their shining tissues in the sun.
JULIA C. R. DORR—*Unanswered.*

The rose is fragrant, but it fades in time:
The violet sweet, but quickly past the prime:

White lilies hang their heads, and
soon decay,
And white snow in minutes melts
away.
DRYDEN—*The Despairing Lover.*

Flowers are the beautiful hieroglyphics of nature, with which she indicates how much she loves us.
GOETHE.

Her modest looks the cottage might
adorn,
Sweet as the primrose peeps beneath
the thorn.
GOLDSMITH—*The Deserted Village.*

The starry, fragile windflower,
Poised above in airy grace,
Virgin white, suffused with blushes,
Shyly droops her lovely face.
ELAINE GOODALE—*The First Flowers.*

The lotus flower is troubled
At the sun's resplendent light;
With sunken head and sadly
She dreamily waits for the night.
HEINE—*Book of Songs.*

They speak of hope to the fainting
heart,
With a voice of promise they come
and part,
They sleep in dust through the wintry
hours,
They break forth in glory—bring
flowers, bright flowers!
FELICIA D. HEMANS—*Bring Flowers.*

Why doe ye weep, sweet babes? Can
tears
Speak griefe in you,
Who were but borne
Just as the modest morne
Teemed her refreshing dew?
HERRICK—*To Primroses.*

Up wi' the flowers o' Scotland,
The emblems o' the free,
Their guardians for a thousand years,
Their guardians still we'll be.
A foe had better brave the de'il
Within his reeky cell,
Than our thistle's purple bonnet,
Or bonny heather bell.
HOGG—*The Flowers of Scotland.*

Jasmine is sweet, and has many loves.
HOOD—*Flowers.*

I remember, I remember
The roses, red and white,
The violets, and the lily-cups,
Those flowers made of light!
The lilacs, where the robin built,
And where my brother set
The laburnum on his birthday,—
The tree is living yet.
HOOD—*I Remember, I Remember.*

'Tis but a little faded flower,
But oh, how fondly dear!
'Twill bring me back one golden hour,
Through many a weary year.
ELLEN C. HOWARTH—*'Tis but a Little Faded Flower.*

Underneath large blue-bells tented
Where the daisies are rose-scented,
And the rose herself has got
Perfume which on earth is not.
KEATS—*Bards of Passion and of Mirth.*

Open afresh your round of starry folds,
Ye ardent marigolds!
Dry up the moisture from your golden
lips.
KEATS—*I Stood Tiptoe upon a Little Hill.*

Here are sweet peas, on tiptoe for a
flight;
With wings of gentle flush o'er delicate white,
And taper fingers catching at all
things,
To bind them all about with tiny rings.
KEATS—*I Stood Tiptoe upon a Little Hill.*

O flower-de-luce, bloom on, and let
the river
Linger to kiss thy feet!
O flower of song, bloom on, and make
forever
The world more fair and sweet.
LONGFELLOW—*Flower-de-Luce.*

Gorgeous flowerets in the sunlight
shining,
Blossoms flaunting in the eye of day,
Tremulous leaves, with soft and silver
lining,
Buds that open only to decay.
LONGFELLOW—*Flowers.*

And I will make thee beds of roses,
And a thousand fragrant posies.
MARLOWE—*The Passionate Shepherd to His Love.*

Oh! roses and lilies are fair to see;
But the wild bluebell is the flower for me.
LOUISA A. MEREDITY—*The Bluebell.*

Flowers of all hue, and without thorn the rose.
MILTON—*Paradise Lost.*

Simplest of blossoms! To mine eye
Thou bring'st the summer's painted sky;
The May-thorn greening in the nook;
The minnows sporting in the brook;
The bleat of flocks; the breath of flowers;
The song of birds amid the bowers;
The crystal of the azure seas;
The music of the southern breeze;
And, over all, the blessed sun,
Telling of halcyon days begun.
MOIR—*The Harebell.*

Dutch tulips from their beds
Flaunted their stately heads.
MONTGOMERY—*The Adventure of a Star.*

Blue thou art, intensely blue;
Flower, whence came thy dazzling hue?
MONTGOMERY—*The Gentianella.*

The tulip's petals shine in dew,
All beautiful, but none alike.
MONTGOMERY — *On Planting a Tulip-Root.*

Eagle of flowers! I see thee stand,
And on the sun's noon-glory gaze;
With eye like his, thy lids expand,
And fringe their disk with golden rays:
Though fix'd on earth, in darkness rooted there,
Light is thy element, thy dwelling air,
The prospect heaven.
MONTGOMERY—*The Sunflower.*

As the sunflower turns on her god when he sets,
The same look which she turn'd when he rose.
MOORE—*Believe Me, If All Those Endearing Young Charms.*

Those virgin lilies, all the night
Bathing their beauties in the lake,
That they may rise more fresh and bright,
When their beloved sun's awake.
MOORE—*Lalla Rookh.*

Yet, no—not words, for they
But half can tell love's feeling;
Sweet flowers alone can say
What passion fears revealing:
A once bright rose's wither'd leaf,
A tow'ring lily broken,—
Oh, these may paint a grief
No words could e'er have spoken.
MOORE—*The Language of Flowers*

Where flowers degenerate man cannot live.
NAPOLEON.

"A milkweed, and a buttercup, and cowslip," said sweet Mary,
"Are growing in mv garden-plot, and this I call my dairy."
PETER NEWELL—*Her Dairy.*

"Of what are you afraid, my child?" inquired the kindly teacher.
"Oh, sir! the flowers, they are wild," replied the timid creature.
PETER NEWELL—*Wild Flowers.*

I sometimes think that never blows so red
The Rose as where some buried Caesar bled;
That every Hyacinth the Garden wears
Dropt in her Lap from some once lovely Head.
OMAR KHAYYÁM—*Rubaiyat.*

One thing is certain and the rest is lies;
The Flower that once has blown for ever dies.
OMAR KHAYYÁM—*Rubaiyat.*

In Eastern lands they talk in flowers,
And they tell in a garland their loves and cares;

Each blossom that blooms in their garden bowers,
On its leaves a mystic language bears.
PERCIVAL—*The Language of Flowers.*

If of thy mortal goods thou art bereft,
And from thy slender store two loaves alone to thee are left,
Sell one, and with the dole
Buy hyacinths to feed thy soul.
SAADI—*Gulistan.*

Here's flowers for you:
Hot lavender, mints, savory, marjoram:
The marigold, that goes to bed wi' the sun,
And with him rises weeping.
SHAKESPEARE—*Winter's Tale.* Act IV. Sc. 4.

And the Naiad-like lily of the vale,
Whom youth makes so fair and passion so pale,
That the light of its tremulous bells is seen,
Through their pavilions of tender green.
SHELLEY—*The Sensitive Plant.* Pt. I.

Broad water-lilies lay tremulously,
And starry river-buds glimmered by,
And around them the soft stream did glide and dance
With a motion of sweet sound and radiance.
SHELLEY—*The Sensitive Plant.*

Floral apostles! that in dewy splendor weep without woe, and blush without a crime.
HORACE SMITH.

Sweet is the rose, but grows upon a brere;
Sweet is the juniper, but sharp his bough;
Sweet is the eglantine, but sticketh nere;
Sweet is the firbloome, but its braunches rough;
Sweet is the cypress, but its rynd is tough;
Sweet is the nut, but bitter is his pill;
Sweet is the broome-flowre, but yet sowre enough;
And sweet is moly, but his root is ill.
SPENSER—*Amoretti.*

Love lies bleeding in the bed whereover
Roses lean with smiling mouths or pleading:
Earth lies laughing where the sun's dart clove her:
Love lies bleeding.
SWINBURNE—*Love Lies Bleeding.*

With roses musky-breathed,
And drooping daffodilly,
And silver-leaved lily.
And ivy darkly-wreathed,
I wove a crown before her,
For her I love so dearly.
TENNYSON—*Anacreontics.*

The Lotos blooms below the barren peak:
The Lotos blooms by every winding creek:
All day the wind breathes low with mellower tone:
Thro' every hollow cave and alley lone,
Round and round the spicy downs the yellow Lotos-dust is blown.
TENNYSON—*The Lotos-Eaters.*

Now folds the lily all her sweetness up,
And slips into the bosom of the lake;
So fold thyself, my dearest, thou, and slip
Into my bosom, and be lost in me.
TENNYSON—*The Princess.*

Where scattered wild the Lily of the Vale
Its balmy essence breathes.
THOMSON—*The Seasons.*

Daffy-down-dilly came up in the cold,
Through the brown mould
Although the March breeze blew keen on her face,
Although the white snow lay in many a place.
ANNA WARNER—*Daffy-Down-Dilly.*

To me the meanest flower that blows can give

Thoughts that do often lie too deep for tears.
WORDSWORTH—*Intimations of Immortality.*

FLY

A fly sat on the chariot wheel
And said "what a dust I raise."
LA FONTAINE.

Baby bye
Here's a fly,
Let us watch him, you and I,
How he crawls
Up the walls
Yet he never falls.
THEODORE TILTON—*Baby Bye.*

FOLLY

The folly of one man is the fortune of another.
BACON—*Of Fortune.*

To swallow gudgeons ere they're catch'd.
And count their chickens ere they're hatch'd.
BUTLER—*Hudibras.*

To stumble twice against the same stone, is a proverbial disgrace.
CICERO—*Epistles.*

He who lives without committing any folly is not so wise as he thinks.
LA ROCHEFOUCAULD.

Folly consists in the drawing of false conclusions from just principles, by which it is distinguished from madness, which draws just conclusions from false principles.
LOCKE.

Answer a fool according to his folly.
Proverbs. XXVI. 5.

'Tis not by guilt the onward sweep
Of truth and right, O Lord, we stay;
'Tis by our follies that so long
We hold the earth from heaven away.
E. R. SILL—*The Fool's Prayer.*

He had been eight years upon a project for extracting sunbeams out of cucumbers, which were to be put in phials hermetically sealed, and let out to warm the air in raw, inclement summers.
SWIFT—*Gulliver's Travels.*

He has spent all his life in letting down empty buckets into empty wells, and he is frittering away his age in trying to draw them up again.
SYDNEY SMITH—*Lady Holland's Memoir.*

FOOL

A fool always finds one still more foolish to admire him.
BOILEAU.

Young men think old men are fools; but old men know young men are fools.
GEORGE CHAPMAN—*All Fools.*

Hain't we got all the fools in town on our side? And ain't that a big enough majority in any town?
S. L. CLEMENS (MARK TWAIN)—*Huckleberry Finn.*

A fool must now and then be right by chance.
COWPER—*Conversation.*

A fool and a wise man are alike both in the starting-place—their birth, and at the post—their death; only they differ in the race of their lives.
FULLER—*Of Natural Fools.*

It is in the half fools and the half wise that the greatest danger lies.
GOETHE.

Even the fool is wise after the event.
HOMER.

It needs brains to be a real fool.
GEORGE MACDONALD.

A learned fool is more foolish than an ignorant fool.
MOLIÈRE.

People are never so near playing the fool as when they think themselves wise.
LADY MONTAGU

If a traveler does not meet with one who is his better or his equal, let him firmly keep to his solitary journey;

there is no companionship with a fool.
MAX MÜLLER.

An old doting fool, with one foot already in the grave.
PLUTARCH.

The right to be a cussed fool
Is safe from all devices human,
It's common (ez a gin'l rule)
To every critter born of woman.
LOWELL—*The Biglow Papers.*

We think our fathers fools, so wise we grow;
Our wiser sons, no doubt, will think us so.
POPE—*Essay on Criticism.*

For fools rush in where angels fear to tread.
POPE—*Essay on Criticism.*

Even a fool, when he holdeth his peace, is counted wise.
Proverbs. XVII. 28.

Though thou shouldest bray a fool in a mortar among wheat with a pestle, yet will not his foolishness depart from him.
Proverbs. XXVII. 22.

The fool hath said in his heart, There is no God.
Psalms. XIV. 1; LIII. 1.

Those who wish to appear wise among fools, among the wise seem foolish.
QUINTILIAN.

If you wish to avoid seeing a fool you must first break your looking-glass.
RABELAIS

The fool doth think he is wise, but the wise man knows himself to be a fool.
SHAKESPEARE—*As You Like It.* Act V. Sc. 1.

I had rather have a fool to make me merry than experience to make me sad: and to travel for it too!
SHAKESPEARE—*As You Like It.* Act IV. Sc. 1.

How ill white hairs become a fool and jester!
SHAKESPEARE—*Henry IV.* Pt. II. Act V. Sc. 5.

A fool's bolt is soon shot.
SHAKESPEARE—*Henry V.* Act III. Sc. 7.

Lord, what fools these mortals be!
SHAKESPEARE—*Midsummer Night's Dream.* Act II. Sc. 2.

This fellow is wise enough to play the fool;
And to do that well craves a kind of wit.
SHAKESPEARE—*Twelfth Night.* Act III. Sc. 1.

A fool is he that comes to preach or prate,
When men with swords their right and wrong debate.
TASSO.

He who thinks himself wise, O heavens! is a great fool.
VOLTAIRE.

At thirty man suspects himself a fool;
Knows it at forty, and reforms his plan.
YOUNG—*Night Thoughts.*

FOOTSTEPS

A foot more light, a step more true,
Ne'er from the heath-flower dashed the dew.
SCOTT—*Lady of the Lake.*

Steps with a tender foot, light as on air,
The lovely, lordly creature floated on.
TENNYSON—*The Princess.*

FORCE

The power that is supported by force alone will have cause often to tremble.
KOSSUTH.

Gentleness succeeds better than violence.
LA FONTAINE.

Force is all-conquering, but its victories are short-lived.
LINCOLN.

Hence it happened that all the armed prophets conquered, all the unarmed perished.
MACHIAVELLI.

At the turning points of history, it is force, and force alone, which makes the crucial decision.

MUSSOLINI—*Speech, 1922.*

Force and not opinion is the queen of the world; but it is opinion that uses the force.

PASCAL.

Where force is necessary, there it must be applied boldly, decisively and completely.

LEON TROTSKY—*What Next?*

FORESIGHT

In life, as in chess, forethought wins.

CHARLES BUXTON.

If a man take no thought about what is distant, he will find sorrow near at hand.

CONFUCIUS.

Those old stories of visions and dreams guiding men have their truth; we are saved by making the future present to ourselves.

GEORGE ELIOT.

Forethought we may have, undoubtedly, but not foresight.

NAPOLEON.

Look ere thou leap, see ere thou go.

THOMAS TUSSER.

FORGETFULNESS

There is nothing new except what is forgotten.

MLLE. BERTIN.

There is no remembrance which time does not obliterate, nor pain which death does not terminate.

CERVANTES.

The pyramids themselves, doting with age, have forgotten the names of their founders.

FULLER—*Holy and Profane States.*

A man must *get* a thing before he can *forget* it.

HOLMES—*Medical Essays.*

And when he is out of sight, quickly also he is out of mind.

THOMAS À KEMPIS.

God of our fathers, known of old,
Lord of our far-flung battle-line,
Beneath whose awful Hand we hold
Dominion over palm and pine—
Lord God of Hosts, be with us yet,
Lest we forget—lest we forget!

The tumult and the shouting dies,
The captains and the kings depart;
Still stands thine ancient sacrifice,
A humble and a contrite heart.
Lord God of Hosts, be with us yet
Lest we forget—lest we forget.

KIPLING—*Recessional Hymn.*

God and the Doctor we alike adore
But only when in danger, not before;
The danger o'er, both are alike requited,
God is forgotten, and the Doctor slighted.

JOHN OWEN—*Epigram.*

If I forget thee, O Jerusalem, let my right hand forget her cunning.

Psalms. CXXXVII. 5.

It is sometimes expedient to forget what you know.

SYRUS.

FORGIVENESS

They who forgive most shall be most forgiven.

BAILEY.

When women love us they forgive everything.

BALZAC.

God pardons like a mother, who kisses the offense into everlasting forgetfulness.

HENRY WARD BEECHER.

Good, to forgive;
Best to forget.

BROWNING—*La Saisiaz.*

He who forgives readily only invites offense.

CORNEILLE.

It is easier to forgive an enemy than a friend.

MME. DELUZY.

May I tell you why it seems to me a good thing for us to remember wrong

that has been done us? That we may forgive it.
DICKENS.

His heart was as great as the world, but there was no room in it to hold the memory of a wrong.
EMERSON—*Letters and Social Aims.*

Bear and forbear.
EPICTETUS.

It is right for him who asks forgiveness for his offenses to grant it to others.
HORACE—*Satires.*

Know all and you will pardon all.
THOMAS À KEMPIS—*Imitation of Christ.*

Oh Thou, who Man of baser Earth
didst make,
And ev'n with Paradise devise the
snake;
For all the Sin wherewith the Face
of Man
Is blackened—Man's forgiveness give
and take!
OMAR KHAYYÁM—*Rubaiyat.*

Forgive us our trespasses, as we forgive them that trespass against us.
The Lord's Prayer.

To love is human, it is also human to forgive.
PLAUTUS—*Mercator.*

Good-nature and good-sense must ever
join;
To err is human, to forgive, divine.
POPE—*Essay on Criticism.*

What if this cursed hand
Were thicker than itself with brother's
blood?
Is there not rain enough in the sweet
heavens
To wash it white as snow?
SHAKESPEARE—*Hamlet.* Act III. Sc. 3.

I pardon him, as God shall pardon me.
SHAKESPEARE—*Richard II.* Act V. Sc. 3.

Forgive others often, yourself never.
SYRUS.

It is manlike to punish but godlike to forgive.
P. VON WINTER.

FORTUNE

If fortune favors you do not be elated; if she frowns do not despond.
AUSONIUS.

Fortune makes him fool, whom she makes her darling.
BACON.

Just for a handful of silver he left us,
Just for a ribbon to stick in his coat,
Found the one gift of which Fortune
bereft us,
Lost all the others she lets us devote.
BROWNING—*The Lost Leader.*

Fortune, the great commandress of the
world,
Hath divers ways to advance her followers:
To some she gives honor without deserving;
To others some, deserving without
honor;
Some wit, some wealth,—and some,
wit without wealth;
Some wealth without wit; some nor
wit nor wealth.
GEORGE CHAPMAN—*All Fools.*

It is fortune, not wisdom, that rules man's life.
CICERO.

Men have made of fortune an all-powerful goddess, in order that she may be made responsible for all their blunders.
MME. DE STAËL.

Fortune truly helps those who are of good judgment.
EURIPIDES.

Fortune, men say, doth give too much
to many,
But yet she never gave enough to any.
SIR JOHN HARRINGTON.

The bitter dregs of Fortune's cup to drain.
HOMER—*Iliad.*

Fortunes made in no time are like shirts made in no time; it's ten to one if they hang long together.

DOUGLAS JERROLD.

Fortune never seems so blind as to those upon whom she confers no favors.

LA ROCHEFOUCAULD.

Men are seldom blessed with good fortune and good sense at the same time.

LIVY.

As long as you are fortunate you will have many friends, but if the times become cloudy you will be alone.

OVID.

Fortune and Love befriend the bold.

OVID.

Luck affects everything; let your hook always be cast; in the stream where you least expect it, there will be a fish.

OVID.

The wheel goes round and round,
And some are up and some are on the down,
And still the wheel goes round.

JOSEPHINE POLLARD—*Wheel of Fortune.*

Fortune in men has some small diff'rence made,
One flaunts in rags, one flutters in brocade;
The cobbler apron'd, and the parson gown'd,
The friar hooded, and the monarch crown'd.

POPE—*Essay on Man.*

Nothing is more dangerous to men than a sudden change of fortune.

QUINTILIAN.

Every man is the architect of his own fortune.

SALLUST.

Fortune cannot take away what she did not give.

SENECA.

Happy the man who can endure the highest and the lowest fortune. He, who has endured such vicissitudes with equanimity, has deprived misfortune of its power.

SENECA.

Whatever fortune has raised to a height, she has raised only to cast it down.

SENECA.

Fortune brings in some boats, that are not steer'd.

SHAKESPEARE—*Cymbeline.* Act IV. Sc. 3.

Will Fortune never come with both hands full,
But write her fair words still in foulest letters?
She either gives a stomach, and no food;
Such are the poor, in health: or else a feast,
And takes away the stomach; such are the rich,
That have abundance, and enjoy it not.

SHAKESPEARE—*Henry IV.* Pt. II. Act IV. Sc. 4.

We are carried up to the heaven by the circling wave, and immediately the wave subsiding, we descend to the lowest depths.

VERGIL—*Aeneid.*

Fortune! There is no fortune; all is trial, or punishment, or recompense, or foresight.

VOLTAIRE.

FOX

The fox has many tricks, the hedgehog only one.

ERASMUS.

A sleeping fox counts hens in his dreams.

Russian Proverb.

The little foxes, that spoil the vines.

Song of Solomon. IV. 15.

FRAILTY

A woman filled with faith in the one she loves is the creation of a novelist's imagination.

BALZAC.

This is the porcelain clay of human kind.

DRYDEN—*Don Sebastian.*

What is man's love? His vows are broke even while his parting kiss is warm.

HALLECK.

All men are frail; but thou shouldst reckon none so frail as thyself.

THOMAS À KEMPIS.

Unthought-of Frailties cheat us in the Wise.

POPE—*Moral Essays.*

Frailty, thy name is woman!

SHAKESPEARE—*Hamlet.* Act I. Sc. 2.

FRANCE

The Frenchman, easy, debonair, and brisk,
Give him his lass, his fiddle, and his frisk,
Is always happy, reign whoever may,
And laughs the sense of mis'ry far away.

COWPER—*Table Talk.*

Ye sons of France, awake to glory!
Hark! Hark! what myriads bid you rise!
Your children, wives, and grandsires hoary,
Behold their tears and hear their cries!

ROUGET DE LISLE—*The Marseilles Hymn.*

France, freed from that monster, Bonaparte, must again become the most agreeable country on earth. It would be the second choice of all whose ties of family and fortune give a preference to some other one, and the first choice of all not under those ties.

JEFFERSON, 1814.

France always has plenty men of talent, but it is always deficient in men of action and high character.

NAPOLEON.

Prince, give praise to our French ladies
For the sweet sound their speaking carries;
'Twixt Rome and Cadiz many a maid is,
But no good girl's lip out of Paris.

SWINBURNE—*Translation from Villon's Ballad of the Women of Paris.*

FRAUD

The first and worst of all frauds is to cheat one's self.

BAILEY—*Festus.*

Though fraud in all other actions be odious, yet in matters of war it is laudable and glorious, and he who overcomes his enemies by stratagem is as much to be praised as he who overcomes them by force.

MACHIAVELLI.

So glistered the dire Snake, and into fraud
Led Eve, our credulous mother, to the Tree
Of Prohibition, root of all our woe.

MILTON.

Perplexed and troubled at his bad success
The Tempter stood, nor had what to reply,
Discovered in his fraud, thrown from his hope.

MILTON—*Paradise Regained.*

His heart as far from fraud as heaven from earth.

SHAKESPEARE—*Two Gentlemen of Verona.* Act II. Sc. 7.

FREEDOM

Freedom all solace to man gives:
He lives at ease that freely lives.

JOHN BARBOUR—*The Bruce.*

The cause of freedom is the cause of God.

BOWLES.

Personal liberty is the paramount essential to human dignity and human happiness.

BULWER-LYTTON.

Here the free spirit of mankind, at length,
Throws its last fetters off; and who shall place
A limit to the giant's unchained strength,
Or curb his swiftness in the forward race?
BRYANT—*The Ages.*

Hereditary bondsmen! Know ye not
Who would be free themselves must strike the blow?
BYRON—*Childe Harold.*

Yet, Freedom! yet thy banner, torn, but flying,
Streams like the thunder-storm *against* the wind.
BYRON—*Childe Harold.*

For Freedom's battle once begun,
Bequeath'd by bleeding sire to son,
Though baffled oft is ever won.
BYRON—*Giaour.*

Hope for a season bade the world farewell,
And Freedom shrieked as Kosciusko fell!

. . .

O'er Prague's proud arch the fires of ruin glow.
CAMPBELL—*Pleasures of Hope.*

In a free country there is much clamor, with little suffering; in a despotic state there is little complaint, with much grievance.
CARNOT.

To freemen, threats are impotent.
CICERO.

I want free life, and I want fresh air;
And I sigh for the canter after the cattle,
The crack of the whip like shots in battle,
The medley of horns, and hoofs, and heads
That wars, and wrangles, and scatters and spreads;
The green beneath and the blue above,
And dash, and danger, and life and love.
F. DESPREZ—*Lasca.*

When Freedom from her mountain height
Unfurled her standard to the air.
She tore the azure robe of night,
And set the stars of glory there.
JOSEPH RODMAN DRAKE.

I am as free as nature first made man,
Ere the base laws of servitude began,
When wild in woods the noble savage ran.
DRYDEN—*Conquest of Granada.*

We grant no dukedoms to the few,
We hold like rights and shall;
Equal on Sunday in the pew,
On Monday in the mall.
For what avail the plough or sail,
Or land, or life, if freedom fail?
EMERSON—*Boston.*

Yes! to this thought I hold with firm persistence;
The last result of wisdom stamps it true;
He only earns his freedom and existence
Who daily conquers them anew.
GOETHE—*Faust.*

Ay, call it holy ground,
The soil where first they trod,
They have left unstained, what there they found,—
Freedom to worship God.
FELICIA D. HEMANS—*Landing of the Pilgrim Fathers.*

I am for freedom of religion and against all maneuvers to bring about a legal ascendancy of one sect over another.
JEFFERSON, 1799.

In the beauty of the lilies Christ was born across the sea,
With a glory in His bosom that transfigures you and me;
As He died to make men holy, let us die to make men free,
While God is marching on.
JULIA WARD HOWE—*Battle Hymn of the Republic.*

All we have of freedom—all we use or know—

This our fathers bought for us, long
and long ago.
KIPLING—*The Old Issue.*

The cause of freedom is identified with the destinies of humanity, and in whatever part of the world it gains ground by and by, it will be a common gain to all those who desire it.
KOSSUTH.

No amount of political freedom will satisfy the hungry masses.
LENIN, 1917.

. . . That this nation, under God, shall have a new birth of freedom.
LINCOLN—*Gettysburg Address.*

Many politicians are in the habit of laying it down as a self-evident proposition that no people ought to be free till they are fit to use their freedom. The maxim is worthy of the fool in the old story who resolved not to go into the water till he had learned to swim.
MACAULAY.

Oh! let me live my own, and die so
too!
(To live and die is all I have to do:)
Maintain a poet's dignity and ease,
And see what friends, and read what
books I please.
POPE—*Prologue to Satires.*

Free soil, free men, free speech, Fremont.
Republican Party Slogan, 1856.

Man is created free, and is free, even though born in chains.
SCHILLER.

Only free peoples can hold their purpose and their honor steady to a common end, and prefer the interests of mankind to any narrow interest of their own.
WOODROW WILSON—*War Address to Congress, 1917.*

We must be free or die, who speak
the tongue
That Shakespeare spake; the faith and
morals hold
Which Milton held.
WORDSWORTH.

FRIEND

Prosperity makes friends and adversity tries them.
ANONYMOUS.

A friend is one who dislikes the same people that you dislike.
ANONYMOUS.

A true friend is one soul in two bodies.
ARISTOTLE.

No friend's a friend till (he shall) prove a friend.
BEAUMONT AND FLETCHER.

There is no man so friendless but what he can find a friend sincere enough to tell him disagreeable truths.
BULWER-LYTTON.

Give me the avowed, the erect, the
manly foe;
Bold I can meet—perhaps may turn
his blow;
But of all plagues, good Heaven, thy
wrath can send,
Save, save, oh! save me from the candid friend.
GEORGE CANNING—*New Morality.*

Greatly his foes he dreads, but more
his friends,
He hurts me most who lavishly commends.
CHARLES CHURCHILL—*The Apology.*

A friend is, as it were, a second self.
CICERO.

Chance makes our parents, but choice makes our friends.
DELILLE.

God save me from my friends, I can protect myself from my enemies.
MARSHAL DE VILLARS.

Forsake not an old friend, for the new is not comparable unto him. A new friend is as new wine: when it is old thou shalt drink it with pleasure.
Ecclesiasticus. IX. 10.

Animals are such agreeable friends—they ask no questions, they pass no criticisms.
GEORGE ELIOT—*Mr. Gilfil's Love-Story.*

A friend may well be reckoned the masterpiece of nature.

EMERSON.

A day for toil, an hour for sport,
But for a friend is life too short.

EMERSON—*Considerations by the Way.*

The only way to have a friend is to be one.

EMERSON—*Of Friendship.*

There are three faithful friends: an old wife, an old dog, and ready money.

FRANKLIN.

'Tis thus that on the choice of friends
Our good or evil name depends.

GAY—*Old Woman and Her Cats.*

An open foe may prove a curse,
But a pretended friend is worse.

GAY—*Shepherd's Dog and the Wolf.*

Two friends, two bodies with one soul inspir'd.

HOMER—*Iliad.*

Two persons will not be friends long if they cannot forgive each other little failings.

LA BRUYÈRE.

Friend of my bosom, thou more than a brother,
Why wert not thou born in my father's dwelling?

LAMB—*The Old Familiar Faces.*

I desire so to conduct the affairs of this administration that if at the end, when I come to lay down the reins of power, I have lost every other friend on earth, I shall at least have one friend left, and that friend shall be down inside of me.

LINCOLN—*Reply to Missouri Committee of Seventy.* (*1864*)

Yes, we must ever be friends; and of all who offer you friendship
Let me be ever the first, the truest, the nearest and dearest!

LONGFELLOW—*Courtship of Miles Standish.*

Ah, how good it feels!
The hand of an old friend.

LONGFELLOW—*John Endicott.*

Friends are like melons. Shall I tell you why?
To find one good, you must a hundred try.

CLAUDE MERMET.

We have been friends together
In sunshine and in shade.

CAROLINE E. S. NORTON.

Trust not yourself; but your defects to know,
Make use of ev'ry friend—and ev'ry foe.

POPE—*Essay on Criticism.*

A man that hath friends must show himself friendly; and there is a friend that sticketh closer than a brother.

Proverbs. XVIII. 24.

He that wants money, means, and content is without three good friends.

SHAKESPEARE—*As You Like It.* Act III. Sc. 2.

Those friends thou hast, and their adoption tried,
Grapple them to thy soul with hoops of steel;
But do not dull thy palm with entertainment
Of each new-hatch'd, unfledg'd comrade.

SHAKESPEARE—*Hamlet.* Act I. Sc. 3.

For by these
Shall I try friends: you shall perceive how you
Mistake my fortunes; I am wealthy in my friends.

SHAKESPEARE—*Timon of Athens.* Act II. Sc. 2.

A friend must not be injured, even in jest.

SYRUS.

Reprove your friends in secret, praise them openly.

SYRUS.

Unless you bear with the faults of a friend you betray your own.

SYRUS.

A man cannot be said to succeed in this life who does not satisfy one friend.

HENRY D. THOREAU.

I choose my friends for their good looks, my acquaintances for their characters, and my enemies for their brains.

WILDE—*The Picture of Dorian Gray.*

A slender acquaintance with the world must convince every man, that actions, not words, are the true criterion of the attachment of friends; and that the most liberal professions of good-will are very far from being the surest marks of it.

WASHINGTON—*Friendship.*

FRIENDSHIP

Great souls by instinct to each other turn,
Demand alliance, and in friendship burn.

ADDISON—*The Campaign.*

Hand
Grasps at hand, eye lights eye in good friendship,
And great hearts expand
And grow one in the sense of this world's life.

BROWNING—*Saul.*

Should auld acquaintance be forgot,
And never brought to mind?
Should auld acquaintance be forgot,
And days o' auld lang syne?

BURNS—*Auld Lang Syne.*

Friendship is Love without his wings!

BYRON.

Friendship makes prosperity brighter, while it lightens adversity by sharing its griefs and anxieties.

CICERO.

True friendship is like sound health, the value of it is seldom known until it be lost.

COLTON.

The highest compact we can make with our fellow is,—Let there be truth between us two forevermore. . . . It is sublime to feel and say of another, I need never meet, or speak, or write to him; we need not reinforce ourselves or send tokens of remembrance; I rely on him as on myself; if he did thus or thus, I know it was right.

EMERSON—*Essays.*

The most violent friendships soonest wear themselves out.

HAZLITT.

Friendship, peculiar boon of Heaven,
The noble mind's delight and pride,
To men and angels only given,
To all the lower world denied.

SAMUEL JOHNSON—*Friendship.*

Rare as is true love, true friendship is rarer.

LA FONTAINE.

Friendship should be in the singular; it can be no more plural than love.

NINON DE LENCLOS.

There is no friendship between those associated in power; he who rules will always be impatient of an associate.

LUCAN.

Forsooth, brethren, fellowship is heaven and lack of fellowship is hell; fellowship is life and lack of fellowship is death; and the deeds that ye do upon the earth, it is for fellowship's sake that ye do them.

WILLIAM MORRIS—*Dream of John Ball.*

Friendship is but a name. I love no one.

NAPOLEON.

As the yellow gold is tried in fire, so the faith of friendship must be seen in adversity.

OVID.

What is thine is mine, and all mine is thine.

PLAUTUS.

Saul and Jonathan were lovely and pleasant in their lives, and in their death they were not divided.

II Samuel. I. 23.

Friendship always benefits; love sometimes injures.

SENECA.

Madam, I have been looking for a person who disliked gravy all my life; let us swear eternal friendship.
Sydney Smith—*Lady Holland's Memoir.*

Be slow to fall into friendship; but when thou art in continue firm and constant.
Socrates.

FRUIT

By their fruits ye shall know them.
Matthew. VII. 20.

But the fruit that can fall without shaking,
Indeed is too mellow for me.
Lady Mary Wortley Montagu.

I don't know how to tell it—but ef such a thing could be
As the angels wantin' boardin', and they'd call around on *me*—
I'd want to 'commodate 'em—all the whole-indurin' flock—
When the frost is on the punkin and the fodder's in the shock.
James Whitcomb Riley—*When the Frost Is on the Punkin.*

The ripest fruit first falls.
Shakespeare—*Richard II.* Act II. Sc. 1.

O,—fruit loved of boyhood!—the old days recalling,
When wood-grapes were purpling and brown nuts were falling!
When wild, ugly faces we carved in its skin,
Glaring out through the dark with a candle within!
When we laughed round the corn-heap, with hearts all in tune,
Our chair a broad pumpkin,—our lantern the moon,
Telling tales of the fairy who travelled like steam
In a pumpkin-shell coach, with two rats for her team!
Whittier—*The Pumpkin.*

FUTURE

God will not suffer man to have the knowledge of things to come; for if he had prescience of his prosperity, he would be careless; and, understanding of his adversity, he would be senseless.
St. Augustine.

The year goes wrong, and tares grow strong,
Hope starves without a crumb;
But God's time is our harvest time,
And that is sure to come.
Lewis J. Bates—*Our Better Day.*

Some day Love shall claim his own
Some day Right ascend his throne,
Some day hidden Truth be known;
Some day—some sweet day.
Lewis J. Bates—*Some Sweet Day.*

When all else is lost, the future still remains.
Bovee.

'Tis the sunset of life gives me mystical lore,
And coming events cast their shadows before.
Campbell—*Lochiel's Warning.*

I never think of the future. It comes soon enough.
Albert Einstein.

Cease to inquire what the future has in store, and to take as a gift whatever the day brings forth.
Horace—*Carmina.*

You'll see that, since our fate is ruled by chance,
Each man, unknowing, great,
Should frame life so that at some future hour
Fact and his dreamings meet.
Victor Hugo—*To His Orphan Grandchildren.*

When Earth's last picture is painted, and the tubes are twisted and dried,
When the oldest colours have faded, and the youngest critic has died,
We shall rest, and faith, we shall need it—lie down for an aeon or two,
Till the Master of All Good Workmen shall set us to work anew.
Kipling—*When Earth's Last Picture Is Painted.*

The present is great with the future.
Leibnitz.

Trust no Future, howe'er pleasant!
Let the dead Past bury its dead!
LONGFELLOW—*A Psalm of Life*.

Go forth to meet the shadowy Future without fear and with a manly heart.
LONGFELLOW—*Hyperion*.

The future is a world limited by ourselves; in it we discover only what concerns us and, sometimes, by chance, what interests those whom we love the most.
MAETERLINCK—*Joyzelle*.

Take therefore no thought for the morrow; for the morrow shall take thought for the things of itself. Sufficient unto the day is the evil thereof.
Matthew. VI. 34.

There was a wise man in the East whose constant prayer was that he might see to-day with the eyes of to-morrow.
ALFRED MERCIER.

There was the Door to which I found no key;
There was the Veil through which I might not see.
OMAR KHAYYÁM—*Rubaiyat*.

After us the deluge.
MME. POMPADOUR.

The mind that is anxious about the future is miserable.
SENECA.

God, if Thy will be so,
Enrich the time to come with smooth-faced peace,
With smiling plenty and fair prosperous days!
SHAKESPEARE—*Richard III*. *Act* V. Sc. 5.

Till the sun grows cold,
And the stars are old,
And the leaves of the Judgment Book unfold.
BAYARD TAYLOR—*Bedouin Song*.

I hear a voice you cannot hear,
Which says, I must not stay;
I see a hand you cannot see,
Which beckons me away.
TICKELL—*Colin and Lucy*.

G

GAMBLING

Whose game was empires, and whose stakes were thrones;
Whose table earth, whose dice were human bones.
BYRON—*The Age of Bronze*.

There is but one good throw upon the dice, which is to throw them away.
CHATFIELD.

By gaming we lose both our time and treasure—two things most precious to the life of man.
FELLTHAM.

Keep flax from fire, youth from gaming.
FRANKLIN.

Shake off the shackles of this tyrant vice;
Hear other calls than those of cards and dice:
Be learn'd in nobler arts than arts of play;
And other debts than those of honour pay.
DAVID GARRICK.

Look round, the wrecks of play behold;
Estates dismember'd, mortgag'd, sold!
Their owners now to jails confin'd,
Show equal poverty of mind.
GAY.

A mode of transferring property without producing any intermediate good.
SAMUEL JOHNSON.

I'll tell thee what it says: it calls me villain, a treacherous husband, a cruel father, a false brother; one lost to nature and her charities; or to say all in one short word, it calls me—gamester.
ED MOORE—*The Gamester*.

How, sir! not damn the sharper, but the dice?
POPE—*Epilogue to the Satires*.

It [gaming] is the child of avarice, the brother of iniquity, and the father of mischief.
WASHINGTON.

GARDEN

My garden is a lovesome thing—God
wot!
Rose plot,
Fringed pool,
Fern grot—
The veriest school
Of peace; and yet the fool
Contends that God is not.—
Not God in gardens! When the sun
is cool?
Nay, but I have a sign!
'Tis very sure God walks in mine.

THOMAS EDWARD BROWN—*My Garden.*

God the first garden made, and the first city Cain.

ABRAHAM COWLEY—*The Garden.* Essay V.

My garden is a forest ledge
Which older forests bound;
The banks slope down to the blue
lake-edge,
Then plunge to depths profound!

EMERSON—*My Garden.*

One is nearer God's heart in a garden
Than anywhere else on earth.

DOROTHY FRANCES GURNEY—*God's Garden.*

GENEROSITY

It is good to be unselfish and generous; but don't carry that too far. It will not do to give yourself to be melted down for the benefit of the tallow-trade; you must know where to find yourself.

GEORGE ELIOT.

How much easier it is to be generous than just! Men are sometimes bountiful who are not honest.

JUNIUS.

If there be any truer measure of a man than by what he does, it must be by what he gives.

SOUTH.

When you give, take to yourself no credit for generosity, unless you deny yourself something in order that you may give.

HENRY TAYLOR.

GENIUS

There is no great genius without a mixture of madness.

ARISTOTLE.

A woman must be a genius to create a good husband.

BALZAC.

Genius is only great patience.

BUFFON.

Many men of genius must arise before a particular man of genius can appear.

ISAAC D'ISRAELI—*Literary Character of Men of Genius.*

But genius must be born, and never can be taught.

DRYDEN.

Genius is one per cent inspiration and ninety-nine per cent perspiration.

EDISON.

When Nature has work to be done, she creates a genius to do it.

EMERSON—*Method of Nature.*

Genius is the power of lighting one's own fire.

JOHN FOSTER.

Genius and its rewards are briefly told:
A liberal nature and a niggard doom,
A difficult journey to a splendid tomb.

FORSTER.

Genius, like humanity, rusts for want of use.

HAZLITT—*Table Talk.*

I know no such thing as genius—genius is nothing but labor and diligence.

HOGARTH.

Nature is the master of talents; genius is the master of nature.

J. G. HOLLAND—*Art and Life.*

Gift, like genius, I often think only means an infinite capacity for taking pains.

ELLICE HOPKINS—*Work amongst Working Men.*

Genius is a promontory jutting out into the infinite.

VICTOR HUGO—*Wm. Shakespeare.*

The true Genius is a mind of large general powers, accidentally determined to some particular direction.
SAMUEL JOHNSON—*Life of Cowley.*

Three-fifths of him genius and two-fifths sheer fudge.
LOWELL—*Fable for Critics.*

Genius does what it must; and talent does what it can.
OWEN MEREDITH.

The lamp of genius burns quicker than the lamp of life.
SCHILLER.

The poets' scrolls will outlive the monuments of stone. Genius survives; all else is claimed by death.
SPENSER—*Shepherd's Calendar.*

GENTLEMAN

When Adam delved and Eve span,
Who was then the gentleman?
ANONYMOUS.

The gentleman is a Christian product.
GEORGE H. CALVERT.

The best of men
That e'er wore earth about him was a sufferer;
A soft, meek, patient, humble, tranquil spirit,
The first true gentleman that ever breathed.
THOMAS DEKKER — *The Honest Whore.* Pt. I. Act I. Sc. 2.

Once a gentleman, always a gentleman.
DICKENS—*Little Dorrit.*

Propriety of manners and consideration for others are the two main characteristics of a gentleman.
DISRAELI.

The flowering of civilization is the finished man, the man of sense, of grace, of accomplishment, of social power—the gentleman.
EMERSON.

To make a fine gentleman, several trades are required, but chiefly a barber.
GOLDSMITH.

The gentleman is solid mahogany; the fashionable man is only veneer.
J. G. HOLLAND.

Since every Jack became a gentleman,
There's many a gentle person made a Jack.
SHAKESPEARE—*Richard III.* Act I. Sc. 3.

And thus he bore without abuse
The grand old name of gentleman,
Defamed by every charlatan
And soiled with all ignoble use.
TENNYSON—*In Memoriam.*

If a man is a gentleman, he knows quite enough, and if he is not a gentleman, whatever he knows is bad for him.
WILDE—*A Woman of No Importance.*

GENTLENESS

Power can do by gentleness that which violence fails to accomplish; and calmness best enforces the imperial mandate.
CLAUDIANUS.

A woman's strength is most potent when robed in gentleness.
LAMARTINE.

Gentleness! more powerful than Hercules.
NINON DE LENCLOS.

Gentle to others, to himself severe.
ROGERS—*Voyage of Columbus.*

GERMANY

Let us put Germany, so to speak, in the saddle! you will see that she can ride.
BISMARCK. In Parliament of Confederation. (1867).

We Germans will never produce another Goethe, but we may produce another Caesar.
OSWALD SPENGLER, 1925.

GIFT

It is more blessed to give than to receive.
Acts. XX. 35.

What is bought is cheaper than a gift.
CERVANTES.

It is not the weight of jewel or plate,
Or the fondle of silk or fur;
'Tis the spirit in which the gift is rich,
As the gifts of the Wise Ones were,
And we are not told whose gift was gold,
Or whose was the gift of myrrh.
EDMUND VANCE COOKE—*The Spirit of the Gift*.

The gift, to be true, must be the flowing of the giver unto me, correspondent to my flowing unto him.
EMERSON—*Essays*.

I make presents to the mother, but think of the daughter.
GOETHE.

Give an inch, he'll take an ell.
HOBBES—*Liberty and Necessity*.

He gives twice who gives quickly.
PUBLIUS MIMUS.

In giving, a man receives more than he gives, and the more is in proportion to the worth of the thing given.
GEORGE MACDONALD—*Mary Marston*.

Or what man is there of you, whom if his son ask bread, will he give him a stone?
Matthew. VII. 9.

All we can hold in our cold dead hands is what we have given away.
Old Sanskrit Proverb.

God has given some gifts to the whole human race, from which no one is excluded.
SENECA.

Win her with gifts, if she respect not words;
Dumb jewels often in their silent kind
More than quick words do move a woman's mind.
SHAKESPEARE—*Two Gentlemen of Verona*. Act III. Sc. 1.

Rich gifts wax poor when givers prove unkind.
SHAKESPEARE—*Hamlet*. Act III. Sc. 1.

I fear the Greeks, even when they bring gifts.
VERGIL—*Aeneid*.

Behold, I do not give lectures or a little charity,
When I give I give myself.
WALT WHITMAN—*Song of Myself*.

Give all thou canst; high Heaven rejects the lore
Of nicely calculated less or more.
WORDSWORTH—*Ecclesiastical Sonnets*.

She gave me eyes, she gave me ears;
And humble cares, and delicate fears;
A heart, the fountain of sweet tears;
And love, and thought, and joy.
WORDSWORTH — *The Sparrow's Nest*.

GLORY

The paths of glory lead but to the grave.
GRAY—*Elegy in a Country Churchyard*.

O how quickly passes away the glory of the earth.
THOMAS À KEMPIS—*Imitation of Christ*.

Who pants for glory, finds but short repose;
A breath revives him, or a breath o'erthrows.
POPE—*Second Book of Horace*.

Sound, sound the clarion, fill the fife!
To all the sensual world proclaim,
One crowded hour of glorious life
Is worth an age without a name.
SCOTT—*Old Mortality*.

Some glory in their birth, some in their skill,
Some in their wealth, some in their bodies' force,
Some in their garments, though newfangled ill;
Some in their hawks and hounds, some in their horse;

And every humor hath his adjunct pleasure,
Wherein it finds a joy above the rest.
SHAKESPEARE—*Sonnet.*

I never learned how to tune a harp, or play upon a lute; but I know how to raise a small and inconsiderable city to glory and greatness.
THEMISTOCLES.

Glories, like glow-worms, afar off shine bright,
But look'd to near have neither heat nor light.
JOHN WEBSTER—*The White Devil.*

We rise in glory, as we sink in pride:
Where boasting ends, there dignity begins.
YOUNG—*Night Thoughts.*

GLOW-WORM

My star, God's glow-worm.
BROWNING—*Popularity.*

Glow-worms on the ground are moving,
As if in the torch-dance circling.
HEINE—*Book of Songs.*

Ye living lamps, by whose dear light
The nightingale does sit so late;
And studying all the summer night,
Her matchless songs does meditate.
MARVELL—*The Mower to the Glow-worm.*

When evening closes Nature's eye,
The glow-worm lights her little spark
To captivate her favorite fly
And tempt the rover through the dark.
MONTGOMERY—*The Glow-worm.*

GOD

Nearer, my God, to Thee—
Nearer to Thee—
E'en though it be a cross
That raiseth me;
Still all my song shall be
Nearer, my God, to Thee,
Nearer to Thee!
SARAH FLOWER ADAMS.

Man thinks, God directs.
ALCUIN.

God helps those who help themselves.
ANONYMOUS.

Man proposes, and God disposes.
ARIOSTO—*Orlando Furioso.*

They that deny a God destroy man's nobility; for certainly man is of kin to the beasts by his body; and, if he be not of kin to God by his spirit, he is a base and ignoble creature.
BACON—*Essays.*

God is the perfect poet,
Who in his person acts his own creations.
BROWNING—*Paracelsus.*

God's in His Heaven—
All's right with the world!
BROWNING—*Pippa Passes.*

Of what I call God,
And fools call Nature.
BROWNING—*The Ring and the Book.*

A picket frozen on duty—
A mother starved for her brood—
Socrates drinking the hemlock,
And Jesus on the rood;
And millions who, humble and nameless,
The straight, hard pathway trod—
Some call it Consecration,
And others call it God.
W. H. CARRUTH—*Evolution.*

How did the atheist get his idea of that God whom he denies?
COLERIDGE.

God hath chosen the foolish things of the world to confound the wise; and God hath chosen the weak things of the world to confound the things that are mighty.
I Corinthians. I. 27

God moves in a mysterious way
His wonders to perform;
He plants his footsteps in the sea
And rides upon the storm.
COWPER—*Hymn.*

Acquaint thyself with God, if thou would'st taste
His works. Admitted once to his embrace,

Thou shalt perceive that thou wast blind before:
Thine eye shall be instructed; and thine heart
Made pure shall relish with divine delight
Till then unfelt, what hands divine have wrought.
COWPER—*The Task.*

My God, my Father, and my Friend,
Do not forsake me in the end.
WENTWORTH DILLON.

'Twas much, that man was made like God before:
But, that God should be made like man, much more.
DONNE—*Holy Sonnets.*

Too wise to err, too good to be unkind,—
Are all the movements of the Eternal Mind.
REV. JOHN EAST—*Songs of My Pilgrimage.*

God is incorporeal, divine, supreme, infinite Mind, Spirit, Soul, Principle, Life, Truth, Love.
MARY BAKER EDDY—*Science and Health.*

He was a wise man who originated the idea of God.
EURIPIDES.

Henceforth the Majesty of God revere;
Fear him and you have nothing else to fear.
FORDYCE.

Whenever I think of God I can only conceive of Him as a Being infinitely great and infinitely good. This last quality of the divine nature inspires me with such confidence and joy that I could have written even a *miserere* in *tempo allegro.*
HAYDN.

O thou, whose certain eye foresees
The fix'd event of fate's remote decrees.
HOMER—*Odyssey.*

Could we with ink the ocean fill,
And were the heavens of parchment made,
Were every stalk on earth a quill,
And every man a scribe by trade;
To write the love of God above,
Would drain the ocean dry;
Nor could the scroll contain the whole,
Though stretch'd from sky to sky.
RABBI MAYIR BEN ISAAC.

An honest God is the noblest work of man.
INGERSOLL—*The Gods.*

God said, "Let us make man in our image." Man said, "Let us make God in our image."
DOUGLAS JERROLD.

Fear that man who fears not God.
ABDL-EL-KADER.

There is no good but God.
The Koran.

The very impossibility in which I find myself to prove that God is not, discloses to me His existence.
LA BRUYÈRE.

"We trust, Sir, that God is on our side." "It is more important to know that we are on God's side."
LINCOLN—*Reply to deputation during Civil War.*

A mighty fortress is our God,
A bulwark never failing,
Our helper he amid the flood
Of mortal ills prevailing.
LUTHER.

A voice in the wind I do not know;
A meaning on the face of the high hills
Whose utterance I cannot comprehend.
A something is behind them: that is God.
GEORGE MACDONALD—*Within and Without.*

Every one is in a small way the image of God.
MANLIUS.

One sole God;
One sole ruler,—his Law;
One sole interpreter of that law—Humanity.
MAZZINI.

What in me is dark,
Illumine; what is low, raise and support;
That to the height of this great argument
I may assert eternal Providence,
And justify the ways of God to men.
MILTON—*Paradise Lost.*

What is it: is man only a blunder of God, or God only a blunder of man?
NIETZSCHE—*The Twilight of the Idols.*

A God-intoxicated man.
NOVALIS (*of Spinoza*).

There is a God within us, and we glow when he stirs us.
OVID.

Fear God. Honour the King.
I Peter. II. 17.

One on God's side is a majority.
WENDELL PHILLIPS.

God is truth and light his shadow.
PLATO.

Lo, the poor Indian! whose untutored mind
Sees God in clouds, or hears him in the wind.
POPE—*Essay on Man.*

To Him no high, no low, no great, no small;
He fills, He bounds, connects and equals all!
POPE—*Essay on Man.*

He mounts the storm, and walks upon the wind.
POPE—*Essay on Man.*

The heavens declare the glory of God; and the firmament showeth his handiwork.
Psalms. XIX. 1.

He maketh me to lie down in green pastures: he leadeth me beside the still waters.
Psalms. XXIII. 2.

God is our refuge and strength, a very present help in trouble.
Psalms. XLVI. 1.

There is no respect of persons with God.
Romans. II. 11. *Acts.* X. 34.

If God be for us, who can be against us?
Romans. VIII. 31.

Give us a God—a living God,
One to wake the sleeping soul,
One to cleanse the tainted blood
Whose pulses in our bosoms roll.
C. G. ROSENBERG—*The Winged Horn.*

Philosophers call God "the great unknown." "The great mis-known" would be more correct.
JOSEPH ROUX.

For the greater glory of God.
Motto of the Society of Jesus.

God tempers the wind to the shorn lamb.
LAURENCE STERNE.

The divine essence itself is love and wisdom.
SWEDENBORG.

God, the Great Giver, can open the whole universe to our gaze in the narrow space of a single lane.
RABINDRANATH TAGORE.

The great world's altar stairs
That slope through darkness up to God.
TENNYSON—*In Memoriam.*

Rock of Ages, cleft for me,
Let me hide myself in thee.
AUGUSTUS TOPLADY—*Living and Dying Prayer.*

God, from a beautiful necessity, is Love.
TUPPER—*Of Immortality.*

I believe that there is no God, but that matter is God and God is matter; and that it is no matter whether there is any God or no.
THE UNBELIEVER'S CREED.

If there were no God, it would be necessary to invent him.
VOLTAIRE.

The God I know of, I shall ne'er
Know, though he dwells exceeding nigh.
Raise thou the stone and find me there,
Cleave thou the wood and there am I.

Yea, in my flesh his spirit doth flow,
Too near, too far, for me to know.
WILLIAM WATSON—*The Unknown God.*

By night an atheist half believes a God.
YOUNG—*Night Thoughts.*

A Deity believed, is joy begun;
A Deity adored, is joy advanced;
A Deity beloved, is joy matured.
Each branch of piety delight inspires.
YOUNG—*Night Thoughts.*

GODS

The Ethiop gods have Ethiop lips,
Bronze cheeks, and woolly hair;
The Grecian gods are like the Greeks,
As keen-eyed, cold and fair.
WALTER BAGEHOT—*Ignorance of Man.*

Ye immortal gods! where in the world are we?
CICERO.

Some thoughtlessly proclaim the Muses nine:
A tenth is Sappho, maid divine.
Greek Anthology.

There's a one-eyed yellow idol to the north of Khatmandu,
There's a little marble cross below the town,
There's a broken-hearted woman tends the grave of Mad Carew,
And the yellow god forever gazes down.
J. MILTON HAYES—*The Green Eye of the Yellow God.*

Yet verily these issues lie on the lap of the gods.
HOMER—*Iliad.*

Nor does Apollo keep his bow continually drawn.
HORACE.

The trident of Neptune is the sceptre of the world.
LEMIERRE.

The gods and their tranquil abodes appear, which no winds disturb, nor clouds bedew with showers, nor does the white snow, hardened by frost, annoy them; the heaven, always pure, is without clouds, and smiles with pleasant light diffused.
LUCRETIUS.

No wonder Cupid is a murderous boy;
A fiery archer making pain his joy.
His dam, while fond of Mars, is Vulcan's wife,
And thus 'twixt fire and sword divides her life.
MELEAGER.

Who knows not Circe,
The daughter of the Sun, whose charmed cup
Whoever tasted, lost his upright shape,
And downward fell into a groveling swine?
MILTON—*Comus.*

My lord Jupiter knows how to gild the pill.
MOLIÈRE—*Amphitryon.*

Man is certainly stark mad; he cannot make a flea, and yet he will be making gods by dozens.
MONTAIGNE.

Even the gods love jokes.
PLATO.

Cupid is a knavish lad,
Thus to make poor females mad.
SHAKESPEARE—*Midsummer Night's Dream.* Act III. Sc. 2.

Atlas, we read in ancient song,
Was so exceeding tall and strong,
He bore the skies upon his back,
Just as the pedler does his pack;
But, as the pedler overpress'd
Unloads upon a stall to rest,
Or, when he can no longer stand,
Desires a friend to lend a hand,
So Atlas, lest the ponderous spheres
Should sink, and fall about his ears,
Got Hercules to bear the pile,
That he might sit and rest awhile.
SWIFT—*Atlas; or, the Minister of State.*

GOLD

You shall not press down upon the brow of labor this crown of thorns—

you shall not crucify mankind upon a cross of gold!

W. J. BRYAN, at Democratic National Convention, 1896.

Gold begets in brethren hate;
Gold in families debate;
Gold does friendship separate;
Gold does civil wars create.

COWLEY—*Anacreontics.*

What female heart can gold despise?
What cat's averse to fish?

GRAY—*On the Death of a Favorite Cat.*

That is gold which is worth gold.

GEORGE HERBERT.

Gold! Gold! Gold! Gold!
Bright and yellow, hard and cold.

HOOD—*Miss Kilmansegg.*

It is observed of gold, by an old epigrammatist, "that to have it is to be in fear, and to want it, to be in sorrow."

SAMUEL JOHNSON.

The lust of gold succeeds the rage of conquest;
The lust of gold, unfeeling and remorseless!
The last corruption of degenerate man.

SAMUEL JOHNSON—*Irene.*

Gold—the picklock that never fails.

MASSINGER.

Gold is, in its last analysis, the sweat of the poor and the blood of the brave.

JOSEPH NAPOLEON.

Truly now is the golden age; the highest honour comes by means of gold; by gold love is procured.

OVID.

Commerce has set the mark of selfishness,
The signet of its all-enslaving power
Upon a shining ore, and called it gold;
Before whose image bow the vulgar great,
The vainly rich, the miserable proud,
The mob of peasants, nobles, priests, and kings,
And with blind feelings reverence the power
That grinds them to the dust of misery.
But in the temple of their hireling hearts
Gold is a living god, and rules in scorn
All earthly things but virtue.

SHELLEY—*Queen Mab.*

Accursed thirst for gold! what dost thou not compel mortals to do?

VERGIL—*Aeneid.*

GOLDEN RULE

My duty towards my neighbor is to love him as myself, and to do to all men as I would they should do unto me.

Book of Common Prayer, 1662.

What you do not want others to do to you, do not do to others.

CONFUCIUS, c. 500 B.C.

Do as you would be done by.

English Proverb.

Whatsoever thou wouldst that men should not do to thee, do not do that to them. This is the whole Law. The rest is only explanation.

HILLEL HA-BABLI, c. 30 B.C.

Whatsoever you require that others should do to you, that do ye to them.

THOMAS HOBBES, 1651.

Do not do to others what would anger you if done to you by others.

ISOCRATES, c. 375 B.C.

As ye would that men should do to you, do ye also to them likewise.

Luke. VI. c. 75.

This is the sum of all true righteousness: deal with others as thou wouldst thyself be dealt by. Do nothing to thy neighbor which thou wouldst not have him do to thee hereafter.

The Mahabharata, c. 150 B.C.

All things whatsoever ye would that men should do to you, do ye even so to them: for this is the law and the prophets.

Matthew. VII. 12, c. 75.

Do not do unto others as you would that they should do unto you. Their tastes may not be the same.

GEORGE BERNARD SHAW, 1903.

What thou thyself hatest, do to no man.

Tobit. IV. c. 180 B.C.

GOOD-HUMOR

A cheerful temper, joined with Innocence, will make beauty attractive, knowledge delightful, and wit good-natured.

ADDISON.

Good-humor makes all things tolerable.

HENRY WARD BEECHER.

The sunshine of the mind.

BULWER-LYTTON.

Good-humor is goodness and wisdom combined.

OWEN MEREDITH.

GOODNESS

What good I see humbly I seek to do,
And live obedient to the law, in trust
That what will come, and must come, shall come well.

EDWIN ARNOLD—*The Light of Asia*.

Because indeed there was never law, or sect, or opinion, did so much magnify goodness, as the Christian religion doth.

BACON—*Essays*.

For the cause that lacks assistance,
The wrong that needs resistance,
For the future in the distance,
And the good that I can do.

GEORGE LINNÆUS BANKS—*What I Live For*.

No good Book, or good thing of any sort, shows its best face at first.

CARLYLE—*Essays*.

Can one desire too much of a good thing?

CERVANTES—*Don Quixote*.

Men in no way approach so nearly to the gods as in doing good to men.

CICERO.

Look around the habitable world, how few
Know their own good, or knowing it, pursue.

DRYDEN—*Juvenal*.

If you wish to be good, first believe that you are bad.

EPICTETUS.

Happy were men if they but understood
There is no safety but in doing good.

JOHN FOUNTAIN.

Experience has convinced me that there is a thousand times more goodness, wisdom, and love in the world than men imagine.

GEHLER.

Can there any good thing come out of Nazareth?

John. I. 46.

As I know more of mankind, I expect less of them, and am ready now to call a man a good man upon easier terms than I was formerly.

SAMUEL JOHNSON.

Be good, sweet maid, and let who will be clever;
Do noble things, not dream them all day long;
And so make life, death, and that vast forever
One grand, sweet song.

KINGSLEY—*Farewell*.

The crest and crowning of all good,
Life's final star, is Brotherhood.

EDWIN MARKHAM—*Brotherhood*.

A real man is he whose goodness is a part of himself.

MENCIUS.

Since good, the more
Communicated, more abundant grows.

MILTON—*Paradise Lost*.

There is no man so good who, were he to submit all his thoughts and actions to the law, would not deserve hanging ten times in his life.

MONTAIGNE.

A glass is good, and a lass is good,
And a pipe to smoke in cold weather;

The world is good, and the people are good,
And we're all good fellows together.
JOHN O'KEEFE—*Sprigs of Laurel.*

He that does good for good's sake seeks neither praise nor reward, though sure of both at last.
WILLIAM PENN.

The fragrance of the flower is never borne against the breeze; but the fragrance of human virtues diffuses itself everywhere.
The Ramayana.

You're good for Madge or good for Cis
Or good for Kate, maybe:
But what's to me the good of this
While you're not good for me?
CHRISTINA G. ROSSETTI—*Jessie Cameron.*

What is beautiful is good, and who is good will soon also be beautiful.
SAPPHO.

There is some soul of goodness in things evil,
Would men observingly distil it out.
SHAKESPEARE—*Henry V.* Act IV. Sc. 1.

I am in this earthly world; where to do harm,
Is often laudable, to do good sometime
Accounted dangerous folly.
SHAKESPEARE—*Macbeth.* Act IV. Sc. 2.

For who is there but you? who not only claim to be a good man and a gentleman, for many are this, and yet have not the power of making others good. Whereas you are not only good yourself, but also the cause of goodness in others.
SOCRATES TO PROTAGORAS.

'Tis only noble to be good.
TENNYSON—*Lady Clara Vere de Vere.*

For the Lord Jesus Christ's sake,
Do all the good you can,
To all the people you can,
In all the ways you can,
As long as ever you can.
Tombstone Inscription in Shrewsbury, England.

Man should be ever better than he seems.
SIR AUBREY DE VERE.

Roaming in thought over the Universe,
I saw the little that is
Good steadily hastening towards immortality,
And the vast all that is called Evil I saw hastening to merge itself and become lost and dead.
WALT WHITMAN—*Roaming in Thought.*

GOOSE

What is sauce for the goose is sauce for the gander.
VARRO, *quoting Gellius.*

The goose gabbles amid the melodious swans.
VERGIL—*Eclogues.* IX. 37.

GOSSIP

Old gossips are usually young flirts gone to seed.
J. L. BASFORD.

Whoever keeps an open ear
For tattlers will be sure to hear
The trumpet of contention.
COWPER—*Friendship.*

You do not know it but you are the talk of all the town.
OVID—*Art of Love.*

He that repeateth a matter separateth very friends.
Proverbs. XVII. 9.

Let the greater part of the news thou hearest be the least part of what thou believest.
QUARLES.

Foul whisperings are abroad.
SHAKESPEARE—*Macbeth.* Act V. Sc. 1.

I heard the little bird say so.
SWIFT—*Letter to Stella.*

Tattlers also and busybodies, speaking things which they ought not.

I Timothy. V. 13.

Report, than which no evil thing of any kind is more swift, increases with travel and gains strength by its progress.

VERGIL—*Aeneid*.

There is only one thing in the world worse than being talked about, and that is not being talked about.

WILDE—*The Picture of Dorian Gray*.

GOVERNMENT

Yesterday the greatest question was decided which was ever debated in America; and a greater perhaps never was, nor will be, decided among men. A resolution was passed without one dissenting colony, that those United Colonies are, and of right ought to be, free and independent States.

JOHN ADAMS—*Letter to Mrs. Adams, 1776*.

The declaration that our People are hostile to a government made by themselves, for themselves, and conducted by themselves, is an insult.

Address to the citizens of Westmoreland Co., Virginia, by John Adams.

States are great engines moving slowly.

BACON—*Advancement of Learning*.

It [Calvinism] established a religion without a prelate, a government without a king.

GEORGE BANCROFT.

Experience teaches us to be most on our guard to protect liberty when the government's purposes are beneficent.

BRANDEIS—*Olmstead vs. U. S.*, 1928.

Well, will anybody deny now that the Government at Washington, as regards its own people, is the strongest government in the world at this hour? And for this simple reason, that it is based on the will, and the good will, of an instructed people.

JOHN BRIGHT.

Government is a contrivance of human wisdom to provide for human wants.

BURKE.

So then because some towns in England are not represented, America is to have no representative at all. They are "our children"; but when children ask for bread we are not to give a stone.

BURKE—*Speech on American Taxation*.

And having looked to Government for bread, on the very first scarcity they will turn and bite the hand that fed them.

BURKE—*Thoughts and Details on Scarcity*.

A thousand years scarce serve to form
 a state;
An hour may lay it in the dust.

BYRON—*Childe Harold*.

Though the people support the government the government should not support the people.

GROVER CLEVELAND.

Whatever was required to be done, the Circumlocution Office was beforehand with all the public departments in the art of perceiving how not to do it.

DICKENS—*Little Dorrit*.

Individualities may form communities, but it is institutions alone that can create a nation.

DISRAELI.

The country has, I think, made up its mind to close this career of plundering and blundering.

DISRAELI.

The best government is not that which renders men the happiest, but that which renders the greatest number happy.

DUCLOS.

If I wished to punish a province, I would have it governed by philosophers.

FREDERICK THE GREAT.

Clouds and darkness are around Him; His pavilion is dark waters and thick clouds; justice and judgment are the establishment of His throne; mercy and truth shall go before His face! Fellow citizens! God reigns and the Government at Washington lives.

JAMES A. GARFIELD—*Address.* April, 1865.

All free governments are managed by the combined wisdom and folly of the people.

JAMES A. GARFIELD.

When constabulary duty's to be done
A policeman's lot is not a happy one.

W. S. GILBERT—*Pirates of Penzance.*

What government is the best? That which teaches us to govern ourselves.

GOETHE.

For just experience tells, in every soil,
That those who think must govern those that toil.

GOLDSMITH—*The Traveller.*

Perish commerce. Let the constitution live!

GEORGE HARDINGE.

Unnecessary taxation is unjust taxation.

ABRAM S. HEWITT.

There was one species of despotism under which he had long groaned, and that was petticoat government.

WASHINGTON IRVING—*Rip Van Winkle.*

The will of the people is the only legitimate foundation of any government, and to protect its free expression should be our first object.

JEFFERSON, 1801.

The safety of the State is the highest law.

JUSTINIAN.

A house divided against itself cannot stand—I believe this government cannot endure permanently half-slave and half-free.

LINCOLN—*Speech. June 17, 1858.*

All your strength is in your union,
All your danger is in discord.

LONGFELLOW—*The Song of Hiawatha.*

The state!—it is I!

Attributed to LOUIS XIV OF FRANCE.

That is the best government which desires to make the people happy, and knows how to make them happy.

MACAULAY.

The principal foundation of all states are good laws and good arms.

MACHIAVELLI.

The government of the Union, then, is emphatically and truly a government of the people. In form and in substance it emanates from them. Its powers are granted by them, and are to be exercised directly on them and for their benefit.

CHIEF JUSTICE JOHN MARSHALL.

Hope nothing from foreign governments. They will never be really willing to aid you until you have shown that you are strong enough to conquer without them.

MAZZINI.

Republics end through luxury; monarchies through poverty.

MONTESQUIEU.

The deterioration of a government begins almost always by the decay of its principles.

MONTESQUIEU.

Democracy is direct self-government, over all the people, for all the people, by all the people.

THEODORE PARKER—*Music Hall, Boston, July 4, 1858.*

In a change of government the poor change nothing but the name of their masters.

PHAEDRUS.

Governments exist to protect the rights of minorities. The loved and the rich need no protection,—they have many friends and few enemies.

WENDELL PHILLIPS.

Today the nations of the world may be divided into two classes—the nations in which the government fears the people, and the nations in which the people fear the government.
AMOS R. E. PINCHOT, 1935.

Three millions of people, so dead to all the feelings of liberty as voluntarily to submit to be slaves, would have been fit instruments to make slaves of the rest.
PITT (The Elder)—*Speech on America.*

Themistocles said, "The Athenians govern the Greeks; I govern the Athenians; you, my wife, govern me; your son governs you."
PLUTARCH.

The labor unions shall have a square deal, and the corporations shall have a square deal, and in addition, all private citizens shall have a square deal.
THEODORE ROOSEVELT.

A hated government does not last long.
SENECA.

No man undertakes a trade he has not learned, even the meanest; yet every one thinks himself sufficiently qualified for the hardest of all trades—that of government.
SOCRATES.

Let us raise a standard to which the wise and honest can repair; the rest is in the hands of God.
WASHINGTON—*Speech to Constitutional Convention, 1787.*

The people's government made for the people, made by the people, and answerable to the people.
DANIEL WEBSTER—*Speech on Foot's Resolution, 1830.*

When my eyes shall be turned to behold, for the last time, the sun in heaven, may I not see him shining on the broken and dishonored fragments of a once glorious Union; on States dissevered, discordant, belligerent; on a land rent with civil feuds, or drenched, it may be, in fraternal blood!
DANIEL WEBSTER—*Speech on Foot's Resolution, 1830.*

The firm basis of government is justice, not pity.
WILSON—*Inaugural Address, 1913.*

GRACE

An outward and visible sign of an inward and spiritual grace.
Book of Common Prayer.

There, but for the grace of God, goes John Bradford.
JOHN BRADFORD, *on seeing a condemned man.*

Ye are fallen from grace.
Galatians. V. 4.

Grace has been defined, the outward expression of the inward harmony of the soul.
HAZLITT.

He does it with a better grace, but I do it more natural.
SHAKESPEARE—*Twelfth Night.* Act II. Sc. 3.

The grace of the spirit comes only from heaven, and lights up the whole bodily presence.
SPURGEON.

Beauty, devoid of grace, is a mere hook without the bait.
TALLEYRAND.

GRASS

We say of the oak, "How grand of girth!"
Of the willow we say, "How slender!"
And yet to the soft grass clothing the earth
How slight is the praise we render.
EDGAR FAWCETT—*The Grass.*

All flesh is grass.
Isaiah. XL. 6.

Nearer the rock, the sweeter the grass.
Scottish Proverb.

GRASSHOPPER

When all the birds are faint with the hot sun,
And hide in cooling trees, a voice will run
From hedge to hedge about the new-mown mead;
That is the grasshopper's—he takes the lead
In summer luxury—he has never done
With his delights, for when tired out with fun,
He rests at ease beneath some pleasant weed.

KEATS—*On the Grasshopper and Cricket.*

GRATITUDE

He who receives a good turn should never forget it; he who does one should never remember it.

CHARRON.

A thankful heart is not only the greatest virtue, but the parent of all the other virtues.

CICERO.

Gratitude is the heart's memory.

French Proverb.

The still small voice of gratitude.

GRAY—*For Music.*

Gratitude is a species of justice.

SAMUEL JOHNSON.

The gratitude of most men is but a secret desire of receiving greater benefits.

LA ROCHEFOUCAULD.

Gratitude is the memory of the heart.

MASSIEU.

Th' unwilling gratitude of base mankind!

POPE—*Second Book of Horace.*

Gratitude is a duty which ought to be paid, but which none have a right to expect.

ROUSSEAU.

"Allah il Allah!" he sings his psalm,
On the Indian Sea, by the isles of balm;
"Thanks to Allah, who gives the palm!"

WHITTIER—*The Palm-Tree.*

I've heard of hearts unkind, kind deeds
With coldness still returning;
Alas! the gratitude of men
Hath often left me mourning.

WORDSWORTH—*Simon Lee.*

GRAVE

By Nebo's lonely mountain,
On this side Jordan's wave,
In a vale in the land of Moab,
There lies a lonely grave;
But no man built that sepulcher,
And no man saw it e'er,
For the angels of God upturned the sod
And laid the dead man there.

CECIL FRANCES ALEXANDER—*Burial of Moses.*

We go to the grave of a friend saying, "A man is dead"; but angels throng about him, saying, "A man is born."

HENRY WARD BEECHER.

Gravestones tell truth scarce forty years.

SIR THOMAS BROWNE—*Hydriotaphia.*

I would rather sleep in the southern corner of a little country churchyard, than in the tombs of the Capulets.

BURKE—*Letter to Matthew Smith.*

And he buried him in a valley in the land of Moab, over against Beth-peor; but no man knoweth of his sepulcher unto this day.

Deuteronomy. XXXIV. 6.

The solitary, silent, solemn scene,
Where Caesars, heroes, peasants, hermits lie,
Blended in dust together; where the slave
Rests from his labors; where th' insulting proud
Resigns his powers; the miser drops his hoard:
Where human folly sleeps.

DYER—*Ruins of Rome.*

Some village Hampden, that, with dauntless breast,
The little tyrant of his fields withstood,
Some mute inglorious Milton here may rest,
Some Cromwell guiltless of his country's blood.
GRAY—*Elegy in a Country Churchyard.*

Fond fool! six feet shall serve for all thy store,
And he that cares for most shall find no more.
JOSEPH HALL—*Satires.*

Green be the turf above thee,
Friend of my better days;
None knew thee but to love thee
Nor named thee but to praise.
FITZ-GREENE HALLECK.

Graves they say are warm'd by glory;
Foolish words and empty story.
HEINE.

Where shall we make her grave?
Oh! where the wild flowers wave
In the free air!
When shower and singing-bird
'Midst the young leaves are heard,
There—lay her there!
FELICIA D. HEMANS—*Dirge.*

The house appointed for all living.
Job. XXX. 23.

Teach me to live that I may dread
The grave as little as my bed.
BISHOP KEN—*Evening Hymn.*

This is the field and Acre of our God,
This is the place where human harvests grow!
LONGFELLOW—*God's Acre.*

There are slave-drivers quietly whipped underground,
There bookbinders, done up in boards, are fast bound,
There card-players wait till the last trump be played,
There all the choice spirits get finally laid,
There the babe that's unborn is supplied with a berth,
There men without legs get their six feet of earth,
There lawyers repose, each wrapped up in his case,
There seekers of office are sure of a place,
There defendant and plaintiff get equally cast,
There shoemakers quietly stick to the last.
LOWELL—*Fables for Critics.*

The temple of silence and reconciliation.
MACAULAY.

There is a calm for those who weep,
A rest for weary pilgrims found,
They softly lie and sweetly sleep
Low in the ground.
MONTGOMERY—*The Grave.*

Dust into dust, and under dust, to lie,
Sans wine, sans song, sans singer, and —sans end.
OMAR KHAYYÁM—*Rubaiyat.*

Oh, how a small portion of earth will hold us when we are dead, who ambitiously seek after the whole world while we are living!
PHILIP, KING OF MACEDON.

The grave unites; where e'en the great find rest,
And blended lie th' oppressor and th' oppressed!
POPE—*Windsor Forest.*

Never the grave gives back what it has won!
SCHILLER—*Funeral Fantasy.*

Lay her i' the earth;
And from her fair and unpolluted flesh
May violets spring!
SHAKESPEARE—*Hamlet.* Act V. Sc. 1.

Gilded tombs do worms infold.
SHAKESPEARE—*Merchant of Venice.* Act II. Sc. 7.

The grave
Is but the threshold of eternity.
SOUTHEY—*Vision of the Maid of Orleans.*

Hark! from the tombs a doleful sound.
WATTS—*Hymns and Spiritual Songs.*

GRAVITY

Gravity is more suggestive than convincing.

DOUGLAS JERROLD.

Gravity is a mysterious carriage of the body invented to cover the defects of the mind.

LA ROCHEFOUCAULD.

To how many blockheads of my time has a cold and taciturn demeanor procured the credit of prudence and capacity!

MONTAIGNE.

GREATNESS

Great warriors, like great earthquakes, are principally remembered for the mischief they have done.

BOVEE.

We have not the love of greatness, but the love of the love of greatness.

CARLYLE—*Essays*.

No man was ever great without divine inspiration.

CICERO.

Everything great is not always good, but all good things are great.

DEMOSTHENES.

No great deed is done
By falterers who ask for certainty.

GEORGE ELIOT—*The Spanish Gypsy*.

All great men come out of the middle classes.

EMERSON.

Nature never sends a great man into the planet, without confiding the secret to another soul.

EMERSON—*Uses of Great Men*.

There was never yet a truly great man that was not at the same time truly virtuous.

FRANKLIN.

But matchless Franklin! What a few
Can hope to rival such as you.
Who seized from kings their sceptred pride
And turned the lightning's darts aside.

PHILIP FRENEAU—*On the Death of Benjamin Franklin*.

No man ever yet became great by imitation.

SAMUEL JOHNSON.

It is the prerogative of great men only to have great defects.

LA ROCHEFOUCAULD.

Great men stand like solitary towers in the city of God.

LONGFELLOW—*Kavanagh*.

It is the age that forms the man, not the man that forms the age.

MACAULAY.

The great are only great because we carry them on our shoulders; when we throw them off they sprawl on the ground.

MONTANDRÉ.

Lives obscurely great.

HENRY J. NEWBOLDT—*Minora Sidera*.

That man is great, and he alone,
Who serves a greatness not his own,
For neither praise nor pelf:
Content to know and be unknown:
Whole in himself.

OWEN MEREDITH—*A Great Man*.

The great are only great because we are on our knees. Let us rise up.

PRUDHOMME.

Farewell! a long farewell, to all my greatness!
This is the state of man: to-day he puts forth
The tender leaves of hope; to-morrow blossoms,
And bears his blushing honours thick upon him:
The third day comes a frost, a killing frost,
And, when he thinks, good easy man, full surely
His greatness is a-ripening, nips his root,
And then he falls, as I do.

SHAKESPEARE—*Henry VIII*. Act III. Sc. 2.

Some are born great, some achieve greatness, and some have greatness thrust upon 'em.
SHAKESPEARE—*Twelfth Night.* Act II. Sc. 5.

Censure is the tax a man pays to the public for being eminent.
SWIFT.

A solemn and religious regard to spiritual and eternal things is an indispensable element of all true greatness.
DANIEL WEBSTER.

GREECE

Fair Greece! sad relic of departed worth!
Immortal, though no more; though fallen great!
BYRON—*Childe Harold.*

The isles of Greece, the isles of Greece!
Where burning Sappho loved and sung.
Where grew the arts of war and peace,—
Where Delos rose, and Phoebus sprung!
Eternal summer gilds them yet,
But all, except their sun, is set.
BYRON—*Don Juan.*

Beware of Greeks bearing gifts.
Latin Proverb.

Athens, the eye of Greece, mother of arts
And eloquence.
MILTON—*Paradise Regained.*

The glory that was Greece.
POE—*To Helen.*

GRIEF

Thank God, bless God, all ye who suffer not
More grief than ye can weep for. That is well—
That is light grieving!
E. B. BROWNING—*Tears.*

There is no grief which time does not lessen and soften.
CICERO.

Grief is the agony of an instant: the indulgence of grief the blunder of a life.
DISRAELI.

Grief is a stone that bears one down, but two bear it lightly.
W. HAUFF.

While grief is fresh, every attempt to divert only irritates. You must wait till grief be digested, and then amusement will dissipate the remains of it.
SAMUEL JOHNSON.

Let us moderate our sorrows. The grief of a man should not exceed proper bounds, but be in proportion to the blow he has received.
JUVENAL.

The only cure for grief is action.
G. H. LEWES—*The Spanish Drama.*

Well has it been said that there is no grief like the grief which does not speak.
LONGFELLOW.

There is a solemn luxury in grief.
WILLIAM MASON—*The English Garden.*

Suppressed grief suffocates, it rages within the breast, and is forced to multiply its strength.
OVID.

Heavy hearts, like heavy clouds in the sky, are best relieved by the letting of water.
RIVAROL.

Every one can master a grief but he that has it.
SHAKESPEARE—*Much Ado about Nothing.* Act III. Sc. 2.

Some griefs show much of love;
But much of grief shows still some want of wit.
SHAKESPEARE—*Romeo and Juliet.* Act III. Sc. 5.

What's gone and what's past help
Should be past grief.
SHAKESPEARE—*Winter's Tale.* Act III. Sc. 2.

GUEST

Every guest hates the others, and the host hates them all.
Albanian Proverb.

Hail, guest, we ask not what thou art;
If friend, we greet thee, hand and heart;
If stranger, such no longer be;
If foe, our love shall conquer thee.
Old Welsh door verse.

No one can be so welcome a guest that he will not annoy his host after three days.
PLAUTUS.

Unbidden guests
Are often welcomest when they are gone.
SHAKESPEARE—*Henry VI.* Pt. I. Act II. Sc. 2.

GUILT

Let no guilty man escape, if it can be avoided. No personal consideration should stand in the way of performing a public duty.
ULYSSES S. GRANT.

What we call real estate—the solid ground to build a house on—is the broad foundation on which nearly all the guilt of this world rests.
HAWTHORNE—*The House of the Seven Gables.*

Men's minds are too ingenious in palliating guilt in themselves.
LIVY.

Nothing is more wretched than the mind of a man conscious of guilt.
PLAUTUS.

It is base to filch a purse, daring to embezzle a million, but it is great beyond measure to steal a crown. The sin lessens as the guilt increases.
SCHILLER.

Let wickedness escape as it may at the bar, it never fails of doing justice upon itself; for every guilty person is his own hangman.
SENECA.

He who flees from trial confesses his guilt.
SYRUS.

H

HABIT

Habit, if not resisted, soon becomes necessity.
ST. AUGUSTINE.

Habit with him was all the test of truth;
"It must be right: I've done it from my youth."
CRABBE—*The Borough.*

Habit is overcome by habit.
THOMAS À KEMPIS.

Habit is a cable. We weave a thread of it every day, and at last we cannot break it.
HORACE MANN.

Nothing is stronger than habit.
OVID.

Sow an act and you reap a habit. Sow a habit and you reap a character. Sow a character and you reap a destiny.
CHARLES READE.

How use doth breed a habit in a man!
SHAKESPEARE—*Two Gentlemen of Verona.* Act V. Sc. 4.

It is easy to assume a habit; but when you try to cast it off, it will take skin and all.
H. W. SHAW.

The fox changes his skin but not his habits.
SUETONIUS.

Unless the habit leads to happiness the best habit is to contract none.
ZIMMERMANN.

HAIR

His hair stood upright like porcupine quills.
BOCCACCIO—*Decameron.*

It is foolish to pluck out one's hair for sorrow, as if grief could be assuaged by baldness.
CICERO.

Bring down my gray hairs with sorrow to the grave.
Genesis. XLII. 38.

Beware of her fair hair, for she excels
All women in the magic of her locks;
And when she winds them round a young man's neck,
She will not ever set him free again.
GOETHE—*Faust*.

One hair of a woman can draw more than a hundred pair of oxen.
JAMES HOWELL.

The very hairs of your head are all numbered.
Matthew. X. 30.

Her head was bare;
But for her native ornament of hair;
Which in a simple knot was tied above,
Sweet negligence, unheeded bait of love!
OVID.

Ere on thy chin the springing beard began
To spread a doubtful down, and promise man.
PRIOR.

The hoary beard is a crown of glory if it be found in the way of righteousness.
Proverbs. XVI. 31.

Ah, thy beautiful hair! so was it once braided for me, for me;
Now for death is it crowned, only for death, lover and lord of thee.
SWINBURNE—*Choriambics*.

HAND

For through the South the custom still commands
The gentleman to kiss the lady's hands.
BYRON—*Don Juan*.

His hand will be against every man, and every man's hand against him.
Genesis. XVI. 12.

The voice is Jacob's voice, but the hands are the hands of Esau.
Genesis. XXVII. 22.

Let not thy left hand know what thy right hand doeth.
Matthew. VI. 3.

'Twas a hand
White, delicate, dimpled, warm, languid, and bland.
The hand of a woman is often, in youth,
Somewhat rough, somewhat red, somewhat graceless in truth;
Does its beauty refine, as its pulses grow calm,
Or as sorrow has crossed the life line in the palm?
OWEN MEREDITH—*Lucile*.

We bear it calmly, though a ponderous woe,
And still adore the hand that gives the blow.
JOHN POMFRET.

They may seize
On the white wonder of dear Juliet's hand.
SHAKESPEARE—*Romeo and Juliet*. Act III. Sc. 3.

God looks at pure, not full, hands.
SYRUS.

HAPPINESS

'Twas a jolly old pedagogue, long ago,
Tall and slender, and sallow and dry;
His form was bent, and his gait was slow,
His long thin hair was white as snow,
But a wonderful twinkle shone in his eye.
And he sang every night as he went to bed,
"Let us be happy down here below;
The living should live, though the dead be dead,"
Said the jolly old pedagogue long ago.
GEORGE ARNOLD—*The Jolly Old Pedagogue*.

Real happiness is cheap enough, yet how dearly we pay for its counterfeit.
HOSEA BALLOU.

The greatest happiness of the greatest number.
BECCARIA.

. . . all who joy would win
Must share it,—Happiness was born a twin.
BYRON—*Don Juan.*

We think a happy life consists in tranquillity of mind.
CICERO.

If solid happiness we prize,
Within our breast this jewel lies,
And they are fools who roam;
The world has nothing to bestow,
From our own selves our bliss must flow,
And that dear hut,—our home.
NATHANIEL COTTON—*The Fireside.*

Happiness lies, first of all, in health.
GEORGE WILLIAM CURTIS.

Who is the happiest of men? He who values the merits of others,
And in their pleasure takes joy, even as though t'were his own.
GOETHE.

The loss of wealth is loss of dirt,
As sages in all times assert;
The happy man's without a shirt.
JOHN HEYWOOD—*Be Merry Friends.*

Happiness grows at our own firesides, and is not to be picked in strangers' gardens.
DOUGLAS JERROLD.

One kind of happiness is to know exactly at what point to be miserable.
LA ROCHEFOUCAULD.

We are never so happy, nor so unhappy, as we suppose ourselves to be.
LA ROCHEFOUCAULD.

We are no longer happy so soon as we wish to be happier.
LANDOR.

What happiness is there which is not purchased with more or less of pain?
MRS. OLIPHANT.

Before he is dead and buried no one ought to be called happy.
OVID.

Fix'd to no spot is Happiness sincere;
'Tis nowhere to be found, or ev'rywhere;
'Tis never to be bought, but always free.
POPE—*Essay on Man.*

Every one speaks of it, few know it.
MME. ROLAND.

The secret of happiness is this: let your interests be as wide as possible, and let your reactions to the things and persons that interest you be as far as possible friendly rather than hostile.
BERTRAND RUSSELL—*The Conquest of Happiness.*

How bitter a thing it is to look into happiness through another man's eyes!
SHAKESPEARE—*As You Like It.* Act V. Sc. 2.

Ye seek for happiness—alas, the day!
Ye find it not in luxury nor in gold,
Nor in the fame, nor in the envied sway
For which, O willing slaves to Custom old,
Severe taskmistress! ye your hearts have sold.
SHELLEY—*Revolt of Islam.*

Wealth I ask not, hope nor love,
Nor a friend to know me;
All I ask, the heavens above,
And the road below me.
STEVENSON—*The Vagabond.*

Man is the artificer of his own happiness.
HENRY D. THOREAU.

Happiness is a good that Nature sells us.
VOLTAIRE.

We're charm'd with distant views of happiness,
But near approaches make the prospect less.
THOMAS YALDEN.

HARVEST

For now, the corn house filled, the harvest home,
Th' invited neighbors to the husking come;

A frolic scene, where work and mirth and play
Unite their charms to cheer the hours away.
JOEL BARLOW—*The Hasty Pudding.*

He that observeth the wind shall not sow; and he that regardeth the clouds shall not reap.
Ecclesiastes. XI. 4.

In the morning sow thy seed, and in the evening withhold not thine hand.
Ecclesiastes. XI. 6.

Whatsoever a man soweth, that shall he also reap.
Galatians. VI. 7.

The harvest truly is plenteous, but the labourers are few.
Matthew. IX. 37.

Who eat their corn while yet 'tis green,
At the true harvest can but glean.
SAADI—*Gulistan.*

HASTE

The more haste, ever the worst speed.
CHARLES CHURCHILL—*The Ghost.*

Fraud and deceit are ever in a hurry. Take time for all things. Great haste makes great waste.
FRANKLIN.

Hurry is only admissible in catching flies.
HALIBURTON.

Haste is of the Devil.
The Koran.

Too great haste leads us to error.
MOLIÈRE.

Stand not upon the order of your going,
But go at once.
SHAKESPEARE—*Macbeth.* Act III. Sc. 4.

He tires betimes that spurs too fast betimes;
With eager feeding food doth choke the feeder.
SHAKESPEARE—*Richard II.* Act II. Sc. 1.

Wisely, and slow; they stumble that run fast.
SHAKESPEARE—*Romeo and Juliet.* Act II. Sc. 3.

HATE

To harbor hatred and animosity in the soul makes one irritable, gloomy, and prematurely old.
AUERBACH.

Now hatred is by far the longest pleasure;
Men love in haste, but they detest at leisure.
BYRON—*Don Juan.*

Whosoever hateth his brother is a murderer.
I John. III. 15.

I like a good hater.
SAMUEL JOHNSON.

But I do hate him as I hate the devil.
BEN JONSON—*Every Man Out of His Humour.*

Life is too short to spare an hour of it in the indulgence of this evil passion.
LAMARTINE.

The hatred we bear our enemies injures their happiness less than our own.
J. PETIT-SENN.

In time we hate that which we often fear.
SHAKESPEARE—*Antony and Cleopatra.* Act I. Sc. 3.

The hatred of relatives is the most violent.
TACITUS.

People hate, as they love, unreasonably.
THACKERAY.

HEALTH

Health and cheerfulness mutually beget each other.
ADDISON—*The Spectator.*

He who has health has hope, and he who has hope has everything.
Arabian Proverb.

Refuse to be ill. Never tell people you are ill; never own it to yourself. Illness is one of those things which a man should resist on principle at the onset.

Bulwer-Lytton.

Health is not a condition of matter, but of Mind.

Mary Baker Eddy—*Science and Health.*

The first wealth is health.

Emerson—*The Conduct of Life.*

Nor love, nor honour, wealth nor pow'r,
Can give the heart a cheerful hour
When health is lost. Be timely wise;
With health all taste of pleasure flies.

Gay.

A cool mouth, and warm feet, live long.

Herbert.

Our prayers should be for a sound mind in a healthy body.

Juvenal.

Preserving the health by too strict a regimen is a wearisome malady.

La Rochefoucauld.

Health lies in labor, and there is no royal road to it but through toil.

Wendell Phillips.

It is part of the cure to wish to be cured.

Seneca.

The fate of a nation has often depended on the good or bad digestion of a prime minister.

Voltaire.

Look to your health; and if you have it, praise God, and value it next to a good conscience.

Izaak Walton.

HEARING

None so deaf as those that will not hear.

Matthew Henry—*Commentaries.* Psalm LVIII.

Little pitchers have wide ears.

George Herbert—*Jacula Prudentum.*

Went in at the one ear and out at the other.

Heywood—*Proverbs.*

We have two ears and only one tongue in order that we may hear more and speak less.

Diogenes Laertius.

He that hath ears to hear, let him hear.

Mark. IV. 9.

Where more is meant than meets the ear.

Milton—*Il Penseroso.*

Friends, Romans, countrymen, lend me your ears.

Shakespeare—*Julius Caesar.* Act III. Sc. 2.

HEART

My heart's in the Highlands, my heart is not here;
My heart's in the Highlands a-chasing the deer.

Robert Burns.

Maid of Athens, ere we part,
Give, oh, give me back my heart!

Byron—*Maid of Athens.*

Soul of fibre and heart of oak.

Cervantes—*Don Quixote.*

Some hearts are hidden, some have not a heart.

Crabbe—*The Borough.*

My peace is gone, my heart is heavy.

Goethe—*Faust.*

A wounded heart can with difficulty be cured.

Goethe—*Torquato Tasso.*

Some people's hearts are shrunk in them, like dried nuts. You can hear 'em rattle as they walk.

Douglas Jerrold.

I caused the widow's heart to sing for joy.

Job. XXIX. 13.

Let not your heart be troubled.

John. XIV. 1.

Still stands thine ancient sacrifice—
An humble and a contrite heart.

Kipling—*Recessional.*

All who know their own minds know not their own hearts.
La Rochefoucauld.

The head is always the dupe of the heart.
La Rochefoucauld.

For his heart was in his work, and the heart
Giveth grace unto every Art.
Longfellow—*The Building of the Ship.*

No one is so accursed by fate,
No one so utterly desolate,
But some heart, though unknown,
Responds unto his own.
Longfellow—*Endymion.*

Where your treasure is, there will your heart be also.
Matthew. VI. 21.

But the beating of my own heart
Was all the sound I heard.
Richard Monckton Milnes—*The Brookside.*

And when once the young heart of a maiden is stolen,
The maiden herself will steal after it soon.
Moore—*Ill Omens.*

Oh, the heart is a free and a fetterless thing,—
A wave of the ocean, a bird on the wing.
Julia Pardoe—*The Captive Greek Girl.*

Hearts are stronger than swords.
Wendell Phillips.

The heart knoweth his own bitterness.
Proverbs. XIV. 10.

A merry heart maketh a cheerful countenance.
Proverbs. XV. 13.

He that is of a merry heart hath a continual feast.
Proverbs. XV. 15.

A man's heart deviseth his way; but the Lord directeth his steps.
Proverbs. XVI. 9.

He fashioneth their hearts alike.
Psalms. XXXIII. 15.

My heart is like a singing bird
Whose nest is in a water'd shoot;
My heart is like an apple-tree
Whose boughs are bent with thick-set fruit;
My heart is like a rainbow shell
That paddles in a halcyon sea;
My heart is gladder than all these,
Because my love is come to me.
Christina G. Rossetti—*A Birthday.*

It is always a poor way of reading the hearts of others to try to conceal our own.
Rousseau—*Confessions.*

It is not flesh and blood but the heart which makes us fathers and sons.
Schiller.

But I will wear my heart upon my sleeve
For daws to peck at; I am not what I am.
Shakespeare—*Othello.* Act I. Sc. 1.

Worse than a bloody hand is a hard heart.
Shelley—*The Cenci.*

My heart, the bird of the wilderness, has found its sky in your eyes.
Tagore—*The Gardener.*

Never morning wore
To evening, but some heart did break.
Tennyson—*In Memoriam.*

Tears may be dried up, but the heart never.
Marguerite de Valois.

The mouth obeys poorly when the heart murmurs.
Voltaire.

HEAVEN

Now he [Nebridius] lives in Abraham's bosom.
St. Augustine—*Confessions.*

Heaven will be inherited by every man who has heaven in his soul.
Henry Ward Beecher.

In hope to merit Heaven by making earth a Hell.
Byron—*Childe Harold.*

The road to heaven lies as near by water as by land.
JEREMY COLLIER.

Heaven means to be one with God.
CONFUCIUS.

And so upon this wise I prayed,—
Great Spirit, give to me
A heaven not so large as yours
But large enough for me.
EMILY DICKINSON—*A Prayer.*

Heaven without good society cannot be heaven.
THOMAS FULLER.

Nothing is farther than earth from heaven; nothing is nearer than heaven to earth.
HARE.

Eye hath not seen it, my gentle boy!
Ear hath not heard its deep songs of joy;
Dreams cannot picture a world so fair—
Sorrow and death may not enter there;
Time doth not breathe on its fadeless bloom,
For beyond the clouds, and beyond the tomb,
It is there, it is there, my child!
FELICIA D. HEMANS—*The Better Land.*

All this, and Heaven too!
PHILIP HENRY.

You will eat bye and bye
In that glorious land above the sky;
Work and pray, live on hay,
You'll get pie in the sky when you die.
JOE HILL—*The Preacher and the Slave.*

There the wicked cease from troubling, and there the weary be at rest.
Job. III. 17.

In my father's house are many mansions.
John. XIV. 2.

When Christ ascended
Triumphantly from star to star
He left the gates of Heaven ajar.
LONGFELLOW—*Golden Legend.*

Lay up for yourselves treasures in heaven.
Matthew. VI. 20.

Love lent me wings; my path was like a stair;
A lamp unto my feet, that sun was given;
And death was safety and great joy to find;
But dying now, I shall not climb to Heaven.
MICHELANGELO—*Sonnet.*

A heaven on earth.
MILTON—*Paradise Lost.*

The hasty multitude
Admiring enter'd, and the work some praise,
And some the architect: his hand was known
In heaven by many a tower'd structure high,
Where scepter'd angels held their residence,
And sat as princes.
MILTON—*Paradise Lost.*

Earth has no sorrow that heaven cannot heal.
MOORE.

A Persian's Heaven is eas'ly made,
'Tis but black eyes and lemonade.
MOORE—*Intercepted Letters.*

The way to heaven out of all places is of like length and distance.
SIR THOMAS MORE—*Utopia.*

Heav'n but the Vision of fulfill'd Desire.
And Hell the Shadow from a Soul on fire.
OMAR KHAYYÁM—*Rubaiyat.*

A day in thy courts is better than a thousand. I had rather be a doorkeeper in the house of my God than to dwell in the tents of wickedness.
Psalms. LXXXIV. 10.

The blessed Damozel lean'd out
From the gold bar of Heaven:
Her eyes knew more of rest and shade
Of waters still'd at even;
She had three lilies in her hand,
And the stars in her hair were seven.
ROSSETTI—*The Blessed Damozel.*

Who seeks for Heaven alone to save his soul
May keep the path, but will not reach the goal;
While he who walks in love may wander far,
Yet God will bring him where the blessed are.
HENRY VAN DYKE—*Story of the Other Wise Man.*

So all we know of what they do above
Is that they happy are, and that they love.
EDMUND WALLER—*On the Death of Lady Rich.*

There is a land of pure delight,
Where saints immortal reign;
Infinite day excludes the night,
And pleasures banish pain.
ISAAC WATTS—*Hymns and Spiritual Songs.*

HELL

Hell is truth seen too late.
H. G. ADAMS.

He fashioned hell for the inquisitive.
ST. AUGUSTINE—*Confessions.*

Hell is the wrath of God—His hate of sin.
BAILEY—*Festus.*

Hell is paved with good intentions.
Attributed to ST. BERNARD OF CLAIRVAUX.

Nor ear can hear nor tongue can tell
The tortures of that inward hell!
BYRON—*The Giaour.*

No hell will frighten men away from sin; no dread of prospective misery; only goodness can cast hell out of any man, and set up the kingdom of heaven within.
HUGH R. HAWEIS.

Hell from beneath is moved for thee to meet thee at thy coming.
Isaiah. XIV. 9.

The dreadful fear of hell is to be driven out, which disturbs the life of man and renders it miserable, overcasting all things with the blackness of darkness, and leaving no pure, unalloyed pleasure.
LUCRETIUS—*De Rerum Natura.*

A dungeon horrible, on all sides round,
As one great furnace, flamed; yet from those flames
No light, but rather darkness visible
Serv'd only to discover sights of woe,
Regions of sorrow, doleful shades, where peace
And rest can never dwell, hope never comes
That comes to all; but torture without end.
MILTON—*Paradise Lost.*

All hell broke loose.
MILTON—*Paradise Lost.*

Myself am Hell;
And, in the lowest deep, a lower deep,
Still threat'ning to devour me, opens wide;
To which the hell I suffer seems a heaven.
MILTON—*Paradise Lost.*

The cunning livery of hell.
SHAKESPEARE—*Measure for Measure.* Act III. Sc. 1.

I think the devil will not have me damned, lest the oil that's in me should set hell on fire.
SHAKESPEARE—*Merry Wives of Windsor.* Act V. Sc. 5.

If there is no Hell, a good many preachers are obtaining money under false pretenses.
WILLIAM A. SUNDAY.

Self-love and the love of the world constitute hell.
SWEDENBORG—*Apocalypse Explained.*

In the throat
Of Hell, before the very vestibule
Of opening Orcus, sit Remorse and Grief,
And pale Disease, and sad Old Age and Fear,
And Hunger that persuades to crime, and Want:
Forms terrible to see. Suffering and Death

Inhabit here, and Death's own brother
Sleep;
And the mind's evil lusts and deadly
War,
Lie at the threshold, and the iron
beds
Of the Eumenides; and Discord wild
Her viper-locks with bloody fillets
bound.
VERGIL—*Aeneid.*

That's the greatest torture souls feel
in hell,
In hell, that they must live, and can-
not die.
JOHN WEBSTER—*Duchess of Malfi.*
Act IV. Sc. 1.

HELP

To the man who himself strives earnestly, God also lends a helping hand.
AESCHYLUS.

If I can stop one heart from breaking,
I shall not live in vain;
If I can ease one life the aching,
Or cool one pain,
Or help one fainting robin
Into his nest again,
I shall not live in vain.
EMILY DICKINSON—*Life.*

Light is the task when many share the toil.
HOMER—*Iliad.*

Make two grins grow where there was only a grouch before.
ELBERT HUBBARD—*Pig-Pen Pete.*

Truths would you teach, or save a
sinking land?
All fear, none aid you, and few understand.
POPE—*Essay on Man.*

In man's most dark extremity
Oft succor dawns from Heaven.
SCOTT—*Lord of the Isles.*

Help me, Cassius, or I sink!
SHAKESPEARE—*Julius Caesar.* Act I.
Sc. 2.

God helps those who help themselves.
ALGERNON SIDNEY.

HERO

If Hero mean *sincere man,* why may not every one of us be a Hero?
CARLYLE—*Heroes and Hero-Worship.*

He's of stature somewhat low—
Your hero always should be tall, you
know.
CHURCHILL—*The Rosciad.*

No man is a hero to his valet.
MME. CORNUEL.

Every hero becomes a bore at last.
EMERSON.

The hero is not fed on sweets,
Daily his own heart he eats;
Chambers of the great are jails,
And head-winds right for royal sails.
EMERSON—*Essays.*

Each man is a hero and an oracle to somebody, and to that person whatever he says has an enhanced value.
EMERSON—*Letters and Social Aims.*

But to the hero, when his sword
Has won the battle for the free,
Thy voice sounds like a prophet's
word,
And in its hollow tones are heard
The thanks of millions yet to be.
FITZ-GREENE HALLECK—*Marco Bozzaris.*

The boy stood on the burning deck
Whence all but him had fled;
The flame that lit the battle's wreck,
Shone round him o'er the dead.
FELICIA D. HEMANS—*Casabianca.*

Hail, Columbia! happy land!
Hail, ye heroes! heaven-born band!
Who fought and bled in Freedom's
cause.
JOSEPH HOPKINSON—*Hail, Columbia!*

The idol of to-day pushes the hero of yesterday out of our recollection; and will, in turn, be supplanted by his successor of to-morrow.
WASHINGTON IRVING—*The Sketch Book.*

The heroes of literary history have been no less remarkable for what they have suffered than for what they have achieved.

Samuel Johnson.

Still the race of hero spirits pass the lamp from hand to hand.

Kingsley—*The World's Age.*

See the conquering hero comes!
Sound the trumpets, beat the drums!

Dr. Thomas Morell.

Take away ambition and vanity, and where will be your heroes or patriots?

Seneca.

HISTORY

History is something that never happened, written by a man who wasn't there.

Anonymous.

Happy is the nation without a history.

Beccaria.

The economic interpretation of history does not necessarily mean that all events are determined solely by economic forces. It simply means that economic facts are the ever recurring decisive forces, the chief points in the process of history.

Edward Bernstein—*Evolutionary Socialism.*

History is a pageant, not a philosophy.

Augustine Birrell.

And history with all her volumes vast,
Hath but *one* page.

Byron—*Childe Harold.*

Histories are as perfect as the Historian is wise, and is gifted with an eye and a soul.

Carlyle—*Cromwell's Letters and Speeches.*

In a certain sense all men are historians.

Carlyle—*Essays.*

History, a distillation of rumor.

Carlyle—*French Revolution.*

History is the witness of the times, the torch of truth, the life of memory, the teacher of life, the messenger of antiquity.

Cicero.

What more would you have? He has invented history.

Madame Du Deffand of Voltaire.

Assassination has never changed the history of the world.

Disraeli.

There is properly no history, only biography.

Emerson—*Essays.*

History is indeed little more than the register of the crimes, follies, and misfortunes of mankind.

Gibbon—*Decline and Fall of the Roman Empire.*

It is not the neutrals or the lukewarms who make history.

Adolf Hitler—*Speech, 1933.*

We must consider how very little history there is—I mean real, authentic history. That certain kings reigned and certain battles were fought, we can depend upon as true; but all the coloring, all the philosophy, of history is conjecture.

Samuel Johnson.

What is history but a fable agreed upon?

Napoleon.

What is public history but a register of the successes and disappointments, the vices, the follies, and the quarrels, of those who engage in contention for power?

Paley.

The historian is a prophet looking backwards.

Schlegel.

The principal office of history I take to be this: to prevent virtuous actions from being forgotten, and that evil words and deeds should fear an infamous reputation with posterity.

Tacitus.

All history is a lie!

Sir Robert Walpole.

HOLINESS

God attributes to place
No sanctity, if none be thither brought
By men who there frequent.
MILTON—*Paradise Lost.*

Whoso lives the holiest life
Is fittest far to die.
MARGARET J. PRESTON—*Ready.*

Holiness is the architectural plan upon which God buildeth up His living temple.
SPURGEON—*Gleanings among the Sheaves.*

HOME

No outward doors of a man's house can in general be broken open to execute any civil process; though in criminal cases the public safety supersedes the private.
BLACKSTONE.

My whinstone house my castle is,
I have my own four walls.
CARLYLE—*My Own Four Walls.*

There is no place more delightful than one's own fireside.
CICERO.

Home is home, though it be never so homely.
JOHN CLARKE—*Paroemiologia.*

For a man's house is his castle.
SIR EDWARD COKE.

I love it, I love it, and who shall dare
To chide me for loving that old arm-chair?
ELIZA COOK—*Old Arm-Chair.*

For the whole world, without a native home,
Is nothing but a prison of larger room.
COWLEY—*To the Bishop of Lincoln.*

He is happiest, be he king or peasant, who finds peace in his home.
GOETHE.

At night returning, every labour sped,
He sits him down, the monarch of a shed;
Smiles by his cheerful fire, and round surveys
His children's looks, that brighten at the blaze;
While his lov'd partner, boastful of her hoard,
Displays her cleanly platter on the board.
GOLDSMITH—*The Traveller.*

To Adam Paradise was home. To the good among his descendants home is paradise.
HARE.

The stately Homes of England,
How beautiful they stand!
Amidst their tall ancestral trees,
O'er all the pleasant land.
FELICIA D. HEMANS—*Homes of England.*

Peace and rest at length have come,
All the day's long toil is past;
And each heart is whispering, "Home,
Home at last!"
HOOD—*Home At Last.*

Stay, stay at home, my heart, and rest;
Home-keeping hearts are happiest,
For those that wander they know not where
Are full of trouble and full of care;
To stay at home is best.
LONGFELLOW—*Song.*

His home, the spot of earth supremely blest,
A dearer, sweeter spot than all the rest.
MONTGOMERY—*West Indies.*

Who has not felt how sadly sweet
The dream of home, the dream of home,
Steals o'er the heart, too soon to fleet,
When far o'er sea or land we roam?
MOORE—*The Dream of Home.*

'Mid pleasures and palaces though we may roam,
Be it ever so humble, there's no place like Home.
J. HOWARD PAYNE—*Home Sweet Home.*

The poorest man may in his cottage bid defiance to all the force of the Crown. It may be frail, its roof may shake; the wind may blow through it; the storms may enter,—the rain may enter,—but the King of England cannot enter; all his forces dare not cross the threshold of the ruined tenement!

WILLIAM PITT (Earl of Chatham).

Home is where the heart is.

PLINY.

Home makes the man.

SAMUEL SMILES.

HONESTY

Honesty is the best policy.

CERVANTES—*Don Quixote.*

Everything that thou reprovest in another, thou must most carefully avoid in thyself.

CICERO.

When rogues fall out, honest men get into their own.

SIR MATTHEW HALE.

He that departs with his own honesty
For vulgar praise, doth it too dearly buy.

BEN JONSON.

Friends, if we be honest with ourselves, we shall be honest with each other.

GEORGE MACDONALD—*The Marquis of Lossie.*

An honest man's the noblest work of God.

POPE—*Essay on Man.*

Rich honesty dwells like a miser, sir, in a poor house; as your pearl in your foul oyster.

SHAKESPEARE—*As You Like It.* Act V. Sc. 4.

Ay, sir; to be honest, as this world goes, is to be one man picked out of ten thousand.

SHAKESPEARE—*Hamlet.* Act II. Sc. 2.

I hope I shall always possess firmness and virtue enough to maintain what I consider the most enviable of all titles, the character of an "Honest Man."

WASHINGTON—*Moral Maxims.*

"Honesty is the best policy," but he who acts on that principle is not an honest man.

ARCHBISHOP WHATELY—*Thoughts and Apothegms.*

HONOR

Better to die ten thousand deaths,
Than wound my honour.

ADDISON—*Cato.*

Dead on the field of honour.

Answer given in the roll-call of La Tour d'Auvergne's *regiment after his death.*

When about to commit a base deed, respect thyself, though there is no witness.

AUSONIUS.

Honor lies in honest toil.

GROVER CLEVELAND.

These were honoured in their generations, and were the glory of the times.

Ecclesiasticus. XLIV. 7.

Give me, kind Heaven, a private station,
A mind serene for contemplation:
Title and profit I resign;
The post of honor shall be mine.

GAY.

For titles do not reflect honor on men, but rather men on their titles.

MACHIAVELLI.

Honour is not won,
Until some honourable deed be done.

MARLOWE—*Hero and Leander.*

When honor comes to you be ready to take it;
But reach not to seize it before it is near.

JOHN BOYLE O'REILLY—*Rules of the Road.*

Honour and shame from no condition rise;
Act well your part, there all the honour lies.

POPE—*Essay on Man.*

But without money honor is nothing but a malady.

RACINE.

What he feels and not what he does honors a man.
SCHILLER.

For Brutus is an honourable man;
So are they all, all honourable men.
SHAKESPEARE—*Julius Caesar.* Act III. Sc. 2.

Let none presume
To wear an undeserv'd dignity.
O, that estates, degrees and offices
Were not deriv'd corruptly, and that clear honour
Were purchas'd by the merit of the wearer!
SHAKESPEARE—*Merchant of Venice.* Act II. Sc. 9.

The nation's honor is dearer than the nation's comfort; yes, than the nation's life itself.
WOODROW WILSON.

HOPE

Hope springs exulting on triumphant wing.
BURNS—*Cotter's Saturday Night.*

Auspicious Hope! in thy sweet garden grow
Wreaths for each toil, a charm for every woe.
CAMPBELL—*Pleasures of Hope.*

To the sick, while there is life there is hope.
CICERO.

Hope! of all ills that men endure,
The only cheap and universal cure.
ABRAHAM COWLEY—*The Mistress.*

Abandon hope, all ye who enter here.
DANTE—*Inferno.*

A woman's hopes are woven of sunbeams; a shadow annihilates them.
GEORGE ELIOT.

Hope, like the gleaming taper's light,
Adorns and cheers our way;
And still, as darker grows the night,
Emits a brighter ray.
GOLDSMITH—*The Captivity.*

Youth fades; love droops, the leaves of friendship fall;
A mother's secret hope outlives them all.
HOLMES—*A Mother's Secret.*

So, when dark thoughts my boding spirit shroud,
Sweet Hope! celestial influence round me shed
Waving thy silver pinions o'er my head.
KEATS—*Hope.*

Hope, deceitful as it is, serves at least to lead us to the end of life along an agreeable road.
LA ROCHEFOUCAULD.

You ask what hope is. He [Aristotle] says it is a waking dream.
DIOGENES LAERTIUS.

Hope says to us constantly, "Go on, go on," and leads us thus to the grave.
MME. DE MAINTENON.

Oh! ever thus, from childhood's hour,
I've seen my fondest hopes decay;
I never loved a tree or flower,
But 'twas the first to fade away.
MOORE—*Lalla Rookh.*

The Worldly Hope men set their Hearts upon
Turns Ashes—or it prospers; and anon,
Like Snow upon the Desert's dusty Face,
Lighting a little hour or two—is gone.
OMAR KHAYYÁM—*Rubaiyat.*

Hope springs eternal in the human breast;
Man never *is,* but always *to be* blest.
POPE—*Essay on Man.*

Hope deferred maketh the heart sick.
Proverbs. XIII. 12.

Who against hope believed in hope.
Romans. IV. 18.

The sickening pang of hope deferr'd.
SCOTT—*Lady of the Lake.*

But hope will make thee young, for Hope and Youth
Are children of one mother, even Love.
SHELLEY—*Revolt of Islam.*

Hope is the poor man's bread.
THALES.

For the living there is hope, for the dead there is none.
THEOCRITUS.

Hope ever urges on, and tells us to-morrow will be better.
TIBULLUS.

Behind the cloud the starlight lurks,
Through showers the sunbeams fall;
For God, who loveth all his works,
Has left his Hope with all.
WHITTIER—*Dream of Summer.*

Hope tells a flattering tale,
Delusive, vain and hollow.
Ah! let not hope prevail,
Lest disappointments follow.
MISS WROTHER—In *The Universal Songster.*

Prisoners of hope.
Zechariah. IX. 12.

HORSE

Gamaun is a dainty steed,
Strong, black, and of a noble breed,
Full of fire, and full of bone,
With all his line of fathers known;
Fine his nose, his nostrils thin,
But blown abroad by the pride within;
His mane is like a river flowing,
And his eyes like embers glowing
In the darkness of the night,
And his pace as swift as light.
"BARRY CORNWALL"—*The Blood Horse.*

You may lead a horse to water but you can't make him drink.
English Proverb.

An two men ride on a horse, one must ride behind.
SHAKESPEARE—*Much Ado about Nothing.* Act III. Sc. 1.

A horse! a horse! my kingdom for a horse!
SHAKESPEARE—*Richard III.* Act V. Sc. 4.

HOSPITALITY

It is not the quantity of the meat, but the cheerfulness of the guests which makes the feast.
CLARENDON.

Let not the emphasis of hospitality lie in bed and board; but let truth and love and honor and courtesy flow in all thy deeds.
EMERSON.

Let me live in my house by the side of the road,
Where the race of men go by;
They are good, they are bad; they are weak, they are strong,
Wise, foolish,—so am I;
Then why should I sit in the scorner's seat,
Or hurl the cynic's ban?
Let me live in my house by the side of the road,
And be a friend to man.
SAM WALTER FOSS—*House by the Side of the Road.*

For 't is always fair weather
When good fellows get together
With a stein on the table and a good song ringing clear.
RICHARD HOVEY—*Spring.*

Oh that I had in the wilderness a lodging-place of wayfaring men!
Jeremiah. IX. 2.

For I, who hold sage Homer's rule the best,
Welcome the coming, speed the going guest.
POPE.

HUMANITY

Our humanity were a poor thing but for the divinity that stirs within us.
BACON.

There is a book into which some of us are happily led to look, and to look again, and never tire of looking. It is the Book of Man. You may open that book whenever and wherever you find another human voice to answer yours, and another human hand to take in your own.

WALTER BESANT.

I love my country better than my family; but I love humanity better than my country.

FÉNELON.

W'en you see a man in woe,
Walk right up and say "hullo."
Say "hullo" and "how d'ye do,"
"How's the world a-usin' you?"

SAM WALTER FOSS—*Hullo*.

He held his seat; a friend to human race.

HOMER—*Iliad*.

Oh, God! that bread should be so dear,
And flesh and blood so cheap!

HOOD—*Song of a Shirt*.

Christianity is the highest perfection of humanity.

SAMUEL JOHNSON.

Every human heart is human.

LONGFELLOW—*Hiawatha*.

Laborin' man an' laborin' woman
Hev one glory an' one shame;
Ev'ythin' thet's done inhuman
Injers all on 'em the same.

LOWELL—*The Biglow Papers*.

It is good to be often reminded of the inconsistency of human nature, and to learn to look without wonder or disgust on the weaknesses which are found in the strongest minds.

MACAULAY—*Warren Hastings*.

Humanity is the Son of God.

THEODORE PARKER.

I am not an Athenian, nor a Greek, but a citizen of the world.

SOCRATES.

The age of chivalry has gone; the age of humanity has come.

CHARLES SUMNER.

I am a man; I count nothing human foreign to me.

TERENCE.

For nothing human foreign was to him.

THOMSON—*To the Memory of Lord Talbot*.

For the interesting and inspiring thing about America, gentlemen, is that she asks nothing for herself except what she has a right to ask for humanity itself.

WOODROW WILSON.

HUMAN NATURE

As there is much beast and some devil in man, so is there some angel and some God in him. The beast and the devil may be conquered, but in this life never wholly destroyed.

COLERIDGE.

In so complex a thing as human nature, we must consider it is hard to find rules without exception.

GEORGE ELIOT.

It is the talent of human nature to run from one extreme to another.

SWIFT.

HUMILITY

Some one called Sir Richard Steele the "vilest of mankind," and he retorted with proud humility, "It would be a glorious world if I were."

BOVEE.

Humility is the root, mother, nurse, foundation, and bond of all virtue.

ST. CHRYSOSTOM.

Humility is the solid foundation of all the virtues.

CONFUCIUS.

'Umble we are, 'umble we have been, 'umble we shall ever be.

DICKENS—*David Copperfield*.

After crosses and losses, men grow humbler and wiser.

FRANKLIN.

In humility imitate Jesus and Socrates.

FRANKLIN.

Humble things become the humble.

HORACE.

God hath sworn to lift on high
Who sinks himself by true humility.

KEBLE—*Miscellaneous Poems*.

One may be humble out of pride.
MONTAIGNE.

Fairest and best adorned is she
Whose clothing is humility.
MONTGOMERY—*Humility.*

I was not born for Courts or great affairs;
I pay my debts, believe, and say my pray'rs.
POPE—*Prologue to Satires.*

I believe the first test of a truly great man is his humility.
JOHN RUSKIN.

Humility is to make a right estimate of one's self. It is no humility for a man to think less of himself than he ought, though it might rather puzzle him to do that.
SPURGEON—*Gleanings among the Sheaves.*

Give place to your betters.
TERENCE.

HUMOR

Unconscious humor.
SAMUEL BUTLER—*Life and Habit.*

Humor has justly been regarded as the finest perfection of poetic genius.
CARLYLE—*Essays.*

Humor is the harmony of the heart.
DOUGLAS JERROLD.

Whenever you find Humor, you find Pathos close by its side.
WHIPPLE.

HUNGER

Hunger is sharper than the sword.
BEAUMONT AND FLETCHER.

Bone and Skin, two millers thin,
Would starve us all, or near it;
But be it known to Skin and Bone
That Flesh and Blood can't bear it.
JOHN BYROM—*Epigram on Two Monopolists.*

Better cross an angry man than a hungry man.
Danish Proverb.

Oliver Twist has asked for more.
DICKENS—*Oliver Twist.*

An empty stomach is not a good political adviser.
ALBERT EINSTEIN—*Cosmic Religion.*

The belly is the teacher of art and the bestower of genius.
PERSIUS—*Satires.*

A hungry people listens not to reason, nor cares for justice, nor is bent by any prayers.
SENECA.

Yond Cassius has a lean and hungry look.
SHAKESPEARE—*Julius Caesar.* Act I. Sc. 2.

HUSBAND

All husbands are alike, but they have different faces so you can tell them apart.
ANONYMOUS.

A good husband is never the first to go to sleep at night or the last to awake in the morning.
BALZAC—*The Physiology of Marriage.*

But O ye lords of ladies intellectual,
Inform us truly, have they not hen-pecked you all?
BYRON—*Don Juan.*

A man should be taller, older, heavier, uglier, and hoarser than his wife.
E. W. HOWE—*Country Town Sayings.*

With thee goes
Thy husband, him to follow thou art bound;
Where he abides, think there thy native soil.
MILTON—*Paradise Lost.*

Men are April when they woo, December when they wed: maids are May when they are maids, but the sky changes when they are wives.
SHAKESPEARE—*As You Like It.* Act IV. Sc. 1.

HYPOCRISY

Saint abroad, and a devil at home.
BUNYAN—*Pilgrim's Progress.*

Be hypocritical, be cautious, be
Not what you *seem* but always what you *see.*
BYRON—*Don Juan.*

And prate and preach about what others prove,
As if the world and they were hand and glove.
COWPER—*Table Talk.*

Every man is a hypocrite.
FREDERICK IV.

A hypocrite is in himself both the archer and the mark, in all actions shooting at his own praise or profit.
FULLER—*The Holy and Profane States.*

The only vice that cannot be forgiven is hypocrisy. The repentance of a hypocrite is itself hypocrisy.
HAZLITT.

Hypocrites do the devil's drudgery in Christ's livery.
MATTHEW HENRY.

To live a life which is a perpetual falsehood is to suffer unknown tortures.
VICTOR HUGO.

Hypocrisy is the homage which vice renders to virtue.
LA ROCHEFOUCAULD.

For neither man nor angel can discern
Hypocrisy, the only evil that walks
Invisible, except to God alone,
By his permissive will, through heav'n and earth.
MILTON—*Paradise Lost.*

He was a man
Who stole the livery of the court of Heaven
To serve the Devil in.
POLLOCK—*Course of Time.*

Not he who scorns the Saviour's yoke
Should wear his cross upon the heart.
SCHILLER—*The Fight with the Dragon.*

O, what may man within him hide,
Though angel on the outward side!
SHAKESPEARE—*Measure for Measure.* Act III. Sc. 2.

When you see a man with a great deal of religion displayed in his shop window, you may depend upon it he keeps a very small stock of it within.
SPURGEON.

How inexpressible is the meanness of being a hypocrite! how horrible is it to be a mischievous and malignant hypocrite.
VOLTAIRE—*A Philosophical Dictionary.*

I hope you have not been leading a double life, pretending to be wicked and being really good all the time. That would be hypocrisy.
OSCAR WILDE—*Importance of Being Earnest.*

I

IDEALS

Be true to your own highest convictions.
WILLIAM ELLERY CHANNING.

God hides some ideal in every human soul. At some time in our life we feel a trembling, fearful longing to do some good thing. Life finds its noblest spring of excellence in this hidden impulse to do our best.
ROBERT COLLYER.

The ideal itself is but truth clothed in the forms of art.
OCTAVE FEUILLET.

What we need most is not so much to realize the ideal as to idealize the real.
F. H. HEDGE.

Every life has its actual blanks, which the ideal must fill up, or which else remain bare and profitless forever.
JULIA WARD HOWE.

All men need something to poetize and idealize their life a little—something which they value for more than its use, and which is a symbol of their emancipation from the mere materialism and drudgery of daily life.

THEODORE PARKER.

Freedom is only in the land of dreams, and the beautiful only blooms in song.

SCHILLER.

We build statues of snow, and weep to see them melt.

SCOTT.

IDEAS

The material universe exists only in the mind.

JONATHAN EDWARDS.

Ideas must work through the brains and the arms of good and brave men, or they are no better than dreams.

EMERSON.

A fixed idea ends in madness or heroism.

VICTOR HUGO.

No army can withstand the strength of an idea whose time has come.

VICTOR HUGO.

An idea, to be suggestive, must come to the individual with the force of a revelation.

WILLIAM JAMES—*The Varieties of Religious Experience.*

We live in an age in which superfluous ideas abound and essential ideas are lacking.

JOUBERT.

Ideas are pitiless.

LAMARTINE.

Ideas often flash across our minds more complete than we could make them after much labor.

LA ROCHEFOUCAULD.

Ideas go booming through the world louder than cannon. Thoughts are mightier than armies. Principles have achieved more victories than horsemen and chariots.

W. M. PAXTON.

To be fossilized is to be stagnant, unprogressive, dead, frozen into a solid. It is only liquid currents of thought that move men and the world.

WENDELL PHILLIPS.

Ideas are like beards: men do not have them until they grow up.

VOLTAIRE.

IDLENESS

Lost time is never found again.

AUGHEY.

Idleness is emptiness; the tree in which the sap is stagnant, remains fruitless.

HOSEA BALLOU.

Idleness is the holiday of fools.

CHESTERFIELD.

There is no remedy for time misspent;
No healing for the waste of idleness,
Whose very languor is a punishment
Heavier than active souls can feel or
guess.

AUBREY DE VERE.

Sloth makes all things difficult, but industry all easy; and he that riseth late must trot all day, and shall scarce overtake his business at night; while laziness travels so slowly that poverty soon overtakes him.

FRANKLIN.

Some people have a perfect genius for doing nothing, and doing it assiduously.

HALIBURTON.

What heart can think, or tongue express,
The harm that groweth of idleness?

JOHN HEYWOOD—*Idleness.*

That destructive siren, sloth, is ever to be avoided.

HORACE.

If idleness do not produce vice or malevolence, it commonly produces melancholy.

SYDNEY SMITH.

He is not only idle who does nothing, but he is idle who might be better employed.

SOCRATES.

Indolence is the sleep of the mind.
VAUVENARGUES.

For Satan finds some mischief still
For idle hands to do.
WATTS—*Against Idleness.*

IGNORANCE

I am not ashamed to confess that I am ignorant of what I do not know.
CICERO.

Ignorance never settles a question.
DISRAELI.

There is nothing more frightful than an active ignorance.
GOETHE.

Where ignorance is bliss,
'Tis folly to be wise.
GRAY—*On a Distant Prospect of Eton College.*

Ignorance, when voluntary, is criminal, and a man may be properly charged with that evil which he neglected or refused to learn how to prevent.
SAMUEL JOHNSON.

Ignorance is the mother of fear.
LORD KAMES.

Nothing is so dangerous as an ignorant friend; a wise enemy is worth more.
LA FONTAINE.

It is with narrow-souled people as with narrow-necked bottles—the less they have in them the more noise they make in pouring it out.
POPE.

From ignorance our comfort flows,
The only wretched are the wise.
PRIOR.

The more we study, we the more discover our ignorance.
SHELLEY.

Everything unknown is magnified.
TACITUS—*Agricola.*

. . . Where blind and naked Ignorance
Delivers brawling judgments, unashamed,
On all things all day long.
TENNYSON—*Idylls of the King.*

ILLUSION

A pleasant illusion is better than a harsh reality.
BOVEE.

Illusion and wisdom combined are the charm of life and art.
JOUBERT.

The loss of our illusions is the only loss from which we never recover.
OUIDA.

In youth we feel richer for every new illusion; in maturer years, for every one we lose.
MME. SWETCHINE.

Illusion is the first of all pleasures.
VOLTAIRE.

IMAGINATION

Thou hast the keys of Paradise, O just, subtle, and mighty opium!
DE QUINCEY—*Confessions of an Opium Eater.*

Imagination is more important than knowledge.
ALBERT EINSTEIN—*On Science.*

Science does not know its debt to imagination. Goethe did not believe that a great naturalist could exist without this faculty.
EMERSON.

There is nothing more fearful than imagination without taste.
GOETHE.

Seem'd washing his hands with invisible soap
In imperceptible water.
HOOD—*Miss Kilmansegg.*

He paints a dolphin in the woods, and a boar in the waves.
HORACE.

He who has imagination without learning has wings but no feet.
JOUBERT.

These are the gloomy comparisons of a disturbed imagination; the melancholy madness of poetry, without the inspiration.
JUNIUS.

When I could not sleep for cold
I had fire enough in my brain,
And builded with roofs of gold
My beautiful castles in Spain!
LOWELL—*Aladdin.*

The human race is governed by its imagination.
NAPOLEON.

Imagination without culture is crippled and moves slowly; but it can be pure imagination, and rich also, as folk-lore will tell the vainest.
OUIDA.

Imagination disposes of everything; it creates beauty, justice, and happiness, which is everything in this world.
PASCAL.

The lunatic, the lover and the poet
Are of imagination all compact.
SHAKESPEARE—*Midsummer Night's Dream.* Act V. Sc. 1.

And as imagination bodies forth
The forms of things unknown, the poet's pen
Turns them to shapes and gives to airy nothing
A local habitation and a name.
SHAKESPEARE—*Midsummer Night's Dream.* Act V. Sc. 1.

IMITATION

Imitation is the sincerest form of flattery.
COLTON.

Men are so constituted that everybody undertakes what he sees another successful in, whether he has aptitude for it or not.
GOETHE.

He who imitates what is evil always goes beyond the example that is set; on the contrary, he who imitates what is good always falls short.
GUICCIARDINI—*Storia d' Italia.*

Imitators are a slavish herd and fools in my opinion.
LA FONTAINE—*Clymène.*

A good imitation is the most perfect originality.
VOLTAIRE.

IMMORTALITY

Fish say, they have their Stream and Pond;
But is there anything Beyond?
RUPERT BROOKE—*Heaven.*

There is nothing strictly immortal, but immortality. Whatever hath no beginning may be confident of no end.
SIR THOMAS BROWNE.

If I stoop
Into a dark tremendous sea of cloud,
It is but for a time; I press God's lamp
Close to my breast; its splendor soon or late
Will pierce the gloom; I shall emerge one day.
BROWNING—*Paracelsus.*

What is human is immortal!
BULWER-LYTTON.

I have been dying for twenty years, now I am going to live.
JAMES DRUMMOND BURNS—*His Last Words.*

A good man never dies.
CALLIMACHUS.

Immortality is the glorious discovery of Christianity.
WILLIAM ELLERY CHANNING—*Immortality.*

No one could ever meet death for his country without the hope of immortality.
CICERO.

There may be beings, thinking beings, near or surrounding us, which we do not perceive, which we cannot imagine. We know very little; but, in my opinion, we know enough to hope for the immortality, the individual immortality, of the better part of man.
SIR HUMPHRY DAVY.

For I never have seen, and never shall see, that the cessation of the evidence of existence is necessarily evidence of the cessation of existence.
WILLIAM DE MORGAN—*Joseph Vance.*

Then shall the dust return to the earth as it was; and the spirit shall return unto God who gave it.
Ecclesiastes. XII. 7.

Oh, may I join the choir invisible
Of those immortal dead who live again.
GEORGE ELIOT—*The Choir Invisible*.

The hope of immortality makes heroes of cowards.
THOMAS GUTHRIE.

'Tis true; 'tis certain; man though dead retains
Part of himself; the immortal mind remains.
HOMER—*Iliad*.

The nearer I approach the end, the plainer I hear around me the immortal symphonies of the worlds which invite me. It is marvelous, yet simple.
VICTOR HUGO.

He ne'er is crowned with immortality
Who fears to follow where airy voices lead.
KEATS—*Endymion*.

Our hope of immortality does not come from any religions, but nearly all religions come from that hope.
INGERSOLL, 1879.

I long to believe in immortality. . . . If I am destined to be happy with you here—how short is the longest life. I wish to believe in immortality—I wish to live with you forever.
KEATS—*Letters to Fanny Brawne*.

And in the wreck of noble lives
Something immortal still survives.
LONGFELLOW—*The Building of the Ship*.

I came from God, and I'm going back to God, and I won't have any gaps of death in the middle of my life.
GEORGE MACDONALD—*Mary Marston*.

Of such as he was, there be few on earth;
Of such as he is, there are few in Heaven:
And life is all the sweeter that he lived,
And all he loved more sacred for his sake:
And Death is all the brighter that he died,
And Heaven is all the happier that he's there.
GERALD MASSEY—*In Memoriam for Earl Brownlow*.

They eat, they drink, and in communion sweet
Quaff immortality and joy.
MILTON—*Paradise Lost*.

And her immortal part with angels lives.
SHAKESPEARE—*Romeo and Juliet*. Act V. Sc. 1.

Ah, Christ, that it were possible,
For one short hour to see
The souls we loved, that they might tell us
What and where they be.
TENNYSON—*Maud*.

Never did Christ utter a single word attesting to a personal resurrection and a life beyond the grave.
TOLSTOY—*What I Believe*.

Go on and increase in valor, O boy! this is the path to immortality.
VERGIL—*Aeneid*.

Happy he whose inward ear
Angel comfortings can hear,
O'er the rabble's laughter;
And, while Hatred's fagots burn,
Glimpses through the smoke discern
Of the good hereafter.
WHITTIER—*Barclay of Ury*.

IMPATIENCE

I have not so great a struggle with my vices, great and numerous as they are, as I have with my impatience.
CALVIN.

Impatience dries the blood sooner than age or sorrow.
CHAPIN.

Nature is methodical, and doeth her work well. Time is never to be hurried.
EMERSON.

Procrastination is hardly more evil than grasping impatience.
KANT.

IMPOSSIBILITY

You cannot make a crab walk straight.
ARISTOPHANES.

It is not a lucky word, this same *impossible;* no good comes of those that have it so often in their mouth.
CARLYLE—*French Revolution.*

You can't get blood out of a turnip.
English Proverb.

You can't make a silk purse out of a sow's ear.
English Proverb.

Few things are impossible to diligence and skill.
SAMUEL JOHNSON—*Rasselas.*

Nothing is impossible; there are ways which lead to everything; and if we had sufficient will we should always have sufficient means.
LA ROCHEFOUCAULD.

Never let me hear that foolish word again.
MIRABEAU.

Impossible is a word only to be found in the dictionary of fools.
NAPOLEON.

To the timid and hesitating everything is impossible because it seems so.
SCOTT.

You cannot make, my Lord, I fear,
A velvet purse of a sow's ear.
JOHN WALCOT—*Lord B. and His Notions.*

IMPROVEMENT

It is necessary to try to surpass one's self always; this occupation ought to last as long as life.
QUEEN CHRISTINA.

Let us strive to improve ourselves, for we cannot remain stationary: one either progresses or retrogrades.
MME. DU DEFFAND.

People seldom improve when they have no other model but themselves to copy after.
GOLDSMITH.

Look up, and not down; look forward, and not back; look out, and not in; and lend a hand.
EDWARD EVERETT HALE.

To hear always, to think always, to learn always, it is thus that we live truly. He who aspires to nothing, who learns nothing, is not worthy of living.
HELPS.

Slumber not in the tents of your fathers. The world is advancing. Advance with it!
MAZZINI.

INCONSTANCY

I hate inconstancy—I loathe, detest,
Abhor, condemn, abjure the mortal made
Of such quicksilver clay that in his breast
No permanent foundation can be laid.
BYRON—*Don Juan.*

O, swear not by the moon, the inconstant moon,
That monthly changes in her circled orb,
Lest that thy love prove likewise variable.
SHAKESPEARE—*Romeo and Juliet.* Act II. Sc. 2.

I loved a lass, a fair one,
As fair as e'er was seen;
She was indeed a rare one,
Another Sheba queen:
But, fool as then I was,
I thought she loved me too:
But now, alas! she's left me,
Falero, lero, loo!
GEORGE WITHER—*I Loved a Lass.*

INCREDULITY

Some men will believe nothing but what they can comprehend; and there are but few things that such are able to comprehend.

St. Evremond.

Nothing is so contemptible as that affectation of wisdom, which some display, by universal incredulity.

Goldsmith.

Incredulity robs us of many pleasures, and gives us nothing in return.

Lowell.

Incredulity is the wisdom of a fool.

H. W. Shaw.

INDEPENDENCE

I never thrust my nose into other men's porridge. It is no bread and butter of mine: Every man for himself and God for us all.

Cervantes—*Don Quixote*.

All we ask is to be let alone.

Jefferson Davis—*First Message to the Confederate Congress, 1861*.

Can anything be so elegant as to have few wants, and to serve them one's self?

Emerson.

When in the course of human events, it becomes necessary for one people to dissolve the political bonds which have connected them with another, and to assume among the powers of the earth the separate and equal station to which the laws of nature and of nature's God entitle them, a decent respect to the opinions of mankind requires that they should declare the causes which impel them to the separation.

Jefferson—*Declaration of Independence*.

The whole trouble is that we won't let God help us.

George MacDonald—*The Marquis of Lossie*.

Voyager upon life's sea:—
To yourself be true,
And whate'er your lot may be,
Paddle your own canoe.

Dr. Edward P. Philpots—*Paddle Your Own Canoe*.

. . . but while
I breathe Heaven's air, and Heaven looks down on me,
And smiles at my best meanings, I remain
Mistress of mine own self and mine own soul.

Tennyson—*The Foresters*.

Hail! Independence, hail! Heaven's next best gift,
To that of life and immortal soul!

Thomson—*Liberty*.

I would rather sit on a pumpkin, and have it all to myself, than to be crowded on a velvet cushion.

Thoreau.

Injustice in the end produces independence.

Voltaire.

Independence *now:* and *independence forever*.

Daniel Webster.

INDIVIDUALITY

We move too much in platoons; we march by sections: we do not live in our vital individuality enough; we are slaves to fashion, in mind and in heart, if not to our passions and appetites.

Chapin.

An institution is the lengthened shadow of one man; as, monachism of the Hermit Anthony, the Reformation of Luther, Quakerism of Fox, Methodism of Wesley, abolition of Clarkson. Scipio, Milton called "the height of Rome"; and all history resolves itself easily into the biography of a few stout and earnest persons. Let a man, then, know his worth, and keep things under his feet.

Emerson.

Every individual has a place to fill in the world, and is important in some respect, whether he chooses to be so or not.

Hawthorne.

The epoch of individuality is concluded, and it is the duty of reformers to initiate the epoch of association

Collective man is omnipotent upon the earth he treads.

MAZZINI.

The worth of a state, in the long run, is the worth of the individuals composing it.

J. S. MILL.

INDOLENCE

A useless life is but an early death.

GOETHE.

Indolence is the devil's cushion.

SAMUEL JOHNSON.

Indolence and stupidity are first cousins.

RIVAROL.

INDUSTRY

The bread earned by the sweat of the brow is thrice blessed bread, and it is far sweeter than the tasteless loaf of idleness.

CROWQUILL.

Earnest, active industry is a living hymn of praise,—a never-failing source of happiness.

MME. DE WALD.

The more we do, the more we can do; the more busy we are, the more leisure we have.

HAZLITT.

Well for the drones of the social hive that there are bees of an industrious turn, willing, for an infinitesimal share of the honey, to undertake the labor of its fabrication.

HOOD.

In this theater of man's life, it is reserved only for God and angels to be lookers-on.

PYTHAGORAS.

INFLUENCE

The humblest individual exerts some influence, either for good or evil, upon others.

HENRY WARD BEECHER.

No human being can come into this world without increasing or diminishing the sum total of human happiness.

ELIHU BURRITT.

The work an unknown good man has done is like a vein of water flowing hidden underground, secretly making the ground green.

CARLYLE—*Essays.*

Be a pattern to others, and then all will go well; for as a whole city is affected by the licentious passions and vices of great men, so it is likewise reformed by their moderation.

CICERO.

He raised a mortal to the skies;
She drew an angel down.

DRYDEN—*Alexander's Feast.*

Blessed influence of one true loving human soul on another.

GEORGE ELIOT—*Janet's Repentance.*

O may I join the choir invisible
Of those immortal dead who live again
In minds made better by their presence; live
In pulses stirred to generosity,
In deeds of daring rectitude, in scorn
For miserable aims that end with self.
In thoughts sublime that pierce the night like stars,
And with their mild persistence urge man's search
To vaster issues.

GEORGE ELIOT.

Nor knowest thou what argument
Thy life to thy neighbor's creed has lent,
All are needed by each one;
Nothing is fair or good alone.

EMERSON—*Each and All.*

A little leaven leaveneth the whole lump.

Galatians. V. 9.

You can only make others better by being good yourself.

HUGH R. HAWEIS.

Our life's a flying shadow, God the pole,
The needle pointing to Him is our soul.
On a slab in Bishop Joceline's crypt in Glasgow Cathedral.

A woman is more influenced by what she divines than by what she is told.
NINON DE LENCLOS.

So when a great man dies,
For years beyond our ken,
The light he leaves behind him lies
Upon the paths of men.
LONGFELLOW—*Charles Sumner.*

No star ever rose or set without influence somewhere.
OWEN MEREDITH—*Lucile.*

If it were in my power, I would be wiser; but a newly felt power carries me off in spite of myself; love leads me one way, my understanding another.
OVID.

If the nose of Cleopatra had been shorter, the whole face of the earth would have been changed.
PASCAL—*Thoughts.*

Thou wert my guide, philosopher, and friend.
POPE—*Essay on Man.*

They are like the deaf adder that stoppeth her ear; which will not hearken to the voice of charmers, charming never so wisely.
Psalms. LVIII. 4, 5.

I am a part of all that I have met.
TENNYSON—*Ulysses.*

INGRATITUDE

Earth produces nothing worse than an ungrateful man.
AUSONIUS.

Brutes leave ingratitude to man.
COLTON.

That man may last, but never lives,
Who much receives, but nothing gives;
Whom none can love, whom none can thank,
Creation's blot, creation's blank.
THOMAS GIBBONS—*When Jesus Dwelt.*

A man is very apt to complain of the ingratitude of those who have risen far above him.
SAMUEL JOHNSON—*Boswell's Life of Johnson.*

Do you know what is more hard to bear than the reverses of fortune? It is the baseness, the hideous ingratitude, of man.
NAPOLEON.

Ingratitude dries up the fountain of all goodness.
RICHELIEU.

This was the most unkindest cut of all;
For when the noble Caesar saw him stab,
Ingratitude, more strong than traitor's arm,
Quite vanquish'd him; then burst his mighty heart;
And, in his mantle muffling up his face,
Even at the base of Pompey's statue,
Which all the while ran blood, great Caesar fell.
SHAKESPEARE—*Julius Caesar.* Act III. Sc. 2.

One ungrateful man does an injury to all who are in suffering.
SYRUS.

INJURY

The injury we do and the one we suffer are not weighed in the same scales.
AESOP—*Fables.*

Recompense injury with justice, and recompense kindness with kindness.
CONFUCIUS.

No man ever did a designed injury to another without doing a greater to himself.
HENRY HOME.

If an injury has to be done to a man it should be so severe that his vengeance need not be feared.

MACHIAVELLI—*The Prince.*

There is no ghost so difficult to lay as the ghost of an injury.

ALEXANDER SMITH.

INJUSTICE

There is but one blasphemy, and that is injustice.

INGERSOLL—*Speech, 1880.*

Extremists are seldom just.

PALEY.

He who commits injustice is ever made more wretched than he who suffers it.

PLATO.

A kingdom founded on injustice never lasts.

SENECA.

INN

You may go to Carlisle's and to Almack's too;
And I'll give you my Head if you find such a Host,
For Coffee, Tea, Chocolate, Butter, or Toast;
How he welcomes at once all the World and his Wife,
And how civil to Folks he ne'er saw in his Life.

ANSTEY—*New Bath Guide.*

He who has not been at a tavern knows not what a paradise it is.

ARETINO.

He who has not been at a tavern knows not what a paradise it is. O holy tavern! O miraculous tavern!—holy, because no carking cares are there, nor weariness, nor pain; and miraculous, because of the spits, which themselves turn round and round!

ARETINO—Quoted by Longfellow in *Hyperion.*

Where'er his fancy bids him roam,
In ev'ry Inn he finds a home.

WILLIAM COMBE—*Dr. Syntax in Search of the Picturesque.*

There is nothing which has yet been contrived by man, by which so much happiness is produced as by a good tavern or inn.

SAMUEL JOHNSON.

Souls of poets dead and gone,
What Elysium have ye known,
Happy field or mossy cavern,
Choicer than the Mermaid Tavern?

KEATS—*Mermaid Tavern.*

A region of repose it seems,
A place of slumber and of dreams.

LONGFELLOW—*Tales of a Wayside Inn.*

INNOCENCE

To see a world in a grain of sand,
And a heaven in a wild flower:
Hold infinity in the palm of your hand,
And eternity in an hour.

WILLIAM BLAKE—*Auguries of Innocence.*

As innocent as a new-laid egg.

W. S. GILBERT—*Engaged.*

They that know no evil will suspect none.

BEN JONSON.

We become innocent when we are unfortunate.

LA FONTAINE.

Innocence finds not near so much protection as guilt.

LA ROCHEFOUCAULD.

The innocence that feels no risk and is taught no caution is more vulnerable than guilt, and oftener assailed.

WILLIS.

INQUISITIVENESS

Shun the inquisitive person, for he is also a talker.

HORACE.

In ancient days the most celebrated precept was, "Know thyself"; in modern times it has been supplanted by the more fashionable maxim, "Know thy neighbor, and everything about him."

JOHNSON.

INSANITY

No excellent soul is exempt from a mixture of madness.
ARISTOTLE.

With curious art the brain, too finely wrought,
Preys on itself, and is destroyed by thought.
CHARLES CHURCHILL.

Much madness is divinest sense
To a discerning eye;
Much sense the starkest madness.
'Tis the majority
In this, as all, prevails
Assent, and you are sane;
Demur,—you're straightway dangerous,
And handled with a chain.
EMILY DICKINSON—*Poems*.

For those whom God to ruin has designed
He fits for fate, and first destroys their mind.
DRYDEN.

Mad as a March hare.
HALLIWELL—*Archaic Dict*.

I teach that all men are mad.
HORACE.

Who then is sane? He who is not a fool.
HORACE.

It is a common calamity; at some one time we have all been mad.
JOH. BAPTISTA MANTUANUS.

Insanity in individuals is something rare—but in groups, parties, nations, and epochs it is the rule.
NIETZSCHE.

My dear Sir, take any road, you can't go amiss. The whole state is one vast insane asylum.
JAMES L. PETIGRU.

That he is mad, 'tis true, 'tis true 'tis pity;
And pity 'tis 'tis true.
SHAKESPEARE—*Hamlet*. Act II. Sc. 2.

Though this be madness, yet there is method in 't.
SHAKESPEARE—*Hamlet*. Act II. Sc. 2.

Whom Jupiter would destroy he first drives mad.
SOPHOCLES—*Antigone*.

Insanity is not a distinct and separate empire; our ordinary life borders upon it, and we cross the frontier in some part of our nature.
TAINE.

INSPIRATION

No man was ever great without divine inspiration.
CICERO.

A writer is rarely so well inspired as when he talks about himself.
ANATOLE FRANCE.

Inspiration and genius—one and the same.
VICTOR HUGO.

Inspiration is solitary, never consecutive.
LAMARTINE.

INSTINCT

Instinct is untaught ability.
BAIN—*Senses and Intellect*.

Instinct is the nose of the mind.
MME. DE GIRARDIN.

A goose flies by a chart which the Royal Geographical Society could not improve.
HOLMES.

A bird sings, a child prattles, but it is the same hymn; hymn indistinct, inarticulate, but full of profound meaning.
VICTOR HUGO.

How instinct varies in the grov'lling swine,
Compar'd, half-reasoning elephant, with thine!
'Twixt that and reason what a nice barrier!
Forever sep'rate, yet forever near!
POPE—*Essay on Man*.

Instinct is intelligence incapable of self-consciousness.

JOHN STERLING.

Brutes find out where their talents lie: a bear will not attempt to fly.

SWIFT.

INSULT

It is very clear that one way to challenge insults is to submit to them.

AIMÉ-MARTIN.

He who allows himself to be insulted deserves to be so; and insolence, if unpunished, increases!

CORNEILLE.

The way to procure insults is to submit to them. A man meets with no more respect than he exacts.

HAZLITT.

What wilt thou do to thyself, who has added insult to injury?

PHAEDRUS.

If you speak insults you will hear them also.

PLAUTUS.

It is often better not to see an insult than to avenge it.

SENECA.

INTELLECT

God has placed no limit to intellect.

BACON.

Works of the intellect are great only by comparison with each other.

EMERSON—*Literary Ethics.*

If a man empties his purse into his head, no one can take it from him.

FRANKLIN.

Glorious indeed is the world of God around us, but more glorious the world of God within us. There lies the Land of Song; there lies the poet's native land.

LONGFELLOW—*Hyperion.*

In the scale of the destinies, brawn will never weigh so much as brain.

LOWELL.

INTEMPERANCE

All the crimes on earth do not destroy so many of the human race, nor alienate so much property, as drunkenness.

BACON.

Man, being reasonable, must get drunk;
The best of life is but intoxication:
Glory, the grape, love, gold, in these are sunk
The hopes of all men and of every nation;
Without their sap, how branchless were the trunk
Of life's strange tree, so fruitful on occasion:
But to return,—Get very drunk; and when
You wake with headache, you shall see what then.

BYRON—*Don Juan.*

A sensual and intemperate youth hands over a worn-out body to old age.

CICERO.

Gloriously drunk, obey the important call.

COWPER—*The Task.*

Then hasten to be drunk, the business of the day.

DRYDEN—*Cymon and Iphigenia.*

Petition me no petitions, Sir, to-day;
Let other hours be set apart for business,
To-day it is our pleasure to be drunk;
And this our queen shall be as drunk as we.

FIELDING—*Tom Thumb the Great.*

Bacchus has drowned more men than Neptune.

GARIBALDI.

What does drunkenness not accomplish? It discloses secrets, it ratifies hopes, and urges even the unarmed to battle.

HORACE.

Touch the goblet no more!
It will make thy heart sore
To its very core!

LONGFELLOW—*Christus.*

The smaller the drink, the clearer the head.

WILLIAM PENN.

Drunkenness is nothing but voluntary madness.

SENECA.

O God, that men should put an enemy in their mouths to steal away their brains! that we should, with joy, pleasance, revel, and applause, transform ourselves into beasts!

SHAKESPEARE — *Othello*. Act II. Sc. 3.

Every inordinate cup is unblessed and the ingredient is a devil.

SHAKESPEARE — *Othello*. Act II. Sc. 3.

He is certainly as guilty of suicide who perishes by a slow, as he who is despatched by an immediate, poison.

STEELE.

INTOLERANCE

The devil loves nothing better than the intolerance of reformers, and dreads nothing so much as their charity and patience.

LOWELL.

It were better to be of no church, than to be bitter for any.

WILLIAM PENN.

INVENTION

A tool is but the extension of a man's hand, and a machine is but a complex tool. And he that invents a machine augments the power of a man and the well-being of mankind.

HENRY WARD BEECHER—*Proverbs from Plymouth Pulpit. Business.*

Want, the mistress of invention.

MRS. CENTLIVRE—*The Busy Body.*

God hath made man upright; but they have sought out many inventions.

Ecclesiastes. VII. 29.

Only an inventor knows how to borrow, and every man is or should be an inventor.

EMERSON—*Letters and Social Aims.*

Electric telegraphs, printing, gas,
Tobacco, balloons, and steam,
Are little events that have come to pass
Since the days of the old *régime*.
And, spite of Lemprière's dazzling page,
I'd give—though it might seem bold—
A hundred years of the Golden Age
For a year of the Age of Gold.

HENRY S. LEIGH—*The Two Ages.*

All our inventions have endowed material forces with intellectual life, and degraded human life into a material force.

KARL MARX—*Speech, 1856.*

INVESTIGATION

Nothing has such power to broaden the mind as the ability to investigate systematically and truly all that comes under thy observation in life.

MARCUS AURELIUS.

Attempt the end and never stand to doubt;
Nothing's so hard but search will find it out.

HERRICK—*Hesperides.*

Hail, fellow, well met,
All dirty and wet:
Find out, if you can,
Who's master, who's man.

SWIFT—*My Lady's Lamentation.*

IRELAND

There's a dear little plant that grows in our isle,
'Twas St. Patrick himself sure that set it;
And the sun on his labor with pleasure did smile,
And with dew from his eye often wet it.
It thrives through the bog, through the brake, and the mireland;
And he called it the dear little shamrock of Ireland—

The sweet little shamrock, the dear little shamrock,
The sweet little, green little, shamrock of Ireland!
ANDREW CHERRY—*Green Little Shamrock of Ireland.*

When Erin first rose from the dark-swelling flood,
God blessed the green island, he saw it was good.
The Emerald of Europe, it sparkled and shone
In the ring of this world, the most precious stone.
WILLIAM DRENNAN—*Erin.*

The groves of Blarney
They look so charming
Down by the purling
Of sweet, silent brooks.
RICHARD ALFRED MILLIKEN—*Groves of Blarney.*

There is a stone there,
That whoever kisses,
Oh! he never misses
To grow eloquent.
'Tis he may clamber
To a lady's chamber
Or become a member
Of Parliament.
FATHER PROUT'S addition to *Groves of Blarney.*

O, love is the soul of a true Irishman;
He loves all that's lovely, loves all that he can,
With his sprig of shillelagh and shamrock so green.
Sprig of Shillelagh.

Whether on the scaffold high
Or on the battle-field we die,
Oh, what matter, when for Erin dear we fall.
T. D. SULLIVAN—*God Save Ireland.*

When law can stop the blades of grass from growing as they grow;
And when the leaves in Summer-time their colour dare not show;
Then will I change the colour too, I wear in my caubeen;
But till that day, plaze God, I'll stick to wearin' o' the Green.
Wearin' o' the Green.

IRRESOLUTION

Nothing of worth or weight can be achieved with half a mind, with a faint heart, and with a lame endeavor.
BARROW.

Don't stand shivering upon the bank; plunge in at once and have it over.
HALIBURTON.

We spend our days in deliberating, and we end them without coming to any resolve.
L'ESTRANGE.

ISLAND

Summer isles of Eden, lying in dark purple spheres of sea.
TENNYSON—*Locksley Hall.*

ITALY

Italy, my Italy!
Queen Mary's saying serves for me—
(When fortune's malice
Lost her Calais)—
Open my heart and you will see
Graved inside of it, "Italy."
ROBERT BROWNING—*Men and Women.*

Beyond the Alps lies Italy.
English Saying.

Italia! O Italia! thou who hast
The fatal gift of beauty, which became
A funeral dower of present woes and past,
On thy sweet brow is sorrow plough'd by shame,
And annals graved in characters of flame.
VINCENZO FILICAJA—*Italia.* English rendering by BYRON—*Childe Harold.*

On desperate seas long wont to roam,
Thy hyacinth hair, thy classic face,
Thy naiad airs have brought me home
To the glory that was Greece
And the grandeur that was Rome.
POE—*Helen.*

My soul to-day
Is far away
Sailing the Vesuvian Bay.
T. B. Read—*Drifting*.

You may have the universe if I may have Italy.
Verdi—*Attila*.

IVY

As creeping ivy clings to wood or stone,
And hides the ruin that it feeds upon.
Cowper—*The Progress of Error*.

J

JANUARY

That blasts of January
Would blow you through and through.
Shakespeare—*Winter's Tale*. Act IV. Sc. 4.

JEALOUSY

He that is not jealous is not in love.
St. Augustine.

Yet he was jealous, though he did not show it,
For jealousy dislikes the world to know it.
Byron—*Don Juan*.

Men are the cause of women not loving one another.
La Bruyère.

In jealousy there is more self-love than love.
La Rochefoucauld.

No true love there can be without
Its dread penalty—jealousy.
Owen Meredith—*Lucile*.

O jealousy,
Thou ugliest fiend of hell! thy deadly venom
Preys on my vitals, turns the healthful hue
Of my fresh cheek to haggard sallowness,
And drinks my spirit up!
Hannah More—*David and Goliath*.

Jealousy is an awkward homage which inferiority renders to merit.
Madame de Puisieux.

O jealousy! thou magnifier of trifles.
Schiller.

But jealous souls will not be answer'd so;
They are not ever jealous for the cause,
But jealous for they are jealous.
Shakespeare — *Othello*. Act III. Sc. 4.

JESTING

A joker is near akin to a buffoon; and neither of them is the least related to wit.
Chesterfield.

A joke's a very serious thing.
Churchill—*Ghost*.

A man who could make so vile a pun would not scruple to pick a pocket.
John Dennis—*The Gentleman's Magazine*.

No time to break jests when the heart-strings are about to be broken.
Fuller—*The Holy and Profane States*.

The jest which is expected is already destroyed.
Samuel Johnson.

Of all the griefs that harass the distress'd,
Sure the most bitter is a scornful jest;
Fate never wounds more deep the generous heart,
Than when a blockhead's insult points the dart.
Samuel Johnson.

Joking decides great things,
Stronger and better oft than earnest can.
Milton—*Horace*.

A jest loses its point when the jester laughs himself.
Schiller.

Alas, poor Yorick! I knew him, Horatio: a fellow of infinite jest, of most excellent fancy.
Shakespeare — *Hamlet*. Act V. Sc. 1.

Jesters do often prove prophets.
SHAKESPEARE—*King Lear.* Act V. Sc. 3.

A bitter jest, when it comes too near the truth, leaves a sharp sting behind it.
TACITUS.

Jesting is frequently an evidence of the poverty of the understanding.
VOLTAIRE.

JEW

The Jews were God's chosen people.
CHRYSOSTOM.

The Jews are among the aristocracy of every land; if a literature is called rich in the possession of a few classic tragedies, what shall we say to a national tragedy lasting for fifteen hundred years, in which the poets and the actors were also the heroes.
GEORGE ELIOT—*Daniel Deronda.*

Nobody can ever make the Americans think ill of the Jews as a class or as a race.
JOHN HAY—*Speech, 1903.*

They are a piece of stubborn antiquity, compared with which Stonehenge is in its nonage. They date beyond the Pyramids.
LAMB.

I will make of thee a great nation, and I will bless thee, and make thy name great.
Genesis. XII. 2.

The Jewish bourgeoisie are our enemies, not as Jews but as bourgeoisie. The Jewish worker is our brother.
LENIN—*Speech, 1918.*

To undo a Jew is charity, and not sin.
MARLOWE—*The Jew of Malta.*

It is not possible for Christians to take part in anti-Semitism. We are Semites spiritually.
POPE PIUS XI.

Still have I borne it with a patient shrug,
(For sufferance is the badge of all our tribe.)
You call me misbeliever, cut-throat dog.
SHAKESPEARE—*Merchant of Venice.* Act I. Sc. 3.

I am a Jew: Hath not a Jew eyes? Hath not a Jew hands, organs, dimensions, senses, affections, passions? fed with the same food, hurt with the same weapons, subject to the same diseases, healed by the same means, warmed and cooled by the same winter and summer, as a Christian is?
SHAKESPEARE—*Merchant of Venice.* Act III. Sc. 1.

JEWEL

January

By her who in this month is born,
No gems save *Garnets* should be worn;
They will insure her constancy,
True friendship and fidelity.

February

The February born will find
Sincerity and peace of mind;
Freedom from passion and from care,
If they the *Pearl* (*also green amethyst*) will wear.

March

Who in this world of ours their eyes
In March first open shall be wise;
In days of peril firm and brave,
And wear a *Bloodstone* to their grave.

April

She who from April dates her years,
Diamonds should wear, lest bitter tears
For vain repentance flow; this stone,
Emblem of innocence is known.

May

Who first beholds the light of day
In Spring's sweet flowery month of May
And wears an *Emerald* all her life,
Shall be a loved and happy wife.

June

Who comes with Summer to this earth
And owes to June her day of birth,
With ring of *Agate* on her hand,
Can health, wealth, and long life command.

July
The glowing *Ruby* should adorn
Those who in warm July are born,
Then will they be exempt and free
From love's doubt and anxiety.

August
Wear a *Sardonyx* or for thee
No conjugal felicity.
The August-born without this stone
'Tis said must live unloved and lone.

September
A maiden born when Autumn leaves
Are rustling in September's breeze,
A *Sapphire* on her brow should bind,
'Twill cure diseases of the mind.

October
October's child is born for woe,
And life's vicissitudes must know;
But lay an *Opal* on her breast,
And hope will lull those woes to rest.

November
Who first comes to this world below
With drear November's fog and snow
Should prize the *Topaz'* amber hue—
Emblem of friends and lovers true.

December
If cold December gave you birth,
The month of snow and ice and mirth,
Place on your hand a *Turquoise* blue,
Success will bless whate'er you do.
ANONYMOUS.

Stones of small worth may lie unseen by day,
But night itself does the rich gem betray.
ABRAHAM COWLEY.

Neither cast ye your pearls before swine.
Matthew. VII. 6.

Pearl of great price.
Matthew. XIII. 46.

On her white breast a sparkling cross she wore,
Which Jews might kiss and Infidels adore.
POPE—*Rape of the Lock*.

JOKE

Jokes are the cayenne of conversation, and the salt of life.
CHATFIELD.

Be not affronted at a joke. If one throw salt at thee, thou wilt receive no harm, unless thou art raw.
JUNIUS.

A joke loses everything when the joker laughs himself.
SCHILLER.

JOURNALISM

Ask how to live? Write, write, write, anything;
The world's a fine believing world, write news.
BEAUMONT AND FLETCHER—*Wit without Money*.

Journalism has already come to be the first power in the land.
SAMUEL BOWLES.

Writing good editorials is chiefly telling the people what they think, not what you think.
BRISBANE.

A would-be satirist, a hired buffoon,
A monthly scribbler of some low lampoon,
Condemn'd to drudge, the meanest of the mean,
And furbish falsehoods for a magazine.
BYRON—*English Bards and Scotch Reviewers*.

The press is the fourth estate of the realm.
CARLYLE.

Burke said there were Three Estates in Parliament; but, in the Reporter's gallery yonder, there sat a fourth estate more important far than they all.
CARLYLE—*Heroes and Hero-Worship*.

Get your facts first, and then you can distort 'em as much as you please.
S. L. CLEMENS (Mark Twain).

The best use of a journal is to print the largest practical amount of important truth,—truth which tends to make mankind wiser, and thus happier.
HORACE GREELEY.

The liberty of the press is the *palladium* of all the civil, political, and religious rights of an Englishman.
JUNIUS—*Dedication to Letters.*

Every newspaper editor owes tribute to the devil.
LA FONTAINE.

Newspapers always excite curiosity. No one ever lays one down without a feeling of disappointment.
CHARLES LAMB—*Essays of Elia.*

I fear three newspapers more than a hundred thousand bayonets.
NAPOLEON.

We live under a government of men and morning newspapers.
WENDELL PHILLIPS.

The press is like the air, a chartered libertine.
PITT—*To Lord Grenville.*

The newspapers! Sir, they are the most villainous — licentious — abominable—infernal—not that I ever read them—no—I make it a rule never to look into a newspaper.
R. B. SHERIDAN—*The Critic.*

JOY

How happy are the pessimists! What joy is theirs when they have proved there is no joy.
MARIE EBNER-ESCHENBACH.

All human joys are swift of wing,
For heaven doth so allot it;
That when you get an easy thing,
You find you haven't got it.
EUGENE FIELD—*Ways of Life.*

There's a hope for every woe,
And a balm for every pain,
But the first joys of our heart
Come never back again!
ROBERT GILFILLAN—*The Exile's Song.*

A thing of beauty is a joy forever.
KEATS.

Joys too exquisite to last,
And yet more exquisite when past.
MONTGOMERY—*The Little Cloud.*

How fading are the joys we dote upon!
Like apparitions seen and gone;
But those which soonest take their flight
Are the most exquisite and strong;
Like angel's visits short and bright,
Mortality's too weak to bear them long.
JOHN NORRIS—*The Parting.*

Sorrows remembered sweeten present joy.
POLLOCK.

I wish you all the joy that you can wish.
SHAKESPEARE—*Merchant of Venice.* Act III. Sc. 2.

Sweets with sweets war not, joy delights in joy.
SHAKESPEARE—*Sonnet.*

I have drunken deep of joy,
And I will taste no other wine to-night.
SHELLEY—*The Cenci.*

There is a sweet joy which comes to us through sorrow.
SPURGEON—*Gleanings among the Sheaves.*

JUDGE

The cold neutrality of an impartial judge.
BURKE.

It is better that a judge should lean on the side of compassion than severity.
CERVANTES.

Judges are but men, and are swayed like other men by vehement prejudices. This is corruption in reality, give it whatever other name you please.
DAVID DUDLEY FIELD.

Judges are apt to be naïve, simple-minded men.
O. W. HOLMES II—*Speech, 1913.*

Let the judges answer to the question of law, and the jurors to the matter of fact.
LAW MAXIM.

The hungry judges soon the sentence sign,
And wretches hang that jurymen may dine.
POPE—*Rape of the Lock.*

If you judge, investigate; if you reign, command.
SENECA.

Heaven is above all yet; there sits a judge,
That no king can corrupt.
SHAKESPEARE—*Henry VIII.* Act III. Sc. 1.

Thieves for their robbery have authority
When judges steal themselves.
SHAKESPEARE—*Measure for Measure.* Act II. Sc. 2.

Four things belong to a judge: to hear courteously, to answer wisely, to consider soberly, and to decide impartially.
SOCRATES.

JUDGMENT

The more one judges, the less one loves.
BALZAC.

Thou art weighed in the balances, and art found wanting.
Daniel. V. 27.

So comes a reck'ning when the banquet's o'er,
The dreadful reck'ning, and men smile no more.
GAY.

One man's word is no man's word; we should quietly hear both sides.
GOETHE.

I know of no way of judging the future but by the past.
PATRICK HENRY, 1775.

We judge ourselves by what we feel capable of doing, while others judge us by what we have already done.
LONGFELLOW—*Kavanagh.*

Give your decisions, never your reasons; your decisions may be right, your reasons are sure to be wrong.
LORD MANSFIELD.

Judge not, that ye be not judged.
Matthew. VII. 1.

There are no judgments so harsh as those of the erring, the inexperienced, and the young.
MULOCK.

Give every man thy ear, but few thy voice;
Take each man's censure, but reserve thy judgment.
SHAKESPEARE—*Hamlet.* Act I. Sc. 3.

Forbear to judge, for we are sinners all.
SHAKESPEARE—*Henry VI.* Pt. II. Act III. Sc. 3.

O judgment! thou art fled to brutish beasts,
And men have lost their reason!
SHAKESPEARE—*Julius Caesar.* Act III. Sc. 2.

The jury, passing on the prisoner's life,
May in the sworn twelve have a thief or two
Guiltier than him they try.
SHAKESPEARE—*Measure for Measure.* Act II. Sc. 1.

A Daniel come to judgment! yea, a Daniel.
SHAKESPEARE—*Merchant of Venice.* Act IV. Sc. 1.

The very thing that men think they have got the most of, they have got the least of; and that is judgment.
H. W. SHAW.

The nature of all men is so formed that they see and discriminate in the affairs of others, much better than in their own.
TERENCE.

One cool judgment is worth a thousand hasty councils. The thing to do is to supply light and not heat. At any rate, if it is heat it ought to be white heat and not sputter, because sputtering heat is apt to spread the fire. There ought, if there is any heat at all, to be that warmth of the heart which makes every man thrust aside his own personal feeling, his own personal interest, and take thought of the welfare and benefit of others.
WOODROW WILSON—*Speech, 1916.*

JULY

Loud is the summer's busy song
The smallest breeze can find a tongue,
While insects of each tiny size
Grow teasing with their melodies,
Till noon burns with its blistering breath
Around, and day lies still as death.
CLARE—*July*.

JUNE

And what is so rare as a day in June?
Then, if ever, come perfect days;
Then Heaven tries earth if it be in tune,
And over it softly her warm ear lays.
LOWELL—*Vision of Sir Launfal*.

It is the month of June,
The month of leaves and roses,
When pleasant sights salute the eyes
And pleasant scents the noses.
N. P. WILLIS—*The Month of June*.

JUSTICE

There is no virtue so truly great and godlike as justice.
ADDISON—*The Guardian*.

Thrice is he armed that hath his quarrel just;
And four times he who gets his fist in fust.
Accredited to JOSH BILLINGS.

It looks to me to be narrow and pedantic to supply the ordinary ideas of criminal justice to this great public contest. I do not know the method of drawing up an indictment against a whole people.
BURKE—*Speech on Conciliation with America*.

Amongst the sons of men how few are known
Who dare be just to merit not their own.
CHARLES CHURCHILL—*Epistle to Hogarth*.

Justice renders to every one his due.
CICERO.

Extreme justice is extreme injustice.
CICERO.

There is no such thing as justice—in or out of court.
CLARENCE DARROW, 1936.

Justice is truth in action.
DISRAELI.

Let justice be done, though the heavens should fall.
Motto of EMPEROR FERDINAND I.

Pity and forbearance should characterize all acts of justice.
FRANKLIN.

Justice without wisdom is impossible.
FROUDE.

That which is unjust can really profit no one; that which is just can really harm no one.
HENRY GEORGE—*The Land Question*.

I have loved justice and hated iniquity; and therefore I die in exile.
POPE GREGORY VII.

The spirits of just men made perfect.
Hebrews. XII. 23.

God's mill grinds slow, but sure.
GEORGE HERBERT.

The love of justice is, in most men, nothing more than the fear of suffering injustice.
LA ROCHEFOUCAULD.

Delay of justice is injustice.
LANDOR.

Man is unjust, but God is just; and finally justice
Triumphs.
LONGFELLOW—*Evangeline*.

I'm armed with more than complete steel,—
The justice of my quarrel.
MARLOWE—*Lust's Dominion*.

Yet I shall temper so
Justice with mercy, as may illustrate most
Them fully satisfied, and thee appease.
MILTON—*Paradise Lost*.

Just are the ways of God,
And justifiable to men.
MILTON—*Samson Agonistes*.

Justice is the insurance which we have on our lives and property; to which may be added, and obedience is the premium which we pay for it.

William Penn.

The path of the just is as the shining light, that shineth more and more unto the perfect day.

Proverbs. IV. 18.

Render therefore to all their dues.

Romans. *XIII*. 7.

He who decides a case without hearing the other side, though he decide justly, cannot be considered just.

Seneca.

Thrice is he arm'd that hath his quarrel just,
And he but naked, though lock'd up in steel,
Whose conscience with injustice is corrupted.

Shakespeare—*Henry VI*. Pt. II. Act III. Sc. 2.

This bond is forfeit;
And lawfully by this the Jew may claim
A pound of flesh.

Shakespeare—*Merchant of Venice*. Act IV. Sc. 1.

Truth is its (justice's) handmaid, freedom is its child, peace is its companion, safety walks in its steps, victory follows in its train; it is the brightest emanation from the gospel; it is the attribute of God.

Sydney Smith—*Lady Holland's Memoir*.

Let justice be done, though the heavens fall.

William Watson, 1602.

Justice, sir, is the great interest of man on earth.

Daniel Webster, 1845.

K

KINDNESS

Have you had a kindness shown?
Pass it on;
'Twas not given for thee alone,
Pass it on:
Let it travel down the years,
Let it wipe another's tears,
'Till in Heaven the deed appears—
Pass it on.

Rev. Henry Burton—*Pass It On*.

It is difficult to tell how much men's minds are conciliated by a kind manner and gentle speech.

Cicero.

Their cause I plead—plead it in heart and mind;
A fellow-feeling makes one wondrous kind.

David Garrick, 1776.

Kindness is the golden chain by which society is bound together.

Goethe.

Wise sayings often fall on barren ground; but a kind word is never thrown away.

Arthur Helps.

Wherever there is a human being there is an opportunity for a kindness.

Seneca.

A little more than kin, and less than kind.

Shakespeare—*Hamlet*. Act I. Sc. 2.

Yet do I fear thy nature;
It is too full o' the milk of human kindness.

Shakespeare — *Macbeth*. Act I. Sc. 5.

Kindness gives birth to kindness.

Sophocles.

If what must be given is given willingly the kindness is doubled.

Syrus.

KISS

Blush, happy maiden, when you feel
The lips which press love's glowing seal;
But as the slow years darklier roll,
Grown wiser, the experienced soul
Will own as dearer far than they
The lips which kiss the tears away.

Elizabeth Akers Allen—*Kisses*.

Some women blush when they are kissed; some call for the police; some

swear; some bite. But the worst are those who laugh.
ANONYMOUS.

Four sweet lips, two pure souls, and one undying affection,—these are love's pretty ingredients for a kiss.
BOVEE.

. . . And when my lips meet thine
Thy very soul is wedded unto mine.
H. H. BOYESEN.

Something made of nothing, tasting very sweet,
A most delicious compound, with ingredients complete;
But if as on occasion the heart and mind are sour
It has no great significance, it loses half its power.
MARY E. BUELL—*The Kiss.*

Gin a body meet a body
Comin' through the rye,
Gin a body kiss a body
Need a body cry?
BURNS.

Come, lay thy head upon my breast,
And I will kiss thee into rest.
BYRON—*The Bride of Abydos.*

A long, long kiss, a kiss of youth, and love.
BYRON—*Don Juan.*

The dearest remembrance will still be the last,
Our sweetest memorial the first kiss of love.
BYRON—*The First Kiss of Love.*

It was thy kiss, Love, that made me immortal.
MARGARET W. FULLER—*Dryad Song.*

Tell me who first did kisses suggest?
It was a mouth all glowing and blest;
It kissed and it thought of nothing beside.
The fair month of May was then in its pride,
The flowers were all from the earth fast springing,
The sun was laughing, the birds were singing.
HEINE—*Book of Songs.*

Give me a kisse, and to that kisse a score;
Then to that twenty, adde a hundred more;
A thousand to that hundred; so kisse on,
To make that thousand up a million;
Treble that million, and when that is done,
Let's kisse afresh, as when we first begun.
HERRICK—*To Anthea.*

What is a kisse? Why this, as some approve:
The sure sweet cement, glue, and lime of love.
HERRICK—*A Kiss.*

Stolen kisses are always sweetest.
LEIGH HUNT.

Jenny kissed me when we met,
Jumping from the chair she sat in;
Time, you thief, who love to get
Sweets into your list, put that in.
Say I'm weary, say I'm sad,
Say that health and wealth have missed me;
Say I'm growing old, but add
Jenny kissed me.
LEIGH HUNT—*Jenny Kissed Me.*

Drink to me only with thine eyes
And I will pledge with mine.
Or leave a kiss but in the cup,
And I'll not look for wine.
BEN JONSON—*To Celia.*

It is delightful to kiss the eyelashes of the beloved—is it not? But never so delightful as when fresh tears are on them.
LANDOR.

When she kissed me once in play,
Rubies were less bright than they;
And less bright were those which shone
In the palace of the Sun.
Will they be as bright again?
Not if kiss'd by other men.
LANDOR—*Rubies.*

The blossom of love.
NINON DE LENCLOS.

I throw a kiss across the sea,
I drink the winds as drinking wine,
And dream they all are blown from thee,
I catch the whisper'd kiss of thine.
JOAQUIN MILLER—*England.*

One kiss the maiden gives, one last,
Long kiss, which she expires in giving.
MOORE—*Lalla Rookh.*

A kiss, when all is said, what is it?
. . . a rosy dot
Placed on the "i" in loving; 'tis a secret
Told to the mouth instead of to the ear.
ROSTAND—*Cyrano de Bergerac.*

Give me kisses! Nay, 'tis true
I am just as rich as you;
And for every kiss I owe,
I can pay you back, you know.
Kiss me, then,
Every moment—and again.
J. G. SAXE—*To Lesbia.*

And steal immortal blessing from her lips;
Who, even in pure and vestal modesty,
Still blush, as thinking their own kisses sin.
SHAKESPEARE—*Romeo and Juliet.* Act III. Sc. 3.

This done, he took the bride about the neck
And kiss'd her lips with such a clamorous smack
That at the parting, all the church did echo.
SHAKESPEARE — *Taming of the Shrew.* Act III. Sc. 3.

See! the mountains kiss high heaven,
And the waves clasp one another;
No sister flower would be forgiven
If it disdained its brother;
And the sunlight clasps the earth,
And the moonbeams kiss the sea:—
What are all these kissings worth,
If thou kiss not me?
PERCY BYSSHE SHELLEY—*Love's Philosophy.*

As in the soft and sweet eclipse,
When soul meets soul on lover's lips.
SHELLEY—*Prometheus Unbound.*

My lips till then had only known
The kiss of mother and of sister,
But somehow, full upon her own
Sweet, rosy, darling mouth,—I kissed her.
E. C. STEDMAN—*The Door-Step.*

Lord! I wonder what fool it was that first invented kissing.
SWIFT—*Polite Conversation.*

Once he drew
With one long kiss my whole soul thro'
My lips, as sunlight drinketh dew.
TENNYSON—*Fatima.*

KNAVERY

Knaves starve not in the land of fools.
CHARLES CHURCHILL.

After a long experience in the world, I affirm, before God, I never knew a rogue who was not unhappy.
JUNIUS.

Zeno first started that doctrine, that knavery is the best defence against a knave.
PLUTARCH.

KNOWLEDGE

Strange how much you've got to know
Before you know how little you know.
ANONYMOUS.

I take all knowledge to be my province.
BACON.

For knowledge, too, is itself a power.
BACON.

That jewel knowledge is great riches, which is not plundered by kinsmen, nor carried off by thieves, nor decreased by giving.
BHAVABHUTI.

Men are four:
He who knows not and knows not he knows not, he is a fool—shun him;
He who knows not and knows he knows not, he is simple—teach him;

He who knows and knows not he knows, he is asleep—wake him;
He who knows and knows he knows, he is wise—follow him!
LADY BURTON—*Life of Sir Richard Burton.*

Knowledge is not happiness, and science
But an exchange of ignorance for that
Which is another kind of ignorance.
BYRON—*Manfred.*

There's lots of people—this town wouldn't hold them;
Who don't know much excepting what's told them.
WILL CARLETON—*City Ballads.*

What is all Knowledge too but recorded Experience, and a product of History; of which, therefore, Reasoning and Belief, no less than Action and Passion, are essential materials?
CARLYLE—*Essays.*

As soon as a true thought has entered our mind, it gives a light which makes us see a crowd of other objects which we have never perceived before.
CHATEAUBRIAND.

Not only is there an art in knowing a thing, but also a certain art in teaching it.
CICERO.

When you know a thing, to hold that you know it; and when you do not know a thing, to allow that you do not know it; this is knowledge.
CONFUCIUS—*Analects.*

Knowledge and Wisdom, far from being one,
Have oft-times no connexion. Knowledge dwells
In heads replete with thoughts of other men,
Wisdom in minds attentive to their own.
COWPER—*The Task.*

Many shall run to and fro, and knowledge shall be increased.
Daniel. XII. 4.

To be conscious that you are ignorant is a great step to knowledge.
DISRAELI—*Sybil.*

He that increaseth knowledge increaseth sorrow.
Ecclesiastes. I. 18.

Our knowledge is the amassed thought and experience of innumerable minds.
EMERSON—*Letters and Social Aims.*

What we do not understand we do not possess.
GOETHE.

We know accurately only when we know little; with knowledge doubt increases.
GOETHE.

One cannot know everything.
HORACE.

A desire of knowledge is the natural feeling of mankind; and every human being whose mind is not debauched, will be willing to give all that he has to get knowledge.
SAMUEL JOHNSON.

Knowledge is of two kinds. We know a subject ourselves, or we know where we can find information upon it.
SAMUEL JOHNSON—*Boswell's Life of Johnson.*

All wish to possess knowledge, but few, comparatively speaking, are willing to pay the price.
JUVENAL.

He knoweth the universe, and himself he knoweth not.
LA FONTAINE.

Half-knowledge is worse than ignorance.
MACAULAY.

It ain't the things you don't know what gets you into trouble; it's the things you know for sure what ain't so.
Negro Saying.

Better know nothing than half-know many things.
NIETZSCHE—*Thus Spake Zarathustra.*

All things I thought I knew; but now confess
The more I know I know, I know the less.
OWEN.

He that hath knowledge spareth his words.
Proverbs. XVII. 27.

What harm in learning and getting knowledge even from a sot, a pot, a fool, a mitten, or a slipper.
RABELAIS—*Pantagruel.*

Then I began to think, that it is very true which is commonly said, that the one-half of the world knoweth not how the other half liveth.
RABELAIS.

If you wish to know yourself observe how others act.
If you wish to understand others look into your own heart.
SCHILLER.

We know what we are, but know not what we may be.
SHAKESPEARE—*Hamlet.* Act IV. Sc. 5.

And seeing ignorance is the curse of God,
Knowledge the wing wherewith we fly to heaven.
SHAKESPEARE—*Henry VI.* Pt. II. Act IV. Sc. 7.

Know thyself.
SOCRATES.

As for me, all I know is that I know nothing.
SOCRATES.

Knowledge comes, but wisdom lingers.
TENNYSON—*Locksley Hall.*

Who loves not Knowledge? Who shall rail
Against her beauty? May she mix
With men and prosper! Who shall fix
Her pillars? Let her work prevail.
TENNYSON—*In Memoriam.*

L

LABOR

He who prays and labours lifts his heart to God with his hands.
ST. BERNARD.

Such hath it been—shall be—beneath the sun
The many still must labour for the one.
BYRON—*The Corsair.*

Not all the labor of the earth
Is done by hardened hands.
WILL CARLETON—*A Working Woman.*

They can expect nothing but their labor for their pains.
CERVANTES—*Don Quixote.*

The labor of a human being is not a commodity or article of commerce.
Clayton Antitrust Act.

A truly American sentiment recognises the dignity of labor and the fact that honor lies in honest toil.
CLEVELAND.

When admirals extoll'd for standing still,
Of doing nothing with a deal of skill.
COWPER—*Table Talk.*

Labour itself is but a sorrowful song,
The protest of the weak against the strong.
F. W. FABER—*The Sorrowful World.*

For as labor cannot produce without the use of land, the denial of the equal right to use of land is necessarily the denial of the right of labor to its own produce.
HENRY GEORGE—*Progress and Poverty.*

How blest is he who crowns in shades like these,
A youth of labour with an age of ease.
GOLDSMITH—*The Deserted Village.*

The labor union is an elemental response to the human instinct for group action in dealing with group problems.
WILLIAM GREEN—*Speech, 1925.*

If little labour, little are our gaines:
Man's fortunes are according to his paines.
HERRICK—*Hesperides.*

To labour is the lot of man below;
And when Jove gave us life, he gave us woe.
HOMER—*Iliad*.

Labor conquers all things.
HOMER.

With fingers weary and worn,
With eyelids heavy and red,
A woman sat in unwomanly rags,
Plying her needle and thread.
HOOD—*Song of the Shirt*.

Why seekest thou rest, since thou art born to labor?
THOMAS À KEMPIS.

Labor, like Israel, has many sorrows. Its women weep for their fallen and they lament for the future of the children of the race.
JOHN L. LEWIS—*Speech, 1937*.

The heights by great men reached and kept
Were not attained by sudden flight,
But they, while their companions slept,
Were toiling upward in the night.
LONGFELLOW—*Birds of Passage*.

The labourer is worthy of his reward.
Luke. X. 7; *I Timothy*. V. 18.

Genius may conceive, but patient labor must consummate.
HORACE MANN.

Bowed by the weight of centuries he leans
Upon his hoe and gazes on the ground,
The emptiness of ages in his face,
And on his back the burden of the world.
EDWIN MARKHAM—*The Man with the Hoe*.

Labor! all labor is noble and holy!
Let thy great deeds be thy prayer to thy God.
FRANCES S. OSGOOD.

And all labor without any play, boys,
Makes Jack a dull boy in the end.
H. A. PAGE.

The duty of labor is written on a man's body: in the stout muscle of the arm, and the delicate machinery of the hand.
THEODORE PARKER.

If you want knowledge, you must toil for it; if food, you must toil for it; and if pleasure, you must toil for it: toil is the law.
RUSKIN.

Many faint with toil,
That few may know the cares and woe of sloth.
SHELLEY—*Queen Mab*.

The Russian Socialist Federated Soviet Republic declares labor the duty of all citizens of the republic.
Soviet Constitution.

Labour of love.
I Thessalonians. I. 3.

Stubborn labor conquers everything.
VERGIL.

Ah, little recks the laborer,
How near his work is holding him to God,
The loving Laborer through space and time.
WALT WHITMAN—*Song of the Exposition*.

LAMB

Mary had a little lamb
Its fleece was white as snow,
And everywhere that Mary went
The lamb was sure to go.
MRS. SARAH J. HALE—*Mary's Little Lamb*.

LANGUAGE

I love the language, that soft bastard Latin,
Which melts like kisses from a female mouth.
BYRON—*Beppo*.

Pedantry consists in the use of words unsuitable to the time, place, and company.
COLERIDGE.

. . . Philologists, who chase
A panting syllable through time and space
Start it at home, and hunt it in the dark,

To Gaul, to Greece, and into Noah's
Ark.
COWPER—*Retirement.*

He Greek and Latin speaks with
greater ease
Than hogs eat acorns, and tame
pigeons peas.
CRANFIELD—*Panegyric on Tom Coriate.*

Who climbs the grammar-tree, distinctly knows
Where noun, and verb, and participle
grows.
DRYDEN.

Language is a city to the building of which every human being brought a stone.
EMERSON—*Letters and Social Aims.*

Language,—human language,—after all, is but little better than the croak and cackle of fowls, and other utterances of brute nature,—sometimes not so adequate.
HAWTHORNE.

But, for my own part, it was Greek to me.
SHAKESPEARE—*Julius Caesar*. Act I. Sc. 2.

There was speech in their dumbness, language in their very gesture.
SHAKESPEARE—*Winter's Tale*. Act V. Sc. 2.

No man fully capable of his own language ever masters another.
GEORGE BERNARD SHAW—*Maxims for Revolutionists.*

Egad, I think the interpreter is the hardest to be understood of the two!
R. B. SHERIDAN—*The Critic.*

I am the King of Rome, and above grammar.
SIGISMUND—*At the Council of Constance.*

Language, as well as the faculty of speech, was the immediate gift of God.
NOAH WEBSTER.

Language is not an abstract construction of the learned, or of dictionary-makers, but is something arising out of the work, needs, ties, joys, affections, tastes, of long generations of humanity, and has its bases broad and low, close to the ground.
WALT WHITMAN—*Slang in America.*

LARK

The merry lark he soars on high,
No worldly thought o'ertakes him.
He sings aloud to the clear blue sky,
And the daylight that awakes him.
HARTLEY COLERIDGE—*Song.*

Rise with the lark, and with the lark to bed.
HURDIS—*The Village Curate.*

To hear the lark begin his flight,
And singing startle the dull Night,
From his watch-tower in the skies,
Till the dappled dawn doth rise.
MILTON—*L'Allegro.*

The bird that soars on highest wing,
Builds on the ground her lowly nest;
And she that doth most sweetly sing,
Sings in the shade when all things
rest;
In lark and nightingale we see
What honor hath humility.
MONTGOMERY—*Humility.*

Lo! here the gentle lark, weary of rest,
From his moist cabinet mounts up on
high,
And wakes the morning, from whose
silver breast
The sun ariseth in his majesty.
SHAKESPEARE—*Venus and Adonis*

Hail to thee blithe Spirit!
Bird thou never wert,
That from Heaven, or near it,
Pourest thy full heart
In profuse strains of unpremeditated
art.
SHELLEY—*To a Skylark.*

Better than all measures
Of delightful sound,
Better than all treasures
That in books are found,
Thy skill to poet were, thou scorner of
the ground!
SHELLEY—*To a Skylark.*

LAUGHTER

To provoke laughter without joining in it greatly heightens the effect.
BALZAC.

I hasten to laugh at everything, for fear of being obliged to weep.
BEAUMARCHAIS.

The man who cannot laugh is not only fit for treasons, stratagems, and spoils, but his whole life is already a treason and a stratagem.
CARLYLE.

Nothing is more silly than silly laughter.
CATULLUS.

The most completely lost of all days is that on which one has not laughed.
CHAMFORT.

The vulgar only laugh, but never smile; whereas well-bred people often smile, but seldom laugh.
CHESTERFIELD—*Letter to His Son.*

What I saw was equal ecstasy:
One universal smile it seemed of all things.
DANTE—*Paradiso.*

As the crackling of thorns under a pot, so is the laughter of a fool.
Ecclesiastes. VII. 6.

Man is the only creature endowed with the power of laughter.
GREVILLE.

Laugh, and be fat, sir, your penance is known.
They that love mirth, let them heartily drink,
'Tis the only receipt to make sorrow sink.
BEN JONSON—*Entertainments.*

Man alone suffers so excruciatingly in the world that he was compelled to invent laughter.
NIETZSCHE—*The Will to Power.*

He laughs best who laughs last.
Old English Proverb.

Laugh at your friends, and if your friends are sore;
So much the better, you may laugh the more.
POPE—*Epilogue to Satire.*

The man that loves and laughs must sure do well.
POPE—*Imitations of Horace.*

Laugh and the world laughs with you,
Weep and you weep alone;
For the sad old earth must borrow its mirth,
But has trouble enough of its own.
ELLA WHEELER WILCOX—*Solitude.*

People who do not know how to laugh, are always pompous and self-conceited.
THACKERAY.

LAUREL

This flower that smells of honey and the sea,
White laurustine, seems in my hand to be
A white star made of memory long ago
Lit in the heaven of dear times dead to me.
SWINBURNE—*Relics.*

LAW

Written laws are like spiders' webs, and will like them only entangle and hold the poor and weak, while the rich and powerful will easily break through them.
ANACHARSIS TO SOLON.

Law is a bottomless pit.
J. ARBUTHNOT—*Title of a Pamphlet.* 1700.

There is but one law for all; namely, that law which governs all law,—the law of our Creator, the law of humanity, justice, equity; the law of nature and of nations.
BURKE.

A good parson once said that where mystery begins religion ends. Cannot I say, as truly at least, of human laws, that where mystery begins, justice ends?
BURKE—*Vindication of Natural Society.*

Who to himself is law, no law doth need,
Offends no law, and is a king indeed.
GEORGE CHAPMAN.

Possession is eleven points in the law.
COLLEY CIBBER.

After an existence of nearly twenty years of almost innocuous desuetude these laws are brought forth.
GROVER CLEVELAND. 1886.

Reason is the life of the law; nay, the common law itself is nothing else but reason. The law which is perfection of reason.
SIR EDWARD COKE—*First Institute.*

Trial by jury itself, instead of being a security to persons who are accused, shall be delusion, a mockery, and a snare.
LORD DENMAN—*In His Judgment of O'Connell, 1894.*

"If the law supposes that," said Mr. Bumble, "the law is a ass, a idiot."
DICKENS—*Oliver Twist.*

Just laws are no restraint upon the freedom of the good, for the good man desires nothing which a just law will interfere with.
FROUDE.

The English laws punish vice; the Chinese laws do more, they reward virtue.
GOLDSMITH.

Laws grind the poor, and rich men rule the law.
GOLDSMITH—*The Traveller.*

I know no method to secure the repeal of bad or obnoxious laws so effective as their stringent execution.
U. S. GRANT—*Address, 1869.*

The verdict acquits the raven, but condemns the dove.
JUVENAL.

Avoid law suits beyond all things; they influence your conscience, impair your health, and dissipate your property.
LA BRUYÈRE.

The laws sometimes sleep, but never die.
Law Maxim.

All things obey fixed laws.
MANILIUS—*Astronomica.*

Render therefore unto Caesar the things which are Caesar's.
Matthew. XXII. 21.

There is no man so good, who, were he to submit all his thoughts and actions to the laws would not deserve hanging ten times in his life.
MONTAIGNE.

Petty laws breed great crimes.
OUIDA—*Wisdom, Wit and Pathos.*

Where law ends, there tyranny begins.
WILLIAM PITT.

It is difficult to make our material condition better by the best laws, but it is easy enough to ruin it by bad laws.
THEODORE ROOSEVELT—*Speech, 1902.*

There is a higher law than the Constitution.
W. H. SEWARD.

'Tis like a breath of an unfee'd lawyer; you gave me nothing for't.
SHAKESPEARE—*King Lear.* Act I. Sc. 4.

The law hath not been dead, though it hath slept.
SHAKESPEARE—*Measure for Measure.* Act II. Sc. 2.

Do as adversaries do in law,
Strive mightily, but eat and drink as friends.
SHAKESPEARE — *Taming of the Shrew.* Act I. Sc. 2.

They have been grand-jurymen since before Noah was a sailor.
SHAKESPEARE—*Twelfth Night.* Act III. Sc. 2.

Still you keep o' the windy side of the law.
SHAKESPEARE—*Twelfth Night.* Act III. Sc. 4.

Laws are generally found to be nets of such a texture, as the little creep through, the great break through, and the middle-sized alone are entangled in.
SHENSTONE—*On Politics.*

LAWYER

Our wrangling lawyers are so litigious and busy here on earth, that I think they will plead their clients' causes hereafter, some of them in hell.
BURTON.

It is a secret worth knowing that lawyers rarely go to law.
MOSES CROWELL.

A lawyer's opinion is worth nothing unless paid for.
English Proverb.

The first thing we do, let's kill all the lawyers.
SHAKESPEARE—*Henry VI.* Pt. II. Act IV. Sc. 2.

Most good lawyers live well, work hard, and die poor.
DANIEL WEBSTER.

LEARNING

Much learning doth make thee mad.
Acts. XXVI. 24.

It is always in season for old men to learn.
AESCHYLUS—*Agamemnon.*

Reading maketh a full man; conference a ready man; and writing an exact man.
BACON—*Essays.*

The three foundations of learning: Seeing much, suffering much, and studying much.
CATHERALL.

Wear your learning like your watch, in a private pocket; and do not pull it out and strike it, merely to show that you have one.
CHESTERFIELD.

Learning without thought is labor lost; thought without learning is perilous.
CONFUCIUS.

Consider that I laboured not for myself only, but for all them that seek learning.
Ecclesiasticus. XXXII. 17.

Whence is thy learning? Hath thy toil
O'er books consum'd the midnight oil?
GAY—*Shepherd and Philosopher.*

And still they gazed, and still the wonder grew,
That one small head should carry all it knew.
GOLDSMITH—*The Deserted Village.*

All wish to be learned, but no one is willing to pay the price.
JUVENAL.

The great man learns only what he wants to learn; the mediocre man can learn what others think he should learn.
GEORGE MOORE.

They have learned nothing, and forgotten nothing.
CHEVALIER DE PANET.

A little learning is a dangerous thing;
Drink deep, or taste not the Pierian spring;
Their shallow draughts intoxicate the brain,
And drinking largely sobers us again.
POPE—*Essay on Criticism.*

Men learn while they teach.
SENECA.

A learned man is an idler who kills time by study.
GEORGE BERNARD SHAW—*Maxims for Revolutionists.*

Each day is the scholar of yesterday.
SYRUS.

Learn to live, and live to learn,
Ignorance like a fire doth burn,
Little tasks make large return.
BAYARD TAYLOR—*To My Daughter.*

LIBERAL

One who has both feet firmly planted in the air.
ANONYMOUS.

Liberalism is trust of the people tempered by prudence; conservatism, distrust of the people tempered by fear.
GLADSTONE.

A liberal is a man who is willing to spend somebody else's money.
CARTER GLASS, 1938.

LIBERALITY

He that defers his charity until he is dead is, if a man weighs it rightly, rather liberal of another man's goods than his own.
BACON.

The liberal soul shall be made fat.
Proverbs. XI. 25.

What's mine is yours, and what is yours is mine.
SHAKESPEARE—*Measure for Measure*. Act V. Sc. 1.

LIBERTY

A day, an hour, of virtuous liberty
Is worth a whole eternity in bondage.
ADDISON—*Cato*.

The tree of liberty grows only when watered by the blood of tyrants.
BARÈRE.

But what is liberty without wisdom, and without virtue? It is the greatest of all possible evils; for it is folly, vice, and madness, without tuition or restraint.
BURKE.

The people never give up their liberties but under some delusion.
BURKE.

Liberty's in every blow!
Let us do or die.
BURNS—*Bruce to His Men at Bannockburn*.

Eternal Spirit of the chainless Mind!
Brightest in dungeons, Liberty! thou art,
For there thy habitation is the heart—
The heart which love of thee alone can bind;
And when thy sons to fetters are consign'd—
To fetters and damp vault's dayless gloom,
Their country conquers with their martyrdom.
BYRON—*Prisoner of Chillon*.

Yes, while I stood and gazed, my temples bare,
And shot my being through earth, sea, and air,
Possessing all things with intensest love,
O Liberty! my spirit felt thee there.
COLERIDGE—*France*.

Where the spirit of the Lord is, there is Liberty.
II Corinthians. III. 17.

Then liberty, like day,
Breaks on the soul, and by a flash from Heaven
Fires all the faculties with glorious joy.
COWPER—*The Task*.

Eternal vigilance is the price of liberty.
JOHN PHILPOT CURRAN—*Dublin, 1808*.

The love of liberty with life is given,
And life itself the inferior gift of Heaven.
DRYDEN—*Palamon and Arcite*.

Those who would give up essential liberty to purchase a little temporary safety deserve neither liberty nor safety.
FRANKLIN.

Where liberty dwells, there is my country.
FRANKLIN.

Give me liberty, or give me death.
PATRICK HENRY.

The God who gave us life, gave us liberty at the same time.
JEFFERSON.

Give me the liberty to know, to think, to believe, and to utter freely according to conscience, above all other liberties.
MILTON.

License they mean when they cry, Liberty!
For who loves that, must first be wise and good.
MILTON.

O liberty! how many crimes are committed in thy name!
MADAME ROLAND.

That treacherous phantom which men call Liberty.
RUSKIN.

So every bondman in his own hand
bears
The power to cancel his captivity.
SHAKESPEARE—*Julius Caesar*. Act I. Sc. 3.

Give me your tired, your poor,
Your huddled masses, yearning to
breathe free,
The wretched refuse of your teeming
shore.
Send these, the homeless, tempest
tossed, to me:
I lift my lamp beside the golden door.
Inscription on Statue of Liberty, New York Harbor.

Liberty, when it begins to take root, is a plant of rapid growth.
WASHINGTON.

God grants liberty only to those who love it, and are always ready to guard and defend it.
DANIEL WEBSTER.

Liberty is the only thing you cannot have unless you are willing to give it to others.
WILLIAM ALLEN WHITE, 1940.

I have always in my own thought summed up individual liberty, and business liberty, and every other kind of liberty, in the phrase that is common in the sporting world, "A free field and no favor."
WOODROW WILSON—*Speech, 1915.*

LIFE

Ofttimes the test of courage becomes rather to live than to die.
ALFIERI—*Oreste.*

I know not if the dark or bright
Shall be my lot;
If that wherein my hopes delight
Be best or not.
HENRY M. ALFORD—*Life's Answer.*

Every man's life is a fairy-tale written by God's fingers.
HANS CHRISTIAN ANDERSEN.

I expect to pass through this world but once. Any good therefore that I can do, or any kindness that I can show to any fellow creature, let me do it now. Let me not defer or neglect it, for I shall not pass this way again.
ANONYMOUS.

Let us live then, and be glad
While young life's before us
After youthful pastime had,
After old age hard and sad,
Earth will slumber over us.
ANONYMOUS.

With aching hands and bleeding feet
We dig and heap, lay stone on
stone;
We bear the burden and the heat
Of the long day, and wish 'twere
done.
Not till the hours of light return
All we have built do we discern.
MATTHEW ARNOLD—*Morality.*

This strange disease of modern life,
With its sick hurry, its divided aims.
MATTHEW ARNOLD—*Scholar-Gypsy.*

They live that they may eat, but he himself (Socrates) eats that he may live.
ATHENAEUS.

It matters not how long we live, but how.
BAILEY—*Festus.*

I live for those who love me,
For those who know me true;
For the heaven so blue above me,
And the good that I can do.
GEORGE LINNAEUS BANKS.

Life is a long lesson in humility.
BARRIE—*Little Minister.*

Our lives are but our marches to the grave.
BEAUMONT and FLETCHER.

It is a misery to be born, a pain to live, a trouble to die.
ST. BERNARD.

Alas, how scant the sheaves for all the trouble,
The toil, the pain and the resolve sublime—
A few full ears; the rest but weeds and stubble,
And withered wild-flowers plucked before their time.
A. B. Bragdon—*The Old Campus.*

There are loyal hearts, there are spirits brave,
There are souls that are pure and true;
Then give to the world the best you have,
And the best will come back to you.
Madeleine Bridges—*Life's Mirror.*

Life, believe, is not a dream,
So dark as sages say;
Oft a little morning rain
Foretells a pleasant day!
Charlotte Brontë—*Life.*

Life is a pure flame, and we live by an invisible sun within us.
Sir Thomas Browne.

The long habit of living indisposeth us for dying.
Sir Thomas Browne.

I count life just a stuff
To try the soul's strength on.
Browning—*In a Balcony.*

O Life! thou art a galling load,
Along a rough, a weary road,
To wretches such as I!
Burns—*Despondency.*

Life is but a day at most.
Burns—*Friars' Carse Hermitage.*

Through life's road, so dim and dirty,
I have dragged to three and thirty;
What have these years left to me?
Nothing, except thirty-three.
Byron—*Diary.*

One life;—a little gleam of Time between two Eternities.
Carlyle.

We come and we cry, and that is life; we yawn and we depart, and that is death!
Ausone de Chancel—*Lines in an Album.*

Life is an incurable disease.
Abraham Cowley.

Men deal with life as children with their play,
Who first misuse, then cast their toys away.
Cowper—*Hope.*

Every moment of life is a step toward the grave.
Crébillon.

Learn to live well, that thou may'st die so too;
To live and die is all we have to do.
Sir John Denham—*Of Prudence.*

One awakens, one rises, one dresses, and one goes forth;
One returns, one dines, one sups, one retires and one sleeps.
De Piis.

For life in general, there is but one decree: youth is a blunder, manhood a struggle, old age a regret.
Disraeli.

When I consider life, 'tis all a cheat;
Yet, fooled with hope, men favour the deceit.
Dryden.

A little rule, a little sway,
A sunbeam in a winter's day,
Is all the proud and mighty have
Between the cradle and the grave.
John Dyer.

A man's ingress into the world is naked and bare,
His progress through the world is trouble and care;
And lastly, his egress out of the world, is nobody knows where.
If we do well here, we shall do well there;
I can tell you no more if I preach a whole year.
John Edwin.

No one is to be despaired of as long as he breathes. (While there is life there is hope.)
Erasmus.

The King in a carriage may ride,
And the Beggar may crawl at his side;

But in the general race,
They are traveling all the same pace.
EDWARD FITZGERALD — *Chrononoros.*

Life is rather a state of embryo,—a preparation for life. A man is not completely born until he has passed through death.
FRANKLIN.

Were the offer made true, I would engage to run again, from beginning to end, the same career of life. All I would ask should be the privilege of an author, to correct, in a second edition, certain errors of the first.
FRANKLIN.

Dost thou love life? Then do not squander time, for that is the stuff life is made of.
FRANKLIN—*Poor Richard.*

How short is life! how frail is human trust!
GAY.

A useless life is an early death.
GOETHE.

For Fate has wove the thread of life with pain,
And twins ev'n from the birth are Misery and Man!
HOMER—*Odyssey.*

Study as if you were to live forever. Live as if you were to die tomorrow.
ISIDORE OF SEVILLE.

All that a man hath will he give for his life.
Job. II. 4.

Human life is everywhere a state in which much is to be endured, and little enjoyed.
SAMUEL JOHNSON.

Catch, then, oh! catch the transient hour,
Improve each moment as it flies;
Life's a short summer—man a flower;
He dies—alas! how soon he dies!
SAMUEL JOHNSON—*Winter.*

Our whole life is like a play.
BEN JONSON.

The short bloom of our brief and narrow life flies fast away. While we are calling for flowers and wine and women, old age is upon us.
JUVENAL.

Life is a tragedy for those who feel, and a comedy for those who think.
LA BRUYÈRE.

Most men employ the first part of life to make the other part miserable.
LA BRUYÈRE.

Love is sunshine, hate is shadow,
Life is checkered shade and sunshine.
LONGFELLOW—*Hiawatha.*

Tell me not, in mournful numbers,
Life is but an empty dream!
LONGFELLOW—*A Psalm of Life.*

Art is long, and Time is fleeting,
And our hearts, though stout and brave,
Still, like muffled drums, are beating
Funeral marches to the grave.
LONGFELLOW—*A Psalm of Life.*

Christian life consists in faith and charity.
LUTHER.

We are always beginning to live, but are never living.
MANILIUS.

To-morrow I will live, the fool does say;
To-day itself's too late, the wise lived yesterday.
MARTIAL.

He most lives who thinks most, feels the noblest, acts the best; and he whose heart beats the quickest lives the longest.
JAMES MARTINEAU.

Wide is the gate and broad is the way that leadeth to destruction.
Matthew. VII. 13.

Strait is the gate and narrow is the way which leadeth unto life.
Matthew. VII. 14.

Life is a mission. Every other definition of life is false, and leads all who accept it astray. Religion, science, philosophy, though still at variance upon many points, all agree in this, that every existence is an aim.
MAZZINI—*Life and Writings.*

To take away life is a power which the vilest of the earth have in common; to give it belongs to gods and kings alone.
METASTASIO.

Were I to live my life over again, I should live it just as I have done. I neither complain of the past, nor do I fear the future.
MONTAIGNE—*Essays on Repentance.*

Life is but jest:
A dream, a doom;
A gleam, a gloom—
And then—good rest!

Life is but play;
A throb, a tear:
A sob, a sneer;
And then—good day.
LEON DE MONTENAEKEN.

'Tis not the whole of life to live;
Nor all of death to die.
MONTGOMERY—*The Issues of Life and Death.*

Vain were the man, and false as vain,
Who said, were he ordained to run
His long career of life again
He would do all that he had done.
MOORE—*My Birthday.*

The longer one lives the more he learns.
MOORE—*Dream of Hindoostan.*

A narrow isthmus 'twixt two boundless seas,
The past, the future, two eternities.
MOORE—*Lalla Rookh.*

Our days begin with trouble here, our life is but a span,
And cruel death is always near, so frail a thing is man.
New England Primer, 1777.

You know how little while we have to stay,
And, once departed, may return no more.
OMAR KHAYYÁM—*Rubaiyat.*

Ah Love! could you and I with him conspire
To grasp this sorry Scheme of Things entire
Would we not shatter it to bits—and then
Re-mould it nearer to the Heart's Desire?
OMAR KHAYYÁM—*Rubaiyat.*

Think, in this batter'd Caravanserai
Whose portals are alternate Night and Day,
How Sultan after Sultan with his Pomp
Abode his destin'd Hour and went his way.
OMAR KHAYYÁM—*Rubaiyat.*

But helpless Pieces of the Game He plays
Upon this Checker-board of Nights and Days;
Hither and thither moves, and checks, and slays,
And one by one back in the Closet lays.
OMAR KHAYYÁM—*Rubaiyat.*

And fear not lest Existence closing your
Account should lose or know the type no more:
The Eternal Saki from that Bowl has poured
Millions of Bubbles like us and will pour.
OMAR KHAYYÁM—*Rubaiyat.*

This life a theatre we well may call,
Where every actor must perform with art,
Or laugh it through, and make a farce of all,
Or learn to bear with grace his tragic part.
PALLADAS.

Let us (since life can little more supply
Than just to look about us and to die)
Expatiate free o'er all this scene of man;
A mighty maze! but not without a plan.
POPE—*Essay on Man.*

Like bubbles on the sea of matter borne,
They rise, they break, and to that sea return.
POPE—*Essay on Man.*

Learn to live well, or fairly make your will;
You've play'd, and lov'd, and ate, and drank your fill:
Walk sober off, before a sprightlier age
Comes titt'ring on, and shoves you from the stage.
POPE—*Second Book of Horace.*

Who breathes must suffer; and who thinks, must mourn;
And he alone is bless'd who ne'er was born.
PRIOR.

So vanishes our state; so pass our days;
So life but opens now, and now decays;
The cradle and the tomb, alas! so nigh,
To live is scarce distinguish'd from to die.
PRIOR.

Half my life is full of sorrow,
Half of joy, still fresh and new;
One of these lives is a fancy,
But the other one is true.
ADELAIDE A. PROCTER—*Dream-Life.*

Lord, make me to know mine end, and the measure of my days, what it is; that I may know how frail I am.
Psalms. XXXIX. 4.

As for man his days are as grass; as a flower of the field so he flourisheth.
Psalms. CIII. 15.

The wind passeth over it, and it is gone; and the place thereof shall know it no more.
Psalms. CIII. 16.

Only deeds give strength to life, only moderation gives it charm.
JEAN PAUL RICHTER—*Titan.*

In speaking to you men of the greatest city of the West, men of the state which gave to the country Lincoln and Grant, men who pre-eminently and distinctly embody all that is most American in the American character, I wish to preach not the doctrine of ignoble ease, but the doctrine of the strenuous life.
THEODORE ROOSEVELT.

This life is but the passage of a day,
This life is but a pang and all is over;
But in the life to come which fades not away
Every love shall abide and every lover.
CHRISTINA G. ROSSETTI—*Saints and Angels.*

Say, what is life? 'Tis to be born,
A helpless Babe, to greet the light
With a sharp wail, as if the morn
Foretold a cloudy noon and night;
To weep, to sleep, and weep again,
With sunny smiles between; and then?
J. G. SAXE—*The Story of Life.*

The May of life blooms once and never again.
SCHILLER—*Resignation.*

His saying was: live and let live.
SCHILLER.

The part of life which we really live is short.
SENECA.

As is a tale, so is life: not how long it is, but how good it is, is what matters.
SENECA.

And so from hour to hour we ripe and ripe,
And then from hour to hour we rot and rot;
And thereby hangs a tale.
SHAKESPEARE—*As You Like It.* Act II. Sc. 7.

Out, out, brief candle!
Life's but a walking shadow.
SHAKESPEARE—*Macbeth.* Act V. Sc. 5.

To make good use of life, one should have in youth the experience of advanced years, and in old age the vigor of youth.
STANISLAUS.

Away with funeral music—set
The pipe to powerful lips—
The cup of life's for him that drinks
And not for him that sips.
STEVENSON. Boulogne, 1872.

Man is an organ of life, and God alone is life.
SWEDENBORG—*True Christian Religion.*

May you live all the days of your life.
SWIFT.

The day is short, the work is much.
BEN SYRA.

Let your life lightly dance on the edges of Time like dew on the tip of a leaf.
RABINDRANATH TAGORE—*Gardener.*

The white flower of a blameless life.
TENNYSON—*Idylls of the King.*

Life is like a game of tables, the chances are not in our power, but the playing is.
TERENCE.

Life is a comedy to him who thinks, and tragedy to him who feels.
HORACE WALPOLE.

Life is a game of whist. From unseen sources
The cards are shuffled, and the hands are dealt.
Blind are our efforts to control the forces
That, though unseen, are no less strongly felt.

I do not like the way the cards are shuffled,
But yet I like the game and want to play;
And through the long, long night will I, unruffled,
Play what I get, until the break of day.
EUGENE F. WARE—*Whist.*

Our life contains a thousand springs,
And dies if one be gone.
Strange! that a harp of thousand strings
Should keep in tune so long.
WATTS—*Hymns and Spiritual Songs.*

I desire to have both heaven and hell ever in my eye, while I stand on this isthmus of life, between two boundless oceans.
JOHN WESLEY—*Letter to Charles Wesley.*

I swear the earth shall surely be complete to him or her who shall be complete,
The earth remains jagged and broken only to him or her who remains jagged and broken.
WALT WHITMAN—*Song of the Rolling Earth.*

Our lives are albums written through
With good or ill, with false or true;
And as the blessed angels turn
The pages of our years,
God grant they read the good with smiles,
And blot the ill with tears!
WHITTIER—*Written in a Lady's Album.*

The days grow shorter, the nights grow longer,
The headstones thicken along the way;
And life grows sadder, but love grows stronger
For those who walk with us day by day.
ELLA WHEELER WILCOX—*Interlude.*

Our lives are songs; God writes the words
And we set them to music at pleasure;
And the song grows glad, or sweet or sad,
As we choose to fashion the measure.
ELLA WHEELER WILCOX—*Our Lives.*

Men know life too early, women know life too late.
WILDE—*A Woman of No Importance.*

Ah! somehow life is bigger after all
Than any painted angel could we see
The God that is within us!
OSCAR WILDE—*Humanitad.*

All the things I really like to do are either immoral, illegal or fattening.
ALEXANDER WOOLLCOTT.

While man is growing, life is in decrease.
And cradles rock us nearer to the tomb:
Our birth is nothing but our death begun.
YOUNG—*Night Thoughts.*

LIGHT

Light is the first of painters. There is no object so foul that intense light will not make it beautiful.
EMERSON—*Nature.*

I shall light a candle of understanding in thine heart, which shall not be put out.
II Esdras. XIV. 25.

And God said, Let there be light: and there was light.
Genesis. I. 3.

Where there is much light, the shadows are deepest.
GOETHE.

The true light, which lighteth every man that cometh into the world.
John. I. 9.

He was a burning and a shining light.
John. V. 35.

Walk while ye have the light, lest darkness come upon you.
John. XII. 35.

He that has light within his own clear breast
May sit i' th' centre and enjoy bright day;
But he that hides a dark soul and foul thoughts
Benighted walks under the mid-day sun.
MILTON—*Comus.*

Lead, kindly Light, amid the encircling gloom,
Lead Thou me on!
The night is dark, and I am far from home—
Lead Thou me on!
Keep Thou my feet; I do not ask to see
The distant scene,—one step enough for me.
JOHN HENRY NEWMAN.

And this I know; whether the one True Light
Kindle to Love, or Wrath consume me quite,
One flash of it within the Tavern caught
Better than in the temple lost outright.
OMAR KHAYYÁM—*Rubaiyat.*

Those having lamps will pass them on to others.
PLATO—*Republic.*

Nature and Nature's laws lay hid in night:
God said, "Let Newton be!" and all was light.
POPE—*Epitaph for Sir Isaac Newton.*

Where God and Nature met in light.
TENNYSON—*In Memoriam.*

LILAC

When lilacs last in the door-yard bloom'd,
And the great star early droop'd in the western sky in the night,
I mourn'd—and yet shall mourn with ever-returning spring.
WALT WHITMAN.

With every leaf a miracle . . . and from this bush in the door-yard,
With delicate-colour'd blossoms, and heart-shaped leaves of rich green
A sprig, with its flower, I break.
WALT WHITMAN.

LILY

I like not lady-slippers,
Nor yet the sweet-pea blossoms,
Nor yet the flaky roses,
Red or white as snow;
I like the chaliced lilies,
The heavy Eastern lilies,
The gorgeous tiger-lilies,
That in our garden grow.
T. B. ALDRICH—*Tiger Lilies.*

. . . Purple lilies Dante blew
To a large bubble with his prophet breath.
E. B. BROWNING—*Aurora Leigh.*

Very whitely still
The lilies of our lives may reassure
Their blossoms from their roots, accessible
Alone to heavenly dews that drop not fewer;
Growing straight out of man's reach, on the hill.
God only, who made us rich, can make us poor.
E. B. BROWNING—*Sonnets from the Portuguese.*

Yet, the great ocean hath no tone of power
Mightier to reach the soul, in thought's hushed hour,
Than yours, ye Lilies! chosen thus and graced!
MRS. HEMANS—*The Lilies of the Field.*

O lovely lily clean,
O lily springing green,
O lily bursting white,
Dear lily of delight,
Spring in my heart agen
That I may flower to men.
MASEFIELD—*Everlasting Mercy.*

Consider the lilies of the field, how they grow; they toil not, neither do they spin.
Matthew. VI. 28.

"Thou wert not, Solomon! in all thy glory
Array'd," the lilies cry, "in robes like ours;
How vain your grandeur! Ah, how transitory
Are human flowers!"
HORACE SMITH—*Hymn to the Flowers.*

But who will watch my lilies,
When their blossoms open white?
By day the sun shall be sentry,
And the moon and the stars by night!
BAYARD TAYLOR—*The Garden of Roses.*

LINCOLN

Some opulent force of genius, soul, and race,
Some deep life-current from far centuries
Flowed to his mind and lighted his sad eyes,
And gave his name, among great names, high place.
JOEL BENTON—*Another Washington.*

If so men's memories not a monument be,
None shalt thou have. Warm hearts, and not cold stone,
Must mark thy grave, or thou shalt lie, unknown.
Marbles keep not themselves; how then, keep thee?
JOHN VANCE CHENEY—*Thy Monument.*

O, Uncommon Commoner! may your name
Forever lead like a living flame!
Unschooled scholar! how did you learn
The wisdom a lifetime may not earn?
Unsainted martyr! higher than saint!
You were a *man* with a man's constraint.
In the world, *of* the world was your lot;
With it and for it the fight you fought,
And never till Time is itself forgot
And the heart of man is a pulseless clot
Shall the blood flow slow, when we think the thought
Of Lincoln!
EDMUND VANCE COOKE—*The Uncommon Commoner.*

And anger, came to North and South
When Lincoln died.
W. J. LAMPTON—*Lincoln.*

That nation has not lived in vain which has given the world Washington and Lincoln, the best great men and the greatest good men whom history can show. . . . You cry out in the words of Bunyan, "So Valiant-for-Truth passed over, and all the trumpets sounded for him on the other side."

HENRY CABOT LODGE—*Lincoln.*

Nature, they say, doth dote,
And cannot make a man
Save on some worn-out plan
Repeating us by rote:
For him her Old World moulds aside she threw
And, choosing sweet clay from the breast
Of the unexhausted West,
With stuff untainted shaped a hero new.

LOWELL—*A Hero New.*

When the Norn-mother saw the Whirlwind Hour,
Greatening and darkening as it hurried on,
She bent the strenuous Heavens and came down
To make a man to meet the mortal need.
She took the tried clay of the common road—
Clay warm yet with the genial heat of Earth,
Dashed through it all a strain of prophecy;
Then mixed a laughter with the serious stuff.
It was a stuff to wear for centuries,
A man that matched the mountains, and compelled
The stars to look our way and honor us.

EDWIN MARKHAM—*Lincoln, the Man of the People.*

Lo, as I gaze, the statured man,
Built up from yon large hand appears:
A type that nature wills to plan
But once in all a people's years.

E. C. STEDMAN—*Hand of Lincoln.*

No Caesar he whom we lament,
A Man without a precedent,
Sent, it would seem, to do
His work, and perish, too.

R. H. STODDARD—*The Man We Mourn Today.*

O captain! my captain! our fearful trip is done;
The ship has weather'd every rack; the prize we sought is won;
The port is near, the bells I hear, the people all exulting,
While follow eyes the steady keel, the vessel grim and daring;
But O heart! heart! heart!
O the bleeding drops of red,
Where on the deck my captain lies,
Fallen cold and dead.

WALT WHITMAN—*O Captain! My Captain!*

LION

The lion is not so fierce as they paint him.

HERBERT.

Do not pluck the beard of a dead lion.

MARTIAL.

It is not good to wake a sleeping lion.

PHILIP SIDNEY—*Arcadia.*

LISTENING

But yet she listen'd—'tis enough—
Who listens once will listen twice;
Her heart, be sure, is not of ice,
And one refusal no rebuff.

BYRON—*Mazeppa.*

A good listener is not only popular everywhere, but after a while he knows something.

WILSON MIZNER.

LITERATURE

The great standard of literature as to purity and exactness of style is the Bible.

BLAIR.

Literature is the thought of thinking Souls.

CARLYLE—*Essays.*

Literature has her quacks no less than medicine, and they are divided into two classes; those who have erudition without genius, and those who have volubility without depth; we shall get

second-hand sense from the one, and original nonsense from the other.
COLTON.

I made a compact with myself that in my person literature should stand by itself, of itself, and for itself.
DICKENS. Speech, 1869.

Literature is an avenue to glory, ever open for those ingenious men who are deprived of honours or of wealth.
ISAAC D'ISRAELI.

The republic of letters.
MOLIÈRE.

The fashion of liking Racine will pass away like that of coffee.
MME. DE SÉVIGNÉ.

Literature always anticipates life. It does not copy it, but molds it to its purpose.
OSCAR WILDE—*The Decay of Lying,* 1891.

LOGIC

Men are apt to mistake the strength of their feeling for the strength of their argument. The heated mind resents the chill touch and relentless scrutiny of logic.
GLADSTONE.

Logic is logic. That's all I say.
O. W. HOLMES—*The One-Hoss Shay.*

The knowledge of the theory of logic has no tendency whatever to make men good reasoners.
MACAULAY.

Grammar is the logic of speech, even as logic is the grammar of reason.
TRENCH.

LONDON

A mighty mass of brick, and smoke, and shipping,
Dirty and dusty, but as wide as eye
Could reach, with here and there a sail just skipping
In sight, then lost amidst the forestry
Of masts; a wilderness of steeples peeping
On tiptoe through their sea-coal canopy;
A huge, dun cupola, like a foolscap crown
On a fool's head—and there is London Town.
BYRON—*Don Juan.*

London is a roost for every bird.
DISRAELI—*Lothair.*

London! the needy villain's general home,
The common sewer of Paris and of Rome!
With eager thirst, by folly or by fate,
Sucks in the dregs of each corrupted state.
SAMUEL JOHNSON—*London.*

LOSS

When wealth is lost, nothing is lost;
When health is lost, something is lost;
When character is lost, all is lost!
ANONYMOUS.

For 'tis a truth well known to most,
That whatsoever thing is lost,
We seek it, ere it comes to light,
In every cranny but the right.
COWPER—*The Retired Cat.*

A wise man loses nothing, if he but save himself.
MONTAIGNE.

What you lend is lost; when you ask for it back, you may find a friend made an enemy by your kindness. If you begin to press him further, you have the choice of two things—either to lose your loan or lose your friend.
PLAUTUS.

Wise men ne'er sit and wail their loss,
But cheerly seek how to redress their harms.
SHAKESPEARE—*Henry VI.* Pt. III. Act V. Sc. 4.

No man can lose what he never had.
IZAAK WALTON—*The Compleat Angler.*

LOVE

Mysterious love, uncertain treasure,
Hast thou more of pain or pleasure!
Endless torments dwell about thee:
Yet who would live, and live without thee!
ADDISON—*Rosamond.*

I seek for one as fair and gay,
But find none to remind me,
How blest the hours pass'd away
With the girl I left behind me.
ANONYMOUS.

Somewhere there waiteth in this world of ours
For one lone soul another lonely soul,
Each choosing each through all the weary hours,
And meeting strangely at one sudden goal,
Then blend they, like green leaves with golden flowers,
Into one beautiful and perfect whole;
And life's long night is ended, and the way
Lies open onward to eternal day.
EDWIN ARNOLD—*Somewhere There Waiteth.*

One sweet, sad secret holds my heart in thrall;
A mighty love within my breast has grown,
Unseen, unspoken, and of no one known;
And of my sweet, who gave it, least of all.
FELIX ARVERS—*Sonnet.*

Ask not of me, love, what is love?
Ask what is good of God above;
Ask of the great sun what is light;
Ask what is darkness of the night;
Ask sin of what may be forgiven;
Ask what is happiness of heaven;
Ask what is folly of the crowd;
Ask what is fashion of the shroud;
Ask what is sweetness of thy kiss;
Ask of thyself what beauty is.
BAILEY—*Festus.*

I cannot love as I have loved,
And yet I know not why;
It is the one great woe of life
To feel all feeling die.
BAILEY—*Festus.*

Love spends his all, and still hath store.
BAILEY—*Festus.*

The sweetest joy, the wildest woe is love.
BAILEY—*Festus.*

Man loves little and often, woman much and rarely.
BASTA.

How many times do I love, again?
Tell me how many beads there are
In a silver chain
Of evening rain
Unravelled from the trembling main
And threading the eye of a yellow star:—
So many times do I love again.
THOMAS LOVELL BEDDOES—*How Many Times.*

Love in France is a comedy; in England a tragedy; in Italy an opera seria; and in Germany a melodrama.
MARGUERITE BLESSINGTON.

Our first and last love is—self-love.
BOVEE.

The first sigh of love is the last of wisdom.
ANTOINE BRET.

Much ado there was, God wot;
He woold love, and she woold not,
She sayd, "Never man was trewe;"
He sayes, "None was false to you."
NICHOLAS BRETON—*Phillida and Corydon.*

In your arms was still delight,
Quiet as a street at night;
And thoughts of you, I do remember,
Were green leaves in a darkened chamber,
Were dark clouds in a moonless sky.
RUPERT BROOKE—*Retrospect.*

Whoever lives true life, will love true love.
E. B. BROWNING—*Aurora Leigh.*

But I love you, sir:
And when a woman says she loves a man,
The man must hear her, though he love her not.
E. B. BROWNING—*Aurora Leigh.*

Who can fear
Too many stars, though each in heaven shall roll—
Too many flowers, though each shall crown the year?
Say thou dost love me, love me, love me—toll
The silver iterance!—only minding, Dear,
To love me also in silence, with thy soul.
E. B. BROWNING—*Sonnets from the Portuguese.*

Unless you can feel when the song is done
No other is sweet in its rhythm;
Unless you can feel when left by one
That all men else go with him.
E. B. BROWNING—*Unless.*

God be thanked, the meanest of his creatures
Boasts two soul-sides, one to face the world with,
One to show a woman when he loves her.
BROWNING—*One Word More.*

To see her is to love her,
And love but her forever;
For nature made her what she is,
And never made anither!
BURNS—*Bonny Lesley.*

The golden hours on angel wings
Flew o'er me and my dearie,
For dear to me as light and life
Was my sweet Highland Mary.
BURNS—*Highland Mary.*

Oh my luve's like a red, red rose,
That's newly sprung in June;
Oh my luve's like the melodie
That's sweetly played in tune.
BURNS—*Red, Red Rose.*

What is life, when wanting love?
Night without a morning;
Love's the cloudless summer sun,
Nature gay adorning.
BURNS—*Thine Am I, My Faithful Fair.*

No cord nor cable can so forcibly draw, or hold so fast, as love can do with a twined thread.
BURTON—*Anatomy of Melancholy.*

What mad lover ever dy'd,
To gain a soft and gentle bride?
Or for a lady tender-hearted,
In purling streams or hemp departed?
BUTLER—*Hudibras.*

Oh Love! young Love! bound in thy rosy band,
Let sage or cynic prattle as he will,
These hours, and only these, redeem Life's years of ill.
BYRON—*Childe Harold.*

O! that the Desert were my dwelling place,
With one fair Spirit for my minister,
That I might all forget the human race,
And, hating no one, love but only her!
BYRON—*Childe Harold.*

Man's love is of man's life a thing apart,
'Tis woman's whole existence: man may range
The court, camp, church, the vessel, and the mart,
Sword, gown, gain, glory, offer in exchange
Pride, fame, ambition, to fill up his heart,
And few there are whom these cannot estrange;
Men have all these resources, we but one,
To love again, and be again undone.
BYRON—*Don Juan.*

In her first passion woman loves her lover;
In all the others, all she loves is love.
BYRON—*Don Juan.*

Yes, Love indeed is light from heaven;
A spark of that immortal fire
With angels shared, by Allah given
To lift from earth our low desire.
BYRON—*The Giaour.*

Then fly betimes, for only they
Conquer love, that run away.
THOMAS CAREW.

Of all the girls that are so smart
There's none like pretty Sally;
She is the darling of my heart,
And lives in our alley.
HENRY CAREY—*Sally in Our Alley.*

What woman says to her fond lover should be written in air or the swift water.
CATULLUS.

There's no love lost between us.
CERVANTES—*Don Quixote.*

Alas! they had been friends in youth;
But whispering tongues can poison truth,
And constancy lives in realms above;
And life is thorny, and youth is vain;
And to be wroth with one we love
Doth work like madness in the brain.
COLERIDGE—*Christabel.*

All thoughts, all passions, all delights,
Whatever stirs this mortal frame,
All are but ministers of Love,
And feed his sacred flame.
COLERIDGE—*Love.*

I have heard of reasons manifold
Why love must needs be blind,
But this is the best of all I hold—
His eyes are in his mind.
COLERIDGE—*To a Lady.*

Heaven has no rage like love to hatred turned.
CONGREVE.

He that can't live upon love deserves to die in a ditch.
CONGREVE.

I know not when the day shall be,
I know not when our eyes may meet;
What welcome you may give to me,
Or will your words be sad or sweet,
It may not be 'till years have passed,
'Till eyes are dim and tresses gray;
The world is wide, but, love, at last,
Our hands, our hearts, must meet some day.
HUGH CONWAY—*Some Day.*

How wise are they that are but fools in love!
JOSHUA COOKE.

A mighty pain to love it is,
And 'tis a pain that pain to miss;
But, of all pains, the greatest pain
Is to love, but love in vain.
ABRAHAM COWLEY.

Love with men is not a sentiment, but an idea.
MADAME DE GIRARDIN.

Love is an ocean of emotions, entirely surrounded by expenses.
LORD DEWAR.

We are all born for love. . . . It is the principle of existence and its only end.
DISRAELI—*Sybil.*

Give, you gods,
Give to your boy, your Caesar,
The rattle of a globe to play withal,
This gewgaw world, and put him cheaply off;
I'll not be pleased with less than Cleopatra.
DRYDEN—*All for Love.*

How happy the lover,
How easy his chain,
How pleasing his pain,
How sweet to discover
He sighs not in vain.
DRYDEN—*King Arthur.*

I have found it impossible to carry the heavy burden of responsibility and to discharge my duties as King as I would wish to do without the help and support of the woman I love.
EDWARD VIII (later the Duke of Windsor) in his farewell address, 1936.

'Tis what I love determines how I love.
GEORGE ELIOT—*The Spanish Gypsy.*

The solid, solid universe
Is pervious to Love;
With bandaged eyes he never errs,
Around, below, above.
His blinding light
He flingeth white
On God's and Satan's brood,
And reconciles
By mystic wiles
The evil and the good.
EMERSON—*Cupido.*

All mankind love a lover.
EMERSON—*Essays.*

But one always returns to one's first loves.
ETIENNE—*Joconde.*

He is not a lover who does not love for ever.
EURIPIDES.

Love is the tyrant of the heart; it darkens
Reason, confounds discretion; deaf to Counsel
It runs a headlong course to desperate madness.
JOHN FORD—*The Lover's Melancholy.*

If you would be loved, love and be lovable.
FRANKLIN.

It's love, it's love that makes the world go round.
French Song.

Love, then, hath every bliss in store;
'Tis friendship, and 'tis something more.
Each other every wish they give;
Not to know love is not to live.
GAY.

Not from the whole wide world I chose thee,
Sweetheart, light of the land and the sea!
The wide, wide world could not inclose thee,
For thou art the whole wide world to me.
R. W. GILDER—*Song.*

Love grants in a moment
What toil can hardly achieve in an age.
GOETHE.

Girls we love for what they are;
Young men for what they promise to be.
GOETHE.

The hawthorn-bush, with seats beneath the shade
For talking age and whispering lovers made!
GOLDSMITH—*The Deserted Village.*

Thus let me hold thee to my heart,
And every care resign:
And we shall never, never part,
My life—my all that's mine!
GOLDSMITH—*The Hermit.*

Man begins by loving love and ends by loving a woman. Woman begins by loving a man and ends by loving love.
REMY DE GOURMONT.

My heart I fain would ask thee
What then is Love? say on.
"Two souls and one thought only
Two hearts that throb as one."
FRIEDRICH HALM.

Love understands love; it needs no talk.
F. R. HAVERGAL.

Whom the Lord loveth he chasteneth.
Hebrews. XII. 6.

It is an ancient story
Yet is it ever new.
HEINE.

You say to me-ward's your affection's strong;
Pray love me little, so you love me long.
HERRICK.

There is a lady sweet and kind,
Was never face so pleased my mind;
I did but see her passing by,
And yet I love her till I die.
HERRICK.

Bid me to live, and I will live
Thy Protestant to be:
Or bid me love, and I will give
A loving heart to thee,
A heart as soft, a heart as kind,
A heart as sound and free
As in the whole world thou canst find,
That heart I'll give to thee.
HERRICK—*To Anthea.*

They do not love that do not show their love.
HEYWOOD—*Proverbs.*

To love is to know the sacrifices which eternity exacts from life.
JOHN OLIVER HOBBES—*School for Saints.*

O, love, love, love!
Love is like a dizziness;
It winna let a poor body
Gang about his biziness!
HOGG—*Love Is Like a Dizziness.*

Soft is the breath of a maiden's Yes:
Not the light gossamer stirs with less;
But never a cable that holds so fast
Through all the battles of wave and blast.
HOLMES—*Songs of Many Seasons.*

For love deceives the best of woman kind.
HOMER—*Odyssey.*

Love's like the measles—all the worse when it comes late in life.
JERROLD.

Greater love hath no man than this, that a man lay down his life for his friends.
John. XV. 13.

There is no fear in love; but perfect love casteth out fear.
I John. IV. 18.

Love in a hut, with water and a crust,
Is—Love, forgive us!—cinders, ashes, dust.
KEATS—*Lamia.*

I wish you could invent some means to make me at all happy without you. Every hour I am more and more concentrated in you; everything else tastes like chaff in my mouth.
KEATS—*Letters.*

When late I attempted your pity to move,
Why seemed you so deaf to my prayers?
Perhaps it was right to dissemble your love
But—why did you kick me downstairs?
J. P. KEMBLE—*Panel.*

The heart of a man to the heart of a maid—
Light of my tents, be fleet—
Morning awaits at the end of the world,
And the world is all at our feet.
KIPLING—*Gypsy Trail.*

Sing, for faith and hope are high—
None so true as you and I—
Sing the Lovers' Litany:
"Love like ours can never die!"
KIPLING—*Lovers' Litany.*

By the old Moulmein Pagoda, lookin' eastward to the sea,
There's a Burma girl a-settin', and I know she thinks o' me;
For the wind is in the palm-trees, and the temple-bells they say:
"Come you back, you British soldier; come you back to Mandalay!"
KIPLING—*Mandalay.*

If Love were jester at the court of Death,
And Death the king of all, still would I pray,
"For me the motley and the bauble, yea,
Though all be vanity, as the Preacher saith,
The mirth of love be mine for one brief breath!"
FREDERIC L. KNOWLES—*If Love Were Jester at the Court of Death.*

Love begins with love.
LA BRUYÈRE.

We never love heartily but once, and that is the first time we love.
LA BRUYÈRE.

O tyrant love, when held by you,
We may to prudence bid adieu.
LA FONTAINE.

The reason why lovers and their mistresses never tire of being together is that they are always talking of themselves.
LA ROCHEFOUCAULD.

Do you know you have asked for the costliest thing
Ever made by the Hand above—
A woman's heart, and a woman's life,
And a woman's wonderful love?
MARY T. LATHROP.

I love a lassie, a bonnie, bonnie lassie,
She's as pure as the lily in the dell.
She's as sweet as the heather,
The bonnie, bloomin' heather,
Mary, ma Scotch Blue-bell.
HARRY LAUDER and GERALD GRAFTON.

Love leads to present rapture,—then to pain;
But all through Love in time is healed again.
LELAND—*Sweet Marjoram.*

Ah, how skillful grows the hand
That obeyeth Love's command!
It is the heart and not the brain
That to the highest doth attain,
And he who followeth Love's behest
Far excelleth all the rest.
LONGFELLOW—*Building of the Ship.*

Like Dian's kiss, unask'd, unsought,
Love gives itself, but is not bought.
LONGFELLOW—*Endymion.*

O, there is nothing holier, in this life of ours, than the first consciousness of love,—the first fluttering of its silken wings.
LONGFELLOW—*Hyperion.*

It is difficult to know at what moment love begins; it is less difficult to know that it has begun.
LONGFELLOW—*Kavanagh.*

That was the first sound in the song of love!
Scarce more than silence is, and yet a sound.
Hands of invisible spirits touch the strings
Of that mysterious instrument, the soul,
And play the prelude of our fate. We hear
The voice prophetic, and are not alone.
LONGFELLOW—*Spanish Student.*

How can I tell the signals and the signs
By which one heart another heart divines?
How can I tell the many thousand ways
By which it keeps the secret it betrays?
LONGFELLOW—*Tales of a Wayside Inn.*

Tell me not, sweet, I am unkind,
That from the nunnery
Of thy chaste breast and quiet mind
To war and arms I fly.

. . .

Yet this inconstancy is such
As you too shall adore:—
I could not love thee, dear, so much,
Loved I not honour more.
LOVELACE—*To Lucasta, on Going to the Wars.*

True love is but a humble, low born thing,
And hath its food served up in earthenware;
It is a thing to walk with, hand in hand,
Through the every-dayness of this workday world.
LOWELL—*Love.*

He who loves not wine, woman, and song,
Remains a fool his whole life long.
Attributed to LUTHER.

As love knoweth no lawes, so it regardeth no conditions.
LYLY.

But thou, through good and evil, praise and blame,
Wilt not thou love me for myself alone?
Yes, thou wilt love me with exceeding love,
And I will tenfold all that love repay;
Still smiling, though the tender may reprove,
Still faithful, though the trusted may betray.
MACAULAY.

Come live with me, and be my love,
And we will all the pleasures prove,
That valleys, groves, or hills, or fields,
Or woods and steepy mountains, yield.
MARLOWE—*The Passionate Shepherd to His Love.*

Love is a flame to burn out human wills,
Love is a flame to set the will on fire,
Love is a flame to cheat men into mire.
MASEFIELD—*Widow in the Bye Street.*

I loved you ere I knew you; know you now,
And having known you, love you better still.
OWEN MEREDITH.

Love is all in fire, and yet is ever freezing;
Love is much in winning, yet is more in leesing:
Love is ever sick, and yet is never dying;
Love is ever true, and yet is ever lying;
Love does doat in liking, and is mad in loathing;
Love indeed is anything, yet indeed is nothing.
THOMAS MIDDLETON—*Blurt, Master Constable.*

He who for love hath undergone
The worst that can befall,
Is happier thousandfold than one
Who never loved at all.
MONCKTON MILNES—*To Myrzha.*

So dear I love him, that with him all deaths
I could endure, without him live no life.
MILTON—*Paradise Lost.*

Love is often a fruit of marriage.
MOLIÈRE.

He loves little who loves by rule.
MONTAIGNE.

Yes, loving is a painful thrill,
And not to love more painful still;
But oh, it is the worst of pain,
To love and not be lov'd again.
MOORE.

I know not, I ask not, if guilt's in that heart,
I but know that I love thee, whatever thou art.
MOORE — *Come, Rest in This Bosom.*

But there's nothing half so sweet in life
As love's young dream.
MOORE.

I've wandered east, I've wandered west,
I've bourne a weary lot;
But in my wanderings far or near
Ye never were forgot.
The fount that first burst frae this heart
Still travels on its way
And channels deeper as it rins
The luve o' life's young day.
WILLIAM MOTHERWELL — *Jeanie Morrison.*

The only victory over love is flight.
NAPOLEON.

So they grew, and they grew, to the church steeple tops
And they couldn't grow up any higher;
So they twin'd themselves into a true lover's knot,
For all lovers true to admire.
Old Ballad.

Thus I am not able to exist either with you or without you; and I seem not to know my own wishes.
OVID.

Jupiter from on high laughs at the perjuries of lovers.
OVID.

He who falls in love meets a worse fate than he who leaps from a rock.
PLAUTUS.

Is it, in Heav'n, a crime to love too well?
To bear too tender or too firm a heart,
To act a lover's or a Roman's part?
Is there no bright reversion in the sky
For those who greatly think, or bravely die?
POPE—*Elegy on an Unfortunate Lady.*

Of all affliction taught a lover yet,
'Tis true the hardest science to forget.
POPE—*Eloisa to Abelard.*

Love, free as air, at sight of human ties,
Spreads his light wings, and in a moment flies.
POPE—*Epistle to Eloisa.*

O Love! for Sylvia let me gain the prize,
And make my tongue victorious as her eyes.
POPE—*Spring.*

Everybody in love is blind.
PROPERTIUS.

If all the world and love were young,
And truth in every shepherd's tongue,
These pretty pleasures might me move
To live with thee, and be thy love.
SIR WALTER RALEIGH — *The Nymph's Reply to the Passionate Shepherd*.

Ah! The seasons of love roll not backward but onward, downward forever.
JEAN PAUL RICHTER—*Hesperus*.

A loving maiden grows unconsciously more bold.
JEAN PAUL RICHTER—*Titan*.

As one who cons at evening o'er an album all alone,
And muses on the faces of the friends that he has known,
So I turn the leaves of Fancy, till in shadowy design
I find the smiling features of an old sweetheart of mine.
JAMES WHITCOMB RILEY—*An Old Sweetheart of Mine*.

The hours I spent with thee, dear heart,
Are as a string of pearls to me;
I count them over, every one apart,
My rosary, my rosary.
ROBERT CAMERON ROGERS — *My Rosary*.

Oh! she was good as she was fair.
None—none on earth above her!
As pure in thought as angels are,
To know her was to love her.
SAMUEL ROGERS—*Jacqueline*.

Love is the fulfilling of the law.
Romans. XIII. 10.

Whither thou goest, I will go; and where thou lodgest, I will lodge: thy people shall be my people, and thy God my God.
Ruth. I. 16.

One always returns to his first love.
ST. JUST.

Thy love to me was wonderful, passing the love of women.
II Samuel. I. 26.

It is not decided that women love more than men, but is indisputable that they love better.
SANIAL-DUBAY.

O that it might remain eternally green,
The beautiful time of youthful love.
SCHILLER.

I have enjoyed earthly happiness,
I have lived and loved.
SCHILLER.

Mortals, while through the world you go,
Hope may succor and faith befriend,
Yet happy your hearts if you can but know,
Love awaits at the journey's end!
CLINTON SCOLLARD—*The Journey's End—Envoy*.

And love is loveliest when embalm'd in tears.
SCOTT—*Lady of the Lake*.

In peace, Love tunes the shepherd's reed;
In war, he mounts the warrior's steed;
In halls, in gay attire is seen;
In hamlets, dances on the green.
Love rules the court, the camp, the grove,
And men below, and saints above;
For love is heaven, and heaven is love.
SCOTT—*Lay of the Last Minstrel*.

True love's the gift which God has given
To man alone beneath the heaven.

. . .

It is the secret sympathy,
The silver link, the silken tie,
Which heart to heart, and mind to mind,
In body and in soul can bind.
SCOTT—*Lay of the Last Minstrel*.

But are you so much in love as your rhymes speak?
Neither rhyme nor reason can express how much.
SHAKESPEARE—*As You Like It*. Act III. Sc. 2.

Men have died from time to time, and worms have eaten them,—but not for love.
SHAKESPEARE—*As You Like It*. Act IV. Sc. 1.

No sooner met but they looked, no sooner looked but they loved, no sooner loved but they sighed, no sooner sighed but they asked one another the reason.
SHAKESPEARE—*As You Like It.* Act V. Sc. 2.

This is the very ecstasy of love,
Whose violent property foredoes itself,
And leads the will to desperate undertakings.
SHAKESPEARE—*Hamlet.* Act II. Sc. 1.

Love thyself last: cherish those hearts that hate thee.
SHAKESPEARE—*Henry VIII.* Act III. Sc. 2.

Ay me! for aught that I ever could read,
Could ever hear by tale or history,
The course of true love never did run smooth.
SHAKESPEARE—*Midsummer Night's Dream.* Act I. Sc. 1.

Friendship is constant in all other things
Save in the office and affairs of love:
Therefore, all hearts in love use their own tongues;
Let every eye negotiate for itself
And trust no agent.
SHAKESPEARE—*Much Ado about Nothing.* Act II. Sc. 1.

Love is a smoke rais'd with the fume of sighs;
Being purg'd, a fire sparkling in a lover's eyes;
Being vex'd, a sea nourish'd with lovers' tears:
What is it else? a madness most discreet,
A choking gall and a preserving sweet.
SHAKESPEARE—*Romeo and Juliet.* Act I. Sc. 1.

Speak but one rhyme, and I am satisfied;
Cry but—"Ay me!" pronounce but "love" and "dove."
SHAKESPEARE—*Romeo and Juliet.* Act II. Sc. 1.

O, Romeo, Romeo! wherefore art thou, Romeo?
SHAKESPEARE—*Romeo and Juliet.* Act II. Sc. 2.

My bounty is as boundless as the sea,
My love as deep; the more I give to thee
The more I have, for both are infinite.
SHAKESPEARE—*Romeo and Juliet.* Act II. Sc. 2.

Therefore love moderately; long love doth so;
Too swift arrives as tardy as too slow.
SHAKESPEARE—*Romeo and Juliet.* Act II. Sc. 6.

Give me my Romeo; and, when he shall die,
Take him, and cut him out in little stars,
And he will make the face of heaven so fine,
And all the world will be in love with night,
And pay no worship to the garish sun.
SHAKESPEARE—*Romeo and Juliet.* Act III. Sc. 2.

They say all lovers swear more performance than they are able, and yet reserve an ability that they never perform.
SHAKESPEARE—*Troilus and Cressida.* Act III. Sc. 2.

Love sought is good, but given unsought is better.
SHAKESPEARE—*Twelfth Night.* Act III. Sc. 1.

Love keeps his revels where there are but twain.
SHAKESPEARE—*Venus and Adonis.*

The fickleness of the woman I love is only equalled by the infernal constancy of the women who love me.
BERNARD SHAW—*The Philanderer.*

It is good to be merry and wise,
It is good to be honest and true,
It is best to be off with the old love,
Before you are on with the new.
Song of England.

Love is strong as death; jealousy is cruel as the grave.
Song of Solomon. VIII. 6.

Many waters cannot quench love, neither can the floods drown it.
Song of Solomon. VIII. 7.

They sin who tell us Love can die:
With life all other passions fly,
All others are but vanity.
SOUTHEY—*Curse of Kehama.*

Love is the emblem of eternity: it confounds all notion of time: effaces all memory of a beginning, all fear of an end.
MADAME DE STAËL—*Corinne.*

Where we really love, we often dread more than we desire the solemn moment that exchanges hope for certainty.
MADAME DE STAËL—*Corinne.*

Love is the history of a woman's life; it is an episode in man's.
MADAME DE STAËL—*Corinne.*

Sweetheart, when you walk my way,
Be it dark or be it day;
Dreary winter, fairy May,
I shall know and greet you.
For each day of grief or grace
Brings you nearer my embrace;
Love hath fashioned your dear face,
I shall know you when I meet you.
FRANK L. STANTON—*Greeting.*

To love her was a liberal education.
STEELE—*Of Lady Elizabeth Hastings.*

And my heart springs up anew,
Bright and confident and true,
And the old love comes to meet me, in the dawning and the dew.
STEVENSON, 1876.

Why so pale and wan, fond lover,
Prithee, why so pale?
Will, when looking well can't move her,
Looking ill prevail?
Prithee, why so pale?
SUCKLING—*Song.*

Love in its essence is spiritual fire.
SWEDENBORG—*True Christian Religion.*

In all I wish, how happy should I be,
Thou grand Deluder, were it not for thee?
So weak thou art that fools thy power despise;
And yet so strong, thou triumph'st o'er the wise.
SWIFT—*To Love.*

If love were what the rose is,
And I were like the leaf,
Our lives would grow together
In sad or singing weather.
SWINBURNE—*A Match.*

Love laid his sleepless head
On a thorny rose bed:
And his eyes with tears were red,
And pale his lips as the dead.
SWINBURNE—*Love Laid His Sleepless Head.*

I that have love and no more
Give you but love of you, sweet;
He that hath more, let him give;
He that hath wings, let him soar;
Mine is the heart at your feet
Here, that must love you to live.
SWINBURNE—*The Oblation.*

Love, as is told by the seers of old,
Comes as a butterfly tipped with gold,
Flutters and flies in sunlit skies,
Weaving round hearts that were one time cold.
SWINBURNE—*Song.*

You must make a lover angry if you wish him to love.
SYRUS.

I love thee, I love but thee,
With a love that shall not die
Till the sun grows cold,
And the stars are old,
And the leaves of the Judgment Book unfold!
BAYARD TAYLOR—*Bedouin Song.*

And on her lover's arm she leant,
And round her waist she felt it fold,
And far across the hills they went
In that new world which is the old.
TENNYSON—*Day Dream.*

'Tis better to have loved and lost,
Than never to have loved at all.
TENNYSON—*In Memoriam.*

There has fallen a splendid tear
From the passion-flower at the gate.
She is coming, my dove, my dear;
She is coming, my life, my fate;

The red rose cries, "She is near, she is near;"
And the white rose weeps, "She is late;"
The larkspur listens, "I hear; I hear;"
And the lily whispers, "I wait."
TENNYSON—*Maud*.

Werther had a love for Charlotte,
Such as words could never utter;
Would you know how first he met her?
She was cutting bread and butter.
THACKERAY—*The Sorrows of Werther*.

Why should we kill the best of passions, love?
It aids the hero, bids ambition rise
To nobler heights, inspires immortal deeds,
Even softens brutes, and adds a grace to virtue.
THOMSON—*Sophonisba*.

Love conquers all things; let us yield to love.
VERGIL.

O, rank is good, and gold is fair,
And high and low mate ill;
But love has never known a law
Beyond its own sweet will!
WHITTIER—*Amy Wentworth*.

"I'm sorry that I spell'd the word;
I hate to go above you,
Because"—the brown eyes lower fell,—
"Because, you see, I love you!"
WHITTIER—*In School-Days*.

O dearer far than light and life are dear.
WORDSWORTH—*Poems Founded on the Affections*.

LUCK

Good luck is a lazy man's estimate of a worker's success.
ANONYMOUS.

Throw a lucky man into the sea, and he will come up with a fish in his mouth.
Arab Proverb.

As ill-luck would have it.
CERVANTES—*Don Quixote*.

Good and bad luck is but a synonyme, in the great majority of instances, for good and bad judgment.
CHATFIELD.

A pound of pluck is worth a ton of luck.
JAMES A. GARFIELD.

A lucky man is rarer than a white crow.
JUVENAL.

Good luck befriend thee, Son; for at thy birth
The fairy ladies danced upon the hearth.
MILTON—*At a Vacation Exercise in the College*.

LUXURY

Luxury possibly may contribute to give bread to the poor; but if there were no luxury there would be no poor.
HENRY HOME.

Avarice and luxury, those pests which have ever been the ruin of every great state.
LIVY.

Luxury is an enticing pleasure, a bastard mirth, which hath honey in her mouth, gall in her heart, and a sting in her tail.
QUARLES.

LYING

Any fool can tell the truth, but it requires a man of some sense to know how to lie well.
SAMUEL BUTLER—*Note-Books*.

And, after all, what is a lie? 'Tis but
The truth in masquerade.
BYRON—*Don Juan*.

Liars are verbal forgers.
CHATFIELD.

A liar is not believed even though he tell the truth.
CICERO.

An experienced, industrious, ambitious, and often quite picturesque liar.
S. L. CLEMENS (Mark Twain).

A good memory is needed once we have lied.

CORNEILLE.

When I err every one can see it, but not when I lie.

GOETHE.

Show me a liar, and I will show thee a thief.

HERBERT.

Sin has many tools, but a lie is the handle which fits them all.

HOLMES—*Autocrat of the Breakfast Table.*

Who dares think one thing, and another tell,
My heart detests him as the gates of hell.

HOMER—*Iliad.*

He who has not a good memory should never take upon him the trade of lying.

MONTAIGNE.

Fell luxury! more perilous to youth
Than storms or quicksands, poverty or chains.

HANNAH MORE—*Belshazzar.*

I said in my haste, All men are liars.

Psalms. CXVI. 11.

He will lie, sir, with such volubility, that you would think truth were a fool.

SHAKESPEARE — *All's Well That Ends Well.* Act IV. Sc. 3.

Lord, Lord, how subject we old men are to the vice of lying!

SHAKESPEARE—*Henry IV.* Pt. II. Act III. Sc. 2.

Whose tongue soe'er speaks false,
Not truly speaks; who speaks not truly, lies.

SHAKESPEARE—*King John.* Act IV. Sc. 3.

The liar's punishment is not in the least that he is not believed, but that he cannot believe any one else.

GEORGE BERNARD SHAW.

That a lie which is half a truth is ever the blackest of lies;
That a lie which is all a lie may be met and fought with outright—
But a lie which is part a truth is a harder matter to fight.

TENNYSON—*The Grandmother.*

M

MAMMON

Maidens, like moths, are ever caught by glare,
And Mammon wins his way where seraphs might despair.

BYRON—*Childe Harold.*

Cursed Mammon be, when he with treasures
To restless action spurs our fate!
Cursed when for soft, indulgent leisures,
He lays for us the pillows straight.

GOETHE—*Faust.*

Ye cannot serve God and Mammon.

Matthew. VI. 24.

Mammon led them on—
Mammon, the least erected Spirit that fell
From Heaven: for even in Heaven his looks and thoughts
Were always downward bent, admiring more
The riches of Heaven's pavement, trodden gold,
Than aught divine or holy else enjoyed
In vision beatific.

MILTON—*Paradise Lost.*

What treasures here do Mammon's sons behold!
Yet know that all that which glitters is not gold.

QUARLES.

MAN

As a rule man is a fool,
When it's hot he wants it cool,
When it's cool he wants it hot,
Always wanting what is not.

ANONYMOUS.

There never was such beauty in another man.

Nature made him, and then broke the mould.
ARIOSTO—*Orlando Furioso.*

Ye children of man! whose life is a span
Protracted with sorrow from day to day,
Naked and featherless, feeble and querulous,
Sickly, calamitous creatures of clay.
ARISTOPHANES—*Birds.*

Let each man think himself an act of God.
His mind a thought, his life a breath of God.
BAILEY—*Festus.*

Man is the nobler growth our realms supply
And souls are ripened in our northern sky.
ANNA LETITIA BARBAULD—*The Invitation.*

A man's a man for a' that!
BURNS.

Man,—whose heaven-erected face
The smiles of love adorn,—
Man's inhumanity to man
Makes countless thousands mourn!
BURNS—*Man Was Made to Mourn.*

But we, who name ourselves its sovereigns, we,
Half dust, half deity, alike unfit
To sink or soar.
BYRON—*Manfred.*

Man!
Thou pendulum betwixt a smile and tear.
BYRON—*Childe Harold.*

And say without our hopes, without our fears,
Without the home that plighted love endears,
Without the smile from partial beauty won,
Oh! what were man?—a world without a sun.
CAMPBELL—*Pleasures of Hope.*

We are the miracle of miracles, the great inscrutable mystery of God.
CARLYLE.

Every man is a volume, if you know how to read him.
CHANNING.

There are times when one would like to hang the whole human race, and finish the farce.
S. L. CLEMENS (Mark Twain)—*A Connecticut Yankee at King Arthur's Court.*

I am made all things to all men.
I Corinthians. IX. 22.

The first man is of the earth, earthy.
I Corinthians. XV. 47.

A self-made man? Yes—and worships his creator.
COWPER.

But strive still to be a man before your mother.
COWPER.

His tribe were God Almighty's gentlemen.
DRYDEN—*Absalom and Achitophel.*

How dull, and how insensible a beast
Is man, who yet would lord it o'er the rest.
DRYDEN—*Essay on Satire.*

Man is a piece of the universe made alive.
EMERSON.

Aye, think! since time and life began
Your mind has only feared and slept;
Of all the beasts they called you man
Only because you toiled and wept.
ARTURO GIOVANNITTI —*The Thinker.*

God give us men. A time like this demands
Strong minds, great hearts, true faith and ready hands!
Men whom the lust of office does not kill,
Men whom the spoils of office cannot buy,
Men who possess opinions and a will,
Men who love honor, men who cannot lie.
J. G. HOLLAND.

The fool of fate, thy manufacture, man.
HOMER—*Odyssey.*

Man passes away; his name perishes from record and recollection; his history is as a tale that is told, and his very monument becomes a ruin.
WASHINGTON IRVING—*The Sketch Book.*

Cease ye from man, whose breath is in his nostrils.
Isaiah. II. 22.

Man that is born of a woman is of few days, and full of trouble.
Job. XIV. 1.

Though I've belted you and flayed you,
By the livin' Gawd that made you,
You're a better man than I am, Gunga Din.
KIPLING—*Gunga Din.*

If you can keep your head when all about you
Are losing theirs and blaming it on you,
If you can trust yourself when all men doubt you,
But make allowance for their doubting too;

. . .

Yours is the Earth and every thing that's in it,
And—which is more—you'll be a man, my son!
KIPLING—*If.* (First and Last Lines)

Make ye no truce with Adam-zad—the Bear that walks like a man.
KIPLING—*The Truce of the Bear.*

It is easier to know mankind in general than man individually.
LA ROCHEFOUCAULD.

Limited in his nature, infinite in his desires, man is a fallen god who remembers the heavens.
LAMARTINE.

Before man made us citizens, great Nature made us men.
LOWELL.

Men, in general, are but great children.
NAPOLEON.

I teach you beyond Man (superman). Man is something that shall be surpassed. What have you done to surpass him?
NIETZSCHE—*Thus Spake Zarathustra.*

'Tis but a Tent where takes his one day's rest
A Sultan to the realm of Death addrest.
A Sultan rises, and the dark Ferrash
Strikes, and prepares it for another Guest.
OMAR KHAYYÁM—*Rubaiyat.*

Man's the bad child of the universe.
JAMES OPPENHEIM—*Laughter.*

God gave man an upright countenance to survey the heavens, and to look upward to the stars.
OVID.

What a chimera, then, is man! what a novelty, what a monster, what a chaos, what a subject of contradiction, what a prodigy! A judge of all things, feeble worm of the earth, depositary of the truth, *cloaca* of uncertainty and error, the glory and the shame of the universe!
PASCAL—*Thoughts.*

We are not more than a bubble.
PETRONIUS.

Chaos of thought and passion, all confused;
Still by himself abused and disabused;
Created half to rise, and half to fall;
Great lord of all things, yet a prey to all;
Sole judge of truth, in endless error hurled;
The glory, jest and riddle of the world!
POPE—*Essay on Man.*

Know then thyself, presume not God to scan;
The proper study of mankind is man.
POPE—*Essay on Man.*

Virtuous and vicious every man must be,
Few in the extreme, but all in the degree.
POPE—*Essay on Man.*

No more was seen the human form divine.
POPE—*Homer's Odyssey*.

Man is the measure of all things.
PROTAGORAS.

Thou hast made him a little lower than the angels.
Psalms. VIII. 5.

Mark the perfect man, and behold the upright.
Psalms. XXXVII. 37.

Quit yourselves like men.
I Samuel. IV. 9.

A man after his own heart.
I Samuel. XIII. 14.

Thou art the man.
II Samuel. XII. 7.

He was a man, take him for all in all,
I shall not look upon his like again.
SHAKESPEARE—*Hamlet*. Act I. Sc. 2.

What a piece of work is a man! how noble in reason! how infinite in faculty! in form and moving how express and admirable! in action how like an angel! in apprehension how like a god! the beauty of the world! the paragon of animals! And, yet, to me, what is this quintessence of dust? man delights not me: no, nor woman neither, though by your smiling, you seem to say so.
SHAKESPEARE—*Hamlet*. Act II. Sc. 2.

Give me that man
That is not passion's slave, and I will wear him
In my heart's core, ay, in my heart of heart
As I do thee.
SHAKESPEARE—*Hamlet*. Act. III. Sc. 2.

This is the state of man: to-day he puts forth
The tender leaves of hope; to-morrow blossoms,
And bears his blushing honours thick upon him:
The third day comes a frost, a killing frost,
And, when he thinks, good easy man, full surely
His greatness is a-ripening, nips his root,
And then he falls, as I do.
SHAKESPEARE—*Henry VIII*. Act III. Sc. 2.

Men at some time are masters of their fates:
The fault, dear Brutus, is not in our stars,
But in ourselves, that we are underlings.
SHAKESPEARE—*Julius Caesar*. Act I. Sc. 2.

His life was gentle, and the elements
So mix'd in him that Nature might stand up,
And say to all the world, This was a man!
SHAKESPEARE—*Julius Caesar*. Act V. Sc. 5.

Why, he's a man of wax.
SHAKESPEARE—*Romeo and Juliet*. Act I. Sc. 3.

I wonder men dare trust themselves with men.
SHAKESPEARE—*Timon of Athens*. Act I. Sc. 2.

Man is of soul and body, formed for deeds
Of high resolve; on fancy's boldest wing.
SHELLEY—*Queen Mab*.

Man is an animal that makes bargains; no other animal does this,—one dog does not change a bone with another.
ADAM SMITH.

Man is man, and master of his fate.
TENNYSON—*Enid*.

Ah God, for a man with heart, head, hand,
Like some of the simple great gone
Forever and ever by,
One still strong man in a blatant land,
Whatever they call him, what care I,
Aristocrat, democrat, autocrat—one
Who can rule and dare not lie.
TENNYSON—*Maud*.

The noble man is only God's image.
LUDWIG TIECK.

I am an acme of things accomplished,
and I am encloser of things to be.
WALT WHITMAN—*Song of Myself.*

When faith is lost, when honor dies,
The man is dead!
WHITTIER—*Ichabod.*

I weigh the man, not his title: 'tis not the king's inscription can make the metal better or heavier.
WYCHERLY—*Plain Dealer.*

Ah! how unjust to nature, and himself,
Is thoughtless, thankless, inconsistent man.
YOUNG—*Night Thoughts.*

MANNERS

He was the mildest manner'd man
That ever scuttled ship or cut a throat.
BYRON—*Don Juan.*

Now as to politeness . . . I would venture to call it benevolence in trifles.
LORD CHATHAM.

A moral, sensible, and well-bred man
Will not affront me, and no other can.
COWPER—*Conversation.*

Fine manners need the support of fine manners in others.
EMERSON—*The Conduct of Life.*

Behavior is a mirror in which every one shows his image.
GOETHE.

The mildest manners with the bravest mind.
HOMER—*Iliad.*

Nothing so much prevents our being natural as the desire of appearing so.
LA ROCHEFOUCAULD.

"What sort of a doctor is he?" "Well, I don't know much about his ability; but he's got a very good bedside manner."
Punch, March 15, 1884.

They ask Lucman, the fabulist, From whom did you learn manners? He answered: From the unmannerly.
SAADI.

What once were vices, are now the manners of the day.
SENECA.

Men's evil manners live in brass; their virtues
We write in water.
SHAKESPEARE—*Henry VIII.* Act IV. Sc. 2.

Politeness goes far, yet costs nothing.
SAMUEL SMILES.

Good manners is the art of making those people easy with whom we converse. Whoever makes the fewest persons uneasy, is the best bred in the company.
SWIFT.

Suit your manner to the man.
TERENCE—*Adelphi.*

MARCH

March comes in like a lion and goes out like a lamb.
English Proverb.

Slayer of the winter, art thou here again?
O welcome, thou that bring'st the summer nigh!
The bitter wind makes not the victory vain,
Nor will we mock thee for thy faint blue sky.
WILLIAM MORRIS—*March.*

The ides of March are come.
SHAKESPEARE—*Julius Caesar.* Act III. Sc. 1.

In fierce March weather
White waves break tether,
And whirled together
At either hand,
Like weeds uplifted,
The tree-trunks rifted
In spars are drifted,
Like foam or sand.
SWINBURNE—*Four Songs of Four Seasons.*

Like an army defeated
The snow hath retreated,
And now doth fare ill
On the top of the bare hill;
The Ploughboy is whooping—anon—anon!
There's joy in the mountains:
There's life in the fountains;

Small clouds are sailing,
Blue sky prevailing;
The rain is over and gone.
WORDSWORTH—*March.*

MARTYR

For a tear is an intellectual thing;
And a sigh is the sword of an angel-king;
And the bitter groan of a martyr's woe
Is an arrow from the Almighty's bow.
WILLIAM BLAKE—*The Grey Monk.*

Who falls for love of God, shall rise a star.
BEN JONSON—*Underwoods.*

It is more difficult, and calls for higher energies of soul, to live a martyr than to die one.
HORACE MANN.

When we read, we fancy we could be martyrs; when we come to act, we cannot bear a provoking word.
HANNAH MORE.

It is the cause, and not the death, that makes the martyr.
NAPOLEON I.

The blood of the martyrs is the seed of the Church.
TERTULLIAN.

MATRIMONY

A man finds himself seven years older the day after his marriage.
BACON.

He that hath a wife and children hath given hostages to fortune; for they are impediments to great enterprises, either of virtue or mischief.
BACON—*Essays.*

No jealousy their dawn of love o'ercast,
Nor blasted were their wedded days with strife;
Each season looked delightful as it past,
To the fond husband and the faithful wife.
JAMES BEATTIE—*The Minstrel.*

To have and to hold from this day forward, for better, for worse, for richer, for poorer, in sickness, and in health, to love and to cherish, till death us do part.
Book of Common Prayer.

To love, cherish, and to obey.
Book of Common Prayer.

With this ring I thee wed, with my body I thee worship, and with all my worldly goods I thee endow.
Book of Common Prayer.

Cursed be the man, the poorest wretch in life,
The crouching vassal, to the tyrant wife,
Who has no will but by her high permission;
Who has not sixpence but in her possession;
Who must to her his dear friend's secret tell;
Who dreads a curtain lecture worse than hell.
Were such the wife had fallen to my part,
I'd break her spirit or I'd break her heart.
BURNS—*The Henpecked Husband.*

Man and wife.
Coupled together for the sake of strife.
CHARLES CHURCHILL—*Rosciad.*

Husbands and wives talk of the cares of matrimony, and bachelors and spinsters bear them.
WILKIE COLLINS.

Thus grief still treads upon the heels of pleasure,
Marry'd in haste, we may repent at leisure.
CONGREVE—*The Old Bachelor.*

A deaf husband and a blind wife are always a happy couple.
Danish Proverb.

Every woman should marry—and no man.
DISRAELI—*Lothair.*

Is not marriage an open question, when it is alleged, from the beginning of the world, that such as are in

the institution wish to get out, and such as are out wish to get in.
EMERSON—*Representative Men.*

The wedlock of minds will be greater than that of bodies.
ERASMUS.

Where there's marriage without love, there will be love without marriage.
FRANKLIN—*Poor Richard.*

It is not good that the man should be alone.
Genesis. II. 18.

Bone of my bones, and flesh of my flesh.
Genesis. II. 23.

Matrimony,—the high sea for which no compass has yet been invented.
HEINE.

Happy and thrice happy are they who enjoy an uninterrupted union, and whose love, unbroken by any complaints, shall not dissolve until the last day.
HORACE.

Marriage is something you have to give your whole mind to.
IBSEN—*The League of Youth.*

Heaven will be no heaven to me if I do not meet my wife there.
ANDREW JACKSON.

I have met with women whom I really think would like to be married to a Poem, and to be given away by a Novel.
KEATS—*Letters to Fanny Brawne.*

You should indeed have longer tarried
By the roadside before you married.
WALTER SAVAGE LANDOR—*To One Ill-mated.*

As unto the bow the cord is,
So unto the man is woman;
Though she bends him she obeys him,
Though she draws him, yet she follows,
Useless each without the other!
LONGFELLOW—*Hiawatha.*

And, to all married men, be this a caution,
Which they should duly tender as their life,
Neither to doat too much, nor doubt a wife.
MASSINGER—*Picture.*

What therefore God hath joined together let not man put asunder.
Matthew. XIX. 6.

To the nuptial bower
I led her, blushing like the morn; all Heaven,
And happy constellations on that hour
Shed their selectest influence; the earth
Gave sign of gratulation, and each hill;
Joyous the birds; fresh gales and gentle airs
Whisper'd it to the woods, and from their wings
Flung rose, flung odours from the spicy shrub.
MILTON—*Paradise Lost.*

Women when they marry buy a cat in the bag.
MONTAIGNE—*Essays.*

Drink, my jolly lads, drink with discerning,
Wedlock's a lane where there is no turning;
Never was owl more blind than a lover,
Drink and be merry, lads, half seas over.
D. M. MULOCK—*Magnus and Morna.*

If thou wouldst marry wisely, marry thine equal.
OVID.

Before I trust my Fate to thee,
Or place my hand in thine,
Before I let thy Future give
Color and form to mine,
Before I peril all for thee,
Question thy soul to-night for me.
ADELAIDE ANN PROCTER—*A Woman's Question.*

My son is my son till he have got him a wife,
But my daughter's my daughter all the days of her life.
Proverb.

A prudent wife is from the Lord.
Proverbs. XIX. 14.

Advice to persons about to marry—Don't.
"Punch's Almanack," 1845.

Marriage is a lottery in which men stake their liberty, and women their happiness.
MME. DE RIEUX.

Men should keep their eyes wide open before marriage, and half shut afterwards.
MLLE. SCUDÉRI.

Men are April when they woo, December when they wed; maids are May when they are maids, but the sky changes when they are wives.
SHAKESPEARE—*As You Like It.* Act IV. Sc. 1.

God, the best maker of all marriages,
Combine your hearts in one.
SHAKESPEARE—*Henry V.* Act I. Sc. 2.

She is not well married that lives married long:
But she's best married that dies married young.
SHAKESPEARE—*Romeo and Juliet.* Act IV. Sc. 5.

To disbelieve in marriage is easy: to love a married woman is easy; but to betray a comrade, to be disloyal to a host, to break the covenant of bread and salt, is impossible.
BERNARD SHAW—*Getting Married.*

What God hath joined together no man shall ever put asunder: God will take care of that.
BERNARD SHAW—*Getting Married.*

The whole world is strewn with snares, traps, gins and pitfalls for the capture of men by women.
BERNARD SHAW—*Man and Superman.*

The reason why so few marriages are happy is because young ladies spend their time in making nets, not in making cages.
SWIFT—*Thoughts on Various Subjects.*

Marriages are made in Heaven.
TENNYSON—*Aylmer's Field.*

Remember, it is as easy to marry a rich woman as a poor woman.
THACKERAY—*Pendennis.*

This I set down as a positive truth. A woman with fair opportunities and without a positive hump, may marry whom she likes.
THACKERAY—*Vanity Fair.*

But happy they, the happiest of their kind!
Whom gentler stars unite, and in one fate
Their Hearts, their Fortunes, and their Beings blend.
THOMSON—*Seasons.*

Men marry because they are tired, women because they are curious: both are disappointed.
OSCAR WILDE.

Marriage is the one subject on which all women agree and all men disagree.
OSCAR WILDE.

MAY

But winter lingering chills the lap of May.
GOLDSMITH—*The Traveller.*

Crimson clover I discover
By the garden gate,
And the bees about her hover,
But the robins wait.
Sing, robins, sing,
Sing a roundelay,—
'Tis the latest flower of Spring
Coming with the May!
DORA READ GOODALE—*Red Clover.*

Oh! that we two were Maying
Down the stream of the soft spring breeze;
Like children with violets playing,
In the shade of the whispering trees.
CHARLES KINGSLEY—*Saint's Tragedy.*

Now the bright morning star, day's harbinger,
Comes dancing from the east, and leads with her
The flowery May, who from her green lap throws

The yellow cowslip, and the pale primrose.
Hail, bounteous May, that doth inspire
Mirth, and youth, and warm desire;
Woods and groves are of thy dressing,
Hill and dale doth boast thy blessing,
Thus we salute thee with our early song,
And welcome thee, and wish thee long.
MILTON—*Song. On May Morning.*

As full of spirit as the month of May.
SHAKESPEARE—*King Henry IV.* Pt. I. Act IV. Sc. 1.

Rough winds do shake the darling buds of May.
SHAKESPEARE—*Sonnet.*

Among the changing months, May stands confest
The sweetest, and in fairest colors dressed.
THOMSON—*On May.*

May, queen of blossoms,
And fulfilling flowers,
With what pretty music
Shall we charm the hours?
Wilt thou have pipe and reed,
Blown in the open mead?
Or to the lute give heed
In the green bowers?
LORD THURLOW—*To May.*

MEDICINE

The physician heals, Nature makes well.
ARISTOTLE.

I find the medicine worse than the malady.
BEAUMONT and FLETCHER—*Love's Cure.*

This is the way that physicians mend or end us,
Secundum artem; but although we sneer
In health—when ill, we call them to attend us,
Without the least propensity to jeer.
BYRON—*Don Juan.*

The best doctor is the one you run for and can't find.
DIDEROT.

Better to hunt in fields for health unbought,
Than fee the doctor for a nauseous draught.
The wise for cure on exercise depend;
God never made his work for man to mend.
DRYDEN.

I firmly believe that if the whole *materia medica* as now used, could be sunk to the bottom of the sea, it would be all the better for mankind and all the worse for the fishes.
HOLMES—*Lecture, Medical Society.*

A sound mind in a sound body is a thing to be prayed for.
JUVENAL.

You behold in me
Only a travelling Physician;
One of the few who have a mission
To cure incurable diseases,
Or those that are called so.
LONGFELLOW—*Christus.*

Physician, heal thyself.
Luke. IV. 23.

A physician is nothing but a consoler of the mind.
PETRONIUS ARBITER—*Satyricon.*

Who shall decide when doctors disagree,
And soundest casuists doubt, like you and me?
POPE—*Moral Essays.*

Trust not the physician;
His antidotes are poison, and he slays
More than you rob.
SHAKESPEARE—*Timon of Athens.* Act IV. Sc. 3.

Doctors are men who prescribe medicines of which they know little, to cure diseases of which they know less, in human beings of whom they know nothing.
VOLTAIRE.

But nothing is more estimable than a physician who, having studied nature from his youth, knows the properties of the human body, the diseases which assail it, the remedies which will benefit it, exercises his art with caution, and pays equal attention to the rich and the poor.

VOLTAIRE—*A Philosophical Dictionary.*

MEDITATION

In maiden meditation, fancy-free.

SHAKESPEARE—*Midsummer Night's Dream.* Act. II. Sc. I.

MEETING

We met—'twas in a crowd.

THOMAS HAYNES BAYLY—*We Met.*

Ships that pass in the night, and speak each other in passing,
Only a signal shown and a distant voice in the darkness:
So on the ocean of life, we pass and speak one another,
Only a look and a voice, then darkness again and a silence.

LONGFELLOW—*Tales of a Wayside Inn.*

Some day, some day of days, threading the street
With idle, heedless pace,
Unlooking for such grace,
I shall behold your face!
Some day, some day of days, thus may we meet.

NORA PERRY—*Some Day of Days.*

When shall we three meet again
In thunder, lightning, or in rain?

SHAKESPEARE—*Macbeth.* Act I. Sc. I.

MELANCHOLY

Melancholy sees the worst of things,—things as they may be, and not as they are. It looks upon a beautiful face, and sees but a grinning skull.

BOVEE.

Melancholy
Is not, as you conceive, indisposition
Of body, but the mind's disease.

JOHN FORD—*The Lover's Melancholy.*

Here rests his head upon the lap of earth,
A youth, to fortune and to fame unknown;
Fair Science frowned not on his humble birth,
And Melancholy marked him for her own.

GRAY—*Elegy in a Country Churchyard.*

There's not a string attuned to mirth
But has its chord in melancholy.

HOOD—*Ode to Melancholy.*

Melancholy is the pleasure of being sad.

VICTOR HUGO.

Employment and hardships prevent melancholy.

SAMUEL JOHNSON.

Hence, all you vain delights,
As short as are the nights
Wherein you spend your folly!
There's nought in this life sweet,
If man were wise to see't,
But only melancholy,
Oh, sweetest melancholy!

DR. STRODE—*Song in Praise of Melancholy.*

MEMORY

Friends depart, and memory takes them
To her caverns, pure and deep.

THOMAS HAYNES BAYLY—*Teach Me to Forget.*

To live in hearts we leave behind,
Is not to die.

CAMPBELL—*Hallowed Ground.*

Memory is the treasury and guardian of all things.

CICERO.

Oh, how cruelly sweet are the echoes that start
When Memory plays an old tune on the heart!

ELIZA COOK—*Journal.*

What peaceful hours I once enjoy'd!
How sweet their memory still!
But they have left an aching void
The world can never fill.

COWPER—*Walking with God.*

Don't you remember sweet Alice, Ben Bolt?
Sweet Alice, whose hair was so brown;
Who wept with delight when you gave her a smile,
And trembl'd with fear at your frown!
THOMAS DUNN ENGLISH—*Ben Bolt.*

A place in thy memory, Dearest!
Is all that I claim:
To pause and look back when thou hearest
The sound of my name.
GERALD GRIFFEN.

I remember, I remember,
The house where I was born,
The little window where the sun
Came peeping in at morn;
He never came a wink too soon,
Nor brought too long a day,
But now, I often wish the night
Had borne my breath away!
HOOD—*I Remember, I Remember.*

We must always have old memories and young hopes.
ARSÈNE HOUSSAYE.

Memory is the primary and fundamental power, without which there could be no other intellectual operation.
SAMUEL JOHNSON.

And when he is out of sight, quickly also is he out of mind.
THOMAS À KEMPIS—*Imitation of Christ.*

The heart hath its own memory, like the mind,
And in it are enshrined
The precious keepsakes, into which is wrought
The giver's loving thought.
LONGFELLOW—*From My Arm-Chair.*

When I remember all
The friends so link'd together,
I've seen around me fall,
Like leaves in wintry weather
I feel like one who treads alone
Some banquet hall deserted,
Whose lights are fled, whose garlands dead,
And all but he departed.
MOORE—*Oft in the Stilly Night.*

All to myself I think of you,
Think of the things we used to do,
Think of the things we used to say,
Think of each happy bygone day,
Sometimes I sigh, and sometimes I smile,
But I keep each olden, golden while
All to myself.
WILBUR D. NESBIT—*All to Myself.*

If I do not remember thee, let my tongue cleave to the roof of my mouth.
Psalms. CXXXVII. 6.

Good things have to be engraved on the memory; bad ones stick there of themselves.
CHARLES READE.

I have a room whereinto no one enters
Save I myself alone:
There sits a blessed memory on a throne,
There my life centres.
CHRISTINA G. ROSSETTI—*Memory.*

Still so gently o'er me stealing,
Mem'ry will bring back the feeling,
Spite of all my grief revealing
That I love thee,—that I dearly love thee still.
SCRIBE—*Opera of La Sonnambula.*

How sharp the point of this remembrance is!
SHAKESPEARE—*Tempest.* Act V. Sc. 1.

Thou comest as the memory of a dream,
Which now is sad because it hath been sweet.
SHELLEY—*Prometheus Unbound.*

The Right Honorable gentleman is indebted to his memory for his jests and to his imagination for his facts.
R. B. SHERIDAN.

O memory, thou bitter sweet,—both a joy and a scourge!
MADAME DE STAËL.

I shall remember while the light lives
yet
And in the night time I shall not
forget.
SWINBURNE—*Erotion*.

A land of promise, a land of memory,
A land of promise flowing with the
milk
And honey of delicious memories!
TENNYSON—*The Lover's Tale*.

As the dew to the blossom the bud to
the bee,
As the scent to the rose, are those
memories to me.
AMELIA B. WELBY—*Pulpit Eloquence*.

Ah! memories of sweet summer eves,
Of moonlit wave and willowy way,
Of stars and flowers, and dewy leaves,
And smiles and tones more dear
than they!
WHITTIER—*Memories*.

MERCY

Among the attributes of God, although they are all equal, mercy shines with even more brilliancy than justice.
CERVANTES.

Mercy to him that shows it, is the rule.
COWPER—*Task*.

We hand folks over to God's mercy, and show none ourselves.
GEORGE ELIOT.

Being all fashioned of the self-same
dust,
Let us be merciful as well as just.
LONGFELLOW—*Tales of a Wayside Inn*.

Think not the good,
The gentle deeds of mercy thou hast
done,
Shall die forgotten all; the poor, the
prisoner,
The fatherless, the friendless, and the
widow,
Who daily owe the bounty of thy
hand,
Shall cry to Heaven, and pull a blessing on thee.
NICHOLAS ROWE—*Jane Shore*.

Open thy gate of mercy, gracious God!
My soul flies through these wounds
to seek out thee.
SHAKESPEARE—*Henry VI*. Pt. III.
Act I. Sc. 4.

The quality of mercy is not strain'd,
It droppeth as the gentle rain from
heaven
Upon the place beneath: it is twice
blest;
It blesseth him that gives and him
that takes;
'Tis mightiest in the mightiest; it becomes
The throned monarch better than his
crown;
His sceptre shows the force of temporal power,
The attribute to awe and majesty,
Wherein doth sit the dread and fear
of kings;
But mercy is above this sceptred sway;
It is enthroned in the hearts of kings,
It is an attribute to God himself;
And earthly power doth then show
liketh God's
When mercy seasons justice.
SHAKESPEARE—*Merchant of Venice*. Act IV. Sc. 1.

We may imitate the Deity in all His attributes; but mercy is the only one in which we can pretend to equal Him. We cannot, indeed, give like God; but surely we may forgive like Him.
STERNE.

MERIT

The sufficiency of my merit is to know that my merit is not sufficient.
ST. AUGUSTINE.

Do not overwork the mind any more than the body; do everything with moderation.
BACON.

The best evidence of merit is a cordial recognition of it whenever and wherever it may be found.
BOVEE.

Every mind was made for growth, for knowledge; and its nature is sinned against when it is doomed to ignorance.

CHANNING.

A well-cultivated mind is, so to speak, made up of all the minds of preceding ages; it is only one single mind which has been educated during all this time.

FONTENELLE.

True merit, like a river, the deeper it is, the less noise it makes.

LORD HALIFAX.

The same principle leads us to neglect a man of merit that induces us to admire a fool.

LA BRUYÈRE.

Nature makes merit, and fortune puts it to work.

LA ROCHEFOUCAULD.

The world rewards the appearance of merit oftener than merit itself.

LA ROCHEFOUCAULD.

As the soil, however rich it may be, cannot be productive without culture, so the mind without cultivation can never produce good fruit.

SENECA.

MERMAID

Who would be
A mermaid fair,
Singing alone,
Combing her hair
Under the sea,
In a golden curl
With a comb of pearl,
On a throne?
I would be a mermaid fair;
I would sing to myself the whole of the day;
With a comb of pearl I would comb my hair;
And still as I comb I would sing and say,
"Who is it loves me? who loves not me?"

TENNYSON—*The Mermaid.*

MERRIMENT

An ounce of mirth is worth a pound of sorrow.

BAXTER—*Self Denial.*

Let us eat, and be merry.

Luke. XV. 23.

Nothing is more hopeless than a scheme of merriment.

SAMUEL JOHNSON—*The Idler.*

A merry heart doeth good like a medicine.

Proverbs. XVII. 22.

MIDNIGHT

I stood on the bridge at midnight,
As the clocks were striking the hour,
And the moon rose over the city,
Behind the dark church tower.

LONGFELLOW—*The Bridge.*

Midnight! the outpost of advancing day!
The frontier town and citadel of night!

LONGFELLOW—*Two Rivers.*

O wild and wondrous midnight,
There is a might in thee
To make the charmed body
Almost like spirit be,
And give it some faint glimpses
Of immortality!

LOWELL—*Midnight.*

Once upon a midnight dreary, while I pondered weak and weary,
Over many a quaint and curious volume of forgotten lore.

POE—*The Raven.*

The iron tongue of midnight hath told twelve;
Lovers, to bed; 'tis almost fairy time.

SHAKESPEARE—*Midsummer Night's Dream.* Act V. Sc. I.

MIND

Measure your mind's height by the shade it casts.

ROBERT BROWNING—*Paracelsus.*

The march of the human mind is slow.

BURKE—*Speech on the Conciliation of America.*

When Bishop Berkeley said "there was no matter,"
And proved it,—'Twas no matter what he said.
BYRON—*Don Juan.*

How fleet is a glance of the mind!
Compared with the speed of its flight,
The tempest itself lags behind,
And the swift-winged arrows of light.
COWPER.

Babylon in all its desolation is a sight not so awful as that of the human mind in ruins.
SCROPE DAVIES.

God is Mind, and God is infinite; hence all is Mind.
MARY BAKER EDDY—*Science and Health.*

The true, strong, and sound mind is the mind that can embrace equally great things and small.
SAMUEL JOHNSON—*Boswell's Life of Johnson.*

What is mind? No matter. What is matter? Never mind.
T. H. KEY.

The mind is its own place, and in itself
Can make a heaven of hell, a hell of heaven.
MILTON—*Paradise Lost.*

The mind alone can not be exiled.
OVID.

The mind's my kingdom.
QUARLES—*School of the Heart.*

Let every man be fully persuaded in his own mind.
Romans. XIV. 5.

A feeble body weakens the mind.
ROUSSEAU—*Émile.*

Man is only miserable so far as he thinks himself so.
SANNAZARE—*Ecloga Octava.*

'Tis but a base, ignoble mind
That mounts no higher than a bird can soar.
SHAKESPEARE—*Henry V.* Act IV. Sc. 1.

For 'tis the mind that makes the body rich.
SHAKESPEARE — *Taming of the Shrew.* Act IV. Sc. 3.

Not body enough to cover his mind decently with; his intellect is improperly exposed.
SYDNEY SMITH—*Lady Holland's Memoir.*

A flower more sacred than far-seen success
Perfumes my solitary path; I find
Sweet compensation in my humbleness,
And reap the harvest of a quiet mind.
TROWBRIDGE—*Twoscore and Ten.*

Mind moves matter.
VERGIL—*Aeneid.*

Minds that have nothing to confer
Find little to perceive.
WORDSWORTH—*Yes! Thou Art Fair.*

MIRACLE

Every believer is God's miracle.
BAILEY—*Festus.*

Man is the miracle in nature. God
Is the One Miracle to man. Behold,
"There is a God," thou sayest. Thou sayest well:
In that thou sayest all. To be is more
Of wonderful, than being, to have wrought,
Or reigned, or rested.
JEAN INGELOW—*Story of Doom.*

The story of the whale swallowing Jonah, though a whale is large enough to do it, borders greatly on the marvelous; but it would have approached nearer to the idea of miracle if Jonah had swallowed the whale.
THOMAS PAINE—*The Age of Reason.*

MISCHIEF

In life it is difficult to say who do you the most mischief, enemies with the worst intentions, or friends with the best.
BULWER-LYTTON

The mischief of children is seldom actuated by malice; that of grown-up people always is.

RIVAROL.

The opportunity to do mischief is found a hundred times a day, and that of doing good once a year.

VOLTAIRE.

MISER

History tells us of illustrious villains, but there never was an illustrious miser.

ST. EVREMOND.

The miser acquires, yet fears to use his gains.

HORACE.

'Tis strange the miser should his cares employ
To gain those riches he can ne'er enjoy;
Is it less strange the prodigal should waste
His wealth to purchase what he ne'er can taste?

POPE—*Moral Essays.*

The life of a miser is a play of which we applaud only the closing scene.

SANIAL-DUBAY.

MISERY

He that is down need fear no fall.

BUNYAN.

The comfort derived from the misery of others is slight.

CICERO.

Misery is so little appertaining to our nature, and happiness so much so, that we in the same degree of illusion only lament over that which has pained us, but leave unnoticed that which has rejoiced us.

RICHTER.

Fire tries gold, misery tries brave men.

SENECA.

Misery acquaints a man with strange bedfellows.

SHAKESPEARE—*Tempest.* Act II. Sc. 2.

MISFORTUNE

After all, our worst misfortunes never happen, and most miseries lie in anticipation.

BALZAC.

Most of our misfortunes are more supportable than the comments of our friends upon them.

C. C. COLTON.

By speaking of our misfortunes we often relieve them.

CORNEILLE.

Fallen, fallen, fallen, fallen,
Fallen from his high estate,
And welt'ring in his blood;
Deserted at his utmost need,
By those his former bounty fed;
On the bare earth expos'd he lies,
With not a friend to close his eyes.

DRYDEN—*Alexander's Feast.*

One more unfortunate
Weary of breath,
Rashly importunate,
Gone to her death.

HOOD—*Bridge of Sighs.*

Little minds are tamed and subdued by misfortune; but great minds rise above it.

WASHINGTON IRVING.

We have all of us sufficient fortitude to bear the misfortunes of others.

LA ROCHEFOUCAULD.

The lowest ebb is the turn of the tide.

LONGFELLOW.

Let us be of good cheer, however, remembering that the misfortunes hardest to bear are those which never come.

LOWELL—*Democracy and Addresses.*

When I was happy I thought I knew men, but it was fated that I should know them in misfortune only.

NAPOLEON.

I never knew any man in my life, who could not bear another's misfortunes perfectly like a Christian.

POPE.

There is nothing so wretched or foolish as to anticipate misfortunes. What madness is it in your expecting evil before it arrives!
SENECA.

The worst is not
So long as we can say "This is the worst."
SHAKESPEARE—*King Lear*. Act IV. Sc. I.

MOB

The mob is man voluntarily descending to the nature of the beast.
EMERSON.

The mob is a sort of bear; while your ring is through its nose, it will even dance under your cudgel; but should the ring slip, and you lose your hold, the brute will turn and rend you.
JANE PORTER.

It has been very truly said that the mob has many heads, but no brains.
RIVAROL.

It is the proof of a bad cause when it is applauded by the mob.
SENECA.

MODERATION

It is best to rise from life as from a banquet, neither thirsty nor drunken.
ARISTOTLE.

Moderation is the keynote of lasting enjoyment.
HOSEA BALLOU.

To live long, it is necessary to live slowly.
CICERO.

This only grant me, that my means may lie
Too low for envy, for contempt too high.
COWLEY.

True happiness springs from moderation.
GOETHE.

A thing moderately good is not so good as it ought to be. Moderation in temper is always a virtue; but moderation in principle is always a vice.
THOMAS PAINE.

In everything the middle course is best: all things in excess bring trouble to men.
PLAUTUS.

He knows to live who keeps the middle state,
And neither leans on this side nor on that.
POPE.

Give me neither poverty nor riches.
Proverbs. XXX. 8.

Give us enough but with a sparing hand.
WALLER—*Reflections*.

MODESTY

Modesty is the conscience of the body.
BALZAC.

Modesty antedates clothes and will be resumed when clothes are no more.
Modesty died when clothes were born.
Modesty died when false modesty was born.
S. L. CLEMENS (Mark Twain).

Immodest words admit of no defence;
For want of decency is want of sense.
WENTWORTH DILLON.

Her modest looks the cottage might adorn,
Sweet as the primrose peeps beneath the thorn.
GOLDSMITH—*The Deserted Village*.

Modesty is the lowest of the virtues, and is a confession of the deficiency it indicates. He who undervalues himself is justly undervalued by others.
HAZLITT.

Modesty is a bright dish-cover, which makes us fancy there is something very nice underneath it.
DOUGLAS JERROLD.

A modest man never talks of himself.
LA BRUYÈRE.

Modesty is to merit, what shade is to figures in a picture; it gives it strength and makes it stand out.
LA BRUYÈRE.

Modesty becomes a young man.
PLAUTUS.

With people of only moderate ability modesty is mere honesty; but with those who possess great talent it is hypocrisy.
SCHOPENHAUER.

MONEY

Money makes the man.
ARISTODEMUS.

Money is a good servant but a bad master.
Quoted by BACON.

Money is a good servant, but a dangerous master.
BOUHOURS.

A fool and his money are soon parted.
GEORGE BUCHANAN.

Penny wise, pound foolish.
BURTON.

The deepest depth of vulgarism is that of setting up money as the ark of the covenant.
CARLYLE.

Wine maketh merry: but money answereth all things.
Ecclesiastes. X. 19.

If you would know the value of money, go and try to borrow some.
FRANKLIN—*Poor Richard's Almanac*.

Money, make money; by honest means if you can; if not, by any means make money.
HORACE.

The almighty dollar, that great object of universal devotion throughout our land, seems to have no genuine devotees in these peculiar villages.
WASHINGTON IRVING—*Creole Village*.

Money and time are the heaviest burdens of life, and the unhappiest of all mortals are those who have more of either than they know how to use.
JOHNSON.

Take care of the pence, and the pounds will take care of themselves.
WILLIAM LOWNDES.

Up and down the City Road,
In and out the Eagle,
That's the way the money goes—
Pop goes the weasel!
W. R. MANDALE.

Ah, take the Cash, and let the Credit go,
Nor heed the rumble of a distant Drum!
OMAR KHAYYÁM—*Rubaiyat*.

The Romans worshipped their standard; and the Roman standard happened to be an eagle. Our standard is only one tenth of an eagle,—a dollar,—but we make all even by adoring it with tenfold devotion.
E. A. POE.

"Get Money, money still!
And then let virtue follow, if she will,"
This, this the saving doctrine preach'd to all,
From low St. James' up to high St. Paul.
POPE—*First Book of Horace*.

O, what a world of vile ill-favour'd faults
Looks handsome in three hundred pounds a year!
SHAKESPEARE—*Merry Wives of Windsor*. Act III. Sc. 4.

Money is not required to buy one necessity of the soul.
THOREAU.

Not greedy of filthy lucre.
I Timothy. III. 3.

The love of money is the root of all evil.
I Timothy. VI. 10.

Money is a new form of slavery, and distinguishable from the old simply by the fact that it is impersonal—that there is no human relation between master and slave.
TOLSTOY—*What Shall We Do?*

Make all you can, save all you can, give all you can.

WESLEY.

No, let the monarch's bags and coffers hold
The flattering, mighty, nay, all-mighty gold.

WOLCOT—*To Kieu Long.*

MONTHS

Thirty days hath September,
April, June, and November;
All the rest have thirty-one
Excepting February alone:
Which hath but twenty-eight, in fine,
Till leap year gives it twenty-nine.

ANONYMOUS.

MONUMENT

If I have done any honorable exploit, that is my monument; but if I have done none, all your statues will signify nothing.

AGESILAUS.

But monuments themselves memorials need.

CRABBE—*The Borough.*

You shall not pile, with servile toil,
Your monuments upon my breast,
Nor yet within the common soil
Lay down the wreck of power to rest,
Where man can boast that he has trod
On him that was "the scourge of God."

EDWARD EVERETT—*Alaric the Visigoth.*

Monuments are the grappling-irons that bind one generation to another.

JOUBERT.

Monuments! what are they? the very pyramids have forgotten their builders, or to whom they were dedicated. Deeds, not stones, are the true monuments of the great.

MOTLEY.

Soldiers, forty centuries are looking down upon you from these pyramids.

NAPOLEON.

MOON

Soon as the evening shades prevail,
The moon takes up the wondrous tale,
And nightly to the listening earth
Repeats the story of her birth.

ADDISON—*Spectator.*

The moon is at her full, and riding high,
Floods the calm fields with light.
The airs that hover in the summer sky
Are all asleep to-night.

BRYANT—*The Tides.*

How like a queen comes forth the lonely Moon
From the slow opening curtains of the clouds
Walking in beauty to her midnight throne!

GEORGE CROLY—*Diana.*

And hail their queen, fair regent of the night.

ERASMUS DARWIN—*Botanic Garden.*

As the moon's fair image quaketh
In the raging waves of ocean,
Whilst she, in the vault of heaven,
Moves with silent peaceful motion.

HEINE—*Book of Songs.*

Such a slender moon, going up and up,
Waxing so fast from night to night,
And swelling like an orange flower-bud, bright,
Fated, methought, to round as to a golden cup,
And hold to my two lips life's best of wine.

JEAN INGELOW—*Songs of the Night Watches.*

Queen and huntress, chaste and fair,
Now the sun is laid to sleep,
Seated in thy silver car,
State in wonted manner keep.
Hesperus entreats thy light,
Goddess, excellently bright!

BEN JONSON—*To Cynthia.*

It is the Harvest Moon! On gilded vanes
And roofs of villages, on woodland crests

And their aerial neighborhoods of nests
Deserted, on the curtained window-panes
Of rooms where children sleep, on country lanes
And harvest-fields, its mystic splendor rests.
LONGFELLOW—*Harvest Moon.*

He should, as he list, be able to prove the moon is green cheese.
SIR THOMAS MORE—*English Works.*

Day glimmer'd in the east, and the white Moon
Hung like a vapor in the cloudless sky.
SAMUEL ROGERS—*Italy.*

Good even, good fair moon, good even to thee;
I prithee, dear moon, now show to me
The form and the features, the speech and degree,
Of the man that true lover of mine shall be.
SCOTT—*Heart of Mid-Lothian.*

That orbed maiden, with white fire laden,
Whom mortals call the moon.
SHELLEY—*The Cloud.*

Art thou pale for weariness
Of climbing heaven, and gazing on the earth,
Wandering companionless
Among the stars that have a different birth,—
And ever changing, like a joyous eye
That finds no object worth its constancy?
SHELLEY—*To the Moon.*

As like the sacred queen of night,
Who pours a lovely, gentle light
Wide o'er the dark, by wanderers blest,
Conducting them to peace and rest.
THOMSON—*Ode to Seraphina.*

Meet me by moonlight alone,
And then I will tell you a tale
Must be told by the moonlight alone,
In the grove at the end of the vale!
You must promise to come, for I said
I would show the night-flowers their queen.
Nay turn not away that sweet head,
'T is the loveliest ever was seen.
J. AUGUSTUS WADE—*Meet Me by Moonlight.*

And suddenly the moon withdraws
Her sickles from the lightening skies,
And to her sombre cavern flies,
Wrapped in a veil of yellow gauze.
OSCAR WILDE.

MORALITY

"Tut, tut, child," said the Duchess. "Everything's got a moral if only you can find it."
LEWIS CARROLL—*Alice in Wonderland.*

Morality may exist in an atheist without any religion, and in a theist with a religion quite unspiritual.
FRANCES POWER COBBE.

Dr. Johnson's morality was as English an article as a beefsteak.
HAWTHORNE—*Our Old Home.*

Turning the other cheek is a kind of moral jiu-jitsu.
GERALD STANLEY LEE—*Crowds.*

To give a man full knowledge of true morality, I would send him to no other book than the New Testament.
LOCKE.

Morality without religion is only a kind of dead reckoning,—an endeavor to find our place on a cloudy sea by measuring the distance we have run, but without any observation of the heavenly bodies.
LONGFELLOW—*Kavanagh.*

We know no spectacle so ridiculous as the British public in one of its periodical fits of morality.
MACAULAY—*On Moore's Life of Lord Byron.*

The health of a community is an almost unfailing index of its morals.
JAMES MARTINEAU.

I find the doctors and the sages
Have differ'd in all climes and ages,
And two in fifty scarce agree
On what is pure morality.
MOORE—*Morality*.

Religious morality is a morality of sacrifice, which is dear to the weak and degenerate, but to all other people is a species of slavery.
MUSSOLINI—*Speech, 1904*.

Do you wish to see that which is really sublime? Repeat the Lord's Prayer.
NAPOLEON BONAPARTE.

Morality is the best of all devices for leading mankind by the nose.
NIETZSCHE—*The Antichrist*.

Do not be too moral. You may cheat yourself out of much life so. Aim above morality. Be not simply good; be good for something.
THOREAU.

All sects are different, because they come from men; morality is everywhere the same, because it comes from God.
VOLTAIRE.

MORNING

The morn is up again, the dewy morn,
With breath all incense, and with cheek all bloom,
Laughing the clouds away with playful scorn,
And living as if earth contained no tomb,—
And glowing into day.
BYRON—*Childe Harold*.

Awake thee, my Lady-Love!
Wake thee, and rise!
The sun through the bower peeps
Into thine eyes.
GEORGE DARLEY—*Sylvia*.

Aurora had but newly chased the night,
And purpled o'er the sky with blushing light.
DRYDEN.

Now from the smooth deep ocean-stream the sun
Began to climb the heavens, and with new rays
Smote the surrounding fields.
HOMER—*Iliad*.

Far off I hear the crowing of the cocks,
And through the opening door that time unlocks
Feel the fresh breathing of To-morrow creep.
LONGFELLOW—*To-morrow*.

Sweet is the breath of morn, her rising sweet,
With charm of earliest birds.
MILTON—*Paradise Lost*.

If I take the wings of the morning, and dwell in the uttermost parts of the sea.
Psalms. CXXXIX. 9.

The cock, that is the trumpet to the morn,
Doth with his lofty and shrill-sounding throat
Awake the god of day.
SHAKESPEARE—*Hamlet*. Act I. Sc. 1.

The grey-ey'd morn smiles on the frowning night,
Chequering the eastern clouds with streaks of light.
SHAKESPEARE—*Romeo and Juliet*. Act I. Sc. 1.

Hail, gentle Dawn! mild blushing goddess, hail!
Rejoic'd I see thy purple mantle spread
O'er half the skies, gems pave thy radiant way,
And orient pearls from ev'ry shrub depend.
WILLIAM SOMERVILLE—*The Chase*.

Now the frosty stars are gone:
I have watched them one by one,
Fading on the shores of Dawn.
Round and full the glorious sun
Walks with level step the spray,
Through his vestibule of Day.
BAYARD TAYLOR—*Ariel in the Cloven Pine*.

Rise, happy morn, rise, holy morn,
Draw forth the cheerful day from night;
O Father, touch the east, and light
The light that shone when Hope was born.
TENNYSON—*In Memoriam.*

MORTALITY

All flesh shall perish together, and man shall turn again unto dust.
Job. XXXIV. 15.

Oh, why should the spirit of mortal be proud?
Like a fast-flitting meteor, a fast-flying cloud,
A flash of the lightning, a break of the wave,
He passes from life to his rest in the grave.
WILLIAM KNOX—*Mortality.*

Consider
The lilies of the field whose bloom is brief;—
We are as they;
Like them we fade away
As doth a leaf.
CHRISTINA G. ROSSETTI—*Consider.*

MOTHER

When God thought of mother, He must have laughed with satisfaction, and framed it quickly—so rich, so deep, so divine, so full of soul, power, and beauty, was the conception.
HENRY WARD BEECHER.

A mother is a mother still,
The holiest thing alive.
COLERIDGE—*The Three Graves.*

Men are what their mothers made them.
EMERSON.

The mother is all living.
Genesis. III. 20.

There is none,
In all this cold and hollow world, no fount
Of deep, strong, deathless love, save that within
A mother's heart.
MRS. HEMANS—*Siege of Valencia.*

One good mother is worth a hundred school masters.
GEORGE HERBERT.

I arose a mother in Israel.
Judges. V. 7.

If I were hanged on the highest hill,
Mother o' mine, O mother o' mine!
I know whose love would follow me still,
Mother o' mine, O mother o' mine!
KIPLING—*Mother o' Mine.*

If the whole world were put into one scale, and my mother into the other, the world would kick the beam.
LORD LANGDALE.

A woman's love
Is mighty, but a mother's heart is weak,
And by its weakness overcomes.
LOWELL—*Legend of Brittany.*

The bravest battle that ever was fought;
Shall I tell you where and when?
On the maps of the world you will find it not;
It was fought by the mothers of men.
JOAQUIN MILLER—*The Bravest Battle.*

Her children arise up and call her blessed.
Proverbs. XXXI. 28.

Who ran to help me when I fell,
And would some pretty story tell,
Or kiss the place to make it well?
My Mother.
ANNE TAYLOR—*My Mother.*

The bearing and the training of a child
Is woman's wisdom.
TENNYSON—*Princess.*

Mother is the name for God in the lips and hearts of children.
THACKERAY—*Vanity Fair.*

They say that man is mighty,
He governs land and sea,
He wields a mighty scepter
O'er lesser powers that be;

But a mightier power and stronger
Man from his throne has hurled,
For the hand that rocks the cradle
Is the hand that rules the world.
WILLIAM ROSS WALLACE—*What Rules the World.*

Sure I love the dear silver that shines in your hair,
And the brow that's all furrowed, and wrinkled with care.
I kiss the dear fingers, so toil-worn for me,
Oh, God bless you and keep you, Mother Machree.
RIDA JOHNSON YOUNG—*Mother Machree.*

MOTIVE

What makes life dreary is the want of motive.
GEORGE ELIOT—*Daniel Deronda.*

The two great movers of the human mind are the desire of good, and the fear of evil.
SAMUEL JOHNSON.

Selfishness is the grand moving principle of nine-tenths of our actions.
LA ROCHEFOUCAULD.

For there's nothing we read of in torture's inventions,
Like a well-meaning dunce, with the best of intentions.
LOWELL—*A Fable for Critics.*

MOUNTAIN

'Tis distance lends enchantment to the view,
And robes the mountain in its azure hue.
CAMPBELL—*Pleasures of Hope.*

Whose sunbright summit mingles with the sky.
CAMPBELL—*Pleasures of Hope.*

To make a mountain of a mole-hill.
HENRY ELLIS—*Original Letters.*

Over the hills, and over the main,
To Flanders, Portugal, or Spain;
The Queen commands, and we'll obey,
Over the hills and far away.
GEORGE FARQUHAR—*The Recruiting Officer.*

The mountain was in labour, and Jove was afraid, but it brought forth a mouse.
TACHOS, King of Egypt.

To pile Ossa upon Pelion.
VERGIL.

MOURNING

Each lonely scene shall thee restore;
For thee the tear be duly shed;
Belov'd till life can charm no more,
And mourn'd till Pity's self be dead.
COLLINS—*Dirge in Cymbeline.*

It is better to go to the house of mourning than to go to the house of feasting.
Ecclesiastes. VII. 2.

Forever honour'd, and forever mourn'd.
HOMER—*Iliad.*

He mourns the dead who lives as they desire.
YOUNG—*Night Thoughts.*

MOUSE

The mouse that hath but one hole is quickly taken.
GEORGE HERBERT.

When a building is about to fall down all the mice desert it.
PLINY THE ELDER.

MOUTH

Some asked me where the rubies grew,
And nothing I did say,
But with my finger pointed to
The lips of Julia.
HERRICK.

As a pomegranate, cut in twain,
White-seeded is her crimson mouth.
OSCAR WILDE.

MURDER

Murder may pass unpunish'd for a time,
But tardy justice will o'ertake the crime.
DRYDEN—*The Cock and the Fox.*

Thou shalt not kill.
Exodus. XX. 13.

Murder, like talent, seems occasionally to run in families.
GEORGE HENRY LEWES—*Physiology of Common Life*.

Absolutism tempered by assassination.
COUNT MÜNSTER.

Murder most foul, as in the best it is;
But this most foul, strange and unnatural.
SHAKESPEARE—*Hamlet*. Act I. Sc. 5.

For murder, though it have no tongue, will speak
With most miraculous organ.
SHAKESPEARE—*Hamlet*. Act II. Sc. 2.

One to destroy is murder by the law,
And gibbets keep the lifted hand in awe;
To murder thousands takes a specious name,
War's glorious art, and gives immortal fame.
YOUNG—*Love of Fame*.

MUSIC

All of heaven we have below.
ADDISON.

Music should strike fire from the heart of man, and bring tears from the eyes of woman.
BEETHOVEN.

God is its author, and not man; he laid
The key-note of all harmonies; he planned
All perfect combinations, and he made
Us so that we could hear and understand.
J. G. BRAINARD—*Music*.

"Music hath charms to soothe the savage beast,"
And therefore proper at a sheriff's feast.
JAMES BRAMSTON—*Man of Taste*.

Soprano, basso, even the contra-alto
Wished him five fathom under the Rialto.
BYRON—*Beppo*.

There's music in the sighing of a reed;
There's music in the gushing of a rill;
There's music in all things, if men had ears:
Their earth is but an echo of the spheres.
BYRON—*Don Juan*.

Music is well said to be the speech of angels.
CARLYLE—*Essays*.

Music is the child of prayer, the companion of religion.
CHATEAUBRIAND.

'Tis God gives skill,
But not without men's hands: He could not make
Antonio Stradivari's violins
Without Antonio.
GEORGE ELIOT—*Stradivarius*.

Why should the devil have all the good tunes?
ROWLAND HILL—*Sermons*.

The musician who always plays on the same string, is laughed at.
HORACE.

When the morning stars sang together, and all the sons of God shouted for joy.
Job. XXXVII. 7.

Heard melodies are sweet, but those unheard
Are sweeter; therefore, ye soft pipes, play on;
Not to the sensual ear, but, more endear'd,
Pipe to the spirit ditties of no tone.
KEATS—*Ode on a Grecian Urn*.

Music is in all growing things;
And underneath the silky wings
Of smallest insects there is stirred
A pulse of air that must be heard;
Earth's silence lives, and throbs, and sings.
LATHROP—*Music of Growth*.

Yea, music is the Prophet's art
Among the gifts that God hath sent,
One of the most magnificent!
LONGFELLOW—*Christus*.

Music is the universal language of mankind.

LONGFELLOW—*Outre-Mer.*

Who, through long days of labor,
And nights devoid of ease,
Still heard in his soul the music
Of wonderful melodies.

LONGFELLOW—*The Day Is Done.*

Such sweet compulsion doth in music lie.

MILTON—*Arcades.*

There let the pealing organ blow,
To the full voiced quire below,
In service high, and anthems clear,
As may with sweetness, through mine ear,
Dissolve me into ecstasies,
And bring all heaven before mine eyes.

MILTON—*Il Penseroso.*

Let me die to the sounds of delicious music.

Last words of MIRABEAU.

The harp that once through Tara's halls
The soul of music shed,
Now hangs as mute on Tara's walls,
As if that soul were fled.

MOORE—*Harp That Once.*

And music too—dear music! that can touch
Beyond all else the soul that loves it much—
Now heard far off, so far as but to seem
Like the faint, exquisite music of a dream.

MOORE—*Lalla Rookh.*

There's a barrel-organ carolling across a golden street
In the city as the sun sinks low;
And the music's not immortal; but the world has made it sweet
And fulfilled it with the sunset glow.

ALFRED NOYES—*Barrel Organ.*

Wagner's music is better than it sounds.

BILL NYE.

When I was young and had no sense
I bought a fiddle for eighteen pence,
And all the tunes that I could play
Was, "Over the Hills and Far Away."

Old Ballad.

One man with a dream, at pleasure,
Shall go forth and conquer a crown
And three with a new song's measure
Can trample a kingdom down.

A. W. E. O'SHAUGHNESSY—*Music Makers.*

Music resembles poetry: in each
Are nameless graces which no methods teach
And which a master-hand alone can reach.

POPE—*Essay on Criticism.*

Light quirks of music, broken and uneven
Make the soul dance upon a jig to Heav'n.

POPE—*Moral Essays.*

Seated one day at the organ,
I was weary and ill at ease,
And my fingers wandered idly
Over the noisy keys.

I do not know what I was playing,
Or what I was dreaming then,
But I struck one chord of music
Like the sound of a great Amen.

ADELAIDE A. PROCTER—*Lost Chord.*

Above the pitch, out of tune, and off the hinges.

RABELAIS—*Works.*

Music is the poetry of the air.

JEAN PAUL RICHTER.

Everything that heard him play,
Even the billows of the sea,
Hung their heads, and then lay by;
In sweet music is such art:
Killing care and grief of heart
Fall asleep, or, hearing, die.

SHAKESPEARE—*Henry VIII.* Act III. Sc. I.

How sweet the moonlight sleeps upon this bank!
Here will we sit and let the sounds of music
Creep in our ears: soft stillness, and the night
Becomes the touches of sweet harmony.

SHAKESPEARE—*Merchant of Venice.* Act V. Sc. I.

The man that hath no music in himself,
Nor is not moved with concord of sweet sounds,
Is fit for treasons, stratagems and spoils.
SHAKESPEARE—*Merchant of Venice.* Act V. Sc. 1.

Music revives the recollections it would appease.
MADAME DE STAËL—*Corinne.*

Music that gentlier on the spirit lies
Than tir'd eyelids upon tir'd eyes.
TENNYSON—*The Lotos Eaters.*

I can't sing. As a singist I am not a success. I am saddest when I sing. So are those who hear me. They are sadder even than I am.
ARTEMUS WARD—*Lecture.*

Bright gem instinct with music, vocal spark.
WORDSWORTH—*A Morning Exercise.*

Sweetest melodies
Are those that are by distance made more sweet.
WORDSWORTH—*Personal Talk.*

The music in my heart I bore,
Long after it was heard no more.
WORDSWORTH — *The Solitary Reaper.*

N

NAME

Oh! no! we never mention her,
Her name is never heard;
My lips are now forbid to speak
That once familiar word.
THOMAS HAYNES BAYLY.

Oh, Amos Cottle!—Phoebus! what a name!
BYRON—*English Bards and Scotch Reviewers.*

Who hath not own'd, with rapture-smitten frame,
The power of grace, the magic of a name.
CAMPBELL—*Pleasures of Hope.*

Ah! replied my gentle fair,
Beloved, what are names but air?
Choose thou whatever suits the line;
Call me Sappho, call me Chloris,
Call me Lalage, or Doris,
Only, only, call me thine.
COLERIDGE—*What's in a Name.*

He lives who dies to win a lasting name.
DRUMMOND—*Sonnet.*

A good name is better than precious ointment.
Ecclesiastes. VII. 1.

There be of them that have left a name behind them.
Ecclesiasticus. XLIV. 8.

The blackest ink of fate was sure my lot,
And when fate writ my name it made a blot.
FIELDING—*Amelia.*

One of the few, the immortal names,
That were not born to die.
FRITZ-GREENE HALLECK—*Marco Bozzaris.*

A nickname is the hardest stone that the devil can throw at a man.
Quoted by HAZLITT.

Fate tried to conceal him by naming him Smith.
HOLMES—*The Boys.*

And, lo! Ben Adhem's name led all the rest.
LEIGH HUNT—*Abou Ben Adhem.*

He left the name, at which the world grew pale,
To point a moral, or adorn a tale.
SAMUEL JOHNSON—*Vanity of Human Wishes.*

But unto you that fear my name shall the Sun of righteousness arise with healing in his wings.
Malachi. IV. 2.

My name is Legion.
Mark. V. 9.

A good name is rather to be chosen than great riches.
Proverbs. XXII. 1.

Your name hangs in my heart like a bell's tongue.
ROSTAND—*Cyrano de Bergerac.*

My foot is on my native heath, and my name is MacGregor!
SCOTT—*Rob Roy.*

I cannot tell what the dickens his name is.
SHAKESPEARE—*Merry Wives of Windsor.* Act III. Sc. 2.

Good name in man and woman, dear my lord,
Is the immediate jewel of their souls:
Who steals my purse steals trash; 'tis something, nothing;
'Twas mine, 'tis his, and has been slave to thousands;
But he that filches from me my good name
Robs me of that which not enriches him,
And makes me poor indeed.
SHAKESPEARE—*Othello.* Act III. Sc. 3.

And the best and the worst of this is
That neither is most to blame,
If you have forgotten my kisses
And I have forgotten your name.
SWINBURNE—*An Interlude.*

The myrtle that grows among thorns is a myrtle still.
The Talmud.

NATURE

All art, all education, can be merely a supplement to nature.
ARISTOTLE.

Nature's great law, and law of all men's minds?—
To its own impulse every creature stirs;
Live by thy light, and earth will live by hers!
MATTHEW ARNOLD—*Religious Isolation.*

At the close of the day, when the hamlet is still,
And mortals the sweets of forgetfulness prove,
When nought but the torrent is heard on the hill,
And nought but the nightingale's song in the grove.
BEATTIE—*The Hermit.*

Nature too unkind;
That made no medicine for a troubled mind!
BEAUMONT and FLETCHER—*Philaster.*

Nature is the most thrifty thing in the world; she never wastes anything; she undergoes change, but there's no annihilation, the essence remains—matter is eternal.
BINNEY.

I trust in Nature for the stable laws
Of beauty and utility. Spring shall plant
And Autumn garner to the end of time.
I trust in God—the right shall be the right
And other than the wrong, while he endures;
I trust in my own soul, that can perceive
The outward and the inward, Nature's good
And God's.
BROWNING—*A Soul's Tragedy.*

Go forth under the open sky, and list
To Nature's teachings.
BRYANT—*Thanatopsis.*

To him who in the love of Nature holds
Communion with her visible forms, she speaks
A various language.
BRYANT—*Thanatopsis.*

I am a part of all you see
In Nature: part of all you feel:
I am the impact of the bee
Upon the blossom; in the tree
I am the sap—that shall reveal
The leaf, the bloom—that flows and flutes
Up from the darkness through its roots.
MADISON CAWEIN—*Penetralia.*

Not without art, but yet to Nature true.
CHARLES CHURCHILL—*The Rosciad.*

Things perfected by nature are better than those finished by art.
CICERO.

Whate'er he did, was done with so much ease,
In him alone 't was natural to please.
DRYDEN—*Absalom and Achitophel.*

For Art may err, but Nature cannot miss.
DRYDEN—*Fables.*

By fate, not option, frugal Nature gave
One scent to hyson and to wall-flower,
One sound to pine-groves and to water-falls,
One aspect to the desert and the lake.
It was her stern necessity: all things
Are of one pattern made; bird, beast, and flower,
Song, picture, form, space, thought, and character
Deceive us, seeming to be many things,
And are but one.
EMERSON—*Xenophanes.*

The woods were made for the hunter of dreams,
The brooks for the fishers of song;
To the hunters who hunt for the gunless game
The streams and the woods belong.
There are thoughts that moan from the soul of pine
And thoughts in a flower bell curled;
And the thoughts that are blown with scent of the fern
Are as new and as old as the world.
SAM WALTER FOSS—*Bloodless Sportsman.*

To me more dear, congenial to my heart,
One native charm, than all the gloss of art.
GOLDSMITH—*Deserted Village.*

Nature is a volume of which God is the author.
HARVEY.

Nature, like a kind and smiling mother, lends herself to our dreams and cherishes our fancies.
VICTOR HUGO.

O what a glory doth this world put on
For him who, with a fervent heart, goes forth
Under the bright and glorious sky, and looks
On duties well performed, and days well spent!
For him the wind, ay, and the yellow leaves,
Shall have a voice, and give him eloquent teachings.
LONGFELLOW—*Autumn.*

And Nature, the old nurse, took
The child upon her knee,
Saying: "Here is a story-book
Thy Father has written for thee.

"Come, wander with me," she said,
"Into regions yet untrod;
And read what is still unread
In the manuscripts of God."
LONGFELLOW—*Fiftieth Birthday of Agassiz.*

So Nature deals with us, and takes away
Our playthings one by one, and by the hand
Leads us to rest so gently, that we go,
Scarce knowing if we wish to go or stay,
Being too full of sleep to understand
How far the unknown transcends the what we know.
LONGFELLOW—*Nature.*

O maternal earth which rocks the fallen leaf to sleep!
E. L. MASTERS—*Spoon River Anthology.*

Accuse not Nature, she hath done her part;
Do thou but thine!
MILTON—*Paradise Lost.*

There is not in the wide world a valley so sweet

As that vale in whose bosom the bright
waters meet.
MOORE—*The Meeting of the Waters.*

And we, with Nature's heart in tune,
Concerted harmonies.
WM. MOTHERWELL—*Jeannie Morrison.*

Seas roll to waft me, suns to light me
rise;
My footstool Earth, my canopy the
skies.
POPE—*Essay on Man.*

All are but parts of one stupendous
whole,
Whose body Nature is, and God the
soul;
That chang'd thro' all, and yet in all
the same,
Great in the earth as in th' ethereal
frame;
Warms in the sun, refreshes in the
breeze,
Glows in the stars, and blossoms in
the trees;
Lives thro' all life, extends thro' all
extent,
Spreads undivided, operates unspent;
Breathes in our soul, informs our mortal
part,
As full, as perfect, in a hair as heart.
POPE—*Essay on Man.*

Slave to no sect, who takes no private
road,
But looks through Nature up to Nature's
God.
POPE—*Essay on Man.*

Nature abhors a vacuum.
RABELAIS—*Gargantua.*

There is religion in everything around
us,—a calm and holy religion in the
unbreathing things of nature, which
man would do well to imitate.
RUSKIN.

To hold, as 'twere, the mirror up to
Nature; to shew virtue her own feature,
scorn her own image, and the
very age and body of the time his
form and pressure.
SHAKESPEARE—*Hamlet.* Act III.
Sc. 2.

One touch of nature makes the whole
world kin.
SHAKESPEARE—*Troilus and Cressida.* Act III. Sc. 3.

A voice of greeting from the wind was
sent;
The mists enfolded me with soft
white arms;
The birds did sing to lap me in content,
The rivers wove their charms,—
And every little daisy in the grass
Did look up in my face, and smile to
see me pass!
R. H. STODDARD—*Hymn to the Beautiful.*

In the world's audience hall, the simple
blade of grass sits on the same carpet
with the sunbeams, and the stars of
midnight.
TAGORE—*Gardener.*

Nothing in Nature is unbeautiful.
TENNYSON—*Lover's Tale.*

O nature! . . .
Enrich me with the knowledge of thy
works;
Snatch me to Heaven.
THOMSON—*Seasons.*

Nature is always wise in every part.
LORD THURLOW—*The Harvest Moon.*

Talk not of temples, there is one
Built without hands, to mankind
given;
Its lamps are the meridian sun
And all the stars of heaven,
Its walls are the cerulean sky,
Its floor the earth so green and fair,
The dome its vast immensity
All Nature worships there!
DAVID VEDDER—*Temple of Nature.*

Nature has always had more force than
education.
VOLTAIRE—*Life of Molière.*

Nature never did betray
The heart that loved her.
WORDSWORTH—*Lines Composed above Tintern Abbey.*

As in the eye of Nature he has lived,
So in the eye of Nature let him die!
WORDSWORTH—*The Old Cumberland Beggar.*

NAVIGATION

O pilot! 'tis a fearful night,
There's danger on the deep.
THOMAS HAYNES BAYLY—*The Pilot.*

O'er the glad waters of the dark blue sea,
Our thoughts as boundless, and our souls as free,
Far as the breeze can bear, the billows foam,
Survey our empire, and behold our home!
BYRON—*The Corsair.*

For they say there's a Providence sits up aloft
To keep watch for the life of poor Jack.
CHARLES DIBDEN—*Poor Jack.*

Skill'd in the globe and sphere, he gravely stands,
And, with his compass, measures seas and lands.
DRYDEN—*Sixth Satire of Juvenal.*

The winds and waves are always on the side of the ablest navigators.
GIBBON—*Decline and Fall of the Roman Empire.*

Oh, I am a cook and a captain bold
And the mate of the *Nancy* brig,
And a bo'sun tight and a midshipmite
And the crew of the captain's gig.
W. S. GILBERT—*Yarn of the "Nancy Bell."*

Thus, I steer my bark, and sail
On even keel, with gentle gale.
MATTHEW GREEN—*Spleen.*

Some love to roam o'er the dark sea's foam,
Where the shrill winds whistle free.
CHARLES MACKAY—*Some Love to Roam.*

Ye gentlemen of England
That live at home at ease,
Ah! little do you think upon
The dangers of the seas.
MARTIN PARKER—*Ye Gentlemen of England.*

Upon the gale she stoop'd her side,
And bounded o'er the swelling tide,
As she were dancing home;
The merry seamen laugh'd to see
Their gallant ship so lustily
Furrow the green sea-foam.
SCOTT—*Marmion.*

Thou bringest the sailor to his wife,
And travell'd men from foreign lands,
And letters unto trembling hands;
And, thy dark freight, a vanish'd life.
TENNYSON—*In Memoriam.*

There were three sailors of Bristol City
Who took a boat and went to sea.
But first with beef and captain's biscuits
And pickled pork they loaded she.
There was gorging Jack and Guzzling Jimmy,
And the youngest he was little Billee.
Now when they got as far as the Equator
They'd nothing left but one split pea.
THACKERAY—*Little Billee.*

NAVY

The royal navy of England has ever been its greatest defence and ornament; it is its ancient and natural strength; the floating bulwark of the island.
BLACKSTONE—*Commentaries.*

Hearts of oak are our ships,
Hearts of oak are our men.
GARRICK.

Now landsmen all, whoever you may be,
If you want to rise to the top of the tree,
If your soul isn't fettered to an office stool,
Be careful to be guided by this golden rule—

Stick close to your desks and *never go to sea,*
And you all may be Rulers of the Queen's Navee.
W. S. GILBERT—*H. M. S. Pinafore.*

Tell that to the Marines—the sailors won't believe it.
Old saying quoted by SCOTT.

NECESSITY

Necessity is often the spur to genius.
BALZAC.

It is necessity and not pleasure that compels us.
DANTE—*Inferno.*

Necessity has no law.
FRANKLIN.

Necessity does not submit to debate.
GARIBALDI.

To make necessity a virtue (a virtue of necessity).
HADRIANUS JULIUS.

Learn on how little man may live, and how small a portion nature requires.
LUCAN.

Necessity is the plea for every infringement of human freedom. It is the argument of tyrants; it is the creed of slaves.
WILLIAM PITT THE ELDER.

He who would eat the kernel, must crack the shell.
PLAUTUS.

Necessity makes even the timid brave.
SALLUST.

The mother of useful arts is necessity; that of the fine arts is luxury. For father, the former has intellect; the latter, genius, which itself is a kind of luxury.
SCHOPENHAUER.

Spirit of Nature! all-sufficing Power!
Necessity, thou mother of the world!
SHELLEY—*Queen Mab.*

I hold that to need nothing is divine, and the less a man needs the nearer does he approach divinity.
SOCRATES.

Necessity knows no law except to conquer.
SYRUS.

Necessity, the mother of invention.
WYCHERLY—*Love in a Wood.*

NEGLECT

Give me a look, give me a face,
That makes simplicity a grace:
Robes loosely flowing, hair as free;
Such sweet neglect more taketh me
Than all the adulteries of art;
They strike mine eyes, but not my heart.
BEN JONSON—*The Silent Woman.*

His noble negligences teach
What others' toils despair to reach.
PRIOR—*Alma.*

NEGRO

The image of God cut in ebony.
FULLER.

We've scrubb'd the negroes till we've nearly kill'd 'em,
And finding that we cannot wash them white,
We mean to gild 'em.
HOOD.

In the negro countenance you will often meet with strong traits of benignity. I have felt yearnings of tenderness towards some of these faces.
LAMB.

The negro is an exotic of the most gorgeous and superb countries of the world, and he has deep in his heart a passion for all that is splendid, rich and fanciful.
MRS. STOWE.

NEUTRALITY

The cold neutrality of an impartial judge.
BURKE.

Neutral men are the devil's allies.
CHAPIN.

Neutrality, as a lasting principle, is an evidence of weakness.
KOSSUTH.

The heart is never neutral.
SHAFTESBURY.

A wise neuter joins with neither, but uses both, as his honest interest leads him.
WILLIAM PENN.

NEW YORK CITY

I like to visit New York, but I wouldn't live there if you gave it to me.
American Saying.

Stream of the living world
Where dash the billows of strife!—
One plunge in the mighty torrent
Is a year of tamer life!
City of glorious days,
Of hope, and labour and mirth,
With room and to spare, on thy splendid bays
For the ships of all the earth!
R. W. GILDER—*The City.*

In dress, habits, manners, provincialism, routine and narrowness, he acquired that charming insolence, that irritating completeness, that sophisticated crassness, that overbalanced poise that makes the Manhattan gentleman so delightfully small in his greatness.
O. HENRY—*Defeat of the City.*

If there ever was an aviary overstocked with jays it is that Yaptown-on-the-Hudson, called New York.
O. HENRY—*The Gentle Grafter.*

Not like the brazen giant of Greek fame,
With conquering limbs astride from land to land;
Here at our sea-washed, sunset gates shall stand
A mighty woman with a torch, whose flame
Is the imprisoned lightning, and her name
Mother of exiles.
EMMA LAZARUS—*The New Colossus.*

Vulgar of manner, overfed,
Overdressed and underbred;
Heartless, Godless, hell's delight,
Rude by day and lewd by night;
Bedwarfed the man, o'ergrown the brute,
Ruled by boss and prostitute;
Purple-robed and pauper-clad,
Raving, rotting, money-mad;
A squirming herd in Mammon's mesh,
A wilderness of human flesh;
Crazed with avarice, lust and rum,
New York, thy name's Delirium.
BYRON R. NEWTON—*Owed to New York.*

NEWNESS

There is nothing new except what is forgotten.
MADEMOISELLE BERTIN (Milliner to Marie Antoinette).

Spick and span new.
CERVANTES—*Don Quixote.*

There is no new thing under the sun.
Ecclesiastes. I. 9.

Is there anything whereof it may be said, See, this is new? It hath been already of old time, which was before us.
Ecclesiastes. I. 10.

Human nature is fond of novelty.
PLINY THE ELDER.

What is valuable is not new, and what is new is not valuable.
DANIEL WEBSTER.

NEWS

If a man bites a dog, that is news.
JOHN BOGART.

By evil report and good report.
II Corinthians. VI. 8.

Ill news is wing'd with fate, and flies apace.
DRYDEN.

Where village statesmen talk'd with looks profound.
And news much older than their ale went round.
GOLDSMITH—*The Deserted Village.*

It is good news, *worthy of all acceptation,* and yet not too good to be true.
MATTHEW HENRY—*Commentaries.* I Timothy. I. 15.

What, what, what,
What's the news from Swat?
Sad news,
Bad news,
Comes by the cable; led
Through the Indian Ocean's bed,
Through the Persian Gulf, the Red
Sea, and the Med-
Iterranean—he's dead;
The Akhoond is dead.
GEORGE THOMAS LANIGAN—*The Akhoond of Swat.*

Who, or why, or which, or what,
Is the Akhond of Swat?
EDWARD LEAR—*The Akhond of Swat.*

As cold waters to a thirsty soul, so is good news from a far country.
Proverbs. XXV. 25.

There's villainous news abroad.
SHAKESPEARE—*Henry IV.* Pt. I. Act II. Sc. 4.

When we hear news we should always wait for the sacrament of confirmation.
VOLTAIRE.

NEWSPAPER

Newspapers are the world's mirrors.
JAMES ELLIS.

In the long, fierce struggle for freedom of opinion, the press, like the Church, counted its martyrs by thousands.
GARFIELD.

In these times we fight for ideas, and newspapers are our fortresses.
HEINE.

Every editor of newspapers pays tribute to the devil.
LA FONTAINE.

Newspapers will ultimately engross all literature.
LAMARTINE.

Four hostile newspapers are more to be feared than a thousand bayonets.
NAPOLEON.

The educators of the common people.
THEODORE PARKER.

Let me make the newspapers, and I care not what is preached in the pulpit or what is enacted in congress.
WENDELL PHILLIPS.

All I know is what I see in the papers.
WILL ROGERS.

The careful reader of a few good newspapers can learn more in a year than most scholars do in their great libraries.
F. B. SANBORN.

NIAGARA

Flow on, forever, in thy glorious robe
Of terror and of beauty. Yea, flow on
Unfathomed and resistless. God hath set
His rainbow on thy forehead: and the cloud
Mantled around thy feet. And He doth give
Thy voice of thunder power to speak of Him
Eternally—bidding the lip of man
Keep silence—and upon thine altar pour
Incense of awe-struck praise.
LYDIA H. SIGOURNEY—*Niagara.*

NIGHT

Night is a stealthy, evil Raven,
Wrapt to the eyes in his black wings.
T. B. ALDRICH—*Day and Night.*

I love night more than day—she is so lovely;
But I love night the most because she brings
My love to me in dreams which scarcely lie.
BAILEY—*Festus.*

The Night has a thousand eyes,
The Day but one;
Yet the light of the bright world dies
With the dying sun.
F. W. BOURDILLON—*Light.*

Most glorious night!
Thou wert not sent for slumber!
BYRON—*Childe Harold.*

For the night
Shows stars and women in a better light.
BYRON—*Don Juan.*

Night's black Mantle covers all alike.
DU BARTAS.

Dark the Night, with breath all flowers,
And tender broken voice that fills
With ravishment the listening hours,—
Whisperings, wooings,
Liquid ripples, and soft ring-dove cooings
In low-toned rhythm that love's aching stills!
Dark the night
Yet is she bright,
For in her dark she brings the mystic star,
Trembling yet strong, as is the voice of love,
From some unknown afar.
GEORGE ELIOT—*Spanish Gypsy.*

O radiant Dark! O darkly fostered ray!
Thou hast a joy too deep for shallow Day.
GEORGE ELIOT—*Spanish Gypsy.*

The smoke ascends
In a rosy-and-golden haze. The spires
Shine and are changed. In the valley
Shadows rise. The lark sings on. The sun
Closing his benediction,
Sinks, and the darkening air
Thrills with the sense of the triumphing night,—
Night with train of stars
And her great gift of sleep.
HENLEY—*Margaritæ Sorori.*

Now deep in ocean sunk the lamp of light,
And drew behind the cloudy vale of night.
HOMER—*Iliad.*

Watchman, what of the night?
Isaiah. XXI. 11.

Night, when deep sleep falleth on men.
Job. IV. 13; XXXIII. 15.

The night cometh when no man can work.
John. IX. 4.

'Tis the witching hour of night,
Orbed is the moon and bright,
And the stars they glisten, glisten,
Seeming with bright eyes to listen—
For what listen they?
KEATS—*A Prophecy.*

O holy Night! from thee I learn to bear
What man has borne before!
Thou layest thy fingers on the lips of Care,
And they complain no more.
LONGFELLOW—*Hymn to the Night.*

And the night shall be filled with music
And the cares, that infest the day,
Shall fold their tents, like the Arabs,
And as silently steal away.
LONGFELLOW—*The Day is Done.*

God makes sech nights, all white an' still
Fur'z you can look or listen,
Moonshine an' snow on field an' hill,
All silence an' all glisten.
LOWELL—*The Courtin'.*

. . . And when night
Darkens the streets, then wander forth the sons
Of Belial, flown with insolence and wine.
MILTON—*Paradise Lost.*

Darkness now rose,
As daylight sunk, and brought in low'ring Night
Her shadowy offspring.
MILTON—*Paradise Regained.*

Night is the time for rest;
How sweet, when labours close,
To gather round an aching breast
The curtain of repose,
Stretch the tired limbs, and lay the head
Down on our own delightful bed!
MONTGOMERY—*Night.*

Then awake! the heavens look bright, my dear;
'Tis never too late for delight, my dear;
And the best of all ways
To lengthen our days
Is to steal a few hours from the night, my dear.
MOORE—*The Young May Moon.*

The wind was a torrent of darkness among the gusty trees,
The moon was a ghostly galleon tossed upon cloudy seas,
The road was a ribbon of moonlight over the purple moor,
And the highwayman came riding.
ALFRED NOYES—*The Highwayman.*

O Night, most beautiful and rare!
Thou giv'st the heavens their holiest hue,
And through the azure fields of air
Bring'st down the gentle dew.
THOMAS BUCHANAN READ—*Night.*

To all, to each, a fair good night,
And pleasing dreams; and slumbers light.
SCOTT—*Marmion.*

Making night hideous.
SHAKESPEARE — *Hamlet.* Act I. Sc. 4.

Light thickens; and the crow
Makes wing to the rooky wood:
Good things of the day begin to droop and drowse;
While night's black agents to their preys do rouse.
SHAKESPEARE—*Macbeth.* Act III. Sc. 2.

The night is long that never finds the day.
SHAKESPEARE—*Macbeth.* Act IV. Sc. 3.

Come, gentle night, come, loving, blackbrow'd night.
SHAKESPEARE—*Romeo and Juliet.* Act III. Sc. 2.

How beautiful this night! the balmiest sigh
Which Vernal Zephyrs breathe in evening's ear
Were discord to the speaking quietude
That wraps this moveless scene.
Heaven's ebon vault,
Studded with stars, unutterably bright,
Through which the moon's unclouded grandeur rolls,
Seems like a canopy which love has spread
To curtain her sleeping world.
SHELLEY—*Queen Mab.*

How beautiful is night!
A dewy freshness fills the silent air;
No mist obscures, nor cloud nor speck nor stain
Breaks the serene of heaven.
SOUTHEY—*Thalaba.*

Dead sounds at night come from the inmost hills,
Like footsteps upon wool.
TENNYSON—*Oenone.*

Come, drink the mystic wine of Night,
Brimming with silence and the stars;
While earth, bathed in this holy light,
Is seen without its scars.
LOUIS UNTERMEYER—*The Wine of Night.*

The summer skies are darkly blue,
The days are still and bright,
And Evening trails her robes of gold
Through the dim halls of Night.
SARAH H. P. WHITMAN—*Summer's Call.*

Night begins to muffle up the day.
WITHERS—*Mistresse of Philarete.*

Night, sable goddess! from her ebon throne,
In rayless majesty, now stretches forth
Her leaden sceptre o'er a slumbering world.
Silence, how dead! and darkness, how profound!
Nor eye, nor list'ning ear, an object finds;
Creation sleeps. 'Tis as the general pulse
Of life stood still, and nature made a pause;
An awful pause! prophetic of her end.
YOUNG—*Night Thoughts.*

NIGHTINGALE

It is the hour when from the boughs
The nightingale's high note is heard;
It is the hour when lovers' vows
Seem sweet in every whisper'd word.
BYRON—*Parisina.*

'Tis the merry nightingale
That crowds, and hurries, and precipitates
With fast thick warble his delicious notes,
As he were fearful that an April night
Would be too short for him to utter forth
His love-chant, and disburthen his full soul
Of all its music!
COLERIDGE—*The Nightingale.*

Sweet bird, that sing'st away the early hours,
Of winter's past or coming void of care,
Well pleasèd with delights which present are,
Fair seasons, budding sprays, sweet-smelling flowers.
DRUMMOND—*To a Nightingale.*

The nightingale appear'd the first,
And as her melody she sang,
The apple into blossom burst,
To life the grass and violets sprang.
HEINE—*Book of Songs.*

Thou wast not born for death, immortal bird!
No hungry generations tread thee down;
The voice I hear this passing night was heard
In ancient days by emperor and clown.
KEATS—*To a Nightingale.*

Soft as Memnon's harp at morning,
To the inward ear devout,
Touched by light, with heavenly warning
Your transporting chords ring out.
Every leaf in every nook,
Every wave in every brook,
Chanting with a solemn voice
Minds us of our better choice.
JOHN KEBLE—*The Nightingale.*

To the red rising moon, and loud and deep
The nightingale is singing from the steep.
LONGFELLOW—*Keats.*

What bird so sings, yet does so wail?
O, 'tis the ravish'd nightingale—
Jug, jug, jug, jug—tereu—she cries,
And still her woes at midnight rise.
LYLY—*The Songs of Birds.*

Sweet bird that shunn'st the noise of folly,
Most musical, most melancholy!
Thee, chauntress, oft, the woods among,
I woo, to hear thy even-song.
MILTON—*Il Penseroso.*

O nightingale, that on yon bloomy spray
Warblest at eve, when all the woods are still;
Thou with fresh hope the lover's heart dost fill
While the jolly hours lead on propitious May.
MILTON—*To the Nightingale.*

Yon nightingale, whose strain so sweetly flows,
Mourning her ravish'd young or much-loved mate,
A soothing charm o'er all the valleys throws
And skies, with notes well tuned to her sad state.
PETRARCH—*To Laura in Death.*

Hark! that's the nightingale,
Telling the self-same tale
Her song told when this ancient earth was young:
So echoes answered when her song was sung
In the first wooded vale.
CHRISTINA G. ROSSETTI—*Twilight Calm.*

The angel of spring, the mellow-throated nightingale.
SAPPHO.

The nightingale, if she should sing by day,
When every goose is cackling, would be thought

No better a musician than the wren.
How many things by season season'd are
To their right praise, and true perfection!

SHAKESPEARE—*Merchant of Venice.* Act V. Sc. 1.

One nightingale in an interfluous wood
Satiate the hungry dark with melody.

SHELLEY — *Woodman and the Nightingale.*

NOBILITY

Noble blood is an accident of fortune; noble actions characterize the great.

GOLDONI—*Pamela.*

Be noble in every thought
And in every deed!

LONGFELLOW—*Christus.*

Be noble! and the nobleness that lies
In other men, sleeping, but never dead,
Will rise in majesty to meet thine own.

LOWELL.

This was the noblest Roman of them all:
All the conspirators save only he
Did that they did in envy of great Caesar;
He only, in a general honest thought
And common good to all, made one of them.

SHAKESPEARE—*Julius Caesar.* Act V. Sc. 5.

NONSENSE

A little nonsense now and then
Is relished by the wisest men.

ANONYMOUS.

For blocks are better cleft with wedges,
Than tools of sharp or subtle edges,
And dullest nonsense has been found
By some to be the most profound.

BUTLER—*Pindaric Ode.*

Conductor, when you receive a fare,
Punch in the presence of the passenjare.
A blue trip slip for an eight-cent fare,
A buff trip slip for a six-cent fare,
A pink trip slip for a three-cent fare,
Punch in the presence of the passenjare!

Chorus

Punch, brothers! punch with care!
Punch in the presence of the passenjare!

S. L. CLEMENS (Mark Twain).

Mingle a little folly with your wisdom; a little nonsense now and then is pleasant.

HORACE.

No one is exempt from talking nonsense; the misfortune is to do it solemnly.

MONTAIGNE.

He killed the noble Mudjokivis.
Of the skin he made him mittens,
Made them with the fur side inside,
He, to get the warm side inside,
Put the inside skin side outside,
He, to get the cold side outside,
Put the warm side fur side inside.
That's why he put the fur side inside,
Why he put the skin side outside,
Why he turned them inside outside.

GEORGE A. STRONG—*The Song of Milkanwatha.*

NOSE

Give me a man with a good allowance of nose, . . . when I want any good head-work done I choose a man—provided his education has been suitable—with a long nose.

NAPOLEON—Related in *Notes on Noses.*

If the nose of Cleopatra had been a little shorter the whole face of the world would have been changed.

PASCAL.

Plain as a nose in a man's face.

RABELAIS.

NOTHINGNESS

Nothing to do but work,
  Nothing to eat but food,
Nothing to wear but clothes,
  To keep one from going nude.

BEN KING—*The Pessimist.*

Nothing's new, and nothing's true, and nothing matters.
Attributed to Lady Morgan.

They laboriously do nothing.
Seneca.

A life of nothing's nothing worth,
From that first nothing ere his birth,
To that last nothing under earth.
Tennyson—*Two Voices.*

NOVEMBER

Fie upon thee, November! thou dost ape
The airs of thy young sisters, . . . thou hast stolen
The witching smile of May to grace thy lip,
And April's rare capricious loveliness
Thou'rt trying to put on!
Julia C. R. Dorr—*November.*

My sorrow when she's here with me,
Thinks these dark days of autumn rain
Are beautiful as days can be;
She loves the bare, the withered tree;
She walks the sodden pasture lane.
Robert Frost—*My November Guest.*

No park—no ring—no afternoon gentility—
No company—no nobility—
No warmth, no cheerfulness, no healthful ease.
No comfortable feel in any member—
No shade, no shine, no butterflies, no bees,
No fruits, no flowers, no leaves, no birds,
November!
Hood—*November.*

O

OATH

You can have no oath registered in heaven to destroy the Government; while I shall have the most solemn one to "preserve, protect, and defend" it.
Lincoln—*First Inaugural Address.*

He that sweareth to his own hurt and changeth not.
Psalms. XV. 4.

'Tis not the many oaths that makes the truth,
But the plain single vow that is vow'd true.
Shakespeare—*All's Well That Ends Well.* Act IV. Sc. 2.

It is a great sin to swear unto a sin,
But greater sin to keep a sinful oath.
Shakespeare—*Henry VI.* Pt. II. Act V. Sc. 1.

An oath, an oath, I have an oath in heaven:
Shall I lay perjury upon my soul?
No, not for Venice.
Shakespeare—*Merchant of Venice.* Act IV. Sc. 1.

I'll take thy word for faith, not ask thine oath;
Who shuns not to break one will sure crack both.
Shakespeare—*Pericles.* Act I. Sc. 2.

I write a woman's oaths in water.
Sophocles.

OBEDIENCE

Obedience alone gives the right to command.
Emerson.

Let thy child's first lesson be obedience, and the second will be what thou wilt.
Franklin.

Women are perfectly well aware that the more they seem to obey the more they rule.
Michelet.

Ascend, I follow thee, safe guide, the path
Thou lead'st me, and to the hand of heav'n submit.
Milton—*Paradise Lost.*

Through obedience learn to command.
Plato.

The eye that mocketh at his father, and despiseth to obey his mother, the ravens of the valley shall pick it out, and the young eagles shall eat it.
Proverbs. XXX. 17.

Let them obey that know not how to rule.
SHAKESPEARE—*Henry VI*. Pt. II. Act V. Sc. 1.

OBSCURITY

I give the fight up; let there be an end,
A privacy, an obscure nook for me,
I want to be forgotten even by God.
BROWNING—*Paracelsus*.

Full many a flower is born to blush unseen,
And waste its sweetness on the desert air.
GRAY—*Elegy in a Country Churchyard*.

He who has lived obscurely and quietly has lived well.
OVID.

How often the highest talent lurks in obscurity!
PLAUTUS.

How happy is the blameless vestal's lot!
The world forgetting, by the world forgot.
POPE—*Eloisa to Abelard*.

Thus let me live, unseen, unknown,
Thus unlamented let me die;
Steal from the world, and not a stone
Tell where I lie.
POPE—*Ode on Solitude*.

How many a rustic Milton has passed by,
Stifling the speechless longings of his heart,
In unremitting drudgery and care!
How many a vulgar Cato has compelled
His energies, no longer tameless then,
To mold a pin, or fabricate a nail!
SHELLEY—*Queen Mab*.

She dwelt among the untrodden ways
Beside the springs of Dove,
A maid whom there were none to praise
And very few to love.
WORDSWORTH.

OBSTINACY

Obstinacy and vehemency in opinion are the surest proofs of stupidity.
BARTON.

People first abandon reason, and then become obstinate; and the deeper they are in error the more angry they are.
BLAIR.

Firmness or stiffness of the mind is not from adherence to truth, but submission to prejudice.
LOCKE.

Obstinacy is ever most positive when it is most in the wrong.
MADAME NECKER.

An obstinate man does not hold opinions, but they hold him.
POPE.

OCCUPATION

I hold every man a debtor to his profession; from the which as men of course do seek to receive countenance and profit, so ought they of duty to endeavor themselves, by way of amends, to be a help and ornament thereunto.
BACON—*Maxims of the Law*.

Blessed is he who has found his work; let him ask no other blessedness. He has a work, a life purpose. Labor is life.
CARLYLE.

The crowning fortune of a man is to be born to some pursuit which finds him employment and happiness, whether it be to make baskets, or broadswords, or canals, or statues, or songs.
EMERSON.

The ugliest of trades have their moments of pleasure. Now, if I were a grave-digger, or even a hangman, there are some people I could work for with a great deal of enjoyment.

DOUGLAS JERROLD—*Ugly Trades.*

No thoroughly occupied man was ever yet very miserable.

LANDOR.

OCEAN

The sea heaves up, hangs loaded o'er the land,
Breaks there, and buries its tumultuous strength.

BROWNING—*Luria.*

Roll on, thou deep and dark blue Ocean—roll!
Ten thousand fleets sweep over thee in vain;
Man marks the earth with ruin—his control
Stops with the shore.

BYRON—*Childe Harold.*

The image of Eternity—the throne
Of the Invisible; even from out thy slime
The monsters of the deep are made; each zone
Obeys thee; thou goest forth, dread, fathomless, alone.

BYRON—*Childe Harold.*

What are the wild waves saying,
Sister, the whole day long,
That ever amid our playing
I hear but their low, lone song?

JOSEPH E. CARPENTER.

The sea! the sea! the open sea!
The blue, the fresh, the ever free!
Without a mark, without a bound,
It runneth the earth's wide regions round;
It plays with the clouds; it mocks the skies;
Or like a cradled creature lies.

BARRY CORNWALL—*The Sea.*

Behold the Sea,
The opaline, the plentiful and strong,
Yet beautiful as is the rose in June,
Fresh as the trickling rainbow of July;
Sea full of food, the nourisher of kinds,
Purger of earth, and medicine of men;
Creating a sweet climate by my breath,
Washing out harms and griefs from memory,
And, in my mathematic ebb and flow,
Giving a hint of that which changes not.

EMERSON—*Sea Shore.*

The sea is flowing ever,
The land retains it never.

GOETHE.

Alone I walked on the ocean strand,
A pearly shell was in my hand;
I stooped, and wrote upon the sand
My name, the year, the day.
As onward from the spot I passed,
One lingering look behind I cast,
A wave came rolling high and fast,
And washed my lines away.

HANNAH FLAGG GOULD—*A Name in the Sand.*

Full many a gem of purest ray serene,
The dark unfathomed caves of ocean bear.

GRAY—*Elegy in a Country Churchyard.*

The breaking waves dashed high
On a stern and rock-bound coast,
And the woods against a stormy sky,
Their giant branches toss'd.

FELICIA D. HEMANS—*The Landing of the Pilgrim Fathers in New England.*

Praise the sea, but keep on land.

GEORGE HERBERT.

Tut! the best thing I know between France and England is the sea.

DOUGLAS JERROLD—*The Anglo-French Alliance.*

Love the sea? I dote upon it—from the beach.

DOUGLAS JERROLD—*Love of the Sea.*

Hitherto thou shalt come, but no further; and here shall thy proud waves be stayed.

Job. XXXVIII. 11.

"Would'st thou,"—so the helmsman answered,
"Learn the secret of the sea?
Only those who brave its dangers
Comprehend its mystery!"

LONGFELLOW—*The Secret of the Sea.*

This precious stone set in the silver sea.
SHAKESPEARE—*Richard II.* Act II. Sc. I.

Thou wert before the Continents, before
The hollow heavens, which like another sea
Encircles them and thee, but whence thou wert,
And when thou wast created, is not known,
Antiquity was young when thou wast old.
R. H. STODDARD—*Hymn to the Sea.*

Break, break, break,
On thy cold gray stones, oh sea!
And I would that my tongue could utter
The thoughts that arise in me.
TENNYSON—*Break, Break, Break.*

Rocked in the cradle of the deep,
I lay me down in peace to sleep.
EMMA WILLARD—*The Cradle of the Deep.*

OCTOBER

October turned my maple's leaves to gold;
The most are gone now; here and there one lingers;
Soon these will slip from out the twig's weak hold,
Like coins between a dying miser's fingers.
T. B. ALDRICH—*Maple Leaves.*

The sweet calm sunshine of October, now
Warms the low spot; upon its grassy mould
The purple oak-leaf falls; the birchen bough
Drops its bright spoil like arrow-heads of gold.
BRYANT—*October* (1866).

There is something in October sets the gypsy blood astir:
We must rise and follow her,
When from every hill of flame
She calls, and calls each vagabond by name.
BLISS CARMAN—*Vagabond Song.*

And close at hand, the basket stood
With nuts from brown October's wood.
WHITTIER—*Snow-bound.*

OPINION

Where an opinion is general, it is usually correct.
JANE AUSTEN—*Mansfield Park.*

Private opinion is weak, but public opinion is almost omnipotent.
HENRY WARD BEECHER.

For most men (till by losing rendered sager)
Will back their own opinions by a wager.
BYRON—*Beppo.*

Popular opinion is the greatest lie in the world.
CARLYLE.

It were not best that we should all think alike; it is difference of opinion that makes horseraces.
S. L. CLEMENS (Mark Twain)—*Pudd'nhead Wilson.*

Stiff in opinion, always in the wrong.
DRYDEN—*Absalom and Achitophel.*

It is the absolute right of the state to supervise the formation of public opinion.
PAUL JOSEPH GOEBBELS, 1933.

Monuments of the safety with which errors of opinion may be tolerated where reason is left free to combat it.
JEFFERSON—*First Inaugural Address.*

Dogmatism is puppyism come to its full growth.
JERROLD—*Man Made of Money.*

Those who never retract their opinions love themselves more than they love truth.
JOUBERT.

How long halt ye between two opinions?
I Kings. XVIII. 21.

He who has no opinion of his own, but depends upon the opinion and taste of others, is a slave.
KLOPSTOCK.

We hardly find any persons of good sense save those who agree with us.
LA ROCHEFOUCAULD.

Public opinion, though often formed upon a wrong basis, yet generally has a strong underlying sense of justice.
LINCOLN.

The foolish and the dead alone never change their opinion.
LOWELL.

Do not think of knocking out another person's brains because he differs in opinion from you. It would be as rational to knock yourself on the head because you differ from yourself ten years ago.
HORACE MANN.

There never was in the world two opinions alike, no more than two hairs, or two grains; the most universal quality is diversity.
MONTAIGNE.

Force and not opinion is the queen of the world; but it is opinion that uses the force.
PASCAL.

Orthodoxy on one side of the Pyrenees may be heresy on the other.
PASCAL.

Some praise at morning what they blame at night,
But always think the last opinion right.
POPE—*Essay on Criticism.*

The feeble tremble before opinion, the foolish defy it, the wise judge it, the skillful direct it.
MME. ROLAND.

There is no process of amalgamation by which opinions, wrong individually, can become right merely by their multitude.
RUSKIN.

I know where there is more wisdom than is found in Napoleon, Voltaire, or all the ministers present and to come—in public opinion.
TALLEYRAND—*In the Chamber of Peers.*

OPPORTUNITY

There is an hour in each man's life appointed
To make his happiness, if then he seize it.
BEAUMONT and FLETCHER.

This could but have happened once,
And we missed it, lost it forever.
BROWNING—*Youth and Art.*

You will never "find" time for anything. If you want time, you must make it.
CHARLES BUXTON.

Do not suppose opportunity will knock twice at your door.
CHAMFORT.

Seek not for fresher founts afar,
Just drop your bucket where you are;
And while the ship right onward leaps,
Uplift it from exhaustless deeps.
Parch not your life with dry despair;
The stream of hope flows everywhere—
So under every sky and star,
Just drop your bucket where you are!
SAM WALTER FOSS—*Opportunity.*

Plough deep while sluggards sleep.
BENJAMIN FRANKLIN.

To improve the golden moment of opportunity, and catch the good that is within our reach, is the great art of life.
JOHNSON.

They do me wrong who say I come no more,
When once I knock and fail to find you in;
For every day I stand outside your door.
And bid you wait, and rise to fight and win.
JUDGE WALTER MALONE—*Opportunity.*

Opportunity is ever worth expecting; let your hook be ever hanging ready.

The fish will be in the pool where you least imagine it to be.
Ovid.

There's place and means for every man alive.
Shakespeare—*All's Well That Ends Well.* Act IV. Sc. 3.

Who seeks, and will not take when once 'tis offer'd,
Shall never find it more.
Shakespeare—*Antony and Cleopatra.* Act II. Sc. 7.

There is a tide in the affairs of men,
Which, taken at the flood, leads on to fortune;
Omitted, all the voyage of their life
Is bound in shallows and in miseries.
Shakespeare—*Julius Caesar.* Act IV. Sc. 3.

Opportunity, to statesmen, is as the just degree of heat to chemists; it perfects all the work.
Suckling.

The opportunity is often lost by deliberating.
Syrus.

When a thief has no opportunity for stealing, he considers himself an honest man.
The Talmud.

The opportunity for doing mischief is found a hundred times a day, and of doing good once in a year.
Voltaire—*Zadig.*

The cleverest of all the devils is Opportunity.
Wieland.

OPPOSITION

He that wrestles with us strengthens our nerves and sharpens our skill. Our antagonist is our helper.
Burke.

No government can be long secure without a formidable opposition.
Disraeli—*Coningsby.*

Nature is upheld by antagonism. Passions, resistance, danger, are educators. We acquire the strength we have overcome.
Emerson.

To make a young couple love each other, it is only necessary to oppose and separate them.
Goethe.

Opposition always inflames the enthusiast, never converts him.
Schiller.

OPTIMIST

An optimist sees an opportunity in every calamity; a pessimist sees a calamity in every opportunity.
Anonymous.

Optimism: A cheerful frame of mind that enables a tea kettle to sing though in hot water up to its nose.
Anonymous.

An optimist is one who buys from Jews and sells to Scotsmen.
Anonymous.

ORANGE

'Twas noon; and every orange bud
Hung languid o'er the crystal flood,
Fain as the lids of maiden eyes
Beneath a lover's burning sighs!
Moore—*I Stole along the Flowery Bank.*

ORATORY

Whatever we conceive well we express clearly, and words flow with ease.
Boileau.

Oratory is the power to talk people out of their sober and natural opinions.
Chatfield.

He mouths a sentence as curs mouth a bone.
Charles Churchill—*The Rosciad.*

There is no power like that of oratory. Caesar controlled men by exciting their fears; Cicero, by captivating their affections and swaying their passions.

The influence of the one perished with its author; that of the other continues to this day.

HENRY CLAY.

Glittering generalities! They are blazing ubiquities.

EMERSON—*Remark on Choate's words.*

What the orators want in depth, they give you in length.

MONTESQUIEU.

When Demosthenes was asked what was the first part of Oratory, he answered, "Action," and which was the second, he replied, "Action," and which was the third, he still answered "Action."

PLUTARCH.

It is a thing of no great difficulty to raise objections against another man's oration,—nay, it is a very easy matter; but to produce a better in its place is a work extremely troublesome.

PLUTARCH.

Fire in each eye, and papers in each hand,
They rave, recite, and madden round the land.

POPE—*Prologue to Satires.*

ORDER

Have a place for everything and have everything in its place.

ANONYMOUS.

Let all things be done decently and in order.

I Corinthians. XIV. 40.

Set all things in their own peculiar place,
And know that order is the greatest grace.

DRYDEN.

For the world was built in order
And the atoms march in tune;
Rhyme the pipe, and Time the warder,
The sun obeys them, and the moon.

EMERSON—*Monadnock.*

Set thine house in order.

Isaiah. XXXVIII. 1.

All are born to observe order, but few are born to establish it.

JOUBERT.

Order is Heaven's first law; and this confess,
Some are and must be greater than the rest.

POPE—*Essay on Man.*

Not chaos-like together crush'd and bruis'd,
But as the world, harmoniously confused:
Where order in variety we see,
And where tho' all things differ, all agree.

POPE—*Windsor Forest.*

It is folly to put the plough in front of the oxen.

RABELAIS—*Gargantua.*

The heavens themselves, the planets and this centre
Observe degree, priority and place,
Insisture, course, proportion, season, form,
Office and custom, in all line of order.

SHAKESPEARE—*Troilus and Cressida.* Act I. Sc. 3.

ORIGINALITY

Great men are more distinguished by range and extent than by originality.

EMERSON.

Great things cannot have escaped former observation.

SAMUEL JOHNSON.

Originality is nothing but judicious imitation.

VOLTAIRE.

OSTENTATION

Ostentation is the signal flag of hypocrisy.

CHAPIN.

Excess in apparel is another costly folly. The very trimming of the vain world would clothe all the naked ones.

WILLIAM PENN.

They used to think they were doing God a favor to print His name in capital letters.
JEAN CHAPIN RICHTER.

OYSTER

It is unseasonable and unwholesome in all months that have not an R in their names to eat an oyster.
BUTLER.

'Twere better to be born a stone
Of rudder shape, and feeling none,
Than with a tenderness like mine
And sensibilities so fine!
Ah, hapless wretch! condemn'd to dwell
Forever in my native shell,
Ordained to move when others please,
Not for my own content or ease;
But toss'd and buffeted about,
Now *in* the water and now *out*.
COWPER—*The Poet, the Oyster and Sensitive Plant.*

Secret, and self-contained, and solitary as an oyster.
DICKENS—*Christmas Carol.*

The world's mine oyster,
Which I with sword will open.
SHAKESPEARE—*The Merry Wives of Windsor.* Act II. Sc. 2.

He was a bold man that first ate an oyster.
SWIFT—*Polite Conversation.*

P

PAIN

Other men's pains are easily borne.
CERVANTES.

A man deep wounded may feel too much pain to feel much anger.
GEORGE ELIOT.

You purchase pain with all that joy can give,
And die of nothing but a rage to live.
POPE—*Moral Essays.*

Ah, to think how thin the veil that lies
Between the pain of hell and Paradise.
G. W. RUSSELL—*Janus.*

One fire burns out another's burning,
One pain is lessen'd by another's anguish.
SHAKESPEARE—*Romeo and Juliet.* Act. I. Sc. 2.

Pain and pleasure, like light and darkness, succeed each other.
LAURENCE STERNE.

The pain of the mind is worse than the pain of the body.
SYRUS.

Nothing begins, and nothing ends,
That is not paid with moan;
For we are born in others' pain,
And perish in our own.
FRANCIS THOMPSON—*Daisy.*

The mark of rank in nature is capacity for pain,
And the anguish of the singer marks the sweetness of the strain.
SARAH WILLIAMS—*Twilight Hours.*

PAINTING

The love of gain never made a painter; but it has marred many.
WASHINGTON ALLSTON.

If we could but paint with the hand as we see with the eye!
BALZAC.

A picture is a poem without words.
CORNIFICIUS.

Hard features every bungler can command:
To draw true beauty shows a master's hand.
DRYDEN—*To Mr. Lee, on His Alexander.*

The mind paints before the brush.
JAMES ELLIS.

Pictures must not be too picturesque.
EMERSON—*Essays.*

"Paint me as I am," said Cromwell,
"Rough with age and gashed with wars;
Show my visage as you find it,
Less than truth my soul abhors."
JAMES T. FIELDS—*On a Portrait of Cromwell.*

One picture in ten thousand, perhaps, ought to live in the applause of mankind, from generation to generation until the colors fade and blacken out of sight or the canvas rot entirely away.
HAWTHORNE—*Marble Faun.*

He paints a dolphin in the woods, a boar in the waves.
HORACE.

A picture is a poem without words.
HORACE.

The only good copies are those which exhibit the defects of bad originals.
LA ROCHEFOUCAULD.

The picture that approaches sculpture nearest is the best picture.
LONGFELLOW—*Michael Angelo.*

I mix them with my brains, sir.
JOHN OPIE, when asked with what he mixed his colors.

He best can paint them who shall feel them most.
POPE—*Eloisa and Abelard.*

The fellow mixes blood with his colors.
GUIDO RENI (about Rubens).

Painting with all its technicalities, difficulties, and peculiar ends, is nothing but a noble and expressive language, invaluable as the vehicle of thought, but by itself nothing.
RUSKIN—*True and Beautiful.*

But who can paint
Like nature? Can imagination boast,
Amid its gay creation, hues like hers?
THOMSON—*Seasons.*

PANSY

The delicate thought, that cannot find expression,
For ruder speech too fair,
That, like thy petals, trembles in possession,
And scatters on the air.
BRET HARTE—*The Mountain Heart's Ease.*

Heart's ease! one could look for half a day
Upon this flower, and shape in fancy out
Full twenty different tales of love and sorrow,
That gave this gentle name.
MARY HOWITT—*Heart's Ease.*

The beauteous pansies rise
In purple, gold, and blue,
With tints of rainbow hue
Mocking the sunset skies.
THOMAS J. OUSELEY—*The Angel of the Flowers.*

Heart's ease or pansy, pleasure or thought,
Which would the picture give us of these?
Surely the heart that conceived it sought
Heart's ease.
SWINBURNE—*A Flower Piece by Fanten.*

PARADISE

In the nine heavens are eight Paradises;
Where is the ninth one? In the human breast.
Only the blessed dwell in th' Paradises,
But blessedness dwells in the human breast.
WILLIAM R. ALGER—*Oriental Poetry.*

Or were I in the wildest waste,
Sae bleak and bare, sae bleak and bare,
The desert were a paradise
If thou wert there, if thou wert there.
BURNS—*Oh! Wert Thou in the Cold Blast.*

In this fool's paradise, he drank delight.
CRABBE—*The Borough Players.*

Unto you is paradise opened.
II Esdras. VIII. 52.

The meanest floweret of the vale,
The simplest note that swells the gale,
The common sun, the air, the skies,
To him are open paradise.
GRAY.

Dry your eyes—O dry your eyes,
For I was taught in Paradise
To ease my breast of melodies.
KEATS—*Fairy Song.*

A Book of Verse underneath the Bough,
A Jug of Wine, a Loaf of Bread—and Thou
Beside me singing in the Wilderness—
Oh, Wilderness were Paradise enow!
OMAR KHAYYÁM—*Rubaiyat.*

The loves that meet in Paradise shall cast out fear,
And Paradise hath room for you and me and all.
CHRISTINA G. ROSSETTI—*Saints and Angels.*

There is no expeditious road
To pack and label men for God,
And save them by the barrel-load,
Some may perchance, with strange surprise,
Have blundered into Paradise.
FRANCIS THOMPSON—*Epilogue.*

PARADOX

For thence,—a paradox
Which comforts while it mocks,—
Shall life succeed in that it seems to fail;
What I aspired to be,
And was not, comforts me:
A brute I might have been, but would not sink i' the scale.
BROWNING—*Rabbi Ben Ezra.*

Then there is that glorious Epicurean paradox, uttered by my friend, the Historian, in one of his flashing moments: "Give us the luxuries of life, and we will dispense with its necessaries."
HOLMES—*The Autocrat of the Breakfast Table.*

PARDON

Nothing in this low and ruined world bears the meek impress of the Son of God so surely as forgiveness.
ALICE CARY.

As we grow in wisdom, we pardon more freely.
MME. DE STAËL.

Pardon others often, thyself never.
SYRUS.

PARENT

There is no friendship, no love, like that of the parent for the child.
HENRY WARD BEECHER.

The first half of our lives is ruined by our parents and the second half by our children.
CLARENCE S. DARROW.

A suspicious parent makes an artful child.
HALIBURTON.

Next to God, thy parents.
WILLIAM PENN.

PARTING

Adieu! 'tis love's last greeting,
The parting hour is come!
And fast thy soul is fleeting
To seek its starry home.
BERANGER—*L'Adieu.*

Such partings break the heart they fondly hope to heal.
BYRON—*Childe Harold.*

Fare thee well! and if for ever,
Still for ever, fare thee well.
BYRON—*Fare Thee Well.*

We two parted
In silence and tears,
Half broken-hearted
To sever for years.
BYRON—*When We Two Parted.*

Kathleen Mavourneen, the gray dawn is breaking,
The horn of the hunter is heard on the hill,
The lark from her light wing the bright dew is shaking—
Kathleen Mavourneen, what, slumbering still?
Oh hast thou forgotten how soon we must sever?

Oh hast thou forgotten this day we must part?
It may be for years and it may be forever;
Oh why art thou silent, thou voice of my heart?
JULIA CRAWFORD.

One kind kiss before we part,
Drop a tear, and bid adieu;
Though we sever, my fond heart
Till we meet shall pant for you.
DODSLEY—*Colin's Kisses.*

The king of Babylon stood at the parting of the way.
EZEKIEL. XXI. 21.

We only part to meet again.
GAY—*Black-eyed Susan.*

Excuse me, then! you know my heart;
But dearest friends, alas! must part.
GAY—*The Hare and Many Friends.*

Good-night! good-night! as we so oft have said
Beneath this roof at midnight, in the days
That are no more, and shall no more return.
Thou hast but taken up thy lamp and gone to bed;
I stay a little longer, as one stays
To cover up the embers that still burn.
LONGFELLOW—*Three Friends of Mine.*

If we must part forever,
Give me but one kind word to think upon,
And please myself with, while my heart's breaking.
THOMAS OTWAY—*The Orphan.*

Say good-bye er howdy-do—
What's the odds betwixt the two?
Comin'—goin'—every day—
Best friends first to go away—
Grasp of hands you'd rather hold
Than their weight in solid gold,
Slips their grip while greetin' you,—
Say good-bye er howdy-do?
JAMES WHITCOMB RILEY—*Good-Bye er Howdy-Do.*

Good-night, good-night! parting is such sweet sorrow.
That I shall say good-night till it be morrow.
SHAKESPEARE—*Romeo and Juliet.* Act II. Sc. 2.

Gone—flitted away,
Taken the stars from the night and the sun
From the day!
Gone, and a cloud in my heart.
TENNYSON—*The Window.*

But fate ordains that dearest friends must part.
YOUNG—*Love of Fame.*

PARTY

Political parties serve to keep each other in check, one keenly watching the other.
HENRY CLAY.

Party honesty is party expediency.
GROVER CLEVELAND, 1889.

He that aspires to be the head of a party will find it more difficult to please his friends than to perplex his foes.
COLTON.

I always voted at my party's call,
And I never thought of thinking for myself at all.
W. S. GILBERT—*H. M. S. Pinafore.*

He serves his party best who serves the country best.
R. B. HAYES—*Inaugural Address. 1877.*

If I could not go to Heaven but with a party I would not go there at all.
THOMAS JEFFERSON, 1789.

Party standards are shadows in which patriotism is buried.
BERNARDIN DE ST. PIERRE.

Now is the time for all good men to come to the aid of the party.
CHARLES E. WELLER, 1867. (Originated as a typing exercise.)

Party spirit enlists a man's virtues in the cause of his vices.
WHATELY.

PASSION

Passion is universal humanity. Without it religion, history, romance and art would be useless.
BALZAC.

The passions are like fire, useful in a thousand ways and dangerous only in one, through their excess.
BOVEE.

Only I discern
Infinite passion, and the pain
Of finite hearts that yearn.
BROWNING—*Two in the Campagna.*

He who is passionate and hasty is generally honest. It is your cool, dissembling hypocrite of whom you should beware.
LAVATER.

The passions do not die out; they burn out.
NINON DE LENCLOS.

Take heed lest passion sway
Thy judgment to do aught, which else free will
Would not admit.
MILTON—*Paradise Lost.*

Passion makes us feel, but never see clearly.
MONTESQUIEU.

In men, we various ruling passions find;
In women two almost divide the kind;
Those only fix'd, they first or last obey.
The love of pleasure, and the love of sway.
POPE—*Moral Essays.*

The ruling passion, be it what it will,
The ruling passion conquers reason still.
POPE—*Moral Essays.*

Give me that man
That is not passion's slave.
SHAKESPEARE—*Hamlet.* Act. III. Sc. 2.

Passion is the drunkenness of the mind.
SOUTH.

We should employ our passions in the service of life, not spend life in the service of our passions.
RICHARD STEELE.

The passions are the gales of life; and it is religion only that can prevent them from rising into a tempest.
DR. WATTS.

PAST

The present contains nothing more than the past, and what is found in the effect was already in the cause.
HENRI BERGSON—*Creative Evolution.*

The age of chivalry is gone.
BURKE—*Reflections on the Revolution in France.*

John Anderson, my jo, John,
When we were first acquent,
Your locks were like the raven,
Your bonny brow was brent.
BURNS—*John Anderson.*

Gone—glimmering through the dream of things that were.
BYRON—*Childe Harold.*

The Present is the living sum-total of the whole Past.
CARLYLE—*Essays.*

Not heaven itself upon the past has power;
But what has been, has been, and I have had my hour.
DRYDEN—*Imitation of Horace.*

Oh! the good times when we were so unhappy.
DUMAS.

O God! Put back Thy universe and give me yesterday.
HENRY ARTHUR JONES—*Silver King.*

The age of chivalry is never past so long as there is a wrong left unredressed on earth.
CHARLES KINGSLEY—*Life.*

Enjoy the spring of love and youth,
To some good angel leave the rest;

For time will teach thee soon the truth,
There are no birds in last year's nest.
LONGFELLOW—*It Is Not Always May.*

The good of other times let people state;
I think it lucky I was born so late.
OVID.

Weep no more, lady, weep no more,
Thy sorrow is in vain,
For violets plucked, the sweetest showers
Will ne'er make grow again.
THOMAS PERCY.

Oh, had I but Aladdin's lamp
Tho' only for a day,
I'd try to find a link to bind
The joys that pass away.
CHARLES SWAIN.

PATIENCE

But there are times when patience proves at fault.
BROWNING—*Paracelsus.*

Patience, shuffle the cards!
CERVANTES.

Patience is a necessary ingredient of genius.
DISRAELI.

A handful of patience is worth more than a bushel of brains.
Dutch Proverb.

Adopt the pace of nature: her secret is patience.
EMERSON.

He that can have patience can have what he will.
FRANKLIN.

By time and toil we sever
What strength and rage could never.
LA FONTAINE.

Still achieving, still pursuing,
Learn to labor and to wait.
LONGFELLOW—*A Psalm of Life.*

All things come round to him who will but wait.
LONGFELLOW—*Tales of a Wayside Inn.*

Patience is bitter, but its fruit is sweet.
ROUSSEAU.

And makes us rather bear those ills we have
Than fly to others that we know not of?
SHAKESPEARE—*Hamlet.* Act III. Sc. 1.

For there was never yet philosopher
That could endure the toothache patiently.
SHAKESPEARE—*Much Ado about Nothing.* Act V. Sc. 1.

How poor are they that have not patience!
What wound did ever heal but by degrees?
SHAKESPEARE—*Othello.* Act II. Sc. 3.

PATRIOTISM

The die was now cast; I had passed the Rubicon. Swim or sink, live or die, survive or perish with my country was my unalterable determination.
JOHN ADAMS—*Works.*

Who would not be that youth? What pity is it
That we can die but once to save our country!
ADDISON—*Cato.*

No man can be a patriot on an empty stomach.
W. C. BRANN—*Old Glory.*

I have already given two cousins to the war, & I stand reddy to sacrifiss my wife's brother ruther'n not see the rebelyin krusht.
C. F. BROWNE (Artemus Ward).

God save our gracious king,
Long live our noble king,
God save the king.
HENRY CAREY—*God Save the King.*

I realize that patriotism is not enough.
I must have no hatred toward any one.
EDITH CAVELL.

Our country is the common parent of all.
CICERO.

I have heard something said about allegiance to the South: I know no South, no North, no East, no West, to which I owe any allegiance.
HENRY CLAY.

Our country! In her intercourse with foreign nations, may she always be in the right; but our country, right or wrong.
STEPHEN DECATUR.

Den I wish I was in Dixie, Hooray! Hooray!
In Dixie Land I'll take my stand
To lib and die in Dixie.
DANIEL D. EMMETT—*Dixie Land.*

I only regret that I have but one life to lose for my country.
NATHAN HALE—(Last Words, 1776).

Strike—for your altars and your fires;
Strike—for the green graves of your sires;
God—and your native land!
FITZ-GREENE HALLECK — *Marco Bozzaris.*

And have they fixed the where, and when?
And shall Trelawny die?
Here's thirty thousand Cornish men
Will know the reason why!
ROBERT STEPHEN HAWKER—*Song of the Wester Men.*

He serves his party best who serves the country best.
RUTHERFORD B. HAYES—*Inaugural Address.*

I am not a Virginian but an American.
PATRICK HENRY.

One flag, one land, one heart, one hand,
One Nation evermore!
HOLMES.

Our federal Union: it must be preserved.
ANDREW JACKSON.

Patriotism is the last refuge of a scoundrel.
SAMUEL JOHNSON—*Boswell's Life of Johnson.*

And how can man die better
Than facing fearful odds,
For the ashes of his fathers
And the temples of his gods?
MACAULAY—*Horatius Keeps the Bridge.*

My country is the world, and my religion is to do good.
THOMAS PAINE—*Rights of Man.*

Millions for defence, but not one cent for tribute.
CHARLES C. PINCKNEY.

PEACE

In time of peace prepare for war.
ANONYMOUS.

The fiercest agonies have shortest reign;
And after dreams of horror, comes again
The welcome morning with its rays of peace.
BRYANT—*Mutation.*

I prefer the most unfair peace to the most righteous war.
CICERO.

Peace rules the day, where reason rules the mind.
COLLINS—*Eclogue II.*

O for a lodge in some vast wilderness,
Some boundless contiguity of shade;
Where rumor of oppression and deceit,
Of unsuccessful or successful war,
Might never reach me more.
COWPER—*The Task.*

Even peace may be purchased at too high a price.
FRANKLIN.

Peace be with you.
Genesis. XLIII. 23.

Let us have peace.
ULYSSES S. GRANT.

I have never advocated war, except as a means of peace.
ULYSSES S. GRANT.

They shall beat their swords into plough-shares, and their spears into pruning-hooks; nation shall not lift up

sword against nation neither shall they learn war any more.
Isaiah. II. 4; *Joel*. III. 10. *Micah*. IV. 3.

The wolf also shall dwell with the lamb, and the leopard shall lie down with the kid.
Isaiah. XI. 6.

Peace, above all things, is to be desired, but blood must sometimes be spilled to obtain it on equable and lasting terms.
ANDREW JACKSON.

We love peace as we abhor pusillanimity; but not peace at any price. There is a peace more destructive of the manhood of living man than war is destructive of his material body. Chains are worse than bayonets.
DOUGLAS JERROLD—*Peace*.

It is thus that mutual cowardice keeps us in peace. Were onehalf of mankind brave and onehalf cowards, the brave would be always beating the cowards. Were all brave, they would lead a very uneasy life; all would be continually fighting; but being all cowards, we go on very well.
SAMUEL JOHNSON—*Boswell's Life*.

I am a man of peace. God knows how I love peace; but I hope I shall never be such a coward as to mistake oppression for peace.
KOSSUTH.

Peace at any price.
LAMARTINE.

Buried was the bloody hatchet;
Buried were all warlike weapons,
And the war-cry was forgotten.
Then was peace among the nations.
LONGFELLOW—*Hiawatha*.

Glory to God in the highest, and on earth peace, good will toward men.
Luke. II. 14.

Peace be to this house.
Matthew. X. 12; *Luke*. X. 5.

Peace hath her victories,
No less renowned than war.
MILTON.

Everlasting peace is a dream, and not even a beautiful one.
HELMUTH VON MOLTKE, 1880.

If they want peace, nations should avoid the pin-pricks that precede cannon-shots.
NAPOLEON.

The peace of God, which passeth all understanding.
Philippians. IV. 7.

Her ways are ways of pleasantness, and all her paths are peace.
Proverbs. III. 17.

Mercy and truth are met together: righteousness and peace have kissed each other.
Psalms. LXXXV. 10.

Peace be within thy walls, and prosperity within thy palaces.
Psalms. CXXII. 7.

People are always expecting to get peace in heaven: but you know whatever peace they get there will be ready-made. Whatever making of peace *they* can be blest for, must be on the earth here.
RUSKIN—*The Eagle's Nest*.

If peace cannot be maintained with honor, it is no longer peace.
LORD JOHN RUSSELL.

Peace won by compromise is usually a short-lived achievement.
WINFIELD SCOTT.

Peace,
Dear nurse of arts, plenties and joyful births.
SHAKESPEARE—*Henry V*. Act V. Sc. 2.

Let the bugles sound the *Truce of God* to the whole world forever.
CHARLES SUMNER.

The war-drum throbb'd no longer, and the battle-flags were furl'd
In the parliament of man, the federation of the world.
TENNYSON—*Locksley Hall*.

To be prepared for war is one of the most effectual means of preserving peace.
WASHINGTON.

As on the Sea of Galilee,
The Christ is whispering "Peace."
WHITTIER—*Tent on the Beach.*

There is such a thing as a man being too proud to fight. There is such a thing as a nation being so right that it does not need to convince others by force that it is right.
WOODROW WILSON. May 10, 1915.

It must be a peace without victory. Only a peace between equals can last: only a peace, the very principle of which is equality, and a common participation in a common benefit.
WOODROW WILSON, January 22, 1917.

PEACH

The ripest peach is highest on the tree.
JAMES WHITCOMB RILEY.

PEN

The pen is mightier than the sword.
BULWER-LYTTON.

Oh! nature's noblest gift—my gray-goose quill!
Slave of my thoughts, obedient to my will,
Torn from thy parent-bird to form a pen,
That mighty instrument of little men!
BYRON—*English Bards and Scotch Reviewers.*

If you give me six lines written by the hand of the most honest of men, I will find something in them which will hang him.
RICHELIEU.

PEOPLE

The voice of the people is the voice of God.
ALCUIN—*Epistles.*

The will of the people is the best law.
ULYSSES S. GRANT.

The people are the only sure reliance for the preservation of our liberty.
JEFFERSON, 1787.

You can fool some of the people all of the time, and all of the people some of the time, but you cannot fool all of the people all the time.
ABRAHAM LINCOLN.

The people are the only sovereigns of any country.
R. D. OWEN.

The second, sober thought of the people is seldom wrong, and always efficient.
MARTIN VAN BUREN.

PERFECTION

The very pink of perfection.
GOLDSMITH—*She Stoops to Conquer.*

There are many lovely women, but no perfect ones.
VICTOR HUGO.

There are no perfect women in the world; only hypocrites exhibit no defects.
NINON DE LENCLOS.

Trifles make perfection, and perfection is no trifle.
MICHELANGELO.

Perfection does not exist. To understand it is the triumph of human intelligence; to desire to possess it is the most dangerous kind of madness.
ALFRED DE MUSSET.

Whoever thinks a faultless piece to see,
Thinks what ne'er was, nor is, nor e'er shall be.
POPE—*Essay on Criticism.*

If a man should happen to reach perfection in this world, he would have to die immediately to enjoy himself.
H. W. SHAW.

The maxims tell you to aim at perfection, which is well; but it's unattainable, all the same.
BAYARD TAYLOR.

PERSECUTION

A religion which requires persecution to sustain it is of the devil's propagation.
HOSEA BALLOU.

The oppression of any people for opinion's sake has rarely had any other effect than to fix those opinions deeper, and render them more important.
HOSEA BALLOU.

The way of this world is, to praise dead saints, and persecute living ones.
REV. N. HOWE.

Wherever you see persecution, there is more than a probability that truth lies on the persecuted side.
LATIMER.

Galileo probably would have escaped persecution if his discoveries could have been disproved.
WHATELY.

Persecution is not wrong because it is cruel; but it is cruel because it is wrong.
WHATELY.

PERSEVERANCE

Attempt the end and never stand to doubt;
Nothing's so hard, but search will find it out.
HERRICK—*Seeke and Finde.*

There is no royal road to anything. One thing at a time, all things in succession. That which grows fast withers as rapidly; that which grows slowly endures.
J. G. HOLLAND.

The waters wear the stones.
Job. XIV. 19.

Great works are performed not by strength but by perseverance.
SAMUEL JOHNSON.

Keep right on to the end of the road;
Keep right on to the end.
HARRY LAUDER—*Song.*

Victory belongs to the most persevering.
NAPOLEON.

We shall escape the uphill by never turning back.
CHRISTINA G. ROSSETTI—*Amor Mundi.*

Many strokes, though with a little axe,
Hew down and fell the hardest-timber'd oak.
SHAKESPEARE—*Henry VI.* Pt. III. Act II. Sc. 1.

PESSIMIST

Pessimist: An optimist who endeavored to practice what he preached.
ANONYMOUS.

A pessimist is a man who happens to live with an optimist.
ANONYMOUS.

A pessimist? A man who thinks everybody as nasty as himself, and hates them for it.
GEORGE BERNARD SHAW.

PHILANTHROPY

Steal the hog, and give the feet for alms.
GEORGE HERBERT.

He is one of those wise philanthropists who, in a time of famine, would vote for nothing but a supply of toothpicks.
DOUGLAS JERROLD.

I was eyes to the blind, and feet was I to the lame.
Job. XXIX. 15.

Who gives himself with his alms feeds three,
Himself, his hungering neighbour, and me.
LOWELL—*The Vision of Sir Launfal.*

He believed that he was born, not for himself, but for the whole world.
LUCAN—*Pharsalia.*

To pity distress is but human; to relieve it is Godlike.
HORACE MANN—*Lectures on Education.*

Take heed that ye do not your alms before men, to be seen of them.
Matthew. VI. 1.

When thou doest alms, let not thy left hand know what thy right hand doeth.
Matthew. VI. 3.

The organized charity, scrimped and iced,
In the name of a cautious, statistical Christ.
JOHN BOYLE O'REILLY—*In Bohemia.*

Being myself no stranger to suffering, I have learned to relieve the sufferings of others.
VERGIL—*Æneid.*

PHILOSOPHY

A little philosophy inclineth man's mind to atheism; but depth in philosophy bringeth men's minds about to religion.
BACON—*Essays.*

The philosophy of one century is the common sense of the next.
HENRY WARD BEECHER.

Philosophy: A route of many roads leading from nowhere to nothing.
BIERCE—*The Devil's Dictionary.*

Queen of arts, and daughter of heaven.
BURKE.

O philosophy, life's guide! O searcher-out of virtue and expeller of vices! What could we and every age of men have been without thee? Thou hast produced cities; thou hast called men scattered about in the social enjoyment of life.
CICERO.

The first step towards philosophy is incredulity.
DENIS DIDEROT—*Last Conversation.*

Philosophy goes no further than probabilities, and in every assertion keeps a doubt in reserve.
FROUDE.

Whence? whither? why? how?—these questions cover all philosophy.
JOUBERT.

Philosophy triumphs easily over past evils and future evils, but present evils triumph over it.
LA ROCHEFOUCAULD.

A pipe is a pocket philosopher,—a truer one than Socrates, for it never asks questions. Socrates must have been very tiresome, when one thinks of it.
OUIDA.

There are more things in heaven and earth, Horatio,
Than are dreamt of in your philosophy.
SHAKESPEARE—*Hamlet.* Act I. Sc. 5.

The philosopher is Nature's pilot. And there you have our difference: to be in hell is to drift: to be in heaven is to steer.
GEORGE BERNARD SHAW—*Man and Superman.*

The discovery of what is true and the practice of that which is good are the two most important objects of philosophy.
VOLTAIRE.

PITY

Of all the paths that lead to a woman's love
Pity's the straightest.
BEAUMONT and FLETCHER—*Knight of Malta.*

More helpful than all wisdom is one draught of simple human pity that will not forsake us.
GEORGE ELIOT—*Mill on the Floss.*

Pity is not natural to man. Children are always cruel; savages are always cruel.
SAMUEL JOHNSON.

We pity in others only those evils which we have ourselves experienced.
ROUSSEAU.

Is there no pity sitting in the clouds,
That sees into the bottom of my grief?
SHAKESPEARE—*Romeo and Juliet.* Act III. Sc. 5.

There are two sorts of pity: one is a balm and the other a poison; the first is realized by our friends, the last by our enemies.
CHARLES SUMNER.

A book or poem which has no pity in it had better not be written.

OSCAR WILDE.

PLAGIARISM

They lard their lean books with the fat of others' works.

BURTON—*Anatomy of Melancholy.*

Most plagiarists, like the drone, have neither taste to select, industry to acquire, nor skill to improve, but impudently pilfer the honey ready prepared, from the hive.

COLTON.

Goethe said there would be little left of him if he were to discard what he owed to others.

CHARLOTTE CUSHMAN.

Plagiarists, at least, have the merit of preservation.

DISRAELI.

Perish those who said our good things before we did.

ÆLIUS DONATUS.

When Shakespeare is charged with debts to his authors, Landor replies, "Yet he was more original than his originals. He breathed upon dead bodies and brought them into life."

EMERSON—*Letters and Social Aims.*

When 'Omer smote 'is bloomin' lyre,
He'd 'eard men sing by land an' sea;
An' what he thought 'e might require,
'E went an' took—the same as me.

KIPLING—*Barrack-Room Ballads.*

Amongst so many borrowed things, I am glad if I can steal one, disguising and altering it for some new service.

MONTAIGNE—*Essays.*

Take the whole range of imaginative literature, and we are all wholesale borrowers. In every matter that relates to invention, to use, or beauty or form, we are borrowers.

WENDELL PHILLIPS—*The Lost Arts.*

Next o'er his books his eyes began to roll,
In pleasing memory of all he stole;
How here he sipp'd, how there he plunder'd snug,
And suck'd all o'er like an industrious bug.

POPE—*Dunciad.*

The seed ye sow, another reaps;
The wealth ye find, another keeps:
The robes ye weave, another wears:
The arms ye forge another bears.

SHELLEY—*To the Men of England.*

Nothing is said nowadays that has not been said before.

TERENCE—*Eunushus.*

All the makers of dictionaries, all compilers who do nothing else than repeat backwards and forwards the opinions, the errors, the impostures, and the truths already printed, we may term plagiarists; but honest plagiarists, who arrogate not the merit of invention.

VOLTAIRE.

PLANT

A filbert-hedge with wild-briar overtwined,
And clumps of woodbine taking the soft wind
Upon their summer thrones.

KEATS—*I Stood Tiptoe Upon a Little Hill.*

Dark-green and gemm'd with flowers of snow,
With close uncrowded branches spread
Not proudly high, nor meanly low,
A graceful myrtle rear'd its head.

MONTGOMERY—*The Myrtle.*

And the woodbine spices are wafted abroad,
And the musk of the rose is blown.

TENNYSON—*Maud.*

PLEASURE

Every age has its pleasures, its style of wit, and its own ways.

NICHOLAS BOILEAU-DESPRÉAUX.

But pleasures are like poppies spread;
You seize the flower, its bloom is shed.
Or like the snow falls in the river,
A moment white—then melts forever.
BURNS—*Tam o' Shanter.*

The rule of my life is to make business a pleasure, and pleasure my business.
AARON BURR—*Letter to Pichon.*

There is a pleasure in the pathless woods,
There is a rapture on the lonely shore,
There is society where none intrudes
By the deep Sea, and music in its roar.
BYRON—*Childe Harold.*

In everything satiety closely follows the greatest pleasures.
CICERO.

Pleasure admitted in undue degree
Enslaves the will, nor leaves the judgment free.
COWPER—*Progress of Error.*

Rich the treasure,
Sweet the pleasure,
Sweet is pleasure after pain.
DRYDEN—*Alexander's Feast.*

The shortest pleasures are the sweetest.
FARQUHAR.

There is no pleasure without a tincture of bitterness.
HAFIZ.

Follow pleasure, and then will pleasure flee,
Flee pleasure, and pleasure will follow thee.
HEYWOOD—*Proverbs.*

Rare indulgence produces greater pleasure.
JUVENAL.

Take all the pleasures of all the spheres,
And multiply each through endless years,
One minute of Heaven is worth them all.
MOORE—*Lalla Rookh.*

God made all pleasures innocent.
MRS. NORTON—*Lady of La Garaye.*

We tire of those pleasures we take, but never of those we give.
J. PETIT-SENN.

Reason's whole pleasure, all the joys of sense,
Lie in three words,—health, peace, and competence.
POPE—*Essay on Man.*

Things forbidden have a secret charm.
TACITUS.

Pleasure is frail like a dewdrop, while it laughs it dies. But sorrow is strong and abiding. Let sorrowful love wake in your eyes.
TAGORE—*Gardener.*

I hold this to be the rule of life,
"Too much of anything is bad."
TERENCE.

Pleasure has its time; so too has wisdom. Make love in thy youth, and in old age attend to thy salvation.
VOLTAIRE.

POET

O brave poets, keep back nothing;
Nor mix falsehood with the whole!
Look up Godward! speak the truth in
Worthy song from earnest soul!
Hold, in high poetic duty,
Truest Truth the fairest Beauty.
E. B. BROWNING—*Dead Pan.*

Most joyful let the Poet be;
It is through him that all men see.
WILLIAM E. CHANNING.

I have never known a poet who did not think himself super-excellent.
CICERO.

Poets by Death are conquer'd but the wit
Of poets triumphs over it.
ABRAHAM COWLEY—*On the Praise of Poetry.*

I can no more believe old Homer blind,
Than those who say the sun hath never shined;

The age wherein he lived was dark, but he
Could not want sight who taught the world to see.
SIR JOHN DENHAM—*Progress of Learning.*

All men are poets at heart.
EMERSON—*Literary Ethics.*

Modern poets mix too much water with their ink.
GOETHE.

Singing and rejoicing,
As aye since time began,
The dying earth's last poet
Shall be the earth's last man.
ANASTASIUS GRÜN—*The Last Poet.*

The man is either mad or he is making verses.
HORACE.

For next to being a great poet is the power of understanding one.
LONGFELLOW—*Hyperion.*

All that is best in the great poets of all countries is not what is national in them, but what is universal.
LONGFELLOW—*Kavanagh.*

For voices pursue him by day,
And haunt him by night,—
And he listens, and needs must obey,
When the Angel says: "Write!"
LONGFELLOW—*The Poet and His Songs.*

Poets are sultans, if they had their will:
For every author would his brother kill.
ORRERY—*Prologues.*

Poets utter great and wise things which they do not themselves understand.
PLATO—*The Republic.*

While pensive poets painful vigils keep,
Sleepless themselves to give their readers sleep.
POPE—*Dunciad.*

Most wretched men
Are cradled into poetry by wrong;
They learn in suffering what they teach in song.
SHELLEY—*Julian and Maddalo.*

I learnt life from the poets.
MADAME DE STAËL—*Corinne.*

Villon, our sad bad glad mad brother's name.
SWINBURNE—*Ballad of François Villon.*

God, eldest of Poets.
WILLIAM WATSON—*England, my England.*

POETRY

For rhyme the rudder is of verses,
With which, like ships, they steer their courses.
BUTLER—*Hudibras.*

Nor florid prose, nor honied lies of rhyme,
Can blazon evil deeds, or consecrate a crime.
BYRON—*Childe Harold.*

Poetry, therefore, we will call Musical Thought.
CARLYLE—*Heroes and Hero Worship.*

Poetry is the music of thought, conveyed to us in music of language.
CHATFIELD.

Prose—words in their best order;—poetry—the best words in their best order.
COLERIDGE—*Table Talk.*

Poetry, the eldest sister of all arts, and parent of most.
CONGREVE.

The finest poetry was first experience.
EMERSON—*Shakespeare.*

Oh love will make a dog howl in rhyme.
JOHN FLETCHER—*Queen of Corinth.*

Poetry is truth dwelling in beauty.
GILFILLAN.

A verse may find him who a sermon flies,
And turn delight into a sacrifice.
GEORGE HERBERT—*The Temple.*

Verses devoid of substance, melodious trifles.
HORACE.

Let your poem be kept nine years.
HORACE.

The essence of poetry is invention; such invention as, producing something unexpected, surprises and delights.

SAMUEL JOHNSON.

A drainless shower
Of light is poesy: 'tis the supreme of power;
'Tis might half slumbering on its own right arm.

KEATS—*Sleep and Poetry.*

These pearls of thought in Persian gulfs were bred,
Each softly lucent as a rounded moon;
The diver Omar plucked them from their bed,
FitzGerald strung them on an English thread.

LOWELL—*In a Copy of Omar Khayyám.*

Curst be the verse, how well soe'er it flow,
That tends to make one worthy man my foe,
Give virtue scandal, innocence a fear,
Or from the soft-eyed virgin steal a tear!

POPE—*Prologue to Satires.*

I consider poetry very subordinate to moral and political science.

SHELLEY—*Letter to Thomas L. Peacock.*

I was promised on a time,
To have reason for my rhyme;
From that time unto this season,
I received nor rhyme nor reason.

SPENSER—*Lines on His Promised Pension.*

Jewels five-words-long,
That on the stretch'd forefinger of all Time
Sparkle for ever.

TENNYSON—*Princess.*

Poetry is the music of the soul, and, above all, of great and feeling souls.

VOLTAIRE.

One merit of poetry few persons will deny: it says more and in fewer words than prose.

VOLTAIRE—*A Philosophical Dictionary.*

POISON

What's one man's poison, signior,
Is another's meat or drink.

BEAUMONT and FLETCHER—*Love's Cure.*

The man recover'd of the bite,
The dog it was that died.

GOLDSMITH—*Elegy on the Death of a Mad Dog.*

To rankling poison hast thou turned in me the milk of human kindness.

SCHILLER—*Wilhelm Tell.*

POLICY

Mahomet made the people believe that he would call a hill to him, and from the top of it offer up his prayers for the observers of his law. The people assembled; Mahomet called the hill to come to him, again and again; and when the hill stood still, he was never a whit abashed, but said, "If the hill will not come to Mahomet, Mahomet will go to the hill."

BACON—*Essays.*

It is easier to catch flies with honey than with vinegar.

English Proverb.

It is better to walk than to run; it is better to stand than to walk; it is better to sit than to stand; it is better to lie than to sit.

Hindu Proverb.

Don't throw a monkey-wrench into the machinery.

PHILANDER JOHNSON.

We shall not, I believe, be obliged to alter our policy of watchful waiting.

WOODROW WILSON—*Annual Message.* 1915.

POLITICS

All political parties die at last of swallowing their own lies.

JOHN ARBUTHNOT.

Man is by nature a civic animal.

ARISTOTLE.

A politician thinks of the next election; a statesman, of the next generation.

JAMES FREEMAN CLARKE.

It is a *condition* which confronts us—not a theory.

GROVER CLEVELAND—*Annual Message, 1877.*

In politics nothing is contemptible.

DISRAELI.

The Right Honorable gentleman [Sir Robert Peel] caught the Whigs bathing and walked away with their clothes.

DISRAELI, House of Commons, 1845.

Damned Neuters, in their Middle way of Steering,
Are neither Fish, nor Flesh, nor good Red Herring.

DRYDEN—*Duke of Guise.*

What is a Communist? One who has yearnings
For equal division of unequal earnings.

EBENEZER ELLIOT—*Corn Law Rhymes.*

I always voted at my party's call,
And I never thought of thinking for myself at all.

W. S. GILBERT—*H. M. S. Pinafore.*

He serves his party best who serves the country best.

RUTHERFORD B. HAYES—*Inaugural Address, 1877.*

Like an armed warrior, like a plumed knight, James G. Blaine marched down the halls of the American Congress and threw his shining lance full and fair against the brazen foreheads of the defamers of his country, and the maligners of his honor.

ROBERT G. INGERSOLL, in nomination of Blaine for President, 1876.

Whenever a man has cast a longing eye on offices, a rottenness begins in his conduct.

JEFFERSON, 1799.

If a due participation of office is a matter of right, how are vacancies to be obtained? Those by death are few; by resignation, none.

JEFFERSON, 1801.

Every time I fill a vacant office I make ten malcontents and one ingrate.

LOUIS XIV.

Free trade, one of the greatest blessings which a government can confer on a people, is in almost every country unpopular.

MACAULAY.

Perhaps I do not know what I was made for; but one thing I certainly never was made for, and that is to put principles on and off at the dictation of a party, as a lackey changes his livery at his master's command.

HORACE MANN.

Those who would treat politics and morality apart will never understand the one or the other.

JOHN MORLEY.

But it is at home and not in public that one should wash one's dirty linen.

NAPOLEON—*On his return from Elba.*

Nothing is politically right which is morally wrong.

DANIEL O'CONNELL.

Great political questions stir the deepest nature of one-half the nation; but they pass far above and over the heads of the other half.

WENDELL PHILLIPS.

Party-spirit, which at best is but the madness of many, for the gain of a few.

POPE—*Letter to Blount.*

A mugwump is a person educated beyond his intellect.

HORACE PORTER.

The Republicans have their splits right after election and Democrats have theirs just before an election.

WILL ROGERS.

There is a homely old adage which runs: "Speak softly and carry a big stick; you will go far." If the Ameri-

can nation will speak softly and yet build and keep at a pitch of the highest training a thoroughly efficient navy, the Monroe Doctrine will go far.
THEODORE ROOSEVELT, 1901.

I am as strong as a bull moose and you can use me to the limit.
THEODORE ROOSEVELT—*Letter to Mark Hanna.*

My hat's in the ring. The fight is on and I'm stripped to the buff.
THEODORE ROOSEVELT, 1912.

The first advice I have to give the party is that it should clean its slate.
LORD ROSEBERRY, 1901.

Something is rotten in the state of Denmark.
SHAKESPEARE—*Hamlet.* Act I. Sc. 4.

O, that estates, degrees, and offices
Were not deriv'd corruptly, and that clear honour
Were purchased by the merit of the wearer!
SHAKESPEARE—*Merchant of Venice.* Act II. Sc. 9.

If nominated I will not accept; if elected I will not serve.
WILLIAM TECUMSEH SHERMAN, 1884.

Congressmen? In Washington they hitch horses to them.
TIMOTHY D. (Big Tim) SULLIVAN, of New York City.

The man who can make two ears of corn or two blades of grass grow on the spot where only one grew before, would deserve better of mankind and render more essential service to the country than the whole race of politicians put together.
SWIFT.

Who is the dark horse he has in his stable?
THACKERAY—*Adventures of Philip.*

As long as I count the votes what are you going to do about it? Say.
WILLIAM M. TWEED—*The Ballot in 1871.*

I am not a politician, and my other habits are good.
ARTEMUS WARD—*Fourth of July Oration.*

Politics I conceive to be nothing more than the science of the ordered progress of society along the lines of greatest usefulness and convenience to itself.
WOODROW WILSON, 1916.

POPPY

Central depth of purple,
Leaves more bright than rose,
Who shall tell what brightest thought
Out of darkness grows?
Who, through what funereal pain,
Souls to love and peace attain?
LEIGH HUNT—*Songs of the Flowers.*

Through the dancing poppies stole
A breeze most softly lulling to my soul.
KEATS—*Endymion.*

Visions for those too tired to sleep,
These seeds cast a film over eyes which weep.
AMY LOWELL—*Sword Blades and Poppy Seed.*

In Flanders' fields the poppies blow
Between the crosses, row on row,
That mark our place, and in the sky,
The larks, still bravely singing, fly
Scarce heard among the guns below.
COL. JOHN MCCRAE—*In Flanders' Fields.*

Let but my scarlet head appear
And I am held in scorn;
Yet juice of subtile virtue lies
Within my cup of curious dyes.
CHRISTINA G. ROSSETTI—*"Consider the Lilies of the Field."*

POPULARITY

Popular applause veers with the wind.
JOHN BRIGHT.

Popularity is like the brightness of a falling star, the fleeting splendor of

a rainbow, the bubble that is sure to burst by its very inflation.
CHATFIELD.

The actor's popularity is evanescent; applauded to-day, forgotten to-morrow.
EDWIN FORREST.

Seek not the favor of the multitude; it is seldom got by honest and lawful means. But seek the testimony of few; and number not voices, but weigh them.
KANT.

There are people who, like new songs, are in vogue only for a time.
LA ROCHEFOUCAULD.

And to some men popularity is always suspicious. Enjoying none themselves, they are prone to suspect the validity of those attainments which command it.
GEORGE HENRY LEWES—*The Spanish Drama.*

There was ease in Casey's manner as he stept into his place,
There was pride in Casey's bearing and a smile on Casey's face,
And when responding to the cheers he lightly doft his hat,
No stranger in the crowd could doubt, 't was Casey at the bat.
ERNEST L. THAYER—*Casey at the Bat.*

POSSESSION

Exclusive property is a theft against nature.
BRISSOT.

When we have not what we love, we must love what we have.
BUSSY-RABUTIN, 1667.

Britannia needs no bulwarks, no towers along the steep:
Her march is o'er the mountain waves; her home is on the deep.
CAMPBELL—*Ye Mariners of England.*

This is the truth as I see it, my dear,
Out in the wind and the rain:
They who have nothing have little to fear,
Nothing to lose or to gain.
MADISON CAWEIN—*The Bellman.*

What is dishonorably got, is dishonorably squandered.
CICERO.

As having nothing, and yet possessing all things.
II Corinthians. VI. 10.

Ah, yet, e'er I descend to th' grave,
May I a *small House* and a *large Garden* have.
And a *few Friends,* and *many Books* both true,
Both wise, and both delightful too.
And since *Love* ne'er will from me flee,
A *Mistress* moderately fair,
And good as *Guardian angels* are,
Only belov'd and loving me.
ABRAHAM COWLEY—*The Wish.*

Of a rich man who was mean and niggardly, he said, "That man does not possess his estate, but his estate possesses him."
DIOGENES LAERTIUS.

Property has its duties as well as its rights.
THOMAS DRUMMOND.

My apple trees will never get across
And eat the cones under his pines, I tell him.
He only says, "Good fences make good neighbors."
ROBERT FROST—*Mending Wall.*

It may be said of them [the Hollanders], as of the Spaniards, that the sun never sets upon their Dominions.
THOMAS GAGE.

Wouldst thou both eat thy cake and have it?
GEORGE HERBERT—*The Church.*

Is it not lawful for me to do what I will with mine own?
Matthew. XX. 15.

Unto every one that hath shall be given, and he shall have abundance; but from him that hath not shall be taken away even that which he hath.
Matthew. XXV. 29.

That dog is mine said those poor children; that place in the sun is mine; such is the beginning and type of usurpation throughout the earth.
PASCAL.

What is yours is mine, and all mine is yours.
PLAUTUS.

Property, it is theft.
PRUD'HON—*Principle of Right.*

Possession, they say, is eleven points of the law.
SWIFT.

Germany must have her place in the sun.
WILHELM II.

POST

He whistles as he goes, light-hearted
wretch,
Cold and yet cheerful; messenger of
grief
Perhaps to thousands, and of joy to
some.
COWPER—(Of the Postman.)

Carrier of news and knowledge,
Instrument of trade and industry,
Promoter of mutual acquaintance,
Of peace and good will
Among men and nations.
CHARLES W. ELIOT—*Inscription on Postoffice,* Washington, D. C.

Neither snow, nor rain, nor heat, nor night stays these couriers from the swift completion of their appointed rounds.
HERODOTUS—*Inscription on Postoffice,* New York City.

A strange volume of real life in the daily packet of the postman. Eternal love and instant payment!
DOUGLAS JERROLD—*The Postman's Budget.*

Good-bye—my paper's out so nearly,
I've only room for, Yours sincerely.
MOORE—*The Fudge Family in Paris.*

I have only made this letter rather long because I have not had time to make it shorter.
PASCAL.

Heav'n first taught letters for some
wretch's aid,
Some banish'd lover, or some captive
maid.
POPE—*Eloisa to Abelard.*

And oft the pangs of absence to re-
move
By letters, soft interpreters of love.
PRIOR—*Henry and Emma.*

A woman seldom writes her Mind, but in her Postscript.
STEELE—*Spectator.*

Go, little letter, apace, apace,
Fly;
Fly to the light in the valley below—
Tell my wish to her dewy blue eye.
TENNYSON—*The Letter.*

POSTERITY

Think of your forefathers! Think of your posterity!
JOHN QUINCY ADAMS, 1802.

As to posterity, I may ask what has it ever done to oblige me?
GRAY—*Letter to Dr. Wharton.*

POTTERY

For a male person *bric-a-brac* hunting is about as robust a business as making doll-clothes.
S. L. CLEMENS (Mark Twain)—*Tramp Abroad.*

Said one among them: "Surely not in
vain
My substance of the common Earth
was ta'en
And to this Figure moulded, to be
broke,
Or trampled back to shapeless Earth
again."
OMAR KHAYYÁM—*Rubaiyat.*

All this of Pot and Potter—Tell me
then,
Who is the Potter, pray, and who the
Pot?
OMAR KHAYYÁM—*Rubaiyat.*

Hath not the potter power over the clay, of the same lump to make one

vessel unto honour, and another unto dishonour?
Romans. IX. 21.

POVERTY

In one important respect a man is fortunate in being poor. His responsibility to God is so much the less.
BOVEE.

Thank God for poverty
That makes and keeps us free,
And lets us go our unobtrusive way,
Glad of the sun and rain,
Upright, serene, humane,
Contented with the fortune of a day.
BLISS CARMAN—*The Word at Saint Kavin's*.

He is now fast rising from affluence to poverty.
S. L. CLEMENS (Mark Twain).

Content with poverty, my soul I arm;
And virtue, though in rags, will keep me warm.
DRYDEN—*Third Book of Horace*.

The greatest man in history was the poorest.
EMERSON—*Domestic Life*.

Poverty possesses this disease; through want it teaches a man evil.
EURIPIDES.

That amid our highest civilization men faint and die with want is not due to the niggardliness of nature, but to the injustice of man.
HENRY GEORGE—*Progress and Poverty*.

The nakedness of the indigent world may be clothed from the trimmings of the vain.
GOLDSMITH—*Vicar of Wakefield*.

Poverty makes people satirical, soberly, sadly, bitterly satirical.
HAINES FRISWELL.

Poverty sits by the cradle of all our great men, and rocks them up to manhood; and this meager foster-mother remains their faithful companion throughout life.
HEINE.

Poverty is no sin.
GEORGE HERBERT.

O God! that bread should be so dear,
And flesh and blood so cheap!
HOOD—*The Song of the Shirt*.

Stitch! stitch! stitch!
In poverty, hunger, and dirt,
And still with a voice of dolorous pitch,
Would that its tone could reach the Rich,
She sang this "Song of the Shirt!"
HOOD—*Song of the Shirt*.

Grind the faces of the poor.
Isaiah. III. 15.

The poor always ye have with you.
John. XII. 8.

They do not easily rise whose abilities are repressed by poverty at home.
JUVENAL.

The lack of wealth is easily repaired; but the poverty of the soul is irreparable.
MONTAIGNE—*Essays*.

He that hath pity upon the poor lendeth unto the Lord.
Proverbs. XIX. 17.

Blessed is he that considereth the poor.
Psalms. XLI. 1.

Not he who has little, but he who wishes for more, is poor.
SENECA.

I am as poor as Job, my lord, but not so patient.
SHAKESPEARE—*Henry IV*. Pt. II. Act I. Sc. 2.

POWER

Give me a lever long enough
And a prop strong enough,
I can single handed move the world.
ARCHIMEDES.

Then, everlasting Love, restrain thy will;
'Tis god-like to have power, but not to kill.
BEAUMONT and FLETCHER—*The Chances*.

Men are never very wise and select in the exercise of a new power.
WILLIAM ELLERY CHANNING—*The Present Age.*

Iron hand in a velvet glove.
CHARLES V.

Power will intoxicate the best hearts, as wine the strongest heads. No man is wise enough, nor good enough to be trusted with unlimited power.
COLTON.

Concentration is the secret of strength in politics, in war, in trade, in short, in all management of human affairs.
EMERSON.

Patience and gentleness is power.
LEIGH HUNT.

Wherever I found a living creature, there I found the will to power.
NIETZSCHE—*Thus Spake Zarathustra.*

The less power a man has, the more he likes to use it.
J. PETIT-SENN.

A partnership with men in power is never safe.
PHAEDRUS.

Power is ever stealing from the many to the few.
WENDELL PHILLIPS.

Unlimited power corrupts the possessor.
PITT, 1770.

The powers that be are ordained of God.
Romans. XIII. 1.

He who has great power should use it lightly.
SENECA.

Power, like a desolating pestilence,
Pollutes whate'er it touches; and obedience,
Bane of all genius, virtue, freedom, truth,
Makes slaves of men, and of the human frame
A mechanized automaton.
SHELLEY—*Queen Mab.*

Lust of power is the most flagrant of all the passions.
TACITUS.

Power is always right, weakness always wrong. Power is always insolent and despotic.
NOAH WEBSTER.

PRAISE

I praise loudly; I blame softly.
CATHERINE II OF RUSSIA.

Earth, with her thousand voices, praises God.
COLERIDGE.

Long open panegyric drags at best,
And praise is only praise when well address'd.
GAY.

Praise from a friend, or censure from a foe,
Are lost on hearers that our merits know.
HOMER—*Iliad.*

We always make our friend appear awkward and ridiculous by giving him a laced suit of tawdry qualifications, which nature never intended him to wear.
JUNIUS.

A refusal of praise is a desire to be praised twice.
LA ROCHEFOUCAULD.

I would have praised you more had you praised me less.
LOUIS XIV.

Approbation from Sir Hubert Stanley is praise indeed.
THOMAS MORTON—*Cure for the Heartache.*

As the Greek said, "Many men know how to flatter, few men know how to praise."
WENDELL PHILLIPS.

To what base ends, and by what abject ways,
Are mortals urg'd through sacred lust of praise!
POPE—*Essay on Criticism.*

With faint praises one another damn.
WYCHERLEY—*Plain Dealer.*

The sweetest of all sounds is praise.
XENOPHON.

PRAYER

I pray the prayer the Easterners do,
May the peace of Allah abide with you;
Wherever you stay, wherever you go,
May the beautiful palms of Allah grow;
Through days of labor, and nights of rest,
The love of Good Allah make you blest;
So I touch my heart—as the Easterners do,
May the peace of Allah abide with you.
ANONYMOUS.

Between the humble and contrite heart and the majesty of heaven there are no barriers; the only password is prayer.
HOSEA BALLOU.

A prayer, in its simplest definition, is merely a wish turned heavenward.
PHILLIPS BROOKS.

God answers sharp and sudden on some prayers,
And thrusts the thing we have prayed for in our face,
A gauntlet with a gift in 't.
E. B. BROWNING—*Aurora Leigh.*

They never sought in vain that sought the Lord aright!
BURNS—*The Cotter's Saturday Night.*

Father of Light! great God of Heaven!
Hear'st thou the accents of despair?
Can guilt like man's be e'er forgiven?
Can vice atone for crimes by prayer?
BYRON—*Prayer of Nature.*

He prayeth well who loveth well
Both man and bird and beast.
COLERIDGE—*Ancient Mariner.*

And Satan trembles when he sees
The weakest saint upon his knees.
COWPER—*Hymns.*

Almighty Father! let thy lowly child,
Strong in his love of truth, be wisely bold,—
A patriot bard, by sycophants reviled,
Let him live usefully, and not die old!
EBENEZER ELLIOTT—*Corn Law Rhymes.*

No man ever prayed heartily without learning something.
EMERSON.

Though I am weak, yet God, when prayed,
Cannot withhold his conquering aid.
EMERSON—*The Nun's Aspiration.*

So a good prayer, though often used, is still fresh and fair in the ears and eyes of Heaven.
FULLER—*Good Thoughts in Bad Times.*

O Lord of Courage grave,
O Master of this night of Spring!
Make firm in me a heart too brave
To ask Thee anything.
JOHN GALSWORTHY—*The Prayer.*

At church, with meek and unaffected grace,
His looks adorn'd the venerable place;
Truth from his lips prevailed with double sway,
And fools, who came to scoff, remain'd to pray.
GOLDSMITH—*The Deserted Village.*

He that will learn to pray, let him go to Sea.
GEORGE HERBERT.

In prayer the lips ne'er act the winning part
Without the sweet concurrence of the heart.
HERRICK—*Hesperides.*

Prayer is the voice of faith.
HORNE.

O God, if in the day of battle I forget Thee, do not Thou forget me.
WILLIAM KING.

My brother kneels, so saith Kabir,
To stone and brass in heathen-wise,
But in my brother's voice I hear

My own unanswered agonies.
His God is as his fates assign
His prayer is all the world's—and mine.
KIPLING—*Song of Kabir.*

I ask and wish not to appear
More beauteous, rich or gay:
Lord, make me wiser every year,
And better every day.
LAMB—*A Birthday Thought.*

Let one unceasing, earnest prayer
Be, too, for light,—for strength to bear
Our portion of the weight of care,
That crushes into dumb despair
One half the human race.
LONGFELLOW—*Goblet of Life.*

Our Father, which art in heaven, Hallowed be thy Name. Thy kingdom come. Thy will be done in earth as it is in heaven. Give us this day our daily bread. And forgive us our debts, as we forgive our debtors. And lead us not into temptation, but deliver us from evil: For thine is the kingdom and the power and the glory, for ever. Amen.
The Lord's Prayer.

O Lord, my God,
I have trusted in Thee;
O Jesu, my dearest One,
Now set me free.
In prison's oppression,
In sorrow's obsession,
I weary for Thee.
With sighing and crying,
Bowed down in dying,
I adore Thee, I implore Thee, set me free.
MARY, QUEEN OF SCOTS.

God warms his hands at man's heart when he prays.
MASEFIELD—*Widow in the Bye Street.*

Ask, and it shall be given you; seek, and ye shall find; knock, and it shall be opened unto you.
Matthew. VII. 7.

Every one that asketh receiveth; and he that seeketh findeth.
Matthew. VII. 8.

Not what we wish, but what we want,
Oh! let thy grace supply,
The good unask'd, in mercy grant;
The ill, though ask'd, deny.
MERRICK—*Hymn.*

Prayer is the soul's sincere desire,
Uttered or unexpressed,
The motion of a hidden fire
That trembles in the breast.
JAMES MONTGOMERY—*What Is Prayer?*

As down in the sunless retreats of the ocean
Sweet flowers are springing no mortal can see,
So deep in my soul the still prayer of devotion
Unheard by the world, rises silent to Thee.
MOORE.

Now I lay me down to take my sleep,
I pray thee, Lord, my soul to keep;
If I should die before I wake,
I pray thee, Lord, my soul to take.
New England Primer, 1814.

Father of All! in every age,
In every clime ador'd,
By saint, by savage, and by sage,
Jehovah, Jove, or Lord!
POPE—*Universal Prayer.*

If I am right, Thy grace impart,
Still in the right to stay;
If I am wrong, O teach my heart
To find that better way!
POPE—*Universal Prayer.*

Earth bears no balsams for mistakes;
Men crown the knave, and scourge the tool
That did his will: but thou, O Lord,
Be merciful to me, a fool.
EDWARD ROWLAND SILL—*The Fool's Prayer.*

Our prayers should be for blessings in general, for God knows best what is good for us.
SOCRATES.

Four things which are not in thy treasury,
I lay before thee, Lord, with this petition:—
My nothingness, my wants,
My sins, and my contrition
SOUTHEY—*Occasional Pieces.*

Pray as if everything depended on God, and work as if everything depended upon man.

ARCHBISHOP FRANCIS J. SPELLMAN.

Prayers are heard in heaven very much in proportion to our faith. Little faith will get very great mercies, but great faith still greater.

SPURGEON—*Gleanings among the Sheaves.*

To pray together, in whatever tongue or ritual, is the most tender brotherhood of hope and sympathy that men can contract in this life.

MADAME DE STAËL—*Corinne.*

Holy Father, in thy mercy,
Hear our anxious prayer.
Keep our loved ones, now far absent,
'Neath Thy care.

ISABELLA S. STEPHENSON—*Hymn.*

Lord, thy most pointed pleasure take,
And stab my spirit broad awake;
Or, Lord, if too obdurate I,
Choose Thou, before that spirit die,
A piercing pain, a killing sin,
And to my dead heart turn them in.

STEVENSON—*Celestial Surgeon.*

My debts are large, my failures great, my shame secret and heavy; yet when I come to ask for my good, I quake in fear lest my prayer be granted.

TAGORE—*Gitanjali.*

Speak to Him thou for He hears, and spirit with spirit can meet—
Closer is He than breathing, and nearer than hands and feet.

TENNYSON—*Higher Pantheism.*

More things are wrought by prayer
Than this world dreams of. Wherefore, let thy voice
Rise like a fountain for me night and day.
For what are men better than sheep or goats
That nourish a blind life within the brain,
If, knowing God, they lift not hands of prayer
Both for themselves and those who call them friend?

TENNYSON—*Morte d'Arthur.*

From compromise and things half done,
Keep me with stern and stubborn pride;
And when at last the fight is won,
God, keep me still unsatisfied.

LOUIS UNTERMEYER—*Prayer.*

God, though this life is but a wraith,
Although we know not what we use,
Although we grope with little faith,
Give me the heart to fight—and lose.

LOUIS UNTERMEYER—*Prayer.*

The Lord's Prayer contains the sum total of religion and morals.

WELLINGTON.

Though smooth be the heartless prayer, no ear in heaven will mind it;
And the finest phrase falls dead, if there is no feeling behind it.

ELLA WHEELER WILCOX—*Art and Heart.*

PREACHING

Do as we say, and not as we do.

BOCCACCIO—*Decameron.*

For the preacher's merit or demerit,
It were to be wished that the flaws were fewer
In the earthen vessel, holding treasure,
But the main thing is, does it hold good measure?
Heaven soon sets right all other matters!

BROWNING—*Christmas Eve.*

Hear how he clears the points o' Faith
Wi' rattlin' an' thumpin'!
Now meekly calm, now wild in wrath,
He's stampin', an' he's jumpin'!

BURNS—*Holy Fair.*

We must judge religious movements, not by the men who make them, but by the men they make.

JOSEPH COOK.

I would express him simple, grave, sincere;
In doctrine uncorrupt; in language plain,

And plain in manner; decent, solemn, chaste,
And natural in gesture; much impress'd
Himself, as conscious of his awful charge,
And anxious mainly that the flock he feeds
May feel it too; affectionate in look,
And tender in address, as well becomes
A messenger of grace to guilty men.
COWPER—*Task*.

The proud he tam'd, the penitent he cheer'd:
Nor to rebuke the rich offender fear'd.
His preaching much, but more his practice wrought;
(A living sermon of the truths he taught;)
For this by rules severe his life he squar'd:
That all might see the doctrines which they heard.
DRYDEN—*Character of a Good Parson*.

Alas for the unhappy man that is called to stand in the pulpit, and *not* give the bread of life.
EMERSON.

I would have every minister of the gospel address his audience with the zeal of a friend, with the generous energy of a father, and with the exuberant affection of a mother.
FÉNELON.

But in his duty prompt at every call,
He watch'd and wept, he pray'd and felt for all.
GOLDSMITH—*Deserted Village*.

Sir, a woman preaching is like a dog's walking on his hind legs. It is not done well: but you are surprised to find it done at all.
SAMUEL JOHNSON, 1763.

Skilful alike with tongue and pen,
He preached to all men everywhere
The Gospel of the Golden Rule,
The New Commandment given to men,
Thinking the deed, and not the creed,
Would help us in our utmost need.
LONGFELLOW—*Prelude to Tales of a Wayside Inn*.

Some plague the people with too long sermons; for the faculty of listening is a tender thing, and soon becomes weary and satiated.
LUTHER.

The Christian ministry is the worst of all trades, but the best of all professions.
NEWTON.

To endeavor to move by the same discourse hearers who differ in age, sex, position and education, is to attempt to open all locks with the same key.
J. PETIT-SENN.

I have taught you, my dear flock, for above thirty years how to live; and I will show you in a very short time how to die.
SANDYS.

Sermons in stones and good in every thing.
SHAKESPEARE—*As You Like It*. Act II. Sc. 1.

It is a good divine that follows his own instructions; I can easier teach twenty what were good to be done, than be one of the twenty to follow mine own teaching.
SHAKESPEARE—*Merchant of Venice*. Act I. Sc. 2.

"Dear sinners all," the fool began, "man's life is but a jest,
A dream, a shadow, bubble, air, a vapour at the best.
In a thousand pounds of law I find not a single ounce of love,
A blind man killed the parson's cow in shooting at the dove;
The fool that eats till he is sick must fast till he is well,
The wooer who can flatter most will bear away the belle."

. . .

And then again the women screamed, and every staghound bayed;

And why? because the motley fool so wise a sermon made.
George W. Thornbury — *The Jester's Sermon.*

The minister's brain is often the "poor-box" of the church.
Whipple.

PREJUDICE

Prejudice squints when it looks, and lies when it talks.
Duchess d'Abrantes.

He hears but half who hears one party only.
Aeschylus.

He who never leaves his country is full of prejudices.
Goldoni—*Pamela.*

Prejudice is the child of ignorance.
Hazlitt.

Opinions founded on prejudice are always sustained with the greatest violence.
Jeffrey.

Every period of life has its peculiar prejudices; whoever saw old age, that did not applaud the past, and condemn the present times?
Montaigne.

Remember, when the judgment's weak,
The prejudice is strong.
Kane O'Hara—*Midas.*

PRETENSION

Pretension almost always overdoes the original, and hence exposes itself.
Hosea Ballou.

Those who quit their proper character to assume what does not belong to them are, for the greater part, ignorant of both the character they leave and of the character they assume.
Burke.

Where there is much pretension, much has been borrowed: nature never pretends.
Lavater.

PRIDE

They are proud in humility, proud in that they are not proud.
Burton—*Anatomy of Melancholy.*

Let pride go afore, shame will follow after.
George Chapman—*Eastward Ho.*

Pride (of all others the most dang'rous fault)
Proceeds from want of sense, or want of thought.
Wentworth Dillon.

Pride that dines on vanity, sups on contempt.
Franklin.

Haughty people seem to me to have, like the dwarfs, the stature of a child and the face of a man.
Joubert.

Oh! Why should the spirit of mortal be proud?
Like a swift-fleeting meteor, a fast flying cloud,
A flash of the lightning, a break of the wave,
Man passes from life to his rest in the grave.
William Knox—*Mortality.*

Pride and weakness are Siamese twins.
Lowell.

In pride, in reas'ning pride, our error lies;
All quit their sphere and rush into the skies.
Pride still is aiming at the bless'd abodes,
Men would be angels, angels would be gods.
Pope—*Essay on Man.*

What the weak head with strongest bias rules,
Is pride, the never-failing vice of fools.
Pope—*Essay on Criticism.*

Pride goeth before destruction, and an haughty spirit before a fall.
Proverbs. XVI. 18.

In general, pride is at the bottom of all great mistakes.
Ruskin—*True and Beautiful.*

When a proud man thinks best of himself, then God and man think worst of him.

HORACE SMITH.

The infinitely little have a pride infinitely great.

VOLTAIRE.

PRINCIPLE

Dangerous principles impose upon our understanding, emasculate our spirits, and spoil our temper.

JEREMY COLLIER.

A precedent embalms a principle.

DISRAELI.

If principle is good for anything, it is worth living up to.

FRANKLIN.

Principle is a passion for truth.

HAZLITT.

I *don't* believe in princerple,
But, oh, I *du* in interest.

LOWELL—*The Biglow Papers.*

Ez to my princerples, I glory
In heven' nothin' o' the sort.

LOWELL—*The Biglow Papers.*

Let us cling to our principles as the mariner clings to his last plank when night and tempest close around him.

ADAM WOOLEVER.

PRINTING

He who first shortened the labor of Copyists by device of *Movable Types* was disbanding hired Armies and cashiering most Kings and Senates, and creating a whole new Democratic world: he had invented the Art of printing.

CARLYLE—*Sartor Resartus.*

Though an angel should write, still 'tis *devils* must print.

MOORE—*The Fudge Family in England.*

I'll print it,
And shame the fools.

POPE—*Prologue to Satires.*

PRISON

In durance vile here must I wake and weep,
And all my frowsy couch in sorrow steep.

BURNS.

Stone walls do not a prison make,
Nor iron bars a cage,
Minds innocent and quiet take
That for an hermitage.

LOVELACE—*To Althea, from Prison.*

I was in prison, and ye came unto me.

Matthew. XXV. 36.

While we have prisons it matters little which of us occupy the cells.

GEORGE BERNARD SHAW—*Maxims for Revolutionists.*

I know not whether laws be right,
Or whether laws be wrong;
All that we know who be in gaol
Is that the wall is strong;
And that each day is like a year,
A year whose days are long.

OSCAR WILDE—*The Ballad of Reading Gaol.*

PROCRASTINATION

By the street of "By and By" one arrives at the house of "Never."

CERVANTES.

Never leave that till to-morrow which you can do to-day.

FRANKLIN.

For yesterday was once to-morrow.

PERSIUS.

Procrastination is the thief of time.

YOUNG.

PROFANITY

Most people who commit a sin count on some personal benefit to be derived therefrom, but profanity has not even this excuse.

HOSEA BALLOU.

Jack was embarrassed—never hero more,
And as he knew not what to say, he swore.

BYRON—*The Island.*

Bad language or abuse
I never, never use,
Whatever the emergency;
Though "Bother it" I may
Occasionally say,
I never never use a big, big D.
W. S. GILBERT—*H. M. S. Pinafore.*

To swear is neither brave, polite, nor wise.
POPE.

The foolish and wicked practice of profane cursing and swearing is a vice so mean and low that every person of sense and character detests and despises it.
WASHINGTON.

PROFIT

Everywhere in life, the true question is not what we *gain,* but what we *do.*
CARLYLE—*Essays.*

And if you mean to profit, learn to please.
CHARLES CHURCHILL—*Gotham.*

Little pains
In a due hour employ'd great profit yields.
JOHN PHILIPS—*Cider.*

As to pay, Sir, I beg leave to assure the Congress that as no pecuniary consideration could have tempted me to accept this arduous employment at the expense of my domestic ease and happiness, I do not wish to make any profit from it.
WASHINGTON—*To Congress on his Appointment as Commander-in-Chief, 1775.*

PROGRESS

Westward the star of empire takes its way.
JOHN QUINCY ADAMS, 1802.

Modern invention has banished the spinning-wheel, and the same law of progress makes the woman of to-day a different woman from her grandmother.
SUSAN B. ANTHONY.

Progress is
The law of life, man is not
Man as yet.
BROWNING—*Paracelsus.*

So long as all the increased wealth which modern progress brings, goes but to build up great fortunes, to increase luxury, and make sharper the contest between the House of Have and the House of Want, progress is not real and cannot be permanent.
HENRY GEORGE—*Progress and Poverty.*

Progress has not followed a straight ascending line, but a spiral with rhythms of progress and retrogression, of evolution and dissolution.
GOETHE.

Nature knows no pause in progress and development, and attaches her curse on all inaction.
GOETHE.

He who moves not forward goes backward!
A capital saying!
GOETHE—*Herman and Dorothea.*

Look up and not down; look forward and not back; look out and not in; and lend a hand.
E. E. HALE.

Some men so dislike the dust kicked up by the generation they belong to, that, being unable to pass, they lag behind it.
HARE.

Every age has its problem, by solving which humanity is helped forward.
HEINRICH HEINE.

Progress,—the stride of God!
VICTOR HUGO.

Nor deem the irrevocable Past
As wholly wasted, wholly vain,
If, rising on its wrecks, at last
To something nobler we attain.
LONGFELLOW—*Ladder of St. Augustine.*

New occasions teach new duties, time makes ancient good uncouth;
They must upward still and onward, who would keep abreast of truth.
LOWELL—*Present Crisis.*

Spiral" the memorable Lady terms
Our mind's ascent.
GEORGE MEREDITH—*The World's Advance.*

That in our proper motion we ascend
Up to our native seat; descent and fall
To us is adverse.
MILTON—*Paradise Lost.*

Every step of progress which the world has made has been from scaffold to scaffold, and from stake to stake.
WENDELL PHILLIPS.

There is a period of life when we go back as we advance.
ROUSSEAU—*Émile.*

If you strike a thorn or rose,
Keep a-goin'!
If it hails or if it snows,
Keep a-goin'!
'Tain't no use to sit and whine
'Cause the fish ain't on your line;
Bait your hook an' keep on tryin',
Keep a-goin'!
FRANK L. STANTON—*Keep a-goin'.*

When old words die out on the tongue, new melodies break forth from the heart; and where the old tracks are lost, new country is revealed with its wonders.
TAGORE—*Gitanjali.*

He who has not the spirit of his age, has all the misery of it.
VOLTAIRE.

Press on!—"for in the grave there is no work
And no device"—Press on! while yet ye may!
N. P. WILLIS.

PROMISE

You never bade me hope, 'tis true;
I asked you not to swear:
But I looked in those eyes of blue,
And read a promise there.
GERALD GRIFFIN—*You Never Bade Me Hope.*

An acre of performance is worth the whole world of promise.
HOWELL.

We promise according to our hopes, and perform according to our fears.
LA ROCHEFOUCAULD.

It is easy to promise, and alas! how easy to forget!
ALFRED DE MUSSET.

He who is the most slow in making a promise is the most faithful in the performance of it.
ROUSSEAU.

PROMPTNESS

Know the true value of time; snatch, seize, and enjoy every moment of it. No idleness, no laziness, no procrastination; never put off till to-morrow what you can do to-day.
LORD CHESTERFIELD.

Timely service, like timely gifts, is doubled in value.
GEORGE MACDONALD.

The keen spirit seizes the prompt occasion.
HANNAH MORE.

PROOF

You may prove anything by figures.
Quoted by CARLYLE.

The burden of proof lies on the plaintiff.
Legal Maxim.

You cannot demonstrate an emotion or prove an aspiration.
JOHN MORLEY—*Rousseau.*

For when one's proofs are aptly chosen,
Four are as valid as four dozen.
PRIOR—*Alma.*

Prove all things; hold fast that which is good.
I Thessalonians. V. 21.

PROPHECY

Be thou the rainbow to the storms of life!
The evening beam that smiles the clouds away,
And tints to-morrow with prophetic ray!
BYRON—*Bride of Abydos.*

Of all the horrid, hideous notes of woe,
Sadder than owl-songs or the mid-night blast;
Is that portentous phrase, "I told you so."
BYRON—*Don Juan*.

The prophet's mantle, ere his flight began,
Dropt on the world—a sacred gift to man.
CAMPBELL—*Pleasures of Hope*.

I shall always consider the best guesser the best prophet.
CICERO.

We know in part, and we prophesy in part.
I Corinthians. XIII. 9.

Thy voice sounds like a prophet's word;
And in its hollow tones are heard
The thanks of millions yet to be.
FITZ-GREENE HALLECK—*Marco Bozzaris*.

Prophet of evil! never hadst thou yet
A cheerful word for me. To mark the signs
Of coming mischief is thy great delight,
Good dost thou ne'er foretell nor bring to pass.
HOMER—*Iliad*.

Don't never prophesy—onless ye know.
LOWELL—*Biglow Papers*.

A prophet is not without honour, save in his own country and in his own house.
Matthew. XIII. 57.

PROSPERITY

It requires a strong constitution to withstand repeated attacks of prosperity.
J. L. BASFORD.

It shows a weak mind not to bear prosperity as well as adversity with moderation.
CICERO.

He that swells in prosperity will be sure to shrink in adversity.
COLTON.

The desert shall rejoice, and blossom as the rose.
Isaiah. XXXV. 1.

They shall sit every man under his vine and under his fig-tree.
Micah. IV. 4.

Length of days is in her right hand and in her left hand riches and honour.
Proverbs. III. 16.

Prosperity makes some friends and many enemies.
VAUVENARGUES.

Take care to be an economist in prosperity; there is no fear of your being one in adversity.
ZIMMERMAN.

PROVERBS

Mind your P's and Q's.
ANONYMOUS.

Neither fish, flesh nor good red herring.
ANONYMOUS.

Eureka! Eureka!
ARCHIMEDES.

The genius, wit, and spirit of a nation are discovered in its proverbs.
BACON.

Right as a trivet.
R. H. BARHAM.

There is no jesting with edge tools.
BEAUMONT and FLETCHER.

Speak boldly, and speak truly, shame the devil.
BEAUMONT and FLETCHER.

One foot in the grave.
BEAUMONT and FLETCHER.

I find the medicine worse than the malady.
BEAUMONT and FLETCHER.

He went away with a flea in 's ear.
BEAUMONT and FLETCHER.

Deeds, not words.
BEAUMONT and FLETCHER.

rom the crown of our head to the
ole of our foot.
BEAUMONT and FLETCHER.

irst come, first served.
BEAUMONT and FLETCHER.

What mare's nest hast thou found?
BEAUMONT and FLETCHER—*Bonduca.*

As cold as cucumbers.
BEAUMONT and FLETCHER—*Cupid's Revenge.*

As high as Heaven, as deep as Hell.
BEAUMONT and FLETCHER—*Honest Man's Fortune.*

One good turn deserves another.
BEAUMONT and FLETCHER—*Little French Lawyer.*

This is a pretty flimflam.
BEAUMONT and FLETCHER—*Little French Lawyer.*

Hit the nail on the head.
BEAUMONT and FLETCHER—*Love's Cure.*

After supper walk a mile.
BEAUMONT and FLETCHER—*Philaster.*

'll have a fling.
BEAUMONT and FLETCHER—*Rule a Wife and Have a Wife.*

Oil on troubled waters.
BEDE.

What is sauce for the goose is sauce
or a gander.
TOM BROWN—*New Maxims.*

Curses are like young chickens,
And still come home to roost!
BULWER.

Dark as pitch.
BUNYAN.

Let us do or die.
BURNS.

Every man for himself, his own ends,
the devil for all.
BURTON.

Make a virtue of necessity.
BURTON.

Penny wise, pound foolish.
BURTON.

Build castles in the air.
BURTON.

As clear and as manifest as the nose
in a man's face.
BURTON.

Set a beggar on horseback, and he
will ride a gallop.
BURTON.

No rule is so general, which admits
not some exception.
BURTON.

Matches are made in heaven.
BURTON.

Comparisons are odious.
BURTON.

Going as if he trod upon eggs.
BURTON—*Anatomy of Melancholy.*

He that has two strings t' his bow.
BUTLER.

Look before you ere you leap.
BUTLER.

He that is down can fall no lower.
BUTLER.

As you sow, y' are like to reap.
BUTLER.

I'll make the fur
Fly 'bout the ears of the old cur.
BUTLER—*Hudibras.*

The point is plain as a pike staff.
JOHN BYROM—*Epistle to a Friend.*

As clear as a whistle.
JOHN BYROM—*Epistle to Lloyd.*

Put himself upon his good behaviour.
BYRON—*Don Juan.*

By all that's good and glorious.
BYRON—*Sardanapalus.*

Better halfe a loafe than no bread.
CAMDEN.

An inch in a miss is as good as an ell.
CAMDEN—*Remains.*

Better a bad excuse, than none at all.
CAMDEN—*Remains.*

No man is a hero to his valet-de-
chambre.
Attributed to MARSHAL CATINAT.

All that glisters is not gold.
CERVANTES.

Can one desire too much of a good thing?
CERVANTES.

Here is the devil-and-all to pay.
CERVANTES.

I can tell where my own shoe pinches me.
CERVANTES.

More knave than fool.
CERVANTES.

Smell a rat.
CERVANTES.

Spick and span new.
CERVANTES.

This peck of troubles.
CERVANTES.

I have other fish to fry.
CERVANTES—*Don Quixote.*

Leap out of the frying pan into the fire.
CERVANTES—*Don Quixote.*

Let the worst come to the worst.
CERVANTES—*Don Quixote.*

Many go out for wool, and come home shorn themselves.
CERVANTES—*Don Quixote.*

Proverbs are short sentences drawn from long and wise experience.
CERVANTES—*Don Quixote.*

Spare your breath to cool your porridge.
CERVANTES—*Don Quixote.*

The more thou stir it the worse it will be.
CERVANTES—*Don Quixote.*

Within a stone's throw of it.
CERVANTES—*Don Quixote.*

Enough is as good as a feast.
GEORGE CHAPMAN.

Let pride go afore, shame will follow after.
GEORGE CHAPMAN.

To put a girdle around the world.
GEORGE CHAPMAN.

Make ducks and drakes with shillings.
GEORGE CHAPMAN—*Eastward Ho.*

The more haste, ever the worst speed.
CHARLES CHURCHILL.

The will for the deed.
COLLEY CIBBER.

Fortune befriends the bold.
CICERO.

The fat's all in the fire.
COBBE—*Prophecies.*

Praise the bridge that carried yo
over.
GEORGE COLMAN (the Younger).

Imitation is the sincerest form c
flattery.
C. C. COLTON.

A thorn in the flesh.
II Corinthians. XII. 7.

He that runs may read.
COWPER.

Cut and come again.
CRABBE.

It is better to wear out than to rus
out.
BISHOP CUMBERLAND.

Turn over a new leaf.
THOMAS DEKKER.

Barkis is willin'.
DICKENS—*David Copperfield.*

Better late than never.
DIONYSIUS.

The mill will never grind with wate
that has past.
SARAH DOWDNEY.

The coast was clear.
MICHAEL DRAYTON—*Nymphidia.*

As sure as a gun.
DRYDEN.

Give the devil his due.
DRYDEN.

He's a sure card.
DRYDEN.

Men are but children of a large
growth.
DRYDEN.

Living from hand to mouth.
DU BARTAS.

Thy will for deed I do accept.
DU BARTAS.

With tooth and nail.
DU BARTAS—*Divine Weekes and Workes.*

Made no more bones.
Du Bartas—*The Maiden Blush.*

Why, then, do you walk as if you had swallowed a ramrod?
Epictetus—*Discourses.*

Life is short, yet sweet.
Euripides.

Tall oaks from little acorns grow.
David Everett.

Needle in a bottle of hay.
Field.

But me no buts.
Henry Fielding—*Rape upon Rape.*

She is no better than she should be.
Henry Fielding.

Faint heart ne'er won fair lady.
Phineas Fletcher.

Diamonds cut diamonds.
John Ford.

Better your room than your company.
Simon Forman.

Moche Crye and no Wull.
Fortescue.

Fools make feasts, and wise men eat them.
Franklin.

If you would be loved, love and be lovable.
Franklin.

Never leave that till to-morrow which you can do to-day.
Franklin.

Three may keep a secret if two of them are dead.
Franklin.

Where there's marriage without love there will be love without marriage.
Franklin.

Glass, China, and Reputation, are easily crack'd and never well mended.
Franklin—*Poor Richard.*

Silence gives consent.
Fuller.

Two of a trade can ne'er agree.
Gay.

Handsome is that handsome does.
Goldsmith.

The very pink of perfection.
Goldsmith.

Out of sight, out of mind.
Googe.

Go West, young man, and grow up with the country.
Horace Greeley.

Oft times many things fall out between the cup and the lip.
Greene.

Not lost, but gone before.
Matthew Henry.

A dwarf on a giant's shoulder sees farther of the two.
George Herbert.

Build castles in Spain.
George Herbert.

Couldst thou both eat thy cake and have it?
George Herbert.

Deceive not thy physician, confessor, nor lawyer.
George Herbert.

God's mills grind slow but sure.
George Herbert.

Half the world knows not how the other half lives.
George Herbert.

It is a poor sport that is not worth the candle.
George Herbert.

Those that God loves, do not live long.
George Herbert.

Thursday come, and the week is gone.
George Herbert.

Whose house is of glass, must not throw stones at another.
George Herbert.

His bark is worse than his bite.
George Herbert—*Country Parson.*

Love, and a Cough, cannot be hid.
George Herbert—*Jacula Prudentum.*

But ne'er the rose without the thorn.
Herrick.

At our wittes end.
Heywood.

God never sendeth mouth but he sendeth meat.
HEYWOOD.

Nought venter nought have.
HEYWOOD.

Robbe Peter and pay Paule.
HEYWOOD.

Set the cart before the horse.
HEYWOOD.

Tell tales out of schoole.
HEYWOOD.

The more the merrier.
HEYWOOD.

Two heads are better than one.
HEYWOOD.

Went in at the one eare and out at the other.
HEYWOOD.

By hook or crook.
HEYWOOD.

Give an inch, he'll take an ell.
HOBBES.

The better day the better deed.
SIR JOHN HOLT.

Bag and baggage.
RICHARD HULOET, 1552.

Rise with the lark and with the lark to bed.
JAMES HURDIS.

Greatest happiness of the greatest number.
HUTCHESON.

He must needes go where the dyvell dryveth.
JOHAN THE HUSBANDE.

Fitted him to a T.
SAMUEL JOHNSON—*Boswell's Life of Johnson.*

See and to be seen.
BEN JONSON.

The burnt child dreads the fire.
BEN JONSON.

Man proposes, but God disposes.
THOMAS À KEMPIS.

A proverb and a byword among all people.
I Kings. IX. 7.

Half as sober as a judge.
CHARLES LAMB.

Neat, not gaudy.
CHARLES LAMB.

Not if I know myself at all.
CHARLES LAMB.

Though this may be play to you,
'Tis death to us.
ROGER L'ESTRANGE.

Facts are stubborn things.
LE SAGE—*Gil Blas.*

Don't cross the bridge till you com[e] to it,
Is a proverb old, and of excellent wit[.]
LONGFELLOW.

There's luck in odd numbers.
SAMUEL LOVER.

As busie as a bee.
LYLY.

There can no great smoke arise, bu[t] there must be some fire.
LYLY.

A new broom sweepeth clean.
LYLY—*Euphues.*

The finest edge is made with the blun[t] whetstone.
LYLY—*Euphues.*

Every tub must stand upon its bottom.
MACKLIN—*Man of the World.*

Where McGregor sits, there is the head of the table.
Attributed to THE MCGREGOR, a Highland Chief.

Have you summoned your wits from wool-gathering?
THOMAS MIDDLETON.

Hold their noses to the grindstone.
THOMAS MIDDLETON—*Blurt, Master Constable.*

On his last legs.
THOMAS MIDDLETON—*The Old Law.*

Hide their diminished heads.
MILTON.

Present company excepted.
O'KEEFE—*London Hermit.*

Ossa on Pelion.
OVID.

No cross, no crown.
St. Paulinus.

So obliging that he ne'er oblig'd.
Pope.

Of two evils I have chose the least.
Prior.

The end must justify the means.
Prior.

A baker's dozen.
Rabelais.

He always looked a given horse in the mouth.
Rabelais.

He did not care a button for it.
Rabelais.

How well I feathered my nest.
Rabelais.

I am just going to leap into the dark.
Rabelais.

Make three bites of a cherry.
Rabelais.

Others set carts before the horses.
Rabelais.

Strike the iron whilst it is hot.
Rabelais.

We'll take the good-will for the deed.
Rabelais.

You shall never want rope enough.
Rabelais.

Every man is the architect of his own fortunes.
Pseudo Sallust.

Wickedness proceedeth from the wicked.
I Samuel. XXIV. 13.

Blood is thicker than water.
Scott.

Fat, fair and forty.
Scott.

Scared out of his seven senses.
Scott—*Rob Roy*.

A little more than kin, and less than kind.
Shakespeare.

All's well that ends well.
Shakespeare.

Although the last, not least
Shakespeare.

Brevity is the soul of wit.
Shakespeare.

But when the fox hath once got in his nose,
He'll soon find means to make the body follow.
Shakespeare.

Delays have dangerous ends.
Shakespeare.

God defend the right.
Shakespeare.

He jests at scars that never felt a wound.
Shakespeare.

He must have a long spoon that must eat with the devil.
Shakespeare.

He will give the devil his due.
Shakespeare.

Ill blows the wind that profits nobody.
Shakespeare.

It is a wise father that knows his own child.
Shakespeare.

Lord, what fools these mortals be.
Shakespeare.

My man's as true as steel.
Shakespeare.

The game is up.
Shakespeare.

The time is out of joint.
Shakespeare.

There's a time for all things.
Shakespeare.

They that touch pitch will be defiled.
Shakespeare.

Unquiet meals make ill digestions.
Shakespeare.

We have scotch'd the snake, not killed it.
Shakespeare.

That was laid on with a trowel.
Shakespeare—*As You Like It*. Act I. Sc. 2.

Every why hath a wherefore.
Shakespeare—*Comedy of Errors*. Act II. Sc. 2.

God save the mark!
SHAKESPEARE—*Henry IV*. Pt. I. Act I. Sc. 3.

I have you on the hip.
SHAKESPEARE—*Merchant of Venice*. Act IV. Sc. 1.

The short and the long of it.
SHAKESPEARE—*Merry Wives of Windsor*. Act II. Sc. 2.

'Tis neither here nor there.
SHAKESPEARE—*Othello*. Act IV. Sc. 3.

Harp not on that string.
SHAKESPEARE—*Richard III*. Act IV. Sc. 4.

Westward-ho!
SHAKESPEARE—*Twelfth Night*. Act III. Sc. 1.

He knew what is what.
SKELTON.

In the name of the Prophet—figs.
HORACE and JAMES SMITH—*Rejected Addresses*.

Go West, young man! Go West.
JOHN L. B. SOULE.

Pity's akin to love.
THOMAS SOUTHERNE.

There, though last, not least.
SPENSER.

A happy accident.
MME. DE STAËL.

Snug as a bug in a rug.
The Stratford Jubilee.

A carpenter's known by his chips.
SWIFT.

Bread is the staff of life.
SWIFT.

I won't quarrel with my bread and butter.
SWIFT.

She watches him as a cat would watch a mouse.
SWIFT.

'Tis nothing when you are used to it.
SWIFT.

Big-endians and small-endians.
SWIFT—*Gulliver's Travels*.

Hail, fellow, well met.
SWIFT—*My Lady's Lamentation*.

Walls have tongues, and hedges ears
SWIFT—*Pastoral Dialogue*.

A fair exterior is a silent recommendation.
SYRUS.

A rolling stone gathers no moss.
SYRUS.

Familiarity breeds contempt.
SYRUS.

Necessity knows no law except to conquer.
SYRUS.

There are some remedies worse than the disease.
SYRUS.

Cut off your nose to spite your face.
TALLEMENT DES REAUX.

Laugh and be fat.
JOHN TAYLOR.

Better fifty years of Europe than a cycle of Cathay.
TENNYSON.

Looked unutterable things.
THOMSON.

A cat may look at a king.
Title of a Pamphlet, 1652.

Much of a muchness.
VANBRUGH—*The Provoked Husband*.

That which is everybody's business is nobody's business.
IZAAK WALTON.

What is the matter with Kansas?
WILLIAM ALLEN WHITE.

I will die in the last ditch.
WILLIAM OF ORANGE.

PROVIDENCE

And pleas'd th' Almighty's orders to perform,
Rides in the whirlwind and directs the storm.
ADDISON—*The Campaign*.

God tempers the cold to the shorn sheep.
ANONYMOUS.

God made bees, and bees made honey,
God made man, and man made money,

Pride made the devil, and the devil made sin;
So God made a cole-pit to put the devil in.
ANONYMOUS.

Fear not, but trust in Providence,
Wherever thou may'st be.
THOMAS HAYNES BAYLY — *The Pilot.*

If heaven send no supplies,
The fairest blossom of the garden dies.
WILLIAM BROWNE—*Visions.*

In some time, his good time, I shall arrive;
He guides me and the bird
In his good time.
BROWNING—*Paracelsus.*

Behind a frowning Providence
He hides a smiling face.
COWPER—*Light Shining Out of Darkness.*

Behind the dim unknown,
Standeth God within the shadow, keeping watch above his own.
LOWELL—*The Present Crisis.*

Eye me, blest Providence, and square my trial
To my proportion'd strength.
MILTON—*Comus.*

Who sees with equal eye, as God of all,
A hero perish, or a sparrow fall,
Atoms or systems into ruin hurl'd,
And now a bubble burst, and now a world.
POPE—*Essay on Man.*

Who finds not Providence all good and wise,
Alike in what it gives, and what denies.
POPE—*Essay on Man.*

The sun shall not smite thee by day, nor the moon by night.
Psalms. CXXI. 6.

For it would have been better that man should have been born dumb, nay, void of all reason, rather than that he should employ the gifts of Providence to the destruction of his neighbor.
QUINTILIAN.

He that doth the ravens feed,
Yea, providently caters for the sparrow,
Be comfort to my age!
SHAKESPEARE—*As You Like It.* Act II. Sc. 3.

There is a divinity that shapes our ends,
Rough-hew them how we will.
SHAKESPEARE—*Hamlet.* Act V. Sc. 2.

For nought so vile that on the earth doth live
But to the earth some special good doth give.
SHAKESPEARE—*Romeo and Juliet.* Act II. Sc. 3.

I firmly believe in Divine Providence. Without belief in Providence I think I should go crazy. Without God the world would be a maze without a clue.
WOODROW WILSON—*Speech, 1919.*

PRUDENCE

Put your trust in God, my boys, and keep your powder dry.
COL. BLACKER.

And it is a common saying that it is best first to catch the stag, and afterwards, when he has been caught, to skin him.
BRACTON.

Dine on little, and sup on less.
CERVANTES.

I recommend you to take care of the minutes, for the hours will take care of themselves.
LORD CHESTERFIELD.

I prefer silent prudence to loquacious folly.
CICERO.

Prudence is the knowledge of things to be sought, and those to be shunned.
CICERO.

Men are born with two eyes, but with one tongue, in order that they should see twice as much as they say.
COLTON.

The first years of man must make provision for the last.

SAMUEL JOHNSON.

Let your loins be girded about, and your lights burning.

Luke. XII. 35.

I won't quarrel with my bread and butter.

SWIFT—*Polite Conversation.*

You will conquer more surely by prudence than by passion.

SYRUS.

That should be long considered which can be decided but once.

SYRUS.

PRUDERY

Some women don buckler and spear to fight dragons which have no existence.

F. A. DURIVAGE.

Prudery is the hypocrisy of modesty.

MASSIAS.

Prudery is the bastard child of virtue.

OUIDA.

There are no greater prudes than those women who have some secret to hide.

GEORGE SAND.

PUBLIC

We would not listen to those who were wont to say the voice of the people is the voice of God, for the voice of the mob is near akin to madness.

ALCUIN.

The tyranny of a multitude is a multiplied tyranny.

BURKE—*To Thomas Mercer.*

The public! why, the public's nothing better than a great baby.

THOMAS CHALMERS.

The public! the public! how many fools does it require to make the public?

CHAMFORT.

The rabble estimate few things according to their real value, most things according to their prejudices.

CICERO.

For who can be secure of private right,
If sovereign sway may be dissolved by might?
Nor is the people's judgment always true:
The most may err as grossly as the few.

DRYDEN—*Absalom and Achitophel.*

He who serves the public is a poor animal; he worries himself to death and no one thanks him for it.

GOETHE.

The public wishes itself to be managed like a woman; one must say nothing to it except what it likes to hear.

GOETHE.

The public have neither shame nor gratitude.

HAZLITT.

The people's voice is odd,
It is, and it is not, the voice of God.

POPE—*To Augustus.*

It is to the middle class we must look for the safety of England.

THACKERAY—*Four Georges.*

The public be damned.

W. H. VANDERBILT.

In a free and republican government, you cannot restrain the voice of the multitude. Every man will speak as he thinks, or, more properly, without thinking, and consequently will judge of effects without attending to their causes.

WASHINGTON.

PUNCTUALITY

The most indispensable qualification of a cook is punctuality. The same must be said of guests.

BRILLAT-SAVARIN.

If I have made an appointment with you, I owe you punctuality; I have no right to throw away your time, if I do my own.

CECIL.

Unfaithfulness in the keeping of an appointment is an act of clear dis-

honesty. You may as well borrow a person's money as his time.
HORACE MANN.

I have always been a quarter of an hour before my time, and it has made a man of me.
LORD NELSON.

PUNISHMENT

Let them stew in their own grease (or juice).
BISMARCK.

Eye for eye, tooth for tooth, hand for hand, foot for foot.
Deuteronomy. XIX. 21.

That is the bitterest of all,—to wear the yoke of our own wrong-doing.
GEORGE ELIOT—*Daniel Deronda*.

My punishment is greater than I can bear.
Genesis. IV. 13.

Whoso sheddeth man's blood, by man shall his blood be shed.
Genesis. IX. 6.

My object all sublime
I shall achieve in time—
To let the punishment fit the crime.
W. S. GILBERT—*Mikado*.

It is more dangerous that even a guilty person should be punished without the forms of law than that he should escape.
JEFFERSON, 1788.

One man meets an infamous punishment for that crime which confers a diadem upon another.
JUVENAL.

The only effect of public punishment is to show the rabble how bravely it can be borne.
LANDOR.

Breach for breach, eye for eye, tooth for tooth.
Leviticus. XXIV. 20.

It were better for him that a millstone were hanged about his neck, and he cast into the sea.
Luke. XVII. 2.

The object of punishment is, prevention from evil; it never can be made impulsive to good.
HORACE MANN.

Unrespited, unpitied, unrepriev'd.
MILTON—*Paradise Lost*.

Just prophet, let the damn'd one dwell
Full in the sight of Paradise,
Beholding heaven and feeling hell.
MOORE—*Lalla Rookh*.

But if the first Eve
Hard doom did receive
When only one apple had she,
What a punishment new
Must be found out for you,
Who eating hath robb'd the whole tree.
POPE—*To Lady Montague*.

He that spareth his rod hateth his son.
Proverbs. XIII. 24.

The time that precedes punishment is the severest part of it.
SENECA.

They spare the rod, and spoil the child.
RALPH VENNING—*Mysteries and Revelations*.

The punishment of criminals should be of use; when a man is hanged he is good for nothing.
VOLTAIRE.

PURITY

The smallest speck is seen on snow.
GAY.

Only the heart without a stain knows perfect ease.
GOETHE.

The stream is always purer at its source.
PASCAL—*Lettres Provinciales*.

Whiter than new snow on a raven's back.
SHAKESPEARE—*Romeo and Juliet*. Act III. Sc. 2.

Unto the pure all things are pure.
Titus. I. 15.

Q

QUACK

Quacks pretend to cure other men's disorders, but fail to find a remedy for their own.

CICERO.

Take the humbug out of this world, and you haven't much left to do business with.

H. W. SHAW.

QUALITY

Things that have a common quality ever quickly seek their kind.

MARCUS AURELIUS—*Meditations.*

The best is the cheapest.

FRANKLIN.

Quality, not quantity, is my measure.

DOUGLAS JERROLD.

Hard as a piece of the nether millstone.

Job. XLI. 24.

Many individuals have, like uncut diamonds, shining qualities beneath a rough exterior.

JUVENAL.

Ye are the salt of the earth: but if the salt have lost his savour, wherewith shall it be salted?

Matthew. V. 13.

Nothing endures but personal qualities.

WALT WHITMAN—*Leaves of Grass.*

QUARRELING

He that blows the coals in quarrels he has nothing to do with has no right to complain if the sparks fly in his face.

FRANKLIN.

Those who in quarrels interpose,
Must often wipe a bloody nose.

GAY—*Fables.*

Quarrels would not last long if the fault was only on one side.

LA ROCHEFOUCAULD.

Those glorious days, when man said to man,
Let us be brothers, or I will knock you down.

LE BRUN.

The quarrels of lovers are like summer storms; everything is more beautiful when they have passed.

MADAME NECKER.

A quarrel is quickly settled when deserted by one party: there is no battle unless there be two.

SENECA.

Let dogs delight to bark and bite,
For God hath made them so;
Let bears and lions growl and fight,
For 'tis their nature too.

But children you should never let
Such angry passions rise,
Your little hands were never made
To tear each other's eyes.

ISAAC WATTS—*Against Quarrelling.*

QUOTATION

One whom it is easier to hate, but still easier to quote—Alexander Pope.

AUGUSTINE BIRRELL.

The wisdom of the wise and the experience of ages may be preserved by quotation.

ISAAC D'ISRAELI — *Curiosities of Literature.*

A book which hath been culled from the flowers of all books.

GEORGE ELIOT — *The Spanish Gypsy.*

Next to the originator of a good sentence is the first quoter of it.

EMERSON — *Letters and Social Aims.*

Every quotation contributes something to the stability or enlargement of the language.

SAMUEL JOHNSON—*Preface to Dictionary.*

Though old the thought and oft exprest,
'Tis his at last who says it best.

LOWELL—*For an Autograph.*

As one might say of me that I have only made here a collection of other people's flowers, having provided nothing of my own but the cord to bind them together.
MONTAIGNE—*Essays.*

The devil can cite Scripture for his purpose.
SHAKESPEARE—*Merchant of Venice.* Act I. Sc. 3.

R

RAIN

After the rain cometh the fair weather.
AESOP—*Fables.*

I think rain is as necessary to the mind as to vegetation. My very thoughts become thirsty, and crave the moisture.
JOHN BURROUGHS.

Nature, like man, sometimes weeps for gladness.
DISRAELI.

She waits for me, my lady Earth,
Smiles and waits and sighs;
I'll say her nay, and hide away,
Then take her by surprise.
MARY MAPES DODGE—*How the Rain Comes.*

How it pours, pours, pours,
In a never-ending sheet!
How it drives beneath the doors!
How it soaks the passer's feet!
How it rattles on the shutter!
How it rumples up the lawn!
How 'twill sigh, and moan, and mutter,
From darkness until dawn.
ROSSITER JOHNSON—*Rhyme of the Rain.*

Be still, sad heart, and cease repining;
Behind the clouds is the sun still shining;
Thy fate is the common fate of all,
Into each life some rain must fall,
Some days must be dark and dreary.
LONGFELLOW—*The Rainy Day.*

It is not raining rain to me,
It's raining daffodils;
In every dimpled drop I see
Wild flowers on distant hills.
ROBERT LOVEMAN—*April Rain.*

He shall come down like rain upon the mown grass.
Psalms. LXXII. 6.

I bring fresh showers for the thirsting flowers,
From the seas and the streams;
I bear light shade for the leaves when laid
In their noonday dreams.
SHELLEY—*The Cloud.*

I know Sir John will go, though he was sure it would rain cats and dogs.
SWIFT—*Polite Conversation.*

Vexed sailors curse the rain for which poor shepherds prayed in vain.
WALLER.

RAINBOW

And, lo! in the dark east, expanded high,
The rainbow brightens to the setting Sun.
BEATTIE—*The Minstrel.*

Triumphal arch, that fill'st the sky
When storms prepare to part,
I ask not proud Philosophy
To teach me what thou art.
CAMPBELL—*To the Rainbow.*

O beautiful rainbow;—all woven of light!
There's not in thy tissue one shadow of night;
Heaven surely is open when thou dost appear,
And, bending above thee, the angels draw near,
And sing,—"The rainbow! the rainbow!
The smile of God is here."
MRS. SARAH J. HALE—*Poems.*

A rainbow in the morning
Is the Shepherd's warning;
But a rainbow at night
Is the Shepherd's delight.
Old Weather Rhyme.

What skilful limner e'er would choose
To paint the rainbow's varying hues,

Unless to mortal it were given
To dip his brush in dyes of heaven?
SCOTT—*Marmion.*

Rain, rain, and sun! a rainbow in the sky!
TENNYSON—*Idylls of the King.*

READING

Reading is to the mind, what exercise is to the body.
ADDISON—*The Tatler.*

Reading maketh a full man.
BACON—*Of Studies.*

Men must read for amusement as well as for knowledge.
HENRY WARD BEECHER.

Read, mark, learn, and inwardly digest.
Book of Common Prayer.

In science, read, by preference, the newest works; in literature, the oldest. The classic literature is always modern.
BULWER-LYTTON.

I should as soon think of swimming across the Charles River when I wish to go to Boston, as of reading all my books in originals, when I have them rendered for me in my mother tongue.
EMERSON.

Our high respect for a well-read man is praise enough of literature.
EMERSON — *Letters and Social Aims.*

My early and invincible love of reading, I would not exchange for the treasures of India.
GIBBON—*Memoirs.*

The first time I read an excellent book, it is to me just as if I had gained a new friend. When I read over a book I have perused before, it resembles the meeting with an old one.
GOLDSMITH—*The Citizen of the World.*

A man ought to read just as inclination leads him; for what he reads as a task will do him little good.
SAMUEL JOHNSON—*Boswell's Life of Johnson.*

I love to lose myself in other men's minds. When I am not walking, I am reading; I cannot sit and think. Books think for me.
CHARLES LAMB—*Last Essays of Elia.*

Many readers judge the power of a book by the shock it gives their feelings.
LONGFELLOW.

And better had they ne'er been born,
Who read to doubt, or read to scorn.
SCOTT—*The Monastery.*

When I am reading a book, whether wise or silly, it seems to me to be alive and talking to me.
SWIFT.

He that runs may read.
TENNYSON—*The Flower.*

REASON

Reason can tell how love affects us but cannot tell what love is.
HENRY WARD BEECHER.

Reason is the mistress and queen of all things.
CICERO.

He who will not reason, is a bigot; he who cannot is a fool; and he who dares not, is a slave.
WILLIAM DRUMMOND.

Reasons are not like garments, the worse for wearing.
EARL OF ESSEX, 1598.

Reason can in general do more than blind force.
CORN GALLUS.

If I go to heaven I want to take my reason with me.
R. G. INGERSOLL.

Come now, and let us reason together.
Isaiah. I. 18.

Human reason is like a drunken man on horseback; set it up on one side, and it tumbles over on the other.
LUTHER.

You know, my friends, with what a brave carouse
I made a second marriage in my house;
Divorced old barren reason from my bed,
And took the daughter of the vine to spouse.
OMAR KHAYYÁM—*Rubaiyat.*

The feast of reason and the flow of soul.
POPE.

Who reasons wisely is not therefore wise;
His pride in reasoning, not in acting lies.
POPE—*Moral Essays.*

Reason is an historian, but the passions are actors.
RIVAROL.

This is our chief bane, that we live not according to the light of reason, but after the fashion of others.
SENECA.

Every why hath a wherefore.
SHAKESPEARE—*Comedy of Errors.* Act II. Sc. 2.

I have no other but a woman's reason.
I think him so because I think him so.
SHAKESPEARE—*Two Gentlemen of Verona.* Act I. Sc. 2.

While Reason drew the plan, the Heart inform'd
The moral page and Fancy lent it grace.
THOMSON—*Liberty.*

Many are destined to reason wrongly; others, not to reason at all; and others, to persecute those who do reason.
VOLTAIRE.

REBELLION

Men seldom, or rather never for a length of time and deliberately, rebel against anything that does not deserve rebelling against.
CARLYLE—*Essays.*

Rebellion to tyrants is obedience to God.
Motto on Jefferson's seal.

A little rebellion now and then . . . is a medicine necessary for the sound health of government.
THOMAS JEFFERSON—*Letter to Madison.*

The only justification of rebellion is success.
THOMAS B. REED—*Speech, 1878.*

REFLECTION

The learn'd reflect on what before they knew.
POPE—*Essay on Criticism.*

REFORM

Reforms should begin at home and stay there.
ANONYMOUS.

At twenty a man is full of fight and hope. He wants to reform the world. When he's seventy he still wants to reform the world, but he knows he can't.
CLARENCE DARROW.

But 'tis the talent of our English nation,
Still to be plotting some new reformation.
DRYDEN.

Sweating, slums, and sense of semi-slavery in labour, must go. We must cultivate a sense of manhood by treating men as men.
LLOYD GEORGE—*Speech, 1919.*

An indefinable something is to be done, in a way nobody knows how, at a time nobody knows when, that will accomplish nobody knows what.
THOMAS B. REED.

REGRET

No simple word
That shall be uttered at our mirthful board,
Shall make us sad next morning; or affright
The liberty that we'll enjoy to-night.
BEN JONSON.

O lost days of delight, that are wasted in doubting and waiting!
O lost hours and days in which we might have been happy!
LONGFELLOW—*Tales of a Wayside Inn.*

For who, alas! has lived,
Nor in the watches of the night recalled
Words he has wished unsaid and deeds undone.
SAMUEL ROGERS—*Reflections.*

RELIGION

Children of men! the unseen Power, whose eye
Forever doth accompany mankind,
Hath look'd on no religion scornfully
That men did ever find.
MATTHEW ARNOLD—*Progress.*

There was never law, or sect, or opinion did so much magnify goodness, as the Christian religion doth.
BACON—*Essays.*

Speak low to me, my Saviour, low and sweet
From out the hallelujahs, sweet and low,
Lest I should fear and fall, and miss Thee so
Who art not missed by any that entreat.
E. B. BROWNING—*Comfort.*

There's naught, no doubt, so much the spirit calms as rum and true religion.
BYRON—*Don Juan.*

His religion at best is an anxious wish, —like that of Rabelais, a great Perhaps.
CARLYLE—*Burns.*

Men will wrangle for religion; write for it; fight for it; die for it; anything but—live for it.
C. C. COLTON—*Lacon.*

Religion, if in heavenly truths attired,
Needs only to be seen to be admired.
COWPER—*Expostulation.*

The Cross!
There, and there only (though the deist rave,
And Atheist, if Earth bears so base a slave);
There and there only, is the power to save.
COWPER—*The Progress of Error.*

"As for that," said Waldenshare, "sensible men are all of the same religion." "Pray, what is that?" inquired the Prince. "Sensible men never tell."
DISRAELI—*Endymion.*

Religion should be the rule of life, not a casual incident of it.
DISRAELI.

You can and you can't,—You shall and you shan't—You will and you won't—And you will be damned if you do—And you will be damned if you don't.
Dow ("Crazy Dow") defining Calvinism.

If men are so wicked with religion, what would they be without it?
FRANKLIN.

Sacrifice is the first element of religion, and resolves itself in theological language into the love of God.
FROUDE—*Short Studies on Great Subjects.*

Am I my brother's keeper?
Genesis. IV. 9.

The best religion is the most tolerant.
MME. DE GIRARDIN.

We do ourselves wrong, and too meanly estimate the holiness above us, when we deem that any act or enjoyment good in itself, is not good to do religiously.
HAWTHORNE—*Marble Faun.*

From Greenland's icy mountains,
From India's coral strand,
Where Afric's sunny fountains
Roll down their golden sand;
From many an ancient river,
From many a palmy plain,
They call us to deliver
Their land from error's chain.
REGINALD HEBER — *Missionary Hymn.*

Religion is not a dogma, nor an emotion, but a service.
ROSWELL D. HITCHCOCK.

No solemn, sanctimonious face I pull,
Nor think I'm pious when I'm only bilious—
Nor study in my sanctum supercilious
To frame a Sabbath Bill or forge a Bull.
HOOD—*Ode to Rae Wilson.*

Should all the banks of Europe crash,
The bank of England smash,
Bring all your notes to Zion's bank,
You're sure to get your cash.
HENRY HOYT—*Zion's Bank, 1857.*

I am for religion against religions.
VICTOR HUGO—*Les Misérables.*

I belong to the Great Church which holds the world within its starlit aisles; that claims the great and good of every race and clime; that finds with joy the grain of gold in every creed, and floods with light and love the germs of good in every soul.
ROBERT G. INGERSOLL.

My creed is this:
Happiness is the only good.
The place to be happy is here.
The time to be happy is now.
The way to be happy is to help make others so.
ROBERT G. INGERSOLL.

Sir, I think all Christians, whether Papists or Protestants, agree in the essential articles, and that their religious differences are trivial, and rather political than religious.
SAMUEL JOHNSON—*Boswell's Life of Johnson.*

To be of no Church is dangerous.
SAMUEL JOHNSON—*Life of Milton.*

Religious contention is the devil's harvest.
LA FONTAINE.

Other hope had she none, nor wish in life, but to follow
Meekly, with reverent steps, the sacred feet of her Saviour.
LONGFELLOW—*Evangeline.*

Puritanism, believing itself quick with the seed of religious liberty, laid, without knowing it, the egg of democracy.
LOWELL—*Among My Books.*

How many evils has religion caused!
LUCRETIUS.

Blessed is the man that hath not walked in the way of the Sacramentarians, nor sat in the seat of the Zwinglians, nor followed the Council of the Zurichers.
LUTHER—*Parody of First Psalm.*

The Puritan hated bear-baiting, not because it gave pain to the bear, but because it gave pleasure to the spectators.
MACAULAY—*History of England.*

No pain, no palm; no thorns, no throne; no gall, no glory; no cross, no crown.
WILLIAM PENN.

The Puritan did not stop to think; he recognized God in his soul, and acted.
WENDELL PHILLIPS.

Religion, blushing, veils her sacred fires,
And unawares Morality expires.
POPE—*The Dunciad.*

So upright Quakers please both man and God.
POPE—*The Dunciad.*

For virtue's self may too much zeal be had;
The worst of madmen is a saint run mad.
POPE—*To Murray.*

I think while zealots fast and frown,
And fight for two or seven,
That there are fifty roads to town,
And rather more to Heaven.
PRAED—*Chant of Brazen Head.*

He that hath no cross deserves no crown.
QUARLES—*Esther.*

Religion is like the fashion, one man wears his doublet slashed, another laced, another plain; but every man has a doublet; so every man has a religion. We differ about the trimming.
JOHN SELDEN—*Table Talk, 1696.*

I always thought
It was both impious and unnatural
That such immanity and bloody strife
Should reign among professors of one faith.

SHAKESPEARE—*Henry VI.* Pt. I. Act V. Sc. 1.

A religious life is a struggle and not a hymn.

MME. DE STAËL—*Corinne.*

Religion has nothing more to fear than not being sufficiently understood.

STANISLAUS (King of Poland)—*Maxims.*

What religion is he of?
Why, he is an Anythingarian.

SWIFT—*Polite Conversation.*

We have enough religion to make us hate, but not enough to make us love one another.

SWIFT—*Thoughts on Various Subjects.*

When I can read my title clear
To mansions in the skies,
I'll bid farewell to every fear,
And wipe my weeping eyes.

WATTS—*Songs and Hymns.*

The world has a thousand creeds, and never a one have I;
Nor church of my own, though a million spires are pointing the way on high.
But I float on the bosom of faith, that bears me along like a river;
And the lamp of my soul is alight with love, for life, and the world, and the Giver.

ELLA WHEELER WILCOX—*Heresy.*

So many gods, so many creeds—
So many paths that wind and wind
While just the art of being kind
Is all the sad world needs.

ELLA WHEELER WILCOX—*The World's Need.*

REMORSE

Remorse turns us against ourselves.

CHAMFORT.

Remorse weeps tears of blood.

COLERIDGE.

God speaks to our hearts through the voice of remorse.

DE BERNIS.

Man, wretched man, whene'er he stoops to sin,
Feels, with the act, a strong remorse within.

JUVENAL.

High minds, of native pride and force,
Most deeply feel thy pangs, Remorse;
Fear, for their scourge, mean villains have,
Thou art the torturer of the brave!

SCOTT—*Marmion.*

REPENTANCE

O ye powers that search
The heart of man, and weigh his inmost thoughts,
If I have done amiss, impute it not!
The best may err, but you are good.

ADDISON—*Cato.*

To err is human, but the contrition felt for the crime distinguishes the virtuous from the wicked.

ALFIERI.

Before God can deliver us from ourselves, we must undeceive ourselves.

ST. AUGUSTINE.

True repentance also involves reform.

HOSEA BALLOU.

What is past is past. There is a future left to all men, who have the virtue to repent and the energy to atone.

BULWER-LYTTON.

If you would be good, first believe that you are bad.

EPICTETUS.

Repentance is not so much remorse for what we have done as the fear of consequences.

LA ROCHEFOUCAULD.

God dropped a spark down into everyone,
And if we find and fan it to a blaze,
It'll spring up and glow, like—like the sun,
And light the wandering out of stony ways.

MASEFIELD—*Widow in the Bye Street.*

The dream is short, repentance long.
SCHILLER.

But with the morning cool repentance came.
SCOTT—*Rob Roy.*

It is never too late to turn from the errors of our ways:
He who repents of his sins is almost innocent.
SENECA.

Repentance is accepted remorse.
MADAME SWETCHINE.

Every one goes astray, but the least imprudent are they who repent the soonest.
VOLTAIRE—*Nanine.*

And while the lamp holds out to burn,
The vilest sinner may return.
ISAAC WATTS—*Hymns and Spiritual Songs.*

REPOSE

What sweet delight a quiet life affords.
DRUMMOND.

When a man finds not repose in himself it is in vain for him to seek it elsewhere.
From the French.

Vulgar people can't be still.
HOLMES.

Too much rest itself becomes a pain.
HOMER.

The best of men have ever loved repose:
They hate to mingle in the filthy fray;
Where the soul sours, and gradual rancour grows,
Imbitter'd more from peevish day to day.
THOMSON—*The Castle of Indolence.*

REPUTATION

It is a maxim with me that no man was ever written out of reputation but by himself.
RICHARD BENTLEY—Monk's *Life of Bentley.*

To disregard what the world thinks of us is not only arrogant but utterly shameless.
CICERO.

How many people live on the reputation of the reputation they might have made!
HOLMES.

That man is thought a dangerous knave,
Or zealot plotting crime,
Who for advancement of his kind
Is wiser than his time.
LORD HOUGHTON (Monckton Milnes)—*Men of Old.*

Reputations, like beavers and cloaks, shall last some people twice the time of others.
DOUGLAS JERROLD.

How many worthy men have we seen survive their own reputation!
MONTAIGNE—*Essays.*

Reputation is an idle and most false imposition; oft got without merit, and lost without deserving.
SHAKESPEARE—*Othello.* Act II. Sc. 3.

The purest treasure mortal times afford
Is spotless reputation; that away,
Men are but gilded loam or painted clay.
SHAKESPEARE—*Richard II.* Act I. Sc. 1.

The way to gain a good reputation is to endeavor to be what you desire to appear.
SOCRATES.

The reputation of a man is like his shadow,—gigantic when it precedes him, and pygmy in its proportions when it follows.
TALLEYRAND.

Associate with men of good quality, if you esteem your own reputation; for it is better to be alone than in bad company.
WASHINGTON.

RESIGNATION

Give what thou canst, without thee we are poor;
And with thee rich, take what thou wilt away.
COWPER—*The Task.*

Dare to look up to God and say, Deal with me in the future as Thou wilt; I am of the same mind as Thou art; I am Thine; I refuse nothing that pleases Thee; lead me where Thou wilt; clothe me in any dress Thou choosest.
EPICTETUS—*Discourses.*

Bends to the grave with unperceived decay,
While resignation gently slopes the way
And, all his prospects brightening to the last,
His heaven commences ere the world be past.
GOLDSMITH—*Deserted Village.*

To will what God doth will, that is the only science
That gives us any rest.
MALHERBE—*Consolation.*

That's best
Which God sends. 'Twas His will: it is mine.
OWEN MEREDITH (Lord Lytton)—*Lucile.*

Let that please man which has pleased God.
SENECA.

It seem'd so hard at first, mother, to leave the blessed sun,
And now it seems as hard to stay—and yet His will be done!
But still I think it can't be long before I find release;
And that good man, the clergyman, has told me words of peace.
TENNYSON—*The May-Queen.*

RESOLUTION

Every tub must stand upon its own bottom.
BUNYAN.

I am in earnest—I will not equivocate—I will not excuse—I will not retreat a single inch *and I will be heard.*
WILLIAM LLOYD GARRISON—*Salutatory of the Liberator, 1831.*

In truth there is no such thing in man's nature as a settled and full resolve either for good or evil, except at the very moment of execution.
HAWTHORNE—*Twice-Told Tales.*

Resolve, and thou art free.
LONGFELLOW.

Tell your master that if there were as many devils at Worms as tiles on its roofs, I would enter.
LUTHER.

Never tell your resolution beforehand.
JOHN SELDEN—*Table Talk.*

REST

In the rest of Nirvana all sorrows surcease:
Only Buddha can guide to that city of Peace
Whose inhabitants have the eternal release.
WILLIAM R. ALGER — *Oriental Poetry.*

Absence of occupation is not rest;
A mind quite vacant is a mind distress'd.
COWPER—*Retirement.*

Rest is not quitting the busy career;
Rest is the fitting of self to its sphere.
JOHN S. DWIGHT—*True Rest.*

Calm on the bosom of thy God,
Fair spirit! rest thee now!
MRS. HEMANS—*Siege of Valencia.*

For too much rest itself becomes a pain.
HOMER—*Odyssey.*

Take rest; a field that has rested gives a bountiful crop.
OVID.

Life's race well run,
Life's work well done,
Life's victory won,
Now cometh rest.
DR. EDWARD HAZEN PARKER.

Master, I've filled my contract, wrought in Thy many lands;
Not by my sins wilt Thou judge me, but by the work of my hands.
Master, I've done Thy bidding, and the light is low in the west,
And the long, long shift is over . . .
Master, I've earned it—Rest.
ROBERT SERVICE—*Song of the Wage Slave.*

The camel at the close of day
Kneels down upon the sandy plain
To have his burden lifted off
And rest again.
ANNA TEMPLE—*Kneeling Camel.*

Thou hadst, for weary feet, the gift of rest.
WILLIAM WATSON—*Wordsworth's Grave.*

RESULT

The thorns which I have reap'd are of the tree
I planted—they have torn me—and I bleed!
I should have known what fruit would spring from such a seed.
BYRON—*Childe Harold.*

As thou sowest, so shalt thou reap.
CICERO.

A bad ending follows a bad beginning.
EURIPIDES.

So comes a reck'ning when the banquet's o'er,
The dreadful reck'ning, and men smile no more.
GAY.

They have sown the wind, and they shall reap the whirlwind.
Hosea. VIII. 7.

By their fruits ye shall know them.
Matthew. VII. 20.

What dire offense from am'rous causes springs,
What mighty contests rise from trivial things.
POPE—*Rape of the Lock.*

Whoso diggeth a pit shall fall therein.
Proverbs. XXVI. 27.

Contentions fierce,
Ardent, and dire, spring from no petty cause.
SCOTT—*Peveril of the Peak.*

RESURRECTION

Earth to earth, ashes to ashes, dust to dust, in sure and certain hope of the resurrection.
Book of Common Prayer—Burial of the Dead.

The last loud trumpet's wondrous sound,
Shall thro' the rending tombs rebound,
And wake the nations under ground.
WENTWORTH DILLON—*On the Day of Judgment.*

The trumpet! the trumpet! the dead have all heard:
Lo, the depths of the stone-cover'd charnels are stirr'd:
From the sea, from the land, from the south and the north,
The vast generations of man are come forth.
MILMAN—*Hymns for Church Service.*

Shall man alone, for whom all else revives,
No resurrection know? Shall man alone,
Imperial man! be sown in barren ground,
Less privileged than grain, on which he feeds?
YOUNG—*Night Thoughts.*

RETALIATION

I am accustomed to pay men back in their own coin.
BISMARCK.

And would'st thou evil for his good repay?
HOMER—*Odyssey.*

RETRIBUTION

Whatsoever a man soweth, that shall he also reap.
Galatians. VI. 7.

They have sown the wind, and they shall reap the whirlwind.
Hosea. VIII. 7.

Though the mills of God grind slowly,
yet they grind exceedingly small;
Though with patience He stands waiting, with exactness grinds He all.
FRIEDRICH VON LOGAU—*Retribution*.

To be left alone
And face to face with my own crime,
had been
Just retribution.
LONGFELLOW—*Masque of Pandora*.

The divine wrath is slow indeed in vengeance, but it makes up for its tardiness by the severity of the punishment.
VALERIUS MAXIMUS.

The way of transgressors is hard.
Proverbs. XIII. 15.

REVELATION

'Tis Revelation satisfies all doubts,
Explains all mysteries except her own,
And so illuminates the path of life,
That fools discover it, and stray no
more.
COWPER—*The Task*.

Nature is a revelation of God;
Art a revelation of man.
LONGFELLOW—*Hyperion*.

REVENGE

The best sort of revenge is not to be like him who did the injury.
MARCUS ANTONINUS.

In taking revenge a man is but equal to his enemy, but in passing it over he is his superior.
BACON.

Revenge is a kind of wild justice; which the more man's nature runs to, the more ought law to weed it out.
BACON—*Of Revenge*.

Women do most delight in revenge.
SIR THOMAS BROWNE — *Christian Morals*.

'Tis more noble to forgive, and more manly to despise, than to revenge an Injury.
FRANKLIN—*Poor Richard*.

Revenge is sweeter than life itself. So think fools.
JUVENAL.

Vengeance is sweet.
WILLIAM PAINTER—*The Palace of Pleasure*.

Not to be provoked is best; but if moved, never correct till the fume is spent; for every stroke our fury strikes is sure to hit ourselves at last.
WILLIAM PENN.

Those who plot the destruction of others often fall themselves.
PHAEDRUS—*Fables*.

Vengeance to God alone belongs;
But, when I think of all my wrongs,
My blood is liquid flame!
SCOTT—*Marmion*.

Revenge is an inhuman word.
SENECA.

REVOLUTION

Revolutions are not about trifles, but spring from trifles.
ARISTOTLE—*Politics*.

A reform is a correction of abuses; a revolution is a transfer of power.
BULWER-LYTTON.

Do you think then that revolutions are made with rose water?
SÉBASTIAN CHAMFORT to Marmontel, on the excesses of the Revolution.

At last I perceive that in revolutions the supreme power finally rests with the most abandoned.
DANTON.

It is not a revolt, it is a revolution.
DUC DE LIANCOURT to Louis XVI, July 14, 1789.

This country, with its institutions, belongs to the people who inhabit it. Whenever they shall grow weary of the existing government they can exercise their constitutional right of amending it, or their revolutionary right to dismember or overthrow it.

LINCOLN—*Inaugural Address, 1861.*

Let the ruling classes tremble at a Communist revolution. The proletarians have nothing to lose but their chains. They have a world to win. Working men of all countries, unite!

KARL MARX and FRIEDRICH ENGELS —*The Communist Manifesto.*

Great revolutions are the work rather of principles than of bayonets, and are achieved first in the moral, and afterwards in the material sphere.

MAZZINI.

I am the signet which marks the page where the revolution has been stopped; but when I die it will turn the page and resume its course.

NAPOLEON to Count Molé.

Revolutions are not made; they come.

WENDELL PHILLIPS.

When Marmontel was regretting the excesses of the period, Chamfort asked: "Do you think that revolutions are made with rose-water?"

WENDELL PHILLIPS.

I know and all the world knows, that revolutions never go backwards.

SEWARD—*Speech on the Irrepressible Conflict.*

RICHES

In this world, it is not what we take up, but what we give up, that makes us rich.

HENRY WARD BEECHER.

The rich fool is like a pig that is choked by its own fat.

CONFUCIUS.

Ah, if the rich were rich as the poor fancy riches!

EMERSON.

A man's true wealth is the good he does in this world.

MOHAMMED.

I am rich beyond the dreams of avarice.

EDWARD MOORE—*The Gamester.*

Nothing is so hard for those who abound in riches as to conceive how others can be in want.

SWIFT.

That man is the richest whose pleasures are the cheapest.

THOREAU.

RIDICULE

If ridicule were employed to laugh men out of vice and folly, it might be of some use.

ADDISON.

Cervantes smiled Spain's chivalry away.

BYRON.

Ridicule more often settles things more thoroughly and better than acrimony.

HORACE.

There is only one step from the sublime to the ridiculous.

NAPOLEON.

The sublime and the ridiculous are often so nearly related that it is difficult to class them separately. One step above the sublime makes the ridiculous, and one step above the ridiculous makes the sublime again.

THOMAS PAINE—*The Age of Reason.*

'Twas the saying of an ancient sage that humour was the only test of gravity, and gravity of humour. For a subject which would not bear raillery was suspicious; and a jest which would not bear a serious examination was certainly false wit.

SHAFTESBURY—*Characteristics.*

I have always made one prayer to God, a very short one. Here it is: "My God, make our enemies very ridiculous!" God has granted it to me.

VOLTAIRE.

RIGHT

The glittering and sounding generalities of natural right which make up the declaration of independence.

RUFUS CHOATE.

Sir, I would rather be right than be President.
HENRY CLAY—*Speech, 1850.*

He will hew to the line of right, let the chips fly where they may.
ROSCOE CONKLING—*Speech, 1880.*

But 'twas a maxim he had often tried,
That right was right, and there he would abide.
CRABBE—*Tales.*

Be sure you are right, then go ahead.
DAVID CROCKETT.

For right is right, since God is God,
And right the day must win;
To doubt would be disloyalty,
To falter would be sin.
F. W. FABER—*The Right Must Win.*

Let us have faith that Right makes Might, and in that faith let us to the end dare to do our duty as we understand it.
ABRAHAM LINCOLN — *Address, 1859.*

With malice toward none, with charity for all, with firmness in the right, as God gives us to see the right.
ABRAHAM LINCOLN—*Second Inaugural Address.*

Might was the measure of right.
LUCAN.

Right is the eternal sun; the world cannot delay its coming.
WENDELL PHILLIPS.

All Nature is but art unknown to thee;
All chance direction, which thou canst not see;
All discord, harmony not understood;
All partial evil, universal good;
And spite of pride, in erring reason's spite,
One truth is clear, Whatever is is right.
POPE—*Essay on Man.*

The proof of a thing's being right is that it has power over the heart; that it excites us, wins us, or helps us.
RUSKIN.

Heaven itself has ordained the right.
WASHINGTON.

No question is ever settled
Until it is settled right.
ELLA WHEELER WILCOX.

RIGHTEOUSNESS

Be not righteous overmuch.
Ecclesiastes. VII. 16.

Every one that useth milk is unskilful in the word of righteousness: for he is a babe.
Hebrews. V. 13.

A righteous man regardeth the life of his beast; but the tender mercies of the wicked are cruel.
Proverbs. XII. 10.

Righteousness exalteth a nation.
Proverbs. XIV. 34.

I have been young, and now am old; yet have I not seen the righteous forsaken, nor his seed begging bread.
Psalms. XXXVII. 25.

The righteous shall flourish like the palm-tree: he shall grow like a cedar in Lebanon.
Psalms. XCII. 12.

RIGHTS

Among the natural rights of the colonists are these: First a right to life, secondly to liberty, thirdly to property; together with the right to defend them in the best manner they can.
SAMUEL ADAMS.

We hold these truths to be self-evident,—that all men are created equal; that they are endowed by their Creator with certain unalienable rights; that among these are Life, Liberty, and the pursuit of happiness.
Declaration of Independence.

Wherever there is a human being, I see God-given rights inherent in that being, whatever may be the sex or complexion.
WILLIAM LLOYD GARRISON.

The equal right of all men to the use of land is as clear as their equal right to breathe the air—it is a right proclaimed by the fact of their existence. For we cannot suppose that some men have a right to be in this world, and others no right.

HENRY GEORGE—*Progress and Poverty.*

Equal rights for all, special privileges for none.

THOMAS JEFFERSON.

Every man has by the law of nature a right to such a waste portion of the earth as is necessary for his subsistence.

MORE—*Utopia.*

RIVER

Is it not better, then, to be alone,
And love Earth only for its earthly sake?
By the blue rushing of the arrowy Rhone
Or the pure bosom of its nursing lake.

BYRON—*Childe Harold.*

And see the rivers how they run
Through woods and meads, in shade and sun,
Sometimes swift, sometimes slow,—
Wave succeeding wave, they go
A various journey to the deep,
Like human life to endless sleep!

JOHN DYER—*Grongar Hill.*

Way down upon de Swanee Ribber,
Far, far away,
Dere's whar ma heart am turning ebber,
Dere's whar de old folks stay.
All up and down the whole creation,
Sadly I roam,
Still longing for de old plantation,
And for de old folks at home.

STEPHEN COLLINS FOSTER — *Old Folks at Home.*

The air grows cool and darkles,
The Rhine flows calmly on;
The mountain summit sparkles
In the light of the setting sun.

HEINE—*The Lorelei.*

Thou hast fair forms that move
With queenly tread;
Thou hast proud fanes above
Thy mighty dead.
Yet wears thy Tiber's shore
A mournful mien:—
Rome, Rome, thou art no more
As thou hast been.

FELICIA D. HEMANS—*Roman Girl's Song.*

It flows through old hushed Egypt and its sands,
Like some grave mighty thought threading a dream.

LEIGH HUNT—*The Nile.*

The Nile, forever new and old,
Among the living and the dead,
Its mighty, mystic stream has rolled.

LONGFELLOW—*Christus.*

He who does not know his way to the sea should take a river for his guide.

PLAUTUS.

Serene yet strong, majestic yet sedate,
Swift without violence, without terror great.

PRIOR—*Carmen Seculare.*

Never did sun more beautifully steep
In his first splendor, valley, rock, or hill;
Ne'er saw I, never felt, a calm so deep!
The river glideth at his own sweet will.
Dear God! the very houses seem asleep;
And all that mighty heart is lying still!

WORDSWORTH — *Composed upon Westminster Bridge.*

ROMANCE

Romances paint at full length people's wooings
But only give a bust of marriages:
For no one cares for matrimonial cooings.
There's nothing wrong in a connubial kiss.
Think you, if Laura had been Petrarch's wife,
He would have written sonnets all his life?

BYRON—*Don Juan.*

Parent of golden dreams, Romance!
Auspicious queen of childish joys,
Who lead'st along, in airy dance,
Thy votive train of girls and boys.
BYRON—*To Romance.*

Romance is the poetry of literature.
MADAME NECKER.

There is no such thing as romance in our day, women have become too brilliant; nothing spoils a romance so much as a sense of humor in the woman.
WILDE—*A Woman of No Importance.*

ROME

If you are at Rome live in the Roman style; if you are elsewhere live as they live elsewhere.
ST. AMBROSE to St. Augustine.

Rome was not built in a day.
ANONYMOUS.

You cheer my heart, who build as if Rome would be eternal.
AUGUSTUS CAESAR to Piso.

All roads lead to Rome; but our antagonists think we should choose different paths.
LA FONTAINE.

Would that the Roman people had but one neck!
SUETONIUS.

ROSE

O rose, who dares to name thee?
No longer roseate now, nor soft, nor sweet,
But pale, and hard, and dry, as stubblewheat,—
Kept seven years in a drawer, thy titles shame thee.
E. B. BROWNING—*A Dead Rose.*

Loveliest of lovely things are they
On earth that soonest pass away.
The rose that lives its little hour
Is prized beyond the sculptured flower.
BRYANT—*A Scene on the Banks of the Hudson.*

I'll pu' the budding rose, when Phoebus peeps in view,
For it's like a baumy kiss o'er her sweet bonnie mou'!
BURNS—*The Posie.*

When love came first to earth, the Spring
Spread rose-beds to receive him.
CAMPBELL—*When Love Came First to Earth.*

It never will rain roses: when we want
To have more roses we must plant more trees.
GEORGE ELIOT—*Spanish Gypsy.*

But ne'er the rose without the thorn.
HERRICK—*The Rose.*

Wild-rose, Sweetbriar, Eglantine,
All these pretty names are mine,
And scent in every leaf is mine,
And a leaf for all is mine,
And the scent—Oh, that's divine!
Happy-sweet and pungent fine,
Pure as dew, and pick'd as wine.
LEIGH HUNT—*Songs and Chorus of the Flowers.*

But the rose leaves herself upon the brier,
For winds to kiss and grateful bees to feed.
KEATS—*On Fame.*

And I will make thee beds of roses,
And a thousand fragrant posies.
MARLOWE—*The Passionate Shepherd to His Love.*

Flowers of all hue, and without thorn the rose.
MILTON—*Paradise Lost.*

Rose of the desert! thou art to me
An emblem of stainless purity;—
Of those who, keeping their garments white,
Walk on through life with steps aright.
D. M. MOIR—*The White Rose.*

Two rose-buds scarcely show'd their hue,
In sweet communion grew,
Together hailed the morning ray
And drank the evening dew.
MONTGOMERY—*The Roses.*

'Tis the last rose of summer,
Left blooming alone.
Moore—*Last Rose of Summer.*

What would the rose with all her pride be worth,
Were there no sun to call her brightness forth?
Moore—*Love Alone.*

Rose! thou art the sweetest flower,
That ever drank the amber shower;
Rose! thou art the fondest child
Of dimpled Spring, the wood-nymph wild.
Moore—*Odes of Anacreon.*

Each Morn a thousand Roses brings, you say;
Yes, but where leaves the Rose of Yesterday?
Omar Khayyám—*Rubaiyat.*

The sweetest flower that blows,
I give you as we part.
For you it is a rose
For me it is my heart.
Frederick Peterson—*At Parting.*

There was never a daughter of Eve but once ere the tale of her years be done,
Shall know the scent of the Eden Rose, but once beneath the sun;
Though the years may bring her joy or pain, fame, sorrow or sacrifice,
The hour that brought her the scent of the Rose, she lived it in Paradise.
Susan K. Phillips—*The Eden Rose.*

There is no gathering the rose without being pricked by the thorns.
Pilpay—*The Two Travellers.*

Like roses, that in deserts bloom and die.
Pope—*Rape of the Lock.*

Little tents of odour, where the bee reposes,
Swooning in sweetness of the bed he dreams upon.
Thomas Buchanan Read—*The New Pastoral.*

The Rose is fairest when 'tis budding new,
And hope is brightest when it dawns from fears;
The rose is sweetest wash'd with morning dew,
And love is loveliest when embalm'd in tears.
Scott—*Lady of the Lake.*

And the rose like a nymph to the bath addrest,
Which unveiled the depth of her glowing breast,
Till, fold after fold, to the fainting air,
The soul of her beauty and love lay bare.
Shelley—*The Sensitive Plant.*

Let us crown ourselves with rosebuds before they be whithered.
Wisdom of Solomon. II. 8.

The year of the rose is brief;
From the first blade blown to the sheaf,
From the thin green leaf to the gold,
It has time to be sweet and grow old,
To triumph and leave not a leaf.
Swinburne—*The Year of the Rose.*

And half in shade and half in sun;
The Rose sat in her bower,
With a passionate thrill in her crimson heart.
Bayard Taylor—*Poems of the Orient.*

The fairest things have fleetest end:
Their scent survives their close,
But the rose's scent is bitterness
To him that loved the rose!
Francis Thompson—*Daisy.*

The garden rose may richly bloom
In cultured soil and genial air,
To cloud the light of Fashion's room
Or droop in beauty's midnight hair,
In lonelier grace, to sun and dew
The sweetbrier on the hillside shows
Its single leaf and fainter hue,
Untrained and wildly free, yet still a sister rose!
Whittier—*The Bride of Pennacook.*

ROYALTY

Ten poor men sleep in peace on one straw heap, as Saadi sings,
But the immensest empire is too narrow for two kings.
WILLIAM R. ALGER — *Oriental Poetry.*

The king reigns but does not govern.
BISMARCK.

That the king can do no wrong is a necessary and fundamental principle of the English constitution.
BLACKSTONE.

Many a crown
Covers bald foreheads.
E. B. BROWNING—*Aurora Leigh.*

Every noble crown is, and on Earth will forever be, a crown of thorns.
CARLYLE—*Past and Present.*

Now let us sing, long live the king.
COWPER—*History of John Gilpin.*

Who made thee a prince and a judge over us?
Exodus. II. 14.

Er Kaiser of dis Faderland,
Und Gott on high all dings commands,
We two—ach! Don't you understand?
Myself—und Gott.
A. M. R. GORDON (McGregor Rose)—*Kaiser & Co.* Later called *Hoch der Kaiser.*

The trappings of a monarchy would set up an ordinary commonwealth.
SAMUEL JOHNSON—*Life of Milton.*

Ah! vainest of all things
Is the gratitude of kings.
LONGFELLOW—*Belisarius.*

I am the State.
LOUIS XIV OF FRANCE.

The King is dead! Long live the King!
PARDOE—*Life of Louis XIV.*

Put not your trust in princes.
Psalms. CXLVI. 3.

Here lies our sovereign lord, the king,
Whose word no man relies on,
Who never said a foolish thing,
And never did a wise one.
ROCHESTER—*To Charles II.*

Uneasy lies the head that wears a crown.
SHAKESPEARE—*Henry IV.* Pt. II. Act III. Sc. 1.

Ay, every inch a king.
SHAKESPEARE—*King Lear.* Act IV. Sc. 6.

I give this heavy weight from off my head,
And this unwieldy sceptre from my hand,
The pride of kingly sway from out my heart;
With mine own tears I wash away my value,
With mine own hands I give away my crown,
With mine own tongue deny my sacred state,
With mine own breath release all duteous oaths.
SHAKESPEARE—*Richard II.* Act V. Sc. 3.

RUIN

While in the progress of their long decay,
Thrones sink to dust, and nations pass away.
EARL OF CARLISLE—*On the Ruins of Paestum.*

The ruins of himself! now worn away
With age, yet still majestic in decay.
HOMER—*Odyssey.*

History fades into fable; fact becomes clouded with doubt and controversy; the inscription moulders from the tablet: the statue falls from the pedestal. Columns, arches, pyramids, what are they but heaps of sand; and their epitaphs, but characters written in the dust?
IRVING—*The Sketch Book.*

Babylon is fallen, is fallen.
Isaiah. XXI. 9.

For such a numerous host
Fled not in silence through the frighted deep
With ruin upon ruin, rout on rout,
Confusion worse confounded.
MILTON—*Paradise Lost.*

Red ruin and the breaking-up of all.
TENNYSON—*Idylls of the King.*

Behold this ruin! 'Twas a skull
Once of ethereal spirit full!
This narrow cell was Life's retreat;
This place was Thought's mysterious seat!
What beauteous pictures fill'd that spot,
What dreams of pleasure, long forgot!
Nor Love, nor Joy, nor Hope, nor Fear,
Has left one trace, one record here.
ANNA JANE VARDILL (Mrs. James Niven). 1816.

Who knows but that hereafter some traveller like myself will sit down upon the banks of the Seine, the Thames, or the Zuyder Zee, where now in the tumult of enjoyment, the heart and the eyes are too slow to take in the multitude of sensations? Who knows but he will sit down solitary amid silent ruins, and weep a people inurned and their greatness changed into an empty name?
VOLNEY—*Ruins.*

I do love these ancient ruins.
We never tread upon them but we set
Our foot upon some reverend history.
JOHN WEBSTER—*The Duchess of Malfi.*

RUMOR

The flying rumours gather'd as they roll'd,
Scarce any tale was sooner heard than told;
And all who told it added something new.
And all who heard it made enlargements too.
POPE—*Temple of Fame.*

I cannot tell how the truth may be;
I say the tale as 'twas said to me.
SCOTT—*Lay of the Last Minstrel.*

Rumour doth double, like the voice and echo,
The numbers of the fear'd.
SHAKESPEARE—*Henry IV.* Pt. II. Act III. Sc. 1.

The rolling fictions grow in strength and size,
Each author adding to the former lies.
SWIFT.

What some invent the rest enlarge.
SWIFT.

Tattlers also and busybodies, speaking things which they ought not.
I Timothy. V. 13.

S

SABBATH

Thou art my single day, God lends to leaven
What were all earth else, with a feel of heaven.
BROWNING—*Pippa Passes.*

Of all the days that's in the week,
I dearly love but one day,
And that's the day that comes betwixt
A Saturday and Monday.
HENRY CAREY—*Sally in Our Alley.*

How still the morning of the hallow'd day!
Mute is the voice of rural labour, hush'd
The ploughboy's whistle, and the milkmaid's song.
JAMES GRAHAME—*The Sabbath.*

Gently on tiptoe Sunday creeps,
Cheerfully from the stars he peeps,
Mortals are all asleep below,
None in the village hears him go;
E'en chanticleer keeps very still,
For Sunday whispered, 'twas his will.
JOHN PETER HEBEL—*Sunday Morning.*

Now, really, this appears the common case
Of putting too much Sabbath into Sunday—
But what is your opinion, Mrs. Grundy?
HOOD—*An Open Question.*

Day of the Lord, as all our days should be!
LONGFELLOW—*Christus.*

The Sabbath was made for man, and not man for the Sabbath.
Mark. II. 27.

So sang they, and the empyrean rung
With Hallelujahs. Thus was Sabbath kept.
MILTON—*Paradise Lost*.

See Christians, Jews, one heavy sabbath keep,
And all the western world believe and sleep.
POPE—*Dunciad*.

SACRIFICE

It is what we give up, not what we lay up, that adds to our lasting store.
HOSEA BALLOU.

You cannot win without sacrifice.
CHARLES BUXTON.

What millions died—that Caesar might be great!
CAMPBELL—*Pleasures of Hope*.

Who lives for humanity, must be content to lose himself.
O. B. FROTHINGHAM.

He is brought as a lamb to the slaughter.
Isaiah. LIII. 7.

It is easier to sacrifice great than little things.
MONTAIGNE.

SADNESS

A feeling of sadness and longing,
That is not akin to pain,
And resembles sorrow only
As the mist resembles the rain.
LONGFELLOW—*The Day Is Done*.

We look before and after,
And pine for what is not,
Our sincerest laughter
With some pain is fraught:
Our sweetest songs are those that tell of saddest thought.
SHELLEY—*To a Skylark*.

SATIRE

A burlesque word is often a powerful sermon.
BOILEAU.

Cervantes smiled Spain's chivalry away.
BYRON.

The guerilla weapon of political warfare.
HORACE GREELEY.

Of a bitter satirist it might be said that the person or thing on which his satire fell shriveled up as if the devil had spit on it.
HAWTHORNE.

Men are more satirical from vanity than from malice.
LA ROCHEFOUCAULD.

Truth is quite beyond the reach of satire. There is so brave a simplicity in her that she can no more be made ridiculous than an oak or a pine.
LOWELL.

Satire should, like a polished razor keen,
Wound with a touch that's scarcely felt or seen.
Thine is an oyster knife, that hacks and hews;
The rage but not the talent to abuse.
LADY MARY WORTLEY MONTAGU.

Damn with faint praise, assent with civil leer,
And without sneering, teach the rest to sneer;
Willing to wound, and yet afraid to strike,
Just hint a fault, and hesitate dislike;
Alike reserv'd to blame, or to commend,
A tim'rous foe, and a suspicious friend.
POPE—*Prologue to Satires*.

Satire or sense, alas! Can Sporus feel?
Who breaks a butterfly upon a wheel?
POPE—*Prologue to Satires*.

Satire's my weapon, but I'm too discreet
To run amuck and tilt at all I meet.
POPE—*Second Book of Horace*.

Satire lies about literary men while they live and eulogy lies about them when they die.
VOLTAIRE.

In my youth I thought of writing a satire on mankind! but now in my age I think I should write an apology for them.

Horace Walpole.

SATISFACTION

Those who seek for much are left in want of much. Happy is he to whom God has given, with sparing hand, as much as is enough.

Horace.

If the crow had been satisfied to eat his prey in silence, he would have had more meat and less quarreling and envy.

Horace.

The fastidious are unfortunate: nothing can satisfy them.

La Fontaine.

He is very foolish who aims at satisfying all the world and his father.

La Fontaine.

My cup runneth over.

Psalms. XXIII. 5.

Enough is as good as a feast.

Joshua Sylvester—*Works.*

SCANDAL

Dead scandals form good subjects for dissection.

Byron—*Don Juan.*

If there is any person to whom you feel dislike, that is the person of whom you ought never to speak.

Cecil.

Scandal is what one-half the world takes pleasure in inventing, and the other half in believing.

Chatfield.

And there's a lust in man no charm can tame
Of loudly publishing our neighbour's shame;
On eagles' wings immortal scandals fly,
While virtuous actions are but born to die.

Juvenal.

I never listen to calumnies, because, if they are untrue, I run the risk of being deceived, and if they are true, of having persons not worth thinking about.

Montesquieu.

He rams his quill with scandal and with scoff,
But 'tis so very foul, it won't go off.

Young—*Epistles to Pope.*

SCIENCE

There are very few persons who pursue science with true dignity.

Sir Humphry Davy—*Consolations in Travel.*

Every great advance in science has issued from a new audacity of imagination.

John Dewey—*The Quest for Certainty.*

Steam is no stronger now than it was a hundred years ago, but it is put to better use.

Emerson.

Science and art belong to the whole world, and before them vanish the barriers of nationality.

Goethe.

Science is simply common sense at its best—that is, rigidly accurate in observation, and merciless to fallacy in logic.

Huxley.

For science is . . . like virtue, its own exceeding great reward.

Charles Kingsley—*Health and Education.*

Science is the systematic classification of experience.

George Henry Lewes.

How index-learning turns no student pale,
Yet hold the eel of science by the tail.

Pope—*Dunciad.*

One science only will one genius fit,
So vast is art, so narrow human wit.

Pope—*Essay on Criticism.*

Science is nothing but developed perception, interpreted intent, common sense rounded out and minutely articulated.

SANTAYANA—*The Life of Reason.*

Science is organized knowledge.

SPENCER—*Education.*

Science when well digested is nothing but good sense and reason.

STANISLAUS (King of Poland)—*Maxims.*

Science falsely so called.

I Timothy. VI. 20.

But beyond the bright searchlights of science,
Out of sight of the windows of sense,
Old riddles still bid us defiance,
Old questions of Why and of Whence.

W. C. D. WHETHAM—*Recent Development of Physical Science.*

SCORN

So let him stand, through ages yet unborn,
Fix'd statue on the pedestal of Scorn.

BYRON—*Curse of Minerva.*

He will laugh thee to scorn.

Ecclesiasticus. XIII. 7.

He hears
On all sides, from innumerable tongues
A dismal universal hiss, the sound
Of public scorn.

MILTON—*Paradise Lost.*

SCOTLAND

Give me but one hour of Scotland,
Let me see it ere I die.

WILLIAM E. AYTOUN.

O Scotia! my dear, my native soil!
For whom my warmest wish to heaven is sent;
Long may thy hardy sons of rustic toil
Be blest with health, and peace, and sweet content.

BURNS—*Cotter's Saturday Night.*

It's guid to be merry and wise,
It's guid to be honest and true,
It's guid to support Caledonia's cause,
And bide by the buff and the blue!

BURNS—*Here's a Health to Them That's Awa'.*

In all my travels I never met with any one Scotchman but what was a man of sense. I believe everybody of that country that has any, leaves it as fast as they can.

FRANCIS LOCKIER—*Scotchmen.*

O Caledonia! stern and wild,
Meet nurse for a poetic child!
Land of brown heath and shaggy wood,
Land of the mountain and the flood,
Land of my sires! what mortal hand
Can e'er untie the filial band,
That knits me to thy rugged strand!

SCOTT—*Lay of the Last Minstrel.*

It requires a surgical operation to get a joke well into a Scotch understanding.

SYDNEY SMITH—*Lady Holland's Memoir.*

SCRIPTURE

A glory gilds the sacred page,
Majestic like the sun,
It gives a light to every age,
It gives, but borrows none.

COWPER—*Olney Hymns.*

One day at least in every week,
The sects of every kind
Their doctrines here are sure to seek,
And just as sure to find.

AUGUSTUS DE MORGAN.

And that the Scriptures, though not everywhere
Free from corruption, or entire, or clear,
Are uncorrupt, sufficient, clear, entire
In all things which our needful faith require.

DRYDEN—*Religio Laici.*

The word unto the prophet spoken
Was writ on tablets yet unbroken:
The word by seers or sibyls told,
In groves of oak or fanes of gold,

Still floats upon the morning wind,
Still whispers to the willing mind.
EMERSON—*The Problem.*

Most wondrous book! bright candle of the Lord!
Star of Eternity! The only star
By which the bark of man could navigate
The sea of life, and gain the coast of bliss
Securely.
POLLOCK—*Course of Time.*

I have more understanding than all my teachers: for thy testimonies are my meditations.
Psalms. CXIX. 99.

Thy word is a lamp unto my feet and a light unto my path.
Psalms. CXIX. 105.

The sweet psalmist of Israel.
II Samuel. XXIII. 1.

Within that awful volume lies
The mystery of mysteries!
Happiest they of human race,
To whom God has granted grace
To read, to fear, to hope, to pray,
To lift the latch, and force the way:
And better had they ne'er been born,
Who read to doubt, or read to scorn.
SCOTT—*Monastery.*

How glad the heathens would have been,
That worship idols, wood and stone,
If they the book of God had seen.
WATTS—*Praise for the Gospel.*

The Bible is a book of faith, and a book of doctrine, and a book of morals, and a book of religion, of especial revelation from God.
DANIEL WEBSTER.

We search the world for truth; we cull
The good, the pure, the beautiful,
From all old flower fields of the soul;
And, weary seekers of the best,
We come back laden from our quest,
To find that all the sages said
Is in the Book our mothers read.
WHITTIER—*Miriam.*

SCULPTURE

Madame de Staël pronounced architecture to be frozen music; so is statuary crystallized spirituality.
ALCOTT.

It was Dante who called this noble art God's grandchild.
WASHINGTON ALLSTON.

A sculptor wields
The chisel, and the stricken marble grows
To beauty.
BRYANT—*The Flood of Years.*

Not from a vain or shallow thought
His awful Jove young Phidias brought.
EMERSON—*The Problem.*

Sculpture is more than painting. It is greater
To raise the dead to life than to create
Phantoms that seem to live.
LONGFELLOW—*Michael Angelo.*

The stone unhewn and cold
Becomes a living mould,
The more the marble wastes
The more the statue grows.
MICHELANGELO—*Sonnet.*

And the cold marble leapt to life a God.
H. H. MILMAN—*The Belvedere Apollo.*

Then marble, soften'd into life, grew warm.
POPE—*Second Book of Horace.*

The sculptor does not work for the anatomist, but for the common observer of life and nature.
RUSKIN—*True and Beautiful.*

SEASONS

Our seasons have no fixed returns,
Without our will they come and go;
At noon our sudden summer burns,
Ere sunset all is snow.
LOWELL.

Autumn to winter, winter into spring,
Spring into summer, summer into fall,—

So rolls the changing year, and so we change;
Motion so swift, we know not that we move.
D. M. MULOCK—*Immutable*.

At Christmas I no more desire a rose
Than wish a snow in May's new-fangled mirth;
But like of each thing that in season grows.
SHAKESPEARE—*Love's Labour's Lost*. Act I. Sc. 1.

January grey is here,
Like a sexton by her grave;
February bears the bier,
March with grief doth howl and rave,
And April weeps—but, O ye hours!
Follow with May's fairest flowers.
SHELLEY—*Dirge for the Year*.

Ah! well away!
Seasons flower and fade.
TENNYSON—*Every Day Hath Its Night*.

SECRECY

For this thing was not done in a corner.
Acts. XXVI. 26.

There is a skeleton in every house.
ANONYMOUS.

A man can hide all things, excepting twain—
That he is drunk, and that he is in love.
ANTIPHANES.

The secret things belong unto the Lord our God.
Deuteronomy. XXIX. 29.

Never inquire into another man's secret; but conceal that which is intrusted to you, though pressed both by wine and anger to reveal it.
HORACE.

Nothing is so oppressive as a secret: women find it difficult to keep one long: and I know a goodly number of men who are women in this regard.
LA FONTAINE.

How can we expect another to keep our secret if we cannot keep it ourselves?
LA ROCHEFOUCAULD.

Nothing is secret which shall not be made manifest.
Luke. VIII. 17.

Tell it not in Gath; publish it not in the streets of Askelon.
II Samuel. I. 20.

Let your left hand turn away what your right hand attracts.
Talmud.

SELF-EXAMINATION

As I walk'd by myself, I talk'd to myself
And myself replied to me:
And the questions myself then put to myself,
With their answers I give to thee.
BARNARD BARTON—*Colloquy with Myself*.

Go to your bosom;
Knock there, and ask your heart what it doth know.
SHAKESPEARE—*Measure for Measure*. Act II. Sc. 2.

Let not soft slumber close your eyes,
Before you've collected thrice
The train of action through the day!
Where have my feet chose out their way?
What have I learnt, where'er I've been,
From all I've heard, from all I've seen?
What have I more that's worth the knowing?
What have I done that's worth the doing?
What have I sought that I should shun?
What duty have I left undone,
Or into what new follies run?
These self-inquiries are the road
That lead to virtue and to God.
ISAAC WATTS—*Self Examination*.

SELF-LOVE

He was like a cock who thought the sun had risen to hear him crow.

GEORGE ELIOT—*Adam Bede*.

He that falls in love with himself will have no rivals.

FRANKLIN.

He who does not think too much of himself is much more esteemed than he imagines.

GOETHE.

A gentleman is one who understands and shows every mark of deference to the claims of self-love in others, and exacts it in return from them.

HAZLITT—*Table Talk*.

Self-love is the greatest of all flatterers.

LA ROCHEFOUCAULD.

Behold the fine appointment he makes with me; that man never did love any one but himself.

MME. DE MAINTENON, when Louis XIV in dying said, "We shall meet again."

I to myself am dearer than a friend.

SHAKESPEARE—*Two Gentlemen of Verona*. Act II. Sc. 6.

I am the most concerned in my own interests.

TERENCE.

This self-love is the instrument of our preservation; it resembles the provision for the perpetuity of mankind: —it is necessary, it is dear to us, it gives us pleasure, and we must conceal it.

VOLTAIRE—*Philosophical Dictionary*.

SELF-RELIANCE

Look well into thyself; there is a source which will always spring up if thou wilt always search there.

MARCUS ANTONINUS.

Doubt whom you will, but never yourself.

BOVEE.

No man should part with his own individuality and become that of another.

CHANNING.

Think wrongly, if you please, but in all cases think for yourself.

LESSING.

I have ever held it as a maxim never to do that through another which it was possible for me to execute myself.

MONTESQUIEU.

Time and I against any two.

PHILIP THE SECOND.

For they can conquer who believe they can.

VERGIL.

SELFISHNESS

No man is more cheated than the selfish man.

HENRY WARD BEECHER.

Every one for his home, every one for himself.

M. DUPIN.

The force of selfishness is as inevitable and as calculable as the force of gravitation.

HILLIARD.

The same people who can deny others everything are famous for refusing themselves nothing.

LEIGH HUNT.

Despite those titles, power, and pelf,
The wretch, concentred all in self,
Living, shall forfeit fair renown,
And, doubly dying, shall go down
To the vile dust from whence he sprung,
Unwept, unhonour'd and unsung.

SCOTT—*Lay of the Last Minstrel*.

To be saved is only this—salvation from our own selfishness.

WHITTIER.

Selfishness is the only real atheism; aspiration, unselfishness, the only real religion.

ZANGWILL—*Children of the Ghetto*.

SENSE

Take care of the sense and the sounds will take care of themselves.
LEWIS CARROLL—*Alice in Wonderland*.

He had used the word in its Pickwickian sense . . . he had merely considered him a humbug in a Pickwickian point of view.
DICKENS—*Pickwick Papers*.

If Poverty is the Mother of Crimes, want of Sense is the Father.
LA BRUYÈRE.

Sensible people find nothing useless.
LA FONTAINE.

Good sense which only is the gift of Heaven,
And though no science, fairly worth the seven.
POPE—*Moral Essays*.

Fool, 'tis in vain from wit to wit to roam:
Know, sense, like charity, begins at home.
POPE—*Umbra*.

SENSIBILITY

Susceptible persons are more affected by a change of tone than by unexpected words.
GEORGE ELIOT—*Adam Bede*.

Do not wish to touch me. Touch me not.
John. XX. 17.

And the heart that is soonest awake to the flowers
Is always the first to be touch'd by the thorns.
MOORE—*O Think Not My Spirits*.

SEPTEMBER

O sweet September, thy first breezes bring
The dry leaf's rustle and the squirrel's laughter,
The cool fresh air whence health and vigor spring
And promise of exceeding joy hereafter.
GEORGE ARNOLD—*September Days*.

SERVICE

When I have attempted to join myself to others by services, it proved an intellectual trick,—no more. They eat your service like apples, and leave you out. But love them, and they feel you, and delight in you all the time.
EMERSON—*Essays*.

Is thy servant a dog, that he should do this great thing?
II Kings. VIII. 13.

Who seeks for aid
Must show how service sought can be repaid.
OWEN MEREDITH—*Siege of Constantinople*.

Servant of God, well done.
MILTON—*Paradise Lost*.

They also serve who only stand and wait.
MILTON—*On His Blindness*.

They serve God well,
Who serve his creatures.
MRS. NORTON—*The Lady of La Garaye*.

My heart is ever at your service.
SHAKESPEARE—*Timon of Athens*. Act I. Sc. 2.

Small service is true service while it lasts:
Of humblest friends, bright Creature! scorn not one;
The Daisy, by the shadow that it casts,
Protects the lingering dew drop from the Sun.
WORDSWORTH—*To a Child*.

SHADOW

Coming events cast their shadows before.
CAMPBELL—*Lochiel's Warning*.

Thus shadow owes its birth to light.
GAY—*The Persian, Sun and Cloud*.

Alas! must it ever be so?
Do we stand in our own light, wherever we go,
And fight our own shadows forever?
OWEN MEREDITH—*Lucile.*

Shadows are in reality, when the sun is shining, the most conspicuous thing in a landscape, next to the highest lights.
RUSKIN—*Painting.*

SHAKESPEARE

This was Shakespeare's form;
Who walked in every path of human life,
Felt every passion; and to all mankind
Doth now, will ever, that experience yield
Which his own genius only could acquire.
AKENSIDE—*Inscription.*

Others abide our question. Thou art free.
We ask and ask—Thou smilest and art still,
Out-topping knowledge.
MATTHEW ARNOLD—*Shakespeare.*

There, Shakespeare, on whose forehead climb
The crowns o' the world. Oh, eyes sublime
With tears and laughter for all time.
E. B. BROWNING—*A Vision of Poets.*

No man is too busy to read Shakespeare.
CHARLES BUXTON.

If I say that Shakespeare is the greatest of intellects, I have said all concerning him. But there is more in Shakespeare's intellect than we have yet seen. It is what I call an unconscious intellect; there is more virtue in it than he himself is aware of.
CARLYLE—*Characteristics of Shakespeare.*

But Shakespeare's magic could not copied be;
Within that circle none durst walk but he.
DRYDEN.

Nor sequent centuries could hit
Orbit and sum of Shakespeare's wit.
EMERSON—*May Day and Other Pieces.*

Now you who rhyme, and I who rhyme,
Have not we sworn it, many a time,
That we no more our verse would scrawl,
For Shakespeare he had said it all!
R. W. GILDER—*The Modern Rhymer.*

Whatever can be known of the heart of man may be found in Shakespeare's plays.
GOETHE.

If we wish to know the force of human genius we should read Shakespeare. If we wish to see the insignificance of human learning we may study his commentators.
HAZLITT—*On the Ignorance of the Learned.*

The stream of Time, which is continually washing the dissoluble fabrics of other poets, passes without injury by the adamant of Shakspere.
SAMUEL JOHNSON—*Preface to Works of Shakspere.*

He was not of an age, but for all time!
And all the Muses still were in their prime,
When, like Apollo, he came forth to warm
Our ears, or like a Mercury to charm!
BEN JONSON—*Lines to the Memory of Shakespeare.*

Shakespeare is not our poet, but the world's,
Therefore on him no speech!
WALTER SAVAGE LANDOR.

Shakespeare has had neither equal nor second.
MACAULAY.

What needs my Shakespeare for his honored bones
The labors of an age in poled stones?
Or that his hallowed reliques should be hid
Under a starre-y-pointing pyramid?

Dear son of Memory, great heir of fame,
What need'st thou such weak witness of thy name?
Thou in our wonder and astonishment
Hath built thyself a living monument.
MILTON—*An Epitaph.*

Shakespeare (whom you and every playhouse bill
Style the divine! the matchless! what you will),
For gain, not glory, wing'd his roving flight,
And grew immortal in his own despite.
POPE—*Imitations of Horace.*

SHAME

Shame is an ornament to the young; a disgrace to the old.
ARISTOTLE.

A nightingale dies for shame if another bird sings better.
BURTON—*Anatomy of Melancholy.*

As soon as she (woman) begins to be ashamed of what she ought not, she will not be ashamed of what she ought.
LIVY—*Annales.*

I count him lost, who is lost to shame.
PLAUTUS.

O shame! Where is thy blush?
SHAKESPEARE—*Hamlet.* Act III. Sc. 4.

We live in an atmosphere of shame. We are ashamed of everything that is real about us; ashamed of ourselves, of our relatives, of our incomes, of our accents, of our opinion, of our experience, just as we are ashamed of our naked skins.
GEORGE BERNARD SHAW—*Man and Superman.*

The most curious offspring of shame is shyness.
SYDNEY SMITH—*Lecture on the Evil Affections.*

SHAMROCK

O, the Shamrock, the green, immortal Shamrock!
Chosen leaf
Of Bard and Chief,
Old Erin's native Shamrock.
MOORE—*O, the Shamrock.*

SHEEP

She walks—the lady of my delight—
A shepherdess of sheep.
Her flocks are thoughts. She keeps them white;
She guards them from the steep.
She feeds them on the fragrant height,
And folds them in for sleep.
ALICE MEYNELL—*The Lady of the Lambs.*

Baa, baa, black sheep,
Have you any wool?
Yes, marry, have I
Three bags full:
One for the master,
And one for my dame,
And one for the little boy
Who lives in the lane.
Nursery Rhyme.

A leap year
Is never a good sheep year.
Old English Saying.

The mountain sheep are sweeter,
But the valley sheep are fatter.
We therefore deemed it meeter
To carry off the latter.
THOMAS L. PEACOCK—*The Misfortunes of Elphin.*

SHIP

She walks the waters like a thing of life,
And seems to dare the elements to strife.
BYRON—*The Corsair.*

For she *is* such a smart little craft,
Such a neat little, sweet little craft—
Such a bright little,
Tight little,
Slight little,
Light little,
Trim little, slim little craft!
W. S. GILBERT—*Ruddigore.*

A great ship asks deep waters.
GEORGE HERBERT.

Being in a ship is being in a jail, with the chance of being drowned.
SAMUEL JOHNSON—*Boswell's Life of Johnson.*

The Liner she's a lady, an' she never looks nor 'eeds—
The Man-o'-War's 'er 'usband an' 'e gives 'er all she needs;
But, oh, the little cargo-boats, that sail the wet seas roun',
They're just the same as you an' me, a-plyin' up an' down.
KIPLING—*The Liner She's a Lady.*

There's not a ship that sails the ocean,
But every climate, every soil,
Must bring its tribute, great or small,
And help to build the wooden wall!
LONGFELLOW—*Building of the Ship.*

They that go down to the sea in ships, that do business in great waters.
Psalms. CVII. 23.

She comes majestic with her swelling sails,
The gallant Ship: along her watery way,
Homeward she drives before the favouring gales;
Now flirting at their length the streamers play,
And now they ripple with the ruffling breeze.
SOUTHEY.

It would have been as though he (Pres. Johnson) were in a boat of stone with masts of steel, sails of lead, ropes of iron, the devil at the helm, the wrath of God for a breeze, and hell for his destination.
EMORY A. STORRS—*Speech in Chicago.*

Whoever you are, motion and reflection are especially for you,
The divine ship sails the divine sea for you.
WALT WHITMAN—*Song of the Rolling Earth.*

Speed on the ship;—But let her bear
No merchandise of sin,
No groaning cargo of despair
Her roomy hold within;
No Lethean drug for Eastern lands,
Nor poison-draught for ours;
But honest fruits of toiling hands
And Nature's sun and showers.
WHITTIER—*The Ship-Builders.*

If all the ships I have at sea
Should come a-sailing home to me,
Ah, well! the harbor would not hold
So many ships as there would be
If all my ships came home from sea.
ELLA WHEELER WILCOX—*My Ships.*

SHIPWRECK

Then rose from sea to sky the wild farewell—
Then shriek'd the timid, and stood still the brave,—
Then some leap'd overboard with fearful yell,
As eager to anticipate their grave.
BYRON—*Don Juan.*

Again she plunges! hark! a second shock
Bilges the splitting vessel on the rock;
Down on the vale of death, with dismal cries,
The fated victims shuddering cast their eyes
In wild despair; while yet another stroke
With strong convulsion rends the solid oak:
Ah Heaven!—behold her crashing ribs divide!
She loosens, parts, and spreads in ruin o'er the tide.
FALCONER—*Shipwreck.*

And fast through the midnight dark and drear,
Through the whistling sleet and snow,
Like a sheeted ghost, the vessel swept
Towards the reef of Norman's Woe.
LONGFELLOW—*The Wreck of the Hesperus.*

Through the black night and driving rain
A ship is struggling, all in vain,
To live upon the stormy main;—
Miserere Domine!

ADELAIDE A. PROCTER—*The Storm.*

A rotten carcass of a boat, not rigged,
Nor tackle, sail, nor mast; the very rats
Instinctively have quit it.

SHAKESPEARE—*Tempest.* Act I. Sc. 2.

Every drunken skipper trusts to Providence. But one of the ways of Providence with drunken skippers is to run them on the rocks.

GEORGE BERNARD SHAW—*Heartbreak House.*

SHOEMAKING

Him that makes shoes go barefoot himself.

BURTON—*Anatomy of Melancholy.*

I can tell where my own shoe pinches me.

CERVANTES—*Don Quixote.*

The shoemaker makes a good shoe because he makes nothing else.

EMERSON—*Letters and Social Aims.*

As he cobbled and hammered from morning till dark,
With the footgear to mend on his knees,
Stitching patches, or pegging on soles as he sang,
Out of tune, ancient catches and glees.

OSCAR H. HARPEL—*The Haunted Cobbler.*

Shoemaker, stick to your last.

Proverb quoted by PLINY THE ELDER.

You cannot put the same shoe on every foot.

SYRUS—*Maxims.*

Rap, rap! upon the well-worn stone,
How falls the polished hammer!
Rap, rap! the measured sound has grown
A quick and merry clamor.
Now shape the sole! now deftly curl
The glassy vamp around it,
And bless the while the bright-eyed girl
Whose gentle fingers bound it!

WHITTIER—*The Shoemakers.*

SICKNESS

The best of remedies is a beefsteak
Against sea-sickness; try it, sir, before
You sneer, and I assure you this is true,
For I have found it answer—so may you.

BYRON—*Don Juan.*

But when ill indeed,
E'en dismissing the doctor don't *always* succeed.

GEORGE COLMAN (the Younger).

Sickness is a belief, which must be annihilated by the divine Mind.

MARY BAKER EDDY—*Science and Health.*

Prevention is better than cure.

ERASMUS—*Adagia.*

Some maladies are rich and precious and only to be acquired by the right of inheritance or purchased with gold.

HAWTHORNE—*The Old Manse.*

The whole head is sick, and the whole heart faint.

Isaiah. I. 5.

SIGH

Implores the passing tribute of a sigh.

GRAY—*Elegy in a Country Churchyard.*

Oh, if you knew the pensive pleasure
That fills my bosom when I sigh,
You would not rob me of a treasure
Monarchs are too poor to buy.

SAMUEL ROGERS.

SIGHT

And finds with keen, discriminating sight,
Black's not so black—nor white so very white.

CANNING—*New Morality.*

Two men look out through the same bars:
One sees the mud, and one the stars.
FREDERICK LANGBRIDGE.

SILENCE

Silence gives consent.
POPE BONIFACE VIII.

Three things are ever silent—Thought, Destiny, and the Grave.
BULWER-LYTTON—*Harold*.

Speech is great; but silence is greater.
CARLYLE—*Essays*.

Silence is more eloquent than words.
CARLYLE—*Heroes and Hero Worship*.

Striving to tell his woes, words would not come;
For light cares speak, when mighty griefs are dumb.
SAMUEL DANIEL—*Complaint of Rosamond*.

Vessels never give so great a sound as when they are empty.
BISHOP JOHN JEWELL.

It is a great misfortune neither to have enough wit to talk well nor enough judgment to be silent.
LA BRUYÈRE.

Silent people are dangerous; others are not so.
LA FONTAINE.

What shall I say to you? What can I say
Better than silence is?
LONGFELLOW—*Morituri Salutamus*.

Blessed are they who have nothing to say, and who cannot be persuaded to say it.
LOWELL.

I have known the silence of the stars and of the sea,
And the silence of the city when it pauses,
And the silence of a man and a maid,
And the silence for which music alone finds the word.
EDGAR LEE MASTERS—*Silence*.

You know
There are moments when silence, prolong'd and unbroken,
More expressive may be than all words ever spoken,
It is when the heart has an instinct of what
In the heart of another is passing.
OWEN MEREDITH—*Lucile*.

That silence is one of the great arts of conversation is allowed by Cicero himself, who says, there is not only an art, but even an eloquence in it.
HANNAH MORE—*Thoughts on Conversation*.

Be silent and safe—silence never betrays you.
JOHN BOYLE O'REILLY—*Rules of the Road*.

Bekker is silent in seven languages.
SCHLEIERMACHER.

Smooth runs the water where the brook is deep.
SHAKESPEARE—*Henry VI*. Pt. II. Act III. Sc. 1.

Silence! Oh, well are Death and Sleep and Thou
Three brethren named, the guardians gloomy-winged,
Of one abyss, where life and truth and joy
Are swallowed up.
SHELLEY—*Silence*.

Macaulay is like a book in breeches . . . He has occasional flashes of silence, that make his conversation perfectly delightful.
SYDNEY SMITH—*Lady Holland's Memoir*.

Woman, to woman silence is the best ornament.
SOPHOCLES—*Ajax*.

The silence that is in the starry sky.
WORDSWORTH—*Song at the Feast of Brougham*.

SIMPLICITY

The greatest truths are the simplest.
HOSEA BALLOU.

Nothing is more simple than greatness; indeed, to be simple is to be great.

EMERSON—*Literary Ethics.*

To me more dear, congenial to my heart,
One native charm, than all the gloss of art.

GOLDSMITH—*Deserted Village.*

Simplicity of character is the natural result of profound thought.

HAZLITT.

Affected simplicity is refined imposture.

LA ROCHEFOUCAULD.

Simplicity is an exact medium between too little and too much.

SIR JOSHUA REYNOLDS.

The fewer our wants, the nearer we resemble the gods.

SOCRATES.

A man is simple when his chief care is the wish to be what he ought to be, that is honestly and naturally human.

CHARLES WAGNER—*Simple Life.*

SIN

Come, now again, thy woes impart,
Tell all thy sorrows, all thy sin;
We cannot heal the throbbing heart
Till we discern the wounds within.

CRABBE—*Hall of Justice.*

O sin, what hast thou done to this fair earth!

DANA.

I couldn't live in peace if I put the shadow of a wilful sin between myself and God.

GEORGE ELIOT—*The Mill on the Floss.*

He that falls into sin is a man; that grieves at it, is a saint; that boasteth of it, is a devil.

FULLER—*Holy State.*

Poverty and wealth are comparative sins.

VICTOR HUGO.

Man-like is it to fall into sin,
Fiend-like is it to dwell therein,
Christ-like is it for sin to grieve,
God-like is it all sin to leave.

FRIEDRICH VON LOGAU.

Yes, every sin is a mistake, and the epitaph for the sinner is, "Thou fool."

ALEXANDER MACLAREN.

Her rash hand in evil hour
Forth reaching to the fruit, she pluck'd, she eat;
Earth felt the wound, and Nature from her seat
Sighing through all her works gave signs of woe
That all was lost.

MILTON—*Paradise Lost.*

Law can discover sin, but not remove,
Save by those shadowy expiations weak.

MILTON—*Paradise Lost.*

So many laws argues so many sins.

MILTON—*Paradise Lost.*

It is not alone what we do, but also what we do not do, for which we are accountable.

MOLIÈRE.

O thou, who didst with pitfall and with gin
Beset the road I was to wander in,
Thou wilt not with predestin'd evil round
Enmesh, and then impute my fall to sin.

OMAR KHAYYÁM—*Rubaiyat.*

Indulgent gods, grant me to sin once with impunity. That is sufficient. Let a second offence bear its punishment.

OVID.

If Jupiter hurled his thunderbolt as often as men sinned, he would soon be out of thunderbolts.

OVID.

My son, if sinners entice thee, consent thou not.

Proverbs. I. 10.

The way of transgressors is hard.

Proverbs. XIII. 15.

The wages of sin is death.

Romans. VI. 23.

Other men's sins are before our eyes; our own behind our backs.

SENECA.

The greater part of mankind are angry with the sinner and not with the sin.

SENECA.

Sin is a state of mind, not an outward act.

SEWELL—*Passing Thoughts on Religion.*

I am a man
More sinn'd against than sinning.

SHAKESPEARE—*King Lear*. Act III. Sc. 2.

They say sin touches not a man so near
As shame a woman; yet he too should be
Part of the penance, being more deep than she
Set in the sin.

SWINBURNE—*Tristram of Lyonesse.*

But he who never sins can little boast
Compared to him who goes and sins no more!

N. P. WILLIS—*The Lady Jane.*

SINCERITY

Of all the evil spirits abroad at this hour in the world, insincerity is the most dangerous.

FROUDE—*Short Studies on Great Subjects.*

Sincerity is impossible, unless it pervade the whole being, and the pretence of it saps the very foundation of character.

LOWELL—*Essay on Pope.*

There is no greater delight than to be conscious of sincerity on self-examination.

MENCIUS.

A little sincerity is a dangerous thing, and a great deal of it is absolutely fatal.

OSCAR WILDE—*The Critic as Artist.*

SINGING

That which is not worth speaking they sing.

BEAUMARCHAIS.

The tenor's voice is spoilt by affectation,
And for the bass, the beast can only bellow;
In fact, he had no singing education,
An ignorant, noteless, timeless, tuneless fellow.

BYRON—*Don Juan.*

At every close she made, th' attending throng
Replied, and bore the burden of the song:
So just, so small, yet in so sweet a note,
It seemed the music melted in the throat.

DRYDEN—*Flower and the Leaf.*

So she poured out the liquid music of her voice to quench the thirst of his spirit.

HAWTHORNE—*Mosses from an Old Manse.*

God sent his Singers upon earth
With songs of sadness and of mirth,
That they might touch the hearts of men,
And bring them back to heaven again.

LONGFELLOW—*The Singers.*

Or bid the soul of Orpheus sing
Such notes as, warbled to the string,
Drew iron tears down Pluto's cheek.

MILTON—*Il Penseroso.*

But would you sing, and rival Orpheus' strain,
The wond'ring forests soon should dance again;
The moving mountains hear the powerful call.
And headlong streams hang listening in their fall!

POPE—*Summer.*

Sing again, with your dear voice revealing
A tone
Of some world far from ours.
Where music and moonlight and feeling
Are one.

SHELLEY—*To Jane.*

SKY

And they were canopied by the blue sky,
So cloudless, clear, and purely beautiful,
That God alone was to be seen in Heaven.
BYRON—*The Dream.*

How bravely Autumn paints upon the sky
The gorgeous fame of Summer which is fled!
HOOD.

When it is evening, ye say it will be fair weather: for the sky is red.
Matthew. XVI. 2.

And that inverted Bowl they call the Sky,
Whereunder crawling coop'd we live and die,
Lift not your hands to it for help—for it
As impotently moves as you or I.
OMAR KHAYYÁM—*Rubaiyat.*

Sometimes gentle, sometimes capricious, sometimes awful, never the same for two moments together; almost human in its passions, almost spiritual in its tenderness, almost Divine in its infinity.
RUSKIN—*The Sky.*

The moon has set
In a bank of jet
That fringes the Western sky,
The pleiads seven
Have sunk from heaven
And the midnight hurries by;
My hopes are flown
And, alas! alone
On my weary couch I lie.
SAPPHO—*Fragment.*

Heaven's ebon vault,
Studded with stars unutterably bright,
Through which the moon's unclouded grandeur rolls,
Seems like a canopy which love has spread
To curtain her sleeping world.
SHELLEY—*Queen Mab.*

Green calm below, blue quietness above.
WHITTIER—*The Pennsylvania Pilgrim.*

The soft blue sky did never melt
Into his heart; he never felt
The witching of the soft blue sky!
WORDSWORTH—*Peter Bell.*

SLANDER

There are . . . robberies that leave man or woman forever beggared of peace and joy, yet kept secret by the sufferer.
GEORGE ELIOT—*Felix Holt.*

I hate the man who builds his name
On ruins of another's fame.
GAY—*The Poet and the Rose.*

If slander be a snake, it is a winged one—it flies as well as creeps.
DOUGLAS JERROLD—*Slander.*

Where it concerns himself,
Who's angry at a slander, makes it true.
BEN JONSON—*Catiline.*

Cut
Men's throats with whisperings.
BEN JONSON—*Sejanus.*

There is no protection against slander.
MOLIÈRE.

Never throw mud. You may miss your mark, but you must have dirty hands.
JOSEPH PARKER.

Your tittle-tattlers, and those who listen to slander, by my good will should all be hanged—the former by their tongues, the latter by the ears.
PLAUTUS.

'Twas slander filled her mouth with lying words;
Slander, the foulest whelp of Sin.
POLLOCK—*Course of Time.*

I am disgrac'd, impeach'd and baffled here,—
Pierc'd to the soul with slander's venom'd spear.
SHAKESPEARE—*Richard II.* Act I. Sc. 1.

A slander is like a hornet; if you cannot kill it dead the first blow, better not strike at it.
H. W. SHAW.

Slanderers do not hurt me, because they do not hit me.
SOCRATES.

Soft-buzzing Slander; silly moths that eat
An honest name.
THOMSON—*Liberty.*

SLAVERY

It (Chinese Labor in South Africa) could not, in the opinion of His Majesty's Government, be classified as slavery in the extreme acceptance of the word without some risk of terminological inexactitude.
WINSTON CHURCHILL in House of Commons, 1906.

I would not have a slave to till my ground,
To carry me, to fan me while I sleep,
And tremble when I wake, for all the wealth
That sinews bought and sold have ever earn'd.
COWPER—*Task.*

I do not see how a barbarous community and a civilized community can constitute a state. I think we must get rid of slavery or we must get rid of freedom.
EMERSON.

Corrupted freemen are the worst of slaves.
DAVID GARRICK.

The compact which exists between the North and the South is a covenant with death and an agreement with hell; involving both parties in atrocious criminality, and should be immediately annulled.
WILLIAM LLOYD GARRISON.

The man who gives me employment, which I must have or suffer, that man is my master, let me call him what I will.
HENRY GEORGE—*Social Problems.*

I believe this government cannot endure permanently half slave and half free.
ABRAHAM LINCOLN—*Speech, 1858.*

In giving freedom to the slave we assure freedom to the free,—honorable alike in what we give and what we preserve.
ABRAHAM LINCOLN—*Annual Message to Congress, 1862.*

They are slaves who fear to speak
For the fallen and the weak;
. . .
They are slaves who dare not be
In the right with two or three.
LOWELL—*Stanzas on Freedom.*

The air of England has long been too pure for a slave, and every man is who breathes it.
LORD MANSFIELD.

Execrable son! so to aspire
Above his brethren, to himself assuming
Authority usurp'd, from God not given.
He gave us only over beast, fish, fowl,
Dominion absolute; that right we hold
By his donation; but man over men
He made not lord; such title to himself
Reserving, human left from human free.
MILTON—*Paradise Lost.*

And ne'er shall the sons of Columbia be slaves,
While the earth bears a plant, or the sea rolls its waves.
ROBERT PAINE—*Adams and Liberty.*

Englishmen never will be slaves; they are free to do whatever the Government and public opinion allow them to do.
GEORGE BERNARD SHAW—*Man and Superman.*

Where Slavery is there Liberty cannot be; and where Liberty is there Slavery cannot be.
CHARLES SUMNER.

They (the blacks) had no right which the white man was bound to respect.
ROGER B. TANEY—*The Dred Scott Case.*

I never mean, unless some particular circumstances should compel me to do it, to possess another slave by purchase, it being among my first wishes to see some plan adopted by which slavery in this country may be abolished by law.
WASHINGTON—*Farewell Address.*

That execrable sum of all villainies commonly called the Slave-trade.
JOHN WESLEY—*Journal.*

What! mothers from their children riven!
What! God's own image bought and sold!
Americans to market driven,
And bartered as the brute for gold!
WHITTIER—*Voices of Freedom.*

SLEEP

What means this heaviness that hangs upon me?
This lethargy that creeps through all my senses?
Nature, oppress'd and harass'd out with care,
Sinks down to rest.
ADDISON—*Cato.*

What probing deep
Has ever solved the mystery of sleep?
T. B. ALDRICH—*Human Ignorance.*

Come to me now! O, come! benignest sleep!
And fold me up, as evening doth a flower,
From my vain self, and vain things which have power
Upon my soul to make me smile or weep.
And when thou comest, oh, like Death be deep.
PATRICK PROCTOR ALEXANDER—*Sleep.*

Sleep on, Baby, on the floor,
Tired of all the playing,
Sleep with smile the sweeter for
That you dropped away in!
On your curls' full roundness stand
Golden lights serenely—
One cheek, pushed out by the hand,
Folds the dimple inly.
E. B. BROWNING—*Sleeping and Watching.*

Sleep is the best cure for waking troubles.
CERVANTES.

Awake thee, my Lady-Love!
Wake thee, and rise!
The sun through the bower peeps
Into thine eyes.
GEORGE DARLEY—*Waking Song.*

Golden slumbers kiss your eyes,
Smiles awake you when you rise.
THOMAS DEKKER.

The sleep of a labouring man is sweet.
Ecclesiastes. V. 12.

Fatigue is the best pillow.
FRANKLIN.

Sleep sweet within this quiet room,
O thou! whoe'er thou art;
And let no mournful Yesterday,
Disturb thy peaceful heart.
ELLEN M. H. GATES—*Sleep Sweet.*

Oh! lightly, lightly tread!
A holy thing is sleep,
On the worn spirit is sleep
And eyes that wake to weep.
FELICIA D. HEMANS—*The Sleeper.*

Great eaters and great sleepers are incapable of anything else that is great.
HENRY IV of France.

One hour's sleep before midnight is worth three after.
GEORGE HERBERT.

I lay me down to sleep,
With little thought or care
Whether my waking find
Me here, or there.
MRS. R. S. HOWLAND (Miss Woolsey)—*Rest.*

I never take a nap after dinner but when I have had a bad night, and then the nap takes me.
SAMUEL JOHNSON—*Boswell's Life of Johnson.*

O magic sleep! O comfortable bird,
That broodest o'er the troubled sea of the mind
Till it is hush'd and smooth! O unconfined
Restraint! imprisoned liberty! great key
To golden palaces.
KEATS—*Endymion.*

Over the edge of the purple down,
Where the single lamplight gleams,
Know ye the road to the Merciful Town
That is hard by the Sea of Dreams—
Where the poor may lay their wrongs away,
And the sick may forget to weep?
But we—pity us! Oh pity us!
We wakeful; Ah, pity us!—
KIPLING—*City of Sleep.*

For I am weary, and am over wrought
With too much toil, with too much care distraught,
And with the iron crown of anguish crowned.
Lay thy soft hand upon my brow and cheek,
O peaceful Sleep!
LONGFELLOW—*Sleep.*

Dreams of the summer night!
Tell her, her lover keeps
Watch! while in slumber light
She sleeps!
My lady sleeps!
Sleeps!
LONGFELLOW—*Spanish Student.*

The timely dew of sleep
Now falling with soft slumb'rous weight inclines
Our eyelids.
MILTON—*Paradise Lost.*

Sleep, rest of nature, O sleep, most gentle of the divinities, peace of the soul, thou at whose presence care disappears, who soothest hearts wearied with daily employments, and makest them strong again for labour!
OVID—*Metamorphoses.*

Sleep, baby, sleep
Thy father's watching the sheep,
Thy mother's shaking the dreamland tree,
And down drops a little dream for thee.
ELIZABETH PRENTISS—*Sleep, Baby, Sleep.*

I will both lay me down in peace, and sleep: for thou, Lord, only makest me dwell in safety.
Psalms. IV. 8.

He giveth the beloved sleep.
Psalms. CXXVII. 2.

I never sleep comfortable except when I am at sermon or when I pray to God.
RABELAIS—*Gargantua.*

She slept the sleep of the just.
RACINE.

"God bless the man who first invented sleep!"
So Sancho Panza said and so say I;
And bless him, also, that he didn't keep
His great discovery to himself, nor try
To make it,—as the lucky fellow might—
A close monopoly by patent-right.
J. G. SAXE—*Early Rising.*

To all, to each, a fair good-night,
And pleasing dreams, and slumbers light.
SCOTT—*Marmion.*

To sleep! perchance to dream; ay, there's the rub;
For in that sleep of death what dreams may come,
When we have shuffled off this mortal coil,
Must give us pause.
SHAKESPEARE—*Hamlet.* Act III. Sc. 1.

Sleep, the fresh dew of languid love, the rain
Whose drops quench kisses till they burn again.
SHELLEY—*Epipsychidion.*

Come, Sleep: O Sleep! the certain knot of peace,
The baiting place of wit, the balm of woe,

The poor man's wealth, the prisoner's release,
Th' indifferent judge between the high and low.
SIR PHILIP SIDNEY—*Astrophel and Stella.*

She sleeps: her breathings are not heard
In palace chambers far apart,
The fragrant tresses are not stirr'd
That lie upon her charmed heart.
She sleeps: on either hand upswells
The gold fringed pillow lightly prest:
She sleeps, nor dreams, but ever dwells
A perfect form in perfect rest.
TENNYSON—*The Sleeping Beauty.*

Hush, my dear, lie still and slumber!
Holy angels guard thy bed!
Heavenly blessings without number
Gently falling on thy head.
WATTS—*Cradle Hymn.*

SMILE

What's the use of worrying?
It never was worth while, so
Pack up your troubles in your old kit-bag,
And smile, smile, smile.
GEORGE ASAF—*Smile, Smile, Smile.*

Smiles form the channels of a future tear.
BYRON—*Childe Harold.*

Her very frowns are fairer far
Than smiles of other maidens are.
HARTLEY COLERIDGE—*She Is Not Fair.*

For smiles from reason flow
To brute deny'd, and are of love the food.
MILTON—*Paradise Lost.*

The thing that goes the farthest towards making life worth while,
That costs the least, and does the most, is just a pleasant smile.
. . . .
It's full of worth and goodness too, with manly kindness blent,
It's worth a million dollars and it doesn't cost a cent.
W. D. NESBIT—*Let Us Smile.*

There is a snake in thy smile, my dear,
And bitter poison within thy tear.
SHELLEY—*Beatrice Cenci.*

'Tis easy enough to be pleasant,
When life flows along like a song;
But the man worth while is the one who will smile
When everything goes dead wrong;
For the test of the heart is trouble,
And it always comes with the years,
But the smile that is worth the praise of earth
Is the smile that comes through tears.
ELLA WHEELER WILCOX—*Worth While.*

A tender smile, our sorrows' only balm.
YOUNG—*Love of Fame.*

SNEER

There was a laughing Devil in his sneer,
That raised emotions both of rage and fear.
BYRON—*Corsair.*

Who can refute a sneer?
WILLIAM PALEY.

It is just as hard to do your duty when men are sneering at you as when they are shooting at you.
WOODROW WILSON—*Speech, 1914.*

SNOW

Announced by all the trumpets of the sky,
Arrives the snow, and, driving o'er the fields,
Seems nowhere to alight: the whited air
Hides hills and woods, the river, and the heaven,
And veils the farmhouse at the garden's end.
The sled and traveller stopped, the courier's feet
Delayed, all friends shut out, the housemates sit
Around the radiant fireplace, enclosed
In a tumultuous privacy of storm.
EMERSON—*The Snow-Storm.*

Out of the bosom of the Air,
Out of the cloud-folds of her garments shaken,
Over the woodlands brown and bare,
Over the harvest-fields forsaken,
Silent, and soft and slow
Descends the snow.
LONGFELLOW—*Snow-Flakes.*

For thou wilt lie upon the wings of night
Whiter than new snow on a raven's back.
SHAKESPEARE—*Romeo and Juliet.* Act III. Sc. 2.

But where are the snows of yesteryear?
VILLON.

O the snow, the beautiful snow,
Filling the sky and earth below;
Over the house-tops, over the street,
Over the heads of the people you meet,
Dancing, flirting, skimming along.
JAMES W. WATSON—*Beautiful Snow.*

SOCIETY

These families, you know, are our upper crust, not upper ten thousand.
COOPER—*The Ways of the Hour.*

For every social wrong there must be a remedy. But the remedy can be nothing less than the abolition of the wrong.
HENRY GEORGE—*Social Problems.*

The wise man sometimes flees from society from fear of being bored.
LA BRUYÈRE.

He might have proved a useful adjunct, if not an ornament to society.
LAMB—*Captain Starkey.*

The Don Quixote of one generation may live to hear himself called the savior of society by the next.
LOWELL—*Don Quixote.*

A system in which the two great commandments were, to hate your neighbour and to love your neighbour's wife.
MACAULAY—*Essays.*

Man is a social animal.
SENECA.

Society is no comfort
To one not sociable.
SHAKESPEARE—*Cymbeline.* Act IV. Sc. 2.

As the French say, there are three sexes,—men, women, and clergymen.
SYDNEY SMITH—*Lady Holland's Memoir.*

It is impossible, in our condition of Society, not to be sometimes a Snob.
THACKERAY—*Book of Snobs.*

Other people are quite dreadful. The only possible society is oneself.
OSCAR WILDE—*An Ideal Husband.*

I suppose Society is wonderfully delightful.
To be in it is merely a bore. But to be out of it is simply a tragedy.
OSCAR WILDE—*Woman of No Importance.*

There is
One great society alone on earth:
The noble Living and the noble Dead.
WORDSWORTH—*The Prelude.*

SOLDIER

God and a soldier all people adore
In time of war, but not before;
And when war is over and all things are righted,
God is neglected and an old soldier slighted.
ANONYMOUS.

The king of France with twenty thousand men
Went up the hill, and then came down again:
The king of Spain with twenty thousand more
Climbed the same hill the French had climbed before.
ANONYMOUS.

See! There is Jackson standing like a stone wall.
BERNARD E. BEE—*Battle of Manassas.*

His breast with wounds unnumber'd riven,
His back to earth, his face to heaven.
BYRON—*Giaour*.

How sleep the brave, who sink to rest,
By all their country's wishes blest!
. . . . .
By fairy hands their knell is rung,
By forms unseen their dirge is sung.
COLLINS—*Ode Written in 1746*.

He stands erect; his slouch becomes a walk;
He steps right onward, martial in his air,
His form and movement.
COWPER—*The Task*.

Under the sod and the dew,
Waiting the Judgment Day;
Love and tears for the Blue,
Tears and love for the Gray.
FRANCIS M. FINCH—*The Blue and the Gray*.

We are coming, Father Abraham, three hundred thousand more.
J. S. GIBBONS.

The broken soldier, kindly bade to stay;
Sat by his fire, and talked the night away,
Wept o'er his wounds, or tales of sorrow done,
Shoulder'd his crutch, and show'd how fields were won.
GOLDSMITH—*Deserted Village*.

Ben Battle was a soldier bold,
And used to war's alarms;
But a cannon-ball took off his legs,
So he laid down his arms.
HOOD—*Faithless Nellie Gray*.

He smote them hip and thigh.
Judges. XV. 8.

Let not him that girdeth on his harness boast himself as he that putteth it off.
I Kings. XX. 11.

As we pledge the health of our general, who fares as rough as we,
What can daunt us, what can turn us, led to death by such as he?
CHARLES KINGSLEY—*A March*.

"For they're hangin' Danny Deever, you can 'ear the Dead March play,
The regiment's in 'ollow square—
They're hangin' him to-day;
They've taken of his buttons off an' cut his stripes away,
An' they're hangin' Danny Deever in the morning."
KIPLING—*Danny Deever*.

So 'ere's to you, Fuzzy-Wuzzy, at your 'ome in the Soudan;
You're a pore benighted 'eathen but a first-class fightin' man;
And 'ere's to you, Fuzzy-Wuzzy, with your 'ay-rick 'ead of 'air;
You big black boundin' beggar—for you broke a British square!
KIPLING—*Fuzzy-Wuzzy*.

For it's Tommy this an' Tommy that, an' "Chuck 'im out, the brute!"
But it's "Savior of 'is country," when the guns begin to shoot.
KIPLING—*Tommy*.

It is not the guns or armament
Or the money they can pay,
It's the close co-operation
That makes them win the day.
It is not the individual
Or the army as a whole,
But the everlastin' teamwork
Of every bloomin' soul.
J. MASON KNOX.

But in a larger sense we cannot dedicate, we cannot consecrate, we cannot hallow this ground. The brave men, living and dead, who struggled here, have consecrated it far above our poor power to add or detract.
LINCOLN—*Gettysburg Address*.

The greatest general is he who makes the fewest mistakes.
NAPOLEON.

The muffled drum's sad roll has beat
The soldier's last tattoo;
No more on Life's parade shall meet
The brave and fallen few.
On Fame's eternal camping-ground
Their silent tents are spread,
And Glory guards, with solemn round
The bivouac of the dead.
THEODORE O'HARA—*The Bivouac of the Dead*.

But off with your hat and three times three for Columbia's true-blue sons;
The men below who batter the foe—the men behind the guns!
JOHN JEROME ROONEY.

I want to see you shoot the way you shout.
THEODORE ROOSEVELT.

Soldier, rest! thy warfare o'er,
Dream of fighting fields no more:
Sleep the sleep that knows not breaking,
Morn of toil, nor night of waking.
SCOTT—*Lady of the Lake.*

Although too much of a soldier among sovereigns, no one could claim with better right to be a sovereign among soldiers.
SCOTT—*Life of Napoleon.*

A soldier is an anachronism of which we must get rid.
GEORGE BERNARD SHAW—*Devil's Disciple.*

When the military man approaches, the world locks up its spoons and packs off its womankind.
GEORGE BERNARD SHAW—*Man and Superman.*

Sleep, soldiers! still in honored rest
Your truth and valor wearing:
The bravest are the tenderest,—
The loving are the daring.
BAYARD TAYLOR—*The Song of the Camp.*

Home they brought her warrior dead.
TENNYSON—*The Princess.*

Oh, a strange hand writes for our dear son—O, stricken mother's soul!
All swims before her eyes—flashes with black—she catches the main words only;
Sentences broken—*gun-shot wound in the breast, cavalry skirmish, taken to hospital;*
At present low, but will soon be better.
WALT WHITMAN—*Drum-Taps.*

No useless coffin enclosed his breast,
Not in sheet nor in shroud we wound him;
But he lay like a warrior taking his rest
With his martial cloak around him.
CHARLES WOLFE—*The Burial of Sir John Moore at Carunna.*

SOLITUDE

In solitude, when we are *least* alone.
BYRON—*Childe Harold.*

Alone, alone, all, all alone,
Alone on a wide, wide sea.
COLERIDGE—*Ancient Mariner.*

I praise the Frenchman; his remark was shrewd,—
"How sweet, how passing sweet is solitude."
But grant me still a friend in my retreat,
Whom I may whisper—Solitude is sweet.
COWPER—*Retirement.*

Oh, for a lodge in some vast wilderness,
Some boundless contiguity of shade,
Where rumour of oppression and deceit,
Of unsuccessful or successful war,
Might never reach me more!
COWPER—*Task.*

We enter the world alone, we leave it alone.
FROUDE.

Far from the madding crowd's ignoble strife.
GRAY—*Elegy in a Country Churchyard.*

Solitude is as needful to the imagination as society is wholesome for the character.
LOWELL—*Among My Books.*

For solitude sometimes is best society,
And short retirement urges sweet return.
MILTON—*Paradise Lost.*

I feel like one who treads alone
Some banquet hall deserted,
Whose lights are fled, whose garlands dead,
And all but he departed.
MOORE—*Oft in the Stilly Night.*

Until I truly loved, I was alone.
MRS. NORTON—*The Lady of La Garaye.*

Now the New Year reviving old Desires,
The thoughtful Soul to Solitude retires.
OMAR KHAYYÁM—*Rubaiyat.*

When, musing on companions gone,
We doubly feel ourselves alone.
SCOTT—*Marmion.*

Solitude is the best nurse of wisdom.
STERNE—*Letters.*

I never found the companion that was so companionable as solitude.
THOREAU—*Solitude.*

O sacred solitude! divine retreat!
Choice of the prudent! envy of the great,
By thy pure stream, or in thy waving shade,
We court fair wisdom, that celestial maid.
YOUNG—*Love of Fame.*

SONG

I can not sing the old songs now!
It is not that I deem them low,
'Tis that I can't remember how
They go.
CHARLES S. CALVERLEY—*Changed.*

Unlike my subject now . . . shall be my song,
It shall be witty and it sha'n't be long!
CHESTERFIELD—*Preface to Letters.*

A song of hate is a song of Hell;
Some there be who sing it well.
Let them sing it loud and long,
We lift our hearts in a loftier song:
We lift our hearts to Heaven above,
Singing the glory of her we love,
England.
HELEN GRAY CONE—*Chant of Love of England.*

A song will outlive all sermons in the memory.
HENRY GILES.

Listen to that song, and learn it!
Half my kingdom would I give,
As I live,
If by such songs you would earn it!
LONGFELLOW—*Tales of a Wayside Inn.*

Such songs have power to quiet
The restless pulse of care,
And come like the benediction
That follows after prayer.
LONGFELLOW—*The Day Is Done.*

Builders, raise the ceiling high,
Raise the dome into the sky,
Hear the wedding song!
For the happy groom is near,
Tall as Mars, and statelier,
Hear the wedding song!
SAPPHO—*Fragments.*

Songs consecrate to truth and liberty.
SHELLEY.

They sang of love and not of fame;
Forgot was Britain's glory;
Each heart recalled a different name,
But all sang "Annie Laurie."
BAYARD TAYLOR—*A Song of the Camp.*

Short swallow-flights of song, that dip
Their wings in tears, and skim away.
TENNYSON—*In Memoriam.*

Soft words, with nothing in them, make a song.
EDMUND WALLER—*To Mr. Creech.*

A careless song, with a little nonsense in it now and then, does not misbecome a monarch.
HORACE WALPOLE.

Bring the good old bugle, boys! we'll sing another song—
Sing it with a spirit that will start the world along—
Sing it as we used to sing it, fifty thousand strong,
While we were marching through Georgia.
HENRY CLAY WORK — *Marching Through Georgia.*

SORROW

Ah, nothing comes to us too soon but sorrow.
BAILEY—*Festus.*

Sorrow preys upon
Its solitude, and nothing more diverts it
From its sad visions of the other world
Than calling it at moments back to this.
The busy have no time for tears.
BYRON—*The Two Foscari.*

Every noble crown is, and on earth will ever be, a crown of thorns.
CARLYLE.

All sorrows are bearable, if there is bread.
CERVANTES.

Men die, but sorrow never dies;
The crowding years divide in vain,
And the wide world is knit with ties
Of common brotherhood in pain.
SUSAN COOLIDGE — *The Cradle Tomb in Westminster Abbey.*

When I was young, I said to Sorrow,
"Come and I will play with thee!"
He is near me now all day,
And at night returns to say,
"I will come again to-morrow—
I will come and stay with thee."
AUBREY THOMAS DE VERE—*Song.*

Who never ate his bread in sorrow,
Who never spent the darksome hours,
Weeping, and watching for the morrow,—
He knows ye not, ye gloomy Powers.
GOETHE—*Wilhelm Meister.*

I walked a mile with Sorrow
And ne'er a word said she;
But, oh, the things I learned from her
When Sorrow walked with me.
ROBERT BROWNING HAMILTON—*Along the Road.*

The sorrowful dislike the gay, and the gay the sorrowful.
HORACE—*Epistles.*

When sparrows build and the leaves break forth
My old sorrow wakes and cries.
JEAN INGELOW—*Song of Old Love.*

Hang sorrow, care'll kill a cat.
BEN JONSON—*Every Man in His Humour.*

To Sorrow
I bade good-morrow,
And thought to leave her far away behind;
But cheerly, cheerly,
She loves me dearly:
She is so constant to me, and so kind.
KEATS—*Endymion.*

Our days and nights
Have sorrows woven with delights.
MALHERBE—*To Cardinal Richelieu.*

Weep on; and, as thy sorrows flow,
I'll taste the luxury of woe.
MOORE—*Anacreontic.*

Sorrows remembered sweeten present joy.
POLLOCK—*Course of Time*

Do not cheat thy Heart and tell her,
"Grief will pass away,
Hope for fairer times in future,
And forget to-day."
Tell her that the lesson taught her
Far outweighs the pain.
ADELAIDE A. PROCTER—*Friend Sorrow.*

Sorrows are like thunderclouds—in the distance they look black, over our heads scarcely gray.
JEAN PAUL RICHTER—*Hesperus.*

When sorrow sleepeth, wake it not,
But let it slumber on.
MISS M. A. STODART—*Song.*

What shall be done for sorrow
With love whose race is run?
Where help is none to borrow,
What shall be done?
SWINBURNE—*Wasted Love.*

The deeper the sorrow, the less tongue hath it.
Talmud.

Joy was a flame in me
Too steady to destroy.
Lithe as a bending reed,
Loving the storm that sways her—
I found more joy in sorrow
Than you could find in joy.
SARA TEASDALE—*The Answer.*

O sorrow, wilt thou rule my blood,
Be sometimes lovely, like a bride,

And put thy harsher moods aside,
If thou wilt have me wise and good.
TENNYSON—*In Memoriam.*

There can be no rainbow without a cloud and a storm.
J. H. VINCENT.

Where there is sorrow, there is holy ground.
OSCAR WILDE—*De Profundis.*

Hang sorrow, care will kill a cat,
And therefore let's be merry.
WITHER—*Christmas.*

SOUL

What sculpture is to a block of marble, education is to the soul.
ADDISON—*Spectator.*

John Brown's body lies a-mouid'ring in the grave,
His soul goes marching on.
THOMAS BRIGHAM BISHOP—*John Brown's Body.*

And I have written three books on the soul,
Proving absurd all written hitherto,
And putting us to ignorance again.
ROBERT BROWNING—*Cleon.*

And he that makes his soul his surety,
I think, does give the best security.
BUTLER—*Hudibras.*

The dome of Thought, the palace of the Soul.
BYRON—*Childe Harold.*

The countenance is the portrait of the soul, and the eyes mark its intentions.
CICERO.

The soul of man is larger than the sky,
Deeper than ocean, or the abysmal dark
Of the unfathomed centre.
HARTLEY COLERIDGE—*To Shakespeare.*

I have a soul that, like an ample shield,
Can take in all, and verge enough for more.
DRYDEN—*Sebastian.*

The one thing in the world, of value, is the active soul.
EMERSON—*American Scholar.*

Gravity is the ballast of the soul, which keeps the mind steady.
FULLER—*Holy and Profane States.*

It matters not how strait the gate,
How charged with punishments the scroll,
I am the master of my fate:
I am the captain of my soul.
HENLEY—*Echoes.*

Build thee more stately mansions, O my soul,
As the swift seasons roll!
Leave thy low-vaulted past!
Let each new temple, nobler than the last,
Shut thee from heaven with a dome more vast,
Till thou at length art free,
Leaving thine outgrown shell by life's unresting sea!
HOLMES—*The Chambered Nautilus.*

The production of souls is the secret of unfathomable depth.
VICTOR HUGO—*Shakespeare.*

Awake, my soul, and with the sun
Thy daily course of duty run.
BISHOP KEN—*Evening Hymn.*

Ah, the souls of those that die
Are but sunbeams lifted higher.
LONGFELLOW—*Christus.*

Soul, thou hast much goods laid up for many years; take thine ease, eat, drink and be merry.
Luke. XII. 19; *Ecclesiastes.* VIII. 15.

In your patience possess ye your souls.
Luke. XXI. 19.

The dust's for crawling, heaven's for flying,
Wherefore, O Soul, whose wings are grown,
Soar upward to the sun!
EDGAR LEE MASTERS—*Spoon River Anthology.*

What is a man profited, if he shall gain the whole world, and lose his own soul?
Matthew. XVI. 26.

I reflected how soon in the cup of desire
The pearl of the soul may be melted away;
How quickly, alas, the pure sparkle of fire
We inherit from heaven, may be quenched in the clay.
MOORE—*A Beam of Tranquillity.*

Lord of myself, accountable to none.
But to my conscience, and my God alone.
JOHN OLDHAM.

I sent my Soul through the Invisible,
Some letter of that After-life to spell,
And by and by my Soul returned to me,
And answered "I Myself and Heav'n and Hell."
OMAR KHAYYÁM—*Rubaiyat.*

The soul, uneasy and confin'd from home,
Rests and expatiates in a life to come.
POPE—*Essay on Man.*

The iron entered into his soul.
Psalms. CV. 18.

Man who man would be
Must rule the empire of himself.
SHELLEY—*Sonnet on Political Greatness.*

Whate'er of earth is form'd, to earth returns,
. . . The soul
Of man alone, that particle divine,
Escapes the wreck of worlds, when all things fail.
W. C. SOMERVILLE—*The Chase.*

What then do you call your soul? What idea have you of it? You cannot of yourselves, without revelation, admit the existence within you of anything but a power unknown to you of feeling and thinking.
VOLTAIRE—*A Philosophical Dictionary.*

Were I so tall to reach the pole,
Or grasp the ocean with my span,
I must be measur'd by my soul:
The mind's the standard of the man.
WATTS—*False Greatness.*

A charge to keep I have,
A god to glorify:
A never-dying soul to save,
And fit it for the sky.
CHARLEY WESLEY—*Hymns.*

I loafe and invite my soul,
I lean and loafe at my ease, observing a spear of summer grass.
WALT WHITMAN—*Song of Myself.*

SOUND

A noise like of a hidden brook
In the leafy month of June,
That to the sleeping woods all night
Singeth a quiet tune.
COLERIDGE—*Ancient Mariner.*

The murmur that springs
From the growing of grass.
POE—*Al Aaraaf.*

The sound must seem an echo to the sense.
POPE—*Essay on Criticism.*

The empty vessel makes the greatest sound.
SHAKESPEARE—*Henry V.* Act IV. Sc. 4.

Hark! from the tombs a doleful sound.
ISAAC WATTS—*Hymns and Spiritual Songs.*

My eyes are dim with childish tears,
My heart is idly stirred,
For the same sound is in my ears
Which in those days I heard.
WORDSWORTH—*The Fountain.*

SPEECH

Discretion of speech is more than eloquence; and to speak agreeably to him with whom we deal is more than to speak in good words or in good order.
BACON—*Essays.*

Hear much; speak little.
BIAS.

That which is repeated too often becomes insipid and tedious.
BOILEAU.

Let him now speak, or else hereafter for ever hold his peace.
Book of Common Prayer.

His speech was a fine sample, on whole,
Of rhetoric, which the learn'd call "*rigmarole.*"
BYRON—*Don Juan.*

The heart seldom feels what the mouth expresses.
CAMPISTRON—*Pompeia.*

Speech is silvern, silence is golden.
CARLYLE—*A Swiss Inscription.*

Speak not at all, in any wise, till you have somewhat to speak; care not for the reward of your speaking, but simply and with undivided mind for the truth of your speaking.
CARLYLE—*Essays.*

Speak briefly and to the point.
CATO.

He mouths a sentence as curs mouth a bone.
CHARLES CHURCHILL—*The Rosciad.*

Let your speech be alway with grace, seasoned with salt.
Colossians. IV. 6.

Congress shall make no law . . . abridging the freedom of speech or of the press.
Constitution of the United States, Amendment I.

Seeing then that we have such hope, we use great plainness of speech.
II Corinthians. III. 12.

But though I be rude in speech, yet not in knowledge.
II Corinthians. XI. 6.

I realize that there are certain limitations placed upon the right of free speech. I may not be able to say all I think, but I am not going to say anything I do not think.
EUGENE V. DEBS—*Speech, 1918.*

A vessel is known by the sound, whether it be cracked or not; so men are proved, by Their speech, whether they be wise or foolish.
DEMOSTHENES.

I will sit down now, but the time will come when you will hear me.
DISRAELI—*Maiden Speech in the House of Commons.*

A sophistical rhetorician, inebriated with the exuberance of his own verbosity.
DISRAELI—*Speech, 1878.*

The hare-brained chatter of irresponsible frivolity.
DISRAELI—*Speech, 1878.*

Miss not the discourse of the elders.
Ecclesiasticus. VIII. 9.

Blessed is the man who having nothing to say, abstains from giving us wordy evidence of the fact.
GEORGE ELIOT—*Impressions of Theophrastus.*

Speech is power: speech is to persuade, to convert, to compel.
EMERSON.

Speech is better than silence; silence is better than speech.
EMERSON—*Essay on Nominalist and Realist.*

In man speaks God.
HESIOD—*Works and Days.*

I love to hear thine earnest voice,
Wherever thou art hid . . .
Thou say'st an undisputed thing
In such a solemn way.
HOLMES—*To an Insect.*

For that man is detested by me as the gates of hell, whose outward words conceal his inmost thoughts.
HOMER—*Iliad.*

His speech flowed from his tongue sweeter than honey.
HOMER—*Iliad.*

Persuasive speech, and more persuasive sighs,
Silence that spoke, and eloquence of eyes.
HOMER—*Iliad.*

In laboring to be concise, I become obscure.
HORACE.

It is never so difficult to speak as when we are ashamed of our silence.
LA ROCHEFOUCAULD.

Speak gently! 'tis a little thing
Dropp'd in the heart's deep well:
The good, the joy, that it may bring
Eternity shall tell.
G. W. LANGFORD—*Speak Gently.*

In general those who nothing have to say
Contrive to spend longest time in doing it.
LOWELL—*To Charles Eliot Norton.*

Woe unto you, when all men shall speak well of you!
Luke. VI. 26.

They think that they shall be heard for their much speaking.
Matthew. VI. 7.

Out of the abundance of the heart the mouth speaketh.
Matthew. XII. 34.

When we are understood, we always speak well, and then all your fine diction serves no purpose.
MOLIÈRE.

If you your lips would keep from slips,
Five things observe with care;
To whom you speak, of whom you speak,
And how, and when, and where.
W. E. NORRIS—*Thirlby Hall.*

Do you wish people to speak well of you? Then do not speak at all yourself.
PASCAL.

Rhetoric is the art of ruling the minds of men.
PLATO.

It is a tiresome way of speaking, when you should despatch the business, to beat about the bush.
PLAUTUS.

And empty heads console with empty sound.
POPE—*Dunciad.*

Let no one be willing to speak ill of the absent.
PROPERTIUS.

A soft answer turneth away wrath.
Proverbs. XV. 1.

God, that all-powerful Creator of nature and Architect of the world, has impressed man with no character so proper to distinguish him from other animals, as by the faculty of speech.
QUINTILIAN.

He replies nothing but monosyllables. I believe he would make three bites of a cherry.
RABELAIS—*Pantagruel.*

Speak after the manner of men.
Romans. VI. 19.

When thought is speech, and speech is truth.
SCOTT—*Marmion.*

Speech was given to the ordinary sort of men, whereby to communicate their mind; but to wise men, whereby to conceal it.
BISHOP SOUTH—*Sermon.*

I have often regretted having spoken, never having kept silent.
SYRUS—*Maxims.*

Speak but little and well, if you would be esteemed as a man of merit.
TRENCH.

I disapprove of what you say, but I will defend to the death your right to say it.
Attributed to Voltaire.

Men use thought only to justify their wrong doings, and employ speech only to conceal their thoughts.
VOLTAIRE.

SPIDER

"Will you walk into my parlour?"
Said a spider to a fly;
"'Tis the prettiest little parlour
That ever you did spy."
MARY HOWITT—*The Spider and the Fly.*

The spider's touch, how exquisitely fine!
Feels at each thread, and lives along the line.
POPE—*Essay on Man.*

SPIRIT

Not of the letter, but of the spirit; for the letter killeth, but the spirit giveth life.
II Corinthians. III. 6.

The spirit indeed is willing, but the flesh is weak.
Matthew. XXVI. 41.

Millions of spiritual creatures walk the earth
Unseen, both when we wake, and when we sleep.
MILTON—*Paradise Lost.*

Ornament of a meek and quiet spirit.
I Peter. III. 4.

He that is slow to anger is better than the mighty; and he that ruleth his spirit than he that taketh a city.
Proverbs. XVI. 32.

A wounded spirit who can bear?
Proverbs. XVIII. 14.

SPORT

By sports like these are all their cares beguil'd,
The sports of children satisfy the child.
GOLDSMITH—*The Traveller.*

When I play with my cat, who knows whether I do not make her more sport, than she makes me?
MONTAIGNE.

If all the year were playing holidays,
To sport would be as tedious as to work.
SHAKESPEARE—*Henry IV.* Pt. I. Act I. Sc. 2.

When a man wants to murder a tiger he calls it sport: when the tiger wants to murder him he calls it ferocity.
GEORGE BERNARD SHAW—*Maxims for Revolutionists.*

SPRING

Now Spring returns; but not to me returns
The vernal joy my better years have known;
Dim in my breast life's dying taper burns,
And all the joys of life with health have flown.
MICHAEL BRUCE—*Elegy, written in Spring.*

Now Nature hangs her mantle green
On every blooming tree,
And spreads her sheets o' daisies white
Out o'er the grassy lea.
BURNS—*Lament of Mary Queen of Scots.*

Spring hangs her infant blossoms on the trees,
Rock'd in the cradle of the western breeze.
COWPER—*Tirocinium.*

If there comes a little thaw,
Still the air is chill and raw,
Here and there a patch of snow,
Dirtier than the ground below,
Dribbles down a marshy flood;
Ankle-deep you stick in mud
In the meadows while you sing,
"This is Spring."
C. P. CRANCH—*A Spring Growl.*

Daughter of heaven and earth, coy Spring,
With sudden passion languishing,
Teaching barren moors to smile,
Painting pictures mile on mile,
Holds a cup of cowslip wreaths
Whence a smokeless incense breathes.
EMERSON—*May Day.*

The spring's already at the gate
With looks my care beguiling;
The country round appeareth straight
A flower-garden smiling.
HEINE—*Book of Songs.*

I come, I come! ye have called me long,
I come o'er the mountain with light and song:
Ye may trace my step o'er the wakening earth,
By the winds which tell of the violet's birth,
By the primrose-stars in the shadowy grass,
By the green leaves, opening as I pass.
FELICIA D. HEMANS—*Voice of Spring.*

For surely in the blind deep-buried roots
Of all men's souls to-day
A secret quiver shoots.
RICHARD HOVEY—*Spring.*

And softly came the fair young queen
O'er mountain, dale, and dell;
And where her golden light was seen
An emerald shadow fell.
The good-wife oped the window wide,
The good-man spanned his plough;
'Tis time to run, 'tis time to ride,
For Spring is with us now.
LELAND—*Spring.*

Came the Spring with all its splendor,
All its birds and all its blossoms,
All its flowers, and leaves, and grasses.
LONGFELLOW—*Hiawatha.*

Thus came the lovely spring with a rush of blossoms and music,
Flooding the earth with flowers, and the air with melodies vernal.
LONGFELLOW—*Tales of a Wayside Inn.*

Awake! the morning shines, and the fresh field
Calls us; we lose the prime, to mark how spring
Our tended plants, how blows the citron grove,
What drops the myrrh, and what the balmy reed.
How nature paints her colours, how the bee
Sits on the bloom, extracting liquid sweet.
MILTON—*Paradise Lost.*

Yet Ah, that Spring should vanish with the Rose.
That Youth's sweetscented manuscript should close!
The Nightingale that in the branches sang
Ah whence and whither flown again, who knows?
OMAR KHAYYÁM—*Rubaiyat.*

Gentle Spring!—in sunshine clad,
Well dost thou thy power display!
For Winter maketh the light heart sad,
And thou,—thou makest the sad heart gay.
CHARLES D'ORLÉANS—*Spring.*

Hark! the hours are softly calling
Bidding Spring arise,
To listen to the rain-drops falling
From the cloudy skies,
To listen to Earth's weary voices,
Louder every day,
Bidding her no longer linger
On her charm'd way;
But hasten to her task of beauty
Scarcely yet begun.
ADELAIDE A. PROCTER—*Spring.*

There is no time like Spring,
When life's alive in everything,
Before new nestlings sing,
Before cleft swallows speed their journey back
Along the trackless track.
CHRISTINA G. ROSSETTI—*Spring.*

I sing the first green leaf upon the bough,
The tiny kindling flame of emerald fire,
The stir amid the roots of reeds, and how
The sap will flush the briar.
CLINTON SCOLLARD—*Song in March.*

For, lo! The winter is past, the rain is over and gone; the flowers appear on the earth; the time of the singing of birds is come, and the voice of the turtle is heard in our land.
The Song of Solomon. II. 11, 12.

Now the hedge meads renew
Rustic odor, smiling hue,
And the clean air shines and twinkles as the World goes wheeling through;
And my heart springs up anew,
Bright and confident and true,
And my old love comes to meet me in the dawning and the dew.
STEVENSON—*Poem written in 1876.*

O tender time that love thinks long to see,
Sweet foot of Spring that with her footfall sows

Late snow-like flowery leavings of the snows,
Be not too long irresolute to be;
O mother-month, where have they hidden thee?
SWINBURNE—*A Vision of Spring in Winter.*

The bee buzz'd up in the heat,
"I am faint for your honey, my sweet."
The flower said, "Take it, my dear,
For now is the Spring of the year.
So come, come!"
"Hum!"
And the bee buzz'd down from the heat.
TENNYSON—*The Forester.*

In the Spring a livelier iris changes on the burnish'd dove;
In the Spring a young man's fancy lightly turns to thoughts of love.
TENNYSON—*Locksley Hall.*

'Tis spring-time on the eastern hills!
Like torrents gush the summer rills;
Through winter's moss and dry dead leaves
The bladed grass revives and lives,
Pushes the mouldering waste away,
And glimpses to the April day.
WHITTIER—*Mogg Megone.*

And all the woods are alive with the murmur and sound of spring,
And the rosebud breaks into pink on the climbing briar,
And the crocus bed is a quivering moon of fire
Girdled round with the belt of an amethyst ring.
OSCAR WILDE—*Magdalen Walks.*

STAR

The spacious firmament on high,
With all the blue ethereal sky,
And spangled heavens, a shining frame,
Their great Original proclaim.
Forever singing, as they shine,
The hand that made us is divine.
ADDISON—*Ode.*

Surely the stars are images of love.
BAILEY—*Festus.*

What are ye orbs?
The words of God? the Scriptures of the skies?
BAILEY—*Festus.*

The sad and solemn night
Hath yet her multitude of cheerful fires;
The glorious host of light
Walk the dark hemisphere till she retires;
All through her silent watches, gliding slow,
Her constellations come, and climb the heavens, and go.
BRYANT—*Hymn to the North Star.*

When stars are in the quiet skies,
Then most I pine for thee;
Bend on me then thy tender eyes,
As stars look on the sea.
BULWER-LYTTON.

And the sentinel stars set their watch in the sky.
CAMPBELL—*The Soldier's Dream.*

No one sees what is before his feet: we all gaze at the stars.
CICERO.

While twilight's curtain gathering far,
Is pinned with a single diamond star.
M'DONALD CLARK—*Death in Disguise.*

Or soar aloft to be the spangled skies
And gaze upon her with a thousand eyes.
COLERIDGE—*Lines on an Autumnal Evening.*

The stars are golden fruit upon a tree
All out of reach.
GEORGE ELIOT—*The Spanish Gypsy.*

Hitch your wagon to a star.
EMERSON—*Society and Solitude.*

Why, who shall talk of shrines, of sceptres riven?
It is too sad to think on what *we* are,
When from its height afar
A world sinks thus; and yon majestic Heaven
Shines not the less for that one vanish'd star!
FELICIA D. HEMANS—*The Lost Pleiad.*

The dawn is lonely for the sun,
And chill and drear;
The one lone star is pale and wan,
As one in fear.
RICHARD HOVEY — *Chanson de Rosemonde.*

When, like an Emir of tyrannic power,
Sirius appears, and on the horizon black
Bids countless stars pursue their mighty track.
VICTOR HUGO—*The Vanished City.*

The morning stars sang together, and all the sons of God shouted for joy.
Job. XXXVIII. 7.

Canst thou bind the sweet influences of Pleiades, or loose the bands of Orion?
Job. XXXVIII. 31

Canst thou guide Arcturus with his sons?
Job. XXXVIII. 32.

When sunset flows into golden glows,
And the breath of the night is new,
Love finds afar eve's eager star—
That is my thought of you.
ROBERT UNDERWOOD JOHNSON—*Star Song.*

Who falls for love of God shall rise a star.
BEN JONSON—*Underwoods.*

The stars in their courses fought against Sisera.
Judges. V. 21.

Just above yon sandy bar,
As the day grows fainter and dimmer,
Lonely and lovely, a single star
Lights the air with a dusky glimmer.
LONGFELLOW—*Chryaor.*

Silently, one by one, in the infinite meadows of heaven,
Blossomed the lovely stars, the forget-me-nots of the angels.
LONGFELLOW—*Evangeline.*

Stars of the summer night!
Far in yon azure deeps
Hide, hide your golden light!
She sleeps!
My lady sleeps!
Sleeps.
LONGFELLOW—*Spanish Student.*

And made the stars,
And set them in the firmament of heav'n
T' illuminate the earth, and rule the day
In their vicissitude, and rule the night.
MILTON—*Paradise Lost.*

Brightest seraph, tell
In which of all these shining orbs hath man
His fixed seat, or fixed seat hath none,
But all these shining orbs his choice to dwell.
MILTON—*Paradise Lost.*

Now the bright morning-star, day's harbinger,
Comes dancing from the east.
MILTON—*Song on May Morning.*

And the day star arise in your hearts.
II Peter. I. 19.

Would that I were the heaven, that I might be
All full of love-lit eyes to gaze on thee.
PLATO—*To Stella.*

No star is ever lost we once have seen,
We always may be what we might have been.
ADELAIDE A. PROCTER—*Legend of Provence.*

Her blue eyes sought the west afar,
For lovers love the western star.
SCOTT—*Lay of the Last Minstrel*

These blessed candles of the night.
SHAKESPEARE—*Merchant of Venice.* Act V. Sc. 1.

He that strives to touch a star,
Oft stumbles at a straw.
SPENSER—*Shepherd's Calendar.*

Twinkle, twinkle, little star!
How I wonder what you are,
Up above the world so high,
Like a diamond in the sky!
ANNE TAYLOR—*Rhymes for the Nursery.*

Each separate star
Seems nothing, but a myriad scattered stars
Break up the Night, and make it beautiful.
BAYARD TAYLOR—*Lars.*

Many a night I saw the Pleiads, rising thro' the mellow shade,
Glitter like a swarm of fire-flies tangled in a silver braid.
TENNYSON—*Locksley Hall.*

You meaner beauties of the night,
That poorly satisfy our eyes.
More by your number than your light;
You common people of the skies,—
What are you when the moon shall rise?
SIR HENRY WOTTON—*On His Mistress, the Queen of Bohemia.*

One sun by day, by night ten thousand shine;
And light us deep into the Deity;
How boundless in magnificence and might.
YOUNG—*Night Thoughts.*

STATESMANSHIP

A disposition to preserve, and an ability to improve, taken together, would be my standard of a statesman.
BURKE—*Reflections on the Revolution in France.*

No statesman e'er will find it worth his pains
To tax our labours and excise our brains.
CHARLES CHURCHILL—*Night.*

The people of the two nations (French and English) must be brought into mutual dependence by the supply of each other's wants. There is no other way of counteracting the antagonism of language and race. It is God's own method of producing an *entente cordiale,* and no other plan is worth a farthing.
RICHARD COBDEN—*Letter to M. Michel Chevalier.* Sept., 1859.

I have the courage of my opinions, but I have not the temerity to give a political blank cheque to Lord Salisbury.
GOSCHEN. *In Parliament, Feb. 19, 1884.*

Ambassadors are the eye and ear of states.
GUICCIARDINI—*Storia d'Italia.*

Learn to think continentally.
ALEXANDER HAMILTON.

Peace, commerce, and honest friendship with all nations—entangling alliances with none.
JEFFERSON—*First Inaugural Address.*

Statesman, yet friend to truth; of soul sincere,
In action faithful, and in honour clear;
Who broke no promise, serv'd no private end,
Who gain'd no title, and who lost no friend;
Ennobled by himself, by all approv'd,
And prais'd, unenvy'd, by the Muse he lov'd.
POPE—*Epistle to Addison.*

It is well indeed for our land that we of this generation have learned to think nationally.
THEODORE ROOSEVELT—*Builders of the State.*

And statesmen at her council met
Who knew the seasons when to take
Occasion by the hand, and make
The bounds of freedom wider yet.
TENNYSON—*To the Queen.*

Why don't you show us a statesman who can rise up to the emergency, and cave in the emergency's head?
ARTEMUS WARD—*Things in New York.*

'Tis our true policy to steer clear of permanent alliances, with any portion of the foreign world—as far, I mean, as we are now at liberty to do it.
WASHINGTON—*Farewell Address.* Sept. 17, 1796.

An ambassador is an honest man sent to lie abroad for the commonwealth.
WOTTON.

STORM

Rides in the whirlwind, and directs the storm.
ADDISON—*The Campaign.*

The earth is rocking, the skies are riven—
Jove in a passion, in god-like fashion,
Is breaking the crystal urns of heaven.
ROBERT BUCHANAN — *Horatius Cogitandibus.*

He used to raise a storm in a teapot.
CICERO.

Bursts as a wave that from the clouds impends,
And swell'd with tempests on the ship descends;
White are the decks with foam; the winds aloud
Howl o'er the masts, and sing through every shroud:
Pale, trembling, tir'd, the sailors freeze with fears;
And instant death on every wave appears.
HOMER—*Iliad.*

The winds grow high;
Impending tempests charge the sky;
The lightning flies, the thunder roars;
And big waves lash the frightened shores.
PRIOR—*The Lady's Looking-Glass.*

Loud o'er my head though awful thunders roll,
And vivid lightnings flash from pole to pole,
Yet 'tis Thy voice, my God, that bids them fly,
Thy arm directs those lightnings through the sky.
Then let the good Thy mighty name revere,
And hardened sinners Thy just vengeance fear.
SCOTT—*On a Thunderstorm.*

Blow, wind, and crack your cheeks! rage! blow!
You cataracts and hurricanoes, spout
Till you have drench'd our steeples.
SHAKESPEARE—*King Lear.* Act III. Sc. 2.

His rash fierce blaze of riot cannot last,
For violent fires soon burn out themselves;
Small showers last long, but sudden storms are short.
SHAKESPEARE—*Richard II.* Act II. Sc. 1.

For many years I was self-appointed inspector of snow-storms and rainstorms and did my duty faithfully.
THOREAU—*Walden.*

STORY-TELLING

A schoolboy's tale, the wonder of an hour!
BYRON—*Childe Harold.*

This story will never go down.
HENRY FIELDING—*Tumble-Down Dick.*

When thou dost tell another's jest, therein
Omit the oaths, which true wit cannot need;
Pick out of tales the mirth, but not the sin.
GEORGE HERBERT—*Temple.*

And what so tedious as a twice-told tale.
HOMER—*Odyssey.*

But that is another story.
KIPLING—*Plain Tales from the Hills.*

It is a foolish thing to make a long prologue, and to be short in the story itself.
II Maccabees. II. 32.

An' all us other children, when the supper things is done,
We set around the kitchen fire an' has the mostest fun
A-list'nin' to the witch tales 'at Annie tells about
An' the gobble-uns 'at gits you
Ef you
Don't
Watch
Out!
JAMES WHITCOMB RILEY—*Little Orphant Annie.*

I cannot tell how the truth may be;
I say the tale as 'twas said to me.
SCOTT—*Lay of the Last Minstrel.*

I could a tale unfold whose lightest word
Would harrow up thy soul, freeze thy young blood,
Make thy two eyes, like stars, start from their spheres,
Thy knotted and combined locks to part
And each particular hair to stand on end,
Like quills upon the fretful porcupine.
SHAKESPEARE—*Hamlet*. Act. I. Sc. 5.

And thereby hangs a tale.
SHAKESPEARE — *Taming of the Shrew*.

For seldom shall she hear a tale
So sad, so tender, yet so true.
SHENSTONE—*Jemmy Dawson*.

STRATEGY

There webs were spread of more than common size,
And half-starved spiders prey'd on half-starved flies.
CHARLES CHURCHILL—*The Prophecy of Famine*.

Strategy is a system of makeshifts.
HELMUTH VON MOLTKE—*Essay on Strategy*.

Those oft are stratagems which errors seem,
Nor is it Homer nods, but we that dream.
POPE—*Essay on Criticism*.

STRENGTH

My strength is made perfect in weakness.
II Corinthians. XII. 9.

As thy days, so shall thy strength be.
Deuteronomy. XXXIII. 25.

A threefold cord is not quickly broken.
Ecclesiastes. IV. 12.

Like strength is felt from hope, and from despair.
HOMER—*Iliad*.

Their strength is to sit still.
Isaiah. XXX. 7.

They go from strength to strength.
Psalms. LXXXIV. 7.

I feel like a Bull Moose.
THEODORE ROOSEVELT. On returning from the Spanish War.

O, it is excellent
To have a giant's strength, but it is tyrannous
To use it like a giant.
SHAKESPEARE—*Measure for Measure*. Act II. Sc. 2.

So let it be in God's own might
We gird us for the coming fight,
And strong in Him whose cause is ours
In conflict with unholy powers,
We grasp the weapons he has given,—
The Light, and Truth, and Love of Heaven.
WHITTIER—*The Moral Warfare*.

STUDENT

Strange to the world, he wore a bashful look,
The fields his study, nature was his book.
BLOOMFIELD—*Farmer's Boy*.

Experience is the best of schoolmasters, only the school-fees are heavy.
CARLYLE—*Miscellaneous Essays*.

The world's great men have not commonly been great scholars, nor its great scholars great men.
HOLMES—*Autocrat of the Breakfast-Table*.

Where should the scholar live? In solitude, or in society? in the green stillness of the country, where he can hear the heart of Nature beat, or in the dark, gray town where he can hear and feel the throbbing heart of man?
LONGFELLOW—*Hyperion*.

He was a scholar, and a ripe and good one;
Exceeding wise, fair-spoken, and persuading;
Lofty and sour to them that lov'd him not;

But to those men that sought him sweet as summer.

SHAKESPEARE—*Henry VIII*. Act IV. Sc. 2.

STUDY

O Granta! sweet Granta! Where studious of ease,
I slumbered seven years, and then lost my degrees.

CHRISTOPHER ANSTEY—*New Bath Guide*.

Histories make men wise; poets, witty; the mathematics, subtile; natural philosophy, deep; morals, grave; logic and rhetoric, able to contend.

BACON—*Of Studies*.

When night hath set her silver lamp on high,
Then is the time for study.

BAILEY—*Festus*.

There are more men ennobled by study than by nature.

CICERO.

These (literary) studies are the food of youth, and consolation of age; they adorn prosperity, and are the comfort and refuge of adversity; they are pleasant at home, and are no incumbrance abroad; they accompany us at night, in our travels, and in our rural retreats.

CICERO.

As turning the logs will make a dull fire burn, so change of studies a dull brain.

LONGFELLOW—*Drift-Wood*.

You are in some brown study.

LYLY—*Euphues*.

Iron sharpens iron; scholar, the scholar.

Talmud.

STUPIDITY

We are growing serious, and, let me tell you, that's a very next step to being dull.

ADDISON—*The Drummer*.

With various readings stored his empty skull,
Learn'd without sense, and venerably dull.

CHURCHILL—*The Rosciad*.

He is not only dull himself, but the cause of dulness in others.

SAMUEL JOHNSON—*Boswell's Life of Johnson*.

The bookful blockhead, ignorantly read,
With loads of learned umber in his head.

POPE—*Essay on Criticism*.

Against stupidity the very gods
Themselves contend in vain.

SCHILLER—*Maid of Orleans*.

Peter was dull; he was at first
Dull,—Oh, so dull—so very dull!
Whether he talked, wrote, or rehearsed—
Still with his dulness was he cursed—
Dull—beyond all conception—dull.

SHELLEY—*Peter Bell the Third*.

STYLE

A chaste and lucid style is indicative of the same personal traits in the author.

HOSEA BALLOU.

One who uses many periods is a philosopher; many interrogations, a student; many exclamations, a fanatic.

J. L. BASFORD.

The least degree of ambiguity which leaves the mind in suspense as to the meaning ought to be avoided with the greatest care.

BLAIR.

Style is the dress of thoughts.

CHESTERFIELD—*Letter to His Son*.

Montesquieu had the style of a genius; Buffon, the genius of style.

BARON GRIMM.

Neat, not gaudy.

LAMB—*Letter to Wordsworth*.

The secret of force in writing lies not so much in the pedigree of nouns and adjectives and verbs, as in having something that you believe in to say, and making the parts of speech vividly conscious of it.

LOWELL.

Expression is the dress of thought, and still
Appears more decent as more suitable;
A vile conceit in pompous words express'd,
Is like a clown in regal purple dress'd.

POPE—*Essay on Criticism.*

Such labour'd nothings, in so strange a style,
Amaze th' learn'd, and make the learned smile.

POPE—*Essay on Criticism.*

Long sentences in a short composition are like large rooms in a little house.

SHENSTONE.

Clearness ornaments profound thoughts.

VAUVENARGUES.

SUCCESS

Be commonplace and creeping, and you attain all things.

BEAUMARCHAIS.

Success is full of promise till men get it; and then it is a last year's nest, from which the bird has flown.

HENRY WARD BEECHER.

Successful minds work like a gimlet,—to a single point.

BOVEE.

That low man seeks a little thing to do,
Sees it and does it:
This high man with a great thing to pursue,
Dies ere he knows it.
That low man goes on adding one to one,
His hundred's soon hit:
This high man, aiming at a million,
Misses an unit.

BROWNING—*Grammarian's Funeral.*

They never fail who die
In a great cause.

BYRON—*Marino Faliero.*

Be it jewel or toy,
Not the prize gives the joy,
But the striving to win the prize.

PISISTRATUS CAXTON (First Earl Lytton)—*The Boatman.*

All you need in this life is ignorance and confidence, and then success is sure.

S. L. CLEMENS (Mark Twain), 1887.

One never rises so high as when one does not know where one is going.

CROMWELL.

Nothing succeeds like success.

DUMAS—*Ange Pitou.*

The race is not to the swift, nor the battle to the strong.

Ecclesiastes. IX. 11.

If a man has good corn, or wood, or boards, or pigs to sell, or can make better chairs or knives, crucibles, or church organs, than anybody else, you will find a broad, hard-beaten road to his house, tho it be in the woods.

EMERSON—*In his Journal* (1855).

If a man write a better book, preach a better sermon, or make a better mouse-trap than his neighbor, tho he build his house in the woods, the world will make a beaten path to his door.

Mrs. Sarah S. B. Yule credits the quotation to EMERSON in her *Borrowings* (1889).

If you wish in this world to advance,
Your merits you're bound to enhance;
You must stir it and stump it,
And blow your own trumpet,
Or trust me, you haven't a chance.

W. S. GILBERT—*Ruddigore.*

The deed is everything, the glory naught.

GOETHE—*Faust.*

Somebody said that it couldn't be done,
But he with a chuckle replied
That "maybe it couldn't," but he would be one
Who wouldn't say so till he'd tried.

So he buckled right in with the trace of a grin
On his face. If he worried he hid it.
He started to sing as he tackled the thing
That couldn't be done, and he did it.
EDGAR A. GUEST—*It Couldn't Be Done.*

There are but two ways of rising in the world: either by one's own industry or profiting by the foolishness of others.
LA BRUYÈRE.

He will succeed; for he believes all he says.
MIRABEAU.

I have always observed that to succeed in the world one should appear like a fool but be wise.
MONTESQUIEU.

Either do not attempt at all, or go through with it.
OVID.

He that will not stoop for a pin will never be worth a pound.
PEPYS—*Diary.*

The race by vigour, not by vaunts, is won.
POPE—*Dunciad.*

Singing and dancing alone will not advance one in the world.
ROUSSEAU—*Confessions.*

Success makes some crimes honorable.
SENECA.

To climb steep hills
Requires slow pace at first.
SHAKESPEARE—*Henry VIII.* Act I. Sc. 1.

And he gave it for his opinion, that whoever could make two ears of corn, or two blades of grass, to grow upon a spot of ground where only one grew before, would deserve better of mankind and do more essential service to his country, than the whole race of politicians put together.
SWIFT—*Gulliver's Travels.*

Nothing succeeds so well as success.
TALLEYRAND.

Not to the swift, the race:
Not to the strong, the fight:
Not to the righteous, perfect grace:
Not to the wise, the light.
HENRY VAN DYKE—*Reliance.*

Faith, mighty faith, the promise sees,
And looks to that alone;
Laughs at impossibilities,
And cries it shall be done.
CHARLES WESLEY—*Hymns.*

Others may sing the song,
Others may right the wrong.
WHITTIER—*My Triumph.*

SUFFERING

Knowledge by suffering entereth,
And Life is perfected by Death.
E. B. BROWNING—*A Vision of Poets.*

I have trodden the wine-press alone.
Isaiah. LXIII. 3.

Ah, yes, the sea is still and deep,
All things within its bosom sleep!
A single step, and all is o'er,
A plunge, a bubble, and no more.
LONGFELLOW—*Christus.*

Have patience and endure; this unhappiness will one day be beneficial.
OVID.

And the poor beetle that we tread upon,
In corporal sufferance finds a pang as great
As when a giant dies.
SHAKESPEARE—*Measure for Measure.* Act III. Sc. 1.

Is it so, O Christ in heaven, that the highest suffer most,
That the strongest wander furthest, and more hopelessly are lost?
SARAH WILLIAMS—*In Twilight Hours.*

SUICIDE

Our time is fixed, and all our days are numbered;
How long, how short, we know not:—this we know,

Duty requires we calmly wait the summons,
Nor dare to stir till Heaven shall give permission.
BLAIR—*The Grave.*

It is cowardice to commit suicide.
NAPOLEON, 1817.

For who would bear the whips and scorns of time,
The oppressor's wrong, the proud man's contumely,
The pangs of despised love, the law's delay,
The insolence of office, and the spurns
That patient merit of the unworthy takes,
When he himself might his quietus make
With a bare bodkin?
SHAKESPEARE—*Hamlet.* Act III. Sc. 1.

There is no refuge from confession but suicide; and suicide is confession.
DANIEL WEBSTER.

SUMMER

One swallow alone does not make the summer.
CERVANTES—*Don Quixote.*

I question not if thrushes sing,
If roses load the air;
Beyond my heart I need not reach
When all is summer there.
JOHN VANCE CHENEY—*Love's World.*

O summer day beside the joyous sea!
O summer day so wonderful and white,
So full of gladness and so full of pain!
Forever and forever shalt thou be
To some the gravestone of a dead delight,
To some the landmark of a new domain.
LONGFELLOW—*A Summer Day by the Sea.*

Where'er you walk cool gales shall fan the glade,
Trees where you sit shall crowd into a shade.
Where'er you tread the blushing flowers shall rise,
And all things flourish where you turn your eyes.
POPE—*Pastorals. Summer.*

Oh, the summer night
Has a smile of light
And she sits on a sapphire throne.
B. W. PROCTER—*The Nights.*

Before green apples blush,
Before green nuts embrown,
Why, one day in the country
Is worth a month in town.
CHRISTINA G. ROSSETTI—*Summer.*

SUN

The sun, centre and sire of light,
The keystone of the world-built arch of heaven.
BAILEY—*Festus.*

Make hay while the sun shines.
CERVANTES—*Don Quixote.*

The glorious lamp of heaven, the radiant sun,
Is Nature's eye.
DRYDEN.

Father of rosy day,
No more thy clouds of incense rise;
But waking flow'rs,
At morning hours,
Give out their sweets to meet thee in the skies.
HOOD—*Hymn to the Sun.*

Whence are thy beams, O sun! thy everlasting light? Thou comest forth, in thy awful beauty; the stars hide themselves in the sky; the moon, cold and pale, sinks in the western wave. But thou, thyself, moves alone.
MACPHERSON—*Ossian.*

And see—the Sun himself!—on wings
Of glory up the East he springs.
Angel of Light! who from the time
Those heavens began their march sublime,
Hath first of all the starry choir
Trod in his Maker's steps of fire!
MOORE—*Lalla Rookh.*

In the warm shadow of her loveli-
ness;—
He kissed her with his beams.
SHELLEY—*The Witch of Atlas.*

Fairest of all the lights above,
Thou sun, whose beams adorn the
spheres,
And with unwearied swiftness move,
To form the circles of our years.
ISAAC WATTS.

SUN DIAL MOTTOES

Let not the sun go down upon your
wrath.
Ephesians. IV. 26.

Give God thy heart, thy service, and
thy gold;
The day wears on, and time is waxing
old.
*Sun Dial in the Garden of Glou-
cester Cathedral.*

The night cometh when no man can
work.
John. IX. 9.

Let others tell of storms and showers,
I'll only mark your sunny hours.
On a Sun Dial at Pittsfield, Mass.

As the long hours do pass away,
So doth the life a man decay.
*On a Sun Dial in the Garden of
the Royal Hotel at Sevenoaks,
Kent, England.*

Time is
Too Slow for those who Wait,
Too Swift for those who Fear,
Too Long for those who Grieve,
Too Short for those who Rejoice,
But for those who Love
Time is not.
HENRY VAN DYKE—*Motto for the
Sun Dial in the Garden of
Yaddo, Saratoga Springs, N. Y.*

SUNRISE

Wake! For the sun who scatter'd into
flight
The stars before him from the field of
night,
Drives night along with them from
heav'n, and strikes
The sultan's turret with a shaft of
light.
OMAR KHAYYÁM—*Rubaiyat.*

See! led by Morn, with dewy feet,
Apollo mounts his golden seat,
Replete with seven-fold fire;
While, dazzled by his conquering
light,
Heaven's glittering host and awful
night
Submissively retire.
THOMAS TAYLOR—*Ode to the Ris-
ing Sun.*

But yonder comes the powerful King
of Day,
Rejoicing in the East.
THOMSON—*Seasons.*

SUNSET

The death-bed of a day, how beautiful!
BAILEY—*Festus.*

It was the cooling hour, just when the
rounded
Red sun sinks down behind the
azure hill,
Which then seems as if the whole
earth is bounded,
Circling all nature, hush'd, and dim,
and still,
With the far mountain-crescent half
surrounded
On one side, and the deep sea calm
and chill
Upon the other, and the rosy sky
With one star sparkling through it
like an eye.
BYRON—*Don Juan.*

The sacred lamp of day
Now dipt in western clouds his part-
ing ray.
FALCONER—*The Shipwreck.*

Softly the evening came. The sun from
the western horizon
Like a magician extended his golden
wand o'er the landscape;
Twinkling vapors arose; and sky and
water and forest
Seemed all on fire at the touch, and
melted and mingled together.
LONGFELLOW—*Evangeline.*

Now in his Palace of the West,
Sinking to slumber, the bright Day,
Like a tired monarch fann'd to rest,
'Mid the cool airs of Evening lay;
While round his couch's golden rim
The gaudy clouds, like courtiers, crept—
Struggling each other's light to dim,
And catch his last smile ere he slept.
MOORE—*The Summer Fête.*

When the sun sets, who doth not look for night?
SHAKESPEARE—*Richard III.* Act II. Sc. 3.

SUPERSTITION

The general root of superstition is that men observe when things hit, and not when they miss; and commit to memory the one, and forget and pass over the other.
BACON.

Foul Superstition! howsoe'er disguised,
Idol, saint, virgin, prophet, crescent, cross,
For whatsoever symbol thou art prized,
Thou sacerdotal gain, but general loss!
Who from true worship's gold can separate thy dross?
BYRON—*Childe Harold.*

Religion is not removed by removing superstition.
CICERO.

There is in superstition a senseless fear of God: religion consists in the pious worship of Him.
CICERO.

A peasant can no more help believing in a traditional superstition than a horse can help trembling when he sees a camel.
GEORGE ELIOT.

Superstition is the poesy of practical life; hence, a poet is none the worse for being superstitious.
GOETHE.

I die adoring God, loving my friends, not hating my enemies, and detesting superstition.
VOLTAIRE.

SUSPICION

Suspicions amongst thoughts are like bats amongst birds, they ever fly by twilight.
BACON.

Suspicion is far more apt to be wrong than right; oftener unjust than just. It is no friend to virtue, and always an enemy to happiness.
HOSEA BALLOU.

Suspicion follows close on mistrust.
LESSING.

As to Caesar, when he was called upon, he gave no testimony against Clodius, nor did he affirm that he was certain of any injury done to his bed. He only said, "He had divorced Pompeia because the wife of Caesar ought not only to be clear of such a crime, but of the very suspicion of it."
PLUTARCH—*Life of Cicero.*

Suspicion always haunts the guilty mind;
The thief doth fear each bush an officer.
SHAKESPEARE—*Henry VI.* Pt. III. Act V. Sc. 6.

A woman of honor should not suspect another of things she would not do herself.
MARGUERITE DE VALOIS.

SWAN

All our geese are swans.
BURTON—*Anatomy of Melancholy.*

Place me on Sunium's marbled steep,
Where nothing save the waves and I
May hear our mutual murmurs sweep;
There, swan-like, let me sing and die.
BYRON—*Don Juan.*

Death darkens his eyes, and unplumes his wings,
Yet the sweetest song is the last he sings:

Live so, my Love, that when death shall come,
Swan-like and sweet it may waft thee home.
G. W. DOANE.

You think that upon the score of fore-knowledge and divining I am infinitely inferior to the swans. When they perceive approaching death they sing more merrily than before, because of the joy they have in going to the God they serve.
SOCRATES.

SWEETNESS

The pursuit of the perfect, then, is the pursuit of sweetness and light.
MATTHEW ARNOLD—*Culture and Anarchy.*

Every sweet hath its sour, every evil its good.
EMERSON—*Compensation.*

Sweet meat must have sour sauce.
BEN JONSON—*Poetaster.*

SWINE

Neither cast ye your pearls before swine.
Matthew. VII. 6.

SYMPATHY

Of a truth, men are mystically united: a mystic bond of brotherhood makes all men one.
CARLYLE—*Essays.*

The man who melts
With social sympathy, though not allied,
Is of more worth than a thousand kinsmen.
EURIPIDES.

He watch'd and wept, he pray'd and felt for all.
GOLDSMITH—*The Deserted Village.*

World-wide apart, and yet akin,
As showing that the human heart
Beats on forever as of old.
LONGFELLOW—*Tales of a Wayside Inn.*

For I no sooner in my heart divin'd,
My heart, which by a secret harmony
Still moves with thine, joined in connection sweet.
MILTON—*Paradise Lost.*

Never elated while one man's oppress'd;
Never dejected while another's blessed.
POPE—*Essay on Man.*

Somewhere or other there must surely be
The face not seen, the voice not heard,
The heart that not yet--never yet—ah me!
Made answer to my word.
CHRISTINA G. ROSSETTI—*Somewhere or Other.*

It (true love) is the secret sympathy,
The silver link, the silken tie,
Which heart to heart, and mind to mind
In body and in soul can bind.
SCOTT—*Lay of the Last Minstrel.*

T

TAILORS

It takes nine tailors to make a man.
Breton Proverb.

TALENT

To do easily what is difficult for others is the mark of talent.
AMIEL.

Concealed talent brings no reputation.
ERASMUS.

Talent without tact is only half talent.
HORACE GREELEY.

The world is always ready to receive talent with open arms.
O. W. HOLMES.

Talent is that which is in a man's power!
Genius is that in whose power a man is.
LOWELL—*Among My Books.*

TALK

"The time has come," the Walrus said,
"To talk of many things:
Of shoes—and ships—and sealing-wax—
Of cabbages—and kings—
And why the sea is boiling hot—
And whether pigs have wings."

LEWIS CARROLL—*Through the Looking Glass.*

But far more numerous was the herd of such,
Who think too little, and who talk too much.

DRYDEN—*Absalom and Achitophel.*

My tongue within my lips I rein;
For who talks much must talk in vain.

GAY—*Introducton to the Fables.*

And the talk slid north, and the talk slid south
With the sliding puffs from the hookah-mouth;
Four things greater than all things are—
Women and Horses and Power and War.

KIPLING—*Ballad of the King's Jest.*

In general those who nothing have to say
Contrive to spend the longest time in doing it.

LOWELL—*An Oriental Apologue.*

Those who have few things to attend to are great babblers; for the less men think, the more they talk.

MONTESQUIEU.

His talk was like a stream which runs
With rapid change from rock to roses;
It slipped from politics to puns;
It passed from Mahomet to Moses;
Beginning with the laws that keep
The planets in their radiant courses,
And ending with some precept deep
For dressing eels or shoeing horses.

PRAED—*The Vicar.*

They never taste who always drink;
They always talk who never think.

PRIOR.

Tut! tut! my lord! we will not stand to prate;
Talkers are no good doers, be assured;
We go to use our hands, and not our tongues.

SHAKESPEARE.

The secret of being tiresome is in telling everything.

VOLTAIRE.

TASTE

Good taste consists first upon fitness.

GEORGE WILLIAM CURTIS

Taste is the mind's tact.

DE BOUFFLERS.

My tastes are aristocratic; my actions democratic.

VICTOR HUGO.

Taste has never been corrupted by simplicity.

JOUBERT.

Good taste is the flower of good sense.

POINCELOT.

The finer impulse of our nature.

SCHILLER.

TAXES

Over-taxation cost England her colonies of North America.

BURKE.

Death and taxes are inevitable.

HALIBURTON.

The power to tax carries with it the power to embarrass and destroy.

SUPREME COURT OF THE UNITED STATES—*Evans vs. Gore,* 1920.

Men who prefer any load of infamy, however great, to any pressure of taxation, however light.

SYDNEY SMITH.

The repose of nations cannot be secure without arms, armies cannot be maintained without pay, nor can the pay be produced except by taxes.

TACITUS.

Taxation is the legitimate support of government.

THIERS.

TEA

Love and scandal are the best sweeteners of tea.

FIELDING.

Thank God for tea! what would the world do without tea? how did it exist? I am glad I was not born before tea.

SYDNEY SMITH—*Lady Holland's Memoir*.

TEACHING

You cannot teach old dogs new tricks.

ANONYMOUS.

The one exclusive sign of a thorough knowledge is the power of teaching.

ARISTOTLE.

What's a' your jargon o' your schools,
Your Latin names for horns and stools;
If honest nature made you fools.

BURNS—*Epistle to J. L——k*.

He is wise who can instruct us and assist us in the business of daily virtuous living.

CARLYLE—*Essays*.

The twig is so easily bended
I have banished the rule and the rod:
I have taught them the goodness of knowledge,
They have taught me the goodness of God;
My heart is the dungeon of darkness,
Where I shut them for breaking a rule;
My frown is sufficient correction;
My love is the law of the school.

CHARLES M. DICKINSON—*The Children*.

You cannot teach a man anything; you can only help him to find it within himself.

GALILEO.

A boy is better unborn than untaught.

GASCOIGNE.

A teacher who is attempting to teach without inspiring the pupil with a desire to learn is hammering on cold iron.

HORACE MANN.

Education is our only political safety.

HORACE MANN.

Speak to the earth, and it shall teach thee.

Job. XII. 8.

He who honestly instructs reverences God.

MOHAMMED.

Public instruction should be the first object of government.

NAPOLEON.

To dazzle let the vain design,
To raise the thought and touch the heart, be thine!

POPE—*Moral Essays*.

The teacher is like the candle which lights others in consuming itself.

RUFFINI.

I am not a teacher: only a fellow-traveller of whom you asked the way. I pointed ahead—ahead of myself as well as of you.

GEORGE BERNARD SHAW—*Getting Married*.

Everybody who is incapable of learning has taken to teaching.

WILDE—*The Decay of Lying*.

TEARS

Dear Lord, though I be changed to senseless clay,
And serve the Potter as he turns his wheel,
I thank Thee for the gracious gift of tears!

T. B. ALDRICH—*Two Moods*.

And friends, dear friends,—when it shall be
That this low breath is gone from me,
And round my bier ye come to weep,
Let One, most loving of you all,
Say, "Not a tear must o'er her fall;
He giveth His beloved sleep."

E. B. BROWNING—*The Sleep*.

Oh! too convincing—dangerously dear—
In woman's eye the unanswerable tear!
That weapon of her weakness she can wield,
To save, subdue—at once her spear and shield.
Byron—*Corsair.*

There is a tear for all who die,
A mourner o'er the humblest grave.
Byron—*Elegiac Stanzas.*

For Beauty's tears are lovelier than her smile.
Campbell—*Pleasures of Hope.*

Nothing dries sooner than a tear.
Cicero.

Words that weep and tears that speak.
Abraham Cowley—*The Prophet.*

Weep no more, nor sigh, nor groan,
Sorrow calls no time that's gone:
Violets plucked the sweetest rain
Makes not fresh nor grow again.
John Fletcher—*Queen of Corinth.*

Never a tear bedims the eye
That time and patience will not dry.
Bret Harte—*Lost Galleon.*

Accept these grateful tears! for thee they flow,
For thee, that ever felt another's woe!
Homer—*Iliad.*

Oh! would I were dead now,
Or up in my bed now,
To cover my head now
And have a good cry!
Hood—*A Table of Errata.*

Jesus wept.
John. XI. 35 (Shortest verse in the Bible).

If the man who turnips cries,
Cry not when his father dies,
'Tis a proof that he had rather
Have a turnip than his father.
Samuel Johnson.

On parent knees, a naked new-born child
Weeping thou sat'st while all around thee smiled;
So live, that sinking in thy last long sleep
Calm thou may'st smile, while all around thee weep.
Sir William Jones—Taken from *Enchanted Fruit. Six Hymns to Hindu Deities.*

Tears are sometimes as weighty as words.
Ovid.

It is some relief to weep; grief is satisfied and carried off by tears.
Ovid.

Sweet drop of pure and pearly light;
In thee the rays of Virtue shine;
More calmly clear, more mildly bright,
Than any gem that gilds the mine.
Samuel Rogers—*On a Tear.*

If you have tears, prepare to shed them now.
Shakespeare—*Julius Caesar.* Act III. Sc. 2.

When that the poor have cried, Caesar hath wept:
Ambition should be made of sterner stuff:
Yet Brutus says he was ambitious;
And Brutus is an honourable man.
Shakespeare—*Julius Caesar.* Act IV. Sc. 3.

Tears, idle tears, I know not what they mean,
Tears from the depths of some divine despair.
Tennyson—*The Princess.*

Two aged men, that had been foes for life,
Met by a grave, and wept—and in those tears
They washed away the memory of their strife;
Then wept again the loss of all those years.
Frederick Tennyson — *The Golden City.*

The tears of the young who go their way, last a day;
But the grief is long of the old who stay.
Trowbridge—*A Home Idyll.*

Tears are the silent language of grief.
Voltaire—*A Philosophical Dictionary.*

When summoned hence to thine eternal sleep,
Oh, may'st thou smile while all around thee weep.
CHARLES WESLEY—*On an Infant.*

TEMPERANCE

The first draught serveth for health, the second for pleasure, the third for shame, and the fourth for madness.
ANACHARSIS.

Temperance to be a virtue must be free, and not forced.
BARTOL.

Every moderate drinker could abandon the intoxicating cup if he would; every inebriate would if he could.
J. B. GOUGH.

Drink not the third glass, which thou canst not tame,
When once it is within thee; but before
Mayst rule it, as thou list: and pour the shame,
Which it would pour on thee, upon the floor.
It is most just to throw that on the ground,
Which would throw me there, if I keep the round.
HERBERT—*Temple. The Church Porch.*

Well observe
The rule of Not too much, by temperance taught
In what thou eat'st and drink'st.
MILTON—*Paradise Lost.*

Drinking water neither makes a man sick, nor in debt, nor his wife a widow.
JOHN NEAL.

Use, do not abuse; neither abstinence nor excess ever renders man happy.
VOLTAIRE.

TEMPTATION

Why comes temptation but for man to meet
And master and make crouch beneath his foot,
And so be pedestaled in triumph?
BROWNING—*The Ring and the Book.*

I may not here omit those two main plagues, and common dotages of human kind, wine and women, which have infatuated and besotted myriads of people: they go commonly together.
BURTON—*Anatomy of Melancholy.*

So you tell yourself you are pretty fine clay
To have tricked temptation and turned it away,
But wait, my friend, for a different day;
Wait till you want to want to!
EDMUND VANCE COOKE—*Desire.*

Thou shalt abstain,
Renounce, refrain.
GOETHE—*Faust.*

Blessed is the man that endureth temptation; for when he is tried, he shall receive the crown of life.
James. I. 12.

Honest bread is very well—it's the butter that makes the temptation.
DOUGLAS JERROLD—*The Catspaw.*

Get thee behind me, Satan.
Matthew. XVI. 23.

But Satan now is wiser than of yore,
And tempts by making rich, not making poor.
POPE—*Moral Essays.*

Never resist temptation: prove all things: hold fast that which is good.
GEORGE BERNARD SHAW—*Maxims for Revolutionists.*

I can resist everything except temptation.
WILDE—*Lady Windermere's Fan.*

THANKFULNESS

When I'm not thank'd at all, I'm thank'd enough,
I've done my duty, and I've done no more.
HENRY FIELDING—*The Life and Death of Tom Thumb the Great.*

Your bounty is beyond my speaking;
But though my mouth be dumb, my heart shall thank you.
NICHOLAS ROWE—*Jane Shore.*

Beggar that I am, I am even poor in thanks.
SHAKESPEARE—*Hamlet.* Act II. Sc. 2.

How sharper than a serpent's tooth it is
To have a thankless child.
SHAKESPEARE—*King Lear.* Act I. Sc. 4.

From too much love of living,
From hope and fear set free,
We thank with brief thanksgiving
Whatever gods may be,
That no life lives forever,
That dead men rise up never;
That even the weariest river
Winds somewhere safe to sea.
SWINBURNE—*The Garden of Proserpine.*

THANKSGIVING DAY

Thanksgiving-day, I fear,
If one the solemn truth must touch,
Is celebrated, not so much
To thank the Lord for blessings o'er,
As for the sake of getting more!
WILL CARLETON—*Captain Young's Thanksgiving.*

Ah! on Thanksgiving day, when from East and from West,
From North and South, come the pilgrim and guest,
When the gray-haired New Englander sees round his board
The old broken links of affection restored,
When the care-wearied man seeks his mother once more,
And the worn matron smiles where the girl smiled before.
What moistens the lips and what brightens the eye?
What calls back the past, like the rich pumpkin pie?
WHITTIER—*The Pumpkin.*

THIEVING

In vain we call old notions fudge
And bend our conscience to our dealing.
The Ten Commandments will not budge
And stealing will continue stealing.
Motto of American Copyright League. Written 1885.

Who steals a bugle-horn, a ring, a steed,
Or such like worthless thing, has some discretion;
'Tis petty larceny: not such his deed
Who robs us of our fame, our best possession.
BERNI—*Orlando Innamorata.*

Kill a man's family, and he may brook it,
But keep your hands out of his breeches' pocket.
BYRON—*Don Juan.*

Stolen sweets are best.
COLLEY CIBBER—*Rival Fools.*

Stolen waters are sweet, and bread eaten in secret is pleasant.
Proverbs. IX. 17.

Stolen sweets are always sweeter:
Stolen kisses much completer;
Stolen looks are nice in chapels:
Stolen, stolen be your apples.
THOMAS RANDOLPH—*Song of Fairies.*

A plague upon it when thieves cannot be true one to another!
SHAKESPEARE—*Henry IV.* Pt. I. Act II. Sc. 2.

Let me tell you, Cassius, you yourself
Are much condemn'd to have an itching palm.
SHAKESPEARE—*Julius Caesar.* Act IV. Sc. 3.

The robb'd that smiles steals something from the thief:
He robs himself that spends a bootless grief.
SHAKESPEARE—*Othello.* Act I. Sc. 3.

You take my house when you do take
the prop
That doth sustain my house; you take
my life
When you do take the means whereby
I live.

SHAKESPEARE—*Merchant of Venice*. Act IV. Sc. 1.

The sun's a thief, and with his great
attraction
Robs the vast sea; the moon's an
arrant thief,
And her pale fire she snatches from
the sun:
The sea's a thief, whose liquid surge
resolves
The moon into salt tears: the earth's
a thief,
That feeds and breeds by a compos-
ture stolen
From general excrement: each thing's
a thief;
The laws, your curb and whip, in their
rough power
Have uncheck'd theft.

SHAKESPEARE—*Timon of Athens*. Act IV. Sc. 3.

THOUGHT

First thoughts are not always the best.

ALFIERI.

Great thoughts, like great deeds,
need
No trumpet.

BAILEY—*Festus*.

The power of Thought,—the magic of the Mind!

BYRON—*Corsair*.

Thought will not work except in silence.

CARLYLE.

My thoughts ran a wool-gathering.

CERVANTES—*Don Quixote*.

Any man may make a mistake; none but a fool will stick to it. Second thoughts are best as the proverb says.

CICERO.

Learning without thought is labor lost.

CONFUCIUS.

I think, therefore I am.

DESCARTES.

Second thoughts, they say, are best.

DRYDEN.

Great men are they who see that spiritual is stronger than any material force, that thoughts rule the world.

EMERSON—*Letters and Social Aims*.

Thoughts that breathe and words that burn.

GRAY—*Progress of Poesy*.

Great thoughts reduced to practice become great acts.

HAZLITT.

The mind grows by what it feeds on.

J. G. HOLLAND.

Why can't somebody give us a list of things that everybody thinks and nobody says, and another list of things that everybody says and nobody thinks?

HOLMES—*Professor at the Breakfast Table*.

He that never thinks never can be wise.

SAMUEL JOHNSON.

That fellow seems to me to possess but one idea, and that is a wrong one.

SAMUEL JOHNSON.

The thoughts that come often unsought, and, as it were, drop into the mind, are commonly the most valuable of any we have, and therefore should be secured, because they seldom return again.

LOCKE.

Thoughts so sudden, that they seem
The revelations of a dream.

LONGFELLOW—*Prelude to Tales of a Wayside Inn*.

All thoughts that mould the age begin
Deep down within the primitive soul.

LOWELL—*An Incident in a Railroad Car*.

A penny for your thought.

LYLY.

As he thinketh in his heart, so is he.

Proverbs. XXIII. 7.

At Learning's fountain it is sweet to drink,
But 'tis a nobler privilege to think.
J. G. Saxe—*The Library.*

Strange thoughts beget strange deeds.
Shelley—*The Cenci.*

A thought by thought is piled, till some great truth
Is loosened, and the nations echo round,
Shaken to their roots, as do the mountains now.
Shelley—*Prometheus Unbound.*

They are never alone that are accompanied with noble thoughts.
Sir Philip Sidney—*Arcadia.*

What a man *thinks* in his spirit in the world, that he *does* after his departure from the world when he becomes a spirit.
Swedenborg—*Divine Providence.*

When a thought is too weak to be expressed simply, it is a proof that it should be rejected.
Vauvenargues.

Great thoughts come from the heart.
Vauvenargues.

THUNDER

Loud roared the dreadful thunder,
The rain a deluge showers.
Andrew Cherry—*Bay of Biscay.*

The thunder,
Wing'd with red lightning and impetuous rage,
Perhaps hath spent his shafts, and ceases now
To bellow through the vast and boundless deep.
Milton—*Paradise Lost.*

That great artillery of God Almighty.
William Temple.

TIDE

The punctual tide draws up the bay,
With ripple of wave and hiss of spray.
Susan Coolidge—*On the Shore.*

The western tide crept up along the sand,
And o'er and o'er the sand,
And round and round the sand,
As far as eye could see
The rolling mist came down and hid the land:
And never home came she.
Kingsley—*The Sands o' Dee.*

The little waves, with their soft, white hands,
Efface the footprints in the sands,
And the tide rises, the tide falls.
Longfellow—*The Tide Rises, the Tide Falls.*

TIME

Backward, turn backward, O Time in your flight;
Make me a child again just for to-night.
Mother, come back from the echoless shore,
Take me again to your heart as of yore.
Elizabeth Akers Allen—*Rock Me to Sleep.*

In time take time while time doth last, for time
Is no time when time is past.
Anonymous.

Why slander we the times?
What crimes
Have days and years, that we
Thus charge them with iniquity?
If we would rightly scan,
It's not the times are bad, but man.
Dr. J. Beaumont—*Original Poems.*

Time flies and draws us with it. The moment in which I am speaking is already far from me.
Boileau.

Time was made for slaves.
John B. Buckstone—*Billy Taylor.*

Time is money.
Bulwer-Lytton—*Money.*

O Time! the beautifier of the dead,
Adorner of the ruin, comforter
And only healer when the heart hath bled—

Time! the corrector where our judgments err,
The test of truth, love, sole philosopher,
For all besides are sophists, from thy thrift
Which never loses though it doth defer—
Time, the avenger! unto thee I lift
My hands, and eyes, and heart, and crave of thee a gift.
BYRON—*Childe Harold.*

The more we live, more brief appear
Our life's succeeding stages;
A day to childhood seems a year,
And years like passing ages.
CAMPBELL—*A Thought Suggested by the New Year.*

Time's fatal wings do ever forward fly;
To every day we live, a day we die.
THOMAS CAMPION—*Come, Cheerful Day.*

The great mystery of Time, were there no other; the illimitable, silent, never-resting thing called Time, rolling, rushing on, swift, silent, like an all-embracing ocean tide, on which we and all the Universe swim like exhalations, like apparitions which *are,* and then *are not:* this is forever very literally a miracle; a thing to strike us dumb,—for we have no word to speak about it.
CARLYLE—*Heroes and Hero Worship.*

There is no remembrance which time does not obliterate, nor pain which death does not put an end to.
CERVANTES—*Don Quixote.*

I recommend you to take care of the minutes, for the hours will take care of themselves.
CHESTERFIELD.

Know the true value of time; snatch, seize, and enjoy every moment of it. No idleness, no laziness, no procrastination: never put off till to-morrow what you can do to-day.
CHESTERFIELD—*Letters to His Son.*

O tempora! O mores!
O what times! what morals!
CICERO.

Now is the accepted time.
II Corinthians. VI. 2.

Touch us gently, Time!
Let us glide adown thy stream
Gently,—as we sometimes glide
Through a quiet dream!
BARRY CORNWALL—*A Petition to Time.*

His time's forever, everywhere his place.
COWLEY—*Friendship in Absence.*

See Time has touched me gently in his race,
And left no odious furrows in my face.
CRABBE—*Tales of the Hall.*

Swift speedy Time, feathered with flying hours,
Dissolves the beauty of the fairest brow.
SAMUEL DANIEL—*Delia.*

Old Time, that greatest and longest established spinner of all! . . . his factory is a secret place, his work is noiseless, and his Hands are mutes.
DICKENS—*Hard Times.*

But what minutes! Count them by sensation, and not by calendars, and each moment is a day and the race a life.
DISRAELI—*Sybil.*

Time, to the nation as to the individual, is nothing absolute; its duration depends on the rate of thought and feeling.
DRAPER—*History of the Intellectual Development of Europe.*

To everything there is a season, and a time to every purpose under the heaven.
Ecclesiastes. III. 1.

Say not thou, What is the cause that the former days were better than these? for thou dost not inquire wisely concerning this.
Ecclesiastes. VII. 10.

Who loses a day loses life.
EMERSON.

Write it on your heart that every day is the best day in the year. No man has learned anything rightly, until he knows that every day is Doomday.

EMERSON—*Society and Solitude.*

Procrastination brings loss, delay danger.

ERASMUS.

Gather ye rose-buds while ye may,
Old Time is still a flying,
And this same flower that smiles to-day,
To-morrow will be dying.

HERRICK—*Hesperides.*

Enjoy the present day, trusting very little to the morrow.

HORACE—*Carmina.*

How short our happy days appear!
How long the sorrowful!

JEAN INGELOW—*The Mariner's Cave.*

My days are swifter than a weaver's shuttle.

Job. VII. 6.

The noiseless foot of Time steals swiftly by
And ere we dream of manhood, age is nigh.

JUVENAL—*Satires.*

Time, which strengthens Friendship, weakens Love.

LA BRUYÈRE.

Better late than never.

LIVY.

Time has laid his hand
Upon my heart, gently, not smiting it,
But as a harper lays his open palm
Upon his harp, to deaden its vibrations.

LONGFELLOW—*The Golden Legend.*

Alas! it is not till Time, with reckless hand has torn out half the leaves from the Book of Human Life to light the fires of human passion with, from day to day, that man begins to see that the leaves which remain are few in number.

LONGFELLOW—*Hyperion.*

We should count time by heart-throbs.

JAMES MARTINEAU.

The signs of the times.

Matthew. XVI. 3.

Who can undo
What time hath done? Who can win back the wind?
Beckon lost music from a broken lute?
Renew the redness of a last year's rose?
Or dig the sunken sunset from the deep?

OWEN MEREDITH—*Orval, or the Fool of Time.*

When time is flown, how it fled
It is better neither to ask nor tell,
Leave the dead moments to bury their dead.

OWEN MEREDITH—*Wanderer.*

For each age is a dream that is dying,
Or one is coming to birth.

ARTHUR O'SHAUGHNESSY—*We Are the Music Makers.*

Neither will the wave which has passed be called back; nor can the hour which has gone by return.

OVID.

Time makes more converts than reason.

THOMAS PAINE.

These are the times that try men's souls.

THOMAS PAINE—*The American Crisis.*

The present is our own; but while we speak,
We cease from its possession, and resign
The stage we tread on, to another race,
As vain, and gay, and mortal as ourselves.

THOMAS LOVE PEACOCK—*Time.*

Time is the wisest counsellor.

PERICLES.

Seize time by the forelock.

PITTACUS OF MITYLENE.

Years following years steal something ev'ry day.
At last they steal us from ourselves away.

POPE—*Imitations of Horace.*

Time conquers all, and we must time obey.

POPE—*Winter*.

A thousand years in thy sight are but as yesterday when it is past, and as a watch in the night.

Psalms. XC. 4.

We spend our years as a tale that is told.

Psalms. XC. 9.

Whilst we deliberate how to begin a thing, it grows too late to begin it.

QUINTILIAN.

Time flies on restless pinions—constant never.
Be constant—and thou chainest time forever.

SCHILLER—*Epigram*.

Upon my lips the breath of song,
Within my heart a rhyme,
Howe'er time trips or lags along,
I keep abreast with time!

CLINTON SCOLLARD—*The Vagrant*.

An age builds up cities: an hour destroys them.

SENECA.

There's a time for all things.

SHAKESPEARE—*Comedy of Errors*. Act II. Sc. 2.

The time is out of joint.

SHAKESPEARE—*Hamlet*. Act I. Sc. 5.

Time's the king of men,
He's both their parent, and he is their grave,
And gives them what he will, not what they crave.

SHAKESPEARE—*Pericles*. Act II. Sc. 3.

O, call back yesterday, bid time return.

SHAKESPEARE—*Richard II*. Act III. Sc. 2.

Yet, do thy worst, old Time; despite thy wrong,
My love shall in my verse ever live young.

SHAKESPEARE—*Sonnet*.

What seest thou else
In the dark backward and abysm of time?

SHAKESPEARE—*Tempest*. Act I. Sc. 2.

Make use of time, let not advantage slip;
Beauty within itself should not be wasted:
Fair flowers that are not gather'd in their prime
Rot and consume themselves in little time.

SHAKESPEARE—*Venus and Adonis*.

Unfathomable Sea! whose waves are years,
Ocean of Time, whose waters of deep woe
Are brackish with the salt of human tears!
Thou shoreless flood, which in thy ebb and flow
Claspest the limits of mortality!
And sick of prey, yet howling on for more,
Vomitest thy wrecks on its inhospitable shore,
Treacherous in calm, and terrible in storm,
Who shall put forth on thee,
Unfathomable sea?

SHELLEY—*Time*.

A wonderful stream is the River Time,
As it runs through the realms of Tears,
With a faultless rhythm, and a musical rhyme,
And a broader sweep, and a surge sublime
As it blends with the ocean of Years.

BENJAMIN F. TAYLOR—*The Long Ago*.

Every moment dies a man,
Every moment one is born.

TENNYSON—*Vision of Sin*.

Once in Persia reigned a king
Who upon his signet ring
Graved a maxim true and wise,
Which if held before the eyes
Gave him counsel at a glance
Fit for every change and chance.
Solemn words, and these are they:
"Even this shall pass away."

THEODORE TILTON—*The King's Ring*.

He was always late on principle, his principle being that punctuality is the thief of time.

OSCAR WILDE—*Picture of Dorian Gray.*

Our time is a very shadow that passeth away.

Wisdom of Solomon. II. 5.

Delivered from the galling yoke of time.

WORDSWORTH—*Laodamia.*

TOASTS

Some hae meat, and canna eat,
And some wad eat that want it;
But we hae meat, and we can eat,
And sae the Lord be thankit.

BURNS—*The Selkirk Grace.*

Here's a sigh to those who love me,
And a smile to those who hate;
And whatever sky's above me,
Here's a heart for every fate.

BYRON—*Letter to Thomas Moore.*

Were't the last drop in the well,
As I gasp'd upon the brink,
Ere my fainting spirit fell,
'Tis to thee that I would drink.

BYRON—*To Thomas Moore.*

Drink to her that each loves best,
And if you nurse a flame
That's told but to her mutual breast,
We will not ask her name.

THOMAS CAMPBELL—*A Toast.*

Here's to the red of it,
There's not a thread of it,
No, not a shred of it,
In all the spread of it,
From foot to head,
But heroes bled for it,
Faced steel and lead for it,
Precious blood shed for it,
Bathing in red.

JOHN DALY—*A Toast to the Flag.*

Ho! stand to your glasses steady!
'Tis all we have left to prize.
A cup to the dead already,—
Hurrah for the next that dies.

BARTHOLOMEW DOWLING—*Revelry in India*

You to the left and I to the right,
For the ways of men must sever,—
And it may be for a day and a night,
And it well may be forever.
But whether we meet or whether we part,
(For our ways are past our knowing)
A pledge from the heart to its fellow heart,
On the ways we all are going!
Here's luck!
For we know not where we are going.

RICHARD HOVEY—*At the Cross-roads.*

Here's to your good health, and your family's good health, and may you all live long and prosper.

IRVING—*Rip Van Winkle.*

Drink to me only with thine eyes,
And I will pledge with mine;
Or leave a kiss but in the cup,
And I'll not look for wine.

BEN JONSON—*To Celia.*

To the old, long life and treasure;
To the young, all health and pleasure.

BEN JONSON.

A glass is good, and a lass is good,
And a pipe to smoke in cold weather;
The world is good and the people are good,
And we're all good fellows together.

JOHN O'KEEFE—*Sprigs of Laurel.*

Here's a health to all those that we love,
Here's a health to all those that love us,
Here's a health to all those that love them that love those
That love them that love those that love us.

Old Toast.

Here's a health to you and yours who have done such thing for us and ours.
And when we and ours have it in our powers to do for you and yours what you and yours have done for us and ours,

Then we and ours *will* do for you and yours what you and yours have done for us and ours.
Old Toast.

Here's to you, as good as you are,
And here's to me, as bad as I am;
But as good as you are, and as bad as I am,
I am as good as you are, as bad as I am.
Old Scotch Toast.

I fill this cup to one made up
Of loveliness alone,
A woman, of her gentle sex
The seeming paragon;
To whom the better elements
And kindly stars have given
A form so fair that, like the air,
'Tis less of earth than heaven.
EDWARD C. PINKNEY—*A Health.*

Here's to the maiden of bashful fifteen;
Here's to the widow of fifty;
Here's to the flaunting, extravagant quean;
And here's to the housewife that's thrifty.
Let the toast pass,—
Drink to the lass,
I'll warrant she'll prove an excuse for the glass.
R. B. SHERIDAN—*School for Scandal.*

May you live all the days of your life.
SWIFT—*Polite Conversation.*

First pledge our Queen this solemn night,
Then drink to England, every guest;
That man's the best Cosmopolite
Who loves his native country best.
TENNYSON—*Hands All Round.*

May all your labors be in vein.
Yorkshire mining toast.

TOBACCO

It's all one thing—both tend into one scope—
To live upon Tobacco and on Hope,
The one's but smoke, the other is but wind.
SIR ROBERT AYTOUN—*Sonnet on Tobacco.*

Little tube of mighty pow'r,
Charmer of an idle hour,
Object of my warm desire.
ISAAC HAWKINS BROWNE—*A Pipe of Tobacco.*

He who doth not smoke hath either known no great griefs, or refuseth himself the softest consolation, next to that which comes from heaven.
BULWER-LYTTON—*What Will He Do With It?*

Some sigh for this and that;
My wishes don't go far;
The world may wag at will,
So I have my cigar.
HOOD—*The Cigar.*

For thy sake, tobacco, I
Would do anything but die.
LAMB—*A Farewell to Tobacco.*

For tho' at my simile many may joke,
Man is but a pipe—and his life but smoke.
Old Ballad.

Tobacco's but an Indian weed,
Grows green at morn, cut down at eve;
It shows our decay, we are but clay.
Think on this when you smoak Tobacco.
Quoted by SCOTT—*Rob Roy.*

Yes, social friend, I love thee well,
In learned doctors' spite;
Thy clouds all other clouds dispel
And lap me in delight.
CHARLES SPRAGUE—*To My Cigar.*

A cigarette is the perfect type of a perfect pleasure. It is exquisite, and it leaves one unsatisfied. What more can you want?
OSCAR WILDE—*Picture of Dorian Gray.*

TO-DAY

Out of Eternity
The new Day is born;
Into Eternity
At night will return.
CARLYLE—*To-day.*

Happy the man, and happy he alone,
He, who can call to-day his own:

He who, secure within, can say,
To-morrow, do thy worst, for I have liv'd to-day.
DRYDEN—*Imitation of Horace.*

One to-day is worth two to-morrows.
FRANKLIN.

What yesterday was fact to-day is doctrine.
JUNIUS.

Nothing that is can pause or stay;
The moon will wax, the moon will wane,
The mist and cloud will turn to rain,
The rain to mist and cloud again,
To-morrow be to-day.
LONGFELLOW—*Kéramos.*

To-morrow life is too late: live to-day.
MARTIAL.

Oh, the nursery is lonely and the garden's full of rain,
And there's nobody at all who wants to play,
But I think if I should only run with all my might and main,
I could leave this dreary country of To-day.
CAROLINE MCCORMICK—*Road to Yesterday.*

Rise! for the day is passing,
And you lie dreaming on;
The others have buckled their armour,
And forth to the fight have gone:
A place in the ranks awaits you,
Each man has some part to play;
The Past and the Future are nothing,
In the face of the stern To-day.
ADELAIDE PROCTER—*Legends and Lyrics.*

To-morrow comes, and we are where?
Then let us live to-day.
SCHILLER.

We know nothing of to-morrow; our business is to be good and happy to-day.
SYDNEY SMITH.

TOLERATION

Has not God borne with you these many years? Be ye tolerant to others.
HOSEA BALLOU.

Every man must get to heaven his own way.
FREDERICK THE GREAT.

We are all of one dying, one immortal family.
HENRY GILES.

Tolerance is the only real test of civilization.
ARTHUR HELPS.

Toleration is the best religion.
VICTOR HUGO.

It is intolerance to speak of toleration. Away with the word from the dictionary!
MIRABEAU.

Let those who celebrate by name, by waxlight at noonday, tolerate such as are content with the light of the sun.
VOLTAIRE.

TO-MORROW

Some say "to-morrow" never comes,
A saying oft thought right;
But if to-morrow never came,
No end were of "to-night."
The fact is this, time flies so fast,
That ere we've time to say
"To-morrow's come," presto! behold!
"To-morrow" proves "To-day."
ANONYMOUS.

Dreaming of a to-morrow, which to-morrow
Will be as distant then as 'tis to-day.
TOME BURGUILLOS—*To-morrow, and To-morrow.*

A shining isle in a stormy sea,
We seek it ever with smiles and sighs;
To-day is sad. In the bland To-be,
Serene and lovely To-morrow lies.
MARY CLEMMER—*To-morrow.*

Defer not till to-morrow to be wise,
To-morrow's Sun to thee may never rise;
Or should to-morrow chance to cheer thy sight
With her enlivening and unlook'd for light,

How grateful will appear her dawning rays!
As favours unexpected doubly please.
CONGREVE—*Letter to Cobham.*

Trust on and think To-morrow will repay;
To-morrow's falser than the former day;
Lies worse; and while it says, we shall be blest
With some new Joys, cuts off what we possest.
DRYDEN—*Aurengzebe.*

One today is worth two tomorrows.
FRANKLIN—*Poor Richard's Almanac.*

Never leave that till to-morrow which you can do to-day.
FRANKLIN—*Poor Richard's Almanac.*

Oh! to be wafted away
From this black Aceldama of sorrow,
Where the dust of an earthy to-day,
Makes the earth of a dusty to-morrow.
W. S. GILBERT—*Heart-Foam.*

There is a budding morrow in midnight.
KEATS.

Tomorrow! the mysterious, unknown guest,
Who cries to me: "Remember Barmecide,
And tremble to be happy with the rest."
And I make answer: "I am satisfied;
I dare not ask; I know not what is best;
God hath already said what shall betide."
LONGFELLOW—*To-morrow.*

To-morrow never yet
On any human being rose or set.
WILLIAM MARSDEN — *What Is Time?*

To-morrow you will live, you always cry;
In what fair country does this morrow lie,
That 'tis so mighty long ere it arrive?
Beyond the Indies does this morrow live?
'Tis so far-fetched, this morrow, that I fear
'Twill be both very old and very dear.
"To-morrow I will live," the fool does say:
To-day itself's too late;—the wise lived yesterday.
MARTIAL—*Epigrams.*

This day was yesterday to-morrow nam'd:
To-morrow shall be yesterday proclaimed:
To-morrow not yet come, not far away,
What shall to-morrow then be call'd?
To-day.
OWEN—*To-Day and To-Morrow.*

To-morrow, what delight is in to-morrow!
What laughter and what music, breathing joy,
Float from the woods and pastures, wavering down
Dropping like echoes through the long to-day,
Where childhood waits with weary expectation.
T. B. READ—*The New Pastoral.*

Where art thou, beloved To-morrow?
When young and old, and strong and weak,
Rich and poor, through joy and sorrow,
Thy sweet smiles we ever seek,—
In thy place—ah! well-a-day!
We find the thing we fled—To-day!
SHELLEY—*To-Morrow.*

To-morrow, to-morrow, not to-day,
Hear the lazy people say.
WEISSE.

A Man he seems of cheerful yesterdays
And confident to-morrows.
WORDSWORTH—*The Excursion.*

TONGUE

The magic of the tongue is the most dangerous of all spells.
BULWER-LYTTON—*Eugene Aram.*

The stroke of the tongue breaketh the bones. Many have fallen by the edge of the sword; but not so many as have fallen by the tongue.

Ecclesiasticus. XXVIII. 17, 18.

Birds are entangled by their feet and men by their tongues.

THOMAS FULLER.

Since word is thrall, and thought is free,
Keep well thy tongue, I counsel thee.

JAMES I OF SCOTLAND—*Ballad of Good Counsel*.

The tongue can no man tame; it is an unruly evil.

James. III. 8.

Though wickedness be sweet in his mouth, though he hide it under his tongue.

Job. XX. 12.

In her tongue is the law of kindness.

Proverbs. XXXI. 26.

Keep thy tongue from evil, and thy lips from speaking guile.

Psalms. XXXIV. 13.

My tongue is the pen of a ready writer.

Psalms. XLV. 1.

Many a man's tongue shakes out his master's undoing.

SHAKESPEARE—*All's Well That Ends Well*. Act II. Sc. 4.

TRAVELING

The traveled mind is the catholic mind educated from exclusiveness and egotism.

AMOS BRONSON ALCOTT—*Table-Talk*.

Travel, in the younger sort, is a part of education; in the elder, a part of experience. He that travelleth into a country before he hath some entrance into the language, goeth to school, and not to travel.

BACON—*Of Travel*.

He travels safest in the dark night who travels lightest.

HERNANDO CORTEZ.

I have been a stranger in a strange land.

Exodus. II. 22.

Know most of the rooms of thy native country before thou goest over the threshold thereof.

FULLER—*The Holy and Profane States*.

A wise traveler never despises his own country.

GOLDONI—*Pamela*.

I am fevered with the sunset,
I am fretful with the bay,
For the wander-thirst is on me
And my soul is in Cathay.

RICHARD HOVEY—*A Sea Gypsy*.

As the Spanish proverb says, "He who would bring home the wealth of the Indies must carry the wealth of the Indies with him." So it is in travelling: a man must carry knowledge with him, if he would bring home knowledge.

SAMUEL JOHNSON—*Boswell's Life of Johnson*.

Down to Gehenna or up to the throne,
He travels the fastest who travels alone.

KIPLING—*The Winners*.

Better sit still where born, I say,
Wed one sweet woman and love her well,
Love and be loved in the old East way,
Drink sweet waters, and dream in a spell,
Than to wander in search of the Blessed Isles,
And to sail the thousands of watery miles
In search of love, and find you at last
On the edge of the world, and a curs'd outcast.

JOAQUIN MILLER—*Pace Implora*.

He who is everywhere is nowhere.

SENECA.

I think it was Jekyll who used to say that the further he went west, the more convinced he felt that the wise men came from the east.

SYDNEY SMITH—*Lady Holland's Memoir*.

I pity the man who can travel from Dan to Beersheba and cry, "'Tis all barren!"

LAURENCE STERNE—*Sentimental Journey.*

O toiling hands of mortals! O wearied feet, travelling ye know not whither! Soon, soon, it seems to you, you must come forth on some conspicuous hill-top, and but a little way further, against the setting sun, descry the spires of El Dorado. Little do ye know your own blessedness; for to travel hopefully is a better thing than to arrive, and the true success is to labour.

STEVENSON—*El Dorado.*

'Tis a mad world (my masters) and in sadness
I travail'd madly in these dayes of madness.

JOHN TAYLOR—*Wandering to See the Wonders of the West.*

Let observation with extended observation observe extensively.

TENNYSON, paraphrasing Johnson.

Good company in a journey makes the way to seem the shorter.

IZAAK WALTON—*The Compleat Angler.*

All human race from China to Peru,
Pleasure, howe'er disguis'd by art, pursue.

THOMAS WARTON—*The Universal Love of Pleasure.*

TREACHERY

There is treachery, O Ahaziah.

II Kings. IX. 23.

Treachery, though at first very cautious, in the end betrays itself.

LIVY.

Et tu Brute! (You too, Brutus!)

SHAKESPEARE—*Julius Caesar.* Act III. Sc. 1.

TREASON

Is there not some chosen curse,
Some hidden thunder in the stores of heaven,
Red with uncommon wrath, to blast the man
Who owes his greatness to his country's ruin?

ADDISON—*Cato.*

With evil omens from the harbour sails
The ill-fated ship that worthless Arnold bears;
God of the southern winds, call up thy gales,
And whistle in rude fury round his ears.

PHILIP FRENEAU—*Arnold's Departure.*

Oh, colder than the wind that freezes
Whose treason, like a deadly blight,
Comes o'er the councils of the brave,
And blasts them in their hour of might!

MOORE—*Lalla Rookh.*

TREE

I think that I shall never scan
A tree as lovely as a man.

. . . .

A tree depicts divinest plan,
But God himself lives in a man.

ANONYMOUS.

The groves were God's first temples. Ere man learned
To hew the shaft, and lay the architrave,
And spread the roof above them,—ere he framed
The lofty vault, to gather and roll back
The sound of anthems; in the darkling wood,
Amidst the cool and silence, he knelt down
And offered to the Mightiest solemn thanks
And supplication.

BRYANT—*A Forest Hymn.*

No tree in all the grove but has its charms,
Though each its hue peculiar.

COWPER—*The Task.*

The monarch oak, the patriarch of
the trees,
Shoots rising up, and spreads by slow
degrees.
Three centuries he grows, and three
he stays
Supreme in state; and in three more
decays.
DRYDEN—*Palamon and Arcite.*

In the place where the tree falleth,
there it shall be.
Ecclesiastes. XI. 3.

Tall oaks from little acorns grow.
DAVID EVERETT.

Willow, in thy breezy moan,
I can hear a deeper tone;
Through thy leaves come whispering
low,
Faint sweet sounds of long ago—
Willow, sighing willow!
FELICIA D. HEMANS—*Willow Song.*

Faire pledges of a fruitful tree
Why do yee fall so fast?
Your date is not so past
But you may stay yet here awhile
To blush and gently smile
And go at last.
HERRICK—*To Blossoms.*

Those green-robed senators of mighty
woods,
Tall oaks, branch-charmed by the
earnest stars,
Dream, and so dream all night without a stir.
KEATS—*Hyperion.*

I think that I shall never see
A poem lovely as a tree.
. . . .
Poems are made by fools like me,
But only God can make a tree.
JOYCE KILMER—*Trees.*

Like two cathedral towers these stately
pines
Uplift their fretted summits tipped
with cones;
The arch beneath them is not built
with stones,
Not Art but Nature traced these lovely
lines,
And carved this graceful arabesque
of vines;
No organ but the wind here sighs
and moans,
No sepulchre conceals a martyr's
bones,
No marble bishop on his tomb re-
clines.
Enter! the pavement, carpeted with
leaves,
Give back a softened echo to thy
tread!
Listen! the choir is singing; all the
birds,
In leafy galleries beneath the eaves,
Are singing! listen, ere the soul be
fled,
And learn there may be worship with-
out words.
LONGFELLOW—*My Cathedral.*

This is the forest primeval.
LONGFELLOW—*Evangeline.*

The tree is known by his fruit.
Matthew. XII. 33.

Cedar, and pine, and fir, and branch-
ing palm,
A sylvan scene, and as the ranks ascend
Shade above shade, a woody theatre
Of stateliest view.
MILTON—*Paradise Lost.*

The tall Oak, towering to the skies,
The fury of the wind defies,
From age to age, in virtue strong,
Inured to stand, and suffer wrong.
MONTGOMERY—*The Oak.*

And the wind, full of wantonness,
woos like a lover
The young aspen-trees till they tremble
all over.
MOORE—*Lalla Rookh.*

Woodman, spare that tree!
Touch not a single bough!
In youth it sheltered me,
And I'll protect it now.
GEORGE P. MORRIS—*Woodman,
Spare That Tree.*

We hanged our harps upon the wil-
lows in the midst thereof.
Psalms. CXXXVII. 2.

So bright in death I used to say,
So beautiful through frost and cold!

A lovelier thing I know to-day,
The leaf is growing old,
And wears in grace of duty done,
The gold and scarlet of the sun.
MARGARET E. SANGSTER—*A Maple Leaf.*

Under the greenwood tree
Who loves to lie with me,
And tune his merry note
Unto the sweet bird's throat,
Come hither, come hither, come hither:
No enemy here shall he see,
But winter and rough weather.
SHAKESPEARE—*As You Like it.* Act II. Sc. 5.

The trees were gazing up into the sky,
Their bare arms stretched in prayer for the snows.
ALEXANDER SMITH—*A Life-Drama.*

Now rings the woodland loud and long,
The distance takes a lovelier hue,
And drowned in yonder living blue
The lark becomes a sightless song.
TENNYSON—*In Memoriam.*

Welcome, ye shades! ye bowery Thickets hail!
Ye lofty Pines! ye venerable Oaks!
Ye Ashes wild, resounding o'er the steep!
Delicious is your shelter to the soul.
THOMSON—*Seasons. Summer.*

In such green palaces the first kings reign'd,
Slept in their shades, and angels entertain'd;
With such old counsellors they did advise,
And by frequenting sacred groves grew wise.
EDMUND WALLER—*On St. James' Park.*

One impulse from a vernal wood
May teach you more of man,
Of moral evil and of good,
Than all the sages can.
WORDSWORTH—*The Tables Turned.*

TRIAL

'Tis a lesson you should heed,
Try, try, try again.
If at first you don't succeed,
Try, try, try again.
W. E. HICKSON—*Try and Try Again.*

But noble souls, through dust and heat,
Rise from disaster and defeat
The stronger.
LONGFELLOW—*The Sifting of Peter.*

These are the times that try men's souls.
THOMAS PAINE—*The Crisis.*

There are no crown-wearers in heaven who were not cross-bearers here below.
SPURGEON—*Gleaning among the Sheaves.*

TRIFLE

Seeks painted trifles and fantastic toys,
And eagerly pursues imaginary joys.
AKENSIDE—*The Virtuoso.*

Little deeds of kindness, little words of love,
Help to make earth happy, like the heaven above.
JULIA FLETCHER CARNEY—*Little Things.*

He that despiseth small things will perish by little and little.
EMERSON—*Prudence.*

Small things are best:
Grief and unrest
To rank and wealth are given;
But little things
On little wings
Bear little souls to Heaven.
REV. F. W. FABER.

For precept must be upon precept, precept upon precept; line upon line, line upon line; here a little, and there a little.
Isaiah. XXVIII. 10.

A little one shall become a thousand, and a small one a strong nation.
Isaiah. IX. 22.

Events of great consequence often spring from trifling circumstances.
LIVY.

For the maintenance of peace, nations should avoid the pin-pricks which forerun cannon-shots.
NAPOLEON to the Czar Alexander.

At every trifle scorn to take offence;
That always shows great pride or little sense.
POPE—*Essay on Criticism*.

And many strokes, though with a little axe,
Hew down and fell the hardest-timber'd oak.
SHAKESPEARE—*Henry VI*. Pt. III. Act. II. Sc. 1.

TROUBLE

Sweet is the remembrance of troubles when you are in safety.
EURIPIDES.

Troubles, like babies, grow larger by nursing.
LADY HOLLAND.

Man is born unto trouble, as the sparks fly upward.
Job. V. 7.

The true way to soften one's troubles is to solace those of others.
MME. DE MAINTENON.

Trouble and perplexity drive us to prayer, and prayer driveth away trouble and perplexity.
MELANCTHON.

Trifling troubles find utterance; deeply felt pangs are silent.
SENECA.

To take arms against a sea of troubles.
SHAKESPEARE—*Hamlet*. Act III. Sc. 1.

There are people who are always anticipating trouble, and in this way they manage to enjoy many sorrows that never really happen to them.
H. W. SHAW.

TRUST

All government is a trust. Every branch of government is a trust, and immemorially acknowledged to be so.
JEREMY BENTHAM.

Government is a trust, and the officers of the government are trustees; and both the trust and the trustees are created for the benefit of the people.
HENRY CLAY—*Speech*.

Public officers are the servants and agents of the people, to execute laws which the people have made and within the limits of a constitution which they have established.
GROVER CLEVELAND.

Trust in God, and keep your powder dry.
CROMWELL.

All power is a trust; that we are accountable for its exercise; that from the people and for the people all springs, and all must exist.
DISRAELI—*Vivian Grey*.

Trust men, and they will be true to you; treat them gently, and they will show themselves great.
EMERSON—*Essays*.

I believe in God, and I trust myself in His hands.
J. A. GARFIELD.

Women are more credulous than men.
VICTOR HUGO.

Thou trustest in the staff of this broken reed.
Isaiah. XXXVI. 6.

When a man assumes a public trust, he should consider himself as public property.
JEFFERSON.

Public office is a public trust.
DAN S. LAMONT.

O holy trust! O endless sense of rest!
Like the beloved John
To lay his head upon the Saviour's breast,
And thus to journey on!
LONGFELLOW—*Hymn*.

To be trusted is a greater compliment than to be loved.
GEORGE MACDONALD—*The Marquis of Lossie.*

I think we may safely trust a good deal more than we do.
THOREAU.

TRUTH

Yet the deepest truths are best read between the lines, and, for the most part, refuse to be written.
AMOS BRONSON ALCOTT—*Concord Days.*

But no pleasure is comparable to the standing upon the vantage ground of Truth.
BACON—*Essays.*

Think truly, and thy thoughts
Shall the world's famine feed.
Speak truly, and each word of thine
Shall be a fruitful seed.
Live truly, and thy life shall be
A great and noble creed.
HORATIUS BONAR—*Hymns of Faith and Hope.*

Truth, like the sun, submits to be obscured; but, like the sun, only for a time.
BOVEE.

Truth is mighty and will prevail.
THOMAS BROOKS, 1662.

If it is not true it is very well invented.
GIORDANO BRUNO.

Truth crushed to earth shall rise again:
Th' eternal years of God are hers;
But Error, wounded, writhes in pain,
And dies among his worshippers.
BRYANT—*The Battle Field.*

Better be cheated to the last,
Than lose the blessed hope of truth.
MRS. BUTLER (Fanny Kemble).

For truth is precious and divine;
Too rich a pearl for carnal swine.
BUTLER—*Hudibras.*

'Tis strange—but true; for truth is always strange,
Stranger than fiction.
BYRON—*Don Juan.*

A man protesting against error is on the way towards uniting himself with all men that believe in truth.
CARLYLE—*Heroes and Hero Worship.*

Every man seeks for truth; but God only knows who has found it.
CHESTERFIELD.

Truths turn into dogmas the moment they are disputed.
G. K. CHESTERTON—*Heretics.*

When fiction rises pleasing to the eye,
Men will believe, because they love the lie;
But truth herself, if clouded with a frown,
Must have some solemn proof to pass her down.
CHARLES CHURCHILL—*Epistle to Hogarth.*

He who has once deviated from the truth, usually commits perjury with as little scruple as he would tell a lie.
CICERO.

Our minds possess by nature an insatiable desire to know the truth.
CICERO.

Tell the truth or trump—but get the trick.
S. L. CLEMENS (Mark Twain)—*Pudd'nhead Wilson.*

"It was as true," said Mr. Barkis, . . . "as taxes is. And nothing's truer than them."
DICKENS—*David Copperfield.*

For truth has such a face and such a mien,
As to be lov'd needs only to be seen.
DRYDEN—*The Hind and the Panther.*

Truth is immortal; error is mortal.
MARY BAKER EDDY—*Science and Health.*

The greater the truth the greater the libel.
LORD ELLENBOROUGH.

Truth is too simple for us; we do not like those who unmask our illusions.
EMERSON.

Great is truth, and mighty above all things.
I Esdras. IV. 41.

Her terrible tale
You can't assail,
With truth it quite agrees;
Her taste exact
For faultless fact
Amounts to a disease.
W. S. GILBERT—*Mikado*.

Truth like a torch, the more 'tis shook, it shines.
SIR WILLIAM HAMILTON—*Discussions on Philosophy*.

One truth discovered is immortal, and entitles its author to be so: for, like a new substance in nature, it cannot be destroyed.
HAZLITT—*The Spirit of the Age*.

Dare to be true, nothing can need a lie;
A fault which needs it most, grows two thereby.
GEORGE HERBERT—*The Temple*.

Don't be "consistent," but be simply true.
HOLMES.

The truth shall make you free.
John. VIII. 32.

There is no truth in him.
John. VIII. 44.

Truth and justice are the immutable laws of social order.
LAPLACE.

It is said that truth is often eclipsed but never extinguished.
LIVY.

To love truth for truth's sake is the principal part of human perfection in this world, and the seed-plot of all other virtues.
LOCKE.

Who dares
To say that he alone has found the truth?
LONGFELLOW—*Christus*.

Truth forever on the scaffold. Wrong forever on the throne.
LOWELL—*The Present Crisis*.

Peace, if possible, but the truth at any rate.
LUTHER.

Children and fools speak true.
LYLY—*Endymion*.

But there is no veil like light—no adamantine armor against hurt like the truth.
GEORGE MACDONALD—*The Marquis of Lossie*.

The language of truth is unadorned and always simple.
AMMIANUS MARCELLINUS.

Truth is as impossible to be soiled by any outward touch as the sunbeam.
MILTON—*Doctrine and Discipline of Divorce*.

I speak truth, not so much as I would, but as much as I dare; and I dare a little the more as I grow older.
MONTAIGNE—*Essays*.

I seem to have been only like a boy playing on the seashore and diverting myself in now and then finding a smoother pebble or a prettier shell than ordinary, whilst the great ocean of truth lay all undiscovered before me.
ISAAC NEWTON—*Statement*.

In the mountains of truth, you never climb in vain.
NIETZSCHE — *Thus Spake Zarathustra*.

We know the truth, not only by the reason, but also by the heart.
PASCAL—*Thoughts*.

When truth or virtue an affront endures,
Th' affront is mine, my friend, and should be yours.
POPE—*Epilogue to Satires*.

To thine own self be true,
And it must follow, as the night the day,
Thou canst not then be false to any man.
SHAKESPEARE—*Hamlet*. Act I. Sc. 3.

Truth is truth
To the end of reckoning.
SHAKESPEARE—*Measure for Measure.* Act V. Sc. 1.

The seeming truth which cunning times put on
To entrap the wisest.
SHAKESPEARE—*Merchant of Venice.* Act III. Sc. 2.

They breathe truth that breathe their words in pain.
SHAKESPEARE—*Richard II.* Act II. Sc. 1.

My man's as true as steel.
SHAKESPEARE—*Romeo and Juliet.* Act II. Sc. 4.

When my love swears that she is made of truth,
I do believe her, though I know she lies.
SHAKESPEARE—*Sonnet.*

All great truths begin as blasphemies.
GEORGE BERNARD SHAW—*Annajanska.*

My way of joking is to tell the truth.
It's the funniest joke in the world.
BERNARD SHAW—*John Bull's Other Island.*

As scarce as truth is, the supply has always been in excess of the demand.
H. W. SHAW.

Truth and, by consequence, liberty, will always be the chief power of honest men.
MME. DE STAËL—*Coppet et Weimar.*

Tell truth, and shame the devil.
SWIFT—*Mary, the Cookmaid's Letter.*

Truth is strengthened by observation and time, pretences by haste and uncertainty.
TACITUS.

It takes two to speak the truth—one to speak, and another to hear.
THOREAU.

There are truths which are not for all men, nor for all times.
VOLTAIRE.

There is nothing so powerful as truth; and often nothing so strange.
DANIEL WEBSTER.

It is one thing to wish to have truth on our side, and another to wish sincerely to be on the side of truth.
ARCHBISHOP WHATELEY.

TURK

The unspeakable Turk should be immediately struck out of the question, and the country be left to honest European guidance.
CARLYLE—*Letter,* 1876.

We have on our hands a sick man,—a very sick man. (The sick man of Europe, the Turk.)
NICHOLAS I, OF RUSSIA.

TWILIGHT

The sunbeams dropped
Their gold, and passing in porch and niche,
Softened to shadows, silvery, pale, and dim,
As if the very Day paused and grew Eve.
EDWIN ARNOLD—*Light of Asia.*

Fair Venus shines
Even in the eye of day; with sweetest beam
Propitious shines, and shakes a trembling flood
Of softened radiance from her dewy locks.
ANNA LETITIA BARBAULD—*A Summer Evening's Meditation.*

The summer day is closed, the sun is set:
Well they have done their office, those bright hours,
The latest of whose train goes softly out
In the red west.
BRYANT—*An Evening Reverie.*

Parting day
Dies like the dolphin, whom each pang imbues

With a new colour as it gasps away,
The last still loveliest, till—'tis gone—
and all is gray.
BYRON—*Childe Harold.*

How lovely are the portals of the night,
When stars come out to watch the daylight die.
THOMAS COLE—*Twilight.*

Beauteous Night lay dead
Under the pall of twilight, and the love-star sickened and shrank.
GEORGE ELIOT—*Spanish Gypsy.*

Sweet shadows of twilight! how calm their repose,
While the dewdrops fall soft in the breast of the rose!
How blest to the toiler his hour of release
When the vesper is heard with its whisper of peace!
HOLMES—*Poems of the Class of '29.*

The gloaming comes, the day is spent,
The sun goes out of sight,
And painted is the occident
With purple sanguine bright.
ALEXANDER HUME—*Story of a Summer Day.*

The sun is set; and in his latest beams
Yon little cloud of ashen gray and gold,
Slowly upon the amber air unrolled,
The falling mantle of the Prophet seems.
LONGFELLOW—*A Summer Day by the Sea.*

The west is broken into bars
Of orange, gold, and gray,
Gone is the sun, come are the stars,
And night infolds the day.
GEORGE MACDONALD—*Songs of the Summer.*

From that high mount of God whence light and shade
Spring both, the face of brightest heaven had changed
To grateful twilight.
MILTON—*Paradise Lost.*

. . . th' approach of night
The skies yet blushing with departing light,
When falling dews with spangles deck'd the glade,
And the low sun had lengthen'd ev'ry shade.
POPE—*Pastorals.*

Twilight's soft dews steal o'er the village-green,
With magic tints to harmonize the scene.
Stilled is the hum that through the hamlet broke
When round the ruins of their ancient oak
The peasants flocked to hear the minstrel play,
And games and carols closed the busy day.
SAMUEL ROGERS—*Pleasures of Memory.*

Her feet along the dewy hills
Are lighter than blown thistledown;
She bears the glamour of one star
Upon her violet crown.
CLINTON SCOLLARD—*Duck.*

The weary sun hath made a golden set,
And, by the bright track of his fiery car,
Gives signal of a goodly day to-morrow.
SHAKESPEARE—*Richard III.* Act V. Sc. 3.

Twilight, ascending slowly from the east,
Entwined in duskier wreaths her braided locks
O'er the fair front and radiant eyes of day;
Night followed, clad with stars.
SHELLEY—*Alastor.*

Now the soft hour
Of walking comes; for him who lonely loves
To seek the distant hills, and there converse
With Nature, there to harmonize his heart,
And in pathetic Song to breathe around
The harmony to others.
THOMSON—*Seasons.*

Her eyes as stars of twilight fair,
Like twilight's too her dusky hair.
WORDSWORTH—*She Was a Phantom of Delight.*

TYRANNY

A king ruleth as he ought, a tyrant as he lists, a king to the profit of all, a tyrant only to please a few.
ARISTOTLE.

The tyrant now
Trusts not to men: nightly within his chamber
The watch-dog guards his couch, the only friend
He now dare trust.
JOANNA BAILLIE—*Ethwald.*

Tyranny
Absolves all faith; and who invades our rights,
Howe'er his own commence, can never be
But an usurper.
HENRY BROOKE—*Gustavus Vasa.*

Bad laws are the worst sort of tyranny.
BURKE.

Think'st thou there is no tyranny but that
Of blood and chains? The despotism of vice—
The weakness and the wickedness of luxury—
The negligence—the apathy—the evils
Of sensual sloth—produce ten thousand tyrants,
Whose delegated cruelty surpasses
The worst acts of one energetic master,
However harsh and hard in his own bearing.
BYRON—*Sardanapalus.*

Unlimited power corrupts the possessor; and this I know, that, where law ends, there tyranny begins.
CHATHAM.

Is there no tyrant but the crowned one?
CHÉNIER—*Caius Cracchus.*

He who strikes terror into others is himself in continual fear.
CLAUDIAN.

Tyrants have not yet discovered any chains that can fetter the mind.
COLTON.

Men are still men. The despot's wickedness
Comes of ill teaching, and of power's excess,—
Comes of the purple he from childhood wears,
Slaves would be tyrants if the chance were theirs.
VICTOR HUGO — *The Vanished City.*

Resistance to tyrants is obedience to God.
JEFFERSON.

Where the hand of tyranny is long we do not see the lips of men open with laughter.
SAADI.

O nation miserable
With an untitled tyrant bloody-scepter'd
When shalt thou see thy wholesome days again?
SHAKESPEARE—*Macbeth.* Act IV. Sc. 3.

'Tis time to fear when tyrants seem to kiss.
SHAKESPEARE—*Pericles.* Act I. Sc. 2.

The sovereign is called a tyrant who knows no laws but his caprice.
VOLTAIRE—*A Philosophical Dictionary.*

Arbitrary power is most easily established on the ruins of liberty abused to licentiousness.
WASHINGTON.

U

UGLINESS

An ugly face and the want of exterior beauty generally increases the interior beauty.
CHATFIELD.

Better an ugly face than an ugly mind.
JAMES ELLIS.

Absolute and entire ugliness is rare.
RUSKIN.

There is a sort of charm in ugliness, if the person has some redeeming qualities and is only ugly enough.
H. W. SHAW.

Nobody's sweetheart is ugly.
J. J. VADÉ.

UNBELIEF

The fearful Unbelief is unbelief in yourself.
CARLYLE—*Sartor Resartus.*

I'm from Missouri; you must show me.
COL. WILLARD D. VANDIVER.

UNCERTAINTY

All human things hang on a slender thread: the strongest fall with a sudden crash.
OVID.

This
I ever held worse than all certitude,
To know not what the worst ahead
might be.
SWINBURNE—*Marino Faliero.*

When the mind is in a state of uncertainty the smallest impulse directs it to either side.
TERENCE—*Andria.*

UNDERSTANDING

Whatever we well understand we express clearly, and words flow with ease.
BOILEAU.

What we do not understand we do not possess.
GOETHE.

The defects of the understanding, like those of the face, grow worse as we grow old.
LA ROCHEFOUCAULD.

The improvement of the understanding is for two ends: first, our own increase of knowledge; secondly, to enable us to deliver and make out that knowledge to others.
LOCKE.

When he to whom one speaks does not understand, and he who speaks himself does not understand, this is metaphysics.
VOLTAIRE.

UNION

When bad men combine, the good must associate; else they will fall, one by one, an unpitied sacrifice in a contemptible struggle.
BURKE.

I never use the word "nation" in speaking of the United States. I always use the word "Union" or "Confederacy." We are not a nation but a *union,* a confederacy of equal and sovereign States.
J. C. CALHOUN.

The Constitution in all its provision looks to an indestructible union composed of indestructible States.
SALMON P. CHASE.

There is no more sure tie between friends than when they are united in their objects and wishes.
CICERO.

Then join in hand, brave Americans
all!
By uniting we stand, by dividing we
fall.
JOHN DICKINSON—*Liberty Song,* 1768.

We must all hang together or assuredly we shall hang separately.
FRANKLIN.

Then none was for a party;
Then all were for the state;
Then the great man helped the poor,
And the poor man loved the great:
Then lands were fairly portioned;
Then spoils were fairly sold:
The Romans were like brothers
In the brave days of old.
MACAULAY — *Lays of Ancient Rome.*

The union of lakes—the union of
lands—
The union of States none can
sever—

The union of hearts—the union of hands—
And the flag of our Union for ever!
GEORGE P. MORRIS—*The Flag of Our Union*.

Behold how good and how pleasant it is for brethren to dwell together in unity.
Psalms. CXXXIII. 1.

By union the smallest states thrive, by discord the greatest are destroyed.
SALLUST.

We are one people and will act as one.
SCHILLER—*Wilhelm Tell*.

Liberty and Union, now and forever, one and inseparable.
DANIEL WEBSTER. 1830.

One Country, one Constitution, one Destiny.
DANIEL WEBSTER. 1837.

UNKINDNESS

Since trifles make the sum of human things,
And half our misery from our foibles springs;
Since life's best joys consist in peace and ease,
And though but few can serve, yet all may please;
Oh, let th' ungentle spirit learn from hence,
A small unkindness is a great offence.
HANNAH MORE—*Sensibility*.

In nature there's no blemish but the mind;
None can be call'd deform'd but the unkind.
SHAKESPEARE—*Twelfth Night*. Act III. Sc. 4.

V

VALOR

Let me die facing the enemy.
BAYARD.

Discretion, the best part of valor.
BEAUMONT and FLETCHER.

But where life is more terrible than death, it is then the truest valour to dare to live.
SIR THOMAS BROWNE.

The mean of true valor lies between the extremes of cowardice and rashness.
CERVANTES.

There is always safety in valor.
EMERSON.

My valor is certainly going!—it is sneaking off!—I feel it oozing out, as it were, at the palms of my hands.
SHERIDAN—*The Rivals*.

VALUE

That ye might learn in us not to think of men above that which is written.
I Corinthians. IV. 6.

We ought not to treat living creatures like shoes or household belonging, which when worn with use we throw away.
PLUTARCH—*Life of Cato the Censor*.

A cynic, a man who knows the price of everything and the value of nothing.
OSCAR WILDE—*Lady Windermere's Fan*.

VANITY

The vain being is the really solitary being.
AUERBACH.

It beareth the name of Vanity Fair, because the town where it is kept is "lighter than vanity."
BUNYAN—*Pilgrim's Progress*.

Oh, wad some power the giftie gie us
To see oursel's as ithers see us!
It wad frae monie a blunder free us,
And foolish notion.
BURNS—*To a Louse*.

Vanity has no sex.
COLTON.

Vanity of vanities, all is vanity.
Ecclesiastes. I. 2; XII. 8.

All is vanity and vexation of spirit.
Ecclesiastes. I. 14.

Vanity is as ill at ease under indifference as tenderness is under a love which it cannot return.
GEORGE ELIOT—*Daniel Deronda.*

That which makes the vanity of others unbearable to us is that which wounds our own.
LA ROCHEFOUCAULD.

We say little if not egged on by vanity.
LA ROCHEFOUCAULD.

She neglects her heart who studies her glass.
LAVATER.

What is your sex's earliest, latest care,
Your heart's supreme ambition? To be fair.
LORD LYTTLETON—*Advice to a Lady.*

Every man at his best state is altogether vanity.
Psalms. XXXIX. 5.

Surely men of low degree are vanity, and men of high degree are a lie: to be laid in the balance they are altogether lighter than vanity.
Psalms. LXII. 9.

Light vanity, insatiate cormorant,
Consuming means, soon preys upon itself.
SHAKESPEARE—*Richard II.* Act. II. Sc. 1.

Vanity makes men ridiculous, pride odious, and ambition terrible.
STEELE.

Vanity is often the unseen spur.
THACKERAY.

It is difficult to esteem a man as highly as he would wish.
VAUVENARGUES.

Maud Muller looked and sighed: "Ah me!
That I the Judge's bride might be!
He would dress me up in silks so fine,
And praise and toast me at his wine."
WHITTIER—*Maud Muller.*

VARIETY

Variety's the very spice of life,
That gives it all its flavour.
COWPER—*The Task.*

Variety's the source of joy below,
From whence still fresh-revolving pleasures flow,
In books and love the mind one end pursues,
And only change the expiring flame renews.
GAY—*Epistles.*

Countless the various species of mankind,
Countless the shades which sep'rate mind from mind;
No general object of desire is known,
Each has his will, and each pursues his own.
WILLIAM GIFFORD—*Perseus.*

Diversity, that is my motto.
LA FONTAINE.

When our old Pleasures die,
Some new One still is nigh;
Oh! fair Variety!
NICHOLAS ROWE.

VENICE

In Venice, Tasso's echoes are no more,
And silent rows the songless gondolier;
Her palaces are crumbling to the shore,
And music meets not always now the ear.
BYRON—*Childe Harold.*

White swan of cities, slumbering in thy nest
So wonderfully built among the reeds
Of the lagoon, that fences thee and feeds,
As sayeth thy old historian and thy guest!
LONGFELLOW—*Venice.*

The sylphs and undines
And the sea-kings and queens
Long ago, long ago, on the waves built a city,
As lovely as seems
To some bard in his dreams,
The soul of his latest love-ditty.
OWEN MEREDITH—*Venice.*

Once did she hold the gorgeous East in fee,
And was the safeguard of the west.
WORDSWORTH.

VICE

Vices of the time; vices of the man.
BACON.

Vice gets more in this vicious world
Than piety.
BEAUMONT and FLETCHER—*Love's Cure.*

One vice worn out makes us wiser than fifty tutors.
BULWER-LYTTON.

What maintains one vice would bring up two children.
FRANKLIN.—*Poor Richard's Almanac.*

Every vice makes its guilt the more conspicuous in proportion to the rank of the offender.
JUVENAL.

We do not despise all those who have vices, but we despise all those who have not a single virtue.
LA ROCHEFOUCAULD.

Saint Augustine! well hast thou said,
That of our vices we can frame
A ladder, if we will but tread
Beneath our feet each deed of shame.
LONGFELLOW—*The Ladder of St. Augustine.*

Spare the person, but lash the vice.
MARTIAL.

Human nature is not of itself vicious.
THOMAS PAINE.

Vice is a monster of so frightful mien,
As to be hated needs but to be seen;
Yet seen too oft, familiar with her face,
We first endure, then pity, then embrace.
POPE—*Essay on Man.*

The heart resolves this matter in a trice.
"Men only feel the smart, but not the vice."
POPE—*Horace.*

Vices are often habits rather than passions.
RIVAROL.

There is no vice so simple but assumes
Some mark of virtue on his outward parts.
SHAKESPEARE—*Merchant of Venice.* Act III. Sc. 2.

Vice lives and thrives best by concealment.
VERGIL.

VICTORY

Hannibal knows how to gain a victory, but not how to use it.
BARCA.

Victories that are cheap are cheap. Those only are worth having which come as the result of hard fighting.
HENRY WARD BEECHER.

How beautiful is victory, but how dear!
BOUFFLERS.

Kings may be blest, but Tam was glorious,
O'er a' the ills o' life victorious.
BURNS—*Tam o' Shanter.*

Out spoke the victor then,
As he hail'd them o'er the wave,
Ye are brothers, ye are men!
And we conquer but to save;
So peace instead of death let us bring;
But yield, proud foe, thy fleet,
With the crews, at England's feet,
And make submission meet
To our King.
CAMPBELL—*The Battle of the Baltic.*

Not one of all the purple host
Who took the flag to-day
Can tell the definition
So clear of victory,
As he, defeated, dying,
On whose forbidden ear
The distant strains of triumph
Break agonized and clear.
EMILY DICKINSON—*Success.*

Our peace must be a peace of victors, not of the vanquished.
GENERAL FOCH.

To the victors belong the spoils.
ANDREW JACKSON.

They see nothing wrong in the rule, that to the victors belong the spoils of the enemy.
W. L. MARCY—*Speech in U. S. Senate*, 1832.

Who overcomes
By force, hath overcome but half his foe.
MILTON—*Paradise Lost.*

There are some defeats more triumphant than victories.
MONTAIGNE.

Victory belongs to the most persevering.
NAPOLEON.

Before this time tomorrow I shall have gained a peerage or Westminster Abbey.
NELSON—*before the Battle of the Nile.*

It is the contest that delights us, and not the victory.
PASCAL.

We have met the enemy and they are ours.
OLIVER HAZARD PERRY.

Woe to the vanquished!
PLAUTUS.

We conquered France, but felt our captives' charms,
Her arts victorious triumph'd o'er our arms.
POPE—*Horace.*

But if
We have such another victory, we are undone.
Attributed to PYRRHUS by BACON—*Apothegms.*

Hail to the Chief who in triumph advances.
SCOTT—*Lady of the Lake.*

With dying hand, above his head,
He shook the fragment of his blade,
And shouted "Victory!—
Charge, Chester, charge; on, Stanley, on!"
Were the last words of Marmion.
SCOTT—*Marmion.*

To whom God will, there be the victory.
SHAKESPEARE—*Henry VI.* Pt. III. Act II. Sc. 5.

"But what good came of it at last?"
Quoth little Peterkin.
"Why, that I cannot tell," said he;
"But 'twas a famous victory."
SOUTHEY—*Battle of Blenheim.*

Victor and vanquished never unite in substantial agreement.
TACITUS.

There is nothing so dreadful as a great victory—except a great defeat.
Quoted as WELLINGTON'S.

It must be a peace without victory. . . . Victory would mean peace forced upon the loser; a victor's terms imposed upon the vanquished. It would be accepted in humiliation, under duress, at an intolerable sacrifice, and would leave a sting, a resentment, a bitter memory upon which terms of peace would rest not permanently, but only as upon quicksand. Only a peace between equals can last: only a peace, the very principle of which is equality, and a common participation in a common benefit.
WOODROW WILSON—*Address to the U. S. Senate, Jan. 22, 1917.*

VILLAINY

Calm, thinking villains, whom no faith could fix,
Of crooked counsels and dark politics.
POPE—*Temple of Fame.*

O villainy! Ho! let the door be lock'd;
Treachery! seek it out.
SHAKESPEARE—*Hamlet.* Act V. Sc. 2.

VIOLET

Early violets blue and white
Dying for their love of light.
EDWIN ARNOLD—*Almond Blossoms.*

Deep violets, you liken to
The kindest eyes that look on you,
Without a thought disloyal.
E. B. Browning—*A Flower in a Letter.*

The modest, lowly violet
In leaves of tender green is set;
So rich she cannot hide from view,
But covers all the bank with blue.
Dora Read Goodale—*Spring Scatters Far and Wide.*

The violets prattle and titter,
And gaze on the stars high above.
Heine—*Book of Songs.*

Welcome, maids of honor,
You doe bring
In the spring,
And wait upon her.
Herrick—*To Violets.*

We are violets blue,
For our sweetness found
Careless in the mossy shades,
Looking on the ground.
Love's dropp'd eyelids and a kiss,—
Such our breath and blueness is.
Leigh Hunt—*Songs and Chorus of the Flowers. Violets.*

Violet! sweet violet!
Thine eyes are full of tears;
Are they wet
Even yet
With the thought of other years?
Lowell—*Song.*

Hath the pearl less whiteness
Because of its birth?
Hath the violet less brightness
For growing near earth?
Moore—*Desmond's Song.*

Steals timidly away,
Shrinking as violets do in summer's ray.
Moore—*Lalla Rookh.*

The violet thinks, with her timid blue eye,
To pass for a blossom enchantingly shy.
Frances S. Osgood—*Garden Gossip.*

The violets whisper from the shade
Which their own leaves have made:
Men scent ou. fragrance on the air,
Yet take no heed
Of humble lessons we would read.
Christina G. Rossetti—*Consider the Lilies of the Field.*

The smell of violets, hidden in the green,
Pour'd back into my empty soul and frame
The times when I remembered to have been
Joyful and free from blame.
Tennyson — *Dream of Fair Women.*

And from his ashes may be made
The violet of his native land.
Tennyson—*In Memoriam.*

Banks that slope to the southern sky
Where languid violets love to lie.
Sarah Helen Whitman — *Wood Walks in Spring.*

A violet by a mossy stone
Half hidden from the eye!
Fair as a star when only one
Is shining in the sky.
Wordsworth—*Nutting.*

VIRTUE

Sweet are the slumbers of the virtuous man!
Addison—*Cato.*

One's outlook is a part of his virtue.
Amos Bronson Alcott—*Concord Days.*

Virtue, the strength and beauty of the soul,
Is the best gift of Heaven: a happiness
That even above the smiles and frowns of fate
Exalts great Nature's favourites: a wealth
That ne'er encumbers, nor can be transferr'd.
Armstrong—*Art of Preserving Health.*

Virtue is like a rich stone, best plain set.
Bacon—*Essays.*

Recommend to your children virtue; that alone can make happy, not gold.
Beethoven.

Virtue alone is the unerring sign of a noble soul.
BOILEAU.

Honor is the reward of virtue.
CICERO.

That which leads us to the performance of duty by offering pleasure as its reward, is not virtue, but a deceptive copy and imitation of virtue.
CICERO.

The more virtuous any man is, the less easily does he suspect others to be vicious.
CICERO.

The whole of virtue consists in its practice.
CICERO.

Virtue is not left to stand alone. *He who practices it* will have neighbors.
CONFUCIUS.

I believe that Virtue shows quite as well in rags and patches as she does in purple and fine linen.
DICKENS.

And virtue, though in rags, will keep me warm.
DRYDEN—*Imitation of Horace.*

The only reward of virtue is virtue.
EMERSON—*Essays.*

Yet why should learning hope success at court?
Why should our patriots' virtues support?
Why to true merit should they have regard?
They know that virtue is its own reward.
GAY—*Epistle to Methuen.*

Our virtues and vices spring from one root.
GOETHE.

The virtuous nothing fear but life with shame,
And death's a pleasant road that leads to fame.
GEORGE GRANVILLE (Lord Lansdowne).

Virtue knowing no base repulse, shines with untarnished honour; nor does she assume or resign her emblems of honour by the will of some popular breeze.
HORACE—*Carmina.*

Silver is less valuable than gold, gold than virtue.
HORACE—*Epistles.*

The good hate sin because they love virtue.
HORACE—*Epistles.*

Virtue is the only and true nobility.
JUVENAL.

To be discontented with the divine discontent, and to be ashamed with the noble shame, is the very germ of the first upgrowth of all virtue.
KINGSLEY—*Health and Education.*

Our virtues are most frequently but vices disguised.
LA ROCHEFOUCAULD.

Virtue is an angel, but she is a blind one, and must ask of Knowledge to show her the pathway that leads to her goal.
HORACE MANN.

Virtue may be assailed, but never hurt,
Surprised by unjust force, but not inthralled;
Yea, even that which mischief meant most harm
Shall in the happy trial prove most glory.
MILTON—*Comus.*

I prefer an accommodation vice to an obstinate virtue.
MOLIÈRE.

I find that the best virtue I have has in it some tincture of vice.
MONTAIGNE—*Essays.*

Virtue is not hereditary.
THOMAS PAINE.

Virtue is health, vice is sickness.
PETRARCH.

He who dies for virtue, does not perish.
PLAUTUS.

Virtue may choose the high or low degree,
'Tis just alike to virtue, and to me;

Dwell in a monk, or light upon a king,
She's still the same belov'd, contented thing.
Pope—*Epilogue to Satires.*

But sometimes virtue starves while vice is fed.
What then? Is the reward of virtue bread ?
Pope—*Essay on Man.*

O let us still the secret joy partake,
To follow virtue even for virtue's sake.
Pope—*Temple of Fame.*

The glory of riches and of beauty is frail and transitory; virtue remains bright and eternal.
Sallust.

For in the fatness of these prusy times
Virtue itself of vice must pardon beg.
Shakespeare—*Hamlet.* Act III. Sc. 4.

Virtue often trips and falls on the sharp-edged rock of poverty.
Eugène Sue.

Heaven made virtue; man, the appearance.
Voltaire.

Good company and good discourse are the very sinews of virtue.
Izaak Walton—*Compleat Angler.*

Virtue alone outbuilds the pyramids:
Her monuments shall last, when Egypt's fall.
Young—*Night Thoughts.*

VISION

Visions of glory, spare my aching sight!
Ye unborn ages, crowd not on my soul.
Gray—*The Bard.*

I have multiplied visions, and used similitudes.
Hosea. XII. 10.

Abou Ben Adhem (may his tribe increase!)
Awoke one night from a deep dream of peace,
And saw, within the moonlight in his room,
Making it rich, and like a lily in bloom,
An angel, writing in a book of gold;
Exceeding peace had made Ben Adhem bold,
And to the presence in the room he said—
"What writest thou?" The Vision raised its head,
And, with a look made all of sweet accord,
Answered, "The names of those who love the Lord."
Leigh Hunt—*Abou Ben Adhem and the Angel.*

And it shall come to pass afterward, that I will pour out my Spirit upon all flesh; and your sons and your daughters shall prophesy, your old men shall dream dreams, your young men shall see visions.
Joel. II. 28; *Acts.* II. 17.

It is a dream, sweet child! a waking dream,
A blissful certainty, a vision bright,
Of that rare happiness, which even on earth
Heaven gives to those it loves.
Longfellow—*Spanish Student.*

An angel stood and met my gaze,
Through the low doorway of my tent;
The tent is struck, the vision stays;
I only know she came and went.
Lowell—*She Came and Went.*

My thoughts by night are often filled
With visions false as fair:
For in the past alone, I build
My castles in the air.
Thomas Love Peacock—*Castles in the Air.*

Hence the fool's paradise, the statesman's scheme,
The air-built castle, and the golden dream,
The maid's romantic wish, the chemist's flame,
And poet's vision of eternal fame.
Pope—*Dunciad.*

Where there is no vision, the people perish.
Proverbs. XXIX. 18.

VOICE

Her voice changed like a bird's:
There grew more of the music, and less of the words.
BROWNING—*Flight of the Duchess.*

The devil hath not, in all his quiver's choice,
An arrow for the heart like a sweet voice.
BYRON—*Don Juan.*

The voice of the people is the voice of God.
HESIOD.

A still, small voice.
I Kings. XIX. 12.

Thy voice
Is a celestial melody.
LONGFELLOW—*Masque of Pandora.*

Her silver voice
Is the rich music of a summer bird,
Heard in the still night, with its passionate cadence.
LONGFELLOW — *The Spirit of Poetry.*

The voice of one crying in the wilderness.
Matthew. III. 3.

The soft contralto notes of a woman's voice are born in the immediate region of the heart.
ALFRED DE MUSSET.

Her voice was like the voice the stars
Had when they sang together.
DANTE GABRIEL ROSSETTI — *The Blessed Damozel.*

Her voice was ever soft,
Gentle and low, an excellent thing in woman.
SHAKESPEARE—*King Lear.* Act V. Sc. 3.

VOWS

Better is it that thou shouldest not vow, than that thou shouldest vow and not pay.
Ecclesiastes. V. 5.

Ease would recant
Vows made in pain, as violent and void.
MILTON—*Paradise Lost.*

W

WANT

It is not from nature, but from education and habits that our wants are chiefly derived.
FIELDING.

Man wants but little here below,
Nor wants that little long.
GOLDSMITH—*The Hermit.*

Constantly choose rather to want less, than to have more.
THOMAS À KEMPIS.

How few our real wants, and how vast our imaginary ones!
LAVATER.

The keener the want, the lustier the growth.
WENDELL PHILLIPS.

Hundreds would never have known want if they had not first known waste.
SPURGEON.

The stoical scheme of supplying our wants by lopping off our desires is like cutting off our feet when we want shoes.
SWIFT.

WAR

War is science of destruction.
JOHN S. C. ABBOTT.

Fifty-four forty (54°40′ N.), or fight.
WILLIAM ALLEN—*In the U. S. Senate,* the Oregon Boundary Question. (1844)

War cannot be put on a certain allowance.
ARCHIDAMUS III.

And by a prudent flight and cunning save
A life, which valour could not, from the grave.

A better buckler I can soon regain;
But who can get another life again?
ARCHILOCHUS.

All quiet along the Potomac they say
Except now and then a stray picket
Is shot as he walks on his beat, to and fro,
By a rifleman hid in the thicket.
ETHEL LYNN BEERS—*The Picket Guard.*

The inevitableness, the idealism, and the blessing of war, as an indispensable and stimulation law of development, must be repeatedly emphasized.
BERNHARDI—*Germany and the Next War.*

Just for a word—"neutrality," a word which in war-time had so often been disregarded—just for a scrap of paper, Great Britain was going to make war on a kindred nation who desired nothing better than to be friends with her.
BETHMANN-HOLLWEG, German Chancellor, 1914.

Better pointed bullets than pointed speeches.
BISMARCK—*Speech, 1850*

(The great questions of the day) are not decided by speeches and majority votes, but by blood and iron.
BISMARCK—*To the Prussian House of Delegates.*

It is magnificent, but it is not war.
GENERAL PIERRE BOSQUET.

He who did well in war just earns the right
To begin doing well in peace.
BROWNING—*Lauria.*

Lay down the axe; fling by the spade;
Leave in its track the toiling plough;
The rifle and the bayonet-blade
For arms like yours were fitter now;
And let the hands that ply the pen
Quit the light task, and learn to wield
The horseman's crooked brand, and rein
The charger on the battle-field.
BRYANT—*Our Country's Call.*

War never leaves, where it found a nation.
BURKE.

Scots, wha hae wi' Wallace bled;
Scots, wham Bruce has aften led,
Welcome to your gory bed,
Or to victory!
BURNS—*Bruce to His Men at Bannockburn.*

Bloody wars at first began,
The artificial plague of man,
That from his own invention rise,
To scourge his own iniquities.
BUTLER—*Upon the Weakness and Misery of Man.*

Hand to hand, and foot to foot:
Nothing there, save death, was mute;
Stroke, and thrust, and flash, and cry
For quarter or for victory,
Mingle there with the volleying thunder.
BYRON—*Siege of Corinth.*

In war events of importance are the result of trivial causes.
JULIUS CAESAR.

Veni, vidi, vici.
I came, I saw, I conquered.
JULIUS CAESAR.

War will never yield but to the principles of universal justice and love, and these have no sure root but in the religion of Jesus Christ.
WILLIAM ELLERY CHANNING.

An army abroad is of little use unless there are prudent counsels at home.
CICERO.

For your altars and your fires.
CICERO.

The law is silent during war.
CICERO.

We made war to the end—to the very end of the end.
CLEMENCEAU—*Message to American People.*

What voice did on my spirit fall,
Peschiera, when thy bridge I crossed?
"'Tis better to have fought and lost,
Than never to have fought at all."
A. H. CLOUGH—*Peschiera.*

War in fact is becoming contemptible, and ought to be put down by the great nations of Europe, just as we put down a vulgar mob.

MORTIMER COLLINS—*Thoughts in My Garden.*

But war's a game, which, were their subjects wise,
Kings would not play at.

COWPER—*The Task.*

General Taylor never surrenders.

THOMAS L. CRITTENDEN—*Reply to Gen. Santa.*

We give up the fort when there's not a man left to defend it.

GENERAL CROGHAN. *At Fort Stevenson.* (1812)

From fear in every guise,
From sloth, from love of pelf,
By war's great sacrifice
The world redeems itself.

J. DAVIDSON—*War Song.*

What argufies pride and ambition?
Soon or late death will take us in tow:
Each bullet has got its commission,
And when our time's come we must go.

CHARLES DIBDIN—*The Benevolent Tar.*

Carry his body hence!
Kings must have slaves:
Kings climb to eminence
Over men's graves:
So this man's eye is dim;
Throw the earth over him!

HENRY AUSTIN DOBSON—*Before Sedan.*

War, he sung, is toil and trouble;
Honour but an empty bubble.

DRYDEN—*Alexander's Feast.*

By the rude bridge that arched the flood,
Their flag to April's breeze unfurl'd;
Here once the embattl'd farmers stood,
And fired the shot heard round the world.

EMERSON—*Hymn sung at the completion of the Concord Monument.*

The essence of war is violence. Moderation in war is imbecility.

Attributed to LORD FISHER.

My right has been rolled up. My left has been driven back. My center has been smashed. I have ordered an advance from all directions.

Attributed to GENERAL FOCH.

Keep the home fires burning, while your hearts are yearning,
Tho' your lads are far away they dream of home.
There's a silver lining through the dark cloud shining;
Turn the dark cloud inside out till the boys come home.

MRS. LENA GUILBERT FORD.

There never was a good war or a bad peace.

FRANKLIN—*Letter to Quincy.*

I . . . purpose to fight it out on this line if it takes all summer.

U. S. GRANT—*Despatch from Spottsylvania.*

Yes; quaint and curious war is!
You shoot a fellow down
You'd treat if met where any bar is,
Or help to half-a-crown.

THOMAS HARDY—*The Man He Killed.*

Hark! I hear the tramp of thousands,
And of armèd men the hum;
Lo, a nation's hosts have gathered
Round the quick alarming drum—
Saying, Come,
Freemen, Come!
Ere your heritage be wasted,
Said the quick alarming drum.

BRET HARTE—*The Reveille.*

Hang yourself, brave Crillon. We fought at Arques, and you were not there.

HENRY IV, *to Crillon after a great victory.*

I war not with the dead.

HOMER—*Iliad.*

Our business in the field of fight
Is not to question, but to prove our might.

HOMER—*Iliad.*

It is not right to exult over slain men.
HOMER—*Odyssey.*

Mine eyes have seen the glory of the coming of the Lord:
He is trampling out the vintage where the grapes of wrath are stored:
He hath loosed the fateful lightning of his terrible swift sword:
His truth is marching on.
JULIA WARD HOWE—*Battle Hymn of the Republic.*

We don't want to fight, but by jingo if we do,
We've got the ships, we've got the men, we've got the money too.
We've fought the Bear before and while we're Britons true,
The Russians shall not have Constantinople.
G. W. HUNT.

He saith among the trumpets, Ha, ha; and he smelleth the battle afar off.
Job. XXXIX. 25.

I have prayed in her fields of poppies,
I have laughed with the men who died—
But in all my ways and through all my days
Like a friend He walked beside.
I have seen a sight under Heaven
That only God understands,
In the battles' glare I have seen Christ there
With the Sword of God in His hand.
GORDON JOHNSTONE—*On Fields of Flanders.*

The Philistines be upon thee, Samson.
Judges. XVI. 9.

The people arose as one man.
Judges. XX. 8.

For heathen heart that puts her trust
In reeking tube and iron shard—
All valiant dust that builds on dust,
And guarding calls not Thee to guard—
For frantic boast and foolish word,
Thy mercy on Thy People, Lord!
KIPLING—*Recessional.*

Modern warfare is an intricate business about which no one knows everything and few know very much.
FRANK KNOX—*Speech, 1942.*

There is no such thing as an inevitable war. If war comes it will be from failure of human wisdom.
BONAR LAW—*Speech before the Great War.*

When Greeks joined Greeks, then was the tug of war!
NATHANIEL LEE — *The Rival Queens.*

O God assist our side: at least, avoid assisting the enemy and leave the rest to me.
PRINCE LEOPOLD OF ANHALT-DESSAU.

The ballot is stronger than the bullet.
LINCOLN. (1856)

To arms! to arms! ye brave!
Th' avenging sword unsheathe,
March on! march on! all hearts resolved
On victory or death!
ROUGET DE LISLE—*The Marseillaise.*

At the Captain's mess, in the Banquet-hall,
Sat feasting the officers, one and all—
Like a sabre-blow, like the swing of a sail,
One raised his glass, held high to hail,
Sharp snapped like the stroke of a rudder's play,
Spoke three words only: "To the day!"
ERNEST LISSAUER—*Song of Hate against England.*

You need only a show of war to have peace.
LIVY—*History.*

Too late in moving here, too late in arriving there, too late in coming to this decision, too late in starting with enterprises, too late in preparing. In this war the footsteps of the allied forces have been dogged by the mocking specter of Too Late! and unless we quicken our movements, damnation will fall on the sacred cause for which so much gallant blood has flowed.
LLOYD GEORGE—Speech, in House of Commons. 1915.

Is it, O man, with such discordant noises,
With such accursed instruments as these,
Thou drownest Nature's sweet and kindly voices,
And jarrest the celestial harmonies?
LONGFELLOW—*Arsenal at Springfield*.

Ez for war, I call it murder,—
Ther you hev it plain and flat;
I don't want to go no furder
Than my Testyment for that.
LOWELL—*The Biglow Papers*.

Here I stand. I can do no other. God help me. Amen.
LUTHER—*Diet of Worms*. 1521.

I beg that the small steamers . . . be spared if possible, or else sunk without a trace being left. (Spurlos versenkt.)
COUNT KARL VON LUXBURG, *Chargé d'Affaires at Buenos Ayres to his Berlin Foreign Office*, 1917.

War in men's eyes shall be
A monster of iniquity
In the good time coming.
Nations shall not quarrel then,
To prove which is the stronger;
Nor slaughter men for glory's sake;—
Wait a little longer.
CHARLES MACKAY — *The Good Time Coming*.

The warpipes are pealing, "The Campbells are coming."
They are charging and cheering. O dinna ye hear it?
ALEXANDER MACLAGAN — *Jennie's Dream*.

Wars and rumours of wars.
Matthew. XXIV. 6.

Take up our quarrel with the foe!
To you from failing hands we throw
The torch; be yours to hold it high.
If ye break faith with us who die
We shall not sleep, though poppies grow
In Flanders' fields.
JOHN MCCRAE — *In Flanders' Fields*.

The brazen throat of war.
MILTON—*Paradise Lost*.

To overcome in battle, and subdue
Nations, and bring home spoils with infinite
Man-slaughter, shall be held the highest pitch
Of human glory.
MILTON—*Paradise Lost*.

When after many battles past,
Both tir'd with blows, make peace at last,
What is it, after all, the people get?
Why! taxes, widows, wooden legs, and debt.
FRANCIS MOORE—*Almanac*.

Providence is always on the side of the last reserve.
Attributed to NAPOLEON.

England expects every officer and man to do his duty this day.
NELSON—*Before the battle of Trafalgar*.

A soldier of the Legion lay dying in Algiers;
There was lack of woman's nursing, there was dearth of woman's tears.
C. E. S. NORTON—*Bingen on the Rhine*.

These are the times that try men's souls. The Summer soldier and the sunshine patriot will, in this crisis, shrink from the service of their country, but he that stands it *now* deserves the love and thanks of man and woman. Tyranny, like Hell, is not easily conquered; yet we have this consolation with us, that the harder the conflict the more glorious the triumph. What we obtain too cheaply we esteem too lightly; it is dearness only that gives everything its value. Heaven knows how to put a proper price upon its goods; and it would be strange indeed if so celestial an article as *freedom* should not be highly rated.
THOMAS PAINE—*The Crisis*.

Hell, Heaven or Hoboken by Christmas.
Attributed to GENERAL JOHN JOSEPH PERSHING. (1918)

They shall not pass.
GENERAL PÉTAIN. (1916)

Don't cheer, boys; the poor devils are dying.
CAPTAIN JOHN W. PHILIP, at the Battle of Santiago.

If I were an American, as I am an Englishman, while a foreign troop was landed in my country I never would lay down my arms,—never! never! never!
WILLIAM PITT THE ELDER. 1777.

It is the province of kings to bring wars about; it is the province of God to end them.
CARDINAL POLE—*To Henry VIII.*

War its thousands slays,
Peace its ten thousands.
PORTEUS—*Death.*

He that fights and runs away,
May turn and fight another day;
But he that is in battle slain,
Will never rise to fight again.
RAY—*History of the Rebellion.*

And he gathered them together into a place called in the Hebrew tongue Armageddon.
Revelation. XVI. 16.

The guard dies but never surrenders.
ROUGEMONT.

He never would believe that Providence had sent a few men into the world, ready booted and spurred to ride, and millions ready saddled and bridled to be ridden.
RICHARD RUMBOLD. *At his execution.* (1685)

"Charge, Chester, charge! On, Stanley, on!"
Were the last words of Marmion.
SCOTT—*Marmion.*

In the lost battle,
Borne down by the flying.
Where mingles war's rattle
With groans of the dying.
SCOTT—*Marmion.*

It's easy to fight when everything's right
And you're mad with the thrill and the glory;
It's easy to cheer when victory's near,
And wallow in fields that are gory.
It's a different song when everything's wrong,
When you're feeling infernally mortal;
When it's ten against one, and hope there is none,
Buck up, little soldier, and chortle!
ROBERT W. SERVICE—*Carry On.*

It is an irrepressible conflict between opposing and enduring forces.
WILLIAM H. SEWARD—*Speech.*

Sound trumpets! let our bloody colours wave!
And either victory, or else a grave.
SHAKESPEARE—*Henry VI.* Pt. III. Act II. Sc. 2.

The arms are fair,
When the intent of bearing them is just.
SHAKESPEARE—*Henry IV.* Pt. I. Act V. Sc. 2.

Lay on, Macduff,
And damn'd be him that first cries, "Hold, enough!"
SHAKESPEARE — *Macbeth.* Act V. Sc. 8.

Conscience avaunt, *Richard's* himself again:
Hark! the shrill trumpet sounds, to horse, away,
My soul's in arms, and eager for the fray.
SHAKESPEARE—*Richard III.* Act V. Sc. 3.

In the arts of life man invents nothing; but in the arts of death he outdoes Nature herself, and produces by chemistry and machinery all the slaughter of plague, pestilence and famine.
GEORGE BERNARD SHAW—*Man and Superman.*

Hold the Fort! I am coming.
GENERAL W. T. SHERMAN. Oct. 5, 1864.

War is hell.
Attributed to W. T. SHERMAN, 1880.

Lafayette, we are here.
COL. C. E. STANTON—*Speech*, July 4, 1917.

War, that mad game the world so loves to play.
SWIFT—*Ode to Sir William Temple.*

Not with dreams, but with blood and with iron
Shall a nation be moulded to last.
SWINBURNE — *A Word for the Country.*

Even war is better than a wretched peace.
TACITUS.

Forward, the Light Brigade!
Was there a man dismayed?
Not tho' each soldier knew
Some one had blunder'd.
Theirs not to make reply,
Theirs not to reason why,
Theirs but to do and die.
Into the valley of death
Rode the six hundred.
TENNYSON—*Charge of the Light Brigade.*

Cannon to right of them,
Cannon to left of them,
Volley'd and thunder'd;
Stormed at with shot and shell,
Boldly they rode and well,
Into the jaws of Death,
Into the mouth of Hell
Rode the six hundred.
TENNYSON—*Charge of the Light Brigade.*

It becomes a wise man to try negotiation before arms.
TERENCE.

Ten good soldiers, wisely led,
Will beat a hundred without a head.
D. W. THOMPSON.

Fight the good fight of faith.
I Timothy. VI. 12

War is elevation, because the individual disappears before the great conception of the state.
TREITSCHKE—*Politics.*

This is the soldier brave enough to tell
The glory-dazzled world that "war is hell."
HENRY VAN DYKE—*On the St. Gaudens' Statue of General Sherman.*

The love of arms and the mad wickedness of war are raging.
VERGIL—*Aeneid.*

It is said that God is always on the side of the heaviest battalions.
VOLTAIRE.

To be prepared for war is one of the most effectual means of preserving peace.
WASHINGTON, 1790.

Nothing except a battle lost can be half so melancholy as a battle won.
WELLINGTON—*Despatch.* (1815)

The battle of Waterloo was won on the playing field of Eton.
Attributed to WELLINGTON.

The whole art of war consists in getting at what is on the other side of the hill.
DUKE OF WELLINGTON.

We seemed to see our flag unfurled,
Our champion waiting in his place
For the last battle of the world,
The Armageddon of the race.
WHITTIER—*Rantoul.*

As long as war is regarded as wicked it will always have its fascinations. When it is looked upon as vulgar, it will cease to be popular.
OSCAR WILDE—*Intentions.*

It is not an army that we must train for war; it is a nation.
WOODROW WILSON—*Speech*, 1917.

But Thy most dreaded instrument
In working out a pure intent,
Is man,—arrayed for mutual slaughter,—
Yea, Carnage is Thy daughter.
WORDSWORTH. Poems dedicated to *National Independence and Liberty.*

WASHINGTON

Simple and brave, his faith awoke
Ploughmen to struggle with their fate;
Armies won battles when he spoke,
And out of Chaos sprang the state.
ROBERT BRIDGES—*Washington.*

While Washington's a watchword, such as ne'er
Shall sink while there's an echo left to air.
BYRON—*Age of Bronze.*

The character, the counsels, and example of our Washington . . . they will guide us through the doubts and difficulties that beset us; they will guide our children and our children's children in the paths of prosperity and peace, while America shall hold her place in the family of nations.
EDWARD EVERETT—*Speech,* 1858.

O Washington! thrice glorious name,
What due rewards can man decree—
Empires are far below thy aim,
And scepters have no charms for thee;
Virtue alone has your regards,
And she must be your great reward.
PHILIP FRENEAU — *Washington's Arrival in Philadelphia.*

Were an energetic and judicious system to be proposed with your signature it would be a circumstance highly honorable to your fame . . . and doubly entitle you to the glorious republican epithet,
The Father of your Country.
HENRY KNOX—*Letter to Washington.*

First in war, first in peace, first in the hearts of his countrymen.
GENERAL HENRY LEE — *Funeral Oration on Washington.*

This is the one hundred and tenth anniversary of the birthday of Washington. . . . We are met to celebrate this day. Washington is the mightiest name on earth—long since mightiest in the cause of civil liberty; still mightiest in moral reformation. On that name an eulogy is expected. It can not be. To add brightness to the sun or glory to the name of Washington is alike impossible. . . . Let none attempt it. In solemn awe pronounce the name and its naked, deathless splendor leave it shining on.
LINCOLN—*Speech,* Feb. 22, 1842.

Oh, Washington! thou hero, patriot sage,
Friend of all climes, and pride of every age!
THOMAS PAINE.

Every countenance seeked to say, "Long live George Washington, the Father of the People."
Pennsylvania Packet, April 21, 1789.

His work well done, the leader stepped aside
Spurning a crown with more than kingly pride.
Content to wear the higher crown of worth,
While time endures, "First citizen of earth."
JAMES J. ROCHE—*Washington.*

'Twas his ambition, generous and great
A life to life's great end to consecrate.
SHELLEY—*Washington.*

Washington—a fixed star in the firmament of great names, shining without winkling or obscuration, with clear, beneficent light.
DANIEL WEBSTER.

That name descending with all time, spreading over the whole earth, and uttered in all the languages belonging to all tribes and races of men, will forever be pronounced with affectionate gratitude by everyone in whose breast there shall arise an aspiration for human rights and liberty.
DANIEL WEBSTER—*Speech.*

WATER

Still waters run no mills.
Quoted by AGLIONBY—*Life of Bickerstaff.*

Pure water is the best of gifts that man to man can bring,
But who am I that I should have the best of anything?
Let princes revel at the pump, let peers with ponds make free,
Whisky, or wine, or even *beer* is good enough for me.
ANONYMOUS.

Pouring oil on troubled water.
BEDE—*Historia Ecclesiastica.*

Water, water, everywhere,
And all the boards did shrink;
Water, water, everywhere,
Nor any drop to drink.
COLERIDGE—*Ancient Mariner.*

The world turns softly
Not to spill its lakes and rivers,
The water is held in its arms
And the sky is held in the water.
What is water,
That pours silver,
And can hold the sky?
HILDA CONKLING—*Water.*

Unstable as water, thou shalt not excel.
Genesis. XLIX. 4.

Water is the mother of the vine,
The nurse and fountain of fecundity,
The adorner and refresher of the world.
CHARLES MACKAY—*The Dionysia.*

Stones are hollowed out by the constant dropping of water.
OVID.

It is wretched business to be digging a well just as thirst is mastering you.
PLAUTUS.

As water spilt on the ground, which cannot be gathered up again.
II Samuel. XIV. 14.

How dear to this heart are the scenes of my childhood,
When fond recollection presents them to view.

. . . . .

The old oaken bucket, the iron-bound bucket,
The moss-covered bucket, which hung in the well.
SAMUEL WOODWORTH—*The Old Oaken Bucket.*

How sweet from the green mossy brim to receive it,
As, poised on the curb, it inclined to my lips!
Not a full blushing goblet could tempt me to leave it,
The brightest that beauty or revelry sips.
SAMUEL WOODWORTH—*The Old Oaken Bucket.*

WEAKNESS

The cord breaketh at last by the weakest pull.
BACON—*On Seditions.*

But the concessions of the weak are the concessions of fear.
BURKE—*Speech on the Conciliation of America.*

Amiable weakness of human nature.
GIBBON—*Decline and Fall of the Roman Empire.*

The mortal race is far too weak not to grow dizzy on unwonted heights.
GOETHE.

And the weak soul, within itself unbless'd,
Leans for all pleasure on another's breast.
GOLDSMITH—*The Traveller.*

If weakness may excuse
What murderer, what traitor, parricide,
Incestuous, sacrilegious, but may plead it?
All wickedness is weakness; that plea, therefore,
With God or man will gain thee no remission.
MILTON—*Samson Agonistes.*

Heaven forming each on other to depend,
A master, or a servant, or a friend,
Bids each on other for assistance call,
Till one man's weakness grows the strength of all.
POPE—*Essay on Man.*

WEALTH

I have mental joys and mental health,
Mental friends and mental wealth,
I've a wife that I love and that loves me;
I've all but riches bodily.
WILLIAM BLAKE—*Mammon.*

But I have learned a thing or two; I know as sure as fate,
When we lock up our lives for wealth, the gold key comes too late.
WILL CARLETON—*The Ancient Miner's Story.*

Midas-eared Mommonism, double-barreled Dilettantism, and their thousand adjuncts and corollaries, are *not* the Law by which God Almighty has appointed this His universe to go.
CARLYLE—*Past and Present.*

Surplus wealth is a sacred trust which its possessor is bound to administer in his lifetime for the good of the community.
ANDREW CARNEGIE—*Gospel of Wealth.*

The foolish sayings of the rich pass for wise saws in society.
CERVANTES—*Don Quixote.*

The savings of many in the hands of one.
EUGENE V. DEBS.

Without a rich heart wealth is an ugly beggar.
EMERSON.

Give no bounties: make equal laws: secure life and prosperity and you need not give alms.
EMERSON—*Wealth.*

If you would be wealthy, think of saving as well as of getting.
FRANKLIN.

If your Riches are yours, why don't you take them with you to t'other world?
FRANKLIN—*Poor Richard.* (1751).

The ideal social state is not that in which each gets an equal amount of wealth, but in which each gets in proportion to his contribution to the general stock.
HENRY GEORGE—*Social Problems.*

Dame Nature gave him comeliness and health,
And Fortune (for a passport) gave him wealth.
W. HARTE—*Eulogius.*

These riches are possess'd, but not enjoy'd!
HOMER—*Odyssey.*

A little farm well tilled,
A little barn well filled,
A little wife well willed—
Give me, give me.
JAMES HOOK—*The Soldier's Return.*

Riches either serve or govern the possessor.
HORACE.

And you prate of the wealth of nations, as if it were bought and sold,
The wealth of nations is men, not silk and cotton and gold.
RICHARD HOVEY—*Peace.*

Life is short. The sooner that a man begins to enjoy his wealth the better.
SAMUEL JOHNSON.

All wealth is the product of labor.
LOCKE.

The rich man's son inherits cares;
The bank may break, the factory burn,
A breath may burst his bubble shares,
And soft, white hands could hardly earn
A living that would serve his turn.
LOWELL—*The Heritage.*

Our Lord commonly giveth Riches to such gross asses, to whom he affordeth nothing else that is good.
LUTHER—*Colloquies.*

The wealth of society is its stock of productive labor.
SIR JAMES MACKINTOSH.

It is easier for a camel to go through the eye of a needle, than for a rich man to enter into the kingdom of God.
Matthew. XIX. 24.

I am rich beyond the dreams of avarice.

EDWARD MOORE—*The Gamester.*

Get place and wealth, if possible, with grace;
If not, by any means get wealth and place.

POPE—*Epistles of Horace.*

Riches certainly make themselves wings.

Proverbs. XXIII. 5.

He that maketh haste to be rich shall not be innocent.

Proverbs. XXVIII. 20.

He heapeth up riches, and knoweth not who shall gather them.

Psalms. XXXIX. 6.

Probably the greatest harm done by vast wealth is the harm that we of moderate means do ourselves when we let the vices of envy and hatred enter deep into our own natures.

THEODORE ROOSEVELT—*Speech,* 1902.

No good man ever became suddenly rich.

SYRUS.

Rich in good works.

I Timothy. VI. 18.

WEDLOCK

There is a French saying: "Love is the dawn of marriage, and marriage is the sunset of love."

DE FINOD.

It destroys one's nerves to be amiable every day to the same human being.

DISRAELI.

Since all the maids are good and lovable, from whence come the evil wives?

LAMB.

The land of marriage has this peculiarity: that strangers are desirous of inhabiting it, while its natural inhabitants would willingly be banished from thence.

MONTAIGNE.

WEEDS

The richest soil, if uncultivated, produces the rankest weeds.

PLUTARCH.

WELCOME

'Tis sweet to hear the watch-dog's honest bark
Bay deep-mouth'd welcome as we draw near home;
'Tis sweet to know there is an eye will mark
Our coming, and look brighter when we come.

BYRON—*Don Juan.*

Come in the evening, or come in the morning,
Come when you're looked for, or come without warning,
Kisses and welcome you'll find here before you,
And the oftener you come here the more I'll adore you.

THOMAS O. DAVIS—*The Welcome.*

Come in the evening, come in the morning,
Come when expected, come without warning;
Thousands of welcomes you'll find here before you,
And the oftener you come, the more we'll adore you.

Irish Rhyme.

Welcome as the flowers in May.

SCOTT—*Rob Roy.*

Welcome ever smiles,
And farewell goes out sighing.

SHAKESPEARE—*Troilus and Cressida.* Act III. Sc. 3.

WICKEDNESS

All wickedness is but little to the wickedness of a woman.

Ecclesiasticus. XXV. 19.

The world loves a spice of wickedness.

LONGFELLOW—*Hyperion.*

The wicked flee when no man pursueth; but the righteous are bold as a lion.

Proverbs. XXVIII. 1.

As saith the proverb of the Ancients, Wickedness proceedeth from the wicked.

I Samuel. XXIV. 13.

'Cause I's wicked,—I is. I's mighty wicked, anyhow, I can't help it.

HARRIET BEECHER STOWE—*Uncle Tom's Cabin*.

WIFE

She would rather be an old man's darling than a young man's warling.

HARRISON AINSWORTH—*Miser's Daughter*.

Wives are young men's mistresses; companions for middle age; and old men's nurses.

BACON—*Of Marriage and Single Life*.

A husband should always know what is the matter with his wife, for she always knows what is not.

BALZAC.

The man who enters his wife's dressing-room is either a philosopher or a fool.

BALZAC.

My fond affection thou hast seen,
Then judge of my regret
To think more happy thou hadst been
If we had never met!

And has that thought been shared by thee?
Ah, no! that smiling cheek
Proves more unchanging love for me
Than labor's words could speak.

THOMAS HAYNES BAYLY—*To My Wife*.

Without thee I am all unblessed,
And wholly blessed in thee alone.

G. W. BETHUNE—*To My Wife*.

In thy face have I seen the eternal.

BARON CHRISTIAN VON BUNSEN—*To His Wife*.

She is a winsome wee thing,
She is a handsome wee thing,
She is a bonny wee thing,
This sweet wee wife o' mine.

BURNS—*My Wife's a Winsome Wee Thing*.

Be thou the rainbow to the storms of life!
The evening beam that smiles the clouds away
And tints to-morrow with prophetic ray!

BYRON—*The Bride of Abydos*.

What is there in the vale of life
Half so delightful as a wife,
When friendship, love, and peace combine
To stamp the marriage-bond divine?

COWPER—*Love Abused*.

The wife of thy bosom.

Deuteronomy. XIII. 6.

In every mess I find a friend,
In every port a wife.

CHARLES DIBDIN—*Jack in His Element*.

An undutiful Daughter will prove an unmanageable Wife.

FRANKLIN—*Poor Richard*.

He knows little who will tell his wife all he knows.

FULLER—*Holy and Profane State*.

One wife is too much for most husbands to bear,
But two at a time there's no mortal can bear.

GAY—*The Beggar's Opera*.

Alas! another instance of the triumph of hope over experience.

SAMUEL JOHNSON, referring to the second marriage of a friend.

Sail forth into the sea of life,
O gentle, loving, trusting wife,
And safe from all adversity
Upon the bosom of that sea
Thy comings and thy goings be!
For gentleness and love and trust
Prevail o'er angry wave and gust;
And in the wreck of noble lives
Something immortal still survives.

LONGFELLOW—*Building of the Ship*.

How much the wife is dearer than the bride.
LORD LYTTLETON—*An Irregular Ode.*

In the election of a wife, as in
A project of war, to err but once is
To be undone forever.
THOMAS MIDDLETON—*Anything for a Quiet Life.*

Awake,
My fairest, my espous'd, my latest found,
Heaven's last best gift, my ever new delight!
MILTON—*Paradise Lost.*

For what thou art is mine:
Our state cannot be sever'd; we are one,
One flesh; to lose thee were to lose myself.
MILTON—*Paradise Lost.*

Giving honour unto the wife as unto the weaker vessel.
I Peter. III. 7.

All other goods by fortune's hand are given,
A wife is the peculiar gift of heaven.
POPE—*January and May.*

She who ne'er answers till a husband cools,
Or, if she rules him, never shews she rules;
Charms by accepting, by submitting sways,
Yet has her humour most when she obeys.
POPE—*Moral Essays.*

She looketh well to the ways of her household, and eateth not the bread of idleness.
Proverbs. XXXI. 27.

It is a woman's business to get married as soon as possible, and a man's to keep unmarried as long as he can.
GEORGE BERNARD SHAW—*Man and Superman.*

My dear, my better half.
SIR PHILIP SIDNEY—*Arcadia.*

Of earthly goods, the best is a good wife;
A bad, the bitterest curse of human life.
SIMONIDES.

Thou art mine, thou hast given thy word,
Close, close in my arms thou art clinging;
Alone for my ear thou art singing
A song which no stranger hath heard:
But afar from me yet, like a bird,
Thy soul in some region unstirr'd
On its mystical circuit is winging.
E. C. STEDMAN—*Stanzas for Music.*

When choosing a wife look down the social scale; when selecting a friend, look upwards.
The Talmud.

The world well tried—the sweetest thing in life
Is the unclouded welcome of a wife.
N. P. WILLIS—*Lady Jane.*

WILL

He that will not when he may,
When he will he shall have nay.
BURTON—*Anatomy of Melancholy.*

The commander of the forces of a large State may be carried off, but the will of even a common man cannot be taken from him.
CONFUCIUS.

Barkis is willin'!
DICKENS—*David Copperfield.*

"When a man says he's willin'," said Mr. Barkis, "it's as much as to say, that man's a-waitin' for a answer."
DICKENS—*David Copperfield.*

Everything in this world depends upon will.
DISRAELI.

There is nothing good or evil save in the will.
EPICTETUS.

A man can do what he ought to do; and when he says he cannot, it is because he will not.
FICHTE.

To deny the freedom of the will is to make morality impossible.
FROUDE.

He who is firm in will molds the world to himself.
GOETHE.

People do not lack strength; they lack will.
VICTOR HUGO.

Man can do everything with himself, but he must not attempt to do too much with others.
WILHELM VON HUMBOLDT.

All theory is against the freedom of the will, all experience for it.
SAMUEL JOHNSON.

The star of the unconquered will,
He rises in my breast,
Serene, and resolute, and still,
And calm, and self-possessed.
LONGFELLOW—*The Light of Stars.*

A boy's will is the wind's will.
LONGFELLOW—*My Lost Youth.*

If you have overcome your inclination and not been overcome by it, you have reason to rejoice.
PLAUTUS.

And binding nature fast in fate,
Left free the human will.
POPE—*The Universal Prayer.*

I have known many who could not when they would, for they had not done it when they could.
RABELAIS—*Pantagruel.*

WIND

Blow, Boreas, foe to human kind!
Blow, blustering, freezing, piercing wind!
Blow, that thy force I may rehearse,
While all my thoughts congeal to verse!
JOHN BANCKS—*To Boreas.*

The faint old man shall lean his silver head
To feel thee; thou shalt kiss the child asleep,
And dry the moistened curls that overspread
His temples, while his breathing grows more deep.
BRYANT—*Evening Wind.*

A breeze came wandering from the sky,
Light as the whispers of a dream;
He put the o'erhanging grasses by,
And softly stooped to kiss the stream,
The pretty stream, the flattered stream,
The shy, yet unreluctant stream.
BRYANT—*The Wind and Stream.*

As winds come whispering lightly from the West,
Kissing, not ruffling, the blue deep's serene.
BYRON—*Childe Harold.*

Perhaps the wind
Wails so in winter for the summer's dead,
And all sad sounds are nature's funeral cries
For what has been and is not.
GEORGE ELIOT—*The Spanish Gypsy.*

The wind moans, like a long wail from some despairing soul shut out in the awful storm!
W. H. GIBSON—*Pastoral Days.*

The wind, the wandering wind
Of the golden summer eyes—
Whence is the thrilling magic
Of its tunes amongst the leaves?
Oh, is it from the waters,
Or from the long, tall grass?
Or is it from the hollow rocks
Through which its breathings pass?
FELICIA D. HEMANS—*The Wandering Wind.*

A little wind kindles, much puts out the fire.
GEORGE HERBERT.

An ill wind that bloweth no man good—
The blower of which blast is she.
JOHN HEYWOOD—*Idleness.*

I hear the wind among the trees
Playing the celestial symphonies;

I see the branches downward bent,
Like keys of some great instrument.
LONGFELLOW—*A Day of Sunshine.*

It's a warm wind, the west wind, full of birds' cries;
I never hear the west wind but tears are in my eyes.
For it comes from the west lands, the old brown hills,
And April's in the West wind, and daffodils.
MASEFIELD—*The West Wind.*

Loud wind, strong wind, sweeping o'er the mountains,
Fresh wind, free wind, blowing from the sea,
Pour forth thy vials like streams from airy mountains,
Draughts of life to me.
D. M. MULOCK—*North Wind.*

Who walketh upon the wings of the wind.
Psalms. CIV. 3.

O the wind is a faun in the spring time
When the ways are green for the tread of the May!
List! hark his lay!
Whist! mark his play!
T-r-r-r-l!
Hear how gay!
CLINTON SCOLLARD—*The Wind.*

Take a straw and throw it up into the air,
You may see by that which way the wind is.
JOHN SELDEN—*Table Talk.*

Ill blows the wind that profits nobody.
SHAKESPEARE—*Henry VI.* Pt. III. Act II. Sc. 5.

O wind,
If Winter comes, can Spring be far behind?
SHELLEY—*Ode to the West Wind.*

Sweet and low, sweet and low,
Wind of the western sea,
Low, low, breathe and blow,
Wind of the western sea!
TENNYSON—*The Princess.*

WINE AND SPIRITS

Firm and erect the Caledonian stood;
Sound was his mutton, and his claret good;
"Let him drink port!" the English statesman cried:
He drank the poison, and his spirit died.
ANONYMOUS.

John Barleycorn was a hero bold,
Of noble enterprise,
For if you do but taste his blood,
'Twill make your courage rise,
'Twill make a man forget his wo;
'Twill heighten all his joy.
BURNS—*John Barleycorn.*

So Noah, when he anchor'd safe on
The mountain's top, his lofty haven,
And all the passengers he bore
Were on the new world set ashore,
He made it next his chief design
To plant and propagate a vine,
Which since has overwhelm'd and drown'd
Far greater numbers, on dry ground,
Of wretched mankind, one by one,
Than all the flood before had done.
BUTLER—*Satire Upon Drunkenness.*

Few things surpass old wine; and they may preach
Who please, the more because they preach in vain,—
Let us have wine and women, mirth and laughter,
Sermons and soda-water the day after.
BYRON—*Don Juan.*

Which cheer the sad, revives the old, inspires
The young, makes Weariness forget his toil,
And Fear her danger; opens a new world
When this, the present, palls.
BYRON—*Sardanapalus.*

From wine what sudden friendship springs?
GAY.

Let schoolmasters puzzle their brain,
With grammar, and nonsense, and learning;
Good liquor, I stoutly maintain,
Gives genius a better discerning.
GOLDSMITH—*She Stoops to Conquer.*

Call things by their right names . . . Glass of brandy and water! That is the current, but not the appropriate name; ask for *a glass of liquid fire and distilled damnation.*
ROBERT HALL.

Sparkling and bright, in liquid light,
Does the wine our goblets gleam in;
With hue as red as the rosy bed
Which a bee would choose to dream in.
CHARLES FENNO HOFFMAN—*Sparkling and Bright.*

And wine can of their wits the wise beguile,
Make the sage frolic, and the serious smile.
HOMER—*Odyssey.*

Claret is the liquor for boys; port for men; but he who aspires to be a hero must drink brandy.
SAMUEL JOHNSON.

There is a devil in every berry of the grape.
The Koran.

If with water you fill up your glasses,
You'll never write anything wise;
For wine is the horse of Parnassus,
Which hurries a bard to the skies.
MOORE.

The Grape that can with Logic absolute
The Two-and-Seventy jarring Sects confute:
The sovereign Alchemist that in a trice
Life's leaden metal into Gold transmute.
OMAR KHAYYÁM—*Rubaiyat.*

Wine is the most healthful and most hygienic of beverages.
LOUIS PASTEUR.

This is the great evil in wine, it first seizes the feet; it is a cunning wrestler.
PLAUTUS.

Look not thou upon the wine when it is red, when it giveth his colour in the cup; . . . at the last it biteth like a serpent, and stingeth like an adder.
Proverbs. XXIII. 31.

Wine that maketh glad the heart of man.
Psalms. CIV. 15.

Day and night my thoughts incline
To the blandishments of wine,
Jars were made to drain, I think;
Wine, I know, was made to drink.
R. H. STODDARD—*A Jar of Wine.*

When the wine's in, murder will out.
The Talmud.

Drink no longer water, but use a little wine for thy stomach's sake.
I Timothy. V. 23.

And must I wholly banish hence
These red and golden juices,
And pay my vows to Abstinence,
That pallidest of Muses?
WILLIAM WATSON—*To a Maiden Who Bade Me Shun Wine.*

WINTER

These Winter nights against my window-pane,
Nature with busy pencil draws designs
Of ferns and blossoms and fine spray of pines,
Oak-leaf and acorn and fantastic vines,
Which she will make when summer comes again—
Quaint arabesques in argent, flat and cold,
Like curious Chinese etchings.
T. B. ALDRICH—*Frost-Work.*

O Winter! bar thine adamantine doors:
The north is thine; there hast thou built thy dark,
Deep-founded habitation. Shake not thy roofs,
Nor bend thy pillars with thine iron car.
WILLIAM BLAKE—*To Winter.*

Look! the massy trunks
Are cased in the pure crystal; each light spray,
Nodding and tinkling in the breath of heaven,
Is studded with its trembling water-drops,
That glimmer with an amethystine light.
BRYANT—*A Winter Piece.*

The tendinous part of the mind, so to speak, is more developed in winter; the fleshy, in summer. I should say winter had given the bone and sinew to literature, summer the tissues and the blood.
JOHN BURROUGHS—*The Snow-Walkers.*

O Winter! ruler of the inverted year,
. . . . .
I crown thee king of intimate delights,
Fireside enjoyments, home-born happiness,
And all the comforts that the lowly roof
Of undisturb'd Retirement, and the hours
Of long uninterrupted evening, know.
COWPER—*The Task.*

Every winter,
When the great sun has turned his face away,
The earth goes down into a vale of grief,
And fasts, and weeps, and shrouds herself in sables,
Leaving her wedding-garlands to decay—
Then leaps in spring to his returning kisses.
KINGSLEY—*Saint's Tragedy.*

But see, Orion sheds unwholesome dews;
Arise, the pines a noxious shade diffuse;
Sharp Boreas blows, and nature feels decay,
Time conquers all, and we must time obey.
POPE—*Ode to Winter.*

Wintry boughs against a wintry sky;
Yet the sky is partly blue
And the clouds are partly bright.
Who can tell but sap is mounting high,
Out of sight,
Ready to burst through?
CHRISTINA G. ROSSETTI—*Spring Signals to Winter.*

Dread Winter spreads his latest glooms,
And reigns, tremendous, o'er the conquer'd Year.
How dead the vegetable kingdom lies!
How dumb the tuneful! Horror wide extends
His desolate domain.
THOMSON—*The Seasons.*

See, Winter comes, to rule the varied year,
Sullen and sad, with all his rising train;
Vapors, and Clouds, and Storms.
THOMSON—*The Seasons.*

Make we here our camp of winter;
And, through sleet and snow,
Pitchy knot and beechen splinter
On our hearth shall glow.
Here, with mirth to lighten duty,
We shall lack alone
Woman's smile and girlhood's beauty,
Childhood's lisping tone.
WHITTIER—*Lumbermen.*

What miracle of weird transforming
Is this wild work of frost and light,
This glimpse of glory infinite?
WHITTIER—*The Pageant.*

WISDOM

To speak as the common people do, to think as wise men do.
ROGER ASCHAM.

The wisdom of our ancestors.
BURKE.

But these are foolish things to all the wise,
And I love wisdom more than she loves me;
My tendency is to philosophise
On most things, from a tyrant to a tree;

But still the spouseless virgin *Knowledge* flies,
What are we? and whence come we? what shall be
Our ultimate existence? What's our present?
Are questions answerless, and yet incessant.
BYRON—*Don Juan.*

Wise men learn more from fools than fools from the wise.
CATO.

Wisdom and goodness are twin-born, one heart
Must hold both sisters, never seen apart.
COWPER—*Expostulation.*

But they whom truth and wisdom lead
Can gather honey from a weed.
COWPER—*Pine-Apple and Bee.*

Knowledge is proud that he has learn'd so much;
Wisdom is humble that he knows no more.
COWPER—*The Task.*

Who are a little wise the best fools be.
DONNE—*The Triple Fool.*

In much wisdom is much grief.
Ecclesiastes. I. 18.

The words of the wise are as goads.
Ecclesiastes. XII. 11.

No one could be so wise as Thurlow looked.
CHARLES JAMES FOX.

Some are weather-wise, some are otherwise.
FRANKLIN—*Poor Richard.*

Wisdom is only found in truth.
GOETHE.

The heart is wiser than the intellect.
J. G. HOLLAND—*Kathrina.*

In youth and beauty wisdom is but rare!
HOMER—*Odyssey.*

How prone to doubt, how cautious are the wise!
HOMER—*Odyssey.*

The price of wisdom is above rubies.
Job. XXVIII. 18.

Days should speak, and multitude of years should teach wisdom.
Job. XXXII. 7.

Great men are not always wise.
Job. XXXII. 9.

It is easier to be wise for others than for ourselves.
LA ROCHEFOUCAULD.

Ripe in wisdom was he, but patient, and simple, and childlike.
LONGFELLOW—*Evangeline.*

Whoever is not too wise is wise.
MARTIAL.

Be wise;
Soar not too high to fall; but stoop to rise.
MASSINGER—*Duke of Milan.*

Be ye therefore wise as serpents, and harmless as doves.
Matthew. X. 16.

Wisdom is justified of her children.
Matthew. XI. 19; *Luke.* VII. 35.

But to know,
That which before us lies in daily life,
Is the prime wisdom.
MILTON—*Paradise Lost.*

A wise man sees as much as he ought, not as much as he can.
MONTAIGNE.

It is good to rub and polish our brain against that of others.
MONTAIGNE.

He gains wisdom in a happy way, who gains it by another's experience.
PLAUTUS.

No man is wise enough by himself.
PLAUTUS.

No one is wise at all times.
PLINY THE ELDER.

Tell (for you can) what is it to be wise?
'Tis but to know how little can be known,
To see all others' faults, and feel our own.
POPE—*Essay on Man.*

Wisdom crieth without; she uttereth her voice in the street.
Proverbs. I. 20.

Go to the ant, thou sluggard; consider her ways, and be wise.
Proverbs. VI. 6.

Wisdom is the principal thing; therefore get wisdom; and with all thy getting get understanding.
Proverbs. VIII. 11.

Be wisely worldly, but not worldly wise.
QUARLES.

It is not wise to be wiser than is necessary.
QUINAULT.

The power is yours, but not the sight;
You see not upon what you tread;
You have the ages for your guide,
But not the wisdom to be led.
EDWIN ARLINGTON ROBINSON—*Cassandra.*

Nine-tenths of wisdom consists in being wise in time.
THEODORE ROOSEVELT — *Speech, 1917.*

We become wiser by adversity; prosperity destroys our appreciation of the right.
SENECA.

I never knew so young a body with so old a head.
SHAKESPEARE—*Merchant of Venice.* Act IV. Sc. 1.

As for me, all I know is that I know nothing.
SOCRATES.

The doorstep to the temple of wisdom is a knowledge of our own ignorance.
SPURGEON—*Gleanings among the Sheaves.*

By Wisdom wealth is won;
But riches purchased wisdom yet for none.
BAYARD TAYLOR—*The Wisdom of Ali.*

True wisdom consists not in seeing what is immediately before our eyes, but in foreseeing what is to come.
TERENCE.

The children of this world are in their generation wiser than the children of light.
I Timothy. XVI. 8.

Wisdom is the gray hair unto men, and an unspotted life is old age.
Wisdom of Solomon. IV. 8.

Wisdom is ofttimes nearer when we stoop
Than when we soar.
WORDSWORTH—*The Excursion.*

Teach me my days to number, and apply
My trembling heart to wisdom.
YOUNG—*Night Thoughts.*

WISH

"Man wants but little here below
Nor wants that little long,"
'Tis not with me exactly so;
But 'tis so in the song.
My wants are many, and, if told,
Would muster many a score;
And were each wish a mint of gold,
I still should long for more.
JOHN QUINCY ADAMS—*The Wants of Man.*

Every wish
Is like a prayer—with God.
E. B. BROWNING—*Aurora Leigh.*

If a man could half his wishes he would double his Troubles.
FRANKLIN—*Poor Richard.*

What one has wished for in youth, in old age one has in abundance.
GOETHE.

And the evil wish is most evil to the wisher.
HESIOD.

Little I ask; my wants are few;
I only wish a hut of stone
(A *very plain* brown stone will do,)
That I may call my own;
And close at hand is such a one
In yonder street that fronts the sun.
HOLMES—*Contentment.*

I wish I knew the good of wishing.
HENRY S. LEIGH—*Wishing.*

If I live to grow old, as I find I go down,
Let this be my fate in a country town;
May I have a warm house, with a stone at my gate,
And a cleanly young girl to rub my bald pate.
May I govern my passions with an absolute sway,
Grow wiser and better as my strength wears away,
Without gout or stone, by a gentle decay.

WALTER POPE—*The Old Man's Wish.*

O, that I were where I would be,
Then would I be where I am not;
For where I am I would not be,
And where I would be I can not.

A. QUILLER-COUCH.

Thy wish was father, Harry, to that thought:
I stay too long by thee, I weary thee.

SHAKESPEARE—*Henry IV.* Pt. II. Act IV. Sc. 5.

I've often wished that I had clear,
For life, six hundred pounds a year,
A handsome house to lodge a friend,
A river at my garden's end,
A terrace walk, and half a rood
Of land, set out to plant a wood.

SWIFT—*Imitation of Horace.*

As you can not do what you wish, you should wish what you can do.

TERENCE.

We cannot wish for that we know not.

VOLTAIRE.

WIT

Sharp wits, like sharp knives, do often cut their owner's fingers.

ARROWSMITH.

Don't put too fine a point to your wit for fear it should get blunted.

CERVANTES—*The Little Gypsy.*

Great wits are sure to madness near allied,
And thin partitions do their bounds divide.

DRYDEN—*Absalom and Achitophel.*

There's many witty men whose brains can't fill their bellies.

FRANKLIN—*Poor Richard's Almanac.*

With little wit and ease to suit them,
They whirl in narrow circling trails,
Like kittens playing with their tails.

GOETHE—*Faust.*

There must be more malice than love in the hearts of all wits.

B. R. HAYDON.

Those who object to wit are envious of it.

HAZLITT.

Wit is the salt of conversation, not the food.

HAZLITT.

This man (Chesterfield) I thought had been a lord among wits; but I find he is only a wit among lords.

SAMUEL JOHNSON—*Boswell's Life of Johnson.*

A man does not please long when he has only one species of wit.

LA ROCHEFOUCAULD.

A small degree of wit, accompanied by good sense, is less tiresome in the long run than a great amount of wit without it.

LA ROCHEFOUCAULD.

Wit should be wit, but never satire.

MADAME LA ROCHEJAQUELEIN.

Avoid witticisms at the expense of others.

HORACE MANN.

Repartee is precisely the touchstone of the man of wit.

MOLIÈRE.

Raillery is a mode of speaking in favor of one's wit at the expense of one's better nature.

MONTESQUIEU.

Whose wit, in the combat, as gentle as bright,
Ne'er carried a heart-stain away on its blade.

MOORE—*Lines on the Death of Sheridan.*

Wit is the most rascally, contemptible, beggarly thing on the face of the earth.
MURPHY—*The Apprentice.*

You beat your pate, and fancy wit will come;
Knock as you please, there's nobody at home.
POPE—*Epigram.*

For wit and judgment often are at strife,
Though meant each other's aid, like man and wife.
POPE—*Essay on Criticism.*

True wit is nature to advantage dress'd,
What oft was thought, but ne'er so well expressed.
POPE—*Essay on Criticism.*

Great men may jest with saints; 'tis wit in them;
But, in the less foul profanation.
SHAKESPEARE—*Measure for Measure.* Act. II. Sc. 2.

Surprise is so essential an ingredient of wit that no wit will bear repetition; —at least the original electrical feeling produced by any piece of wit can never be renewed.
SYDNEY SMITH.

One wit, like a knuckle of ham in soup, gives a zest and flavour to the dish, but more than one serves only to spoil the pottage.
SMOLLETT—*Humphrey Clinker.*

Wit consists in knowing the resemblance of things which differ, and the difference of things which are alike.
MADAME DE STAËL.

It is with wits as with razors, which are never so apt to cut those they are employed on as when they have lost their edge.
SWIFT—*Tale of a Tub.*

Wit does not take the place of knowledge.
VAUVENARGUES.

WOE

He scorns his own who feels another's woe.
CAMPBELL.

Not suffering, but faint heart, is worst of woes.
LOWELL.

So perish all whose breast ne'er learned to glow
For other's good or melt at other's woe.
POPE—*Elegy to an Unfortunate Lady.*

One woe doth tread upon another's heel
So fast they follow.
SHAKESPEARE—*Hamlet.* Act IV. Sc. 7.

Woe brings woe upon woe.
SOPHOCLES.

WOMAN

Loveliest of women! heaven is in thy soul,
Beauty and virtue shine forever round thee,
Bright'ning each other! thou art all divine!
ADDISON—*Cato.*

I think Nature hath lost the mould
Where she her shape did take;
Or else I doubt if Nature could
So fair a creature make.
ANONYMOUS.

Oh, the shrewdness of their shrewdness when they are shrewd,
And the rudeness of their rudeness when they're rude;
But the shrewdness of their shrewdness and the rudeness of their rudeness,
Are as nothing to their goodness when they're good.
ANONYMOUS.

Women give themselves to God when the devil wants nothing more to do with them.
SOPHIE ARNOULD.

Woman has this in common with angels, that suffering beings belong especially to her.

BALZAC.

Oh the gladness of their gladness when they're glad,
And the sadness of their sadness when they're sad;
But the gladness of their gladness, and the sadness of their sadness,
Are as nothing to their badness when they're bad.

J. M. BARRIE—*Rosalind.*

You see, dear, it is not true that woman was made from man's rib; she was really made from his funny bone.

J. M. BARRIE—*What Every Woman Knows.*

Women are a new race, recreated since the world received Christianity.

HENRY WARD BEECHER.

Their tricks and craft have put me daft,
They've ta'en me in, and a' that,
But clear your decks, and—Here's the sex!
I like the jads for a' that.

BURNS—*Jolly Beggars.*

Heart on her lips, and soul within her eyes,
Soft as her clime, and sunny as her skies.

BYRON—*Beppo.*

I love the sex, and sometimes would reverse
The tyrant's wish, "that mankind only had
One neck, which he with one fell stroke might pierce";
My wish is quite as wide, but not so bad,
And much more tender on the whole than fierce;
It being (not *now,* but only while a lad)
That womankind had but one rosy mouth,
To kiss them all at once, from North to South.

BYRON—*Don Juan.*

What a strange thing is man! and what a stranger
Is woman! What a whirlwind is her head,
And what a whirlpool full of depth and danger
Is all the rest about her.

BYRON—*Don Juan.*

The world was sad; the garden was a wild;
And man, the hermit, sigh'd—till woman smiled.

CAMPBELL—*Pleasures of Hope.*

Of all the girls that are so smart,
There's none like pretty Sally.

HENRY CAREY—*Sally in Our Alley.*

Heaven has no rage like love to hatred turned,
Nor hell a fury like a woman scorned.

CONGREVE—*The Mourning Bride.*

But what is woman? Only one of nature's agreeable blunders.

COWLEY.

Her air, her manners, all who saw admired;
Courteous though coy, and gentle, though retired:
The joy of youth and health her eyes display'd,
And ease of heart her every look convey'd.

CRABBE—*Parish Register.*

Whoe'er she be,
That not impossible she,
That shall command my heart and me.

CRASHAW—*Wishes to His (Supposed) Mistress.*

Men *say* of women what pleases them; women *do* with men what pleases them.

DE SEGUR.

Women always have some mental reservation.

DESTOUCHES.

But were it to my fancy given
To rate her charms, I'd call them heaven;
For though a mortal made of clay,
Angels must love Ann Hathaway;
She hath a way so to control,
To rapture the imprisoned soul,

And sweetest heaven on earth display,
That to be heaven Ann hath a way;
She hath a way,
Ann Hathaway,—
To be heaven's self Ann hath a way.
CHARLES DIBDIN—*A Love Dittie.*

A woman's counsel brought us first to woe,
And made her man his paradise forego,
Where at heart's ease he liv'd, and might have been
As free from sorrow as he was from sin.
DRYDEN—*Cock and the Fox.*

Cherchez la femme.
Find the woman.
DUMAS—*Les Mohicans de Paris.*

When greater perils men inviron,
Then women show a front of iron;
And, gentle in their manner, they
Do bold things in a quiet way.
THOMAS DUNN ENGLISH—*Betty Zane.*

There is no worse evil than a bad woman; and nothing has ever been produced better than a good one.
EURIPIDES.

Only the men who do not care about women are interested in women's dresses. And the men who like them never notice what they wear.
ANATOLE FRANCE.

Where is the man who has the power and skill
To stem the torrent of a woman's will?
For if she will, she will, you may depend on't;
And if she won't, she won't; so there's an end on't.
From the Pillar Erected in Dane John Field, Canterbury.

If the heart of a man is depressed with cares,
The mist is dispell'd when a woman appears.
GAY—*The Beggar's Opera.*

There are only two good women in the world; one of them is dead, and the other is not to be found.
German Proverb.

The society of women is the foundation of good manners.
GOETHE.

Most men who run down women are running down one woman only.
REMY DE GOURMONT.

Woman would be more charming if one could fall into her arms without falling into her hands.
REMY DE GOURMONT.

Mankind, from Adam, have been women's fools;
Women, from Eve, have been the devil's tools:
Heaven might have spar'd one torment when we fell;
Not left us women, or not threatened hell.
GEORGE GRANVILLE (Lord Lansdowne)—*She-Gallants.*

Women forgive injuries, but never forget slights.
THOMAS C. HALIBURTON.

The crown of creation.
HERDER.

Man has his will,—but woman has her way.
HOLMES—*Autocrat of the Breakfast Table.*

O woman, woman, when to ill thy mind
Is bent, all hell contains no fouler fiend.
HOMER—*Odyssey.*

It is God who makes woman beautiful, it is the devil who makes her pretty.
VICTOR HUGO.

O woman! thou wert fashioned to beguile:
So have all sages said, all poets sung.
JEAN INGELOW—*The Four Bridges.*

In that day seven women shall take hold of one man.
Isaiah. IV. 1.

I am very fond of the company of ladies. I like their beauty, I like their delicacy, I like their vivacity, and I like their silence.
SAMUEL JOHNSON.

I met a lady in the meads
Full beautiful—a faery's child,
Her hair was long, her foot was light,
And her eyes were wild.
KEATS—*La Belle Dame sans Merci.*

For the female of the species is more deadly than the male.
KIPLING.

An' I learned about women from 'er.
KIPLING—*The Ladies.*

The colonel's lady and Judy O'Grady
Are sisters under their skins.
KIPLING—*The Ladies.*

A rag and a bone and a hank of hair.
KIPLING—*The Vampire.*

There are no ugly women; there are only women who do not know how to look pretty.
LA BRUYÈRE.

Women are extreme in all points. They are better or worse than men.
LA BRUYÈRE.

There is a woman at the beginning of all great things.
LAMARTINE.

Nature intended that woman should be her masterpiece.
LESSING.

I have always said it—Nature meant woman to be her masterpiece.
LESSING.

The life of woman is full of woe,
Toiling on and on and on,
With breaking heart, and tearful eyes,
The secret longings that arise,
Which this world never satisfies!
Some more, some less, but of the whole
Not one quite happy, no, not one!
LONGFELLOW—*Christus.*

Earth's noblest thing, a Woman perfected.
LOWELL—*Irene.*

Woman is a miracle of divine contradictions.
MICHELET.

O woman, born first to believe us;
Yea, also born first to forget;
Born first to betray and deceive us,
Yet first to repent and regret.
JOAQUIN MILLER—*Charity.*

Too fair to worship, too divine to love.
MILMAN—*Apollo Belvedere.*

Grace was in all her steps, heaven in her eye,
In every gesture dignity and love.
MILTON—*Paradise Lost.*

Disguise our bondage as we will,
'Tis woman, woman rules us still.
MOORE—*Sovereign Woman.*

My only books
Were women's looks,
And folly's all they've taught me.
MOORE—*The Time I've Lost in Wooing.*

What mighty ills have not been done by woman!
Who was't betray'd the Capitol? A woman;
Who lost Mark Antony the world? A woman;
Who was the cause of a long ten years' war,
And laid at last old Troy in ashes? Woman;
Destructive, damnable, deceitful woman!
THOMAS OTWAY—*The Orphan.*

O woman! lovely woman! Nature made thee
To temper man: we had been brutes without you;
Angels are painted fair, to look like you:
There's in you all that we believe of Heaven,
Amazing brightness, purity, and truth,
Eternal joy, and everlasting love.
THOMAS OTWAY—*Venice Preserved.*

To chase the clouds of life's tempestuous hours,

To strew its short but weary way with flow'rs,
New hopes to raise, new feelings to impart,
And pour celestial balsam on the heart;
For this to man was lovely woman giv'n,
The last, best work, the noblest gift of Heav'n.
THOMAS LOVE PEACOCK—*The Visions of Love.*

Those who always speak well of women do not know them sufficiently; those who always speak ill of them do not know them at all.
GUILLAUME PIGAULT-LEBRUN.

Most women have no characters at all.
POPE—*Moral Essays.*

Offend her, and she knows not to forgive;
Oblige her, and she'll hate you while you live.
POPE—*Moral Essays.*

O! bless'd with temper, whose unclouded ray
Can make to-morrow cheerful as today;
She who can own a sister's charms, or hear
Sighs for a daughter with unwounded ear;
She who ne'er answers till a husband cools,
Or, if she rules him, never shows she rules.
Charms by accepting, by submitting sways,
Yet has her humour most when she obeys.
POPE—*Moral Essays.*

Woman's at best a contradiction still.
POPE—*Moral Essays.*

Give God thy broken heart, He whole will make it.
Give woman thy whole heart, and she will break it.
EDMUND PRESTWICH—*The Broken Heart.*

It is better to dwell in a corner of the housetop than with a brawling woman in a wide house.
Proverbs. XXI. 9.

If she undervalue me,
What care I how fair she be?
SIR WALTER RALEIGH.

That, let us rail at women, scorn and flout 'em,
We may live with, but cannot live without 'em.
FREDERICK REYNOLDS—*My Grandfather's Will.*

A woman is the most inconsistent compound of obstinacy and self-sacrifice that I am acquainted with.
JEAN PAUL RICHTER.

O wild, dark flower of woman,
Deep rose of my desire,
An Eastern wizard made you
Of earth and stars and fire.
C. G. D. ROBERTS—*The Rose of My Desire.*

It is easier for a woman to defend her virtue against men than her reputation against women.
ROCHEBRUNE.

Angels, listen when she speaks;
She's my delight, all mankind's wonder;
But my jealous heart would break
Should we live one day asunder.
EARL OF ROCHESTER.

And one false step entirely damns her fame.
In vain with tears the loss she may deplore,
In vain look back on what she was before;
She sets like stars that fall, to rise no more.
ROWE—*Jane Shore.*

Men who flatter women do not know them; men who abuse them know them still less.
MME. DE SALM.

He ploughs the waves, sows the sand, and hopes to gather the wind in a net, who places his hopes on the heart of woman.
SANNAZARO.

Such, Polly, are your sex—part truth, part fiction;
Some thought, much whim, and all contradiction.

RICHARD SAVAGE—*To a Young Lady.*

Honor women! they entwine and weave heavenly roses in our earthly life.

SCHILLER.

The weakness of their reasoning faculty also explains why women show more sympathy for the unfortunate than men; . . . and why, on the contrary, they are inferior to men as regards justice, and less honourable and conscientious.

SCHOPENHAUER—*On Women.*

O Woman! in our hours of ease,
Uncertain, coy, and hard to please,
And variable as the shade
By the light quivering aspen made;
When pain and anguish wring the brow,
A ministering angel thou!

SCOTT—*Marmion.*

Age cannot wither her, nor custom stale
Her infinite variety.

SHAKESPEARE—*Antony and Cleopatra.* Act II. Sc. 2.

Frailty, thy name is woman!

SHAKESPEARE—*Hamlet.* Act I. Sc. 2.

Two women plac'd together makes cold weather.

SHAKESPEARE—*Henry VIII.* Act I. Sc. 4.

Ah me, how weak a thing
The heart of woman is!

SHAKESPEARE—*Julius Caesar.* Act II. Sc. 4.

From women's eyes this doctrine I derive:
They sparkle still the right Promethean fire;
They are the books, the arts, the academes,
That show, contain, and nourish all the world.

SHAKESPEARE—*Love's Labour's Lost.* Act IV. Sc. 3.

You are pictures out of doors,
Bells in your parlours, wild-cats in your kitchens,
Saints in your injuries, devils being offended,
Players in your housewifery, and housewives in your beds.

SHAKESPEARE—*Othello.* Act II. Sc. 1.

In the beginning, said a Persian poet —Allah took a rose, a lily, a dove, a serpent, a little honey, a Dead Sea apple, and a handful of clay. When he looked at the amalgam—it was a woman.

WILLIAM SHARP.

Woman reduces us all to the common denominator.

GEORGE BERNARD SHAW—*Great Catherine.*

The fickleness of the woman I love is only equalled by the infernal constancy of the women who love me.

GEORGE BERNARD SHAW—*Philanderer.*

Woman's dearest delight is to wound Man's self-conceit, though Man's dearest delight is to gratify hers.

GEORGE BERNARD SHAW—*Unsocial Socialist.*

She is pretty to walk with,
And witty to talk with,
And pleasant too, to think on.

SUCKLING—*Brennoralt.*

Daphne knows, with equal ease,
How to vex and how to please;
But the folly of her sex
Makes her sole delight to vex.

SWIFT—*Daphne.*

A woman either loves or hates: she knows no medium.

SYRUS.

O Woman, you are not merely the handiwork of God, but also of men; these are ever endowing you with beauty from their own hearts. . . .

You are one-half woman and one-half dream.
TAGORE—*Gardener.*

A rosebud set with little wilful thorns,
And sweet as English air could make her, she.
TENNYSON—*The Princess.*

When I say that I know women, I mean that I know that I don't know them. Every single woman I ever knew is a puzzle to me, as I have no doubt she is to herself.
THACKERAY—*Mr. Brown's Letters.*

Regard the society of women as a necessary unpleasantness of social life, and avoid it as much as possible.
TOLSTOY—*Diary.*

Woman is more impressionable than man. Therefore in the Golden Age they were better than men. Now they are worse.
TOLSTOY—*Diary.*

He is a fool who thinks by force or skill
To turn the current of a woman's will.
SIR SAMUEL TUKE.

A woman is always changeable and capricious.
VERGIL—*Aeneid.*

Very learned women are to be found, in the same manner as female warriors; but they are seldom or never inventors.
VOLTAIRE—*A Philosophical Dictionary.*

Not from his head was woman took,
As made her husband to o'erlook;
Not from his feet, as one designed
The footstool of the stronger kind;
But fashioned for himself, a bride;
An equal, taken from his side.
CHARLES WESLEY.

There are only two kinds of women, the plain and the coloured.
OSCAR WILDE—*Picture of Dorian Gray.*

A perfect Woman nobly planned
To warn, to comfort, and command.
WORDSWORTH—*She Was a Phantom of Delight.*

She was a Phantom of delight
When first she gleamed upon my sight;
A lovely Apparition, sent
To be a moment's ornament.
WORDSWORTH—*She Was a Phantom of Delight.*

And beautiful as sweet!
And young as beautiful! and soft as young!
And gay as soft! and innocent as gay.
YOUNG—*Night Thoughts.*

WONDER

A schoolboy's tale, the wonder of an hour!
BYRON—*Childe Harold.*

If a man proves too clearly and convincingly to himself . . . that a tiger is an optical illusion—well, he will find out he is wrong. The tiger will himself intervene in the discussion, in a manner which will be in every sense conclusive.
G. K. CHESTERTON.

Men love to wonder and that is the seed of our science.
EMERSON—*Works and Days.*

The things that have been and shall be no more,
The things that are, and that hereafter shall be,
The things that might have been, and yet were not,
The fading twilight of joys departed.
LONGFELLOW—*Christus.*

Wonder (said Socrates) is very much the affection of a philosopher; for there is no other beginning of philosophy than this.
PLATO.

WOOING

Thrice happy's the wooing that's not long adoing,
So much time is saved in the billing and cooing.
R. H. BARHAM—*Sir Rupert the Fearless.*

"Yes," I answered you last night;
"No," this morning, sir, I say:
Colors seen by candle-light
Will not look the same by day.
E. B. BROWNING—*The Lady's "Yes."*

Woo the fair one when around
Early birds are singing;
When o'er all the fragrant ground
Early herbs are springing:
When the brookside, bank, and grove
All with blossom laden,
Shine with beauty, breathe of love,
Woo the timid maiden.
BRYANT—*Love's Lessons.*

And let us mind, faint heart ne'er wan
A lady fair.
Wha does the utmost that he can
Will whyles do mair.
BURNS—*To Dr. Blacklock.*

Do proper homage to thine idol's eyes;
But not too humbly, or she will despise
Thee and thy suit, though told in moving tropes:
Disguise even tenderness, if thou art wise.
BYRON—*Childe Harold.*

There is a tide in the affairs of women
Which, taken at the flood, leads—God knows where.
BYRON—*Don Juan.*

'Tis enough—
Who listens once will listen twice;
Her heart be sure is not of ice,
And one refusal no rebuff.
BYRON—*Mazeppa.*

Better be courted and jilted
Than never be courted at all.
CAMPBELL—*The Jilted Nymph.*

Never wedding, ever wooing,
Still a lovelorn heart pursuing,
Read you not the wrong you're doing
In my cheek's pale hue?
All my life with sorrow strewing;
Wed or cease to woo.
CAMPBELL—*The Maid's Remonstrance.*

Perhaps if you address the lady
Most politely, most politely,
Flatter and impress the lady
Most politely, most politely,
Humbly beg and humbly sue,
She may deign to look on you.
W. S. GILBERT—*Princess Ida.*

The surest way to hit a woman's heart is to take aim kneeling.
DOUGLAS JERROLD—*Douglas Jerrold's Wit.*

Follow a shadow, it still flies you,
Seem to fly, it will pursue:
So court a mistress, she denies you;
Let her alone, she will court you.
Say are not women truly, then,
Styled but the shadows of us men?
BEN JONSON—*The Forest Song.*

A fool there was and he made his prayer
(Even as you and I!)
To a rag and a bone and a hank of hair
(We called her the woman who did not care)
But the fool he called her his lady fair—
(Even as you or I!)
KIPLING—*The Vampire.*

If I am not worth the wooing, I surely am not worth the winning.
LONGFELLOW—*Courtship of Miles Standish.*

Why don't you speak for yourself, John?
LONGFELLOW—*Courtship of Miles Standish.*

Come live in my heart and pay no rent.
LOVER.

That you are in a terrible taking,
By all these sweet oglings I see;
But the fruit that can fall without shaking,
Indeed is too mellow for me.
LADY MARY WORTLEY MONTAGU.

Let this great maxim be my virtue's guide:
In part she is to blame that has been tried;

He comes too near that comes to be denied.
LADY MARY WORTLEY MONTAGU—*The Lady's Resolve.*

If I speak to thee in friendship's name,
Thou think'st I speak too coldly;
If I mention Love's devoted flame,
Thou say'st I speak too boldly.
MOORE—*How Shall I Woo?*

The time I've lost in wooing,
In watching and pursuing
The light that lies
In woman's eyes,
Has been my heart's undoing.
MOORE—*The Time I've Lost in Wooing.*

Ye shall know my breach of promise.
Numbers. XIV. 34.

They dream in courtship, but in wedlock wake.
POPE—*Wife of Bath.*

The way of an eagle in the air; the way of a serpent upon a rock; the way of a ship in the midst of the sea; and the way of a man with a maid.
Proverbs. XXX. 19.

But in vain did she conjure him
To depart her presence so,
Having a thousand tongues t'allure him,
And but one to bid him go.
SIR WALTER RALEIGH—*Dulcina.*

A heaven on earth I have won by wooing thee.
SHAKESPEARE—*All's Well That Ends Well.* Act IV. Sc. 2.

She's beautiful and therefore to be woo'd:
She is a woman, therefore to be won.
SHAKESPEARE—*Henry VI.* Pt. I. Act V. Sc. 3.

We cannot fight for love, as men may do;
We should be woo'd and were not made to woo.
SHAKESPEARE—*Midsummer Night's Dream.* Act II. Sc. 1.

Sigh no more, ladies, sigh no more,
Men were deceivers ever,
One foot in sea and one on shore;
To one thing constant never.
SHAKESPEARE—*Much Ado about Nothing.* Act II. Sc. 3.

O gentle Romeo,
If thou dost love, pronounce it faithfully.
Or if thou think'st I am too quickly won,
I'll frown and be perverse and say thee nay,
So thou wilt woo: but else, not for the world.
SHAKESPEARE—*Romeo and Juliet.* Act II. Sc. 2.

Men prize the thing ungain'd more than it is.
SHAKESPEARE—*Troilus and Cressida.* Act I. Sc. 2.

Win her with gifts, if she respect not words;
Dumb jewels often in their silent kind
More than quick words do move a woman's mind.
SHAKESPEARE—*Two Gentlemen of Verona.* Act III. Sc. 1.

Take no repulse, whatever she doth say;
For, "get you gone," she doth not mean, "away."
Flatter and praise, commend, extol their graces;
Though ne'er so black, say they have angels' faces.
That man that hath a tongue, I say, is no man,
If with his tongue he cannot win a woman.
SHAKESPEARE—*Two Gentlemen of Verona.* Act III. Sc. 1.

Bring therefore all the forces that ye may,
And lay incessant battery to her heart;
Playnts, prayers, vowes, truth, sorrow, and dismay;
Those engins can the proudest love convert:
And, if those fayle, fall down and dy before her;
So dying live, and living do adore her.
SPENSER.

Full little knowest thou that hast not tried,
What hell it is in suing long to bide:
To loose good dayes, that might be better spent;
To waste long nights in pensive discontent;
To speed to-day, to be put back to-morrow;
To feed on hope, to pine with feare and sorrow.
SPENSER.

WORD

Words of truth and soberness.
Acts. XXVI. 25.

Words, as a Tartar's bow, do shoot back upon the understanding of the wisest, and mightily entangle and pervert the judgment.
BACON—*Advancement of Learning.*

Words of affection, howsoe'er express'd,
The latest spoken still are deem'd the best.
JOANNA BAILLIE.

'Tis a word that's quickly spoken,
Which being restrained, a heart is broken.
BEAUMONT and FLETCHER—*The Spanish Curate.*

'Twas he that ranged the words at random flung,
Pierced the fair pearls and them together strung.
BIDPAI (Pilpay)—*Anvar-i Suhaili.*

A very great part of the mischiefs that vex this world arises from words.
BURKE.

Words writ in waters.
GEORGE CHAPMAN—*Revenge for Honour.*

Fair words butter no parsnips.
CLARKE—*Paraemiologia.*

Mum's the word.
GEORGE COLMAN THE YOUNGER—*Battle of Hexham.*

Without knowing *the force* of words, it is impossible to know men.
CONFUCIUS—*Analects.*

Words that weep, and tears that speak.
COWLEY—*The Prophet.*

Father is rather vulgar, my dear. The word Papa, besides, gives a pretty form to the lips. Papa, potatoes, poultry, prunes and prism are all very good words for the lips; especially prunes and prism.
DICKENS—*Little Dorrit.*

But words once spoke can never be recall'd.
WENTWORTH DILLON.

I trade both with the living and the dead for the enrichment of our native language.
DRYDEN.

Let thy words be few.
Ecclesiastes. V. 2.

Our words have wings, but fly not where we would.
GEORGE ELIOT—*The Spanish Gypsy.*

Let no man deceive you with vain words.
Ephesians. V. 6.

The arrow belongs not to the archer when it has once left the bow; the word no longer belongs to the speaker when it has once passed his lips, especially when it has been multiplied by the press.
HEINE—*Religion and Philosophy.*

Words are women, deeds are men.
HERBERT.

How forcible are right words!
Job. VI. 25.

Who is this that darkeneth counsel by words without knowledge?
Job. XXXVIII. 2.

I am not yet so lost in lexicography, as to forget that words are the daughters of earth, and that things are the sons of heaven.
SAMUEL JOHNSON—*Preface to His Dictionary.*

Words are the most powerful drug used by mankind.

KIPLING—*Speech, 1923.*

We should have a great many fewer disputes in the world if words were taken for what they are, the signs of our ideas only, and not for things themselves.

LOCKE—*Essay on the Human Understanding.*

Speaking words of endearment where words of comfort availed not.

LONGFELLOW—*Evangeline.*

My words are little jars
For you to take and put upon a shelf.
Their shapes are quaint and beautiful,
And they have many pleasant colours and lustres
To recommend them.
Also the scent from them fills the room
With sweetness of flowers and crushed grasses.

AMY LOWELL—*A Gift.*

There comes Emerson first, whose rich words, every one,
Are like gold nails in temples to hang trophies on.

LOWELL—*A Fable for Critics.*

A single little word can strike him dead.

LUTHER (Of the Pope).

His words, . . . like so many nimble and airy servitors, trip about him at command.

MILTON—*Apology for Smectymnuus.*

And to bring in a new word by the head and shoulders, they leave out the old one.

MONTAIGNE—*Essays.*

The word impossible is not in my dictionary.

NAPOLEON.

Things were first made, then words.

SIR T. OVERBURY—*A Wife.*

Ah me! how easy it is to indulge in brave words in another person's trouble.

OVID.

Words will build no walls.

PLUTARCH.

Words are like leaves; and where they most abound,
Much fruit of sense beneath is rarely found.

POPE—*Essay on Criticism.*

In words, as fashions, the same rule will hold:
Alike fantastic, if too new, or old:
Be not the first by whom the new are tried,
Nor yet the last to lay the old aside.

POPE—*Essay on Criticism.*

A word spoken in good season, how good is it!

Proverbs. XV. 23.

A word fitly spoken is like apples of gold in pictures of silver.

Proverbs. XXV. 11.

The words of his mouth were smoother than butter, but war was in his heart; his words were softer than oil, yet were they drawn swords.

Psalms. LV. 21.

One of our defects as a nation is a tendency to use what have been called "weasel words." When a weasel sucks eggs the meat is sucked out of the egg. If you use a "weasel word" after another there is nothing left of the other.

THEODORE ROOSEVELT—*Speech, 1916.*

O! many a shaft, at random sent,
Finds mark the archer little meant!
And many a word, at random spoken,
May soothe or wound a heart that's broken!

SCOTT—*Lord of the Isles.*

My words fly up, my thoughts remain below:
Words without thoughts never to heaven go.

SHAKESPEARE—*Hamlet.* Act III. Sc. 3.

But yesterday the word of Caesar might
Have stood against the world; now lies he there,
And none so poor to do him reverence.

SHAKESPEARE—*Julius Caesar.* Act III. Sc. 2.

Taffeta phrases, silken terms precise,
Three-piled hyperboles, spruce affectation,
Figures pedantical.
SHAKESPEARE — *Love's Labour's Lost*. Act V. Sc. 2.

Words pay no debts, give her deeds.
SHAKESPEARE—*Troilus and Cressida*. Act III. Sc. 2.

But from sharp words and wits men pluck no fruit;
And gathering thorns they shake the tree at root;
For words divide and rend,
But silence is most noble till the end.
SWINBURNE—*Atalanta*.

I sometimes hold it half a sin
To put in words the grief I feel;
For words, like Nature, half reveal
And half conceal the Soul within.
TENNYSON—*In Memoriam*.

A word to the wise is sufficient.
TERENCE.

Hold fast the form of sound words.
I Timothy. I. 13.

He utters empty words, he utters sound without mind.
VERGIL—*Aeneid*.

You (Pindar) who possessed the talent of speaking much without saying anything.
VOLTAIRE.

For of all sad words of tongue or pen,
The saddest are these: "It might have been!"
WHITTIER—*Maud Muller*.

WORK

When Adam dolve, and Eve span,
Who was then the gentleman?
JOHN BALL in *Wat Tyler's Rebellion*.

Tools were made and born were hands,
Every farmer understands.
WILLIAM BLAKE—*Proverbs*.

The best verse hasn't been rhymed yet,
The best house hasn't been planned,
The highest peak hasn't been climbed yet,
The mightiest rivers aren't spanned;
Don't worry and fret, faint-hearted,
The chances have just begun
For the best jobs haven't been started,
The best work hasn't been done.
BERTON BRALEY—*No Chance*.

Get leave to work
In this world,—'tis the best you get at all.
E. B. BROWNING—*Aurora Leigh*.

Free men freely work:
Whoever fears God, fears to sit at ease.
E. B. BROWNING—*Aurora Leigh*.

And still be doing, never done.
BUTLER—*Hudibras*.

It is the first of all problems for a man to find out what kind of work he is to do in this universe.
CARLYLE—*Address* (1866).

With hand on the spade and heart in the sky
Dress the ground and till it;
Turn in the little seed, brown and dry,
Turn out the golden millet.
Work, and your house shall be duly fed:
Work, and rest shall be won;
I hold that a man had better be dead
Than alive when his work is done.
ALICE CARY—*Work*.

All Nature seems at work, slugs leave their lair—
The bees are stirring—birds are on the wing—
And Winter, slumbering in the open air,
Wears on his smiling face a dream of Spring!
And I the while, the sole unbusy thing,
Nor honey make, nor pair, nor build, nor sing.
COLERIDGE—*Work Without Hope*.

Every man's work shall be made manifest.
I Corinthians. III. 13.

Work thou for pleasure—paint or sing or carve
The thing thou lovest, though the body starve—
Who works for glory misses oft the goal;
Who works for money coins his very soul.
Work for the work's sake, then, and it may be
That these things shall be added unto thee.
KENYON COX—*Our Motto.*

Better to wear out than to rust out.
BISHOP CUMBERLAND.

The workers are the saviors of society, the redeemers of the race.
EUGENE V. DEBS—*Speech, 1905.*

The Lord had a job for me, but I had so much to do,
I said, "You get somebody else—or wait till I get through."
I don't know how the Lord came out, but He seemed to get along:
But I felt kinda sneakin' like, 'cause I know'd I done Him wrong.
One day I needed the Lord—needed Him myself—needed Him right away,
And He never answered me at all, but I could hear Him say
Down in my accusin' heart, "Nigger, I'se got too much to do,
You get somebody else or wait till I get through."
PAUL LAURENCE DUNBAR—*The Lord Had a Job.*

All things are full of labour; man cannot utter it: the eye is not satisfied with seeing, nor the ear filled with hearing.
Ecclesiastes. I. 8.

I never did anything worth doing by accident, nor did any of my inventions come by accident; they came by work.
EDISON.

'Tis toil's reward, that sweetens industry,
As love inspires with strength the enraptur'd thrush.
EBENEZER ELLIOT—*Corn Law Rhymes.*

Too busy with the crowded hour to fear to live or die.
EMERSON—*Nature.*

A ploughman on his legs is higher than a gentleman on his knees.
FRANKLIN—*Poor Richard.*

Handle your tools without mittens.
FRANKLIN—*Poor Richard.*

"Men work together," I told him from the heart,
"Whether they work together or apart."
ROBERT FROST—*Tuft of Flowers.*

In every rank, or great or small,
'Tis industry supports us all.
GAY—*Man, Cat, Dog, and Fly.*

In the sweat of thy face shalt thou eat bread.
Genesis. III. 19.

Joy to the Toiler!—him that tills
The fields with Plenty crowned;
Him with the woodman's axe that thrills
The wilderness profound.
BENJAMIN HATHAWAY—*Songs of the Toiler.*

Light is the task when many share the toil.
HOMER—*Iliad.*

When Darby saw the setting sun
He swung his scythe, and home he run,
Sat down, drank off his quart and said,
"My work is done, I'll go to bed."
"My work is done!" retorted Joan,
"My work is done! Your constant tone,
But hapless woman ne'er can say
'My work is done' till judgment day."
ST. JOHN HONEYWOOD—*Darby and Joan.*

Keep doing some kind of work, that the devil may always find you employed.
ST. JEROME.

I like work; it fascinates me. I can sit and look at it for hours. I love to keep it by me: the idea of getting rid of it nearly breaks my heart.

JEROME K. JEROME—*Three Men in a Boat.*

For men must work and women must weep,
And the sooner it's over the sooner to sleep,
And good-bye to the bar and its moaning.

KINGSLEY—*Three Fishers.*

But till we are built like angels, with hammer and chisel and pen,
We will work for ourself and a woman, for ever and ever, Amen.

KIPLING—*Imperial Rescript.*

And only the Master shall praise us, and only the Master shall blame;
And no one shall work for money, and no one shall work for fame;
But each for the joy of the working, and each, in his separate star,
Shall draw the Thing as he sees It, for the God of Things as They Are!

KIPLING—*L'Envoi.* In *Seven Seas.*

Who first invented work, and bound the free
And holyday-rejoicing spirit down . . .
To that dry drudgery at the desk's dead wood?
Sabbathless Satan!

LAMB—*Work.*

The finest eloquence is that which gets things done; the worst is that which delays them.

LLOYD-GEORGE.

No man is born into the world whose work
Is not born with him; there is always work,
And tools to work withal, for those who will;
And blessed are the horny hands of toil!

LOWELL—*A Glance Behind the Curtain.*

Why do strong arms fatigue themselves with frivolous dumb-bells? To dig a vineyard is a worthier exercise for men.

MARTIAL.

Man hath his daily work of body or mind
Appointed.

MILTON—*Paradise Lost.*

I am of nothing and to nothing tend,
On earth I nothing have and nothing claim,
Man's noblest works must have one common end,
And nothing crown the tablet of his name.

MOORE—*Ode upon Nothing.*

Study until twenty-five, investigation until forty, profession until sixty, at which age I would have him retired on a double allowance.

WILLIAM OSLER.

Many hands make light work.

WILLIAM PATTEN. 1547.

Hard toil can roughen form and face,
And want can quench the eye's bright grace.

SCOTT—*Marmion.*

A day's work is a day's work, neither more nor less, and the man who does it needs a day's sustenance, a night's repose, and due leisure, whether he be painter or ploughman.

GEORGE BERNARD SHAW—*Unsocial Socialist.*

How many a rustic Milton has passed by,
Stifling the speechless longings of his heart,
In unremitting drudgery and care!
How many a vulgar Cato has compelled
His energies, no longer tameless then,
To mould a pin, or fabricate a nail!

SHELLEY—*Queen Mab.*

A workman that needeth not to be ashamed.

II Timothy. II. 15.

Heaven is blessed with perfect rest but the blessing of earth is toil.

HENRY VAN DYKE—*Toiling of Felix.*

Too long, that some may rest,
Tired millions toil unblest.

WILLIAM WATSON—*New National Anthem.*

There will be little drudgery in this better ordered world. Natural power harnessed in machines will be the general drudge. What drudgery is inevitable will be done as a service and duty for a few years or months out of each life; it will not consume nor degrade the whole life of anyone.
H. G. WELLS—*Outline of History.*

Thine to work as well as pray,
Clearing thorny wrongs away;
Plucking up the weeds of sin,
Letting heaven's warm sunshine in.
WHITTIER—*The Curse of the Charter-Breakers.*

WORLD

The wrecks of matter, and the crush of worlds.
ADDISON—*Cato.*

Naked came we into the world, and naked shall we depart from it.
AESOP—*Fables.*

This is the best world, that we live in,
To lend and to spend and to give in:
But to borrow, or beg, or to get a man's own,
It is the worst world that ever was known.
ANONYMOUS.

Wandering between two worlds, one dead,
The other powerless to be born,
With nowhere yet to rest my head,
Like these, on earth I wait forlorn.
MATTHEW ARNOLD—*Stanzas from the Grande Chartreuse.*

The verdict of the world is conclusive.
ST. AUGUSTINE.

This world's a bubble.
BACON.

Earth took her shining station as a star,
In Heaven's dark hall, high up the crowd of worlds.
BAILEY—*Festus.*

Believe everything you hear said of the world; nothing is too impossibly bad.
BALZAC.

God is the author, men are only the players. These grand pieces which are played upon earth have been composed in heaven.
BALZAC.

He who best knows the world will love it least.
BALZAC.

Fly away, pretty moth, to the shade
Of the leaf where you slumbered all day;
Be content with the moon and the stars, pretty moth,
And make use of your wings while you may.
THOMAS HAYNES BAYLY.

This world is God's workshop for making men in.
HENRY WARD BEECHER.

The world is like a board with holes in it, and the square men have got into the round holes, and the round into the square.
BISHOP BERKELEY.

The pomps and vanity of this wicked world.
Book of Common Prayer.

In this bad, twisted, topsy-turvy world,
Where all the heaviest wrongs get uppermost.
E. B. BROWNING—*Aurora Leigh.*

O world as God has made it! All is beauty.
BROWNING—*Guardian Angel.*

The wide world is all before us—
But a world without a friend.
BURNS—*Strathallan's Lament.*

I have not loved the world, nor the world me;
I have not flatter'd its rank breath, nor bow'd
To its idolatries a patient knee.
BYRON—*Childe Harold.*

Well, well, the world must turn upon its axis,
And all mankind turn with it, heads or tails,

And live and die, make love and pay our taxes,
And as the veering winds shift, shift our sails.

BYRON—*Don Juan.*

Such is the world. Understand it, despise it, love it; cheerfully hold on thy way through it, with thy eye on highest loadstars!

CARLYLE—*Essays.*

Socrates, indeed, when he was asked of what country he called himself, said, "Of the world"; for he considered himself an inhabitant and a citizen of the whole world.

CICERO.

Such stuff the world is made of.

COWPER—*Hope.*

Come, follow me, and leave the world to its babblings.

DANTE.

Since every man who lives is born to die,
And none can boast sincere felicity,
With equal mind, what happens let us bear,
Nor joy nor grieve too much for things beyond our care.
Like pilgrims, to th' appointed place we tend;
The world's an inn, and death the journey's end.

DRYDEN—*Palamon and Arcite.*

Good-bye, proud world! I'm going home;
Thou art not my friend; I am not thine.

EMERSON—*Good-bye, Proud World!*

But in this world nothing is sure but death and taxes.

FRANKLIN—Letter to M. Leroy, 1789.

But it does move.

GALILEO—*Before the Inquisition.*

The world is a beautiful book, but of little use to him who cannot read it.

GOLDONI—*Pamela.*

Ill fares the land, to hastening ills a prey,
Where wealth accumulates, and men decay;
Princes and Lords may flourish, or may fade—
A breath can make them, as a breath has made—
But a bold peasantry, their country's pride,
When once destroy'd can never be supplied.

GOLDSMITH—*Deserted Village.*

Earth is but the frozen echo of the silent voice of God.

HAGEMAN—*Silence.*

The world's a theatre, the earth a stage,
Which God and nature do with actors fill.

HEYWOOD—*Dramatic Works.*

Let the world slide, let the world go;
A fig for care and a fig for woe!
If I can't pay, why I can owe,
And death makes equal the high and low.

HEYWOOD—*Be Merry Friends.*

There are two worlds; the world that we can measure with line and rule, and the world that we feel with our hearts and imaginations.

LEIGH HUNT—*Men, Women, and Books.*

The nations are as a drop of a bucket.

Isaiah. XL. 15.

World without end.

Isaiah. XLV. 17.

It takes all sorts of people to make a world.

DOUGLAS JERROLD—*Story of a Feather.*

This world, where much is to be done and little to be known.

SAMUEL JOHNSON—*Prayers and Meditations.*

If there is one beast in all the loathsome fauna of civilization I hate and despise, it is a man of the world.

HENRY ARTHUR JONES—*The Liars.*

The world is God's world, after all.

CHARLES KINGSLEY.

The world goes up and the world goes down,
And the sunshine follows the rain;
And yesterday's sneer and yesterday's frown
Can never come over again,
Sweet wife.
No, never come over again.
CHARLES KINGSLEY—*Dolcino to Margaret.*

If all the world must see the world
As the world the world hath seen,
Then it were better for the world
That the world had never been.
LELAND—*The World and the World.*

It is an ugly world. Offend
Good people, how they wrangle,
The manners that they never mend,
The characters they mangle.
They eat, and drink, and scheme, and plod,
And go to church on Sunday—
And many are afraid of God—
And more of Mrs. Grundy.
FREDERICK LOCKER-LAMPSON—*The Jester's Plea.*

O what a glory doth this world put on
For him who, with a fervent heart, goes forth
Under the bright and glorious sky, and looks
On duties well performed, and days well spent!
LONGFELLOW—*Autumn.*

Glorious indeed is the world of God around us, but more glorious the world of God within us. There lies the Land of Song; there lies the poet's native land.
LONGFELLOW—*Hyperion.*

One day with life and heart,
Is more than time enough to find a world.
LOWELL—*Columbus.*

The world in all doth but two nations bear,
The good, the bad, and these mixed everywhere.
MARVELL—*The Loyal Scot.*

This world is full of beauty, as other worlds above,
And if we did our duty, it might be as full of love.
GERALD MASSEY—*This World.*

A mad world, my masters.
MIDDLETON.

Hanging in a golden chain
This pendent world, in bigness as a star
Of smallest magnitude close by the moon.
MILTON—*Paradise Lost.*

Then stayed the fervid wheels, and in his hand
He took the golden compasses, prepared
In God's eternal store, to circumscribe
This universe and all created things:
One foot he centred, and the other turned
Round through the vast profundity obscure,
And said, "Thus far extend, thus far thy bounds,
This be thy just circumference, O World."
MILTON—*Paradise Lost.*

This world is all a fleeting show,
For man's illusion given;
The smiles of joy, the tears of woe,
Deceitful shine, deceitful flow,—
There's nothing true but Heaven.
MOORE—*This World Is All a Fleeting Show.*

Think, in this battered Caravanserai,
Whose Portals are alternate Night and Day,
How Sultán after Sultán with his Pomp
Abode his destined Hour, and went his way.
OMAR KHAYYÁM—*Rubaiyat.*

Love to his soul gave eyes; he knew things are not as they seem.
The dream is his real life: the world around him is the dream.
F. T. PALGRAVE—*Dream of Maxim Wledig.*

They who grasp the world,
The Kingdom, and the power, and the glory,
Must pay with deepest misery and spirit,
Atoning unto God for a brief brightness.

STEPHEN PHILLIPS—*Herod.*

The world is a great ocean, upon which we encounter more tempestuous storms than calms.

POE.

But as the world, harmoniously confused,
Where order in variety we see;
And where, tho' all things differ, all agree.

POPE—*Windsor Forest.*

All nations and kindreds and people and tongues.

Revelation. VII. 9.

The world delights to tarnish shining names,
And to trample the sublime in the dust.

SCHILLER.

All the world's a stage,
And all the men and women merely players.

SHAKESPEARE—*As You Like It.* Act II. Sc. 7.

Why, then, the world's mine oyster,
Which I with sword will open.

SHAKESPEARE—*Merry Wives of Windsor.* Act II. Sc. 2.

You'll never have a quiet world till you knock the patriotism out of the human race.

GEORGE BERNARD SHAW—*O'Flaherty, V. C.*

The world's great age begins anew,
The golden years return,
The earth doth like a snake renew
Her winter weeds outworn.

SHELLEY—*Hellas.*

This world surely is wide enough to hold both thee and me.

STERNE—*Tristram Shandy.*

There was all the world and his wife.

SWIFT—*Polite Conversation.*

A mad world, my masters.

JOHN TAYLOR—*Western Voyage.*

So many worlds, so much to do,
So little done, such things to be.

TENNYSON—*In Memoriam.*

The world is a looking-glass, and gives back to every man the reflection of his own face. Frown at it and it will in turn look sourly upon you; laugh at it and with it, and it is a jolly kind companion.

THACKERAY—*Vanity Fair.*

Everything is for the best in this best of all possible worlds.

VOLTAIRE—*Candide.*

This world is a comedy to those who think, a tragedy to those who feel.

HORACE WALPOLE—*Letter to Sir Horace Mann.*

The world is too much with us; late and soon,
Getting and spending we lay waste our powers;
Little we see in Nature that is ours.

WORDSWORTH—*Miscellaneous Sonnets.*

WORSHIP

Ah, why
Should we, in the world's riper years, neglect
God's ancient sanctuaries, and adore
Only among the crowd and under roofs
That our frail hands have raised?

BRYANT—*A Forest Hymn.*

Man always worships something; always he sees the Infinite shadowed forth in something finite; and indeed can and must so see it in any finite things, once tempt him well to fix his eyes thereon.

CARLYLE—*Essays.*

It is only when men begin to worship that they begin to grow.

CALVIN COOLIDGE—*Speech, 1922.*

And what greater calamity can fall upon a nation than the loss of worship.

EMERSON.

I don't like your way of conditioning and contracting with the saints. Do this and I'll do that! Here's one for t'other. Save me and I'll give you a taper or go on a pilgrimage.
ERASMUS—*The Shipwreck.*

Ay, call it holy ground,
The soil where first they trod.
They have left unstained, what there they found—
Freedom to worship God.
FELICIA D. HEMANS—*The Landing of the Pilgrim Fathers.*

As the skull of the man grows broader, so do his creeds.
And his gods they are shaped in his image and mirror his needs.
And he clothes them with thunders and beauty,
He clothes them with music and fire,
Seeing not, as he bows by their altars,
That he worships his own desire.
D. R. P. MARQUIS (Don Marquis) —*The God-Maker, Man.*

How often from the steep
Of echoing hill or thicket have we heard
Celestial voices to the midnight air,
Sole, or responsive each to other's note,
Singing their great Creator?
MILTON—*Paradise Lost.*

So shall they build me altars in their zeal,
Where knaves shall minister, and fools shall kneel:
Where faith may mutter o'er her mystic spell,
Written in blood—and Bigotry may swell
The sail he spreads for Heav'n with blasts from hell!
MOORE—*Lalla Rookh.*

Yet, if he would, man cannot live all to this world. If not religious, he will be superstitious. If he worship not the true God, he will have his idols.
THEODORE PARKER.

WORTH

This was the penn'worth of his thought.
BUTLER—*Hudibras.*

Nothing common can seem worthy of you.
CICERO to Caesar.

We are valued either too highly or not high enough; we are never taken at our real worth.
MARIE EBNER-ESCHENBACH.

Worth begets in base minds envy; in great souls, emulation.
FIELDING.

He has paid dear, very dear, for his whistle.
FRANKLIN—*The Whistle.*

The game is not worth the candle.
French Proverb.

Too good for great things and too great for good.
FULLER—*Worthies.*

Of whom the world was not worthy.
Hebrews. XI. 38.

It is easier to appear worthy of a position one does not hold, than of the office which one fills.
LA ROCHEFOUCAULD.

Worth makes the man, and want of it the fellow;
The rest is all but leather and prunello.
POPE—*Essay on Man.*

A pilot's part in calms cannot be spy'd,
In dangerous times true worth is only tri'd.
STIRLING—*Doomes-day.*

All human things,
Of dearest value hang on slender strings.
EDMUND WALLER.

But though that place I never gain,
Herein lies comfort for my pain:
I will be worthy of it.
ELLA WHEELER WILCOX.

It is easy enough to be prudent,
When nothing tempts you to stray;

When without or within no voice of sin
Is luring your soul away;
But it's only a negative virtue
Until it is tried by fire,
And the life that is worth the honor of earth,
Is the one that resists desire.
ELLA WHEELER WILCOX—*Worth While.*

WOUND

What deep wounds ever closed without a scar?
The hearts bleed longest, and but heal to wear
That which disfigures it.
BYRON—*Childe Harold.*

Thou hast wounded the spirit that loved thee
And cherish'd thine image for years;
Thou hast taught me at last to forget thee,
In secret, in silence, and tears.
MRS. DAVID PORTER.

I was wounded in the house of my friends.
Zechariah. XIII. 6.

WRONG

The multitude is always in the wrong.
WENTWORTH DILLON.

Brother, brother; we are both in the wrong.
GAY—*Beggar's Opera.*

It is better to suffer wrong than to do it, and happier to be sometimes cheated than not to trust.
JOHNSON.

Wrong is but falsehood put in practice.
LANDOR.

Truth forever on the scaffold, wrong forever on the throne.
LOWELL.

Alas! how easily things go wrong!
A sigh too deep, or a kiss too long,
And then comes a mist and a weeping rain,
And life is never the same again.
GEORGE MACDONALD—*A Fairy Story.*

A man finds he has been wrong at every preceding stage of his career, only to deduce the astonishing conclusion that he is at last entirely right.
STEVENSON—*Crabbed Age.*

The remedy for wrongs is to forget them.
SYRUS.

Higher than the perfect song
For which love longeth,
Is the tender fear of wrong,
That never wrongeth.
BAYARD TAYLOR.

Wrongs unredressed, or insults unavenged.
WORDSWORTH—*The Excursion.*

Y

YOUTH

Young men soon give and soon forget affronts;
Old age is slow in both.
ADDISON—*Cato.*

Young men are fitter to invent than to judge; fitter for execution than for counsel; and fitter for new projects than for settled business.
BACON—*Of Youth and Age.*

Our youth we can have but to-day;
We may always find time to grow old.
BISHOP BERKELEY.

Ah! happy years! once more who would not be a boy!
BYRON—*Childe Harold.*

As I approve of a youth that has something of the old man in him, so I am no less pleased with an old man that has something of the youth. He that follows this rule may be old in body, but can never be so in mind.
CICERO.

I remember my youth and the feeling that will never come back any more—

the feeling that I could last forever, outlast the sea, the earth, and all men.
JOSEPH CONRAD—*Youth.*

Be it a weakness, it deserves some praise,
We love the play-place of our early days;
The scene is touching, and the heart is stone,
That feels not at that sight, and feels at home.
COWPER.

In youth we learn; in age we understand.
MARIE EBNER-ESCHENBACH.

Wine and youth are fire upon fire.
FIELDING.

Reckless youth makes rueful age.
FRANKLIN.

Over the trackless past, somewhere,
Lie the lost days of our tropic youth,
Only regained by faith and prayer,
Only recalled by prayer and plaint,
Each lost day has its patron saint!
BRET HARTE—*Lost Galleon.*

There is a feeling of Eternity in youth which makes us amends for everything. To be young is to be as one of the Immortals.
HAZLITT—*Table Talk.*

Youth! youth! how buoyant are thy hopes! they turn,
Like marigolds, toward the sunny side.
JEAN INGELOW—*The Four Bridges.*

All the world's a mass of folly,
Youth is gay, age melancholy:
Youth is spending, age is thrifty,
Mad at twenty, cold at fifty;
Man is nought but folly's slave,
From the cradle to the grave.
W. H. IRELAND—*Modern Ship of Fools.*

Towering inconfidence of twenty-one.
SAMUEL JOHNSON—*Letter to Bennet Langton.*

When all the world is young, lad,
And all the trees are green;
And every goose a swan, lad,
And every lass a queen;
Then hey, for boot and horse, lad,
And round the world away;
Young blood must have its course, lad,
And every dog his day.
CHARLES KINGSLEY—*Water Babies.*

Our youth began with tears and sighs,
With seeking what we could not find;
We sought and knew not what we sought;
We marvel, now we look behind:
Life's more amusing than we thought.
ANDREW LANG—*Ballade of Middle Age.*

Youth comes but once in a lifetime.
LONGFELLOW—*Hyperion.*

How beautiful is youth! how bright it gleams
With its illusions, aspirations, dreams!
Book of Beginnings, Story without End,
Each maid a heroine, and each man a friend!
LONGFELLOW—*Morituri Salutamus.*

'Tis now the summer of your youth: time has not cropped the roses from your cheeks, though sorrow long has washed them.
EDWARD MOORE—*The Gamester.*

The smiles, the tears
Of boyhood's years,
The words of love then spoken.
THOMAS MOORE—*Oft in the Stilly Night.*

The atrocious crime of being a young man.
WILLIAM PITT to Walpole.

When the brisk minor pants for twenty-one.
POPE—*Epistle I.*

We think our fathers fools, so wise we grow;
Our wiser sons, no doubt, will think us so.
POPE—*Essay on Criticism.*

If youth but knew, and age were able,
Then poverty would be a fable.
Proverb.

Keep true to the dreams of thy youth.
SCHILLER.

My salad days;
When I was green in judgment.
SHAKESPEARE—*Antony and Cleopatra.* Act I. Sc. 5.

Crabbed age and youth cannot live together;
Youth is full of pleasance, age is full of care;
Youth like summer morn, age like winter weather;
Youth like summer brave, age like winter bare.
Youth is full sport, age's breath is short;
Youth is nimble, age is lame;
Youth is hot and bold, age is weak and cold;
Youth is wild, age is tame.
Age, I do abhor thee; youth, I do adore thee.
SHAKESPEARE—*The Passionate Pilgrim.*

Live as long as you may, the first twenty years are the longest half of your life.
SOUTHEY.

For God's sake give me the young man who has brains enough to make a fool of himself.
STEVENSON—*Crabbed Age.*

All sorts of allowances are made for the illusions of youth; and none, or almost none, for the disenchantments of age.
STEVENSON—*Virginibus Puerisque.*

A youth to whom was given
So much of earth, so much of heaven.
WORDSWORTH—*Ruth.*

YUKON

There's a land where the mountains are nameless
And the rivers all run God knows where;
There are lives that are erring and aimless,
And deaths that just hang by a hair;
There are hardships that nobody reckons;
There are valleys unpeopled and still;
There's a land—oh, it beckons and beckons,
And I want to go back—and I will.
ROBERT W. SERVICE—*Spell of the Yukon.*

Z

ZEAL

There is no greater sign of a general decay of virtue in a nation, than a want of zeal in its inhabitants for the good of their country.
ADDISON—*Freeholder.*

Through zeal knowledge is gotten, through lack of zeal knowledge is lost; let a man who knows this double path of gain and loss thus place himself that knowledge may grow.
BUDDHA.

For zeal's a dreadful termagant,
That teaches saints to tear and cant.
BUTLER—*Hudibras.*

Motives by excess reverse their very nature, and instead of exciting, stun and stupefy the mind.
COLERIDGE.

Awake, my soul! stretch every nerve,
And press with vigour on;
A heavenly race demands thy zeal,
And an immortal crown.
PHILIP DODDRIDGE.

There is no zeal blinder than that which is inspired with a love of justice against offenders.
FIELDING.

It is good to be zealously affected always in a good thing.
Galatians. IV. 18.

Blind zeal can only do harm.
LICHTWER.

Not the zeal alone of those who seek Him proves God, but the blindness of those who seek Him not.
PASCAL.

To be furious in religion is to be irreligiously religious.
WILLIAM PENN.

Poets heap virtues, painters gems, at will,
And show their zeal, and hide their want of skill.
POPE—*Moral Essays.*

Zeal is very blind, or badly regulated, when it encroaches upon the rights of others.
PASQUIER QUESNEL.

A zeal of God, but not according to knowledge.
Romans. X. 2.

My hat is in the ring.
THEODORE ROOSEVELT.

Zeal is fit for wise men, but flourishes chiefly among fools.
TILLOTSON.

Terms ill defined, and forms misunderstood,
And customs, when their reasons are unknown,
Have stirred up many zealous souls
To fight against imaginary giants.
TUPPER—*Proverbial Philosophy.*

Press bravely onward!—not in vain
Your generous trust in human kind;
The good which bloodshed could not gain
Your peaceful zeal shall find.
WHITTIER—*To the Reformers of England.*

ZEPHYRS

Let Zephyr only breathe
And with her tresses play.
DRUMMOND—*Phoebus, Arise.*

While the wanton Zephyr sings,
And in the vale perfumes his wings.
DYER—*Gronger Hill.*

Fair laughs the morn, and soft the zephyr blows.
GRAY—*The Bard.*

And on the balmy zephyrs tranquil rest
The silver clouds.
KEATS—*Posthumous Poems.*

Soft is the strain when zephyr gently blows.
POPE—*Essay on Criticism.*

The balmy zephyrs, silent since her death,
Lament the ceasing of a sweeter breath.
POPE—*Winter.*

INDEX

A

C

D

E

K

L

M

N

O

P